5/02

Baedeker's

GREAT BRITAIN

Hints for using the Guide

Following the tradition established by Karl Baedeker in 1844, buildings and works of art, places of natural beauty and sights of particular interest, as well as hotels and restaurants of especially high quality, are distinguished by one ★ or two ★★.

To make it easier to locate the various places listed in the "A to Z" section of the Guide, their co-ordinates are shown in red at the head of each entry: e.g., Coventry K 8.

Coloured lines down the right-hand side of the page are an aid to finding the main heading in the Guide: blue stands for the Introduction (Nature, Culture, History, etc.), red for the "A to Z" section, and yellow indicates Practical Information.

Only a selection of hotels, restaurants and shops can be given; no reflection is implied therefore on establishments not included.

In a time of rapid change it is difficult to ensure that all the information given is entirely accurate and up-to-date, and the possibility of error can never be entirely eliminated.

Although the publishers can accept no responsibility for inaccuracies and omissions, they are constantly endeavouring to improve the quality of their Guides and are therefore always grateful for criticisms, corrections and suggestions for improvement.

Preface

This guide to Great Britain and Northern Ireland is one of the new generation of Baedeker guides.

Illustrated throughout in colour they are designed to meet the needs of the modern traveller. They are quick and easy to consult, with the principal sights described in alphabetical order, and practical details and useful tips shown in the margin. The information is presented in a format that is both attractive and easy to follow.

The guide is in three parts. The first part gives a general account of the country, its topography, climate, flora and fauna, population, language, state and society, education, economy, transport, history, famous people and art and culture. A brief selection of quotations and some suggested routes lead into the second part, in which the principal places of tourist interest are described in detail. The third part contains a variety of practical information designed to help visitors to find thier way about and make the most of their stay. Both the sights and the practical information sections are listed in alphabetical order

A British Tradition: Old-timer cars and country houses – Langshott Manor, south of London

The new Baedeker guides are noted for their concentration on essentials and their convenience of use. They contain numerous specially drawn plans and colour illustrations; and at the end of the book is a large map making it easy to locate the various places described in the "A to Z" section of the guide with the help of the co-ordinates given at the head of each entry.

Contents

Baedeker Specials

Britain is

"A jewel in the silver sea" was how continental visitors described these islands two hundred years ago. "Lush meadows, lovely villages, delightful country houses set amidst parks and lakes" – a hymn of praise no less appropriate today and indeed easily added to. From Kent to Cornwall, from Land's End to the Shetland Islands, from the East of England to westernmost Wales, Britain reveals an intriguing, man-made landscape, and with it this island kingdom's distinctive face, at once akin to continental Europe but at the same time wondrously different. "The English Channel is not a waterway" declared Winston Churchill "but an outlook". Even the advent of the Eurotunnel has made little impact on this island mentality. The United Kingdom's special charm lies in the way its Norse, Celtic, Anglo-Saxon and Norman inheritance combines to produce a richly varied whole, everything from Stone Age sites such as Stonehenge and Callanish to medieval fortresses, magnificent country houses and elegant spas, delightful little market towns and thatched farm cottages amid green hedgerows and a mosaic of fields. How better to learn something of the islands' chequered history than by touring its castles, perhaps in search of King Arthur and the Knights of the Round Table, or the sites of savage battles between fiercely rival clans. Or why not embark on a literary trail through the land of William Shakespeare, Sir Walter Scott and that most prolific of Victorian novelists Charles Dickens, or follow in the footsteps of highwaymen and smugglers or any one of a host of notable characters such as Lawrence of Arabia or Mary Queen of Scots whose tragic destiny made her a legend in

London
Britain's capital city with style

Leeds Castle
for over 300 years was a royal residence

British pubs
are more than an institution

Great

her lifetime. Here too, in the country that gave birth to the industrial revolution, are some of the oldest monuments of the machine age, as well as enchanting ruined abbeys and a panoply of splendid cathedrals shown off to perfection in their open, often lawned settings. As for the world of nature, lonely heaths and moorland complement breathtaking cliffs and rocky coasts, fine sandy beaches and gently undulating hills, while extravagant displays of flowers adorn innumerable delightful gardens and parks. British sportsmanship being renowned, a stay in Britain is also an invitation to enjoy an active holiday. Golf tops the list of the nation's favourite sports and

there are almost 2000 golf courses throughout the country, the most famous of them at St Andrews, traditional "home" of the game. As for getting to know the people, look no further than the local pub. This is where folk meet over a pint of bitter for a chat or a game of pool or darts. Pubs are a real British institution; but they are much more besides. Homely and comfortable, if occasionally smoke-filled, they provide an agreeable refuge from the changeable British weather. Where else but in Britain, though, is rain so easily forgiven – after all, what self-respecting ghost would haunt a sun-drenched castle! Last but by no means least there is British hospitality, as traditional among this friendly island people as their celebrated sense of humour and unfailing politeness, attributes which contribute enormously to the pleasing quality of British life. Set out to explore Great Britain in all its fascinating variety and this "jewel in the silver sea" will quickly have you under its spell.

Melrose

Jewel of the Scottish border region

Golf

a popular sport

Stone-age village
Skara Brae in the Orkney Islands

Facts and Figures

General

The United Kingdom of Great Britain lies to the north-west of mainland Europe, between latitude 50° (Isles of Scilly) and 61° N (Shetland Islands), and between longitude 8°W (Northern Ireland) and 2° E (Lowestoft in Suffolk). Further south lie the Channel Islands which however – like the Isle of Man in the Irish Sea – are largely independent with their own parliaments and laws and are linked directly with the Crown. As a result of its insular situation – the mainland alone has over 4600 miles of coastline – Great Britain has only one land border, that between Northern Ireland and the Republic of Ireland. In the North Sea, the English Channel, the Irish Sea and the Atlantic limits within which each country is permitted to operate in such fields as oil and gas exploitation and fishing, for example, have been laid down in agreements made with Norway, Denmark, Germany, the Netherlands, Belgium, France and Ireland.

Great Britain and Northern Ireland

© Baedeker

At its nearest point the British mainland is only 22 miles from that of Europe (Dover–Calais).

Area

The United Kingdom covers a total area of 94,250 sq. miles including over 1200 sq. miles of inland waterways. The mainland obviously accounts for most of this, namely 84,200 sq. miles, followed by Northern Ireland with 5452 sq. miles, the Hebrides with 2598 sq. miles, the Shetland Islands and the Orkney Islands. Other islands include the Isles of Wight off the south coast of English and the island of Anglesey off the north coast of Wales.

In length, the mainland extends more than 600 miles from north to south; at its broadest point, in the south, it spans less than 300 miles. Because of its shape, and the many inlets and estuaries (such as those of the rivers Thames, Mersey, Severn and Humber, for example) which penetrate inland, all Britain's large towns (and many smaller ones) are located little more than an hour's journey-time from the sea – an accident of geography which has proved advantageous both to trade and transport and to holidaymakers from Britain and overseas.

Topography

The British Isles lie on the continental shelf of the European land mass, to which they were connected by a land bridge until the Mesolithic period (about 6000–5000 BC). In consequence many features in British topography represent a continuation of continental land-forms. The post-glacial vegetation is similar to that of Europe and the prehistoric inhabitants of Britain belonged to the same cultural systems as those of the Continent.

◀ *Stirling Castle, the chief residence of the Stuarts*

Britain has been physically separated from Europe for long enough, however, for its inhabitants to have developed a sense of standing apart – for example, many still think of crossing the Channel as "a voyage to Europe". For many centuries this feeling of isolation from Europe was reinforced by Britain's links with its widespread colonies, and it is only quite recently, after the loss of the colonies began and Britain joined the European Community in 1973, that its attention has been turned slowly in the direction of Europe.

Natural regions

The British landscape is a patchwork of different elements, all relatively small, and is therefore notable for its rich variety. Two main regions can be distinguished: in the north and west the highland zone, and in the east the lowland zone, based on more recent geological formations. These two zones are roughly defined by an imaginary line running from the mouth of the River Exe in the south-west to that of the Tees in the north-east.

Lowland zone

Lowland Britain is composed mainly of layers of sedimentary deposits from the Mesozoic and Tertiary periods. The latter are found principally in the low-lying plains and basins such as the Hampshire and the London Basins, frequently covered with Ice Age deposits. When the Alps were formed the Mesozoic layers (Trias, Jurassic, Cretaceous) tilted and fell away largely to the east, becoming slightly raised in the south-east. This was followed by a succession of hard stone deposits, producing areas of richly structured scarpland, many parts of which have been designated "areas of outstanding natural beauty".

Jurassic

The Jurassic layers extend eastward from Dorset, in south-west England, by way of the Cotswold Hills (up to 1070 ft above sea-level), Northampton and Lincoln as far as the Cleveland Hills (up to 660 ft) in the north. The various levels differ considerably in form and appearance, because the sequence of clay, sand and chalk varies as the result of differing geological elevations. The major rocks thus produced include the massive limestone and sandstone Dogger formations and the sandstone and limestone malm to the south of Oxford. Where two layers of friable stone meet, on the other hand, the strata layer is replaced by wide, deep valleys with a clay subsoil which forms the basis of the brick and ceramic industry in such areas. The ferruginous layers sandwiched within the Jurassic strata were until very recently of considerable importance in the production of iron ore in, for example, the Northampton and Leicester region.

Cretaceous

East of the Jurassic system lie the Cretaceous systems, which also extend eastwards. They stretch from Salisbury Plain in the south in a north-easterly direction by way of the Chiltern Hills (up to 840 ft) and the Anglian Heights as far as the Wash. North of the Lincoln Wolds and the York Wolds the Cretaceous layer re-appears. In south-east England sandstone re-emerges in The High Weald. To the north and south lie valleys of Weald clay, forming fertile agricultural land.

The cretaceous limestone of the North and South Downs forms the edge of the south-eastern land terrace. The chalk of the South Downs has been eroded by the sea in the Straits of Dover to produce the famous White Cliffs of Dover.

Highland zone

The highland areas of Scotland, Northern Ireland, the north of England and North Wales have a geological structure which can be seen as a westward continuation (but at a lower level) of the Scandinavian highlands. Their surface topography is strongly marked by glacial action.

The highland regions of Great Britain, north and west of the imaginary

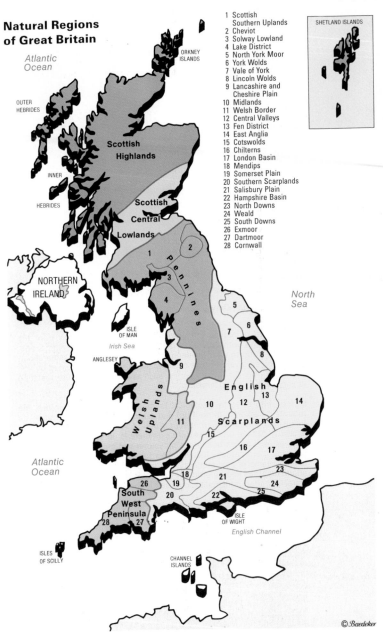

Topography

Natural Regions of Great Britain

1 Scottish Southern Uplands
2 Cheviot
3 Solway Lowland
4 Lake District
5 North York Moor
6 York Wolds
7 Vale of York
8 Lincoln Wolds
9 Lancashire and Cheshire Plain
10 Midlands
11 Welsh Border
12 Central Valleys
13 Fen District
14 East Anglia
15 Cotswolds
16 Chilterns
17 London Basin
18 Mendips
19 Somerset Plain
20 Southern Scarplands
21 Salisbury Plain
22 Hampshire Basin
23 North Downs
24 Weald
25 South Downs
26 Exmoor
27 Dartmoor
28 Cornwall

Atlantic Ocean

SHETLAND ISLANDS

ORKNEY ISLANDS

OUTER HEBRIDES

INNER

HEBRIDES

Scottish Highlands

Scottish Central Lowlands

NORTHERN IRELAND

ISLE OF MAN

Irish Sea

ANGLESEY

Pennines

North Sea

Welsh Uplands

English Scarplands

Atlantic Ocean

South West Peninsula

ISLES OF SCILLY

ISLE OF WIGHT

English Channel

CHANNEL ISLANDS

© Baedeker

Beachy Head, an outlier of the South Downs

line referred to earlier, are dominated by rock formations from the Palaeozoic age, with some even going back to the pre-Cambrian period, especially in north-west Scotland. In many places, too, the general pattern of folded layers of rock and crystalline slate is punctuated by volcanic rock from the Tertiary period, such as basalt and granite, resulting in very varied natural landscapes.

Pennines

Divided into three by geological faults and valleys the Pennines, the mountain backbone of northern and central England, are a straticulate bulge dating from the Carboniferous period. While the edge of the range is clearly defined on the western side there is no such clear line to the east, as here the carboniferous limestone and the millstone/sandstone covering it are partially hidden under further carboniferous layers containing seams of coal and ore. As a result coal has been mined in the adjoining areas and by-products manufactured since time immemorial, especially after industrialisation came in the 18th c.

Scottish Highlands

In contrast to the Pennines, almost all the remaining highland areas of Great Britain resulted from the Caledonian folding and run from south-west to north-east. Valleys, some deeply slashed, divide the main highland regions of North Wales, the Southern Uplands of Scotland and the Scottish Highlands into individual hill and mountain ranges. Thus, the mountains of Scotland fall into three parts; the Southern Uplands are separated from the Highlands by the rift valley of the Central Lowlands, the latter containing two-thirds of Scotland's population and most of its larger towns. A geological fault, known as the Highland Boundary Fault, marks the link with the Scottish Highlands, which in turn are divided by the Great Glen Fault into the Grampian Mountains and the Northern Highlands. In the Grampians rise the highest peaks in Britain, Ben Nevis (4408 ft) and Ben Macdhui (4296 ft). In the valley of the Great Glen Fault

Topograph

SHETLAND ISLANDS

Atlantic Ocean

ORKNEY ISLANDS

High-

Inverness
Loch Ness

Spey

Aberdeen

l a n d s

HEBRIDES

Ben Nevis
▲1343 m

Mountains

Dee

North Sea

Grampian

Tay

Glasgow

Firth of Forth

Edinburgh

Firth of Clyde

Clyde

Britain's Principal Mountains, Hills and Rivers

Bann

Lough Neagh

Lough Erne

Belfast

Mourne Mts.

S o u t h e r n   U p l a n d s

Tweed

Cheviot Hills

Newcastle

Tyne

Cumbrian Mts.

Tees

P e n n i n e s

Ure

York

Wharfe

Hull

ISLE OF MAN

Irish Sea

Humber

Manchester

ANGLESEY

Liverpool

Trent

Witham

The Wash

Cambrian Mountains

Severn

Birmingham

Nen

Ouse

Norwich

Wye

Avon

Chiltern Hills

Usk

Cotswold Hills

LONDON
(Themse)

Atlantic Ocean

Cardiff

Severn

Bristol

Thames

North Downs

Dover

South Downs

Southampton

Brighton

ISLE OF WIGHT

Plymouth

English Channel

ISLES OF SCILLY

CHANNEL ISLANDS

© Baedeker

13

Topography

Loch Assynt in the North-west Highlands

lie a string of three lakes, with depths of up to 750 ft, the best known being the famous Loch Ness. The Caledonian Canal was built in the first half of the 18th c. to form an artificial link between Moray Firth in the north-east and the Forth of Lorm in the west. Since then the canal has become of less economic importance, and now northern Scotland's major link-road runs parallel to it.

Cheviot Hills Cumbrian Mountains

To the west lie the beautiful hills of Cumbria and the Lake District, formed in the Ice Age; the latter's famous lakes and glaciated valleys make it one of Britain's favourite tourist areas.

Welsh mountains

Formed in the Palaeozoic period, the Welsh mountains are the foothills of the higher Cambrian range and possess similar geological, petrographic and morphological features. North Wales is famous mainly for the glacial region of Snowdonia, a magnificent national park dominated by its highest peak, Snowdon (3560 ft); in Mid and South Wales are extensive areas of moor and heathland.

South-western peninsula

The rock masses of the south-western peninsula (Devon and Cornwall) have been levelled down into a plateau out of which rise areas of higher ground, notably Dartmoor and Exmoor.

Northern Ireland

The relief of Ireland is closely allied to that of the British mainland. Most of Northern Ireland is a westward continuation of the Scottish mountain ranges, although their surface topography is strongly marked by erosion. Those areas which were once covered in ice are studded with moraines and glacial lakes, Lough Neagh being the largest lake in Great Britain. The "Giant's Causeway", a stretch of columnar basalt forming a promontory on the north coast of Ireland, is similar in structure to the Inner Hebrides.

In the Grampian mountains ...

... "pure nature"

In Snowdonia

Romney Marsh

Ice Age

The effect of glacial torrents during the Ice Age can be seen in the Highlands in the north of Scotland, the Grampian Mountains, the Lake District, the Cheviot Hills and the upper ranges of the Pennines. From these central points the ice-masses moved out to the North Sea, the Atlantic, the Irish Sea and towards the English lowlands; in the east of England they joined up with the glacial torrents pouring down from Scandinavia. The southernmost edge of the ice deposits passed across southern England about 130,000 years ago, in the Wolstonian Ice Age. The latest ice-surge, known as the "Loch Lomond Readvance", occurred about 10,000 BC and created the most recent glacial forms, as evidenced by the numerous corries found high up in the Scottish Highlands and in Wales. Existing reliefs became deepened and lakes formed in the basins and fjords. In the Lake District the valleys became glaciated and U-shaped; often side valleys led off the main valleys. In many places glacial activity was further evidenced by the presence of debris at the ends, sides and bottoms of the clefts. The landscape took on almost an Alpine character, even though the mountains were not so high. During the whole of the Ice Ages the English lowlands were a periglacial region.

Coastal formation

All these various geological and structural changes resulted in the formation of some very attractive coastlines in Great Britain. Fjord-like coasts are to be found in the north of Scotland, whereas those of south Wales are characterised by long narrow inlets formed by the partial submergence of river valleys. Some sections of the coastline of southern England display cliffs composed of a variety of rocks, whereas others consist of flat marshland. In the north of Scotland and Northern Ireland, in particular, raised coastlines at levels of up to 100 ft above sea-level are evidence of more recent land heaves. In Wales, too, and as far north as the Isle of Man, there are many fossil sand beaches which are some twelve to sixteen feet above sea-level. In the south, on the other hand, world-wide rises in sea-levels combined with a relative fall in land level has led to the formation of estuaries, such as the mouth of the Thames. Promontories, spits and hooks are (historically speaking) the most recent developments along the coasts; they are found mainly along the south coast of England and are the result of sand movements caused by the north-east winds. Along a 125 mile strip of coast between Chichester in the west and Ramsgate in the east, twelve harbours which were in use during the Middle Ages have been made unusable as the result of such sand movement.

Main watershed

Britain has a watershed running from north to south. As the line of this is west of centre it follows that those rivers which flow eastwards to the North Sea are generally longer than those to the west and also have a more gentle fall. The nature of the watershed favoured the building of canals during the period of the Industrial Revolution of the 19th c., but only the Manchester Ship Canal remained economically viable until the middle of the 20th c. Whilst possessing high water levels most rivers are too short for shipping and fall too gently to be able to produce hydro-electric power; only those rivers with estuaries, like the Thames, have harbours which are suitable for deep-sea and coastal shipping.

Climate

The British Isles, lying between the Atlantic in the west and the North Sea in the east, have a mid-oceanic climate. On the side facing the Atlantic the air is also warmed in winter by the benign currents of the Gulf Stream, and the effects of the sea are felt inland, too, as Britain lies at right angles to the prevailing west winds and the coast is studded with numerous bays and inlets.

This oceanic climate results in low temperature variations between

day and night and between summer and winter, together with comparatively high rainfall throughout the year and high winds, especially in
winter.

The limited daily fluctuations in temperature mean that in the lowlands
night temperatures seldom fall below freezing point, and that on the
other hand they are rarely unbearably high during the day. The minor
variations between summer and winter arise from the fact that the seas
conserve warmth – in spring the increasing sunshine is "swallowed" by
the sea, with the result that the land can warm up only slowly; in
autumn, as the strength of the sun reduces, the sea releases this stored
heat, the land cools down slowly and winters remain mainly mild. As a
result, growing periods are long and cattle can graze for much of the
year. Snow seldom falls in the lowland areas and does not lie for long.
The oceanic climate also causes rain to fall throughout the year, on average every other day. Periods of drought are comparatively rare.

Areas of low pressure, or depressions, moving in from the west have
a major effect on the weather. These frequently bring rain followed
equally quickly by brighter periods as the depressions pass through.
Cloud amounts do not change so very much during the course of the
year, either, and the sun shines in winter more often than might be
expected; Oxford, for example, enjoys some 51 hours of sunshine in
December. On the other hand, in summer the sun often hides behind the
clouds. As the lowest rainfall of the year is normally in March and April
these can be good months in which to holiday, especially in the lowlands of the south.

As depressions pass through they often cause a build-up of storms
over the Atlantic, the unreduced effect of which is then felt over the
British Isles. The constant winds have an adverse effect on vegetation,
namely cooling down, increased evaporation and – on the coast – by
depositing salt; nevertheless, in spite of high humidity, they help to dry
hay and corn.

In those areas lying further to the west the daily and annual temperature
variations are less, amounts of rainfall greater and storms more frequent
than in the east.

Generally speaking, temperatures in the north are lower than those in
the south; for example, the average January temperature in Lerwick in
the Shetland Islands is 7.2°C (45°F), in Edinburgh 8.7°C (47.7°F), and in
Plymouth 10.8°C (51.4°F).

The higher the land the lower the temperatures tend to be, normally
dropping by some 0.5°C (0.9°F) every 330 ft, and rainfall, cloud amounts
and the period of snow in winter are all greater. In the northern
Pennines, at a height of 820 ft, there is a covering of snow for at least 30
days in the year; above 2600 ft this increases to 100 to 140 days. As snow
conditions are usually good the Scottish Highlands west of Aberdeen
have become popular with skiers.

Some idea of the rainfall and temperature patterns throughout the year
can be obtained from the climatic diagrams. The blue rainfall columns
show the amounts of rain (in mm) per month, as indicated by the figures
in blue on the right. The temperatures are represented by an orange
band, the upper edge of which shows the maximum average daytime
temperatures and the lower edge the minimum night temperatures, as
shown by the red figures on the right.

With the help of the general indications listed below it should be possible roughly to estimate the climate expected in the regions in between
the places shown.

Lerwick represents the high-oceanic climate of the islands to the north
of Scotland, **Oban** the exposed north-western coastal regions of
Scotland, **Belfast** the somewhat milder climate in the east of Ireland,
Edinburgh the north-eastern coast of Britain, **Plymouth** the mild and

Seven typical regional climates

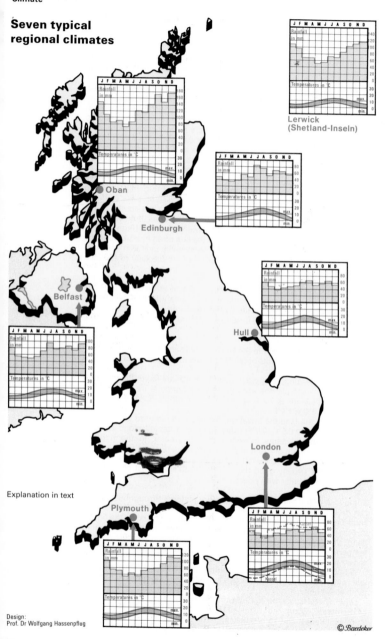

Lerwick
(Shetland-Inseln)

Oban

Edinburgh

Belfast

Hull

London

Explanation in text

Plymouth

Design:
Prof. Dr Wolfgang Hassenpflug

© Baedeker

warm climate of the south-western coast, and **London** and **Hull** that of the south and east respectively.

The **Shetland Islands** have a high-oceanic climate, i.e. high annual rainfall (over 40in.) and extremely low variations in temperatures both daily 5°C (9°F) and annually 9°C (16°F); thus the temperature band on the diagram is narrow and comparatively flat. Moving south to the coasts of Scotland winter temperatures scarcely increase at all, remaining at about 1–2°C (2–4°F) above freezing point. In summer, however, maximum temperatures and daily variations do increase.

Northern Ireland, lying in the rain-shadow, is much drier than the west coast of Scotland across the North Channel, but with similar temperatures.

The climate of the **west coast of Scotland** – including the many off-shore islands making up the Hebrides – is determined by the rain-bearing winds coming in from the Atlantic which produce the highest rainfall in the country, often accompanied by violent storms.

The Atlantic air-masses rise up against the mountains in the west of the **Scottish Highlands**, resulting in heavy rain, which lessens as they move east. Temperatures on the higher ground are lower than those on the coast; snow falls frequently and lies longer.

North-east England, more protected from the winds, is warmer and drier than the Scottish Highlands, but much cooler than the south of the country.

The industrial central area of England witnesses a changeover in climatic conditions. Smoke and waste gases tend to produce more fog and smog, although such conditions are less frequent here than in some other areas abroad.

Temperatures in Wales lie between those of Oban and Plymouth, being relatively lower in the more mountainous regions. Like the rest of the exposed western costs of Britain, rainfall is high.

The south and, in particular, the south-west coasts of England are the best from a weather point of view. Winters are extremely mild and vegetables can be grown in the open in winter. On the other hand, maximum summer temperatures, although good, are some 4°C (7°F) less than those of central Europe.

South-east England experiences greater variations of temperature than does the south-west; summers are warmer and winters cooler, as indicated by the wider and more curved temperature band on the climatic diagram for London. As a result of its position in the lee of hills the east enjoys considerably less rainfall.

Flora and Fauna

As Great Britain has been quite heavily populated and intensively farmed for thousands of years little of its original vegetation remains. In the lowland regions, in particular, most of the native forests of oak and beech disappeared back in the early Middle Ages, to be replaced by further woodland or agricultural land. Today, in spite of intense post-war reafforestation programmes involving the planting mainly of coniferous trees, only 7–8 per cent of the country is woodland. However, this lack of forests is largely offset by the large areas of fields and pastures so typical of England. As well as the parkland settings for castles and country houses there are beautiful fields and grazing meadows, some dotted with trees and surrounded by hedges.

Flora
Parkland and green fields

Moors, heath and open grassland are also very typical of Britain. On the flatlands of east and south-east England, in particular, lime-loving grasses now cover large areas of what was once forest, contrasting with the acid grassland found on the rough pastures of the more mountainous regions. These latter expanses of grass are often studded with areas

Heath and moorland

of heathland and ferns; large areas of heather are to be found especially on the porous soil of the more mountainous regions. Heathers of the generae erica and calluna predominate, often interspersed with grass and gorse. Moorland. with species of sphagnum, acid-loving grasses and rushes, is commonly found in those mountainous regions which are strongly influenced by the Atlantic Ocean; as well as flat moorland, high plateaux of impoverished soil on peat subsoil and – especially in the highly humid climate of the Scottish Highlands – tableland cover large areas. A peculiarity of some lower hilly areas are the English "moors" covered in heather and moisture-loving plants growing in acid peat soil;

Heath and moorland vegetation on Dartmoor

as well as Exmoor and Dartmoor, for example, such moors cover large areas of the Grampians and the Pennines.

Mediterranean flora

Finally mention should be made of the Mediterranean, even sub-tropical vegetation which flourishes in protected places on the south and south-west coast favoured by the warm Gulf Stream.

Fauna

The native fauna of Britain is more or less the same as that of western and central Europe, although many of its typical forest-dwellers and larger mammals have reduced considerably in number. The country boasts a great variety of birds, ranging from seabirds to the songbirds of the open countryside and the birds of prey seen on the heaths and moors. Many kinds of fish are to be found in the seas around Britain, although their numbers have been decimated by over-fishing. Animals which are reared include cattle, pigs and especially sheep, large flocks of

Scottish cattle in Galloway

which are to be seen on the mountainsides of northern England and Scotland.

The rough mountain regions are home to many breeds of cattle suited to the conditions, such as the Scottish Highland cattle or "Galloways", found on the Southern Uplands of Scotland.

Population

The 1991 census indicates that some 55.5 million people live in the United Kingdom, equal to 609 per sq. mile. Only 8 per cent live in rural areas. All the districts with the highest population are in England. The most densely populated is a zone of urban conurbations stretching north-west from London towards Liverpool; these include Greater London (10,448 per sq. mile), Birmingham (9093 per sq. mile), Liverpool (10,274 per sq. mile) and Manchester (9083 per sq. mile), as well as Leeds and Bradford (3134 per sq. mile). Other densely populated cities include Bristol (8718 per sq. mile), Sheffield (3515 per sq. mile), Newcastle-upon-Tyne (5447 per sq. mile) and Glasgow (8275 per sq. mile). The most thinly populated district is the Scottish highland region around Inverness, with only 21 per sq. mile).

Population groups

The largest single entity within the United Kingdom is **England**, with a population of 47.1 million and covering by far the largest area; however, Scots, Irish and above all the Welsh will react strongly if labelled as "Englishmen". Although they regard themselves as British the people of Scotland, Northern Ireland and Wales tend to cherish their own separate histories and traditions, and have different mentalities. In addition, the Welsh in particular (not forgetting some parts of Scotland and Ireland as well) have preserved their own Celtic language (see Language) – still the living tongue of a considerable proportion of the population of Wales. In the economic and social spheres many Scots, Irish and Welsh feel disadvantaged, and this has led to a resurgence of parties seeking some degree of devolution.

Scotland has a population of 5.1 million, spread over an area equal to almost a third of the whole United Kingdom, at a density of only 166 to the sq. mile. It has its own historic capital in Edinburgh, its own Church, parliament and legal system, its own educational traditions and issues its own banknotes and postage stamps. Most Scottish domestic matters are the responsibility of the separate Scottish parliament based in Edinburgh and headed by a Scottish First Minister. This parliament was established in 1999 after a referendum of the Scottish electorate.

Scotsmen left their homeland at the rate of between 20,000 and 40,000 a year in the 1960s. In spite of the discovery of oil in the North Sea off Scotland living standards remained generally speaking lower than those in England until the 1990s, when many of the Scottish cities, particularly Glasgow, underwent an economic and cultural transformation.

Wales, with a population of 2.8 million, has been joined to England since 1536. Like Scotland, it has felt economically disadvantaged, with a high rate of unemployment following closure of many of the coalmines. Welsh nationalism also has a large cultural element; almost a quarter of the population speaks Welsh, and a movement – the "Cymdeithas yr Jaith Gymraeg" – to promote the spread and official recognition of the language has been active since 1962. Welsh writers, dramatists and musicians have been encouraged to develop their creative talents, and the traditional Welsh festival of music and poetry, the Eisteddfod, has been revived. Welsh is used as the medium of instruction in some schools; there is a Welsh-language newspaper; and Welsh is used in some radio and television programmes. Since 1967 Welsh has shared equal status with English in the administration of justice and the conduct of government business, and in 1972 bilingual street names and road signs were introduced. A separate Welsh parliament was established in 1999 after a narrow vote in favour in the referendum.

Northern Ireland, the former province of Ulster, which remained part of the United Kingdom after the establishment of the Irish Free State in 1921 and is governed direct from London, has a population of 1,600,000. Most of the people are Protestants, descendants of Scottish and English settlers in the 17th c., with some 35 per cent Roman Catholics. The latter minority have for many years been excluded from important posts by the Protestant "Orangemen" and generally socially disadvantaged. This is the root cause of much of the current trouble in Northern Ireland between the Catholic IRA (Irish Republican Army) on the one hand and the Protestant UDA (Ulster Defence Army) on the other. Since the outbreak of "the troubles" in 1969 more than 2900 people have lost their lives. At the end of the 20th c., however, there were signs that a peaceful settlement might finally be reached.

When the British Empire came to an end after the Second World War many people from the new **Commonwealth States**, especially India, Pakistan and the Caribbean, emigrated to Britain; the British Nationality Act of 1948 stated that there was to be no discrimination between citizens of the United Kingdom and the Commonwealth States, and moreover workers were needed in post-war Britain. However, the numbers of immigrants began to get out of hand, and in 1971 it was found necessary to introduce a law requiring entry visas to be obtained by all citizens of the Indian subcontinent and some African states, and in 1981 citizenship requirements were further tightened up. Nevertheless, illegal immigration remains a problem. Today there are some 2.6 million members of ethnic minorities living in Britain, of which 1.2 million are from India, Pakistan or Bangladesh, 520,000 from the Caribbean and a similar number from other countries. About a half of them were born in Britain.

Most of the 115,000 **Chinese** living in Britain came from Hong Kong, and many are in the restaurant trade. A further 50,000 Chinese from Hong Kong were granted full British citizenship when the colony was handed over to China in 1997.

Religion

More than half the UK population nominally belongs to the established Anglican Church, the Church of England, of which the Queen is the head. The number of Roman Catholics now amounts to some 7 million, centred mainly around Merseyside, Central Clydeside and in Northern Ireland. The Church of Scotland is Presbyterian, with about 1.3 million adherents; in England most of the Congregationalists have combined with the Presbyterians to form the United Reformed Church. In England there are also active Nonconformist groups (dissenting from the established church), mainly Methodists (about 450,000), Baptists and Quakers.

Non-Christian religious communities include a million or so Moslems and 500,000 Sikhs. There are also more than 300,000 Jews in Britain, of whom two-thirds live in London.

Employment structure

Although Britain was the birthplace of the Industrial Revolution in the 19th c., only 22.5 per cent of the working population are currently employed in the production sector, with 69.6 per cent being in the service sectors. Agriculture employs only 1.3 per cent, the building industry 4.8 per cent and the water and energy sectors 2.0 per cent. The average rate of unemployment for Britain as a whole is 8.1 per cent; in Northern Ireland it is significantly higher, at 13.8 per cent. At present the unemployment situation, especially in the north-east of England and in Scotland, continues to give cause for concern, although there are now slight signs of an end to the recession and of the "green shoots" of economic recovery.

Language

Apart from Chinese, English is now the world's most widely-spoken language, being the mother tongue of more than 300 million people, mainly in Great Britain, Ireland, USA, Canada, South Africa, Australia and New Zealand. In many parts of the world it serves as a lingua franca in the fields of science and technology and has thus become the major universal foreign language. The English language also forms a bond between the United Kingdom and the Commonwealth and the United States of America.

The first documented language used in Britain was Celtic. The Roman period of occupation which lasted until the 5th c. AD left comparatively few linguistic traces. English as we know it today belongs to the Germanic group of the Indo-European family of languages, being most closely related to Friesian, Dutch and Low German. Its roots go back to the 5th c. AD when Angles, Saxons and Jutes conquered Britain and pushed the native Celts to the "edge" (Celtic Fringe). Viking invaders and Danish settlers also imposed their stamp on the language in the 9th and 10th c. Following the Norman invasion in 1066, however, French was for centuries the (official) language of the ruling class, and numerous French words became absorbed into the language. The number of words of Romanic origin grew as Latin became increasingly used in religious and academic circles. As a result the vocabulary now often includes both an Anglo-Saxon and a Romance word for the same thing – e.g., freedom (Anglo-Saxon) and liberty (from the French); in such cases, the Romance word usually has the more abstract meaning.

History

The evolution of the language can be divided into three sections – Old English (up to the 11th c.), Medieval English (up to the 15th c.) and Modern English. The principal differences between the spoken and written word arise mainly from the fact that whereas the written form had more or less been finalised by the end of the 15th c., the spoken word continued to evolve and change.

Many different dialects will be heard in Britain, most dating back to Anglo-Saxon times, but Oxford English, or the Queen's English, spoken without dialect, is still considered "correct" and used as a standard form of speech. Some degree of snobbery persists, however, and there is a tendency for such dialects as those of the industrial Midlands, the north-east (Geordie) and the London "Cockney" dialect to be regarded in some quarters as a sign of a less educated person. Today the introduction of "BBC English" performs an important function in standardising the spoken language, so that the often exaggerated "Oxford" English has to a certain extent declined in favour. Fears are currently being expressed that over-standardisation will lead to dialects dying out, something that would be found most regrettable in the eyes of many people.

Standard English

Other languages have survived in multinational Britain, especially in the Celtic Fringe mentioned above. Linguistically, the Scots can be divided into three – those speaking English (with or without a Scottish accent), Lowland Scots, speaking the dialect of the region lying between the Scottish border and the Highlands, and those who use Scots Gaelic, the Celtic language of the Highlands and the Scottish islands, now spoken by some 100,000 people, most of whom are bilingual. The Catholic minority in Northern Ireland tends to identify itself to a large degree with Erse (or Gaelic), the official language of the Republic of Ireland. Although Irish (Erse) is now spoken only by a small minority as their sole language, it remains a compulsory subject in all Irish schools.

Celtic languages

The Celtic language most used today is Welsh (Cymric); national campaigns have succeeded in obtaining Welsh TV and radio channels, and Welsh is spoken by almost a million people. On the other hand, the

Cornish language spoken in Cornwall in the 18th c. has now died out. The Celtic languages can be divided into two groups – "p-Celtic" (Irish, Scots Gaelic and Manx, the original tongue spoken in the Isle of Man) and "q-Celtic" (Cymric, Cornish and Breton).

State and Society

The United Kingdom of Great Britain and Northern Ireland comprises the four countries of England, Scotland (including the Orkney and Shetland Islands), Wales and Northern Ireland. In addition there are the "Dependencies of the Crown", namely, the Isle of Man, the Channel Islands and remnants of the Empire such as Gibraltar, Hong Kong (to be handed back to China in 1997) and several islands and groups of islands in the Atlantic, Caribbean, Indian and Pacific Oceans.

The United Kingdom is a parliamentary democracy with a hereditary monarchy of the House of Windsor. The sovereign (Queen Elizabeth II since 1952) must be a member of the Church of England and is not allowed to marry a Catholic. The right of succession rests with the monarch's eldest son, or with a daughter if there is no son.

The flag of the United Kingdom is the "Union Jack" (see page 27), made up of the crosses of the patron saints of England (St George), Scotland (St Andrew) and Ireland (St Patrick). The flag of Northern Ireland consists of the Cross of St George together with the Star symbolising the Provinces and the Red Hand of Ulster. Since 1837 the royal coat-of-arms has depicted a shield with the three English lions, the Scottish lions and the Irish harp, surrounded by the Ribbon of the Order of the Garter with its motto "Honi soit qui mal y pense" (shame on him who thinks evil of it). The shield is supported by an English lion and the Scottish unicorn, standing on a field with the emblems of England (the rose), Scotland (the thistle) and Ireland (the shamrock); below this is the royal motto "Dieu et mon droit" (God and my right). The Scottish shield differs in layout and mottoes. The Red Dragon of Wales does not appear on the national flag or in the coat-of-arms.

Based on a 17th c. song, the British national anthem was established as such in 1745, making it the oldest in the world.

Constitution

As the oldest of the great democracies, Britain has no written constitution. This is a defect more apparent than real, for the principles of the constitution are firmly established in the consciousness of the British public and of the politicians they elect. The lack of any basic or fundamental law of the constitution is the consequence of the country's gradual development from a feudal to a liberal and democratic state, achieved by a process of reform over centuries rather than by revolution. Consequently the principles of the British constitution have been built up over the centuries on the basis of "common law", determined by a succession of legal judgements which have elaborated the law and modified previous judgements in line with the prevailing climate of opinion. In modern times there has been a great proliferation of statutory law – incorporated in Acts of Parliament. Nevertheless the unwritten "laws and customs of the constitution" have continued to regulate the behaviour of the Crown and Cabinet and of the government and opposition. It might be thought that this leaves the British constitution open to unfortunate influences and developments and this might be so were it not protected by two unshakeable principles – the "Rule of Law" and the sovereignty of Parliament. Nevertheless, there have been increased rumblings in recent years proposing far-reaching constitutional reforms.

Certain written documents are, however, honoured as the cornerstones of the British constitution, most of which came into being as the result of struggles between the Crown and Parliament or its predecessors. Prime among these historical documents stands the Magna Carta, which King John was compelled by his nobles to sign in 1215. In it he guaranteed to safeguard the common law and to recognise the right of the barons to force him to do so, and in Article 39 the liberty of the individual is guaranteed.

From the time of the Stuarts came the Petition of Rights in 1628 (in which Charles I was obliged to agree to a list of basic rights in return for financial assistance from Parliament), the Act of Habeas Corpus 1679, which provided protection against arbitrary imprisonment, and finally the Bill of Rights 1689, in which William of Orange and Mary confirmed various basic rights of the individual, such as freedom of expression and the right to petition. Other important constitutional legislation includes several laws allowing voting rights, which were passed between 1832 and 1969, the Parliament Acts of 1911 and 1949, and the law effecting British membership of the EEC (1973).

Many major facets of the British constitution are not laid down in writing at all, but are based simply on "conventions", a system of understandings and agreements which has grown up over the years and under which precedents have been established just as they have been under common law. Perhaps the most striking example of such a "convention" is the fact that the office of Prime Minister and the formation of the cabinet have never actually been laid down in law.

The monarch is Head of State and also Head of the Commonwealth of Nations and of 17 of the 51 independent Commonwealth States. Although in theory still endowed with considerable power, in practice the monarch's parliamentary role is now almost entirely ritual – the opening and closing of the sessions of Parliament, the dissolution of Parliament, the formal appointment of the prime minister and members of the government, the granting of royal assent to laws passed by Parliament. In practice the monarch must act on ministerial advice, but has a right to be kept informed of the work of the cabinet of ministers, and this is provided in the course of a weekly audience granted to the prime minister. Although the power now wielded by the monarchy is largely symbolic this is nevertheless still of considerable importance in upholding the unwritten constitution of the nation.

The Crown

The Privy Council (see below), the chief advisory body during the reign of the Stuarts, has since been largely superseded by the "Cabinet". The cabinet as it is known today first came into being as a decisive factor in British politics during the reign of George I, led by Sir Robert Walpole, the first "real" prime minister. The members of the cabinet, numbering twenty or so, are chosen by the prime minister; these always include the Chancellor of the Exchequer, the Home Secretary, the Foreign Secretary, the Minister of Defence and the Lord Chancellor, together with a number of other ministers and aides. The actual government is made up of 80 to 100 members.

Cabinet and prime minister

The Prime Minister, appointed by the monarch, must be a member of the House of Commons and is normally the leader of the party which won the previous general election. He possesses very full powers; in particular, he can choose and dismiss ministers at his discretion, ask the monarch (without previous discussion with his cabinet if he so desires) to dissolve Parliament to enable him to go to the country in fresh elections at a time he considers favourable to himself and his party, and make certain important decisions without the prior consent of his ministers or of the House of Commons (for example, prime minister John Major sent the British army into the Gulf War without consulting Parliament). He is also the leader of his party in the Lower House and the ruling figure in British politics; now – especially after the three periods of office held by Margaret Thatcher between 1979 and 1990 – people often speak of "prime ministerial government" having superseded "cabinet government".

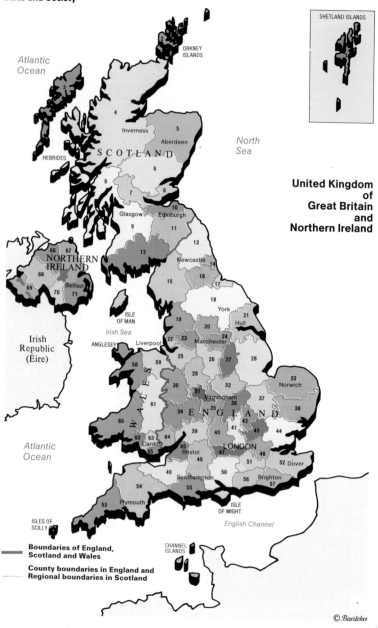

SHETLAND ISLANDS

Atlantic
Ocean

ORKNEY
ISLANDS

HEBRIDES

Inverness

Aberdeen

S C O T L A N D

North
Sea

**United Kingdom
of
Great Britain
and
Northern Ireland**

Glasgow

Edinburgh

NORTHERN
IRELAND

Belfast

Newcastle

ISLE
OF MAN

Irish Sea

York

Hull

Irish
Republic
(Éire)

ANGLESEY

Liverpool

Manchester

Norwich

W A L E S

E N G L A N D

Birmingham

Atlantic
Ocean

Cardiff

Bristol

LONDON

Dover

Southampton

Brighton

ISLE
OF WIGHT

Plymouth

ISLES OF
SCILLY

English Channel

CHANNEL
ISLANDS

Boundaries of England,
Scotland and Wales

County boundaries in England and
Regional boundaries in Scotland

© Baedeker

26

Scotland (Regions)

1 Shetland Islands Area
2 Orkney Islands Area
3 Western Islands Area
4 Highland Region
5 Grampian Region
6 Tayside Region
7 Central Region
8 Fife Region
9 Strathclyde Region
10 Lothian Region
11 Borders Region
12 Dumfries & Galloway Region

England (Counties)

13 Northumberland
14 Tyne & Wear
15 Cumbria
16 Durham
17 Cleveland
18 North Yorkshire
19 Lancashire
20 West Yorkshire
21 Humberside
22 Merseyside
23 Greater Manchester
24 South Yorkshire
25 Cheshire
26 Derbyshire
27 Nottinghamshire
28 Lincolnshire
29 Staffordshire
30 Salop
31 West Midlands
32 Leicestershire
33 Norfolk
34 Hereford & Worcester
35 Warwickshire
36 Northamptonshire

37 Cambridgeshire
38 Suffolk
39 Gloucestershire
40 Oxfordshire
41 Buckinghamshire
42 Bedfordshire
43 Hertfordshire
44 Essex
45 Avon
46 Wiltshire
47 Berkshire
48 Greater London
49 Somerset
50 Hampshire
51 Surrey
52 Kent
53 Cornwall
54 Devon
55 Dorset
56 West Sussex
57 East Sussex

Wales (Counties)

58 Gwynedd
59 Clwyd
60 Dyfed
61 Powys
62 West Glamorgan
63 Mid Glamorgan
64 Gwent
65 South Glamorgan

Northern Ireland (Counties[1])

66 Londonderry
67 Antrim
68 Tyrone
69 Fermanagh
70 Armagh
71 Down

[1] In 1973 the six counties of Northern Ireland were replaced by 26 districts.

United Kingdom

England

Scotland

Ireland

Wales

Northern Ireland

Coat of Arms

Privy Council

The Privy Council has lost much of its former power, but nevertheless its role should not be underestimated, for it is through the medium of this body that the government can shorten the legislative process by means of "Orders in Council". The Privy Council has 350 "Right Honourable" members chosen by the prime minister, made up of the members of the cabinet, members of the clergy and High Court judges.

Parliament

Parliament consists of the House of Commons, or Lower House, and the House of Lords, or Upper House. In fact the House of Lords has little real political power nowadays, so when people speak of "Parliament" they are really referring to the House of Commons.

The role of Parliament has changed considerably over the years. For many centuries it found itself in dispute with the monarch of the day and this finally came to a head in the 17th c. with the execution of Charles I. It could be said that Parliament enjoyed its heyday during the 19th c., since when its power has to a certain extent been undermined by that of the cabinet, which normally succeeds in carrying the day – for the government to be defeated in debate is a rare event. This can be clearly seen from the fact that over 90 per cent of draft bills are successfully introduced by the government.

The **House of Commons** has 651 members, corresponding to the total number of electoral constituencies (524 in England, 72 in Scotland, 38 in Wales and 17 in Northern Ireland); they are directly elected by majority vote for the life of a Parliament (maximum five years). The two-party system has a long tradition in Britain, and during most of this century there has been fairly regular alternation between Labour and Conservative governments. Members of the governing party sit on one side of the "House" and "Her Majesty's Opposition" sits on the opposite side. On the floor in front of each party are red lines – traditionally "two sword-lengths and a foot" apart – which members are not allowed

A debate in the House of Commons

to cross. In the front rows sit the cabinet ministers or, in the case of the Opposition, the "shadow cabinet"; these are known as "front-benchers". Behind them sit the other members of the party, known as "back-benchers". Between the two sides of the House stands a table at the head of which, on a raised platform, sits the "Speaker", who pre-sides over proceedings and, on election to an office going back to medieval times, withdraws from party political activity. An important role is also played by the party "Whips", who seek to maintain party discipline and to ensure the presence of members at important debates.

Until 1999 there were 1191 members of the **House of Lords**. It was com-posed of hereditary peers (lords temporal and lords spiritual), "life peers" appointed by the government of the day, and the "law lords". The system is undergoing reform, with the first stage (removal of 600 hereditary peers) completed in November 1999. The power of the House of Lords is limited, as measures of which it disapproves can only be delayed but not finally countermanded.

The British legal system differs in many respects from that of most other European states. It is based on common law, equity and statute law, the most important of which is common law, with its origins going back to the time of the Norman kings. This is based on case law, with some 350,000 precedents on which to base decisions. Equity is also based on legal precedent, but only in the sphere of civil law. Finally, statute law is the law as laid down in Acts of Parliament, decrees and ordinances. In Scotland the system is based on Roman law.

Legal system

The lower courts in England and Wales are the magistrates' courts (for both criminal and civil matters), with crown courts (criminal) and county courts (civil) at the next higher level. There are appeals to the High Court, which sits in London, and to the Supreme Court of Justice, and a right of appeal to the House of Lords can be sought. Most minor cases, including 80-90 per cent of criminal cases, are dealt with simply at local level by Justices of the Peace. An important role is played by the "jury" of "twelve good men and true" chosen at random from the electoral roll and who are sworn to decide the facts of a case and reach a verdict in a court of law. Judges – who still wear the traditional robes and wigs – cannot be dismissed once appointed by the monarch and have a wide freedom of decision-making.

Following revelations of a number of cases of gross injustice the British legal system has recently been the subject of considerable criticism. For example, in 1991 the "Birmingham Six" were released after having spent sixteen years in prison on a charge of attempted IRA bombings which they did not commit. It transpired that for years judges had chosen to ignore evidence, and the prisoners were finally released thanks only to the efforts of a journalist and a former member of parliament.

Local government

Since the 1974 administrative reforms there have been 47 counties in England plus six metropolitan counties, with eight counties in Wales, 26 districts in Northern Ireland and twelve regions in Scotland. In addition Great Britain has 85 independent towns and cities. The counties, known as administrative counties, are divided into municipal boroughs and county districts; these in turn are broken down into over 10,000 individ-ual parishes.

The policing system is also interesting; 80 per cent of the British police are organised on a regional level in 52 police districts. At the head of each district is a Chief Constable, elected by the county police commit-tee; he is completely independent in the way in which he chooses to run his district and receives no directives from the Home Secretary. The London Metropolitan Police are, however, answerable to the Home Secretary. The London "bobby" gets his name from Sir Robert ("Bobby") Peel (1788–1850), Home Secretary and later prime minister who founded the modern police force.

Education

Parties

The struggle between King and Parliament in the 17th c. resulted in the emergence of two main political parties, the "Whigs" and the "Tories" (both originally swear-words!). The Whigs were mainly landowners and merchants who supported a strong House of Commons, while the Tories were mostly landed gentry who favoured the monarchy. In the 19th c. these two parties became the Liberals and the Conservatives. In 1906 the Labour party was founded. Since the split in the Liberal party in 1931 the Conservatives and Labour have alternated in government fairly regularly, as it can be argued that the British electoral system tends to favour the larger parties. At the parliamentary elections in May 1997 Tony Blair's "new" Labour party – now tending more to the centre – gained its greatest success so far by ousting the Conservatives after 18 years of government. The third largest party are now the Liberal Democrats. Other parties represented in the House of Commons include the Scottish National Party, Plaid Cymru (Wales), the Ulster Unionist Party, the Ulster Popular Unionist Party, the Democratic Unionist Party and the Social Democratic and Labour Party. Sinn Fein, the political wing of the IRA, is no longer represented in the House of Commons.

Trades unions

Trades unions, too, have a long tradition. The Trades Union Congress (T.U.C.), the voluntary umbrella organisation of some of the individual trade unions, was formed in 1868. Of the total of 360 trades unions 73, representing 8.2 million members, belong to the T.U.C.; 38 per cent of all British workers are members of trade unions. The largest individual unions are the Transport and General Workers (1.2 million) and the General Municipal, Boilermakers and Allied Trades Union (0.9 million). Until the beginning of the Thatcher era the trades unions were very powerful, as demonstrated by their readiness to strike; under Margaret Thatcher, however, their power was considerably reduced and there were far fewer strikes. During the 1980s membership of trades unions fell by some 25 per cent.

Army

The British army, steeped in tradition, has been a volunteer professional force since conscription was abolished in 1960. It now numbers 317,000 men and women, and responsibility for it falls upon the cabinet. All sections of the forces possess nuclear weapons.

Membership of international organisations

The United Kingdom is a member of the United Nations (UN), with a permanent seat on the Security Council, as well as of the European Union (EU), the West European Union (WEU), the Council of Europe, OECD and NATO.

Education

Until 1989 education in Great Britain was largely the responsibility of the Local Education Authorities, but following the Education Reform Act of 1988 central government was given considerably more control. The Department of Education and Science in London is now responsible for all British universities and for schools in England; schools in Scotland, Wales and Northern Ireland have their own government departments.

School system

Education is compulsory from the ages of five to sixteen. It is necessary to distinguish between state maintained schools and independent schools. Apart from Northern Ireland, the school systems are basically similar in all parts of the country.

State schools

Primary schools, providing education from the ages of five to eleven years, are divided into Infant Schools and Junior Schools. Alternatively, a few areas in England have First Schools for five to eight year-olds, followed by a transitional Middle School, aimed at preparing pupils for the step up to Secondary Education at the age of eleven.

In 1964 the Labour government abolished the much-criticised "11-plus" examination and introduced the "comprehensive school" system. Grammar Schools still exist in a few places, together with comprehensive Secondary Modern Schools and Technical Schools (some of which are to be replaced by the controversial City Technology Colleges). The top forms in secondary schools, the sixth forms, may be found either as part of the secondary school itself, as separate Sixth Form Colleges or within Colleges of Further Education.

Outside the state system there are at present some 2500 independent schools of varying quality, most of them privately endowed. All these establishments charge quite high fees and most are boarding-schools catering for all age-groups. At the higher level students have to take an entrance examination, although in the final analysis the school governors have a free hand in deciding whom to accept, usually reserving a number of free places for gifted children of parents who cannot afford the fees.

Independent schools

Such academies cater for only about 6.5 per cent of the school population, but nevertheless are of considerable importance, especially the "public schools", which still provide the key to successful careers in politics, law and economics for the elite. They are a sensitive political issue and frequently criticised as being an anachronism, politically divisive and out of date. The somewhat confusing term of "public schools" stems from the oldest among them which descend from medieval grammar schools most of which were supported by the church. These, known as the "Clarendon Schools" (Winchester, Eton, Westminster, Harrow, Shrewsbury, Charterhouse, Rugby, St Paul's, Merchant Taylors), together with the more modern Radley College near Oxford and

The University of St Andrews

Oxford: Christ Church College

Gordonstoun in Scotland, comprise the "crème de la crème" among the elite schools, opening the door to a promising career for most who graduate from them.

School-leaving examinations

In the final years of their school career, at both state and independent schools, most pupils sit for the General Certificate of Secondary Education (GCSE). candidates being awarded one of seven grades in each subject. If a pupil stays on at school for a further two years in the sixth form he or she will then sit for the GCSE A-level (Advanced), success in which is a normal prerequisite for entry to a university or college of further education. This can then be followed by sitting for the Advanced Supplementary Level (GCE AS) examination. In Scotland pupils sit for the Scottish Certificate of Education (SCE) at Ordinary Grade or Higher Grade.

Universities and colleges

Britain has a total of 47 universities – 36 in England, eight in Scotland, two in Northern Ireland and one in Wales. The two ancient English universities, Oxford and Cambridge, were founded in the 12th and 13th c. respectively, and the oldest Scottish universities of St Andrews, Glasgow, Aberdeen and Edinburgh date from the 15th and 16th c.; all the other colleges date either from the 19th and early 20th c. – the "redbrick universities" – or the 1960s – technical colleges and the "concrete universities". As with schools, there are considerable differences between the universities. Oxford and Cambridge are, of course, world-famous and are traditional rivals, as illustrated in the annual boat race held on the River Thames; Cambridge is regarded as being pre-eminent in the sciences, Oxford in the arts. Of the less traditional colleges London University is the largest; founded in 1828, it was intended as a rival to the older universities which were then open only to those of the Anglican persuasion. The 30 Polytechnics, a product of the 1960s, concentrate on business management and commercial and industrial courses. The division between universities and polytechnics has recently been removed and polytechnics are now calling themselves universities.

University degrees and their importance vary with the university. In England, Wales and Northern Ireland a student may initially graduate as a Bachelor of Arts (BA) or Bachelor of Science (BSc), and then possibly go on to become a Master of Arts (MA), Master of Science (MSc) or Doctor of Philosophy (PhD); in Scotland, on the other hand, a Master of Arts degree is equivalent to a BA degree in England.

Cambridge: King's College

The Open University provides tuition by television and radio, sup-   Open University
plemented by postal courses, for those – usually older people – who
have not had an opportunity of going to a conventional university.

Economy

No other country in the world is so closely linked with the concept of
industrialisation as Britain, the country in which the industrial revolution
in the late 18th and 19th c. led to a complete restructuring of production
methods and a new way of life. However, whereas 100 years ago Britain
had attained high growth rates and was offering plenty of employment,
as the leading industrial nation was producing half the world's industrial
output, and had the largest merchant navy in the world, it went through
a period of economic crisis after the First World War which – in spite of
brief boom periods after the Second World War – still basically lingers
on. In the mid-19th c. Britain was by far the world's leading industrial
nation and major exporter; today it ranks only seventh on the basis of its
gross national product and fifth in the world trade league. Between the
comparatively prosperous and more densely populated centres of
London and the south-east on the one hand and the economically
deprived old industrial areas of northern England, Scotland, Wales and
Northern Ireland on the other there exist serious differences in income
and living standards, rates of unemployment and future economic outlook.

There are a number of reasons for the growing social and economic
problems and regional differences, especially the increasing
"north–south divide". The beginnings of this economic crisis can be
traced back to the break-up of the British Empire, which once covered a
quarter of the earth's surface and embraced a quarter of its population.
Britain thereafter gradually lost its sources of cheap materials and its
world-wide markets. The former colonies, by now members of the
Commonwealth, began seeking aid from the mother country, and in that
sense the Empire had become a liability rather than an asset. Britain was
now faced with stiff competition in world markets from the United
States, Japan and many other countries. These difficulties are now
aggravated by the need to re-equip industry with modern technology,
especially in the old "industrial heartlands" and the effects of strikes and
continuous disputes between employers and unions.

It was not until the 1980s, under the premiership of Margaret Thatcher,
that strenuous efforts were made thoroughly to modernise British industry and to make it competitive once again in the markets of the world.
Measures taken included curtailing the power of the trade unions, limit-
ing state subsidies in old and non-viable branches of industry (such as
coal and iron-ore mining, the iron, steel and textile industries, docks,
etc.), allowing them to run down and be replaced by more "high-tech"
forms of production with a more promising future, privatising many
state concerns, promoting the service sector and taking numerous
measures to encourage the economic re-development of many run-
down urban areas, such as the schemes undertaken in Birmingham,
Liverpool, Manchester, the East End of Glasgow and in the Docklands
area of London. Although these measures met with a considerable
degree of success they were not sufficient to prevent Britain going into
recession in 1990 largely because of the worldwide economic decline.
As a result its gross domestic product grew only very slightly in the early
1990s; by 1992 the rate of unemployment had risen to 9 per cent (more
than 15 per cent in many problem areas) and inflation rose to over 7 per
cent).

One result of the measures taken during the Thatcher era – which are
frequently referred to as the "policies of inequality" and which concentrated on developing private ownership and those areas with economic

St Catherine's Dock in London's Docklands

potential – has been a further widening of the existing geographical and social disparities.

Industry

In 1971 9.9 million people, equal to 46 per cent of all those in work, were engaged in production. In 1991 this figure had fallen to 22.5 per cent. The only branch of industry able to maintain or increase its workforce was the electronics industry which had come to the fore in the 1970s and 1980s. Even though the government attempted to counteract this marked trend towards "de-industrialisation" by encouraging the service sectors and new growth areas the general labour market trends remained relatively unfavourable. In spite of this reduction in importance British industry remains extraordinarily varied, ranging from a highly-developed food industry to chemical, electrical and technical trades and iron and steel production. The following are examples of some of the structural changes which have taken place in recent years.

Iron and steel industry

Since the 1970s the British Steel Corporation was subjected to a large number of factory closures and rationalisation measures as a result of a worldwide slump in sales and a declining home market. Far-reaching programmes involving centralisation and partial privatisation introduced when the Conservatives came to power in 1979 did succeed in increasing productivity to a considerable degree, but increasing imports of finished products such as motor vehicles together with a fall in the volume of exports led to a further reduction in the demand for steel. The resultant fall in the number of men employed in the steel industry particularly affected the traditional regions of south Wales, north-east England and central Scotland. Largely as the result of an increase in the volume of imported cars, even the automobile industry – once acknowledged as the perfect example of a growth industry profiting from new technology – suffered drastic falls in production (1970: 1.64 million cars,

1989: 1.25 million, compared with four times as many in Germany) and a reduction in the workforce (1979: 450,000, 1989: 250,000 workers). Most affected by this was the traditional motor manufacturing area around Birmingham in the once prosperous West Midlands.

The relatively modern electrical and electronic industry has displayed a marked upward trend ever since the end of the Second World War. Even though as in other industries, the total number of employees has reduced in recent years (1972: 780,000, 1982: 624,000, 1990: about 600,000), certain specialised branches, especially those concerned with microelectronics, computers and new information technology have continued to expand to a marked degree. Although some firms have elected to move to other parts of the country most of the electronic industry, with 40 per cent of its work force, is still concentrated in the south-east region where most of the research establishments are situated. It is in that region, too, with the advantages of being with easy reach of London and with access to a large force of highly-qualified workers, that a number of small private and high-tech firms have set up (around Cambridge, for example), while mass production firms are tending to move to outlying development areas.

Electrical and electronic industries

As recently as 60 years ago British textiles were famous and sought after throughout the world. Today the textile industry is but a fraction of its former size and importance, with high rates of unemployment, a serious population drain and increasing socio-economic problems. Just after the First World War the textile industry provided 30 per cent of the country's total exports and employed a quarter of all industrial workers (about 1.32 million). Since then – with the exception of a brief upturn after the Second World War – their number has fallen radically, and by 1990 only some 220,000 were employed in the industry. Some of the

Textile industry

Slate quarrying near Blaenau

"Big Pit", former iron foundry, South Wales

specific reasons for this downturn include a failure to adapt quickly enough to a changing market, a delay in converting from work-intensive to capital-intensive methods, and outdated equipment and factories. In areas such as East Lancashire and West Yorkshire only a small minority of those who lost their jobs were able to find employment in new industries, many of the latter being far away in the Midlands and southern England. The modern British textile industry is really little more than a relic of the old industrial era, an example of the apparently unstoppable "de-industrialisation process" now taking place in Britain.

Mining and Energy

Metallic ores have been mined in Britain since time immemorial, including iron-ore in central England and tin in Cornwall, for example; in latter years, however, it has been found unprofitable and most mines have closed. Boring and mining for energy supplies, on the other hand, has gained in importance. The United Kingdom has greater sources of energy (crude oil, natural gas, coal) than any other member of the European Union and as a result of continued North Sea oil production it has become self-sufficient energy-wise to a considerable extent since 1980 and is also able to export.

Coal

The decline in the importance of the British coal industry is due mainly to the high production costs incurred by the predominantly small mining firms, their low standards of mechanisation and rationalisation, increasingly cheap imports from the United States, South Africa and Australia, electrification, the anti-pollution laws and the increasing use of other energy sources in place of coal. After an expansion period in the 1950s, recession and loss of markets to imported energy suppliers in the 1960s and renewed investment programmes under the Labour government following the oil-price shock of 1973–74, a free energy market was encouraged after the Conservatives came to power. This tended to concentrate on a few high-tech "super-pits" in the central coalfields in Yorkshire, East Midlands and South Midlands, which met more than a quarter of the demand – at the end of the 1980s the newly opened mining complex at Selby was producing 10 million tonnes a year, and in 1990 a total of 98 million tonnes was mined in Britain – while more and more of the less productive coal-fields with smaller mines (Scotland, North East, Western and South Wales) were forced to close. When the coal-mines were nationalised in 1947 there were still 718,000 miners employed in 958 pits; after the miners' strike in 1985 there were only 160 mines left with 100,000 men; in 1992 there were only 50 mines still operating with less than 50,000 miners. North Nottinghamshire has for years been the most profitable field owned by the National Coal Board (NCB). With more and more power stations now deciding to rely on natural gas, however, the government has elected to close even more pits, much to the dismay of the mining communities, and it is estimated that by the year 2000 there may be less than ten pits still operating.

National coal deposits are estimated at 190 billion tonnes, of which about 45 billion tonnes are currently considered to be accessible.

Oil and natural gas

The oil industry is one of the few branches of industry which is increasing production and taking on more workers. Scotland is profiting most from North Sea oil; as early as 1983 more than 100,000 Scottish workers were employed in "oil activities", equal to 5–6 per cent of the total work force, most of which were concentrated in the Grampian region of north Scotland and at Aberdeen, the "oil capital of the north". In 1990 93.5 million tonnes of crude oil were extracted from the British continental shelf (UKCS). The largest offshore storage sites are Brent and Forties, and total stocks are shown to be some 800 million tonnes. Overall, however, there appears to be a slowing down in oil production and boring activities have been moved further north. Latest developments are linked to the maintenance and repair depots at Cromarty Firth north of Inverness. On-shore production, concentrated at Wyth Farm in Dorset, is of far less

Eggborough Power Station (North Humberside)

importance. The United Kingdom's natural gas needs can be met almost entirely from local off-shore fields, where in 1990 the major fields of Leman, Frogg (UK), Indefatigable, Hewett, Viking and West Sole produced 1677 billion cu.ft of natural gas.

In 1989 energy production amounted to approx. 312 billion kilowatt-hours, 80 per cent of which came from conventional power stations and some 18 per cent from nuclear stations. Drax power station in North Yorkshire was until 1986 the largest coal-powered station in Europe (4000 megawatts). The gigantic pumped-storage hydro-electric power station at Dinorwig in Gwynedd, North Wales, was completed in 1984 with a production of 1680 megawatts. A nuclear power station at Calder Hall in Cumbria was producing electricity as long ago as 1956. The first generation of nine Magnox power stations was followed in 1976 onwards by five modern gas-cooled reactors with capacities of at least 1200 megawatts. By 1991 there were 31 nuclear power stations in operation. Like other countries, Britain has not yet solved the problems associated with the re-cycling and disposal of nuclear materials, and the recycling plant at Sellafield is constantly open to criticism.

Various research stations are studying the feasibility of alternative sources of energy such as wind, tides and geothermal energy.

Energy production

British agriculture is known for its efficiency and productivity. Although it employed only 1.3 of the working population in 1990 it produced almost two-thirds of the country's food needs, and contributes around 2 per cent per annum to the gross domestic product. Over three-quarters of the total area of Britain, equal to some 46 million acres, is used for agriculture, about twice as much as in the former West Germany. This is largely accounted for by the fact that the area of forest and woodland is comparatively small (only 5.2 million acres) and meets only 10 per cent of Britain's timber requirements. In 1990 there were about 230,000 farms averaging 175 acres, 13 per cent of which were large farms accounting for a half of the total production; however, the valuable contribution made by small farmers in Wales and Northern Ireland should not be underestimated.

Agricultural and Fishing

As a result of the general trend towards specialisation the number of mixed farms has reduced considerably, and almost 60 per cent of farms in full production have specialised in milk and livestock. Most sheep and cattle are kept on large meadows in the mountains and moors of

Livestock

Scotland, Wales, Northern Ireland and north and south-west England. Many well-known breeds, such as Hereford and Jersey cattle and Large White pigs, have been bred in Britain. Farmers and the meat industry are now anxiously awaiting the end of the BSE affair which led to a European import ban on British beef in 1996. So far neither the problem of slaughtering affected herds nor the question of compensation payments by the Government has been resolved, and there is still debate about what is the actual cause of the disease.

Arable farming and horticulture

Most of those farms which specialise in arable farming, pigs, poultry and horticulture are to be found in eastern and central-southern England and in the east of Scotland. Large quantities of potatoes and other vegetables are grown in the Fens, in the alluvial regions along the Thames and in south Lancashire. South-west Wales, Kent and south-west England are famous for their early potatoes, whereas Scotland and Northern Ireland produce seed potatoes of high quality. Increased corn production has meant that at present 25 per cent of the wheat and barley crop is exported. Sugar made from locally-grown sugar-beet meets 50 per cent of the country's total demand. Horticulture is practised in most parts of the country; in 1990 some 625,000 acres of land were cultivated in this way, 40 per cent of the production being vegetables grown in fields. Tomatoes, cucumbers, lettuces, flowers, etc., are raised in greenhouses.

The British government is anxious to promote and expand the exporting of agricultural products to the major markets in Western Europe, North America and the Near East. Great Britain is also a major exporter of agricultural machinery.

Fishing

The United Kingdom is one of Europe's major fishing countries. The fishing industry contributes some two-thirds of the country's needs and constitutes an important source of employment and income in many ports, such as Fleetwood, Grimsby and Lowesto ft, for example. About 75 per cent of the total catch (920,000 tonnes in 1988) comes from coastal waters. In recent years a fall in profits has made it necessary for deep-sea fleets to reduce the number of their boats (about 200). Above all, extension of the territorial fishing limits enjoyed by other countries together with reduced stocks caused by over-fishing and sea pollution have had a serious adverse effect on British fishermen.

Service Sector

In 1991 the expanding service sector accounted for nearly 70 per cent of all jobs and contributed about two-thirds of the gross national product. The highest rates of growth were seen in the sectors dealing with commerce, finance, education and health. "Central Business Direct" of London dealt worldwide with the largest groups of banks (accounting for 255 of the total international credit volume) and insurance companies, as well as an unprecedented portfolio of stocks and shares. After Zurich, London is Europe's major centre for world dealings in gold and also the leading currency market.

Tourism

Since the 1970s in particular tourism has developed into a major industry in Britain, and both central and local governments are doing all in their power to encourage further growth. Many regions have installed computerised booking systems and substantially improved tourist advice and service facilities. In 1996 over 20 million overseas tourists visited Britain, of whom 3.3 million came from the USA and about 3 million from Germany. In addition to London and other sights many tourists – both from Britain and abroad – are attracted to the beautiful national parks and mountainous regions such as Snowdonia. the Lake District and the Scottish Highlands. While many Britons also favour seaside resorts, for example Blackpool, Brighton and Torquay/Torbay, a large proportion of overseas tourists restrict

Floors Castle – a fairytale castle belonging to the Duke of Roxburgh (Borders Region)

themselves to London, which is also a favourite place for short breaks.

Britain's main environmental problems stem from the intensive industrialisation programmes of the past, which have left their legacy in the form of contaminated ground around old factories and sites, poisonous slagheaps or natural water systems despoiled as the result of mines dug without any concern for the surrounding countryside, all signs of widespread environmental damage in these old industrial regions. The marked "de-industrialisation" following the Second World War led to a considerable improvement in the environmental situation, while the widespread conversion of old forms of coal-fired heating to oil or gas did much to improve the air quality in towns and cities and the notorious "smog" became largely a thing of the past. However, as in most other European countries, the major environmental problems of today are those arising from poisonous traffic exhaust fumes, contamination of water through inadequate filtering and pollution of the soil by the excessive and irresponsible use of fertilisers and pesticides. Another problem, the full effects of which are not yet known, is that of the pollution of the North Sea caused by the entry of harmful substances and waste from oil extraction.

Environment

The economic future of Britain is above all inextricably linked with the country's ties with the European Union. Although in many quarters there remains considerable scepticism as to the wisdom of further integration with Europe under the terms of the Maastricht Treaty, the majority of the population appears in favour of at least some form of economic union in Europe. A pressing problem, and one to which an answer must soon be found, is that of the economic disparities existing between various regions of the country, something which could seriously endanger the solidarity of Britain if allowed to remain unsolved.

Future Prospects

Transport

Road traffic

Great Britain has some of the heaviest road traffic anywhere in the world. In 1988 21.2 million vehicles were licensed for use on the country's 230,000 miles of roads, which include 1900 miles of motorway. The final sections of the M25, the great motorway encircling London, were opened in 1986. The current motorway programme gives priority to providing links between the major industrial areas and the coast.

Railway

The United Kingdom gave birth to the railways back in 1825, when the first steam railway line in the world, the Stockton and Darlington Railway, was opened.

On average, British railways carry some 650 million passengers a year. The construction of main lines for express trains has meant that travel times on the InterCity routes have been reduced considerably. In addition faster trains have been brought into service. Electrification of the railway network, which began in 1974 with the main London–Glasgow line, is being continued. On the other hand, many of the smaller lines in rural areas have been closed down since the Second World War and passengers now travel largely by bus – although there is a move to re-establish rural rail links as part of an integrated transport policy.

Goods trains now play a comparatively minor role, having largely been replaced by long-distance lorries.

Eurotunnel

Over the last century there have been many suggestions put forward for some form of "fixed link" across the English Channel, including tunnels, bridges, and combinations of the two. Early in 1986 Britain and France signed an agreement for the construction of a "double-barrelled" tunnel under the Channel. The largest building project in Europe, it will be 31 miles long and cost an estimated £10 billion. The two halves of the tunnel met in mid-Channel in 1991, and it is expected to open in 1994, in spite of accusations of delaying tactics on the part of the construction companies. After being linked up to the European high-speed network the travel time from London to Paris is expected to be reduced from 5½ to 2¼ hours, and that from London to Frankfurt from 10½ to 4¾ hours.

Over the Firth of Forth by rail or ferry

Black taxis and double-decker buses are typical of London

The United Kingdom is still one of the leading shipping nations, even though the British trading fleet has suffered considerably as a result of the recession and international competition (1975: 33.2 million g.r.t., 1991: 5.7 million g.r.t.). Almost all the 30 million or so passengers who embark from British ports each year travel to Europe or the Republic of Ireland. The largest British passenger lines are Stena-Sealink UK Ltd and P&O European Ferries. Hoverspeed Ltd. operates hovercraft between Dover and Calais, and these take only one third as long as conventional ships to make the crossing. Passenger and freight ferries travel regularly to the islands off the coast.

Britain has more than 300 harbours and ports, most of which are small ones of only local significance. About 450 million tonnes of freight are handled every year, more than a half being fuel, mainly oil and oil products.

Three radical changes during the last 20 years have affected the development of British ports. On the one hand, several traditional large ports, such as London, Liverpool and Manchester, lost a considerable proportion of their container freight to ports such as Dover and Felixstowe which had constructed special equipment to deal with it following the worldwide switch to container and "roll-on roll-off" traffic. A further important change occurred when Britain joined the Common Market in 1973; as more and more British trade switched to the continent of Europe, ports along the south and east coasts found themselves handling increased volumes of freight at the expense of those on the west coast. Finally, since the mid-1970s, special terminals for North Sea oil have been built at Hound Point on the Forth, on the Tees, in Flotta and at Sullom Voe, now one of the world's largest oil ports, with an annual turnover of 60 to 70 million tonnes. Three berths in Sullom Voe can service oil tankers of up to 350,000 gross tonnage, and a fourth is used for the export of crude oil, taking tankers of up to 26,500 register tons capacity.

Almost 60 per cent of the freight conveyed on inland waterways is found in the south-east, mainly on the Thames. Of the 2000 miles or so of navigable canals and rivers in Britain only 350 miles now serve as commercial waterways; most canals are now used only by holiday barges and house-boats.

Air travel

In 1990 about 90 million passengers flew from or to the United Kingdom and – value-wise – 20 per cent of all imports and exports went by air. Of those routes served by British airlines British Airways had a share of about 70 per cent, while the charter market was operated mainly by private firms.

In the early 1990s some 95 per cent of all international flights used the airports around London, while less than 5 per cent flew from Manchester, the second largest British airport outside the main south-east region.

London's Heathrow airport is one of the world's busiest (1989: 39.6 million passengers and 692,150 tonnes of freight). Gatwick is the second largest in the London area (1989: 21.2 million passengers), and since 1988 has had a new terminal, the North terminal, which will increase capacity to 25 million passengers a year. Other major airports include those at Birmingham, Manchester, Stansted and Glasgow.

History

Pre- and Early History (before 60,000–1 BC)

Palaeolithic period (Old Stone Age). The earliest found implements of flaked stone belong to the Acheulian culture, and the Swanscombe skull indicates that the Acheulian people belonged to the pre-sapiens group.

Before 60,000 BC

An important cultural phase is the Clactonian, named after a site at Clacton-on-Sea in Essex.

During the Mesolithic (Middle Stone Age) incomers from northern and western Europe reach the British Isles. After 3000 BC these immigrants belong to a Neolithic farming culture, known as the Windmill Hill culture after the site at Avebury, established on the chalk soils of southern England. These peoples, mostly of Iberian origin, develop the megalithic culture with its imposing chambered tombs, dolmens and standing stones.

About 8000 to 1800 BC

At the beginning of the 2nd millennium BC several waves of the Beaker peoples from the Low Countries begin to arrive in Britain. Recent research suggests that these peoples were responsible for the erection of the great stone circles of Stonehenge (c. 19th–15th c. BC) and the first mining of copper in England.

Beginning of the Bronze Age. After further waves of newcomers the Wessex culture is established, owing its wealth to the trade in tin as far afield as the Mediterranean region.

About 1660 BC

In the 14th c. BC the Urnfield culture develops. Accompanied by the growing of wheat and barley, it spreads from England into Scotland and Ireland.

From 900 BC onwards the first group of Celts, the Goidels (hence, perhaps, the term "Gaelic"), arrives in Britain.

900–600 BC

Beginning of the Iron Age, with a new influx of Celts from the northern coast of France. Another group of Celts, the Brythons ("Britons"), arrive about 300 BC These Celts live in tribes without any overall leaders; only the Druids assume a position of power.

500–300 BC

Belgian Celtic tribes from the Rhein-Maas region settle in southern England under the first organised state-like system.

About 75 BC

The Romans in Britain (55 BC–AD 412)

The Romans under Julius Caesar cross the Channel and land north-east of what is now Dover. The second invasion meets resistance from the Celts under Cassivelaunus and retreats.

55 and 54 BC

South-east England is conquered by four legions and becomes a Roman province.

AD 43

After repressing a rising by the Iceni, led by their Queen Boudica or Boadicea, the Romans advance westward and northward. In 78 Julius Agricola begins a campaign of conquest which ends with his victory at Mons Graupius in Scotland in 84, bringing the whole of England and part of Scotland (Caledonia) under Roman control.

61–84

History

After 122	Hadrian's Wall is built between Wallsend-on-Tyne and Maryport, West Cumbria, as a defence against the warlike peoples of the north.
286–291	The Roman general Carausius proclaims a Brito-Roman empire independent of Rome, but is defeated.
About 290	Defences are built against the Romans on the south-east coast of England
360–67	Raids by Picts and Scots from Ireland. Hadrian's Wall is breached but later rebuilt.
410	Individual towns are responsible for defending themselves against the Picts and Scots. Final withdrawal of the Roman legions from Britain.

Middle Ages – from the Anglo-Saxons to the House of York

Anglo-Saxon period (449–1066)	The Britons, unable to withstand Pictish attacks without Roman aid, appeal to the Angles, Saxons and Jutes for help; these land in Britain but turn against the Britons, some of whom withdraw to the mountainous west coast of Wales, while others emigrate to Armorica in Gaul (now Brittany).
	The Anglo-Saxon conquerors found seven kingdoms in England – Kent, Sussex, Essex, East Anglia, Wessex, Mercia and Northumbria.
516	Resistance to the invaders continues for more than a hundred years. About 516 a British general named Arthur is believed to have defeated them at a place called Mons Badonicus. This is the origin of the legend of King Arthur and the Knights of the Round Table.
596	Pope Gregory I sends the monk Augustine from Rome to convert the Anglo-Saxons. Christianity is also spread in the north by Celtic monks of the Iro-Scottish church, which is independent of Rome and is founded on Iona by St Columba in 563.
664	The Whitby Synod decides to adopt the ceremonies and customs of the Roman church.
About 800–39	Raids by the Norsemen. King Egbert of Wessex unites the Anglo-Saxons in a single kingdom.
871–99	King Alfred the Great defeats the Danes and in 885 signs a treaty under which England north-east of a line from London to Chester remains in Danish hands. "Shires" are formed, governed by "sheriffs" appointed by the king.
About 1000	During the reign of Ethelred the Unready (978–1016) there are renewed Danish raids. In order to raise money to appease the Danes he introduces "Danegeld", the first general tax to be levied by a medieval kingdom.
1016–42	England is a Danish kingdom under Canute (Knut) the Great and his sons.
1042–66	Edward the Confessor favours the Normans but is obliged to bend to Anglo-Saxon pressure.
1066	Following the death of Edward, Duke William of Normandy ("William the Conqueror") lands with his army and defeats King Harold at the Battle of Hastings on October 14th.

Representation of the Battle of Hastings on the Bayeaux Tapestry

William I the Conqueror (1066–87) establishes control over the whole of England by 1071, while simultaneously ruling Normandy. He introduces the harsh Norman feudal system. The Anglo-Saxon landowners are replaced by Norman barons, and Norman bishops are appointed. This ruling class speaks French and writes Latin, while Anglo-Saxon remains the language of the uneducated.

Norman Dynasty
(1066–1138)

Henry I establishes the Treasury, the first institution of its kind in Europe. After his son is drowned Henry names his daughter Matilda heiress to the throne and marries her to Geoffrey Plantagenet, Count of Anjou (the family name being derived from planta genista, the Latin name of the broom sprig worn in humility by Geoffrey when a pilgrim to the Holy Land). Following the death of Henry, Stephen Earl of Blois claims the vacant throne; on his death Henry, son of Matilda and Geoffrey, becomes king and founds a new dynasty.

1101–35

Henry II (1154–89) rules over England, Normandy, Brittany, Touraine, Poitou, Guyenne and Gascony, known as the "Angevin Empire". Under his rule common law begins to form.

House of Plantagenet
(1138–1399)

Henry comes into conflict with Thomas à Becket, archbishop of Canterbury, over the respective powers of church and state. Becket excommunicates the king's supporters, and is murdered in Canterbury Cathedral in 1170 by four of the king's knights.

1170

Henry's campaign against Ireland marks the beginning of the conquest of that country by England.

1171

Richard I, Coeur-de-Lion, takes a prominent part in the third Crusade and is taken prisoner on his way home from the Holy Land in 1192 and held by the German emperor Henry VI until 1194.

1189–99

Richard's successor King John (known as Lackland) loses Normandy, Anjou and all the French possessions of the English crown. The powerful English barons force him to sign the Magna Carta on June 15th 1215.

1199–1216

Henry III (1216–72) makes war on the rebellious barons led by Simon de Montfort. After winning some initial victories Montfort is defeated and killed by Henry's son Edward at the battle of Evesham.

1258–65

Edward I continues the reforms introduced by Simon de Montfort; in particular, he allows ordinary citizens and the lower clergy to enter the

1272–1307

new "Model Parliament" (1295). Lawyers are instructed in "Inns of Court". Edward completes the conquest of Wales; from 1301 the heir to the throne takes the title of Prince of Wales.

In the contest for the Scottish throne Edward supports John Balliol, who swears allegiance to him, but claims the throne himself when Balliol breaks his oath. The Scots rise up under William Wallace but are defeated in 1298. Robert the Bruce, Scottish king since 1306, pursues a kind of guerilla war.

1314–27

Edward II (1307–27) is defeated at Bannockburn in 1314 by the Scottish army led by Robert the Bruce. Scottish independence is thus secured. Edward is deposed and murdered.

1327–77

Edward III advances his claim to the French throne, thereby unleashing the Hundred Years' War (1339–1453). The English are victorious in a naval battle at Sluys and in the land battles of Crécy (1346) and Poitiers (1356), thanks to a novel strategy combining infantry and cavalry. At Poitiers the French king is taken prisoner by Edward's son, the Black Prince. After the death of the Black Prince all the English possessions in France except Calais and Gascony are lost.

The Lower House of Parliament breaks away from the Upper House, and the cry "no taxation without representation" is heard. The nobility re-adopts the English language in preference to French.

1349–50

The plague kills 1.5 million of England's population of 4 million.

1377–99

Richard II, son of the Black Prince, faces opposition to ecclesiastical authority from John Wycliffe and the Lollards. War against France continues without success.

1381

A poll tax imposed to finance the war leads to the Peasants' Revolt under their leaders Wat Tyler and John Ball. They enter London on June 13th, ransack the Tower and sack the homes of the King's ministers. Tyler is later killed and some 1500 perish on the gibbet.

1399

Henry Bolingbroke, Duke of Lancaster, leads an uprising against the king and takes him prisoner, thus bringing to an end a period of autocratic reign.

House of Lancaster (1399–1461)

Henry IV (Bolingbroke) establishes his claim to the throne and defeats a rising by the nobility.

Henry V (1413–22) renews the English claim to the French throne and conquers northern France.

Henry VI is only one year old when he becomes king. In 1431 he is crowned King of France in Paris. His regents are John of Bedford in France and the Duke of Gloucester in England. The French gradually regain their territory. In 1453 the Hundred Years' War comes to an end. England has lost all its French possessions except Calais.

1455–85

Outbreak of the Wars of the Roses, a conflict between the House of Lancaster (the red rose) and the House of York (the white rose). Henry VI has become mentally deranged, and Richard, Duke of York, Edward III's great-grandson, claims the throne in opposition to Margaret of Anjou, Henry's queen, and allies himself with the "King-maker", the Earl of Warwick. Although Richard is defeated and killed at Wakefield his son Edward defeats the Lancasters at Towton in 1461 and becomes king.

House of York (1461–85)

After a series of battles and temporary flight to Holland, Edward IV (1461–83) decisively defeats the Lancasters at Tewkesbury and establishes himself on the throne. Henry VI dies in the Tower.

1483

The 12 year-old boy Edward V is declared illegitimate and, with his younger brother, murdered in the Tower. The Duke of Gloucester ascends the throne as Richard III (1483–85).

Richard in turn is defeated at Bosworth by Henry Tudor, Earl of Richmond, a scion of the House of Lancaster. By marrying Elizabeth, daughter of Edward IV, he unites the Houses of Lancaster and York, thus bringing the Wars of the Roses to an end, and – as Henry VII (1485–1509) – founds the House of Tudor.   1485

From the Middle Ages to the Modern Era (1485–1714)

Henry VII is succeeded by the enigmatic Henry VIII (1509–47), who mar-   **House of Tudor**
ries six times.   (1485–1603)

Wales is annexed by order of Parliament.   1536

In order to legitimise his divorce from Catharine of Aragon Henry breaks   1542
with the Church of Rome and declares himself head of the Anglican
church. Dissolution of the monasteries follows. Henry adopts the title of
King of Ireland. The Calvinist Reformation, led by John Knox, spreads in
Scotland.

Edward VI supports the Reformed church.   1547–53

His successor, Mary I, marries Philip of Spain, restores Catholicism as   1553–58
the established faith and initiates a bloody persecution of Protestants.

Under Elizabeth I the reformed church is re-established. There is an econ-   1558–1603
omic upsurge and science and the arts flourish in the "Elizabethan Age".

Sir Francis Drake is the second man, after Magellan of Portugal, to cir-   1577–80
cumnavigate the globe.

Sir Walter Raleigh founds Virginia, the first British colony in North   1584
America.

The Scottish queen Mary Stuart, who fled to England in 1569 and dis-   1587
puted Elizabeth's right to the throne, is executed on a charge of high
treason.

Destruction of the Spanish Armada in the English Channel establishes   1588
English naval supremacy.

The foundation of the East India Company heralds the beginning of   1600
England's rise as a colonial power.

James I (James VI of Scotland), son of Mary Queen of Scots, unites   **House of Stuart**
England and Scotland under his rule (1603–25). Persecution of Puritans   (1603–1714)
and Roman catholics.

The "Gunpowder Plot", in which Guy Fawkes and his confederates try to   1605
blow up Parliament.

Charles I attempts to rule on his own against the will of Parliament.   1625–49

The "Long Parliament" (1640–53) accuses Charles' advisor, the Earl of   1641
Strafford, of usurpation and he is executed.
   The "Roundheads", supporting Parliament, and the "Cavaliers", faith-
ful to the king, are formed.

The failed attempt by Charles I to arrest five members of Parliament   1642–49 leads to the outbreak of the Civil War between the Roundheads and the Cavaliers. Roundhead leader Oliver Cromwell and his "Ironsides" defeat the Royalists at Marston Moor (1644) and Naseby (1645). The king flees to Scotland but is handed over to the Parliamentary forces, tried and executed in 1649.

1649–60	England is a Republic.
1649–50	Ireland is completely subjugated.
1651–54	The Navigation Act, which allows goods from and to England to be carried in English ships only, leads to naval warfare with the Netherlands.
1653–60	Cromwell becomes Lord Protector in 1653, but has difficulty in securing Parliamentary agreement to his policies. He is succeeded in 1658 by his son Richard, who soon withdraws, allowing Charles II to return to the throne with the help of General Monk.
1660–85	Charles II persecutes the Catholics. Many Puritans emigrate to America. War with Holland.
1662	The Royal Society is founded.
1666	The Great Fire of London destroys four-fifths of the city.
1673	The Test Act excludes all non-Anglicans from official positions.
1679	Habeas Corpus Act protects the freedom of the individual.
1685–88	James II loses the confidence of the people by his preference for Catholicism, is unable to prevent the landing of his nephew and son-in-law William of Orange. James flees to France unharmed – the "Glorious Revolution".
House of Orange and Stuart (1688–1714)	William III (1688–1702) rules Great Britain and Holland jointly with his wife Mary II, daughter of James II. The "Declaration of Rights" recognises the rights of Parliament. In the "Act of Settlement" (1701) the Stuarts give up their right of succession to the throne in favour of the House of Hannover. Queen Anne (1702–14), James II's younger daughter, completes the incorporation of Scotland into the United Kingdom by the Union of the English and Scottish Parliaments (1707). Victories by Marlborough in the War of the Spanish Succession. Gibraltar is captured.

Rise to a World Power (1714–1914)

House of Hannover (1714–1901)	Under George I (1714–27) Sir Robert Walpole, with the support of Parliament and the king, becomes the first "Prime Minister" in the modern sense of the word.
1727–60	In the reign of George II (1726–60) a further Stuart uprising in Scotland, led by "Bonnie Prince Charlie", is finally crushed at the battle of Culloden (1746).
1760–1820	Under George III Britain becomes the world's major colonial power.
After 1760	The Industrial Revolution begins, with factory production aided by the invention of the steam engine in 1769 and the mechanical weaving-loom in 1790.

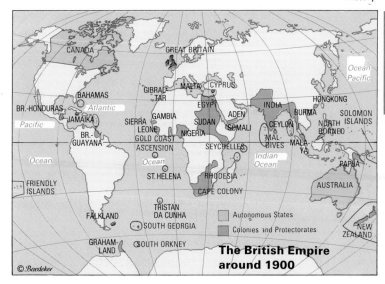

The British Empire
around 1900

Autonomous States

Colonies and Protectorates

© Baedeker

England is on the side of Prussia in the Seven Years' War. The Peace of Paris concludes the war, and Britain expands its overseas territories to include Canada, Louisiana, Florida and former French possessions in West Africa and southern India.	1756–63
Robert Clive and Warren Hastings colonise the East Indies.	1757–80
James Cook discovers Australia.	1770
Britain loses its American colonies in the War of American Independence. Florida is ceded back to Spain.	1775–83
Britain is one of the major opponents of the French Revolution. In 1798 Nelson defeats the French fleet at Aboukir, and his subsequent victory in the battle of the Nile enables Pitt the Younger to form the Second Coalition against France. In the Third Coalition against Napoleon Admiral Nelson defeats the Franco-Spanish fleet at the battle of Trafalgar, but is himself killed. In 1806 Napoleon sets up a commercial blockade of England, known as the Continental System. In 1808 French troops invade Spain and Portugal but are forced out by Wellington in 1814. At the battle of Waterloo on June 18th 1815 the combined British, Dutch and Prussian armies under Wellington and Blücher finally defeat the French.	1789–1815
Until the mid-19th c. Scotland is subjected to the "Highland Clearances", whereby almost two-thirds of the Highland crofters are forced to move to the coasts (or to emigrate) to work at processing seaweed for the lords of the manor and to provide room in the Highlands for their flocks of sheep.	About 1800–50
The British and Irish parliaments are joined.	1801
After serious social rioting freedom of the press and freedom of assembly are curtailed. In 1824 the formation of trades unions is once again permitted, but many workers emigrate.	1819–24

49

1829	Catholics are again allowed to hold state posts.

1837–1901 During the long "Victorian Age" under Queen Victoria, who married her cousin Prince Albert of Saxe-Coburg-Gotha in 1840, Britain enjoys a period of industrial and political expansion and great prosperity, becoming the most powerful nation in the world and making the transition to a modern state.

The British Empire expands to include Hong Kong, Burma, Cyprus, Egypt, the Sudan, East Africa, South Africa and Rhodesia. Parliamentary reforms extend the suffrage. Workers suffer under early capitalist conditions. Sir Robert Owen fights against the employment of children in factories, etc. and controlling legislation is passed. Slavery is abolished in the colonies.

In Parliament the two-party system evolves, Conservatives (Disraeli) versus Liberals (Gladstone).

1838 The Chartist Movement lists the needs and demands of the working class.

1845–46 Failure of the potato crop in Ireland leads to a million people dying from starvation, and a further million emigrate, many to the USA.

1858 Following the suppression of the Indian Mutiny the power of government in India passes from the East India Company to the British crown.

1869 Under the premiership of Benjamin Disraeli (1874–80) Britain obtains a majority shareholding in the Suez Canal.

1377 Queen Victoria assumes the title of "Empress of India".

1880 Boer uprising in South Africa.

1899–1902 In the Second Boer War the Boers are defeated and their Free States forfeited.

1901 After the death of Victoria her son Edward VII succeeds to the throne. Old-age pensions are introduced.

1904 "Entente Cordiale" between Britain and France in the event of war with Germany.

1906 The Labour Party is founded.

1912 The House of Lords loses its right of veto. Relations with Germany become tense as the German fleet grows in size.

1914 Third Home Rule Act for Ireland; Ulster declines to accept it.

Great Britain between 1914 and 1945

First World War (1914–18) George V on the throne from 1910. Germany enters neutral Belgium and Britain declares war on Germany on August 4th 1914. Battles in Flanders soon develop into positional warfare. A Liberal, Conservative and Labour coalition cabinet under Asquith deals with the business of government (1915).

General conscription introduced in 1916. Easter Uprising of April 24th 1916 in Dublin is put down with much bloodshed but signals the start of the movement for Irish independence. Both navies suffer heavily at the battle of Jutland.

For the first time in history tanks are used by the British army and prove a decisive weapon.

The royal family takes the name of Windsor.

The end of the war finds Britain economically exhausted. The colonies strive for independence, and the British Empire becomes the British Commonwealth of Nations. There are pressing social problems.

Establishment of the Irish Free State with the status of a dominion. The six counties of Ulster (Northern Ireland) remain part of the United Kingdom.   1921

First Labour cabinet under Ramsay Macdonald lasts from January to November.   1924

Indian independence movement led by Mahatma Gandhi.   1930

A parliamentary statute defines the status of the dominions forming part of the Commonwealth.

In the midst of a world economic crisis more than two million Britons are out of work.   1931

Anglo-German Fleet Agreement allows the German fleet to be armed.   1935

Death of King George V.

George V is succeeded by Edward VIII but – in the light of his unaccept-   1936–38
able decision to marry Mrs Simpson, an American divorcee – he abdi-
cates in favour of his brother, George VI. Neville Chamberlain's policy of
appeasement towards Nazi Germany fails.

Provoked by the German attack on Poland, Britain enters the war on   **Second World**
September 3rd 1939. Winston Churchill, First Lord of the Admiralty,   **War**
becomes Prime Minister at the head of an all-party government. He   (1939–45)
delivers his famous "blood, sweat and tears" speech.

The remainder of the British Expeditionary Force in France escapes back to England from Dunkirk.

The Battle of Britain rages in the skies above Britain until May 1941. German and British ships fight in the Atlantic. On May 14th Churchill and Roosevelt sign the Atlantic Charter.

Between 1942 and 1944 Bomber Command, led by Sir Arthur Harris, attacks targets in Germany.

In May 1943 the British Eighth Army under Montgomery defeats the German Afrikakorps, lands in Sicily and invades the southern toe of Italy in September.

On June 6th ("D-Day") allied troops land in Normandy. On June 13th 1944 the first of over 9000 V1 and V2 rockets are launched in retaliation against Britain. On May 4th 1945 the northern section of the German army surrenders at Montgomery's headquarters near Lüneburg.

Although on the winning side Britain has lost its international standing by the end of the war, and the USA and Russia take the important decisions.

After the Second World War

In the first post-war elections the Conservatives under Churchill are   1945
defeated by the Labour party led by Clement Attlee.

India becomes independent.   1947

The National Health Service comes into effect.   1948

Britain joins the Western European Union, the Council of Europe and   1949
NATO.

History

1952	Accession of Queen Elizabeth II on February 6th. First British atomic bomb is exploded in the South Pacific on October 3rd.
1956	Anglo-French invasion of Suez.
1957	A large number of the British colonies start to campaign for independence, especially in Africa; at the same time large numbers emigrate to Britain from the Commonwealth. The army is equipped with atomic weapons, and conscription is abolished.
1966	The Labour government of Harold Wilson begins the withdrawal (completed by 1971) from all British bases east of Suez.
1969	Outbreak of religious and social disturbances in Northern Ireland and the despatch of British troops there to enforce security.
1970	Conservative government led by Edward Heath. A new Industrial Relations Act fails to solve the country's industrial and economic problems.
1972	Stormont government abolished in Northern Ireland. National miners' strike; state of emergency declared.
1973	Britain enters the European Common Market.
1974	Labour party under Wilson wins election and lifts state of emergency, but unable to solve economic problems.
1975	Popular referendum confirms British membership of the Common Market.
1976	James Callaghan succeeds Harold Wilson as Prime Minister. "Social contract" between the government and the trade unions on wage and price limitation, in an attempt to improve the country's economic situation.
1979	After a Conservative election victory Margaret Thatcher becomes the first woman Prime Minister of Britain. Under her government many state concerns are privatised, social insurance benefits cut, trade union powers restricted, private investment simplified and private house-buying encouraged.

1981	Social Democrat Party (SDP) founded by former Labour ministers.
	    Prince Charles marries Lady Diana Spencer. Racial unrest in several towns and cities.
	    Ten die of starvation in IRA hunger strike in the Maze prison in Belfast.

1982	Britain defeats Argentina in war over the Falkland Islands.
	    Four million are unemployed.
	    IRA carries out the first acts of terrorism on the mainland of Britain.

1983	General election: Mrs Thatcher's Conservative government is returned with an absolute majority.
1984	Miners' strike, involving 130,000 workers, against the planned closure of 20 pits. Britain and China sign an agreement whereunder Hong Kong will be handed back to China in 1997.
1985	End of the miners' strike.

The Anglo-Irish "Hillsborough" Agreement is signed proposing involvement of the Dublin government in the affairs of Northern Ireland if the majority wish it.

The frontier between Spain and Gibraltar, closed since 1969, is re-opened.

Kings and Queens of England (before 1603) and the United Kingdom (since 1603)

Anglo-Saxon and Danish kings

Alfred the Great	871–899
Edward the Elder	899–924
Athelstan	924–939
Edmund	939–946
Edred	946–955
Edwy	955–959
Edgar	959–975
Edward the Martyr	975–978
Ethelred	978–1016
Edmund Ironside	1016
Knut (Canute)	1016–1035
Harold Harefoot	1035–1040
Harthaknut	1040–1042
Edward the Confessor	1042–1066
Harold II Godwinson	1066

Norman kings

William I, The Conqueror	1066–1087
William II	1087–1100
Henry I	1100–1135
Stephen	1135–1154

House of Anjou-Plantagenet

Henry II, Curtmantel	1154–1189
Richard I, Cœur-de-Lion	1189–1199
John Lackland	1199–1216
Henry III	1216–1272
Edward I	1272–1307
Edward II	1307–1327
Edward III	1327–1377
Richard II	1377–1399

House of Lancaster

Henry IV	1399–1413
Henry V	1413–1422
Henry VI	1422–1461

House of York

Edward IV	1461–1483
Edward V (never crowned)	1483
Richard III	1483–1485

House of Tudor

Henry VII	1485–1509
Henry VIII	1509–1547
Edward VI	1547–1553
Mary I	1553–1558
Elizabeth I	1558–1603

House of Stuart

James I	1603–1625
Charles I	1625–1649

Commonwealth and Protectorate (1649–1659)

Oliver Cromwell, Lord Protector	1653–1658
Richard Cromwell, Lord Protector	1658–1659

House of Stuart (restored)

Charles II	1660–1685
James II	1685–1688
William III and Mary II	1689–1702
Anne	1702–1714

House of Hannover

George I	1714–1727
George II	1727–1760
George III	1760–1820
George IV	1820–1830
William IV	1830–1837
Victoria	1837–1901

House of Saxe-Coburg

Edward VII	1901–1910

House of Windsor

George V	1910–1936
Edward VIII	1936
George VI	1936–1952
Elizabeth II	since 1952

1986 Great Britain and France sign the agreement (February) to build a twin rail tunnel between the two countries.

1987 Capsizing of the British Channel ferry "Herald of Free Enterprise" outside the Belgium port of Zeebrugge, with the loss of nearly 200 lives (March).
The Conservatives win the General Election for the third time (June).

1988 The oil rig "Piper Alpha" off the Scottish coast catches fire and explodes, with the loss of 167 lives.
In the "Lockerbie disaster", a jumbo jet explodes killing 259 passengers and 11 villagers.

1989   The Hillsborough disaster: at a football match in Sheffield too many people are allowed into the stadium, resulting in 95 being crushed to death.

1990   Introduction of the "poll tax" provokes massive protests.
In November Margaret Thatcher is forced to resign and is replaced by John Major.
The two sections of the Channel Tunnel meet (December 1st).
The government grants full citizenship to 50,000 Hong Kong Chinese.

1991   Gulf war against Iraq.

1992   Fourth consecutive Conservative victory at the April General Election, but with a reduced majority.
In September Britain leaves the European Monetary System.
The IRA lodges a series of attacks in London in the autumn.
In November there are mass protests against the government's pit closure plans.
The synod of the Church of England agrees to admit women to the priesthood.
At the end of November a part of Windsor Castle is burnt down.
On December 9th John Major formally announces to Parliament the separation of Prince Charles and Princess Diana.

1993   In early January the Liberian oil tanker "Braer" is stranded on the southern tip of the Shetland Islands, spilling many thousand tonnes of crude oil.

1994   Official opening (May) of the Channel Tunnel/Le Shuttle by Her Majesty Queen Elizabeth II and President François Mitterand.

1995   In February, British Prime Minister John Major and his Irish counterpart John Bruton publish a "framework document" for negotiations aimed at a settlement in Northern Ireland.

1996   In mid February the supertanker 'Sea Empress' runs aground off the coast of Wales and spills almost 40,000 tonnes of crude oil.
New bomb attacks by the IRA shatter hopes of lasting peace in Northern Ireland.
A European import ban is imposed on British beef with efforts throughout Europe to stem the spread of BSE.

1997   At the parliamentary elections in May the Labour party, now in the political centre, achieves the greatest election success of its history. The 43-year old solicitor Tony Blair becomes the new British prime minister.

Famous People

The following alphabetical list of names includes personalities who are associated with Great Britain through birth, residence, influence or death and have achieved international recognition.

Thomas Becket (or à Becket), son of a London merchant, was initially a favourite of Henry II, who appointed him Lord Chancellor in 1154 and Archbishop of Canterbury in 1162. Becket remained "the King's man" until he refused to allow the clergy to submit to the civil courts. Henry triumphed at the Council of Clarendon in 1164, at which he presented the bishops with a clear statement – the Constitutions of Clarendon – of the king's customary rights over the Church, but Becket subsequently defied him on this issue and was forced to forfeit his estates and flee to France. It was six years before he was able to return from exile, when he again proved a thorn in Henry's flesh. Henry's heated words "Of all the cowards who eat my bread, are there none to rid me of this turbulent priest?" were taken all too literally by four of his knights, Hugh de Moreville, Richard Brito, Reginald Fitz Urse and William de Tracy, who – anxious to win the king's favour – murdered the Archbishop in his own cathedral of Canterbury. Two days after his death there occurred the first of 700 miracles which led to his early canonisation in 1173 by Pope Alexander II. Becket's shrine in Canterbury cathedral soon became a place of pilgrimage and was described by Geoffrey Chaucer in his "Canterbury Tales", written c. 1385–87.

Thomas Becket
(1118–70)

The British-American physiologist and inventor Alexander Graham Bell is known as the "father of the telephone". Born in Edinburgh, he worked there as a teacher of deaf-mutes until he emigrated to Canada in 1870. In 1873 he was awarded a professorship at Boston University. While there Bell concentrated on experiments to convert sound vibrations into electrical current or voltage fluctuations which could be passed along cables and converted back into sound vibrations. The apparatus he developed in the course of these experiments proved to be the first functioning telephone, which he patented in 1876. Although it was later improved on by T. A. Edison with his carbon-microphone it still formed the basis of the telephone we know today. The Bell Telephone Company, founded in 1877, became the American Telephone and Telegraph Company (AT and T), now the largest private telephone company in the world.

Alexander
Graham Bell
(1847–1922)

Born in Lowestoft in Suffolk, Britten was one of the major British composers of the 20th c. A student of F. Bridge and J. Ireland, he was only 24 years old when he attracted attention with his "Orchestral Variations for Strings". Between 1939 and 1942 he lived in the United States, in 1947 became the co-founder of the English Opera Company and in 1948 of the famous Aldeburgh Festival. His best-known operas include "Peter Grimes" (1945) and "The Turn of the Screw" (1954), and are distinguished by their dramatic statements and lyrical atmosphere. In addition to his operas and orchestral and choral works, his song-cycles and ballads were also well received. For the dedication of the new Coventry Cathedral after the old had been destroyed by enemy bombing during the Second World War he composed the famous "War Requiem" in 1962. Among his fellow professionals Britten was highly respected as a conductor and pianist. In a period of innovative music, which included such people as Arnold Schönberg in Vienna who broke entirely new ground with his twelve-tone system of music, Britten too contributed to the development of a new musical language with mature tonal qualities

Edward Benjamin
Britten
(1913–76)

Famous People

Robert Burns

Charlie Chaplin

Sir Winston Churchill

and stylistic contrasts whilst retaining an overall power of expression. In 1976 he was made a life peer, being the first musician or composer to be elevated to the peerage.

Robert Burns (1759–96)

Apart from Sir Walter Scott, Robert Burns, born in Alloway in Ayrshire, was Scotland's greatest poet. The son of a poor peasant farmer, he taught himself the rudiments of the literary skills. Following the loss of one job after another together with a difficult love affair he was on the point of emigrating when, at the age of 27, his first published book of poems, "Poems chiefly in the Scottish dialect", made him famous almost overnight. This was followed by invitations to visit Edinburgh where he was royally received by renowned Scottish writers. Two years later he married his former lover Jean Armour and for a short time managed a farm and then worked as a tax collector. He declined the offer of a post as lecturer at Edinburgh and moved to Dumfries, where he wrote his magnificent "Melodies of Scotland". Inspired by old Scottish folk-songs and legends, Burns used mainly traditional, popular subjects as the themes of his verses, most of which were written in local dialect. He composed simple and original ballads, like that describing the daring ride of "Tam O'Shanter", wrote graphic lyrics about nature and love-songs full of feeling, such as the well-known "A red, red rose". Deep national pride found expression in "My heart's in the Highlands" and, of course, "Auld lang syne", now sung at the end of happy gatherings all over the world, and in his moving poem "The Cotter's Saturday Night".

Burns' sympathies with the ideals of the French Revolution and his keen satires against the puritanical despotism of the clergy led to criticism from his patrons. His fame spread abroad, however, and he received acclaim from such worthies as Goethe and Herder. While opening the doors to popular understanding and breathing fresh life into the ballad, it was his lyrics which helped prepare the way to British Romanticism.

Charles Spencer Chaplin (1889–1977)

With shoes and trousers too big for him, and jacket too tight, moustache, bowler hat and walking cane, the famous tramp portrayed by "Charlie" Chaplin as the little man suffering all the injustices the world can throw at him and yet retaining true feelings for his fellow man, produced a figure destined to be immortal in film history.

"Charlie" Chaplin was born in London the son of a poor variety artist and appeared on the stage when still only a child; during a tour of the United States in 1913 he was offered an engagement by the Keystone film company. In the film "The Tramp" in 1915 he first appeared in the role which was to make him world-famous during the 1920s and which he retained in such films as "The Child" and "The Gold Rush" produced by United Artists, a film company he founded in 1919 together with Mary Pickford, Douglas Fairbanks and D. W. Griffith. Chaplin continued his career when the "talkies" arrived and produced such films as "Modern Times" and above all his undisputed masterpiece "The Great Dictator". After the Second World War his political affiliations during the McCarthy era brought him before the Un-American Activities Committee; following a visit to Britain he was refused re-entry into the United States, and subsequently settled in Switzerland. In his later films he portrayed different characters, such as that of the polygamous wife-murderer in "Monsieur Verdoux". Although he gained fame in the United States he remained a British citizen all his life. Chaplin died in Vevey near Lake Geneva in 1977.

Historians continue to argue about the character of Oliver Cromwell. Some consider him a bigoted tyrant, others regard him as a great reformer and one of those who built Britain into a world power. His own religious fanaticism and puritanical way of life were to govern the way men lived for a number of years.

Oliver Cromwell
(1599–1658)

Born in Huntingdon as the son of a small landowner, he received a strict Puritan education and studied at Cambridge. In 1628 he entered Parliament where he rose to become leader of those who opposed the absolutist policies of King Charles I. He organised the Parliamentary Army and formed the "Ironsides", his famous troop of cavalry recruited almost entirely from Independents who had shown themselves faithful to him and who were mainly members of the unorthodox Congregationalist church. During the Civil War, with the help of these troops, he was victorious over the Royalist forces at the battles of Marston Moor in 1644 and Naseby in 1645. Following the execution of Charles I in 1649 the Commonwealth was declared and England became a Republic. At its head stood Cromwell, with scant regard to the wishes of Parliament, so that in many ways the Republic was like a military dictatorship. In 1650 he defeated the uprisings in Ireland and Scotland; in 1651 he passed the Navigation Acts and in a naval war lasting three years finally defeated the Dutch. The new constitution of 1653 made Cromwell Lord Protector. War with Spain 1655-60 resulted in the acquisition of Jamaica. In 1657 Parliament offered Cromwell the title of King but he refused and remained Lord Protector, while nominating his own House of Lords. On his death in 1658 he was succeeded by his son Richard.

Winston Leonard Spencer Churchill was without doubt the ruling figure in British politics during the first half of the 20th c. Having had a seat in Parliament since 1900, he was First Lord of the Admiralty between 1911 and 1915, when he was mainly responsible for arming the British fleet against the expansionist aims of the German Kaiser. Between 1917 and 1929 he held a large number of different Cabinet posts, including that of Minister of War between 1918 and 1921, and finally became Chancellor of the Exchequer. In the 1930s his political star began to wane somewhat, but at the outbreak of the Second World War he was the man who immediately came to mind and he was made First Lord of the Admiralty. In 1940, as Prime Minister of an all-party government, Churchill at last entered No. 10 Downing Street.

Sir Winston
Churchill
(1874–1965)

He and President Roosevelt drew up the Atlantic Charter in 1941, and at the conferences of the "Big Three" (USA, USSR and Great Britain) it was he who put forward the guidelines governing the order of things in post-war Europe. Although he was successful in leading his country to victory, a lack of a satisfactory economic and financial policy resulted in the Conservative government being defeated in the 1945 General Election. However, he did return once more as Prime Minister between 1951 and 1955. Highly regarded as a painter, Churchill also received the

Nobel Prize for Literature in 1953 for his account of the Second World War. It was through his prediction that an "Iron Curtain" would divide Europe from north to south that he left his mark on the period of the Cold War.

Charles Robert Darwin (1809–82)

Born in The Mount near Shrewsbury, Darwin was the founder of the modern theory of evolution. At the request of his father he began to study medicine at Edinburgh University, but in 1827 changed over to theological studies which he completed at Cambridge in 1831. During this time he was already becoming interested in natural science, especially geological and biological research. On the recommendation of his professor of botany, J. S. Henslow, Darwin obtained a post as naturalist on board HMS "Beagle" on a five-year voyage which took him to Cape Verde Islands, the east and west coasts of South America and thence by way of the Galapagos Islands and Tahiti to New Zealand and finally back to England via Mauritius and Cape Town. He then initially settled in Cambridge and later in London, before moving to his Down House estate in 1842.

Inspired by his voyage and in particular by the singular and bizarre fauna of the Galapagos Islands, Darwin settled down to an intensive study of the origin of the species. He was able to describe a vast number of birds, plants and insects hitherto unknown, and supported Lyell's theory of actualism in the field of geology, namely, that the past can be explained through that which is observable in the present. After leaving his theory for eight years Darwin was forced to go into print with his ideas after receiving a memoir from A. R. Wallace embodying similar theories, and his "On the Origin of Species by Means of Natural Selection or the Preservation of Favoured Races in the Struggle for Life", published in 1859 some twenty years after he had first conceived his ideas, was presented to the Linnean Society whose members lent it their full support. Darwin's theories, which seek to explain the evolutionary process through the principles of natural and sexual selection, remain at the centre of much biological research to this day and form the basis of modern genetics. His findings also had a considerable influence on the political and intellectual developments of his time.

Charles Dickens (1812–70)

Born in Portsea, Hampshire. the son of a clerk, Charles Dickens was always acutely aware of the social and economic abysses of Victorian society – he had experienced them at first hand in the port area of London when his father was imprisoned for debt in 1824 as a result of which he was able to receive little in the way of formal education. Dickens worked his way up from being a lawyer's clerk to parliamentary stenographer, journalist and finally to becoming the most successful writer of his time as well as the editor of the "Daily News". He became famous in 1837 for his "Pickwick Papers", followed by such novels as "Oliver Twist", "Nicholas Nickleby" and "David Copperfield". London is always the scene in which the needs of the poor and the injustices they suffer are portrayed in such detail, yet often with brilliant touches of humour. His books are still read with much pleasure by many throughout the world. He is buried in Westminster Abbey in London.

Benjamin Disraeli (1804–81)

Benjamin Disraeli, Earl of Beaconsfield, was the son of an Italo-Jewish family living in London. In a fit of pique following a dispute with the local authorities his father had young Benjamin and his sisters baptised in 1817, something that was to prove very important in Disraeli's political career, because until 1858 Jews were not allowed to sit in Parliament. After a period in a solicitor's office Disraeli wrote a number of novels, including "Vivian Grey" 1826 and "Contarini Fleming" 1832, dealing with the social problems of the day, while pursuing an extravagant and debt-ridden lifestyle. He was able to pay off his debts following his marriage to a rich widow in 1839.

On finally entering Parliament as a Conservative in 1837 after four unsuccessful attempts he was laughed at as a dandy, but soon made a name for himself by his opposition to the ideals of the Conservative prime minister Robert Peel, and when the latter fell from power Disraeli became the leader of the opposition party in the House of Commons. He was Chancellor of the Exchequer and leader of the Commons in the short-lived minority governments led by Lord Derby between 1852 and 1868. In 1867 he attempted to obtain credit for widening the franchise by introducing the Reform Bill. Following Derby's retirement in 1868 Disraeli was made Prime Minister, but his party was defeated by the Liberals in the subsequent General Election. During six years in opposition he ruled his party with an iron glove, published another novel, "Lothair" 1870, and established Conservative Central Office, the prototype of modern party organisation.

In 1874 the Conservatives won the General Election and Disraeli's great hour was at hand; until 1880 he dominated British politics. He enjoyed the close friendship and confidence of Queen Victoria, and the outstanding feature of the government's policy was its imperialism.

Undoubtedly the most famous naval hero of the Elizabethan Age was the English admiral Sir Francis Drake, who was born in Crowndale near Plymouth in Devon. When quite young he went to sea on a coaster, in 1565 joined a voyage to Guinea and two years later was given his first command, of the "Judith". In the years that followed he enriched himself as a pirate against Spanish interests in the Caribbean. In 1577 he sailed in the "Pelican" with four other ships, was the first to round Cape Horn and followed the coasts of Chile and Peru up to the northern end of California, where Drake Bay north of San Francisco still bears his name. From there he sailed west across the Pacific, his ship having now been renamed the "Golden Hind", and in 1579 landed on the island of Ternate. Passing Java and the Cape of Good Hope in June 1580 he finally arrived back in England in September 1580, after an absence of almost three years. The Queen knighted him on the deck of the "Golden Hind" in April 1581, and he became mayor of Plymouth in that same year.

When Britain went to war against Spain Sir Francis Drake was given command of a fleet of twenty ships in 1585; between then and the following year he carried out a number of highly successful raids on Spanish ships and possessions in the Cape Verde Islands and the West Indies. In a raid on Cadiz in 1587 he burned 10,000 tons of shipping. In 1588 Drake served as a vice-admiral under Lord Howard of Effingham in the "Revenge" when the Spanish armada was decisively beaten in the battle in the English Channel. In January 1596 he died of dysentery off the town of Portobello, Panama.

The long reign of Elizabeth, daughter of Henry VIII and his second wife Anne Boleyn, became known as the "Elizabethan Age". It was during this era that England established herself as a world power, trade prospered and the arts and literature, symbolised by the name of Shakespeare, flourished. Elizabeth became Queen in 1558 following the death of her sister Mary. Through the Acts of Supremacy and Uniformity of 1559 the Anglican church was re-established with Elizabeth as "supreme governor". When the Scottish Queen Mary Stuart laid claim to the throne fresh conflict broke out between Catholics and Protestants, culminating in Elizabeth being ex-communicated by Pope Pius V in 1570. This led to even harsher treatment of the Catholics.

The conflict with Spain dominated foreign policy. England supported French intervention in the Netherlands and Sir Francis Drake was permitted to indulge in a privateering war against Spain, ending with the decisive victory over the Spanish armada in the English Channel in 1588. Spain was no longer a rival on the high seas, and England began to develop as a world power. In honour of The Virgin Queen, as the unmar-

Sir Francis Drake
(c. 1540/43–96)

Elizabeth I
(1533–1603)

Famous People

Charles Dickens

Elizabeth I

Henry VIII

ried Elizabeth became known, Sir Walter Raleigh named his acquisitions in North America "Virginia". On her deathbed she named James VI of Scotland, the son of her rival Mary Stuart whom she had had executed in 1587, as her successor to the English throne.

Sir Alexander
Fleming
(1881–1955)

In 1928 the Scottish bacteriologist Alexander Fleming of St Mary's Medical School at London University made a remarkable discovery. He found an unusual mould growing on a neglected culture dish, which he isolated and grew into a pure culture; this led to the discovery of penicillin, the most important advance ever made in the fight against infection. Fleming received the Nobel Prize for medicine in 1945 for his discovery.

Henry VIII
(1491–1547)

Henry VIII of the House of Tudor reigned over England from 1509 to 1547. He has become celebrated in history as the founder of the Anglican Church, and also because of his dissipated life-style and his six wives. Born in Greenwich, Henry was being prepared to take over the throne as early as 1502. Educated in the humanities and theology, he was extremely polite, a very good dancer and hunter and, outwardly at least, a most imposing figure. Thanks largely to the efforts of his chancellor Wolsey, the early years of his reign appeared to live up to expectations. In recognition of a theological treatise in Latin which he (with the assistance of Thomas More) compiled criticising Luther and defending the seven sacraments of the Church of Rome, Pope Leo X bestowed upon him the title of "Defender of the faith". When his marriage to Catharine of Aragon failed to provide him with the son he craved Henry wished to divorce her, but the Pope refused permission. The resultant dispute ended with Henry breaking with papal authority and declaring himself head of the Anglican church in England. Henry then married Anne Boleyn, who was subsequently executed in 1536, ostensibly for adultery, followed by Jane Seymour (died 1537), Anne of Cleves (quickly divorced), Catherine Howard (beheaded 1542) and finally Catherine Parr, who survived him. In the latter years of his life, after he had executed his chancellors Thomas More and Thomas Cromwell, he became a lonely man, filled with distrust of all around him and persecuting Catholics and Protestants alike.

Alfred Hitchcock
(1899–1980)

Alfred Hitchcock was born in London and became a US citizen in 1955. He was master of the suspense thriller, not in the conventional sense of "who dunnit?" but rather by arousing tension within the audience as they watch normal people on the screen becoming involved in completely irrational and threatening situations which leave the audience equally unsuspecting (for example, in "The Invisible Man" or "Rear Window") or, conversely, lets the audience know more than the actor does (in "Psycho", for instance), with the effect further enhanced by excellent montage and camera work.

Educated in a Jewish seminary and a student of aesthetics and engineering, Hitchcock is today recognised as one of the greatest film producers of all time. His first two films were made in Munich in 1926, and his "Blackmail" 1929 was the first successful British talking film. In the 1930s he worked in England ("Thirty-nine Steps" and "The Lady Vanishes") and from the 1940s onwards in the USA. In such films as "Rebecca", "Dial M for Murder", "The Birds", "Strangers on a Train" and "Vertigo" many of the major Hollywood stars worked for him.

William Hogarth trained in London as a silversmith, while in his spare time he taught himself to draw, paint and engrave, skills which he later honed to perfection as a student of James Thornhill. His art was based on the observation of life as it happened. His moralising genre scenes, many full of irony, made him one of the harshest critics of his day and the true founder of English caricature. He established St Martin's Lane Academy, the leading art school of the time, and also made a name for himself as a writer of books on art, such as "The Analysis of Beauty" 1753. In 1757 he was made court painter.

William Hogarth
(1697–1764)

The great African explorer David Livingstone was born in Blantyre in Scotland. Having decided to become a missionary in China he went to Glasgow in 1834 where he spent two years studying Greek, theology and medicine. However, the China project fell through and in 1841 he went to South Africa as a missionary instead. His zeal and thirst for exploration and knowledge led him to go further into darkest Africa than any white man had gone before, and took him as far as Lake Ngami in what is now Botswana. His second expedition was to the Zambesi and thence north-west as far as Luanda in 1854. In the following two years he was the first European to traverse the African continent from the Atlantic in the west to the Indian Ocean in the east. In November 1855 he discovered the mighty falls on the Zambesi river which he named Victoria Falls in honour of Queen Victoria. On returning home he gave lectures which proved immensely popular.

David Livingstone
(1813–73)

On his next expedition along the Zambesi between 1858 and 1864 he discovered Lake Nyassa (now Lake Malawi). Two years later he set out again determined to find the source of the Nile, and reached Lake Tanganyika in 1869. However, he was taken ill, his companions quarrelled and supplies ran out, and people in Britain feared he was dead. Henry Morton Stanley, correspondent on the New York Herald, was sent by his editor to find Livingstone, whom he finally tracked down on the shores of Lake Tanganyika on October 28th 1871 and is said to have greeted with the immortal words "Dr Livingstone, I presume?". They explored Lake Tanganyika together, following which Livingstone decided not to return to Britain. He died in Chitambo (Zambia) in 1873 and his body was taken back to London and buried in Westminster Abbey.

Mary Stuart, also known as Mary Queen of Scots, was the daughter of King James V of Scotland and his French wife Mary of Guise, and the grand-daughter of Henry VII of England. At the age of five she was sent to the French court and brought up like a French princess. When sixteen she married Francis II of France, but he died only two years later. She then returned to Protestant Scotland in 1561, to be regarded by many as a Catholic stranger. Her cousin Queen Elizabeth I of England regarded her as her most serious rival for the English throne, being next in line and favoured by those in England who regarded Elizabeth as an illegitimate offspring of Henry VIII. Mary suffered further as a result of her marriage with Henry Stuart, Earl of Darnley, a depraved

Mary Stuart
(1542–87)

good-for-nothing; early passion soon turned into hatred when Darnley murdered her advisor David Rizzio in 1566. Following the birth of her son James she tried to obtain a separation from her husband and found an ally in the Earl of Bothwell. In February 1567 the house in which Darnley was staying blew up, taking him with it. A mere three months later Mary married Bothwell, who was clearly the prime suspect in the explosion, and this put her beyond the pale as far as the Scottish nobility were concerned; the couple were separated and Mary was banished to an island in Loch Leven, from where she succeeded in fleeing to England in 1569. There – ostensibly for having been involved in Darnley's murder but in truth because she represented a danger to Elizabeth's throne – she was thrown into prison. She remained incarcerated for the next eighteen years of her life, and was the pawn in the struggle between Catholics and Protestants for the throne of England. The discovery in 1586 of a plot to assassinate Elizabeth provided an excuse for accusing Mary of high treason – she was sentenced to death and beheaded at Fotheringhay Castle in Northamptonshire.

Bernard Law
Montgomery
(1887–1976)

Bernard Law, 1st Viscount Montgomery of Alamein, received his military training at Sandhurst. In August 1942 he took command of the 8th Army, then barring the German advance on Cairo. "Monty" reorganised his troops, defeated Rommel at the battle of El Alamein in November 1942 and pushed the German army back into Tunisia, where it surrendered in May 1943. The 8th Army then took part in the invasion of Sicily and the advance through southern Italy. Under the supreme command of the US General Eisenhower Montgomery led the invasion of Normandy on June 6th 1944 and, now promoted to Field Marshal, marched his British and Canadian units through northern France, Belgium and the Netherlands as far as north Germany, where on Lüneberg Heath on May 4th 1945 he accepted the surrender of the German army. After the end of the war he was in command of the British Forces of Occupation in Germany until February 1946, when he was appointed Chief of the Imperial General Staff and then given a high military post in NATO. He retired from active service in 1958.

Henry Moore
(1898–1986)

Henry Moore, son of a miner from Castleford in Yorkshire, is regarded as one of the major sculptors of the 20th c., whose work reflected his revolutionary style. He was a student at the Royal College of Art in London, and then taught there from 1926 to 1932 before moving on to the Chelsea Art School where he tutored until 1939. As his individual style unfolded Moore was influenced as much by the art forms of primitive peoples as by his own close affiliation with nature. The main subjects of his mainly huge sculptures is Man himself, frequently portrayed as recumbent individual figures or in groups, especially those comprising mother and child. At first Moore worked in stone and wood, but mainly in bronze after 1945. During the Second World War he produced his "Shelter Drawings", coloured sketches depicting in a most vivid way the life experienced by the people of London as they sought shelter in the London Underground from enemy bombing. Moore also produced a number of etchings and lithographs, although sculpture was his forte. Moore's figures developed from a tense interplay of rhythmic and structural principles, with internal and external forms frequently intertwined. Abstract works stand next to natural sculptures, free-standing statues complement architectural work. His best-known works include the mystical royal couple in the Southern Uplands on the border between England and Scotland, his "Bronze Warrior" 1953–54 in front of the Kunsthalle in Mannheim (Germany), his "Reclining Figure" 1963–65 in stone outside the UNESCO building in Paris, that in bronze 1963–65 outside the Lincoln Art Center in New York, the "Large Two Forms" erected in 1966 in front of the Federal Chancellery In Bonn, and the large "Marble Arch" 1980 in Kensington Gardens in London. Collections of the artist's work can be seen in London's Tate Gallery.

Son of a London judge, More was educated at the best school in the capital – St Anthony's – before going on to study Greek, Latin, French, theology and music at Oxford and law at Lincoln's Inn. His many friends included Erasmus of Rotterdam, who visited him quite often. In December 1516 he published his novel "Utopia", in which the traveller Raphael Hythloday describes the ordered society that exists in this imaginary state. In total contrast to the England or France of the day, Utopia is a state in which reason and good sense prevail, all are equal and exploitation and envy play no part. The book was soon translated into several languages and is still regarded as the first Utopian novel.

As well as being a humanist writer More found favour at the court of Henry VIII and became the king's confidant. He wrote Henry's speeches and treatises and acted as intermediary between him and Wolsey, the Lord Chancellor. In 1523 More was elected speaker of the Lower House and in 1529 succeeded Wolsey as Lord Chancellor. His disagreement with Henry came about because – as a fervent Catholic – he would not agree to Henry's divorce from Catharine of Aragon and subsequent marriage to Anne Boleyn. In 1534 he refused to take the oath of supremacy acknowledging Henry VIII as head of the church; in April of that year he was thrown into the Tower of London and sentenced to death in July 1535. He was allowed five days in which to change his mind but still refused to take the oath and so was executed. More was canonised by Pope Pius XI in 1935.

Thomas More
(1477–1535)

Horatio Nelson, the sixth of eleven children of the vicar of the village of Burnham Thorpe in Norfolk, went to sea with his uncle following the death of his mother. At the age of twenty he was awarded his master's certificate and given command of a frigate in the War of American Independence. In the Revolutionary Wars against France he first distinguished himself in the bombardment of Toulon and in the battle of Cape St Vincent, and became a national hero, adding yet further to his reputation by successfully evacuating King Ferdinand IV from the besieged city of Naples. Under the command of Sir Hyde Parker he won a decisive victory over Denmark at the battle of Copenhagen in 1801. The Peace of Amiens brought a temporary lull in hostilities, but war broke out again in 1803. Nelson was given command of the Mediterranean fleet and blockaded Toulon for nearly two years. When a Franco-Spanish fleet assembled in the autumn of 1805 in preparation for the invasion of England Nelson took up position near Cape Trafalgar off the Atlantic coast of Andalusia. Before the battle he addressed his crews with the famous words "England expects that every man this day will do his duty". The French were defeated, but Nelson was fatally wounded on the deck of his flagship "Victory". In the annals of the British navy Horatio Nelson is noted for his abandonment of rigid tactical doctrines in favour of commanding on his own initiative. His love-life caused almost as much sensation as his naval exploits; although married, he made no secret of his passionate affection for Lady Emma Hamilton, the wife of the British consul in Naples. While dying after Trafalgar he dictated a letter of farewell to his mistress, which today can be seen in the Graphology Room of the British Library.

Horatio Nelson
(1758–1805)

Sir Isaac Newton is recognised as the father of physics as a theoretical discipline and – together with Galileo – of modern science. As a student and later as a professor at Cambridge he discovered the law of gravity in 1666 and in his major work "Philosophiae naturalis principia mathematica" (1686) he laid down the three standard laws of motion still in use today, those of inertia, action and interaction. He proved that these laws also apply to heavenly bodies and thus established the mechanics of bodies in orbit. As a mathematician he discovered the binomial theorem and differential and integral calculus. He also proved that white light is composed of all the colours of the spectrum. Newton was not just a scientist; he also represented Cambridge University in Parliament, was

Sir Isaac Newton
(1643–1727)

Famous People

Isaac Newton

Florence Nightingale

Sir Walter Scott

made Master of the Royal Mint in 1699 and President of the Royal Society in 1703.

Florence
Nightingale
(1820–1910)

Born in Florence (hence her Christian name), Florence Nightingale was recognised as something of an expert on public health when still only a young woman. When the Crimean War broke out in March 1854 she immediately took a team of nurses to Turkey and set up a field hospital at Scutari (now Üsküdar). Her main interests soon rested less on actual nursing and more on improving the standards of medical care in the British army, and she was made inspector general of all nurses in the military hospitals. The founding of the Army Medical School in 1857 was largely the result of her efforts. In 1860 she established the Nightingale School and Home for Nurses in London, the first of its kind in the world, thus setting a precedent for the training of young ladies in nursing as a profession. From then until her death Florence Nightingale lived in London and pursued her cause with great energy, in spite of being confined to bed although no physical illness could be diagnosed. She became blind in 1901.

Robert I the Bruce
(1274–1329)

Robert I, Robert the Bruce (also known as Robert VIII) is Scotland's national hero. After he had defeated Edward II at Bannockburn in 1314, the Treaty of Northampton 1328 finally recognised Scotland's independence from England and Robert as king.

His grandfather, Robert VI, had claimed the Scottish throne, but in 1209 the English king Edward I made John de Balliol ruler in order to maintain control of the country. In 1306 Bruce and his followers murdered Balliol's nephew and possible rival for the throne, John "the Red" Comyn, in the church at Dumfries. Shortly after that Bruce was crowned king of Scotland at Scone. The years that followed brought constant battles with the English garrisons until Bannockburn decided the issue once and for all. The rest of his reign was devoted to uniting his country and eliminating those who supported England.

Ernest Rutherford
(1871–1937)

Born in New Zealand, Ernest Rutherford was a pioneer of modern atomic physics. In 1897 he discovered alpha, beta and gamma rays. In 1903 this led him, together with F. Soddy, to publish the atomic decay theory, and in 1911 he and Niels Bohr produced a new model of atomic structure, now known as the Bohr model. He received the Nobel Prize for Chemistry in 1908, and this was followed by numerous other honours, including being made President of the Royal Society in 1925 and Baron Rutherford of Nelson in 1931.

Scott was born in Edinburgh to an old Scottish family. He became a lawyer like his father, and was later appointed sheriff of Selkirk and finally a judge in his home city. While studying law Scott became interested in German literature, and translated Bürger's "Leonore" and Goethe's "Götz von Berlichingen". In 1802 he produced his "Minstrelsy of the Scottish Border", a collection of embellished Anglo-Scottish ballads. Henceforth he combined the practice of literature with his legal profession, and wrote a number of novels in verse combining the descriptiveness of the Scottish ballad with the romance of medieval chivalry; these included "The Lay of the Last Minstrel" (1805), "Marmion" (1808) and "The Lady of the Lake" (1810). After that he turned to prose fiction and wrote, anonymously at first, 27 historical novels in rapid succession, the famous "Waverley Novels", which met with great success and were said to have influenced such great writers as Dumas, Hugo, Balzac, Hauff and Manzoni.

From the proceeds he was able to buy and refurbish the house at Abbotsford on the Tweed in 1812–14. Scott's romantic novels reflect over 500 years of Anglo-Scottish history between 1200 and 1700; while the author chose fictitious heroes for his tales they fought against backgrounds involving famous historical figures. Most of his novels are set in 17th and 18th c. Scotland ("The Heart of Midlothian" 1818, "The Legend of Montrose" 1819, "Chronicles of the Conangate" 1827, etc.), some in the England of the Crusades (for example, "Ivanhoe" 1820) or in the France of Louis XIV (such as "Quentin Durward" 1823). At the height of his success Scott was knighted in 1820. Six years later he found himself deeply in debt as a result of the bankruptcy of his publishing firm, and his last years were marked by frantic writing to pay off his creditors. He died from a heart attack in the autumn of 1832 and was buried in Dryburgh Abbey.

Sir Walter Scott
(1771–1831)

Born in Stratford-upon-Avon, the son of a wool-dealer and mayor, it is likely that he came to London as a member of a wandering troupe of players and stayed to work as a writer, actor and director. In 1597 he became part-owner of the Globe Theatre where he put on many of his plays, including "Henry IV". By this time he was already quite wealthy. In 1603 James I made him patron of the royal theatre group, henceforth to be known as "The Kings Men". About 1610 Shakespeare sold his share in the Globe Theatre and returned to Stratford.

As a writer he tried his hand at all three literary genres. Although his short epics are less well-known, the sonnets written in 1609 on the subjects of love and friendship displayed his great literary skills. It was as a dramatist and playwright, however, that he was unrivalled both during his lifetime and since. The 35 plays he is known to have written can be divided into historical plays (including "Richard II" and "Henry VI", for example), light comedies ("The Taming of the Shrew") and dark comedies "Troilus and Cressida"), the later fairytale romances ("The Tempest"), and finally the tragedies (the "Roman" plays and "Macbeth", "Hamlet", "Othello", etc.).

Shakespeare's characters and dramatic ideas are based largely on the powers of the imagination, as seen in the struggles between order and chaos, appearance and reality, personality and fate. For a number of years the authorship of his plays was in doubt, and it was not until the 18th c. that his work was fully researched; even today there exist sceptics who argue that at least some of his plays may be attributable to other writers.

William
Shakespeare
(1564–1616)

George Stephenson was born in Wylam in Northumberland and soon showed a keen interest in everything mechanical, a passion inherited from his father who was a mechanic operating a steam-driven engine in a coal-mine. Young George never went to school, because he had to go out to work at an early age; at 19 he was already in charge of a steam engine. It was not until later that he was able to attend evening classes, where he learned to read and write and to repair almost anything in order to earn some money. Finally he was made chief engineer at Killingworth coal mine.

George
Stephenson
(1781–1848)

Shakespeare   *George Stephenson*   *Queen Victoria*

A colleague in a neighbouring mine built a portable steam engine to carry coal from the mine, but it was bedevilled with faults and problems. Stephenson set out to improve on it, and built the "Blücher", the first locomotive, which could pull eight coal wagons. When proposals were put forward to build a horse-drawn railway from Stockton to Darlington, Stephenson persuaded the investors to substitute his engine for the horses, and so it was that on September 27th 1825 the first steam locomotive with 450 people on board travelled along 15 miles of track. Shortly after that he was commissioned to build a stretch of railway between Liverpool and Manchester. For this he constructed the "Rocket", the prototype for many future engines. From then onwards there was nothing standing in the way of the progress of the railways, and Stephenson found himself in great demand as advisor and builder. He was supported in his work by his nephew George Robert (1819–1905) and his son Robert (1803–59), who became famous for constructing railway bridges, such as the high-level bridge at Newcastle-upon-Tyne and the Menai and Conway tubular bridges in Wales.

Joseph Mallord
William Turner
(1775–1851)

William Turner's first works were landscape drawings and townscapes. After visiting the London Academy he found himself profoundly influenced by the works of the Classical landscape painters, such as Reynolds, Gainsborough and Claude Lorrain. He then travelled widely in Europe between 1802 and 1819 and his landscapes became increasingly Romantic in style. Much of his work dwelt on mythological themes, with the subject often transformed in scale and flooded with brilliant, hazy light, especially in the case of his water-colours. Many of his later works portrayed varying weather situations and visions bordering on Impressionism. Making good use of his deep knowledge of the theory of colour Turner developed a hitherto unknown degree of purity and power in his coloration. His later work is typified by visionary forms almost lost in strong, shimmering floods of light. His best-known works include "The Landing Stage at Calais" 1802, "The Death of Lord Nelson" 1808, "Rain, Steam and Speed" 1844 (one of the first railway paintings) and "Light, Colour, Shadow and Darkness" 1843 (depicting the Great Flood).

In 1987 the Clore Gallery extension to the Tate Gallery, London, was opened to display the collection of his works which he left to the nation.

Victoria
(1819–1901)

Like Elizabeth, Queen Victoria gave her name to a whole epoch. The only daughter of Edward, Duke of Kent, she came to the throne in 1837 in succession to her uncle William IV, and in 1840 married Prince Albert of Saxe-Coburg, a marriage which proved to be a very happy one until his premature death in 1861, after which she withdrew more and more from public life. During her long reign Britain developed into one of the world's major political and economic powers, She died at Osborne House on the Isle of Wight and was buried at Windsor.

The inventor James Watt came from Greenock on the Firth of Clyde. He studied precision engineering in Glasgow and London and from 1759 he devoted himself to developing the steam engine. He made Thomas Newcomen's steam engine vastly more efficient by cooling the used steam in a condenser separate from the main engine, and was awarded a patent for it in 1769. In partnership with Matthew Boulton Watt founded the Boulton and Watt factory near Birmingham in 1775 where, from the mid-1780s onwards, low-pressure rotary steam engines employing governors, centrifugal regulators, throttle valves, sun and planet gears and other devices of his invention were successfully built and proved vital to the Industrial Revolution.

James Watt
(1736–1819)

Born in Dublin, the son of the Earl of Mornington, the future Duke of Wellington won his first military honours in India, for which he was knighted. After returning to Europe he took part in the first expedition against Denmark. From 1808 to 1813 as commander in the Peninsular War he expelled the French from Portugal, for which he was given the title Viscount of Wellington, and also defeated them at the battle of Salamanca. In the battle of Victoria, June 1813, he was victorious over the army of Marshal Jourdan and forced the French to withdraw from Spain. This success gained him the title of Duke of Wellington. Following Napoleon's banishment to the island of Elba Wellington was appointed British consul in Paris, but when Napoleon escaped and reassumed power in 1815 Wellington returned to the battlefield; in the famous battle at Waterloo south of Brussels on June 18th 1815 the combined British, Dutch and Prussian armies finally defeated Napoleon once and for all. Wellington, nicknamed "The Iron Duke", became one of the most honoured men in Europe, and this played no small part in helping him to become Prime Minister in 1828. However, his political career was somewhat less successful than his military one had been; he became unpopular for his opposition to parliamentary reform and lack of opposition to Catholic emancipation, and his government fell in 1830. Wellington is buried next to Lord Nelson in St Paul's Cathedral in London.

Arthur Wellesley,
Duke of
Wellington
(1769–1852)

William was the illegitimate son of Duke Robert the Devil and his mistress Arlette; at first this made it difficult for him to be accepted by the French nobility, but having gained their confidence he then concentrated on events happening outside France. After succeeding his father as Duke of Normandy he claimed that his relative Edward the Confessor had bequeathed him the English throne and that the latter's brother-in-law, Harold of Wessex, had agreed to this. However, when Edward died in January 1066 Harold was made king. William promptly raised an army and landed near Hastings on the south coast of England in September 1066, where on October 13th he encountered the army led by Harold, who had previously defeated other pretenders to his throne, including his brother Tostig and Harold Hardrada of Norway. William defeated Harold at the Battle of Hastings, thus ending the rule of the Anglo-Saxons. On Christmas Day 1066 he was crowned king of England in Westminster Abbey. In the years that followed all the important positions in the land were filled by Normans and the feudal system established. From 1073 onwards, however, Harold spent little time in England and entrusted the affairs of government to Lanfranc, Archbishop of Canterbury. In 1086 the "Domesday Book" (*liber iuducarius Angliae*) was compiled, a detailed record of land and property belonging to the throne and now constituting one of the major sources of reference relating to English social and economic history in the Middle Ages.

William I, the
Conqueror
(c. 1028–87)

William was mainly concerned, however, with making secure the boundaries of Normandy; during the siege of Mantes in 1087 he was thrown from his horse and died later in Rouen. He is buried in Caen.

Art and Culture

History of Art

During the Palaeolithic period Britain was occupied by immigrants from western Europe, hunters and collectors of the Acheulian culture who made implements of carefully-flaked stone. The Clactonian, a Palaeolithic culture named after the site discovered in Essex, is also represented by skilfully made flint implements. Ivory and shell decoration from the Late Palaeolithic age were found in the "Red Lady" burial-cave in South Wales. Examples of the Middle Stone Age Maglemosian culture from Denmark have been discovered at Star Carr, Yorkshire. A farming culture entered Britain from western Europe during the Neolithic period in the 4th c. BC, from which numerous examples of stone and clay pots have been unearthed; these were made in the pottery centres in Cornwall, for example, and used in bartering. After 3000 BC "causeway camps" – collective camps built in circular form on high ground with a wall and moat – such as those at Henbury in Devon were constructed; similar earthworks found near Avebury (Windmill Hill) are considered by some experts as having been cattle compounds. Near the camps there were frequently long barrows, mounds of earth between 100 and 330 ft long and some 10 ft high used as collective graves for a kinship group or overlords.

Extensive excavations on the Orkney Islands have shown that the Megalithic culture developed there from *c.* 3000 BC; examples are the domed tomb of Maes Howe and Neolithic dwellings at Skara Brae. In south-west England the first large stone tombs were built some centuries later in the Cotswolds. In south-west Scotland we find the "horned cairn" type of tomb, named after the semi-circular forecourt from which runs a corridor with burial chambers leading from it. Particularly impressive is the megalithic tomb at West Kennet near Avebury, dating from *c.* 2500 BC, a four-roomed building with a stone gallery some 43 ft long and 8 ft high. As well as tombs, tall upright stones (menhirs) and stone circles (cromlechs) served an important cult purpose.

After *c.* 2200 BC several waves of the "Beaker people" (characterised by beaker-like cups, reddish in colour with patterned bands) also arrived in Britain from the Low Countries during the period of transition from the Neolithic to the Bronze Age. As well as many tombs with grave-goods made from precious metals (such as the Rillaton beaker in hammered gold, now in the British Museum), the Neolithic tradition remained in the form of imposing megalithic constructions, including the Henge monuments in southern England, numbers of standing stones set in avenues or circles, surrounded by ditches and earth-walls, probably used as solar temples. The best example is Stonehenge, built in several phases between 2000 and 1500 BC An extensive network of trade in tin and gold led to contact being made with other cultures as far afield as Eastern Europe and Mycenae and gave rise to the highly-developed Wessex culture in southern England. The Late Bronze Age Deverel-Rimbury, or Urnfield, culture developed in the 14th c. BC, accompanied by the growing of wheat and barley and the rearing of cattle. Finds of weapons and the remains of defensive walls point to warlike events at this time. In the 8th and 7th c. BC there was clearly more contact with North European and Scandinavian cultures.

About 600 BC the Iron Age began in Britain, influenced by the Hallstatt culture. Finds of weapons and walls again suggest that considerable

◀ *Brighton: the Royal Pavilion*

Roman Inscription of the 2nd c. AD, High Rochester

fighting took place. In Scotland the Abernathy culture, related to the Marne culture on the European mainland, came into existence, while in eastern and southern England independent groups displaying the La Tène culture were formed. Between the 4th and 1st c. BC immigrants from Europe introduced the Celtic culture; early Celtic handmade goods with interlaced designs were followed by scabbards and bronze mirrors with stylised circular ornamentation, as well as valuable neck and arm torques in gold (many such finds are displayed in the British Museum in London).

About 75 BC Belgians entered Britain, set up trading posts and gold exchanges and introduced to the island the first organised "municipal" system known as the Oppidum civilisation.

Roman Period

Although earlier attempts had been made in 54 BC, it was AD 43 before Roman troops finally landed in the south of England; by AD 57 they had brought the whole country, with the exception of northern Scotland, under their control. By the 3rd c. AD the mining of tin had brought to the Roman province of Britain a period of cultural and economic prosperity, with cultural centres in Camulodunum (Colchester), Londinium (London), Eburacum (York), Glevum (Gloucester), Lindum Colonia (Lincoln), Aquae Sulis (Bath) and Verulamium (St Albans), as can be seen at the local archaeological digs and museums. The many towns whose names end in "chester" indicate their Roman origin (Latin castrum, or fortress). There are numerous remains of luxurious Roman villas in the milder south-east of England, such as those at Lullingstone (4th c.) and Fishbourne in Sussex, where the Roman Palace (75 BC and later) contains some important mosaics. Most impressive, too, are the Roman fortifications such as the square castle at Portchester on Portsmouth harbour with its 20 ft high surrounding walls dating from the 3rd c. still in good condition. The most striking Roman structure is in the north of England – Hadrian's Wall, built between AD 122 and 128 between Newcastle and Carlisle as a defence against the Picts and Scots. Along Hadrian's Wall can still be seen the line of the fortifications and the remains of several castles which give an insight into the lives of the Roman soldiers. Finds dug from Hadrian's Wall are on display in the Museum of Antiquities in Newcastle-upon-Tyne, while some everyday items, glass, gold and silverware from the Late Roman period (4th c. AD) can be seen in the British Museum in London.

Early Middle Ages

Around 450 the Anglo-Saxons conquered Britain and brought with them Germanic culture and techniques. The Anglo-Saxon period can be divided into two artistic phases – the early period from the 7th to the 9th c., and the later period after Viking raids abated, from the early 10th c. until the Norman conquest in 1066. In Scotland Pict culture flourished in the 7th and 8th c., to be superseded by that of the Irish Scots by the middle of the 9th c.

Early Anglo-Saxon buildings showed a mingling of traditional Celtic and Roman methods. Of the many buildings constructed solely of wood few remain, but they formed the model for the first stone churches built at the end of the 6th c., with simple, long rectangular naves terminating in a short, square chancel. Plain wooden roofs covered the narrow, high interiors. Some of the 7th churches which survive are those at Escomb (Durham), Wing (Buckinghamshire), Brixworth (Northamptonshire) and that of St Lawrence in Bradford-upon-Avon in Wiltshire. The 10th c. saw churches with impressive west towers, such as those at Worth (Sussex), Monkwearmouth (Durham), Sompting (Sussex), Earls Barton (Northamptonshire) and Barton-upon-Humber (Humberside); the latter two boast rich stone-work decoration on the towers, including long and short work, corner stones and stone balusters.

Architecture

The book illumination of the Anglo-Saxon and Irish period is of outstanding quality, much of it the work of nomadic Irish monks. The earliest known work is the "Book of Durrow", dating from 680 and now housed in Trinity College, Dublin, with rich ornamentation used in forming the initial letters and the apostolic symbols which is closely resembles gold and silver work. The "Book of Lindisfarne" (c. 700, British Museum in London) combines interlaced ribbon-ornament with Anglo-Saxon animal and spiral forms and naturalistic portraits of the Apostles showing an Italian influence. In Canterbury in the 8th c. the "Vespasian Psalter" (British Museum, London) and the "Codex Aureus" (Royal Library, Stockholm) were written and illuminated. Book illumination blossomed again during the second half of the 10th c. in a number of different schools; these include Glastonbury Abbey, an example of its work being "Dunstan's Classbook" (c. 950, now in Bodleian Library, Oxford) with freehand drawings, as well as the Winchester School, whose richly decorated "Benedictional of St Aethelwold" (c. 975, now in the British Museum) displays Carolingian influences in its acanthus leaf patterns and the fine robes and drapes. As well as Old Testament scripts such as the "Caedmon Genesis" (c. 1000, Bodleian Library, Oxford) there are also early Christian manuscripts such as the "Prudentius Psychomachia" and astrological texts like the "Aratea".

Painting

In stone sculpture, from the late 7th c. onwards the most notable forms were the stone crosses, about 16 ft high, erected as monuments, votive symbols or – more rarely – as holy places. Although there were many local variations, most of the 8th c. high crosses found in the north of England had figural, mainly Biblical adornment in the Romanesque-Byzantine style with inscriptions round the edge and vine ornamentation; those from Ruthwell, Bewcastle and Hexham are particularly impressive. Many of the crosses erected c. 800 on the island of Iona in the Hebrides show plant ornamentation and the characteristic pierced circular shape at the top. Later crosses dating from 800 to 1050 are strongly influenced by Viking art (Collingham, Ilkley, Walton, Middleton). Scottish crosses, such as those at Hilton of Cadboll, Thornhill, Abercorn, also have vine ornamentation, while those on the Isle of Man have interlaced ornament. Celtic influence is seen in the decoration on Welsh crosses, such as the 11th c. Nevern Celtic Cross.

Some fine examples of architectural sculpture are to be found in many Anglo-Saxon churches; examples are the angel reliefs at Bradford-upon-Avon, parts of a crucifixion in Romsey and Breamore, and a superb frieze with human and animal figures at Breedon-on-the-Hill. Much carving in ivory was also done, often using expensive walrus bone, some-

Sculpture

71

times whalebone. The Franconian Casket, showing scenes of Christian, Germanic and Roman customs, was carved about 750 (British Museum, London), and a very sensitive interpretation of the Birth of Christ, dating from about 200 years later, can be seen in the Merseyside County Museum in Liverpool. The wrought gold and silver work is also magnificent. The ship burial (probably of the East Anglian king Aethelhere, d. 655), an oared vessel some 85 ft long, found at Sutton Hoo in Suffolk in 1939 and now in the British Museum, contained one of the richest collections of Germanic burial artefacts ever discovered, much of it gold and silver work employing the cloisonné, niello and millefiori techniques. Magnificent figural and decorative embroidery work on communion robes dating from the early 10th c. have been preserved at Durham Cathedral.

Pictish art in Scotland is found mainly in the form of stone sculpture, originally with animal carvings, such as the 7th c. bull relief at Burghhead, Morayshire, and later with stone slabs carved in rich relief with crucifixes and vine ornamentation (cross in the cemetery at Nigg, Ross and Cromarty, late 8th c.). The treasure from St Ninian's Isle (National Museum of Antiquities, Edinburgh) shows Pictish metallurgical art of high quality.

Romanesque

Following the Norman conquest of 1066 and the subsequent reordering of the dioceses by moving the episcopal sees to the cities and large towns resulted in a wave of building, and numerous cathedrals and abbey churches were altered or re-built in the Norman or Romanesque style. Most cathedrals stand detached, surrounded by lawns and a spacious cathedral close, and have very long naves.

Religious architecture

The earliest Romanesque minsters are of massive, simple construction and enormous length, cruciform in plan with triple aisles and a twin--towered front, distinctive transepts, massive crossing-towers and square chancels. The aisles are separated by pillars or masonry columns with massive round arches, and the tripartite walls were at first somewhat heavy in appearance but this was later alleviated by means of windows stretching the full height with engaged columns and graduated arches as well as by the use of a double-skinned form of wall construction incorporating galleries. The usual Romanesque barrel-vaulting developed into cross barrel-vaulting and thence to cross groin-vaulting, and flat wooden ceilings became more common. In the south choir of Durham Cathedral can be seen the first ribbed vault in England (from 1096), showing the transition to Early Gothic. Of particular architectural interest are the cathedrals and churches of St Albans (1077–88), Ely (1083–), Bury St Edmunds (1085–), Tewkesbury (1087–), Gloucester (1089–), Peterborough (1118–), Southwell (1108–), Canterbury (1067–), Winchester (1079–), Chichester (1089–), Durham (1093–) and Norwich (1096–). In most of the churches only the naves display the Anglo-Norman style, but in Winchester the transept does so too, while Norwich is almost entirely Norman apart from the Gothic vaulting; Durham is notable for its sheer size and Peterborough for its painted flat ceiling (1220).

Secular architecture

In the field of secular architecture mention should first be made of Norman military edifices. Malling Castle in Kent, the White Tower in London and Colchester Castle all date from the late 11th c., Castle Heddingham (Essex), Castle Rising (Norfolk) and the keep of Rochester castle from the middle of the 12th c. The fortifications at Richmond, Scarborough, Dover and Chester were built in the reign of Henry II (1154–89). 12th c. Norman town houses of stone can still be seen in Lincoln and other places.

Sculpture

Architectural sculpture of the period centres on doorways, friezes and capitals of columns. Cross arches built into walls, folded capitals and

Winchester Bible (12th c.)

zig-zag friezes are frequently found. In addition, mention must be made of the two expressive reliefs depicting the story of Lazarus (1120) in Chichester Cathedral, the Prior's Doorway in Ely Cathedral (1135), the stone frieze showing scenes from the Old Testament and the Jaws of Hell on the west front of Lincoln Cathedral (c. 1150), the doorway of the little church of Kilpeck in Hertfordshire with its fantastic mingling of human and animal figures and monsters (second half of the 12th c.), as well as the doors and friezes of Barfreston church in Kent, the west door of Rochester Cathedral (c. 1160) and the sculpture in the south porch of Malmesbury Abbey (c. 1160).

Of the many Norman baptismal fonts, mainly round or cup-shaped, which are frequently found in churches in Cornwall (an especially fine example is in the church of St Petroc in Bodmin) and elsewhere. Mention should be made of that at Winchester, which is square with a relief of St Nicholas and made from black marble from Tournai in Belgium. In addition to fine carved ivorywork much exquisite gold and silver wrought decoration dates from this period – the Gloucester Sconce (early 12th c., now in the Victoria and Albert Museum in London) with its intertwined fabulous ornamentation is a prime example.

Painting

Irish and Anglo-Saxon book illumination with its linear style developed once more under Franco-Norman influence in the 12th c. (Bayeux Tapestry, see below) and attained a style full of expression and suspense, especially in the schools of St Albans (Alban Psalter, 1123) and Bury St Edmunds (Vita Sancti Edmundi, pre-1135). Byzantine influence is seen in the works produced in the scriptoria of Canterbury (Lambeth Bible, mid-12th c.) and Winchester (Winchester Bible, end of the 12th c.). Of the few wall-paintings which survive, those in St Anselm's Chapel (c. 1160) and in the crypt of Canterbury Cathedral as well as those in the sanctum of Winchester Cathedral (late 12th c.) still bear witness to this great age of Romanesque wall-painting. A special form of narrative painting is represented by the embroidery known as the "Bayeux Tapestry" (Bayeux Museum, Normandy), which depicts the Norman Conquest of England in 1066 and is said to have been worked by William the Conqueror's wife, Mathilde, about 1080.

Gothic

Gothic architecture in Britain is seen less as a unified style than as a sequence of three phases – Early English (1180–1250), Decorated (1250–1350) and Perpendicular (1350–1530) – corresponding very roughly to the Early Gothic, High Gothic and Late Gothic phases recognised in the architecture of continental Europe.

Church architecture

The first example of this new style was the choir of Canterbury Cathedral (1175–84) when it was rebuilt by Guillaume de Sens following a fire. Although the French technique of limb structure was adopted, the Early English style did not display the very high naves,

Harlech Castle

light and delicate walls or polygonal apses seen in France. The west front is often of great breadth, the nave long with a protruding west transept; the chancel is frequently lengthened by the addition of a Lady Chapel, replacing the apse. The walls are normally divided into three by horizontal ledges and galleries and the arches are lancet-shaped; hence the phrase Pointed style, sometimes used instead of Early English. At first the vaulting was in quartered ribbed form, but this was later superseded by ornamental combinations of star, net and fan vaulting which served to bring the separate roof sections together into one harmonious whole. The rectangular cloisters and the elaborate development of the chapterhouse are English characteristics. Salisbury Cathedral (1220–66) is a superb example of the Early English style. Other cathedrals to note include Ripon (begun between 1153 and 1181), Chichester (rebuilt after 1186), Lincoln (St Hugo choir *c.* 1200), Wells (nave and transepts 1180–1239), Peterborough (vaulting and west front *c.* 1220), Worcester (choir begun in the early 13th c., nave and transepts 1317–77) and Southwell (choir, second quarter of 13th c.).

The **Decorated style** in church architecture is notable for the rich tracery of the windows and wall surfaces. The finest examples of this period are Westminster Abbey in London (choir begun 1245), the Angel Choir of Lincoln Cathedral (*c.* 1280), the nave, Lady Chapel, west front and chapterhouse of Lichfield Cathedral (*c.* 1250–1330), the nave and chapterhouse of York Minster (*c.* 1290–1340), the west front (after 1230) and rebuilt part of the choir (early 14th c.) of Wells Cathedral, the choir of Bristol Cathedral (1298–1332) and the choir of Gloucester Cathedral (1329–37).

Although perhaps somewhat less exuberant than the Decorated, the **Perpendicular style** in church architecture also breaks up wall surfaces and windows with an elaborate lattice-work of tracery consisting chiefly of vertical members, two or four arc arches, lavishly decorated vaulting (one of the earliest examples being the Gloucester Cathedral cloisters, 1351–1407) and use of traceried panels. The three great masterpieces of the Perpendicular style are the nave of Winchester Cathedral (begun 1394), King's College Chapel in Cambridge (begun 1446) and the Henry VII Chapel in Westminster Abbey (1503–19). Other fine examples of Perpendicular architecture are the chapel of New College, Oxford (1383), the choir of Tewkesbury Abbey (c. 1350) and St George's Chapel in Windsor Castle (1460–83, seriously damaged by fire in 1992), the nave of Sherborne Abbey, the choir of Christchurch Priory and the parish church of St Mary Redcliff in Bristol.

Religious building was not carried out on a similar scale in Scotland. A number of Gothic buildings were heavily restored in the 19th c. Those of architectural interest include St Machar Cathedral in Aberdeen (15th c.), St Giles Cathedral in Edinburgh (15th c.), Glasgow Cathedral (15th c.) and St Magnus Cathedral in Kirkwell (12th–14th c.).

Notable religious buildings in Wales include the Romanesque-Gothic St David's Cathedral (12th–15th c., beautiful wooden ceiling) and the Late Gothic St Deiniol Cathedral (15th c.) in Bangor.

During the reign of Edward I many massive castles were built between 1270 and 1295 to defend the Welsh borders, such as Conway, Caernarvon, Harlech and Caerphily. Stokesay Castle (c. 1300), Penshurst Place (c. 1340), Bodiam Castle (1385) and Tattershall Castle (1434–45) are all prime examples of a combined fortress and family seat. One of the finest Late Gothic country seats built in the half-timbered style is Ockwells (c. 1465).

Secular architecture

In the towns large structures such as Westminster Hall (1393–99) and the Guildhall in London were built, together with many town-halls and residences in stone and half-timber construction, such as those in Chester, as well as the college buildings at Oxford and Cambridge.

One of most important collections of medieval sculpture in England is to be seen on the west front of Wells Cathedral, where more than 300 individual figures are housed in niches (1230–39). On the front of Salisbury Cathedral robed figures are lined up in blind arcades, while above the main door of Lincoln Cathedral kings sit in judgement on their thrones (1220–30) and the west façade of Exeter Cathedral displays a cycle of angels, apostles, prophets and judges (14th c.). Other major sculptural works can be seen in the Angel Choir (c. 1280) of Lincoln Cathedral and the Lady Chapel (1321–49) in Ely Cathedral. Many chantries (chapels endowed for priests to sing masses for the founders' souls) boast some rich sculpture, notable among which are the Despenser Chantries in Tewkesbury Abbey, the Chantry of Prince Arthur in Worcester Cathedral, the Chantry of Henry V in Westminster Abbey and the Kirkham Chantry in the parish church at Paignton in Devon. Other objects on which the mason has exercised his skills are the numerous roof-bosses and corbel-stones (best examples are in Exeter Cathedral) and rood screens, of which there are fine examples to be seen at Canterbury (1411–30) and York (1480–1500). The Easter Sepulchre at Hawton, Nottinghamshire (early 14th c.) is also a fine piece of sculpture. Grave sculpture is also worthy of note, ranging from raised stone slabs to finely carved brasses and superb works in bronze, such as the tomb of Henry III (c. 1291) in Westminster Abbey, the figure of the Earl of Warwick in gilded copper (1448) at St Mary's in Warwick, as well as expressive alabaster figures such as the tomb of Edward II (c. 1330) in Gloucester Cathedral, and memento mori reminders such as the tomb of Bishop Fleming (c. 1435) in Lincoln Cathedral. Other unique pieces of medieval work are the Eleanor Crosses (1291–94, Waltham, Hardingstone), finely carved and

Sculpture

clothed figures in memory of Eleanor of Castille, wife of Edward I. Much reliquary art was destroyed during the Reformation, but some small items in gold and silver, such as liturgical regalia, goblets and jewellery, can still be found in local museums. The woodcarver's art is seen at its best in many choir-stalls of the period; Exeter Cathedral, for example, boasts some comical misericords (13th c.) and an imposing Bishop's Throne carved in oak; Lincoln (late 13th c.), Winchester (c. 1310) and Wells (c. 1340) also have richly-carved choir-stalls. The monument to the Norman duke Robert in Gloucester Cathedral is an important wood-carving from the late 12th c.

Only a few major examples of medieval sculpture are to be found in Scotland; the statue of the Virgin Mary at Melrose (14th c.) and the stone frieze in Roslin Chapel, Lothian (c. 1450) show a certain French influence combined with archaic figuration.

In Wales, too, little medieval work has been preserved. Some beautiful 13th/14th c. grave-sculptures can be seen in Abergavenny, Betws-y-coed and St Asaph, and St David's Cathedral boasts a 14th c. stone altar with a crucifixion and statue of the saint. Llananno Church in Powys has a richly carved wooden rood screen (c. 1500).

Painting

Book illumination achieved a final period of brilliance up to the end of the 15th c., among the most prized being those from the famous St Albans School, led by the monk Matthew Paris (1236–59), including the "Historia Anglorum" (1236–59, in the British Museum in London) drawn in a most zestful style with fantasy decoration. Mention should also be made of the "Life of St Edward" (c. 1250). The "Ormesby Psalter", "Queen Mary's Psalter", the "Peterborough Psalter" and the "Luttrell Psalter" (c. 1340), all from the East Anglian School, as well as the "Queen Isabella Psalter" from Nottinghamshire. Gothic wall and panel painting, on the other hand, developed only slowly. There are some important frescoes to be seen on the nave pillars in St Albans Cathedral, including a crucifixion dated 1220. Figural panel paintings from the late-15th c. can still be viewed in the church at Horsham St Faith in Norfolk, and there are a few remnants of the important frescoes in St Stephen's Chapel (1350–75) in Westminster Palace (destroyed in 1834, the rest are in the British Museum). The portrayal of the Apocalypse (c. 1400) in the chapterhouse of Westminster Abbey is in the international Gothic style, while the grisaille paintings (in grey monochrome imitating relief) depicting the "Miracles of the Virgin Mary" (1470–80) in Eton College show an early transition to Renaissance art.

Panel painting reached its first peak with the Westminster Reredos (c. 1280, Westminster Abbey), which portrays Christ and the Apostles, only to be overshadowed by that at Thornham Parva in Suffolk (c. 1330), followed by a fresh flowering during the reign of the art-loving King Richard II, whose portrait (late 14th c.) in Westminster Abbey is one of the earliest to be found anywhere in England. The "Wilton Diptych" (c. 1400, National Gallery, London) shows Richard and saints before the Virgin Mary. A further masterpiece, the Norwich Reredos (c. 1390) in Norwich Cathedral shows scenes from Christ's Passion. Stained glass work was also of a high standard; some important examples can be seen in Coventry and York Cathedrals.

English embroidery and tapestry work became admired throughout Europe in the 13th and 14th c. as "opus anglicum". Examples of such work are the "Clare Chasuble" (1272–94), the "Syon Pluvial" (first quarter of the 14th c.) and the "Butler-Bowden Pluvial" (second half of the 14th c.), all to be found in the Victoria and Albert Museum in London.

Tudor, Elizabethan and Jacobean Styles

The transition from the Late Gothic or Perpendicular c. 1500 to the beginning of Neo-Classicism c. 1620, combining Renaissance influences brought into the country from Italy, Germany and Holland with the tastes expressed by Henry VIII, Elizabeth and James I, produced –

in the Tudor, Elizabethan and Jacobean styles – new and typically English forms.

Architecture

During the time of the Reformation church building almost came to a halt; thanks to the wealth of the new aristocracy, on the other hand, secular building flourished in the form of palaces and country houses, much of it in the half-timbered style, often in conjunction with stone. Modelled on the castles built in the Loire valley, most of these new buildings were designed either with three wings surrounding a courtyard or in the shape of an "E". Most had a long and symmetrical main section, together with striking gate-houses, flat roofs with decorative chimneys, fronts with a large number of windows and carved oriels and bays; examples are Hampton Court Palace in Middlesex (1544 ff.), Longleat House, Wiltshire (by Giovanni da Padova,1567–69), Burghley House, Lincolnshire (1555–87), Montacute House, Somerset (begun 1588), Wollaton Hall, Nottinghamshire (designed by Robert Smythson, 1580–88) and Hatfield House, Herefordshire (1607–12). Many towns still have streets of pretty half-timbered houses, such as those found in Chester and Stratford-on-Avon, while Little Moreton Hall, Cheshire (c. 1560) is an imposing three-storey country seat.

Sculpture

Renaissance sculptural forms were brought to England mainly by immigrant Italian sculptors, some of whom had trained in France. Some major examples of such work are the tomb sculptures (1512–18) of Henry VII and his queen in Westminster Abbey by Pietro Torrigiani (1472–1528), and works by Benedetto da Rovezzano (carved oak choir screen in King's College Chapel, Cambridge, 1533–36), who worked in England from 1524 to 1535, and by Giovanni da Maiano (terracotta reliefs on the Anne Boleyn Gate 1521 and decoration on the Wolsey Cabinet in Hampton Court Palace), who worked as a sculptor in England from about 1521 onwards. When many statues and pictures were removed from churches or destroyed during the Reformation, sculpture understandably went into decline about 1550, but some notable carvings were still produced in the alabaster workshops in central England. A good example being the tomb sculptures (1543–) of the Earl of Rutland in Bottesford. Leicestershire, which were begun by Richard Parker and completed by Nicholas Johnson of Southwark following Parker's death in 1571.

Painting

The greatest painter of the Tudor period was the German Hans Holbein the Younger (1497–1543), who painted in England from 1526 to 1528 and again from 1532 until his death, being appointed court painter to Henry VII in 1536. His portraits are very natural in appearance against a neutral background, Holbein had no natural successor, but John Bettes (d. before 1576) and George Gower (d. 1596) continued to work in his style.

Nicholas Hilliard (1547–1619) worked as a miniaturist, recording the spirit of the Elizabethan period in his intimate costume portraits. Isaac Oliver (1556–1617), a French Huguenot, continued Hilliard's style in a psychologically sensitive but less poetic form.

Neo-Classical to Neo-Gothic

The 17th and 18th c. Continental styles of Mannerism, Baroque and Rococo in architecture did not develop in the same way in Britain – in its place a Neo-Classical style, influenced by the Italian Andrea Palladio (1500–80) came to the fore in the shape of villas, palaces and churches displaying imitations of Classical columns and pilasters. The later period of English Neo-Classicism in the 18th c. became known as the Georgian style, after the kings who ruled from 1714. By 1760, however, enthusiasm for the ancient Classical forms had declined somewhat, to be replaced by the Gothic Revival style which found full expression in the 19th c.

Architecture

The design drawn up in 1616 by Inigo Jones (1573–1652) for the Queen's

Nicholas Hilliard: "Elizabeth I" (c. 1574)   *Oxford: the Radcliffe Camera*

House in Greenwich (completed in 1635) ushered in an era of elegantly simple and substantial buildings in a strict Classical and Palladian style. Between 1619 and 1622 he built the Banqueting House in Whitehall (London), constructed in the form of a double cube with a nine-section coffered ceiling and in which paintings by Paul Rubens depicting the apotheosis of James I were hung in 1635. A masterpiece of palace architecture is Wilton House near Salisbury, with a strictly Neo-Classical exterior and magnificent rooms similar to that of the Baroque interiors of many French palaces; one room, the Double Cube Room (1649–50) was designed by Inigo Jones and John Webb, who incorporated portraits painted by van Dyck. John Webb (1611–72), a pupil of Jones, was responsible for the first Classical temple portico to be incorporated into the design of a country house (The Vyne, 1654, Hampshire), the rustic north wing of Lamport Hall in Northamptonshire (1655) and the main section of Greenwich Palace (1664–69), now the Royal Naval College.

Sir Christopher Wren (1632–1723), the greatest exponent of Neo-Classical architecture, was presented after the Great Fire of London in 1666 with an opportunity such as few architects have enjoyed. In London alone he is said to have built more than 50 churches, not all of which have survived, as well as numerous secular buildings. His greatest achievements include his masterpiece St Paul's Cathedral (1675–1711) in London, modelled on St Peter's in Rome, the London parish churches of St Bride's (1671–78), St Stephen Walbrook (1672–79) and St Clement Danes (1680–82), Trinity College Library (1676–84) in Cambridge, Fountains Court (1689–94) at Hampton Court Palace, and the Hospital for Sailors in Greenwich (1696–1716). While Wren worked almost exclusively for his royal masters his contemporaries designed Baroque country houses for private owners, such as Chatsworth House (south and east front, 1687–96) and Dayton House (main front 1702) by William Talman (1650–1719), or the imposing Baroque residences of Blenheim

Palace (1705–16) and Castle Howard (1699) by John Vanburgh (1664–1726); Nicholas Hawksmoor (1661–1736) built the unusual towers at Christ Church, Spitalfields, St George-in-the-East and St Mary Woolnoth in London. Thomas Archer (c. 1668–1743), who journeyed extensively in Europe, came near to imitating West European Baroque, as can be seen from the north front of Chatsworth House (1704) and the Pavilion in Wrest Park (1709–10). James Gibbs (1682–1754), on the other hand, employed a strict Neo-Classical style with the frequent use of lines of columns, examples being St Mary-le-Strand (1714–17) and St Martin-in-the Fields (1720–26), both churches in London, The Radcliff Camera (1737–48), a rotunda-shaped library in Oxford, and the drawing room at Ragley Hall (1750–58). Chiswick House (1723–29) in London and The Assembly Rooms (1731–32) in York are examples of the strict Palladian designs of Lord Burlington. William Kent (1685–1748) was responsible for Holkham Hall in Norfolk, an imposing country house of four wings surrounding a compact central building, as well as the Treasury (1733–37) in London and Horse Guards Building (1748–) in Whitehall. Kent also designed a number of famous gardens, including the park of Blenheim Palace, and together with Lancelot "Capability" Brown (gardens of Stourhead House and many others) and William Chambers (Kew Gardens, London) ranks as one of the pioneers of English landscape gardening. William Chambers (1732–96) also designed Somerset House (1776–96) in London. John Wood the Elder (1704–54) and his son John (1728–81) designed many of the famous features of the spa city of Bath, including The Circus (1754–) and The Royal Crescent, where for the first time detached houses were constructed behind a palace-like semicircular façade. Robert Adam (1728–92) devoted himself primarily to internal design and created such opulent room settings as those in Syon House (1762-69) near London, Saltram House (1768–69) near Plymouth and Kedleston Hall (c. 1760) in Derbyshire. In the second half of the 18th century the slender and delicate lines of Neo-Gothic came to the fore, the earliest example being the Hall (1755) at Lacock Abbey in Wiltshire; its most committed exponents included Horace Walpole (1717–97), designer of the famous Neo-Gothic villa at Strawberry Hill (1750–90) and James Wyatt (1746–1813) with Fonthill Abbey, which was in fact never completed.

In the early 17th c. Epiphanius Evesham (1570–1633) and Nicholas Stone (1583–1647) introduced a greater sense of feeling into their busts and other forms of Renaissance sculpture. Mannerist and Neo-Classical forms merged in the work of Grinling Gibbons (1648–1721), who was responsible for the equestrian statue of James II (1686) and the monument to Sir C. Shovel (1707) in Westminster Abbey as well as for numerous amazingly natural-looking wood-carvings commissioned to decorate the drawing rooms of the nobility. About 1720 immigrant Flemish artists such as John M. Rysbrack (1694–1770) and Peter Scheemakers (1691–1781) provided a fresh impetus in the shape of many monuments to famous people in Westminster Abbey. Rococo sculpture was brought to England by the Frenchman Louis Francois Roubiliac (1702 or 1705–62), examples of his work being the Bishop Hough Tomb (1746) in Worcester Cathedral and the Nightingale Monument (1761) in Westminster Abbey. Henry Cheere was another champion of the Rococo style, as seen in his Sausmarez Monument (c. 1750) in Westminster Abbey. John Flaxman (1755–1826) was an exponent of Neo-Classicism and designed much Wedgwood stoneware and Lord Nelson's Tomb in St Paul's Cathedral.

Sculpture

The decorative arts were promoted as a result of the new middle-class concern with the elegance and comfort of their houses. Thomas Chippendale (1707–79), George Hepplewhite (d. 1788) and Thomas Sheraton (1751–1806) produced high-quality furniture, while Josiah Wedgwood (1730–95) created his famous ceramics, including the cream

Decorative arts

Queen's ware and his famous jasperware, which was coloured by metallic oxides and was used particularly in relief work (white on a blue background), medallions and vases. The factories at Derby, Worcester and Chelsea produced fine porcelain.

Painting

British Baroque painting was largely the legacy of foreign artists such as Anthony van Dyck (1599–1641), who was court painter to Charles I from 1632 and whose use of line and expression in portraiture remained influential in Britain until the end of the 18th century. Among van Dyck's contemporaries and successors were Samuel Cooper (1608–72), famous for his miniature portraits, William Dobson (1610–46), the Dutchman Peter Lely (1618–80) and the German Godfrey Kneller (1646 or 1649–1723), all fine portrait painters. James Thronhill (1675–1734), Antonio Verio (1639–1707) and Louis Laguerre (1663–1721) were masters of large-scale decorative painting.

William Hogarth (1697–1764), originally an engraver, became one of the leading painters of the 18th century and an unsparing critic and commentator on contemporary manners and morals. The Scot Gawen Hamilton (1697–1737) competed with him in the painting of so-called "conversation pieces", a genre which was later developed further by Francis Hayman (1708–76). Frances Cotes (1726–70) produced some charming pastel portraits and the Scot Allan Ramsay painted elegant Baroque likenesses. In the second half of the 18th century portrait painting reached a new pinnacle with the sensitive interpretations by Sir Joshua Reynolds (1723–92). Samuel Scott (1702–72) painted seascapes, Thomas Gainsborough (1727–88) was a fashionable portraitist with a certain pre-Impressionist style and also a considerable landscape artist whose pictures appear flooded with light, while Richard Wilson (c. 1713–82) combined idealistic with natural landscapes. Other contemporary portrait painters included George Romney (1734–1802), the German John Zoffany (or Johann Zeuffely, 1735–1810) and the Scot Sir Henry

William Hogarth: "David Garrick as Richard III" (1745)

Raeburn (1756–1823). Among the many great painters of rural life were George Morland (1763-1804) and George Stubbs (1724–1806), a superb painter of horses. James Seymour (c. 1702–1752) and John Wootton (1682–1764) competed in the field of sporting paintings involving horses. Joseph Wright (1734–1797) used light to great effect in his experimental natural history scenes, landscapes and interiors. The historical and portrait painter John Opie (1761–1807), the "Cornish wonder" and the landscapists John Crome (1768–1821) and John Sell Cotman (1782–1842) from the Norwich School (founded in 1803) were adherents of natural painting. Henry Walton (1746–1813) was an exponent of genre painting.

The poet, painter and visionary William Blake (1757–1827), illustrated works by Hiob, Virgil, Dante and Chaucer's Songs of Innocence in a manner linked to Neo-Classicism, while the Swiss John Fuseli (1741–1825), Director of the Royal Academy in London from 1779, used material from Baroque drama with a cruel and grotesque content (such as "Nightmare") and a strong literary impact when illustrating works by Homer, Dante, Shakespeare, Milton, etc.

Among the masters of watercolour were Paul Sandby (1730–1809), who worked in a Classical style, and Thomas Girtin (1775–1805) and David Cox (1783–1859) with their semi-Impressionist work, while Thomas Hearne (1744–1806) painted naturalistic watercolour landscapes.

Satirical wit is the keynote of the caricatures painted by James Gilray (1756–1815), Thomas Rowlandson (1756–1827) and George Cruickshank (1792–1878).

Engraving in mezzotint (also known as the "English manner") and other forms of colour engraving became very popular in the 18th century.

The architecture of the end of the 18th century and the first half of the 19th was characterised by the continuing juxtaposition of Classical and Gothic revival styles, whereas the Victorian age which followed also saw the beginnings of modern architecture.

19th century
Architecture

One of the best examples of Neo-Gothic church architecture is Truro Cathedral in Cornwall, built after 1880 in the Anglo-French 13th century Gothic style by J. L. Pearson (1817–97), others being Liverpool Cathedral (1904–) by Giles Gilbert Scott (1880–1960), and the church of All Saints, Margaret St., London, by William Butterfield (1814–1900). G. E. Street (1824–81) designed the church of St Andrew in East Heslerton (Yorkshire) in the stocky Italian Gothic style and in 1868 R. H. Carpenter began the Neo-High Gothic chapel at Lancing College in West Sussex. A. W. N. Pugin (1812–52) built the beautiful Neo-Gothic churches of St Giles (1840–6) in Cheadle (Staffordshire) and St Augustine (1845–50) in Ramsgate (Kent). John Francis Bentley (1839–1902) designed the grand Catholic Cathedral of Westminster (1894–1903), and a jewel in the Art Nouveau style is the Cemetery Chapel (1896–1901) in Compton (Surrey) by Watts and his wife.

Church building

Some prime examples of secular buildings in the Classical style include the Bank of England in London by John Soane (1753–1837), the British Museum (1823–) by Robert Smirke (1781–1864), the Fitzwilliam Museum (1834–47) in Cambridge by George Basevi (1794–1845), St George's Hall (designed 1839–40) in Liverpool by Harvey Lonsdale Elmes (1814–47) and the Town Hall (1853–58) in Leeds by Cuthbert Brodrick (1822–1905).

Secular
architecture

The Gothic revival style can be seen in the Houses of Parliament (1837–) and Big Ben (1858) in London, designed by Charles Barry (1795–1860) in collaboration with Augustus Pugin (1812–52), the Town Hall (1867–68) in Manchester by Alfred Waterhouse (1830–1905), and the richly decorated interior of Cardiff Castle in Wales by William Burgess (1827–81).

HillHouse – Art Nouveau villa by Charles Rennie Mackintosh

A marked oriental influence can be seen in the flamboyantly decorative Royal Pavilion in Brighton by John Nash (1752–1835), who also planned Regent Street and Marble Arch in London in the Neo-Classical style.

The buildings and engineering works of the Industrial Revolution – bridges, canals, factories, glass-houses, railway stations and bridges such as Brunel's Clifton Suspension Bridge near Bristol – and above all the Crystal Palace, a structure of cast-iron and glass built by Sir Joseph Paxton (1803–65) for the Great Exhibition of 1851, contain all the necessary elements of 20th century architecture.

A leading architect of the Victorian period (1837–1901), in addition to Sir Charles Barry and Paxton, was George Gilbert Scott (1811–78). Although he did design some major Neo-Classical buildings, such as the Foreign Office in London (1857–61), his main work centred on numerous churches and country houses – such as Kelham Hall, Nottinghamshire, for example – all in the Gothic revival style. The South Kensington Museum in London is another prime example of the mingling of historical styles, as are the Victoria and Albert and the Natural History Museums in London. Philip S. Webb (1831–1915) designed such country houses as "Red House" in Bexleyheath (1859–60) and "Clouds" in Wiltshire (1876–9), while Richard Norman Shaw (1831–1912) busied himself with town mansions such as those at Bedford Park, London (1875) as well as country houses. Charles Rennie Mackintosh (1868–1928) built the Glasgow School of Art (1896–9 and 1907–9), a mingling of Art Nouveau and Functionalism, and left behind in Glasgow and its surroundings some most impressive Art Nouveau villas, such as Hill House, Helensburgh.

Sculpture

During the first half of the 19th century British sculpture was largely on Classical lines – Francis Legatt Chantrey (1781–1841) produced natural-looking busts, John Gibson (1790–1866) was influenced by Roman sculpture, Richard Westmacott (1775–1856) combined stylistic and classical forms (for example, in his memorial to James Fox, 1810–23, in Westminster Abbey in London), Alfred Stevens (1817–75) adopted the monumental Roman style (monument to the Duke of Wellington, 1856, St Paul's Cathedral in London). In the second half of the century Victorian memorial sculpture reached its height with the Albert Memorial (1872–76), designed by George Gilbert Scott, while the New Sculpture movement (after 1875) under Albert Gilbert (1854–1934) attempted to make symbolic and expressive statements.

The Arts and Crafts Movement led by William Morris (1834–96) aimed at promoting traditional decorative art and crafts in the face of increasing mechanisation and mass production. The designer C. Dresser produced precise shapes in metal and ceramics, A. H. Mackmurdo (1851–1942) designed textiles, and C. R. Mackintosh was a maker of Art Nouveau furniture and an interior designer. W. Morris and Edward Burne-Jones produced some superb stained glass in the Pre-Raphaelite style for a number of churches in southern England.

In the early 19th century John Constable (1776–1837) was a master of realistic landscape painting based on the direct observation of nature, a form which also strongly influenced French painting (Delacroix). The Bristol School (c. 1820) under Francis Danby (1793–1861) produced poetical landscapes. J. M. W. Turner carried landscape painting to further heights of achievement; influenced by Claude Lorrain, he painted landscapes which were sometimes a true depiction of nature and sometimes peopled with mythological figures, and in the end the representational aspect became totally dissolved in fantasies of light and colour. His attempts to reproduce the effects of light filtering through the atmosphere, the play of colours and reflections in water have led him to be regarded, probably in error, as a forerunner of Impressionism.

Painting

William Turner: "Stirling" (c. 1834)

Ford Madox Brown: "The last of England" (c. 1852)

Portraiture was considerably enriched by the relaxed and sensitive style adopted by Thomas Lawrence (1769–1830). John Singer Sargent (1856–1925) was the outstanding portraitist of the second half of the century.

William Dyce (1806–1864) produced a number of religious paintings, while John Linell (1792–1882) painted natural landscapes and the Scot Horatio McCulloch (1805–67) was renowned for his Scottish highland scenes. Pastoral landscapes were the speciality of Samuel Palmer (1805–81), one of the Kent group known as the Shoreham painters (c. 1820–30). The sensitive animal studies of Edwin Landseer (1802–73) were very popular, John Martin (1789–1854) created mysterious scenes containing numerous figures, and William Bly (1787–1849) made a name for himself as an historical artist. As genre painters, David Wilkie (1785–1841) and William Quiller Orchardson (1832–1910) were outstanding. William Powell Frith (1819–1909) was a bold recorder of the Industrial Age, and George Frederick Watts (1817–1904) became known for his allegorical pictures and portraits of his contemporaries.

The imaginative art of Blake and Fuseli prepared the way for the pre-Raphaelites, or the "pre-Raphaelite Brotherhood", established by a group of young artists in 1848 and which was directed against the Royal Academy and what they regarded as the pretentious or trivial attitude to art adopted by such painters as Sir Lawrence Alma-Tadema and Sir Edwin Landseer. The leaders of the movement, who sought to return to the period before Raphael (before, that is, the High Renaissance), were Sir John Everett Millais (1829–96), the poet and painter Dante Gabriel

Rossetti (1828–82), William Holman Hunt (1827–1910), Ford Madox Brown (1821–93) and Edward Burne-Jones (1833–98).

Albert Moore (1841–93), influenced by the Parthenon sculptures (British Museum, London), mingled Classical and pre-Raphaelite forms in his works. Symbolic, abstract and sometimes very humorous pictures were the hallmark of the "Glasgow Boys", who included Joseph Crawhall (1861–1913), George Henry (1858–1913) and Edward A. Hornel (1864–1933).

Frederick Leighton (1830–96) tended to pander to the over-sentimental tastes of the age with his Classical Greek subjects. Aubrey Beardsley (1872–98) impressed the fin de siècle stamp on Victorian art with his decadently decorative and fantastic illustrations, such as those for Oscar Wilde's "Salome". The American-born painter James McNeill Whistler (1834–1903), who spent most of his life in Britain, was one of the first to discover the beauty of the Japanese coloured woodcut. His pictures were conceived wholly in terms of colour harmony and include his famous "Arrangement in Grey and Black: Portrait of the Painter's Mother" 1871. Founded in 1886, the New English Art Club had as members Walter R. Sickert (1860–1942) and Philip Wilson Steer (1860–1942) and promoted progressive painting forms. As well as painting portraits and landscapes, William Nicholson (1872–1949) was responsible for some very expressive woodcuts.

After its promising upsurge in the earlier part of the 19th century, architecture now fell back into a traditional mould in the early years of the 20th century, as exemplified by Edwin Lutyens (1896–1944) in Britannica House, 1920–24, the London Midland Bank, 1924, and the Viceroy's House, New Delhi. In the 1920s and 1930s new urban developments and schools and universities showed the influences of Art Deco from France, Expressionism and Bauhaus from Germany and Functionalism (De Stijl)

20th century
Architecture

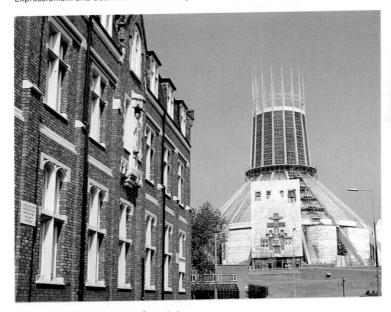

Liverpool: the Roman Catholic Cathedral

from Holland. After the Second World War New Brutalism (an expression coined by Le Corbusier to describe buildings using *béton brut* (concrete exposed at its roughest, with the structures often prominently visible) found its way into British architecture through such exponents as Alison and Peter Smithson.

In church architecture special mention should be made of the Roman Catholic Cathedral in Liverpool and Coventry Cathedral (1951–62, architect Basil Spence) as unique modern creations.

In the 1960s the Archigram Group experimented with futuristic ideas and produced a form which became mirrored in Richard Rogers' Lloyds Building in London (1977) and Norman Foster's Sainsbury Centre at the University of East Anglia in Norwich (1978). Other important examples of modern architecture are the Runcorn New Town development (1968–74) and the Cambridge History Faculty Building by James Stirling, who also designed the extension to the Tate Gallery in London and its branch in Albert Dock in Liverpool. Further modernistic buildings of this category are Gonville and Caius College in Cambridge (1959–61) by L. Martin and C. St John Wilson, the University of East Anglia in Norwich (1962–68) and the National Theatre in London (1967–76) by Denys Lasdun as well as the University of Essex (1960–) by Basil Spence.

Sculpture

The sculpture of the first half of the 20th century is represented by the American-born Jacob Epstein (1880–1958), who lived in London from 1905 and whose work was futuristic with mechanical figures, Roland Penrose (1900–84) and Eileen Agar (b. 1904) with their surrealistic sculptures. Barbara Hepworth (1903–75) produced work of a more abstract kind, with her sleek stone steles and hollow shapes. Henry Moore (1898–1986), above all, created figures of massive solidity, with a preference for reclining figures and carrying abstraction to its extreme. David Smith (1906–65) welded pre-formed steel sections and old iron together to form totem-pole-like monuments. Kenneth Armitage (b. 1916) forms

Augustus John: "George Bernard Shaw"

S. Spencer: "The Glen, Port Glasgow 1952"

a kind of sculptural screen out of groups of his highly abstract, idol-like bronze figures with thin, insect-like limbs. Lynn Chadwick (b. 1914) creates abstracts combining animal and human forms, while Reginald Butler (1913–81) produced abstract figures in metal. The abstract work of Tony Smith (b. 1912) and Philip King (b. 1934) approaches Minimalism. In his early days William Turnbull (b. 1922) created natural, unaffected sculptures, but later changed to simple abstract, coloured work. Minimalistic influences can be seen in the metal creations of William Tucker (b. 1935). Anthony Caro (b. 1924) works with painted sheets of metal which he arranges horizontally and vertically in an attempt to obtain an interaction between them and the space surrounding them. Eduardo Paolozzi (b. 1924) initially made "pop art" collages and then moved on to technoid figures intended to underline the relationship between man and technology. Barry Flanagan (b. 1941) concentrates on "process art", intended to illustrate creative processes in a manner which touches on the fields of conceptual and "land art". Another representative of "land art" is Richard Long (b. 1945), whose concentric stone circles mirror mythical ancient cultures. Stuart Brisley (b. 1933) has made a name for himself as a "performance artist" in conjunction with "body art". Bill Woodrow (b. 1948), Richard Deacon (b. 1949), Tony Cragg (b. 1949) and Julian Opie (b. 1958) use everyday objects in an unfamiliar way in their sculptures.

Early 20th century painting in Britain lacked the unity of innovation and approach shown by, for example, contemporary French painting, as expressed in Fauvism, Expressionism, Cubism, Futurism, Dadaism and Surrealism. Among the important artists of this period, caught between the claims of tradition and change, were Augustus John (1878–1961) with his post-Impressionist pictures and later his sensitive portraits, his sister Gwen John (1876–1939) with her small, simple likenesses and still-lifes, and Duncan Grant (1885–1978), whose work shows a mingling of late-Impressionist, Realist and Abstract-Decorative elements. Percy Wyndham Lewis (1882–1957) was a co-founder of the Vorticism school, a futuristic English school using "vortices" of modern civilisation as a basis, one which was translated into dynamic and abstract forms in the paintings of David Bomberg (1890–1957). The work of Matthew Smith (1874–1959) came close to the French Fauvism. Paul Nash (1889–1946) and Edward Wadsworth (1889–1949) approached the borders of Surrealism with their disturbing landscapes, and so in the widest sense did Stanley Spencer (1891–1959), whose pictures mingling fantasy and realism later tended more towards religious pathos. Ben Nicholson (1894–1982), with his geometrical and lyrical colour forms, was a member of the "Abstraction-Création" group. Victor Pasmore (b. 1908) originally painted representational objects and then moved on to abstract compositions. Vanessa Bell (1879–1961) also trod the path to abstract painting with her flat wash work. In the 1930s the members of the Euston Road School, such as William Coldstream (b. 1908) and Graham Bell (1910–43) attempted to revive representational art, seeking to portray reality. Graham Sutherland (1903–80) used plant and mineral shapes to decorative effect in his landscapes, and during the Second World War adopted rather frightening metaphors in his paintings. In the late 1940s he turned increasingly to characterful portraiture of contemporary figures; his portrait of Winston Churchill (1954) was disliked by his subject and subsequently burned on instructions from Lady Churchill. Francis Bacon (1909–92) painted pictures of maltreated and deformed bodies and people in nightmarish situations. Roger Hilton (1911–75) used flat washes with outline sketches of human figures. The landscapes of Peter Lanyon (1918–64) betray the influence of Cubism and Constructivism, while Alan Davie (b. 1920) concentrates on abstract-expressive painting with emblematic figures. Richard Smith (b. 1931) is also an abstract painter experimenting with shaped canvases. Howard Hodgkin (b. 1932), Leon Kossof (b. 1926) and Frank Auerbach (b. 1931)

Painting

all work with strong colours in an abstract style, while Lucian Freud (b. 1922) leans towards expressive Realism. Exponents of pop art include Richard Hamilton (b. 1922), who uses the collage technique to criticise consumer behaviour, David Hockney (b. 1937) with his "pool pictures" and photographic collages, as well as Allan Jones (b. 1937) who specialises in erotica. Bridget Riley (b. 1931) paints pictures which are most confusing to the observer and put her in the field of "op art". Bruce McLean (b. 1944) relies on photography and videos. The Performance artists Gilbert (b. 1943) and George (b. 1942) have since turned to Photorealism, as has Ben Johnson (b. 1946), while Peter Blake (b. 1932) specialises in painting over photographs.

Literature

Medieval and Renaissance

7th–9th century

The earliest works of literature of the Anglo-Saxon period, before the Norman Conquest, are the poems of Caedmon (7th c.) and Cynewulf (8th c.). At the end of the 9th century Alfred the Great ordered various theological and historical works to be translated, and the Abbot Aelfric produced a translation of the Old Testament.

1066 to the 14th century

After the Norman Conquest in 1066 the Old English written language fell into disuse, and it was not until the 13th century that Middle English took its place as a literary language alongside French and Latin: there was a great flowering of romances on Arthurian themes. The 14th c. was the great period which produced Geoffrey Chaucer's "Canterbury Tales" (c. 1387) and William Langland's "Piers Plowman". Wycliffe's translation of the Bible (1383) and "Mandeville's Travels" are both notable examples of the prose writing of the period.

15th and 16th centuries

Outstanding personalities of the 15th and 16th centuries were Sir Thomas More (1477–1535; see Famous People), Lord Chancellor in the reign of Henry VIII and a friend of Erasmus, with his humanist writings, particularly "Utopia", and Edmund Spenser (1552–99), author of "The Faerie Queene", an unfinished Arthurian epic, and the pastoral "Shepheard's Calendar".

William Shakespeare

At the end of the 16th century came the greatest English poet and dramatist of all time, William Shakespeare (1564–1616; see Famous People). Although his verse tales, "Venus and Adonis" and "The Rape of Lucrece", and even his sonnets, are now seldom read, his plays have lost little of their dramatic effectiveness on the modern stage. This is true no matter whether they be the "king" plays, tragedies such as "Romeo and Juliet", "Hamlet", "Macbeth" and "King Lear", comedies – "A Midsummer Night's Dream", "The Merchant of Venice", "The Taming of the Shrew", "The Two Gentlemen of Verona", "As You Like It", "The Merry Wives of Windsor", "The Comedy of Errors", "Much Ado About Nothing", "Twelfth Night" and "All's Well That Ends Well" – or romances such as "Cymbeline", "The Winter's Tale" and "The Tempest".

Forerunners of Shakespeare

Forerunners of Shakespeare were dramatists such as Robert Greene (1558–92) and Christopher Marlowe (1564–93), who translated Ovid's "Amores" and wrote such tragedies as "Tamburlaine the Great", "The Jew of Malta" and "The Tragical History of Dr Faustus". Among Shakespeare's contemporaries was Ben Jonson (1573–1637), who wrote poems, essays and plays including "Volpone, or The Fox" (1606).

Notable prose writers of the period include John Lyly (1554–1606), author of the didactic romance "Eupheus or the Anatomy of Wit", and

Sir Philip Sidney (1554–86), who wrote the "Arcadia" romances, and Thomas Nash (1567–1601), who created the first English adventure story and whose "Unfortunate Traveller" introduced the picaresque novel into English literature.

Baroque

Shakespeare's successors in the field of drama included Francis Beaumont (1584–1616) and John Fletcher (1579–1625), who jointly wrote some 50 plays and had more success with their contemporary audiences than Shakespeare; John Webster (1580–1625), with his horror tragedies; and Philip Massinger (1584–1640), author of serious and romantic dramas.

Drama

In 1642 all theatres were closed down by the Puritans, bringing Renaissance drama to a sudden end. A characteristic representative of Puritanism was John Milton (1608–74), with his great epic "Paradise Lost". At almost the same time John Bunyan (1626–88) wrote "The Pilgrim's Progress".

Puritanism
John Milton

After Charles II's return to the throne in 1660 art and drama revived, and French literature began to make an impact on Britain's intellectual life. John Dryden (1631–1700) sought to imitate the French heroic play. Typical of the period, however, are the witty and sometimes risqué Restoration Comedies, among the major exponents of which were William Congreve (1670–1729; "The Way of the World"), Sir George Etherege (1635–91; She Would if She Could" and "The Man of Mode, or Sir Fopfling Flutter") and William Wycherley (1640–1717; "The Country Wife"). The Irishman George Farquhar (1677–1726; "The Beaux' Strategem") headed the transition from Restoration to sentimental comedy. Alexander Pope (1688–1744) introduced the rationalism of the Enlightenment into English literature with his pastoral "The Rape of the Lock". Jonathan Swift (1667–1745), the founder of literature in Ireland written in the English language, became world-famed for his satirical "Gulliver's Travels", and Daniel Defoe (1660–1713) with "Robinson Crusoe".

The Restoration

Rationalism, Sensibility and Romanticism

The second half of the 18th century was the great age of Realism and Sensibility. Leading representatives of these trends were Samuel Johnson (1709–84), an influential critic and compiler of the great "Dictionary of the English Language", Laurence Sterne (1713–68), creator of the comic anti-hero "Tristram Shandy" in the whimsical and bawdy novel "The Life and Opinions of Tristram Shandy", and Oliver Goldsmith (1728–74), with the "Vicar of Wakefield". The tone of the novel during this period was set by the realistic and humorous novels of Henry Fielding (1707–54; "Tom Jones") and Tobias Smollett (1721–71; "The Expedition of Humphrey Clinker").

Rationalism
Samuel Johnson

At the beginning of the 19th century came the witty and psychologically perceptive novels of Jane Austen (1775–1817; "Emma") and the true to life historical novels of Maria Edgeworth (1767–1849; "Castle Rackrent").
  The plays of Richard Sheridan (1751–1816) were comedies of manners akin to the Restoration Comedies ("The Rivals" and "School for Scandal"). Thomas Percy (1729–1811), an Anglican bishop, published "Reliques of Ancient English Poetry", which led to a wave of interest in the old English ballads.

Jane Austen

The "Lyrical Ballads" of William Wordsworth (1771–1850) and Samuel Taylor Coleridge (1772–1834) brought English literature into the mainstream of the great European Romantic movement. In deliberately

Romanticism
William
Wordsworth

simple language Wordsworth observed and described the divine element which he saw in nature, and wrote more than 500 sonnets, a form of which he was a master.

The second generation of Romantic poets tended to die young – Lord Byron (1788–1824), Percy Bysshe Shelley (1792–1822) and John Keats (1795–1821), none of whom lived to be older than thirty-six. Byron's principal works, "Childe Harold's Pilgrimage" and "Manfred", reflect his world-weariness, melancholy and passion. The central theme of Shelley's poems, "Ode to the West Wind" and "Prometheus Unbound", is his quest for harmony and union with nature. His wife Mary Wollstonecraft (1797–1851) wrote "Frankenstein or the Modern Prometheus", a vivid novel expressing the Romanticists' fear of the inexorable growth of technology as exemplified in Professor Frankenstein's monster. Keats made his mark in the lyrical field.

Sir Walter Scott

Sir Walter Scott (1771–1832; see Famous People) collected and composed ballads and verse romances, translated many German poems and Goethe's play "Götz von Berlichingen." He also wrote more than forty historical novels, vivid creations of life in earlier centuries, particularly Scotland in the 17th and 18th centuries. His work laid the foundations of the historical novel of the 19th and 20th centuries. The best of a number of such novels written by Edward Bulwer-Lytton (1803–73), "The Last Days of Pompeii", remains popular to this day.

19th century

Realism

The Victorian period was an age of Realism, beginning with the poetry of Alfred Lord Tennyson (1809–92), Poet Laureate, who had a remarkable feeling for rhythm and the music of words ("In Memoriam", "Idylls of the King", "Poems by Two Brothers" and other collections), and the works of Robert Browning (1812–61) which included "The Ring and the Book", "Pippa Passes" and "Men and Women". His adored wife Elizabeth Barret-Browning (1806–61) was renowned as a sensitive poet, one well-known example of her work being "Sonnets from the Portuguese", Matthew Arnold (1822–88), the critic and writer, wrote "Rugby Chapel", "Thyrsis" and "Dover Beach".

Charles Dickens

Charles Dickens (1812–70) introduced the novel of social criticism, pillorying the social abuses of the new industrial society but covering a wide range of mood, examples of his books being "David Copperfield" (with a strong autobiographical element), "Hard Times", "Pickwick Papers" and "A Christmas Carol". Benjamin Disraeli's (1804–81; see Famous People) "Sybil, or The Two Nations" and "Coningsby", and Elizabeth Gaskell's (1810–65) "Mary Barton" are also novels criticising the social conditions of the age.

William Thackeray

The second most important novelist of the period after Dickens was William Makepeace Thackeray (1811–63), whose strength lies in social satire: "Vanity Fair", "The Newcomers", "Barry Lyndon". Others followed him and produced a series of political novels, such as the "Barchester" novels of Anthony Trollope (1815–82).

The Brontë sisters

The three sisters Charlotte (1816–55), Emily (1818–48) and Ann Brontë (1820–49) wrote novels of life on the Yorkshire moors, depicting finely drawn female characters ("Jane Eyre", "Wuthering Heights", "The Tenant of Wildfell Hall").

Pre-Raphaelites

In 1948 a number of young artists and writers joined together to form the Pre-Raphaelite Brotherhood, a group intent on defying the London Academy by shunning the influence of painters and writers who came after the Italian artist Raphael. One of its main adherents in the literary field was Dante Gabriel Rossetti (1828–82) with his ballads (such as "Sister Helen") and poems ("The House of Life"). The greatest poet of this generation was Algernon Charles Swinburne (1837–1909), who was influenced by ancient literature and French poetry. He wrote plays (including a trilogy on Mary Queen of Scots), poems and ballads which gave rise to some criticism in the strictly moral world of Victorian Britain, novels and lyrical dramas, such as "Atalanta in Calydon".

George Eliot, the pseudonym of Mary Ann Evans (1819–80), an unusually emancipated woman for her time, wrote psychological novels of social concern, such as "Adam Bede", "Silas Marner" and others, which are convincing portrayals of simple people and their problems. The best known novel dealing with life in the schools of the day – the model for a whole succession of other works – was "Tom Brown's Schooldays" by the Christian social reformer Thomas Hughes (1822–96).

George Eliot

A leading critic of the art and manners of the day was Thomas Carlyle (1795–1881), later rector of Edinburgh University, who attacked the materialism of his time ("Sartor Resartus", "Past and Present", "Chartism" and a number of historical works). John Ruskin (1819–1900) began as an art critic ("The Stones of Venice") but later turned to social criticism ("Modern Painters", "A Joy for Ever"). Another critic and writer was Arthur Symons (1865–1945), a representative of Symbolism and author of "The Symbolist Movement in Literature". Thomas Babington Macaulay (1800–59), a leading historian of the Victorian period, wrote brilliant essays and an unfinished "History of England".

Thomas Carlyle

Two writers rather outside the mainstream of literature but with a niche of their own and whose work still strongly influences similar writers today were Edward Lear and Lewis Carroll. Edward Lear (1812–88), the landscape painter who created the genre of nonsense literature (limericks, nonsense poems and ballads) has had many imitators. Lewis Carroll, the pseudonym of Charles L. Dodgson (1832–98), professor of mathematics at Oxford, is best known for "Alice's Adventures in Wonderland", "Alice Through the Looking Glass" and his long nonsense poem "The Hunting of the Snark".

Edward Lear
Lewis Carroll

At the end of the 19th century George Meredith (1828–1909) was the most famous representative of the psychological and philosophical novel; his major works include "The Egoist" and "Diana on the Crossways". Thomas Hardy (1840–1928) wrote mostly tragic novels in which pastoral descriptions played a considerable part ("Tess of the d'Urbervilles", "The Return of the Native", "Far from the Madding Crowd", "The Mayor of Casterbridge" and "Jude the Obscure"). Samuel Butler (1835–1902) described a satirical Utopia in his "Erewhon" and "Erewhon Revisited", and wrote a fine autobiographical novel "The Way of All Flesh".

The turn of the century
Thomas Hardy

Robert Louis Stevenson (1850–94) wrote adventure novels such as "Treasure Island" and "Kidnapped", which are still very popular, "The Strange Case of Dr Jekyll and Mr Hyde" and "The New Arabian Nights".

Robert Louis
Stevenson

Rudyard Kipling (1865–1936), the first Englishman to win the Nobel Prize for Literature, wrote stories with an Indian background and a number of books which are still popular with children, including "Kim" and "The Jungle Book".

Rudyard Kipling

Oscar Wilde (1856–1900) gave expression to an aestheticism allied to the French decadent movement in his novel "The Picture of Dorian Gray". While in prison following his trial on homosexual charges he wrote "The Ballad of Reading Gaol", perhaps his finest poem. He is principally remembered today for his pungent comedies, which include "Lady

Oscar Wilde

Windermere's Fan", "A Woman of No Importance", "An Ideal Husband" and "The Importance of Being Ernest".

Plays with a content based on social realism were the hallmark of Sir Arthur Wing Pinero (1855–1934), for thirty years London's most successful dramatist ("The Second Mrs Tanqueray", "The Notorious Mrs Ebbsmith"), the briefly very popular Thomas William Robertson (1829–71; "Caste" and "Society"), and Henry Arthur Jones (1851–1929), author of some 60 plays, including "Saints and Sinners" and "The Liars".

20th century

Lyric poetry

The literature of the 20th century shows a variety of conflicting trends, with more marked differences between that of England, Scotland, Wales and Ireland.

Ireland

Lyric poetry, for example, was strongly influenced by the newly awakened Celtic consciousness. The leading exponent of this school, and the most important lyric poet of the first half of the 20th century, was William Butler Yeats (1865–1939), author of dramas ("Cathleen Ni Houlihan", "The Countess Cathleen"), numerous poems, including "The Lake Isle of Inishfree", "Easter 1916", "Sailing to Byzantium", and essays. His contemporary, George William Russell (1867–1935) was also inspired by Irish mythology in, for example, "Voices of the Stones" and "Midsummer Eve". Yeats was followed by such poets as Austin Clarke (1896–1974), who also revived verse drama, and Patrick Kavanagh (1904–67), author of "The Great Hunger". Contemporary scenes are vividly portrayed by such Northern Ireland lyricists as John Montague (b. 1929; "The Rough Field", "Mount Eagle"), John Hewitt (1907–1987), Michael Longley (b. 1939), Derek Mahon (b. 1941), Paul Muldoon (b. 1951), Tom Paulin (b. 1949) and Medbh McGuckian (b. 1950; "Venus and the Rain"). The major contemporary Irish poet writing in the English language also hails from Northern Ireland: Seamus Heaney (b. 1939; "Death of a Naturalist", "North", "Field Work", "Station Island"), professor of poetry at Oxford University. The Dubliner Thomas Kinsella (b. 1928), with his translations from the Irish and his poems lamenting the break in Irish linguistic tradition, has made a name for himself, together with Eavan Boland (b. 1944) whose diverse subjects ranging from Irish myths to the everyday life of women in Ireland have ensured her a wide readership.

England
T. S. Eliot

A major modern lyric poet, and also a dramatist, was Thomas Stearns Elliot (1888–1965) who, in 1948, won the Nobel Prize for Literature and also held a number of honorary degrees. His works include "The Waste Land", "The Hollow Men" and his most important lyric poem, "Four Quartets".

Another outstanding lyric poet was Dame Edith Sitwell (1887–1964), whose later poems were principally concerned with the insoluble problem of human existence. She also wrote critical essays and novels.

Pylon Poets

Wystan Hugh Auden (1907–73) was the leader of a group of young left-wing students known as the "Pylon poets". His work shows a mingling of old heroic songs and psychoanalysis, mystery plays and Symbolism ("The Age of Anxiety"). Other members of his circle were Stephen Spender (b. 1909), author of works of social criticism as well as poems, Louis MacNeice (1907–63) and Cecil Day-Lewis (1904–72).

Ezra Pound

The Imagist school was launched in London in 1912 with a manifesto written by Ezra Pound (1885–1972). Other members of his group were T. E. Hulme (1883–1917), regarded as the father of Imagism, Richard Aldington (1892–1962), Frank Stuart Flint (1885–1960) and Sir Herbert Read (1893–1968), who was mainly active as an art critic.

There was also a Neo-Romantic trend in lyric poetry, a leading representative of which was John Masefield (1878–1967), author of "Salt Water Ballads", inspired by the old sea-shanties. Neo-Romantic poetry, much of it written by poets of Welsh or Irish origin, largely prevailed over the more intellectual trend of T. S. Eliot's followers.

The most famous of the Neo-Romantics was Dylan Thomas (1914–53), whose "Under Milk Wood" was a very successful television play. His most important lyrical work was "Deaths and Entrances". Other Neo-Romantic poets included Walter de la Mare (1873–1956), the Anglo-Welsh writer W. H. Davies (1871–1940; "Autobiography of a Supertramp"), Laurie Lee (b. 1914), George Granville Barker (b. 1913), Lawrence Durrell (1912–91; "The Alexandria Quartet"), Vernon Watkins (1906–67), a friend of Dylan Thomas and a fellow Welshman who also sang of Wales in his poems, and Kathleen Raine (b. 1908), a successor to the metaphysical poets of the 17th century, who glorifies the wonders of Creation.

Dylan Thomas

Hugh MacDiarmid (the pseudonym of Christopher Murray Grieve, 1892–1973), was the main influence in the "Scottish Renaissance". His lengthy poem "A Drunk Man Looks at the Thistle", for example, ranks in importance with the works of Yeats, Eliot or Ezra Pound. Other Scottish Renaissance writers are Norman MacCraig (b. 1910) and the outstanding poet in the Gaelic language, Sorley MacLean (b. 1911), the novelists Neil Gunn (1891–1973) and Lewis Grasic Gibbon (pseudonym of James Leslie Mitchell, 1901–35) and the lyricist, novelist and translator Edwin Muir (1887–1959). One of the younger generation is Crichton Smith (b. 1928), who writes in both Gaelic and English.

Scotland

In the 20th century the novel turns from descriptive to harsh realism; psychoanalysis plays an increasingly important role; and society's outsiders become the heroes. The subconscious, the world of dreams and science fiction come to the fore. The mode of expression becomes sparer; humour is replaced by the grotesque; description gives way to allusion; and flashbacks and the recollection of characters and events are favourite techniques. It becomes almost impossible to assign writers to this or that group.

Prose

One of the best-known novelists of the early decades of the century was John Galsworthy (1867–1933), who received the Nobel Prize for Literature in 1932; his fame was founded on the sequence of novels which he called "The Forsyte Saga". Another popular author was Sir Hugh Walpole (1884–1941), author of the "Jeremy" books and "The Dark Forest", but even he was exceeded in popularity by A. J. Cronin (1896–1981), whose novel "The Citadel" became an international best-seller, as did "How Green is my Valley" by Richard Llewellyn (1907–1983). A very versatile writer was J. B. Priestley (1894–1974), dramatist, novelist, essayist and critic, whose works included "The Good Companions" and "An Inspector Calls".

John Galsworthy

W. Somerset Maugham (1874–1965) deals with psychological problems in his novels and his brilliant short stories, which include "Liza of Lambeth", "The Moon and Sixpence", "Cakes and Ale" and "Of Human Bondage".

William Somerset Maugham

An intelligent critic of his time, who inspired many successors, was Aldous Huxley (1894–1963), grandson of the famous scientist T. H. Huxley, whose "Brave New World" and "Brave New World Revisited" satirised society's belief in progress. Another sharply satirical writer was Evelyn Waugh (1903–66), author of "Decline and Fall", "Vile Bodies" and "The Loved One", whose most popular novel was without doubt "Brideshead Revisited".

Aldous Huxley

Literature

William Golding

William Golding (b. 1911), the "Grand Old Man" of the contemporary novel ("Lord of the Flies", "The Rites of Passage"), received the Nobel Prize for Literature in 1983.

Joseph Conrad

One of the most brilliant English story-tellers was Joseph Conrad (1857–1924), born in the Ukraine of Polish parents, who learned English only in adulthood. He was a sailor for many years, and the sea, adventure, the irresistible force of the elements and the longing for distant places are the most important features of his novels ("Lord Jim", "Heart of Darkness", "The Rover", "An Outcast of the Islands").

Impressions gained from travel also play an important part in the work of Edward Morgan Forster (1879–1970). Among his best novels are "Howards End" and "A Passage to India". In the novels of Joyce Cary (1888–1957) events are frequently seen through the eyes of the narrator – a device employed in modern fiction – and the central characters are often children ("The House of Children", "The Horse's Mouth").

Victoria Sackville-West

Among the numerous modern women novelists are Victoria Sackville-West (1892–1962; "The Edwardians"), Elizabeth Bowen (1899–1973; "The Death of the Heart") and the New Zealand-born Katherine Mansfield (1888–1923; "The Garden Party").

A distinctive category of modern writing is the "stream of consciousness" novel – concerned not with action but with what goes on in the characters' minds.

James Joyce
Virginia Woolf

Leading exponents of this genre are James Joyce (1822–1941), who had a great influence on the European novel with "Ulysses" and "Finnegan's Wake", and Virginia Woolf (1882–1941; "Mrs Dalloway", "Orlando", "To the Lighthouse"), a shining light among women authors.

H. G. Wells
George Orwell

World-famous authors of Utopian novels were H. G. Wells (1886–1946; "The Time Machine", "The Invisible Man"), and George Orwell, the pseudonym of Eric Blair (1903–50), who wrote "Animal Farm" and "Nineteen Eighty Four". He also wrote enthralling social commentaries such as "The Road to Wigan Pier", essays and reflections on the Spanish Civil War ("Homage to Catalonia").

Graham Greene

Religious themes are common in the work of Graham Greene (1904–1991), who also wrote books for children and light fiction ("The Power and the Glory", "The Heart of the Matter", "The Third Man"), and Bruce Marshall (1899–1987; "All Glorious Within").

D. H. Lawrence

An advocate of natural, healthy sensuality was David Herbert Lawrence (1855–1930), who wrote essays, plays and poems as well as novels. His best work, "Sons and Lovers", has many autobiographical elements. The explicitly sexual novel, "Lady Chatterley's Lover", banned until 1960, was the subject of a celebrated court case.

G. K. Chesterton

The English humorous novel is represented by Gilbert Keith Chesterton (1874–1936), known primarily for his "Father Brown" stories. The outstanding humorist of the 20th century, however, was undoubtedly Sir Pelham Grenville ("P.G.") Wodehouse, whose "Blandings" novels and tales of the accident-prone world of the socialite Bertie Wooster and his manservant Jeeves have guaranteed him immortality.

Detective novels

In the special genre of the detective novel and criminal thriller a leading place has long been held by English writers, ranging from Sir Arthur Conan Doyle (1859–1930), author of the Sherlock Holmes stories, through Edgar Wallace (1875–1957) and P. D. James (b. 1920) to Dame Agatha Christie (1890–1976), who created the two legendary detectives Hercule Poirot and Miss Jane Marple.

The generation of such novelists and short story-writers as Iris Murdoch (b. 1919), Doris Lessing (b. 1919; "The Golden Notebook"), Muriel Spark (b. 1918) and Sir Angus Wilson (1913–91) is followed by that of David Lodge (b. 1935; "Changing Places"), Malcolm Bradbury (b. 1932; "The History Man"), John Braine (1922–86; "Room at the Top"), and Kingsley Amis (b. 1922), one of the "Angry Young Men" with his novel "Lucky Jim"; and also Alan Sillitoe (b. 1928; "The Loneliness of the Long Distance Runner"), Anthony Burgess (b. 1917; "A Clockwork Orange"), Margaret Drabble (b. 1939), John Fowles (b. 1926; "The French Lieutenant's Woman"), Penelope Lively (b. 1933), Anita Brookner (b. 1928; "Hotel du Lac"), the feminist Fay Weldon (b. 1933) and Julian Barnes (b. 1946; "Flaubert's Parrot"), who – under the pseudonym Dan Kavanagh – has also written four amusing thrillers starring the detective Duffy.

In Glasgow, in particular, the 1970s and 1980s saw something approaching a second cultural Renaissance, centred around such novelists as Alasdair Gray (b. 1934), whose large-scale work "Lanark" can be considered on a par with the writings of James Joyce, and James Kelman (b. 1947). Ian McEwan (b. 1948) is another writer whose novels "The Child in Time" and "The Ploughman's Lunch" have been the subject of much debate as a result of the frank and open way in which they treat such matters as sexuality, perversion, passion and politics. The works of Rosamund Pilcher (b. 1924), who lives near Dundee, are also popular abroad. In addition to the rise in the amount of feminist literature and novels geared to certain regions, bi-cultural and multi-cultural authors are coming more and more to the fore; examples of the latter are the Nigerian Ben Okri (b. 1959) or the Bombay-born Salman Rushdie (b. 1947; "The Midnight's Children"), whose "magic realism" was inspired by the work of James Joyce and Günther Grass, and who has been under sentence of death by order of the Ayatollah Khomeini of Iran since the publication of his "Satanic Verses".

Irish writers have played a considerable role in the recent history of the modern novel. Mention must first be made of the "Three O's" – Liam O'Flaherty (1897–1984), best known for his unsentimental and lyrical short stories and for his novel based on the fight for Irish independence, "The Informer"; Frank O'Connor (the pseudonym of Michael Francis O'Donovan, 1903–66), who also worked as a dramatist at the Abbey Theatre; and Sean O'Faolain (1900–91), who published the most influential Irish literary magazine, "The Bell", and was also a biographer. All three contributed to the worldwide regard enjoyed by Irish short stories since George Moore (1852–1933; "The Untilled Field") and James Joyce ("Dubliners"). Another shining light was Flann O'Brien (1911–66; actually Brian O'Nolan, pseudonym Myles na Gopaleen), who contributed witty commentaries on his fellow countrymen to the Irish Times and whose madly funny novels ("At Swim Two Birds") have found avid readers in Britain and elsewhere. The Irish tradition for novels and short stories is being preserved by such writers as Francis Stuart (b. 1902; "Black List, section H"), Mary Lavin (b. 1912), William Trevor (b. 1921; "The Ballroom of Romance", "Fools of Fortune"), Brian Moore (b. 1921; "The Lonely Passion of Judith Hearne", "Lies of Silence"), John Banville (b. 1945; "Birchwood", "Kepler"), Jennifer Johnston (b. 1930; daughter of the dramatist Denis Johnston; wrote "The Captains and the Kings"), Julia O'Faolain (b. 1932; "No Country for Young Men"), Edna O'Brian (b. 1932; "The Country Girls"), John McGahern (b. 1935; "The Pornographer", "Amongst Women"), James Plunkett (b. 1920; "Strumpet City"), Bernard MacLaverty (b. 1945; "Cal, Lamb"), Desmond Hogan (b. 1951; "A Curious Street") and the lyricist, dramatist, novelist and publisher Dermot Bolger (b. 1959; "The Journey Home").

In recent decades the influence of British and Irish playwrights has been a predominant one in the theatre throughout the Western world. In

Literature

association with Yeats and the Abbey Theatre founded in Dublin in 1904, such Irish dramatists as John Millington Synge (1871–1909; "The Playboy of the Western World", "Riders to the Sea"), Lady Augusta Gregory (1852–1932; "The Rising of the Moon") and later Sean O'Casey (1880–1964; "The Shadow of a Gunman", "Juno and the Paycock" and "The Plough and the Stars") have gained international renown.

G. B. Shaw

One of the major figures of the early years was George Bernard Shaw (1856–1950), who received the Nobel Prize for Literature in 1925, and whose plays "Arms and the Man", "Pygmalion", "St Joan" and "Heartbreak House" still feature in the theatre repertoire today.

Other major playwrights of the period are William Somerset Maugham (1874–1965), Noel Coward (1899–1973) with "Blithe Spirit" and "Private Lives", T. S. Eliot (1888–1965), who achieved international fame with "Murder in the Cathedral" (conceived as a kind of mystery play like "Everyman"), Christopher Fry (b. 1907; "The Lady is not for Burning") and Terence Rattigan (1911–77; "The Deep Blue Sea").

"Angry Young Men"
John Osborne

The "angry young men" of the 1950s also left their mark on the theatre, with their vigorous criticisms of society which, mainly in their plays but also in their novels, was expressed in language designed to shock. The original angry young man was John Osborne (b. 1929), with his "Look Back in Anger"; others were Arnold Wesker (b. 1932; "Chicken Soup with Barley"), Shelagh Delaney (b. 1938; "A Taste of Honey") and John Arden (b. 1930; "Sergeant Musgrave's Dance"). In the plays of Harold Pinter (b. 1930; "The Birthday Party") and Norman F. Simpson (b. 1919) the influence of English naturalism is combined with that of the *théâtre de l'absurde* of Samuel Beckett (1906–89), an Irishman who lived in France and wrote many of his plays in French and then translated them into English ("Waiting for Godot", "Endgame").

Samuel Beckett
Brendan Behan

The major Irishman to write plays for the English stage in the 1950s was Brendan Behan (1923–64; "The Hostage"). Since the 1960s Brian Friel, born in 1929 in Northern Ireland, has become a leading playwright with such plays as "Philadelphia, Here I Come" and "Translations or Dancing at Lughnasa". Thomas Murphy (b. 1935; "A Whistle in the Dark", "The Gigli Concert") is difficult to fit into any definite genre but, like John Brendan Keane (b. 1928; "The Field") deals primarily with the radical changes taking place in modern Irish society. Polished dialogue and originality are the hallmarks of Hugh Leonard (actually John Keyes Byrne, b. 1926), who does a lot of work for both Irish and English television. The younger generation includes Frank McGuiness (b. 1953) who, in "Observe the Sons of Ulster Marching Towards the Somme", tries to get at the root of the Northern Ireland conflict. The civil war smouldering in Ireland is also the main subject of works by John Boyd (b. 1912; "The Flats"), Graham Reid (b. 1945) and Martin Lynch (b. 1950), as well as of the two leading female Irish dramatists, Anne Devlin (b. 1950; "Ourselves Alone") and Christina Reid ("Joyriders").

Alan Ayckbourn

One of Britain's most popular writers for the stage during recent years has been Alan Ayckbourn (b. 1939), with such plays as "Absurd Person Singular" or "Bedroom Farce", which border on light theatre. Edward Bond (b. 1934; "Saved") frequently appears on European stages. The short career of Joe Orton (1933–67; "What the Butler Saw", "Entertaining Mr Sloane") was marred by violence and scandals. Elements of farce and satire are mingled in a most amusing way in the plays of Tom Stoppard (b. 1937), such as "Rosencrantz and Guildenstern are Dead" and "Travesties".

Peter Shaffer

International hits were scored by Michael Frayn (b. 1933) with his "farce on top of farce" "Noises Off" and Peter Shaffer (b. 1926) with "Equus" and "Amadeus". The politically leftish "68 Generation" includes such now established writers as David Edgar (b. 1948), Howard Brenton (b. 1942; "The Romans in Britain"), David Hare (b. 1947),

Trevor Griffiths (b. 1935: "The Party") and Howard Barker (b. 1946). The Scot Tom McGrath (b. 1935; "The Cheviot, the Stag and the Black", "Black Oil") has made a considerable impact on popular political theatre. Pam Gems (b. 1925; "Piaff") and Caryl Churchill (b. 1938; "Top Girls") have introduced decisive trends into the feminist theatre.

Music

Although Britain cannot be compared with Germany or Italy in the field of classical music it has nevertheless made a considerable contribution to the history of music in Europe and has produced a number of great composers, such as Purcell, Elgar and Britten. Its real importance, however, lies less in its creative compositions and more in its highly cultivated styles of playing, something which proved irresistible to such famous foreign-born composers as Handel, who became a British subject in 1726 and died in London in 1759, Johann Christian Bach, who died in London in 1782, Haydn and Mendelssohn.

Classical Music

In the Middle Ages the monasteries and later the churches and cathedrals devoted much attention to plainsong, and their influence spread to the Continent of Europe. As early as the 10th century Winchester Cathedral had an organ with more than 400 pipes. Settings for several voices are found in church and secular music from the 11th century onwards (*Sumer is icumen in*, early 13th c.). Fauxbourdon (a simple form of harmonisation) occurs from the first half of the 15th century onwards, but was probably used earlier as a harmonic technique in improvisation.

Middle Ages

The leading European master in the 15th century was John Dunstable (*c.* 1385–1453). An important contribution was made during the Elizabethan period by music for virginals (portable spinets), which influenced instrumental music in general. Hugh Aston (d. 1522) and Thomas Tallis (d. 1585) were followed at the end of the 16th century by composers of madrigals including William Byrd, Orlando Gibbons and the great lutenist John Dowland (1562–1626). They were particularly fond of variations and used many folk tunes in their music. The madrigal rose to great heights in the work of John Blow (1649–1708), still more so in that of his pupil Henry Purcell (1658–95), one of the best-known of all English composers, who also wrote vocal and instrumental music and operas (Dido and Aeneas).

Virginals and madrigals

With Handel (George Frederick Handel), who became director of the Haymarket Opera House in London in 1719, the Germanic influence reached Britain. His major compositions date from the time he spent in London – the "Water Music", "Messiah", "Judas Maccabaeus", "Music for the Royal Firework". Johann Christian Pepusch from Berlin composed the music for John Gay's "Beggar's Opera" in 1728. In the second half of the 18th century Johann Christian Bach, Johann Sebastian's son, became music master to the family of George III and founded the Bach-Abel concerts in collaboration with the German viola virtuoso Karl Friedrich Abel. In the last decade of the century Haydn was enthusiastically feted in London before achieving full recognition in Vienna.

18th century

In the middle of the 19th century there was another great flowering of music in Britain. Arthur Sullivan (1842–1900) composed the music for the ever-popular light operas including the "Mikado", with libretti by W. S. Gilbert. Sidney Jones was another successful composer of operettas. Around 1880 a number of notable musicians came to the fore – Hubert

19th and 20th centuries

Parry (1848–1914), Charles Villiers Stanford (1852–1924) and Alexander Mackenzie (1847–1935). One of the most important British composers since Purcell was Sir Edward Elgar (1857–1934), whose music has a strongly national emphasis. Frederick Delius (1863–1934) composed operas and orchestral and choral works characterised by rich tonal colour. Another composer who achieved international success was Cyril Scott. One of the leading musical personalities of recent times was Ralph Vaughan Williams (1872–1958), who composed symphonic music and operas; he was also a leader of the folk-song movement. Other important composers included Frank Bridge (1879–1941) and Gustav Holst (1874–1935), whose orchestral suite "The Planets" has become more and more popular in recent years.

Among composers born around the turn of the century some, like Sir Arthur Bliss (1891–1975), have achieved international recognition. These include William Walton (1902-83), Michael Tippet (b. 1905), Edmund Rubbra (b. 1901) and Constant Lambert (b. 1905). An outstanding 20th century composer was Benjamin Britten (1913–76; see Famous People), remembered above all for his operas "Peter Grimes" and "Albert Herring", as well as for his impressive "War Requiem". Born slightly later (1920), Peter Racine Fricker is noted as a composer of symphonies.

Britain has made relatively little contribution to the most recent developments in music, including the electronic field. Practitioners of dodecaphonic music include Elizabeth Lutyens (b. 1906) and H. Searle (b. 1926), a pupil of Webern, also respected as a theorist. A more moderate trend is represented by F. Burt (b. 1926) and A. Goehr (b. 1932); C. Cardew (b. 1936), on the other hand, belongs to the avant-garde.

The world of music

The quality of the facilities offered and of the music demanded by audiences in many provincial centres such as Cardiff and Glasgow, for example, as well as in London, continues to attract many international stars who come to give guest performances or even decide to settle here

The Beatles on receiving their MBEs from the Queen

permanently. Of the native virtuosos special mention should be made of the eccentric punk violinist Nigel Kennedy and of Simon Rattle, the conductor of the Birmingham Symphony Orchestra. The Scottish National Opera in Glasgow and the Welsh National Opera in Cardiff have also made their mark in recent years.

Britain has been well represented in the popular music scene in the last few decades. The word "musicals" has become almost synonymous with the name of Andrew Lloyd-Webber, the composer of "Cats" and "The Phantom of the Opera" and commercially the most successful composer of his time. Jazz has always produced some first-class bands, such as those led by Chris Barber and Monty Sunshine, for example.

Light and Popular Music
Musicals and jazz

It is in the field of beat, pop and rock music, however, that Britain has excelled. Growing out of the skiffle music of the 1950s, starring Lonnie Donegan, and rock'n roll from America, the "Swinging Sixties" became the decade of the Beatles, the group of four young men from Liverpool who rocketed to fame almost overnight and whom John Lennon described as "more popular than Jesus" when they were at their height. Fresh from playing in cellar-bars in their native city, John Lennon, Paul McCartney, George Harrison and Ringo Starr produced a number of classics and were responsible for extending the scope of pop music worldwide. They and other British groups combined elements of classical with electronic and Far Eastern music.

Beat, pop and rock
The Beatles

The other rock'n roll institution are the Rolling Stones with Mick Jagger and Keith Richard. Formed in 1962, and once notorious as the "bad boys" of rock, they are still performing on stage even though some of the original members have gone.

The Rolling Stones

In addition to the Beatles and the "Stones" the golden age of beat music brought forth such groups as The Kinks (with the brothers Ray and Dave Davies), The Who (with Pete Townsend and Roger Daltry), The Small Faces, Eric Burdon and the Animals (linked to "blues" music in their early days, like The Cream or Rory Gallagher) and Pink Floyd, a group always ready to experiment.

In the early 1970s music became harder and more stringent, with groups such as Led Zeppelin and Uriah Heep. Musical styles became more varied – heavy metal, hard rock, mainstream, pub rock, glamour and disco became everyday words. Groups, including Slade, Sweet and T. Rex, dominated the charts. The disco wave enabled the Bee Gees to make a comeback. The "bombastic rock" of the late 1970s, with Queen, Emerson, Lake and Palmer, Pink Floyd, Genesis and Yes, was followed by a radical return to the "three chords" of rock'n roll.

"Punk rock" then burst onto the scene, often obscene, always disrespectful, intent on forcing its rebellious style of music on to what it regarded as the smug and self-satisfied world of the music business. Its main exponents were the Sex Pistols, The Stranglers, The Clash and The Jam.

Punk

The short-lived punk revolt evolved in the early 1980s into "New Wave" music, with musical skills again coming to the fore and with such outstanding bands as The Police, Simple Minds and U2, the Irish group. At the same time computerised electronic music was the forte of groups such as Duran Duran, Culture Club and Frankie Goes to Hollywood. Dire Straits and Thin Lizzy played solid or "adult" rock, suggesting that their fans had grown up with the bands. The link between pop and rock music and society in general is underlined by such events as the "Live Aid Concert" organised by Bob Geldorf in 1985 to provide aid to the starving in Africa. Outstanding singers and songwriters include Van Morrison from Northern Ireland, Sting (an ex-member of Police), Peter Gabriel and Phil Collins (Genesis). Music aimed at teenagers and for the hit parade includes a multitude of styles such as "hip hop", "rap", "rave", "house" and "techno".

Films

From the very beginning the British film industry has been over-shadowed by that of the USA. Although various laws imposing restrictions on the numbers of films which could be imported, such as the Cinematograph Films Act of 1927, have helped the British film industry to some extent, they related largely to quantity rather than quality; the notorious "quota quickies" of the 1930s were an example of this. Nevertheless, since the film industry was first established here at the end of the 19th century a typically British film tradition has developed.

Pre-World War II

In 1909 the Cinematograph Act was passed, and in 1912 the Board of Film Censors was set up. One of the first directors to treat films as an artistic medium was Cecil Hepworth, with such films as "Black Beauty" (1907), "David Copperfield" (1913) and "Hamlet" (1913). In the First World War films were used to distribute propaganda, and this in effect sowed the seeds of the great British tradition in the field of documentary films, which enjoyed a heyday in the 1930s with John Grierson and the Crown Film Unit. Documentary films of high quality such as "Coal Face" (1936) and "Night Mail" (1936) still accurately portray the world of industry.

In the 1920s the career of Alfred Hitchcock (see Famous People) began with "The Pleasure Garden", and in 1919 he made his first talkie, "Blackmail". A series of thrillers made Hitchcock a star among directors – "The Man Who Knew Too Much" (1934), "The Thirty-Nine Steps" (1935) and "Sabotage" (1936).

One of the most influential personalities in British films in the 1930s and 1940s was the Hungarian immigrant Alexander Korda, who built his own studios at Denham, known as London Films, and produced such successful films as "The Private Life of Henry VIII" (1933), "The Scarlet Pimpernel" (1934) and "Things to Come" (1936).

During the Second World War some powerful propaganda films were made, such as "London Can Take It" (1940) and "Coastal Command" (1942). Outstanding, however, were Laurence Olivier's Shakespeare films ("Henry V", 1944), which he directed and in which he played the major role and which helped to instil a deep feeling of patriotism in many English hearts. David Lean and Carol Reed were two more directors who established themselves during the war. Lean made "Brief Encounter" in 1945, and Reed was responsible for the Northern Ireland drama "Odd Man Out" in 1947 and one of the century's great films, "The Third Man" (1949), filmed in the bombed city of Vienna with Orson Welles in the starring role.

The post-war period

War films remained popular in the 1950s – "The Colditz Story" (1955) and "Bridge on the River Kwai" (1957). Films showing typical British humour were made at Ealing Studios in the late 1940s and 1950s, such as "Kind Hearts and Coronets" (1947) and "Ladykillers" (1955) – both starring Alec Guiness – as well as "The Man in the White Suit" (1951) and Alexander Mackendruck's hit set on an island off Scotland, "Whisky Galore" (1949). Very popular, too, were films based on the Sherlock Holmes novels of Conan Doyle and the detective novels written by Agatha Christie, starring Peter Ustinov as Hercule Poirot and Margaret Rutherford as Miss Marple. In the face of intense competition from television, the Film Industry Defence Organisation (FIDO) was formed in 1958, with the aim of preventing cinema films being shown on television. At that time, too, basic changes were taking place in British films; the "angry young man" syndrome moved from books to films, and scenes from working-class life, the "concrete jungles" of British industrial areas, class differences and sexuality all appeared on the screen. The way was opened up by films such as Jack Clayton's "Room at the Top" (1958) or the film of John Osborne's book "Look Back in Anger" by

Tony Richardson. Edgar Reisz followed with "Saturday Night and Sunday Morning" (1960). Lindsay Anderson with "This Sporting Life" (1963) and John Schlesinger with "A Kind of Loving" (1962).

Tony Richardson introduced a "new naturalism" with "Tom Jones" (1963), a sparkling comedy and one of the great screen successes of the 1960s. About the same time Terence Young produced "Dr No" (1962), with Sean Connery, the first of the series of James Bond films.

Partly under pressure from the McCarthy regime in America, partly as the result of large-scale foreign investment in the British film industry, a number of foreign directors and producers came to work in England in the 1960s. These included Joseph Losey ("Accident", 1967), Richard Lester and his Beatles films, Stanley Kubrick ("2001: A Space Odyssey", 1968; "A Clockwork Orange", 1971; "Barry Lyndon", 1975) and Roman Polanski ("Dance of the Vampires", 1967). On the other hand, many British producers went to America, ranging from Alfred Hitchcock to Alan Parker, and made such films as "Fame", "Angel Heart", "Birdy" and "The Commitments" (1991).

The success enjoyed by British pop and musical films continued with that of the rock-opera "Tommy" (1975). The new generation of producers in the 1970s included John Boorman ("Zardoz", 1974; "Excalibur", 1981), Ken Russell ("Mahler", 1974; "Lisztomania", 1975) and Ken Loach ("Kes", 1970), who won the European Film Prize for "Riffraff" in 1992.

The present day

A completely individual type of film humour appeared in the Monty Python films including "Monty Python and The Holy Grail" (1974) and "The Life of Brian" (1979). When they split up the members of the Monty Python team pursued their individual careers, and John Cleese and Michael Palin appeared in "A Fish Called Wanda" in 1988. Film spectaculars reached new heights in the hands of Richard Attenborough with his epic "Gandhi" (1982) and David Lean and James Ivory with their elegant films of E. M. Forster's "A Passage to India", 1984 and "A Room With a View", 1985).

Co-operation between the film industry and television (especially Channel 4) now goes without saying. In the 1980s the internationally recognised New British Cinema came into being, mainly working to criticise the Thatcher era. Its films included those of the Scot Bill Forsyth ("Gregory's Girl", 1981; "Local Hero", 1983), multicultural films such as Stephen Frear's "My Beautiful Launderette" (1985; script by Hanif Kureishi) or Chris Bernard's "Letter to Brezhnev" (1985), those of Neil Jordan ("Mona Lisa", 1986) and the opulently bizarre work of Peter Greenaway ("The Draughtsman's Contract", 1982; "Drowning By Numbers", 1987; "The Cook, The Thief, His Wife and Her Lover", 1990), Peter Yates' film version of "The Dresser" (1983) and the frivolous and nostalgic "Wish You Were Here" (1987) by David Leland. George Harrison's Hand Made Films produced such clips as the exquisite satire "Water" (1985) by Dick Clement. The New British Cinema reached a temporary peak with its new production of "Henry V" in 1989, by the Northern Irish writer, actor and director Kenneth Branagh who also successfully filmed Shakespeare's comedies.

In spite of the huge competition from Hollywood British and Irish films made a refreshing, and unique, contribution to European films during the last decade with such works as Peter Ormrod's "Eat The Peach" (1985), Jim Sheridan's "My Left Foot" (1989) as well as Thaddeus O'Sullivan's "December Bride" (1991) and the hugely successful cult comedy "Four Weddings and A Funeral" (1994), the Scotland epic, "Braveheart" (1995) which gained an Oscar, and the films of Jane Austen's "Sense and Sensibility" (1995) and "Pride and Prejudice" (1996). The British Tourism Centre (see Practical Information) publishes a "Movie Map – Film & Locations in Britain" which gives a guide to famous places and filming locations.

Great Britain and Northern Ireland in Quotations

England
Francis Bacon
(1561–1626)

The trivial prophecy, which I heard when I was a child, and queen Elizabeth was in the flower of her years, was
> When hempe is sponne
> England's done

Whereby it was generally conceived, that after the princes had reigned which had the principal letters of that word hempe (which were Henry, Edward, Mary, Philip and Elizabeth), England should come to utter confusion; which, thanks be to God, is verified only in the change of the name; for that the King's style is now no more that of England, but of Britain.
"Essays", 1597–1625

Joseph Addison
(1672–1719)

We have in England a particular Bashfulness in every thing that regards Religion. A well-bred Man is obliged to conceal any Serious Sentiment of this Nature, and very often appear to a greater Libertine than he is, that he may keep himself in Countenance among the Men of Mode.
"Spectator" (no. 485), August 15th 1712

George Berkeley
(1685–1753)

God grant the time be not near when men shall say: "This island was once inhabited by a religious, brave, sincere people, of plain uncorrupt manners, respecting inbred wealth rather than titles and appearances, asserters of liberty, lovers of their country, jealous of their own rights, and unwilling to infringe the rights of others; improvers of learning and useful arts, enemies to luxury, tender of other men's lives and prodigal of their own; inferior in nothing to the old Greeks or Romans, and superior to each of those people in the perfections of the other. Such were our ancestors during their rise and greatness; but they degenerated, grew servile flatterers of men in power, adapted Epicurean notions, became venal, corrupt, injurious, which drew upon them the hatred of God and man, and occasioned their final ruin."
An Essay Towards Preventing the Ruin of Great Britain, 1721

Jonathan Swift
(1667–1745)

Say, Britain, could you ever boast
Three poets in an age at most?
Our chilling climate; hardly bears
A sprig of bays in fifty years
"On Poetry", 1733

James Boswell
(1740–1822)

I breakfasted with Burnett on Scots oatmeal pottage and English porter. This is one of the best methods that can be taken to render the union truly firm.
"Journal", September 16th 1764

Napoleon I
(1769–1821)

You were greatly offended with me for having called you a nation of shopkeepers. Had I meant by this that you were a nation of cowards, you would have had reason to be displeased; but no such thing was ever indented. I meant that you were a nation of merchants, and that all your great riches, and your grand resources arose from commerce, which is true. What else constitutes the riches of England?
"A Voice from St Helena", Barry O'Meara, May 30th 1817

I travelled among unknown men,
In lands beyond the sea;
Nor, England! did I know till then
What love I bore to thee

William
Wordsworth
(1770–1850)

But that vast portion, lastly, of the working-class which is now issuing from its hiding-place to assert an Englishman's heaven-born privilege of doing as he likes, and is beginning to perplex us by marching where it likes, meeting where it likes, bawling what it likes, breaking what it likes – to this vast residuum we may with great propriety give the name of Populace.
   Thus we have got three distinct terms, Barbarians, Philistines, Populace, to denote roughly the three great classes into which our society is divided.
"Culture and Anarchy", 1869

Matthew Arnold
(1822–88)

Coaches:
There is now practically nothing in England or Wales corresponding to the diligence of the Continent, as the railway net has substantially covered the entire island. In some of the most frequented tourist districts, however, such as Wales, the Lakes, Devon and Cornwall, coaches with two or four horses run regularly in the season, affording a very pleasant mode of locomotion in fine weather. In some places (e.g. between New Quay and Bideford) coaches afford the only regular communication. Coaches also ply from London to various points in the vicinity. The coaches are generally well-horsed and the fares reasonable. The best places are on the box-seat, beside the driver, who usually expects a small gratuity.

Baedeker's "Great Britain"
(1864)

Scotland
Shall I tire you with a description of this unfruitfull country? where I must lead you over their hills all brown with heath, or their valleys scarce able to feed a rabbet? Man alone seems to be the only creature who has arrived to the naturall size in this poor soil; every part of the country presents the same dismall landscape, no grove nor brook lend their musick to cheer the stranger, or make the inhabitants forget their poverty; yet with all these disadvantages to call him down to humility, a scotchman is one of the prowdest things alive.
"Letter to Robert Bryanton", September 26th 1753

Oliver Goldsmith
(1730–74)

Breathes there a man with soul so dead,
Who never to himself hath said,
This is my own, my native land!
Whose heart hath ne'er within him burn'd
As home his footsteps he hath turn'd
From wandering on a foreign strand!
"The Lay of the Last Minstrel", 1805

Sir Walter Scott
(1771–1832)

There is no special loveliness in that grey country, with its rainy, sea-belt archipelago; its fields of dark mountains; its unsightly places, black with coal; its treeless, sour, unfriendly-looking cornlands; its quaint, grey, castled city, where the bells clash of a Sunday, and the wind squalls, and the salt showers fly and beat. I do not even know if I desire to live there; but let me hear, in some far land, a kindred voice sing out, "O why left I my hame?" and it seems at once as if no beauty under the kind heavens, and no society of the wise and good, can repay me for my absence from my country. And though I think I would rather die elsewhere, yet in my heart of hearts I long to be buried among good Scots clods. I will say it fairly, it grows on me with every year: there are no stars so lovely as Edinburgh streetlamps.
"The Silverado Squatters", 1883

Robert Louis
Stevenson
(1850–94)

Wales

Henry Parrot
(17th century)

A Welshman and an Englishman disputed
Which of their lands maintained the greatest state;
The Englishman the Welshman quite confuted
Yet would the Welshman naught his brags abate.
"Ten cooks," quoth he, "In Wales one wedding sees."
"True," quoth the other, "each man toasts his cheese."
C. 1613

Daniel Defoe
(1660–1731)

They value themselves much upon their antiquity: The antient race of their houses, and families and the like; and above all, upon their antient heroes: their King Caractacus Owen ap Tudor, Prince Lewellin, and the like noblemen and princes of British extraction; and as they believe their country to be the pleasantest and most agreeable in the world, so you cannot oblige them more, than to make them think you believe so too.
"A Tour through the Whole Island of Great Britain", 1724–27

James Boswell

All that I heard him say of it was, that instead of bleak and barren mountains, there were green and fertile ones; and that one of the castles in Wales would contain all the castles that he had seen in Scotland.
"Life of Johnson", October 1774

Charles Kingsley
(1819–79)

Leave to Robert Browning
Beggars, fleas and vines;
Leave to squeamish Ruskin
Popish Apennines,
Dirty stones of Venice
And his gas-lamps seven;
We've got the stones of Snowdon
And the lamps of heaven.
"The Invitation", 1856

Ireland

Edmund Spenser
(1552–99)

Ffor that parte of the northe sometyme was as populous and plentifull as any parte in England.... Suer it is yett a moste bewtifull and sweete Country as any is under heaven, seamed thoroughout with many godly rivers, replenished with all sortes of fishe most aboundantlie: sprinkled with verie many sweete Ilandes and goodlie lakes, like little inland seas, that will carrie even shippes upon theire waters, adorned with goodlie woodes, fitt for building of houses and shippes so commodiouslie, as that if some princes in the world had them, they would soone hope to be lordes of all the seas, and er longe of all the worlde; also full of verie good portes and havens, opening upon England and Scotland, as invitinge us to come unto them, to see what excellent commodities that Countrie can afforde, besides the soyle it selfe most fertile, fitt to yelde all kynde of fruit that shal be comitted there unto. And lastly the heavens most milde and temperate, though some what more moyste than the partes towardes the West.
"A Veue of the Present State of Ireland", 1596

Jonathan Swift

I will define Ireland a Region of good eating and drinking, of tolerable Company, where a Man from England may sojourn some years with Pleasure, make a Fortune, and then return home, with the spoyls he had got by doing us all the Mischeif he can, and by that make a Merit at Court.
"Letter to John Gay", November 20th 1729

W. M. Thackeray
(1811–63)

They call Belfast the Irish Liverpool. If people are for calling names, it would be better to call it the Irish London at once – the chief city of the kingdom at any rate. It looks hearty, thriving and prosperous, as if it had money in its pockets, and roast-beef for dinner: it has no pretensions to fashion, but looks mayhap better in its honest broadcloth than some people in their shabby brocade. The houses are as handsome as at Dublin, with this advantage, that the people seem to live in them.
"The Irish Sketch Book of 1842", 1843

Suggested Itineraries

The following are merely suggested itineraries, and are not intended to take the place of any individually planned excursions. Places which have a separate entry in the A to Z section of this Guide are shown in **bold** type.

The routes are designed to take in the major cities, beauty spots and places of interest in the countryside. Many of the places described, however, can be reached only on side roads off the main routes. The map at the end of the book will help in detailed planning.

The distances shown are approximate and relate to direct routes.

South-East England

London–Rochester–Canterbury–Dover–Eurotunnel–North/South Downs–London (180 miles)

Leave **London** on the A2 to travel south-east to the county of Kent. After 31 miles the A2 passes the cathedral town of **Rochester** on the Medway, which links with the naval base at Chatham and its historic dry docks, which are worth a visit. The next town of Faversham, with its breweries, shows that Kent is famous for its hops. From there it is only 7 miles to the famous walled cathedral city of **Canterbury**. A few miles north-west on the A290 lies the colourful sailing resort of Whitstable. The coast road continues via Herne Bay to the Isle of Thanet and the popular seaside

Leeds Castle, the favourite residence of Edward I

resort of Margate. By the crossing to Pegwell Bay lies Ramsgate, the Royal Harbour of which is well-known as forming part of the London–Ramsgate–Calais yacht race. Sandwich, the northernmost of the Cinque Ports, and Deal with its two castles lie on the road to the port of **Dover**, the historical gateway to England. Near the massive castle and high above the famous chalk cliffs stands a lighthouse, the oldest Roman edifice on British soil. 7 miles from Dover lies the ferry port of Folkestone, with the **Eurotunnel** providing an alternative means of travel under the Channel to Calais. From Folkestone an excursion can be made to the resort of Hythe, with its long shingle beach and clusters of pretty cottages.

The hills of the **North Downs** lying inland form the backbone of Kent; they fall away steeply in the south but far more gently to the north, where they are broken up by charming dry valleys. Keen walkers can enjoy the North Downs Way leading from Folkestone; this was followed by pilgrims since time immemorial, it goes all the way to Guildford in Surrey. Roughly parallel to it is the M20 motorway to Ashford, with the Palladian country seat of Mersham-le-Hatch designed by Robert Adam. A further 20 miles further north-west lies the county capital of Maidstone, and a short distance from there stands Leeds Castle, in a rural setting surrounded by a moat, and the favourite residence of King Edward I. The A25 now traverses the Low Weald to the south of the Downs, with some interesting walks along ancient towpaths. A good way of exploring the area is to follow the well-signposted "Heart of Kent Country Tour", a circular trip of some 50 miles. At the edge of Greensand Hills the A25 continues to Sevenoaks, where the magnificent Knole Park with one of England's most important country houses awaits the visitor. A little to the north is the M25 motorway for the return journey to London.

London–North/South Downs–Hastings–Brighton–Chichester–Portsmouth(–Isle of Wight)–Guildford–London (280 miles)

The second suggested journey through south-east England begins south of **London** at Westerham, in the centre of which stands a memorial to Sir Winston Churchill, the town's most famous citizen. The visitor can now follow in the footsteps of Henry VIII by travelling south through the **North Downs** to Hever and the castle of the same name, where Anne Boleyn spent her youth. In the wooded High Weald on the border with Sussex will be found the romantic gardens forming part of the magnificent Penshurst Place estate. The A21 then passes through Tunbridge Wells, with its fine old shopping streets, the "Pantiles", and on to the little village of Lamberhurst, with its row of typical "Wealden" houses. The picture-book villages around here lie in countryside covered with apple and cherry orchards. In the Isle of Oxney to the south the traveller will cross the ancient Saxon Store Way. The journey continues between Romney and Walland Marshes to the sandy beaches on the **South Coast**. From Hythe to Dungeness, Europe's longest shingle beach, runs one of the country's smallest miniature railways. From New Romney, one of the Cinque Ports in the reign of Edward the Confessor, return along the same road to Romney Marsh and then turn west onto the A259 to Rye, once an important port until the coast became silted up. The modern port of Hastings was also once one of the Cinque Ports which defended English legal and trading rights in the Channel during the 11th–15th centuries. A must for the tourist is the wall tapestry in the Town Hall containing 81 important dates in Britain's history. From Hastings it is worth making a short detour to the market town of Battle, where the abbey was built on the battlefield shortly after the Battle of Hastings in 1066. Return to the coast and to the chain of hills known as the **South Downs**, near the popular holiday resort of Eastbourne. A favourite drive from here is to the high chalk cliffs of Beachy Head to the west.

The tour continues to **Brighton** which – together with Hove – is the largest seaside resort in Sussex, famous for its Royal Pavilion, built in an exotic oriental style, and the picturesque "Lanes" in the pedestrian quarter. Following the coast road then brings the visitor to Worthing, with its 3 mile-long promenade to Bognor Regis, which earned its name from the time when King George V spent a convalescent holiday there in 1929. About 7 miles to the west lies **Chichester**, the charming capital of West Sussex with a Late Gothic market cross and a beautiful cathedral. The next stop is the major port of **Portsmouth**, where HMS "Victory", Lord Nelson's flagship in the Battle of Trafalgar 1805 and the Tudor man-of-war, the "Mary Rose", can be seen by visitors. If time permits a trip to the charming **Isle of Wight** is recommended. To return to **London**, proceed northward to Guildford (which boasts one of the steepest high streets anywhere in England) and past Clandon Park with its Palladian mansion to Epsom, where Derby Day, the highlight of the racing season, is held at the end of May or early June, and thence back to the capital.

Central Southern England

London–Winchester–Southampton(–Isle of Wight)–Salisbury (–Stonehenge)–Shaftesbury–Bath–Bristol
(200 miles)

First take the A3 out of **London** to Guildford and then west along the A31 to Farnham, where the castle was the seat of the bishops of Winchester from the 12th century. Continue on the A31 through forest-covered hills to the little village of Chawton, with its museum dedicated to the authoress Jane Austin. Our route then passes parallel to the Mid Hants Railway (a picturesque little steam railway from Alton to New Alresford)

Curious cliff formations, Isle of Wight …   *… and English vine (Barton Manor)*

to **Winchester**, which for many years was the capital of England. Its cathedral is an amalgam of almost all English building styles. The A33 then leads directly to **Southampton**, one of Britain's major ports the history of which is documented in the Maritime Museum. It was from Southampton harbour that the Pilgrim Fathers originally set sail for the New World in 1620 (although bad weather forced them ashore again and they finally sailed from Plymouth). From here visitors can take the ferry across the Solent to the beautiful **Isle of Wight**.

Now drive north-west to the county capital of **Salisbury**, with its famous cathedral built between 1220 and 1286. Some 2 miles north of the present city Old Sarum shows where the city once stood. From here the A345 leads to Salisbury Plain and **Stonehenge**, the most important pre-historical cult monument in Britain. After returning to Salisbury, take the A30 to magnificent Wilton House, seat of the Earls of Pembroke. Shaftesbury is the next stop on the route. Visitors may care to wander through tranquil Blanchmoor Vale before setting off again north-west to visit Stourhead, one of England's loveliest country gardens situated outside Stourton. The B3092 leads to Longleat House built in Tudor times with beautiful park gardens designed by "Capability" Brown.

Proceeding east to Warminster, take the A36 to **Bath**, the only British spa town with hot springs. The remains of the Roman Baths and the Georgian Royal Crescent are delightful. The next section of the journey is on the A4, parallel to the River Avon, to the port of **Bristol** on the Severn Estuary, with its beautiful 14th c. church of St Mary Redcliffe and Brunel's Clifton Suspension Bridge above the Avon Gorge.

Bristol–Cotswolds–Avebury–Windsor–London (125 miles)

The fastest route from **Bristol** to London is the M4 motorway via Swindon and Reading. However, those with time to spare are advised to take the A420 through the romantic **Cotswolds** to Chippenham, from where it is worth visiting Sheldon Manor. The A4 then continues past Bowood House and the White Horse of Cherwill to **Avebury**, which boasts Europe's largest stone circle. After passing through the pretty little town of Marlborough in the centre of the charming Marlborough Downs, the A4 takes the visitor to Newbury and Reading before the B3024 leads to Eton, with its famous Public School, and thence to **Windsor** on the south bank of the Thames. Windsor Castle has been a royal residence since the time of William the Conqueror. Finally the A4 passes north of Heathrow Airport to the City of **London**.

South-West England

Southampton–New Forest–Bournemouth–Dorchester–Exeter (–Dartmoor–Plymouth; 50 miles)–Torbay–Plymouth–Cornwall (330 miles)

From **Southampton** drive south on the A336 and A35 through the glorious **New Forest**, once a royal hunting preserve. Near Dipden Purlieu the B3054 branches off to Beaulieu (with the National Motor Museum) and the picturesque port of Bucklers Hard at the mouth of the River Beaulieu. To the south-west then appear the port of Lymington and Christchurch, a centre for yachts and boats, with the remarkable Tucktonia model village. The resort of Bournemouth to the west, framed by 100 ft high cliffs, stretches around Poole Bay as far as Sandbanks, where the ferries leave for the Isle of Purbeck. The A351 now skirts the Purbeck peninsula and continues to Swanage, a mixture of old stone houses and modern buildings. A ride on the narrow-gauge Swanage Railway, a visit to Corfe Castle, some 5 miles inland, or a walk to Smedmore manor house, west of St Aldhelm's Head (with its splendid views) are to be recommended. Our next destination is the old harbour town of Weymouth, from where ferries leave for the **Channel Islands**. After visiting Portland Bill and Rufus Castle, either take the coast road along Lyme Bay to Bridport or make a detour by way of the impressive Maiden Castle and the market town of **Dorchester** to Lyme Regis, the favourite holiday resort of the authoress Jane Austin (1775–1817). The steep coastal road, with its superb panoramic views, continues to Exmouth at the wide mouth of the River Exe, with a beautiful beach set against a backcloth of tall, red cliffs. Our next destination is the historic cathedral city of **Exeter**.

When leaving Exeter the visitor may elect to take the route through **Dartmoor** National Park, the vast area of heath and moorland in the heart of Devon so steeped in legend, driving through Moretonhamstead and passing Princetown. with its notorious prison, and to Tavistock, site of the Morwellham Quay Open Air Museum and once described as "the largest copper port in Queen Victoria's Empire". The famous seafarer Sir Francis Drake was born in nearby Crowndale in 1540. The A386 then leads along the east bank of the River Tamar to **Plymouth**, with its Hoe made famous by Sir Francis Drake and his legendary game of bowls. Plymouth Sound is full of white yacht-sails in summer.

The other route to Plymouth takes the visitor from **Exeter** via Powderham, with its fine castle to the wide Torbay, along which stretches 22 miles of magnificent **South Coast** scenery, the "English Riviera" with the resort of Torquay. In the neighbouring village of Cockington the tiny thatched cottages will be found very attractive. Centrally situated in Tor Bay lies the holiday resort of Paignton, with its impressive Old Mansion House (1871) owned by the Singer sewing-machine company. At the south end of the crescent-shaped bay is the pretty fishing village of Brixham, where William of Orange landed in 1688 to claim the English throne as William III. A walk to Berry Head and Sharkham Point will be rewarded with some fantastic views. To the south lies Dartmouth, dominated by its massive castle, which can be reached by means of the Torbay–Dartmouth Railway. The route then follows the coast along Start Bay on the A379 and by way of Kingsbridge to Bigbury Bay with its small fishing harbours and seaside resorts which are ideal for water-sports, and on to **Plymouth** on the border between the counties of Devon and **Cornwall**.

Eastern England

London–Cambridge(–Ely)–Huntingdon–Peterborough– Grantham–Lincoln–Leeds (260 miles)

Leave London on the A1 to the historical market town of Hatfield, where magnificent Hatfield House, built in the Jacobean style in the 17th century, stands surrounded by superb parkland. Continue by way of Welwyn Garden City, a little to the east of the mansion known as Shaw's Corner, and Knebworth, which also boasts a fine country house, to the market town of Stevenage and then on to Letchworth. Here the A505 turns off north-east to Royston, from where the A10 leads straight to the county town of **Cambridge**. The famous colleges of the 12th century University, together with those of its rival Oxford, are among the most famous in Europe. About 16 miles to the north-east lies the charming city of Ely, with the third largest cathedral in England which towers high in the sky and can be seen for miles across the low-lying **Fen District** surrounding it. After returning to Cambridge take the A604 north-westward for 18 miles to Huntingdon, the birthplace of Oliver Cromwell. The next stop is **Peterborough**, with its splendid Norman cathedral. If time permits, a journey through the romantic Nene Valley on the little Nene

Valley Railway can be recommended. After a further 18 miles the A1 reaches Stamford and Burghley House, a fine Elizabethan manor and seat of the Marquis of Exeter. Continue on the A1 past Woolsthorpe Manor, the house in which the great naturalist Isaac Newton was born, to **Grantham**, in the centre of an intensively-cultivated agricultural area. Grantham's gingerbread has an excellent reputation. Proceed to the picturesque town of Newark-on-Trent, with the imposing Castle of the Bishops of Lincoln where King John died in 1216. Southwell, a short distance to the west, is a favourite setting-out place for strolls through Sherwood Forest near **Nottingham**, made famous by the tales of Robin Hood. From Newark-on-Trent the A46 leads to the historically important city of **Lincoln** on the River Witham which has made its way through the limestone crests. Old town houses, steep flights of stone steps and a wonderful cathedral make a tour of Lincoln well worthwhile. Then take the A57 westward and just before reaching **Sheffield** turn north and proceed via Barnsley, with its interesting monastery, to the university city of **Leeds**. A walk through the well-tended parks, a stroll along Park Row or a visit to the Palladian Town Hall can all be recommended.

Central England (The Midlands)

London–St Albans–Northampton–Leicester–Nottingham–Derby–Sheffield–Manchester (220 miles)

This route commences by leaving **London** on the A5183 in a north-westerly direction, with the first stop being at the old market town of **St Albans**, with its massive cathedral, originally built in the Norman style. Near the River Ver lie extensive remains of the fortifications around the old Roman camp of Verulamium. Now take the A1057 east for 4 miles to

Launches on the Thames

Hatfield, with its imposing 17th c. Jacobean manor house. Then turn north-west once more and follow the River Lea on the B653 to the industrial town of Luton, where Sir Harold Wernher's famous art collection is housed at Luton Hoo in a country house designed by Robert Adam. From Luton the A6 heads north past Wrest Park manor with its superb gardens and on to **Bedford**, the county town, on the River Ouse which offers good fishing. From here the A428 leads to the industrial centre of Northampton 21 miles away on the north bank of the Nene. A few miles east of the town the tourist can drive to the Elizabethan Castle Ashby, seat of the Marquis of Northampton, with its valuable art collection. Northampton's attractions include the Church of the Holy Sepulchre, one of the four round churches in England. Continue then along the A508 past the beautiful Lamport Hall to the little town of Market Harborough and then take the A6 to the historical industrial and commercial centre of **Leicester**, the birthplace of mass tourism as we know it today, for it was from here that Thomas Cook, founder of the firm of that name, arranged the first organised outing to Loughborough, just 15 miles away. To the north-west lies charming Charnwood Forest, a paradise for birds of passage.

The next section of the journey on the A6 crosses the Main Line Steam Trust Railway and then, beyond Loughborough, passes the country seat of Whatton with its beautiful parklands. Finally, after passing Long Eaton on the north bank of River Trent, the visitor will arrive in the university city of Nottingham, known as "The Queen of the Midlands". Sherwood Forest to the north is famous as the legendary home of the folk hero Robin Hood and his Merry Men. About 9 miles north lies Newstead Abbey, Lord Byron's ancestral seat. From here take the A52 west to the industrial town of **Derby**, home of the Rolls-Royce motor car company and of some long-standing porcelain works. Nearby Kedleston Hall, perhaps the most beautiful English country house built in the Robert Adam style, is worth a visit. Then take the A38 via Alfreton and the A61 via Chesterfield (with its magnificent Revolution House) along the foot of the Derbyshire Hills to **Sheffield**, a popular setting-out point for walks in the beautiful **Peak District**, the first English National Park and a favourite excursion spot for people from the conurbations of Manchester, Sheffield and Derby. The unusual design of Sheffield Cathedral is the result of a number of additions and changes over the centuries. Continuing through High Peak – which is crossed to the south by the "Pennine Way", a favourite with long-distance walkers – our route takes us to **Manchester**, the birthplace of the English cotton industry and one of the country's great industrial cities. A stroll through the recently redeveloped area of Castlefield can be recommended, as can a visit to the famous John Rylan's Library, which houses some very old books.

London–Oxford–Stratford-upon-Avon–Warwick– Coventry–Birmingham–Lichfield–Stoke-on- Trent–Liverpool (230 miles)

From **London** take the M40 or A40 westward to the market town of High Wycombe, with its splendid Hughenden Manor, and from there to **Oxford**, one of Europe's oldest and most famous university towns with its many imposing colleges. It is worth fitting into the schedule a tour of Abingdon, some 6 miles to the south, a charming town with an interesting Market Hall and a massive Benedictine Abbey. On returning to Oxford, take the A34 to Woodstock, 8 miles away, with the famous Baroque Blenheim Palace, family seat of the Dukes of Marlborough. The A4095 joins up with the A4260; follow this, past Rousham manor-house near Lower Heyford, to the market town of Banbury.

From here it is worth making a trip to Upton House, to the north-west near Lower Tysoe, on the A422. This road then continues to **Stratford- upon-Avon**, the town which centres around the life of Shakespeare. A visit to the house in which he was born is recommended; the performances given by the Shakespeare Theatre are also very popular. About 4 miles to the east lies Charlecote Park – where Shakespeare is alleged to have gone poaching in his youth – with the manor house of the Lucy family. Now take the A46 to the county town of **Warwick**, with the massive Warwick Castle towering over the River Avon. Nearby Leamington Spa has some fine parks and gardens in which visitors can enjoy a walk. Continue on the A46 and go through Kenilworth, with its castle of red sandstone, to the historic city of **Coventry**, the centre of the British car industry, with its new Cathedral of glass and concrete, built between 1956 and 1962 to replace the old one destroyed during the Second World War. The A45 ends in Birmingham, the second largest city in Britain, with a Museum and Art Gallery housing some of the country's major art collections. Leave **Birmingham** by the A453 to the north and then, from Sutton Coldfield, follow the A51 to the pleasant little town of Lichfield, the birthplace of Samuel Johnson, author of the "Dictionary of the English Language". Beyond the market town of Rugeley the A51 passes the interesting Shugborough Hall near Stafford. Near Stone take the A34 to the industrial towns of Stoke-on-Trent and Newcastle-under-Lyme, the centres of the English china industry. The Gladstone Pottery Museum in Stoke-on-Trent contains exhibits describing early Victorian production methods, while the Mining Museum portrays the industrial development of the area. A little way from Rode Hall the A50 runs parallel to the M6 motorway as far as Warrington on the River Mersey, a town which forms part of the metropolitan county of Merseyside. The M62 or A57 then lead direct to **Liverpool**, while the A562/A561 passes along the north bank of the Mersey close to Speke Hall and thence to Liverpool city centre from the south. This great port at the mouth of the Mersey was the birthplace of the Beatles, whose legendary career fills whole museums here, including the "Beatles Story" in the former Albert Docks, where old ships also lie at anchor.

Manchester: Air Space Gallery ...   *... and a film set in Granada TV studios*

"Boneshaker", Birmingham Museum of Art   *Museum of Labour History in Liverpool*

Bristol–Gloucester(–Cotswolds)–Worcester–Birmingham (95 miles)

This itinerary commences in the beautiful port and industrial city of **Bristol,** known for its parish church of St Mary Redcliffe and Brunel's Clifton Suspension Bridge. Leave the city on the M5 motorway or on the A38 and proceed north, parallel to the Severn Estuary, to **Gloucester**, the county town, with its historic harbour dating back to the 19th century. There are charming excursions to be made from here to the **Cotswolds**, the Forest of Dean and the romantic Wye Valley. Just 10 miles to the east lies the residential town of Cheltenham, with many Regency houses. From Cheltenham the A4019 soon joins the A38; follow this northward to **Worcester**, with its beautiful half-timbered Tudor houses and magnificent Cathedral of red sandstone. Some 7 miles north near Droitwich take the B4090/4091 in order to visit the interesting Avoncroft Museum of Buildings near Bromsgrove, before finally taking the A38 to **Birmingham**, the great industrial city the centre of which has been considerably enhanced in recent years. The Malvern Hills around the city are an example of Mother Nature at her best.

Wales

North Wales, Mid Wales, South Wales

See A to Z

North-West England

See A to Z

Lancaster–Kirkby Stephen–Penrith(–Lake District)–Carlisle(–Hadrian's Wall) (85 miles)

Taking the M6 from **Lancaster**, turn north-east onto the A683 to Kirkby Londsdale in the Lune valley, immortalised by Turner the artist and Ruskin the author. Continue to Sedbergh, which forms part of the **Yorkshire Dales** National Park. From here it is 14 miles to Kirkby Stephen in the upper Eden valley, with many farms and winding streets which are under preservation orders. Passing through Brough, at the foot of Stainmore and dominated by castle ruins, the A66 leads along the River Eden to Appleby in Westmoreland with its impressive castle, once the home of Lady Anne Clifford, so admired by the local people. Now follow the ever-widening River Eden to Temple Sowerby and thence to Penrith, where most of the buildings are in red sandstone, and visits are recommended to the Georgian parish church and the Gloucester Arms, where the Duke of Gloucester and later Richard III once stayed. To the east the A686 climbs some 1770 ft to Alston, the highest market town in England, which owed its development to a lead mine which was once worked nearby. From the hills there is a superb view as far as the Solway. It is well worthwhile visiting Haweswater and Ullswater to the south-west of Penrith, two of the most beautiful lakes in the **Lake District**. The 9 mile trip on a steamer on Ullswater from Pooley Bridge to Glenridding is also recommended.

After returning to Penrith the visitor can chose either the M6 motorway or the A6 to travel to **Carlisle**. The county town of Cumbria, where a visit to the Norman castle and **Hadrian's Wall** will be found most interesting.

Lake District

See A to Z

North-East England

Leeds–Harrogate–Richmond–Durham–Newcastle-upon-Tyne (120 miles)

Leaving **Leeds**, with its numerous museums and well-tended parks, take the A61 – passing Harewood House, designed by Robert Adam for the Earl of Harewood – to the spa town of Harrogate, situated in the foothills of the Yorkshire Moors. On the way to the little town of Biron, to the north the visitor will pass the delightful Newby Hall after about 14 miles; famous for its tapestries, Newby was also designed by Robert Adam. Beyond Biron, take the A1 to the romantic town of **Richmond**, with the second oldest Theatre Royal in England. from where there are some magnificent walks to be had in the Pennines. The next stop is Darlington, with its famous rail link to Stockton-on-Tees on which was made the first ever journey by a passenger train hauled by a steam locomotive in 1825. The A167 then passes through the beautiful cathedral city of **Durham** and then, after a further 11 miles north, the town of Washington, with the family house of George Washington, first president of the United States, and finally leads to the county capital of **Newcastle-upon-Tyne**, in the heart of Tyne and Wear. The city was once an important coal-mining centre; now heavy industry predominates. The old bridges over the River Tyne are very interesting.

Newcastle-upon-Tyne–Southern Uplands–Edinburgh

(110 miles or 125 miles)

On leaving **Newcastle-upon-Tyne**, the traveller can either choose the shortest route along the A69/A68, first crossing the Cheviot Hills with the Northumberland National park and then drive north through the **Scottish Uplands** in the Scottish Borders through the historic wool centres of Jedburgh and Melrose with their famous abbeys as far as Galashields and then take the A7 for a further 34 miles to **Edinburgh**, or alternatively elect to follow the coast road running parallel to the North Sea. This leads from **Newcastle-upon-Tyne** for more than 77 miles to the Scottish capital. Those who have sufficient time can follow the B1068 to the seaside resort of Amble, with Warkworth Castle, and then continue north to the castles near Embleton and Bamburgh and then join up west of Belford on the Scottish border with the A1, the main road from Newcastle-upon-Tyne to Berwick-upon-Tweed. From Berwick continue north parallel to the coast, first along the Merse valley and then through the Lammaermuir Hills watched over by some majestic castles. Finally, the A1 continues via the elegant town of Haddington to **Edinburgh** on the south bank of the Firth of Forth.

Scotland

Carlisle–Dumfries–Glenluce(–Kilmarnock–Glasgow; 140 miles) –Stranraer–Ayr–Arran–Kintyre–Islay–Jura–Inverary–Loch Lomond–Glasgow (370 miles)

From **Carlisle** the A74 leads past Gretna Green (where runaway marriages were legal from 1754 until they were banned in 1940) through romantic countryside to Dumfries, an important centre in Nithsdale on the "Burns Heritage Trail" and in which stands the house where Robert Burns, the great Scottish poet, was born. After making a detour south to see the impressive ruins of Caerlaverock Castle and Sweetheart Abbey, take the A75 to Castle Douglas, an attractive little town in Galloway with Threave Castle, and then on to the sailing centre of Kircudbright on the Solway Firth, where a visit can be made to Broughton House and MacLellan's Castle. A little way to the south-west lies Dundreddan Abbey, where Mary Stuart is said to have spent her last night on Scottish soil. After a few miles on the A75 Gatehouse of Fleet on the coast of Wigtown Bay will come into view, offering some superb walks and the chance to visit Cardoness Castle. The A75 then hugs the coast as far as Newton Stuart, where a tour of Galloway Forest Park can be enjoyed if desired. The A714 then leads inland to Wigtown in the Machars, in the heart of one of Scotland's earliest Christianised regions. Some 11 miles to the south trips can be made to the Drumtroddan Standing Stones and Whithorn Priory, while the A747 will take the visitor westward by way of Port William to the exciting ruins of Glenluce Abbey.

From Glenluce take the A75 back to Newton Stewart and then proceed on the A712/A702 via New Galloway – a spot favoured by mountain-walkers, fishermen and bird-watchers – to Moniaive by Cairn Wate, known for its colourful cottages and the last "Covenant martyr", James Renwick. After passing Maxwellton House (1641) and Drumlanrig Castle take the A76 to Sanguhar, said to have the oldest post-office (1763) in Britain. Nearby Mennock Pass leads to Wanlockhead and Leadhills, once the centre of the Scottish lead-mining industry, as shown by the local museums. Continuing by way of Cumnock the A76 re-joins the "Burns Heritage Trail" in Mauchline and Kilmarnock, both these towns having close connections with the poet. The A71 now leads north-east to Hamilton, surrounded by such interesting places to visit as Strathclyde

Gretna Green: the smithy where couples used to be married

Loch Long in the Scottish Highlands

Park, the castles of Cadzow and Bothwell, Hamilton Mausoleum and the David Livingstone Memorial in Blantyre. Here it is worthwhile making a diversion along the River Clyde to Lanark, on the edge of the Pentland and Tinto Hills where they fall away to form the fruit-growing region along the Clyde. There are some interesting examples of industrial archaeology to be seen in New Lanark, and further north can be seen the ruins of Craignethan Castle, the Corehouse Nature Reserve and the waterfalls at Cora Linn. Hamilton is linked by the M74 motorway with **Glasgow**, the industrial and financial centre with much to offer in the way of entertainment, interesting buildings dating from the Victorian period and some first-class museums, including the Burrell Collection. The city is an ideal base for trips in Ayrshire, the Trossachs, to Loch Lomond and the Firth of Clyde.

Alternatively, instead of driving inland from Glenluce, the visitor can go by way of Castle Kennedy – with some of the most beautiful gardens to be found anywhere in Scotland – to Stranraer on the edge of Loch Ryan, the gateway to Ireland and to the **Isle of Man**. From here the A77 hugs the charming scenic coastline of the North Channel for more than 51 miles, with a detour from Culzean Castle and Country Park near Dunure to Ayr, one of Scotland's largest seaside resorts. In Alloway, just south of Ayr, is Burn's Cottage. The A78 continues to follow the coast to Adrossan, from where ferries leave for the island of Arran, where bare mountains form a contrasting backcloth to some superb sandy beaches. After arriving in Brodick, dominated by its massive castle, take the A841 to Lochranza, where a ferry crosses Kilbrannan Sound to the peninsula known as the Mull of Kintyre; its main town is Campbeltown in the south, with St Kiren's Cave and the Marihanish golf course on the west coast. In the north, Saddell Abbey and Carradale House Gardens are worth a visit.

With Loch Fyne in the east and Loch Tarbert in the west, the A83 then passes along West Loch Tarbert to the port of Kennacraig, where ships

Edinburgh: the panorama from Calton Hill

117

leave for the islands of Islay and Jura. On Gigha Island (accessible from Tayinloan), the neighbouring, fertile "Island of God", some rare species of rhododendrums are grown in the gardens of Achomore House. The ferry also goes to Port Ellen on the Island of Islay, famous for its excellent whisky and fine beaches. The A846 ends in Port Askaig, where travellers can take the ferry to Feolin on Jura Island. This relatively thinly-populated "Island of the Deer" can boast only one road, some spectacular caves and large numbers of red deer.

From Feolin return by ferry to Kennacraig on Kintyre, from where there is a pleasant drive along Loch Fyne northward to Lochgilphead. This region offers excellent facilities for water sports and such historical relics as those at Dunadd, for example. Following the A83, pass the pretty gardens at Crarae and the large Agricultural Museum in Auchindrain; after covering some 47 miles the visitor will come to the 18th c. village of Inverary, dominated by a castle belonging to the Duke of Argyll, head of the Campbell clan. The next stop is Arrochar on the edge of Argyll Forest Park. Close by is the pass known as "Rest and be thankful", which leads to Inverary and Oban. While the A82 heads along the banks of Loch Lomond via Balloch, where the excursion steamers dock, and thence direct to the town of Dumbarton, the A814 passes through the sailing centre of Helensburgh, at the mouth of Gare Loch. Nearby Hill House, designed by Mackintosh, will prove an attraction for those interested in Art Nouveau. Dumbarton, the ancient capital of the kings of Strathclyde, lies under a rock massif on the edge of the Firth of Clyde. Following the River Clyde upstream finally brings the visitor to **Glasgow**.

Edinburgh–Perth–Dundee(–Montrose–Stonehaven)–Brechin–Stonehaven–Aberdeen (135 miles)

After having allowed ample time for a tour of the Scottish capital of **Edinburgh**, cross the Firth of Forth and follow the M90 motorway to Kinross, with its castle and magnificent gardens built on an island in Loch Leven. The M90 continues north to the town and exhibition centre of Perth where, in the parish church of St John, the reformer John Knox once delivered his inflammatory sermons. Scone Palace, a little way to the north, is worth a visit. It is then a further 22 miles along the A85 to **Dundee**, in the harbour of which the "Discovery", the ship of the famous polar explorer Robert Falcon Scott, lies at anchor.

The visitor now has the choice of either taking the A929/A94, the quickest route to Aberdeen, or taking the coast road to Buddon Ness; the latter commences with a drive along the A930 to Broughty Ferry and the seaside resort of Minifieth. Broughty Castle houses an interesting Whaling Museum. The neighbouring town of Carnoustie is also well known as a venue for the British Open Golf Championships. Continue by way of Arbroath to Montrose, with its beautiful sandy beach. Nearby lies the St Cyrus nature reserve. The coast road (A92) finally reaches Stonehaven, where the harbour with the Tolbooth Museum on the quayside, and Dunnottar Castle on a rock to the south are of interest. It is then some 9 miles to the prosperous oil city of **Aberdeen**, capital of the northeast, with much to offer in the way of entertainment and a very interesting Old Town area.

The other road from **Dundee** to Aberdeen leads through the fertile region of Strathmore to Forfar. Here it is worth making a detour to the impressive Glamis Castle to the west, with the neighbouring Angus Folk Museum, and along the A926 to the house in Kirriemuir where the playwright and novelist J. M. Barrie was born. If the visitor follows this road further west to the foot of the Glenisla he will find Alyth, one of the rich little farming towns in Howe of Strathmore, the Scottish raspberry-growing region. Meigle, to the south, has a museum with prehistoric stone carvings done by the Picts. After returning to Forfar continue to the nearest Strathmore town of Brechin and tour the Angus Glens. Then take the A94 back to the coast at Stonehaven and finally on to **Aberdeen**.

Aberdeen–Elgin–Inverness (110 miles)

The coast road from **Aberdeen** to the north is initially the A92/A975 along Cruden Bay to the busy oil and fishing town of Peterhead, which boasts a beautiful golf-course. Fishing is the subject of most exhibits in its Arbuthnot Museum. Places of interest in the vicinity include the rock-crevice known as Bullens of Buchan, and the ruins of Slains Castle, used in the Dracula films. The A952 leads to the northern tip of Buchan and to the fishing port of Fraserburgh, with good fishing, golf-courses and tennis courts. The A98 then continues west along the coast, through several small harbour towns, to Cullen, with its beautiful beach and excellent golf-courses. Near Fochabers on the Spey the A98 joins the A96 from Aberdeen.

Those preferring to go straight from Aberdeen to Fochabers should first take the A947 to the little farming town of Old Meldrum, near Pitmeden Garden, a rare example of a formally laid-out Scottish park dating from the 17th century. Also worth a visit are Haddo House and the grand Villa Tolquhon. This route then continues north via Colpy to Huntly, seat of the Fordon family; the visitor is strongly recommended to visit Huntly Castle, Leith Hall a little to the south with its beautiful gardens, and the medieval church of St Mary in Auchindoir. After passing through the whisky town of Keith the A96 leads to Fochabers and thence to Elgin in the Moray region. Here the ruins of the once magnificent cathedral are known as the "Lantern of the North". Spynie Palace and Duffus Castle to the north-west will be found interesting. A detour can also be made from Elgin on the A941 to the popular golf and water-sports centre of Lossiemouth on the Moray coast. The road to Forres

Stills for distilling whisky ...   *... at the Glenfiddich Distillery*

passes just north of the beautiful Plusgarden Abbey, before the visitor is faced with the choice near Findhorn Bay between the Falconer Museum or Swen Stones. Other attractions in the vicinity include Grant Park, Cluny Hills and Brodie Castle. From Forres the B9011 leads round the east bank of Findhorn Bay to the holiday resort of the same name, with its wide sandy beaches and excellent facilities for water sports. From there take the A96 to Inverness, the capital of the Highland Region, where the famous bagpipe competitions are held.

Edinburgh–Perth–Dunkeld–Pitlochry–Kinguissie– Inverness (155 miles)

Take the M90 motorway north from **Edinburgh** by way of Kinross – where the island castle boasts some beautiful gardens – to Perth, with its Neo-Classical Round House, a water tower designed by Adam Anderson. Scone Palace to the north, seat of the Earls of Mansfield, is well worth a visit. It is also worth making detours to the west to see the superb parkland surrounding Drummond Castle and the Scottish Tartans Museum in Comrie.

After returning to Perth, take the A9 to the delightful village of Dunkeld, with its lovely little cottages which have been restored by the Scottish National Trust. Osprey still breed by the Loch of Lowes nearby. Our route then continues north-west and detours at Ballinluig to Aberfeldy, famous for the regattas held on the River Tay and for the General Wade Bridge. Anyone planning a longish stay here can enjoy some superb drives up to Glen Lyon, along Loch Rannoch and Loch Tay, and to Castle Menzies in Weem. Return to the A9. Just past Ballkinluig lies the town of Pitlochry, situated in the midst of breathtaking Highland scenery and with a well-known Festival Theatre. Other attractions here are the beautiful woodland walks and stretches of water for canoeing, as well as nearby Loch Fascally and the salmon-leap on Loch Tummel. The next destination is the Highland village of Blair Atholl, famous for the white, towered building of Blair Castle. The A9 now makes a wide sweep around the Forest of Atholl and continues north-west to Newtonmore, with Clan MacPherson House, to Kinguissie with its excellent Highland Folk Museum. The Clan Tartan Centre in Aviemore will provide information about the history and manufacture of tartans, kilts and plaids. 5 miles further on the A 95 enters the valley of the River Spey, where the "Malt Whisky Trail" means there some famous distilleries can be visited. The A9 now leads north-west to Inverness, the capital of the Highlands, surrounded by such history-filled places as prehistoric Clava Cairns in the east and the legendary battlefield of Culloden, where Bonnie Prince Charlie, the pretender to the Scottish throne, was decisively beaten by the English under the Duke of Cumberland, or Cawdor Castle with its Macbeth associations.

Northern Ireland

Belfast–Larne–Glenarm(–Slemish)–Ballycastle–Giant's Causeway–Coleraine–Limavady–Londonderry (85 miles)

From **Belfast**, the capital of Northern Ireland since 1920, follow the A2 along the north bank of the River Lagan to its mouth beyond Carrickfergus. Castle Carrickfergus, the construction of which was begun by the Norman John de Courcy at the end of the 12 c., stands proudly on a spur of black basalt rock. After passing through the popular resort of Whitehead the road leads to the promontory known as Island Magee, with its interesting cliffs, the "Gobbins", which are nearly 260 ft high. Quarries and cement works line the road to the industrial town of Larne, from where ferries leave for Stranraer in Scotland. Ships also sail from here to Island Magee. There is a very romantic coast road through Black Cave Tunnel and around the basalt rock of Ballygalley Head to the seaside resort of the same name and then on to Glenarm, where stands the castle of the Earls of Antrim.

To the west rises the extinct volcano known as the Slemish (1437 ft), where St Patrick is said to have tended swine for his master Miluic, and which has for centuries been visited by pilgrims on St Patrick's Day (March 17th). From Broughshare, by the River Braid, signs point the way to the car park about 660 ft below the summit; it is well worth climbing to the top to enjoy the panoramic view of the ruins of Skerry Church and of a hill which was probably the site of Miluic's fortress. Beyond Glenarm, the road leads past white chalk cliffs to the seaside resort of Carnlough, with its good sandy beach, and thence on to Waterfoot on Red Bay on the magical Antrim coast. The sandstone cliffs at Waterfoot are reminiscent of a fantasy-filled amphitheatre. To the south-west stretches one of Antrim's most beautiful gorges, Glenariff, bordered by Red Bay on the seaward side. Walks through Glenariff Forest park, where magnificent waterfalls tumble down into the valley, are very popular. Adjoining Waterfoot to the north is the resort of Cushendall, renowned for its cottages which, like the rest of the village, are under the protection of the National Trust.

The A2 then reaches the northern section of the coast and the port of Ballycastle, famous for the "Out Lammas Fair" held every August and the national "fleadh" (music festival) in June. From here ferries ply to the offshore island of Rathlin, once an important Viking stronghold. Continue on the A2 by way of Ballintoy to White Park Bay, join the "Ulster Way" path, and thence go on to Bushmills, site of the oldest legal whiskey distillery in the world, dating from 1608. Our next destination is the Giant's Causeway, almost reminiscent of a lunar landscape. According to legend, the 40,000 or so basalt columns were created by the Ulster Giant Finn McCool. The next step of the tour takes in Portrush, with Dunluce Castle built in the 14th century, and then on to Coleraine, where the massive Mountsandel Fort is well worth a visit. This lively town is known for its salmon, distilleries and linen-mills. Near Downhill, at the mouth of the River Bann and on a promontory whipped by the wind, can be seen the ruins of a palace built by the eccentric Earl and Bishop of Derry, Frederick Hervey, in the 18th century; only the Mussenden Temple, intended as a library, still remains. Then drive along the fertile Foe Valley to the beautifully situated Georgian town of Limavady, where Miss Jane Ross is said to have learned the now famous melody, the "Londonderry Air", from a passing fiddler and written it down for posterity. Passing through the charming village of Eglinton, the A2 finally enters Northern Ireland's second largest town of Londonderry, with its port and industry, lying at the mouth of the River Foyle. Its Old Town is surrounded by one of the best-preserved town walls to be found anywhere in the United Kingdom.

Sights from A to Z

Aberdeen I 3

Scotland
Region: Grampian
Altitude: 869 ft
Population: 213,000

Aberdeen, known as "the Flower of Scotland", is situated picturesquely on the North Sea coast between the rivers Don and Dee. In the years since the oilfields offshore were first exploited in the late sixties, the city, Scotland's largest fishing port, has developed into one of the oil "capitals" of Europe. With good transport links, well-developed infrastructure and large labour force, combined with a favourable mid-way position on the eastern coastal plain, relatively close to the oil producing areas in the British sector of the North Sea, it was a natural choice early on in the exploration phase of the oil boom for the major centre of onshore activities.

Boasting a rich cultural tradition to complement its modern services and broadly based economy, Aberdeen today is an important commercial and tourist centre with many interesting old buildings and well-tended parks. Its superb flower borders have several times won the city first place in the "Britain in Bloom" competition. Locally quarried grey granite is the traditional building material, used for example in St Machar's, the oldest granite cathedral in the world.

Aberdeen's Dyce Airport is located 6 miles north-west of the city centre. Rail services from Aberdeen Station to London via Edinburgh

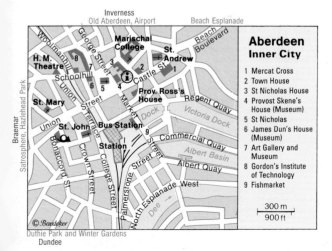

Aberdeen Inner City

1 Mercat Cross
2 Town House
3 St Nicholas House
4 Provost Skene's House (Museum)
5 St Nicholas
6 James Dun's House (Museum)
7 Art Gallery and Museum
8 Gordon's Institute of Technology
9 Fishmarket

300 m
900 ft

© Baedeker

◄ *Modern architecture in the former London dock area*

Aberdeen: the oil port

and Dundee are good. Regular ferry sailings to the Orkneys and Shetlands (see entries) depart from Jamieson Quay.

History The origins of the Celtic chapel of St Machar (who probably died in 594) can be traced back to the 6th c. The cathedral which succeeded it was founded in 1136, although the earliest work in the present building dates only from the 14th c. The building of the famous bridge which spans the Don in a steep Gothic arch, the Brig o'Balgownie, was begun in 1285 but not completed until 1320. The municipal records have been preserved almost without a break since 1398. Mary Queen of Scots (see Famous People) is said to have watched the execution of her cousin and admirer John Gordon from the Earl Marischal's town house in 1562. The "Montrose Field", first of many British oilfields in Scottish waters, came on stream early in 1969 and by 1992 there were almost 50 fields in production. Aberdeen in consequence experienced a tremendous boom. Numerous oil-related organisations established their headquarters in the city, which quickly became the chief supply base for oil platforms in the North Sea.

Sights

Castlegate

Castlegate, now Castle Street, was the old main street of the town, and most of the municipal buildings are still here. The castle itself has disappeared, the oldest building being the tower of the **Tolbooth**, formerly the prison. Nearby stands the elaborate **Mercat Cross** (or City Cross) , erected in 1685 by the Merchants' Guild and bearing portraits of the Scottish kings from James I to James VII. Also in Castlegate is the **Lead Man**, a statue (1706) commemorating the first public water supply in Aberdeen.

A short distance away are **Provost Ross' House** (1593), now a marine museum with an interesting section on oil rigs, and **Provost Skene's House** (1545). The latter, the oldest dwelling house in the city, belonged to Sir George Skene, provost of Aberdeen from 1676 to 1685. It too is now a museum, furnished in period style.

Marischal College, much admired as the largest and most imposing granite building in the country, was founded in 1593 by George Keith, 5th Earl Marischal. The oldest of the present buildings date from 1840, however, the complex being further enlarged between 1890 and 1906; notable features are the Mitchell Tower (235 ft) and the Mitchell Hall (housing the anthropological museum). In 1860 Marischal College was amalgamated with King's College (founded 1494–95), situated 1 mile to the north. King's College has preserved its original chapel with a beautiful dome, carved stalls and a remarkable timber roof.

★Marischal College, King's College

St Nicholas' Church, better known as the East and West Churches, is Scotland's largest parish church. It was divided into two at the time of the Reformation. The West Church contains four fine 17th c. tapestries. -

St Nicholas'

The Art Gallery opposite has an excellent collection with the accent on works by modern Scottish artists.

Art Gallery

The docks are on the other side of Market Street. The early morning **fish market** (located between Commercial Quay and the Albert Basin) is well worth seeing.

Docks

The area north of King's College is known as Old Aberdeen and includes the University, founded in 1494. Several interesting medieval buildings are found in the vicinity of the High Street, most being situated between the Old Town and St Machar's.
  St Machar's Cathedral is believed to occupy the site of a small chapel erected by St Machar in 581. The present building was begun in 1378 and completed in 1552. Note especially the striking towers on the West front, with sandstone spires dating from 1518–30; also the 16th c. wooden ceiling painted with coats of arms.

Old Aberdeen

Surroundings

About 10 miles west of Aberdeen stands the third oldest tower-house in Scotland, Drum Castle, which was begun in 1286.

Drum Castle

The picturesque Crathes Castle (16th c.) just 10 miles further to the West is an excellent example of the Scottish Baronial style; it has valuable furniture and painted wooden ceilings.

Crathes Castle

1½ miles south of Aberdeen, on a crag jutting out into the sea, is Dunnottar Castle, an imposing stronghold protected on three sides by water and on the landward side by a cleft in the rock. The rectangular keep is well preserved, and some idea of Dunnottar's past magnificence can be gained from the remains of the castle and its chapels – ranges of roofless buildings, towers and turrets, arched doorways and halls. During a siege of the castle in 1652 the regalia of Scotland, which were in safe-keeping here, were smuggled out by the wife of the minister of Kinneff church (6½ miles south), as a monument erected in her honour records.

Dunnottar Castle

Castle Frazer (16th/17th c.) lies about 16 miles north-west of Aberdeen with attractive corner turrets, round oriels and dainty conical roofs. A further 10 miles lies the fairytale Craigievar Castle, its first deeds show-

**Castle Frazer
Craigievar Castle**

ing it to have belonged to the Mortimer family in 1457 which at the end of the 16th c. commenced building the L-shaped keep.

Leith Hall

Leith Hall (a little under 10 miles further on), home of the Leith family since 1650, has a Z-shaped keep from the 17th c., its wings (18th/19th c.) encompassing a lovely inner courtyard.

Fyvie Castle

Between the 12th and 19th c. five families dictated the history of the imposingly large, Baronial-style Fyvie Castle (25 miles north-west of Aberdeen) which is endowed with a fine collection of 13 Raeburn paintings and Brussels tapestries.

Haddo House

William Adam drew up the plans for Haddo House in 1731 (10 miles south-east of Fyvie) and the elegant "Adam Revival" interior was designed by Wright and Mansfield in 1880.

Pitmedden Garden

Pitmedden Garden (18 miles north of Aberdeen) laid out by Sir Alexander Seton in 1675 is considered a masterpiece of Baroque garden design and has delightful small pavilions, clipped box hedges and artful planting patterns around the central main fountain.

Newburgh, Cruden Bay

To the north, at the mouth of the River Ythan, is the fishing village of Newburgh. A pearl from one of the mussels which are found in abundance here is set in the Scottish crown. Beyond Newburgh is the seaside resort of Cruden Bay (pop: 490), with a sandy beach and golf course. The Bullers of Buchan, a rocky chasm near here, impressed Dr Johnson as did **Slains Castle**, now a ruin, which Johnson declared was the finest he had ever seen.

Anglesey (Isle of)   G 7

Menai Suspension Bridge

Wales. County: Gwynedd

The Isle of Anglesey, separated from the mainland by the ¾ mile-wide Menai Strait, is spanned by two imposing bridges; the Menai Suspension Bridge (1818–26), built by Telford and a two-level bridge, opened in 1970 which has the roadway above the railway and which rests on the pillars of a former structure. Along the coast are a series of small seaside resorts which have grown out of fishing villages. Apart from five market towns there are only tiny villages, linked by narrow roads on the island.

In addition to its mild climate and fresh sea air, Anglesey is blessed with over a hundred miles of exceedingly attractive coastline. The rugged cliffs are interrupted at intervals by picturesque sandy bays while, inland, hills provide fertile pasture for vast flocks of sheep.

Holyhead

The principal town is Holyhead on the neighbouring Holy Island to the west, from which there are ferry services to Dublin (Republic of Ireland). Holy Island, which is linked with Anglesey by two bridges, is an increasingly popular holiday resort. Two promenades, one being on the 1½ mile-long breakwater, and Salt Island afford interesting views of the rocky coast where large numbers of seabirds nest.

Beaumaris Castle, Edward I's frontier fortress

A splendid panorama can also be enjoyed from Holyhead Mountain (710 ft), on the top of which are a fort and the remains of a small chapel (the only survivor of six or seven which originally stood here). These chapels are said to have earned the island its name of "Holy"; but this interpretation is open to doubt, since in earlier times the local people were predominantly Welsh-speaking, as many still are. There is, similarly, doubt about the interpretation of Anglesey as the "Island of Angels".

Also of historical interest are the **Cytiau'r Gwyddelod** on Holy Island, remains of stone dwellings dating from pre-Christian times.

Trearddur Bay (2½ miles from Holyhead; pop. 1500), is a well-known seaside resort with a good golf course. The direct road across the island to Holyhead from Bangor via the small town of Menai Bridge, is not of interest, and it is preferable to take the road round the coast.

Beaumaris (pop. 2080), about 10 miles north-east of Bangor, is a popular seaside resort and yachting centre (regatta in August). Its castle, a magnificent moated edifice with sturdy walls and defensive towers, is well worth visiting. Begun in 1295 it was the last and largest of the fortresses which Edward I built in Wales (a display in the chapel tower details the story of their construction). Ring walls some 16½ ft thick with solid corner towers enclose the square inner courtyard. Other features of interest in the town are the parish church (14th c. nave), County Hall (1614) and the Old Gaol.

★ **Beaumaris Castle**

About 5 miles away is Penmon Priory (Early Norman). The little off-shore island of Priestholm (also called Puffin Island) is the nesting-place of countless seabirds.

The route continues via Pentreath (pop. 690), with a beautiful sandy beach, and the little seaside resort of Benllech in **Red Wharf Bay**. 1 mile away is the quiet and unspoiled fishing village of **Moelfre**.

Pentreath

127

Llangefni	Within easy reach are the little market towns of Llanerchymedd and Llangefni, the administrative centre of Anglesey, and Lligwy, with a fortified village of the late Roman period.

Amlwch	Amlwch, another little market town and a seaside resort (pop. 2910), was of some importance in the early 19th c. as the port of shipment for the copper from the Parys mines, which were already being worked in Roman times. **Bull Bay** offers excellent bathing and fishing.
	    West of Bull Bay the coast becomes higher and more rugged. There are good bathing beaches between the rocks in **Cemaes Bay**.
	    The coast is particularly wild at **Carmel Head**, the north-west tip of the island.

Rhosneigr	The next seaside resort of any size is Rhosneigr, with sand dunes and rocky bays (boating, fishing, golf). Llangwyfan Old Church can be reached on foot at low tide.
Aberffraw	Further along the coast there is good bathing at Aberffraw and Malltraeth Bay.
Newborough Warren	Newborough Warren is an interesting nature reserve with sand dunes and maritime plants in abundance.
Llanfairpwllgwyn-gyllgogerych-wyrndrobwllllanty-siliogogogoch	Anglesey claims the village with the longest name in Britain: Llanfairpwllgwyngyllgogerychwyrndrobwllllantysiliogogogoch (58 letters; ½ mile from Menai Bridge). Roughly translated the name means "by the church of St Mary in the hollow of white aspen over a rapid whirlpool and St Tysilio's Church close to the red cave". It is usually known as Llanfair PG.
Plas Newydd	Plas Newydd, a 15th c. mansion standing in spacious parkland just 2 miles south-west, came into the possession of the Earls of Uxbridge and later the Marquises of Anglesey in 1784. At the end of the 18th c. the house was extensively rebuilt by James Wyatt, who also designed the very elaborate fan vaulting in the music room and the hall. Among several museum pieces in the house are a mural by the English artist Rex Whistler and the patented "Anglesey leg", a wooden leg made for the first Marquis of Anglesey after the Battle of Waterloo. It was one of the earliest artificial limbs.

Antonine Wall   G/H 4/5

Scotland. Regions: Strathclyde and Central

The Antonine Wall, traditionally known as Grim's Dyke or Graham's Dyke, was a Roman fortification extending from Bo'ness on the Firth of Forth to Dunglass Castle on Dunglass Point (near Clydebank) on the Firth of Clyde, a total distance of 39 miles. The wall was built of turf and earth on a stone base, and was originally about 10 ft high and 14 ft wide. To the north was a ditch 20 ft deep and 40 ft across, and there were nineteen forts situated at intervals along the wall. A paved road ran along the south side.

History The wall was constructed by Roman legionaries in AD 142. As well as artefacts found in the forts, the Hunterian Museum in Glasgow (see entry) possesses a model showing which sections were built by the different units. The wall was designed to afford protection against attacks from the north.

    Scotland, unlike England, was never firmly under Roman control, but was partly occupied on a temporary basis to protect the province of Britannia. Agricola advanced into Scotland in AD 80, and in 84 inflicted a

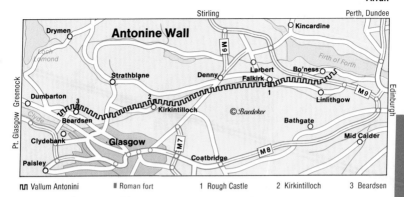

Stirling　　　　　　　　　　　　　　　Perth, Dundee

Antonine Wall

ꖦꖦ Vallum Antonini　　■ Roman fort　　1 Rough Castle　　2 Kirkintilloch　　3 Beardsen

crushing defeat on the natives at Mons Graupius, a site yet to be identified with any certainty but most probably somewhere in southern
Perthshire. Agricola built a number of forts but the wall, named after the
reigning emperor Titus Aurelius Antoninus, was erected by his successor Quintus Lollius Urbicus. The forts along the wall were manned by
Gauls and Belgians, Syrians and Thracians. The wall was abandoned in
about 185, only 40 years after its completion.

While little is left of the wall itself, the ditch has survived well in places
and six of the forts have been excavated. The best preserved forts are at
Kirkintilloch (pop. 23,200; also known as Caerpentulach) and **Rough
Castle**, the latter being not far from the coal mining/iron foundry town of
Falkirk (pop. 42,800). Such pieces of the wall as do remain can best be
seen at Callendar House, a short distance east of the town, and to the
north-west and north-east of **Bearsden** (pop. 26,000), another town
north-west of Glasgow.

Arran (Isle of)　　　　　　　　　　　　　　　　F 5

Scotland. Region: Strathclyde

The 165 sq. mile Isle of Arran is the largest of the islands in the Firth
of Clyde as well as being the most varied scenically. The northern part
is the more mountainous, characterised by the island's highest summits of granite, volcanic rock and red sandstone as well as by deep
valleys, moor and heathland. South of the Highland Boundary Fault
the scenery takes on a more lowland character, with fertile soil and
gentle hills.
　Lying some 12 miles off the Ayrshire coast, Arran (pop. 3,600) is 20
miles long and 11 miles across. Often called "Scotland in miniature"
the island is of great interest to geologists, being composed of almost
every kind of rock found in Britain. For the archaeologically inclined
there are numerous burial cairns, standing stones and Iron Age and
medieval remains. Many rare species of plant are to be found in the
mountains.
Car ferries cross from Ardrossan to Brodick several times a day. In summer
there are additional services from Claonaig (Kintyre) and Lochranza.

Brodick (pop. 850), the island's principal harbour, lies on the east coast
in the delightful setting of Brodick Bay. Here the Arran Heritage Museum
offers an insight into the island's history. 2 miles to the north can be seen

★**Brodick Castle**

The beautiful gardens of Brodick Castle

the red sandstone walls of Brodick Castle, rebuilt several times since the 13th c. It has fine interior furnishings including paintings by Watteau, Gainsborough and Turner (see Famous People) as well as superb silver and porcelain. Magnolias and rhododendrons in a pleasing variety of shades ornament the gardens.

Goatfell

The island's highest peak, Goatfell (2866 ft), can be climbed from Brodick; in good weather there are magnificent panoramic views from the top. The climb takes about five hours there and back; alternatively the descent can be made to Corrie.

Glen Rosa

It is also possible to go round by the very beautiful Glen Rosa.

Holy Island

Holy Island, 1 mile in length, guards the mouth of Lamlash Bay 5 miles south of Brodick. It is an island of varied scenery, rising to a height of 1030 ft. Its name reflects the tradition that St Molaise, a disciple of St Columba, lived here. The cave which the saint is said to have occupied can still be seen, its walls covered with inscriptions of various dates including large runic signs. A large block of sandstone surrounded by artificial depressions in the rock is known as the Saint's Chair.

Lamlash

Lamlash (pop. 620), the second largest community, is a popular seaside resort with a sailing school (Arran Yacht Club) and a beautiful bay which offers good bathing.

Whiting Bay

At the south end of the bay is Kingscross, beyond which is Whiting Bay (golf course). Immediately south is Glen Ashdale, with two waterfalls.

Kildonan Castle

Kildonan Castle was a royal hunting lodge in the days when Arran was Crown property and the Scottish kings came here to hunt; the red deer which were then introduced into Arran can still be seen on the island. The castle is now a picturesque ruin, situated in an exposed position on the coast.

On Brennan Head, the most southerly point on the island, are the Struey rocks, which are well worth a visit. Here too is the Black Cave, 80 ft deep and extending into the cliffs for some 150 ft. **Brennan Head**

The road continues by way of the restful little holiday place of Lagg to beautiful Glen Monarmore and Sliddery, on the coast, with remains of a watch-tower on Castle Hill. **Lagg**

On the south-west coast, looking out to Kilbrennan Sound, is the seaside resort of Blackwaterfoot, with a golf course and good fishing. **Blackwaterfoot**

On King's Hill, at the north end of Drumadoon Bay, are a number of caves in which Robert the Bruce (see Famous People), one of Scotland's national heroes who was crowned king in 1306 and won a resounding victory over Edward II in 1314, is said to have hidden with his men. The largest of the caves is known as the King's Cave. **King's Cave**

3 miles north of Blackwaterfoot stand six Bronze Age stone circles, the Machrie Moor Stones, access to which is along Moss Farm Road by Machrie Water. The stones are of granite and old red sandstones and were erected in about 1600 BC **Machrie Moor**

More prehistoric remains known as the Standing Stones of Tormore are found at Tormore, about 2½ miles north of Blackwaterfoot. **Standing Stones of Tormore**

The road continues by way of the small villages of Auchencar and Catacol to Lochranza, in a very beautiful bay, with a golf course and the remains of the 17th c. Lochranza Castle. The most northerly point on the island is the Cock of Arran, 2 miles from Lochranza. **Lochranza**

From Lochranza the road runs through Glen Chalmadale and Glen Sannox, the wildest of Arran's glens, to Corrie (golf course) and Brodick (6 miles). **Glen Sannox, Corrie**

Avebury   K 9

Southern England. County: Wiltshire
Altitude: 500 ft. Population: 540

Surrounded by the rolling landscape of the North Wessex Downs the little village of Avebury stands right in the centre of a truly remarkable Neolithic cult site dating from the end of the 3rd millennium BC. There is much to see in the village including the pretty 12th–15th c. church of St James (restored in the 19th c., Norman font), the Museum of Wiltshire Life housed in an old barn, and Avebury Manor, an Elizabethan house with 17th c. furnishings. The Alexander Keiller Museum is a collection of models, displays and archaeological finds shedding light on what is one of the largest megalithic monuments in Europe. All the places of interest mentioned below lie within a radius of 1¼–2 miles of Avebury and are well signposted; some, however, can only be reached on foot.

Sights

Viewing the complex of Neolithic stone circles at Avebury today it is hard to imagine how they must originally have looked. Extending over **★Avebury Circle** an area of about 27 acres, the site was surrounded by a 49 ft-high earth rampart and a ditch, with breaks at the four points of the compass. A hundred massive sandstone blocks (sarsens) each weighing up to 50 tonnes, hauled all the way from the Marlborough Downs 5½ miles distant, stood in a circle around the inner perimeter of the earthworks. Two further stone circles, both with diameters in excess of 330 ft, flanked the holy of holies, the inner sanctuary. Enclosed by the northern ring was a U-shaped arrangement of huge stone blocks, while the southern ring encircled equally large stones in a Z-shaped configuration. Archaeologists have estimated that 200 men working 60 hours a week for three years would have been needed to construct the vast complex. The site fell into decline after about 1000 years, later generations using it as a source of building materials.

The 1½ mile-long, 49 ft-wide **Kennet Avenue**, marked out by some 200 stones arranged in pairs, linked the southern exit of Avebury Circle with the Sanctuary on **Overton Hill**. Here there were yet more circles – six concentric stone and timber rings, the latter probably being uprights supporting wooden roofs. Pottery finds suggest the site continued in use as late as the Bronze Age.

Windmill Hill

In Neolithic times livestock were herded into the Windmill Hill enclosure, which takes the form of three concentric rings of earthworks and ditches, prior to the annual autumn slaughter. So great was the number of finds made here that archaeologists refer to an early phase of the Neolithic period in England as "the Windmill Hill culture".

Silbury Hill

This conical hill, almost 130 ft high and 590 ft in diameter, was constructed around 2500 BC Its Stone Age builders, equipped only with reindeer antler picks and shovels fashioned from the shoulder blades of oxen, shifted altogether some 46,000 cu.yd of earth and gravel, the work being carried out in several stages. Its raison d'être remains something of a mystery, excavation having yielded no grave goods or other evidence of use as a burial site. As some form of ritual significance seems the most likely alternative, archaeologists tend to assume that Silbury was either a religious site or possibly served some calendrical purpose.

West Kennet
★ Long Barrow

The 3rd c. BC West Kennet Long Barrow is one of the most outstanding megalithic tombs in England. The arrangement of the stones in the construction of the barrow's several burial chambers and passageways, in which 40 skeletons were uncovered, is particularly impressive.

Surroundings

Marlborough

Marlborough (7 miles east; pop. 6500), an old market town on the River Kennet, has some charming Georgian houses along the High Street. In 1843, what had been a 16th c. manor house, itself constructed from the remains of a Norman castle, became a school, having previously been put to a variety of uses. Marlborough College now has more than 900 pupils and is one of the country's leading public schools.

Bowood House

Set in a large park with old trees, terraced gardens and borders designed by Lancelot "Capability" Brown, Bowood House (8 miles west), seat of the Marquis of Landsdowne, has several interesting features. Inside the house is the laboratory where Joseph Priestley discovered oxygen in 1774 and where in 1779 Jan Ingenhouse discovered photosynthesis. Classical sculptures, porcelain and 18th c. English paintings, including some by Reynolds and Gainsborough, can be seen in the galleries together with a number of curiosities such as the Albanian costume in which Lord Byron was painted in 1814.

Devizes

The old cloth town of Devizes (8 miles south-west; pop. 10,600) has a distinctive sickel-shaped market place with a fountain and cross (19th c.)

bordered by several 18th c. town houses. The portrait painter Thomas Lawrence (1769–1830) was son of the landlord of The Bear Inn and launched himself on his career by drawing sketches of the guests. Also worth seeing is St John's Church with its Norman central tower. The Devises Museum in Long Street has a particularly interesting archaeological section containing, in addition to local finds, models of the development of Avebury and Stonehenge (see entry).

Swindon

Swindon (12 miles north-east; pop. 91,000), otherwise undistinguished, was once a major junction on the Great Western Railway and still owes its chief attractions to the Age of Steam. The **Great Western Railway Museum** and **Railway Village Museum** (both in Faringdon Road) provide a fascinating insight not only into the railways of the period between 1831 and 1948 (with models as well as original rolling-stock) but also the lives and working conditions of railwaymen.

Savernake Forest

From Norman times to the Tudor period this ancient forest (8 miles south-east) was the hunting preserve of England's kings, teeming with wild boar and red deer. In the 18th c. the landscape architect "Capability" Brown planted it with deciduous trees. Today the forest's pleasant paths and picnic places offer visitors the opportunity to relax. The Grand Avenue with its splendid old beeches is particularly lovely.

Ridgeway Path

Also highly recommended is a walk along a stretch of the 85 mileRidgeway (signposted with an acorn symbol). This long-distance footpath goes from Overton Hill at Avebury, via Uffington White Horse, to the Ivinghoe Beacon near Tring. It makes its way across delightful chalk downland with distant views and past ancient sites redolent with history from the Stone Age to the days of Roman rule.

★Uffington White Horse

Every tourist should be sure to visit this most famous of White Horses, cut in the turf of a hillside near Uffington (on the B4507 between Swindon and Wantage). The 374 ft-long horse is of uncertain date. One suggestion is that it was a tribal totem of the Iceni (1st or 2nd c. BC) – a theory supported by the presence of an Iron Age fort (probably 2nd c. BC) known as Uffington Castle on the hill-top. The figure shows some resemblance to the horses depicted on late Iron Age coins. Wiltshire's other white horses are of more recent origin, cut in the 18th and 19th centuries.

Bath   I 9

Southern England. Unitary Authority of Bath
Altitude: 98 ft. Population: 84,500

Bath was, and still is, the most celebrated spa in England, the only resort to boast hot springs and one of England's most elegant and attractive towns. Lying sheltered in the valley of the Avon between the Cotswolds and the Mendip Hills, the city, with its well-proportioned Georgian houses built of honey-coloured stone, its attractive squares and its parks, has a townscape unsurpassed in Britain. Since 1998 it has featured on the UNESCO world cultural heritage list. Some 500 of its buildings are statutorily protected as being of historical or architectural importance and almost every other house carries a plaque with the name of some eminent, usually 18th or 19th c., figure whose home or visiting place it once was.

History Geological research shows there have been thermal springs bubbling from the ground here for at least 100,000 years. According

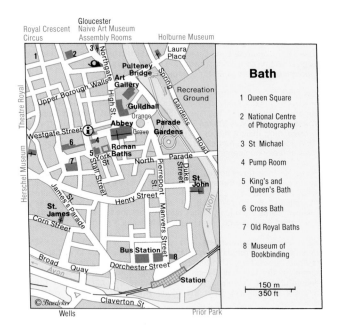

Gloucester
Royal Crescent Naive Art Museum
Circus Assembly Rooms Holburne Museum

Bath

1 Queen Square

2 National Centre
of Photography

3 St Michael

4 Pump Room

5 King's and
Queen's Bath

6 Cross Bath

7 Old Royal Baths

8 Museum of
Bookbinding

150 m
350 ft

© Baedeker

Wells Prior Park

to tradition the healing powers of the waters were first discovered about 500 BC by Prince Bladud, who had been banished from court because of leprosy. While roaming the countryside as a swineherd he allowed his pigs to wallow in the warm mud and took to bathing in the mud himself. This cured him of his leprosy; now able to return to court with his health restored he eventually became king. It was the Romans who first accorded the springs proper recognition as a spa, building a town with extensive baths known from AD 75 onwards as Aquae Sulis. Once the Romans had left Britain, however, the baths fell into disrepair. In the 7th c. the Saxons built an abbey and small settlement within the Roman walls, and in the 12th c. the Norman bishop John de Villula began building a new, grander episcopal priory church which was never completed. During the late Middle Ages Bath was a centre of the wool trade, a status reflected in Chaucer's "Wife of Bath's Tale". It only became widely appreciated again as a spa in 1702 when Queen Anne visited it, bringing the English nobility in her train. Among those whom fashion drew to Bath was the wealthy young Richard Nash, known as "Beau Nash", the greatest dandy of the 18th c. Taking up residence in the city he was largely responsible for establishing the canons of taste and etiquette observed by genteel society. From 1738 Bath itself was virtually rebuilt, the classically-inspired architect John Wood designing suitably elegant buildings in the Palladian style, the stone for which came from quarries belonging to the wealthy Ralph Allen who also owned the sites. The city emerged from this redevelopment very much as seen today.

In addition to its architecture Bath is renowned for its cultural tradition, music in particular, hosting the highly regarded Bath International Festival.

Sights

The Roman Baths and the Temple of Sulis Minerva, built in about 75 BC around the largest of the three hot springs, are extraordinarily impressive. The water, containing some 43 different minerals, gushes from a depth of 9800 ft at a rate of 275,000 gallons a day, with a constant temperature of 46.5°C (116°F).

A model of the Roman Baths

The Romans named the temple after the Celtic goddess Sul who they associated with their own goddess Minerva. The complex of buildings around the spring served not only to supply the baths with mineral water but also for worship of the two deities, many votive offerings being recovered from the wells. Systematic excavations began in the late 19th c., the most recent being conducted between 1981 and 1983.

Many of the artefacts found in the baths, temples and sacred springs are on display in the museum although some have also been left in situ. Visitors should give priority to seeing the Great Bath, which measures 39 × 78 ft and is nearly 6 ft deep. In Roman times it was roofed over with barrel vaulting and equipped with side ducts. The statues and balustrades are of a later date. Other items of interest include the Gorgon's head on the temple pediment, altar-stones, mosaics, votive offerings (including tablets inscribed with curses) and various fragments of sculpture, among them part of a gilded bronze figure of Minerva.

The Classical-style **Pump Room** dates from Georgian times. As well as its gilded decoration it is embellished with a statue of Beau Nash and a clock by Tompion. The terrace overlooks the King's Bath, a medieval structure from about 1100 much altered in the 19th c. The many brass rings were tokens of gratitude from appreciative beneficiaries of Bath's waters.

The late-Gothic cathedral of the Bishop of Bath and Wells is known simply as "the Abbey", a reflection of the long history of abbey churches preceding it on the site. The present building was started by Bishop Oliver King who, on his consecration in 1495, dreamed of angels ascending and descending ladders to and from heaven, at the same time hearing a voice declare that "the crown should plant an olive tree and the king restore the church". This he interpreted as a sign to rebuild the church. His dream is immortalised in stone on the west front where, above olive trees encircled by crowns, angels can be seen ascending and descending tall ladders surrounded by apostles. The figure of Christ appears high up in the tympanum.

The interior of the church has three aisles and unusually shallow transepts. Superb fan-vaulting by the Vertue brothers adorns the chancel and side aisles (1504–18). When building was finally completed at the end of the 16th c. (after several lengthy interruptions), there were insufficient resources to vault the nave. Its fan tracery consequently dates only from the late 19th c. Flying buttresses were added at the same time to give increased strength.

The somewhat plain interior is chiefly distinguished by the tombs of various 16th and 17th c. bishops, as well as by numerous tablets and memorials.

The Georgian architecture for which Bath is famous is found chiefly in the north-west of the city. **Queen Square** with its beautifully

Bath: Royal Crescent, a palatial Georgian building

symmetrical façades (1729–36), a popular place for taking the air, Gay Street, and the perfectly proportioned, classically modelled **Circus** (1754 onwards), were all designed by John Wood the Elder (1704–54).

★**Royal Crescent**, a monumental 600 ft semi-circular sweep of residential town houses with a breathtakingly uniform, palace-like façade, was the work of his son, John Wood the Younger (1728–81) whose inspired masterpiece dispensed for the first time with the classic town square in the interests of integrating nature and urban architecture.

The elegant **Assembly Rooms** (built 1769–71, restored 1991) where visitors would gather for the evening's entertainment, are also by the younger Wood. Today they house a delightful collection of costumes.

The charming **Pulteney Bridge** spanning the River Avon was built by Robert Adam for Sir William Pulteney in about 1770, prior to Pulteney's development of the east bank. The bridge, with three arches and lined on either side with little shops, opens onto the dignified rows of Neo-Classical houses in Great Pulteney Street.

Sally Lunn's	This medieval house, the oldest in Bath, is now a museum and tea room, serving delicious "Sally Lunn's buns" made to ancient recipes. An old fashioned kitchen can be seen in the basement.
Naïve Art Museum	The Museum of English Naïve Art opened in this 19th c. schoolhouse in 1987. On display are primitive English paintings from between 1750 and 1900.
National Centre of Photography	The RPS photographic museum possesses a comprehensive collection on the history of photography. The Centre also regularly mounts special exhibitions of photographic art.
Holburne Museum	The Holburne Museum's fine collection originally belonged to Sir Thomas Holburne, who died in 1874. It includes paintings by Gainsborough, Reynolds and Stubbs, miniatures, 18th c. silver, Wedgwood porcelain, Renaissance bronzes and medallions and early period furniture.
Herschel House	Now a museum it was in this house that the musician and astronomer William Herschel lived. His discovery of the planet Uranus was made from the garden in 1781.

Surroundings

A further two fine 18th c. residential streets are found on the outskirts of Bath. Camden Crescent was built by John Eveleigh between 1786 and 1792, remaining uncompleted because of structural problems. The Baroque sweep of John Palmer's Landsdown Crescent (1794), several hundred metres long, represented quite an innovation in urban architecture, twisting in serpentine conformity to the contours of the site.

Camden Crescent, Landsdown Crescent

Claverton Manor (2½ miles south-east), built by Sir Jeffry Wyatville in 1820, now houses an American Museum with evocative period reconstructions of interiors from American homes (17th–19th c.). There are special sections on the American West and the American Indians.

Claverton Manor

Prior Park (2 miles south-east) was built between 1735 and 1750 for Ralph Allen, to plans by John Wood. It is a fine example of a Palladian mansion, with a magnificent colonnaded portico. There is also a lovely Palladian bridge in the landscaped grounds. The park but not the house is open to the public.

Prior Park

Dyrham Park (8 miles north) is a 17th c. mansion set in more than 250 acres of parkland and gardens, with delightful views. The interior contains fine furniture, paintings, etc.

Dyrham

Battle   M 10

Southern England
County: East Sussex
Altitude: 230 ft. Population: 4700

The delightful little market town of Battle is situated just 6 miles from the South Coast, north of Hastings. Although nearly every schoolchild is taught that the battle in which William the Conqueror (see Famous People) defeated the Saxon king Harold in 1066 was fought at Hastings, in fact this most notorious of encounters on English soil took place here, on the site of the town later named after it. To commemorate his victory, and in atonement for all the blood shed during his invasion, William built an abbey where his rival Harold fell. The finest portrayal of the battle itself is found on the famous Bayeux Tapestry, embroidered in the 11th c.
    Starting from the abbey gatehouse a round walk tours the battlefield. Events on that fateful day – 14th October 1066 – can be followed with the help of topographical models sited at intervals along the way. The lower terrace of the abbey commands a sweeping view over the scene of battle.

The 223 ft Benedictine abbey church was consecrated in 1094, its high altar marking the spot where Harold died. In 1539, at the time of the Reformation, Henry VIII gave the abbey to his Master of the Horse, Sir Anthony Browne, following which large parts of it were torn down. The Norman church was demolished and the west wing converted by Sir Anthony for use as his private residence. Altered in 1857 in Neo-Gothic style, this latter is now a girls' school and closed to the public. The gatehouse, completed in 1339, and the ruins of the monks' dormitory (1120), remain particularly impressive today.
    The tomb of Sir Anthony Browne (died 1548), a splendid Renaissance sarcophagus, can be seen in St Mary's, the parish church a little to the north.

Battle Abbey

Buckleys "Yesterday World" at 90 High Street offers a nostalgic glimpse of by-gone days with shop interiors and fittings from 1850 to 1950. The Memorial Hall houses the Battle and District Historical Society Museum.

Museums

In the Benedictine abbey at Battle

Surroundings

★Herstmonceux Castle

Herstmonceux Castle (10 miles) west) is a splendid 15th c. moated and fortified, red brick manor house. Until 1990 it was the home of the Royal Observatory, which moved there from its original site in Greenwich and has now been transferred to Cambridge.

★Bodiam Castle

Built on the northern slopes of the Rother valley between 1385 and 1389, Bodiam Castle (8 miles north-east of Battle) is one of the country's best preserved medieval moated castles. It is also widely regarded as one of the most romantic castle ruins in England (a reputation it acquired in the 19th c. due in no small measure to J. Fuller). Never having endured a siege, Bodiam retains much of its original character, an outstanding example of a medieval fortress from a time when domestic comfort began to be prized as well as security. The unusually wide moat creates the appearance of a lake, in which the square castle with its sturdy, round, battlemented corner towers, stands as if on an island.

Bedford   L 8

Central England
County: Bedfordshire
Altitude: 93 ft. Population: 75,700

Bedford, situated on the River Ouse 26 miles west of Cambridge, is the county town of Bedfordshire. Despite its various thriving industries it has a quiet residential air, with many attractive parks and gardens. The Ouse offers excellent angling and boating. The town is noted for its schools and its association with John Bunyan (1628–88).

History In 1552 Sir William Harpur (1496–1573), a cloth merchant who became Lord Mayor of London (1561–62), founded a school in Bedford, his native town. The Harpur Trust now runs some four schools with a total of 3500 pupils. John Bunyan was born in the neighbouring village of Elstow, the son of a tinker. After marrying a pious woman he became an itinerant preacher, joining a Nonconformist sect. Although banned from preaching he continued to do so nevertheless and was thereupon confined to the county gaol from 1660 to 1672, preaching to his warders and fellow prisoners. In 1675 he was arrested once more and committed to the town prison, where most of "The Pilgrim's Progress" was written.

St Paul's Church, near the bridge over the Ouse, has a 14th c. pulpit. A statue of John Howard (1726–90), the great prison reformer, stands in St Paul's Square.

St Paul's

At the end of the High Street, looking towards the site of the old county gaol, is a statue of John Bunyan by Joseph Boehm.

Statue of Bunyan

The Cecil Higgins Art Gallery and Museum in Castle Close possesses a notable collection of English and Continental porcelain, glass, furniture and watercolours. Nearby is the Bedford Museum, devoted to local history from the Ice Age to the present day.

Museums

St Peter's Church has a Norman tower incorporating some Saxon work.

St Peter's

The Howard Congregational Church in Mill Street was founded by John Howard in 1772. The Bunyan Meeting, also in Mill Street, has ten scenes from "The Pilgrim's Progress" adorning its bronze doors (1876). It stands on the site of a barn where Bunyan used to preach. The museum and library contain many Bunyan memorabilia as well as various editions of his works.

Mill Street
Bunyan Meeting

The adjacent Howard House belonged to John Howard, who moved to Cardington, 3 miles south-east, in 1858.

Howard House

Luton (pop. 170,000), an industrial town with an **airport** serving London, has an interesting church, the 13th c. **St Mary's**, built largely in the Decorated style. Also noteworthy are the canopied stone font and wooden choir screen in the Wenlock Chapel (1461; William Wenlock was a prebendary of St Paul's Cathedral in London).
   Luton Hoo (2½ miles south-east), a handsome country mansion begun by Robert Adam in 1767 and completed by Smirke in 1816, was rebuilt between 1903 and 1907 following a fire. It now houses a splendid art collection assembled by Sir Harold Wernher.

Luton

Belfast   E/F 6

Northern Ireland
County: Antrim. District: Belfast
Altitude: 59 ft. Population: 292,000

Belfast, capital since 1920 of the six counties of Northern Ireland (reorganised into 26 districts in 1973), is an important industrial city and port. It lies beautifully situated on Belfast Lough in the north-east of Ireland, at the mouth of the River Lagan, the county boundary between Down and Antrim. Belfast's shipyards are among the most modern in Europe and for many years Harland and Wolff's dry dock was the largest in the world. Here as elsewhere, however, the world-wide crisis in shipbuilding has left its mark.

The city has numerous fine buildings and about 170 churches and small chapels. The central pedestrianised area on the west bank of the River Lagan makes a pleasant place to stroll, with several department stores, shopping arcades, pubs and restaurants. In November each year the city plays host for three weeks to one of the biggest cultural festivals in the British Isles (second only to the Edinburgh Festival). There is excellent access to the coast, the surrounding countryside and Lough Neagh, Ireland's largest lake, all of which are very attractive.

Transport Belfast International Airport is at Aldergrove, 15 miles to the north-west, from where buses run a shuttle service to the city centre (Glengall Street/Great Victoria Street Bus Station, Oxford Street Bus Station). The City Airport (4 miles) north of the centre) only handles flights to and from destinations in the UK. In addition to the Stranraer and Cairnryan (Scotland) car ferry services, which leave from Larne (rail connection from York Road station), there are ferries (from Donegal Quay) to the Isle of Man and to Liverpool (see entries). Rail services from the Central Station are good.

History Belfast ("Beal feirste" = "Sandy Ford") already possessed a fort in the early Middle Ages, but this was destroyed in 1177. Thereafter a castle was built, the possession of which was often disputed between the native Irish and the English conquerors. In 1613 the town which had grown up around the castle was granted a charter by James I. The manufacture of linen had long been an important industry in Belfast, and it received additional impetus in the latter part of the 17th c. when Huguenots fleeing from France introduced improved industrial methods. The newcomers gave the life of the town a French stamp and contributed to the development of its intellectual life. Following the 1800 Act of Union and Ireland's formal integration with Great Britain, Belfast grew rapidly into the most important industrial city in Ireland. Its prosperity was founded on rope manufacture, shipbuilding and tobacco as well as linen. The magnificence of its 19th c. buildings earned the city the soubriquet "Athens of the North".

Since 1968–69 when an eruption of civil strife prompted the British government to send troops to the province, Belfast has suffered repeatedly from terrorist violence associated with the Northern Ireland conflict. **The "troubles"**, as the bloody sectarian dispute over Ulster's future is known, have decisively shaped the everyday life and economic fortunes of the city. Outside the city centre the boundaries between Catholic and Protestant districts are not always as obvious as they are in mainly Catholic West Belfast, where barbed wire and walls separate the two communities. Segregation extends to schools, pubs and other areas of social life.

After the start of the IRA ceasefire on September 1st 1994 the situation in Belfast improved markedly and the military and police presence was scaled down. In September 1994 the European Union provided some 2.4 million Ecu for the promotion of projects intended to bridge the gap between Ulster's Catholic and Protestant communities.

In February 1996 an explosion at Canary Wharf in London ended the IRA ceasefire. In spite of intense efforts this was not restored in time to enable Sinn Fein to attend the all-party talks in June 1996. Efforts continue to bring about a lasting peace.

Note: Tourists should take care to avoid the "control zones" where parking is in any case prohibited; unattended vehicles may be treated as suspicious and dealt with accordingly. Drivers should be prepared for the occasional vehicle check and pedestrians, whether local people or visitors, may be asked for proof of identity.

Sights

Donegall Square

The central feature of Belfast is the **City Hall**, a huge Neo-

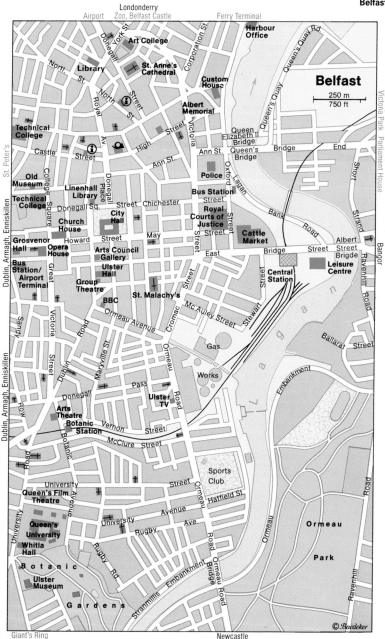

Belfast

Londonderry
Airport Zoo, Belfast Castle   Ferry Terminal

Harbour Office

Belfast

250 m
750 ft

Bangor
Victoria Park Parliament House

Bangor

York St.
Donegall
Corporation St.
North St.
Art College
North St.
Library
Royal Av.
St. Anne's Cathedral
Custom House
Queen's Quay Rd
Queen's Quay

Technical College
Castle Street
High Street
Victoria Street
Albert Memorial
Queen Elizabeth II Bridge
Ann St.
Queen's Bridge
End
Short Strand

Old Museum
College Square
Linenhall Library
Donegall Place
Donegall Sq.
Chichester Street
Police
Oxford Street
Lagan
Bridge
Bangor

Technical College
Church House
City Hall
Street
May Street
Bus Station
Royal Courts of Justice
Bank Road
Cattle Market
Albert Street Brigde
Ravenhill Road

Grosvenor Hall
Opera House
Howard Street
Arts Council Gallery
Ulster Hall
East Street
Bridge Street
Leisure Centre

Bus Station/ Airport Terminal
Great Victoria Street
Group Theatre
BBC
St. Malachy's
Cromac Street
Mc Auley Street
Stewart Street
Central Station
L a g a n

Sandy Row
Dublin Road
Ormeau Avenue
Pass
Gas Works
Embankment
Ballarat Street

Maryville St.
Donegall
Ulster TV
Ormeau Road

Arts Theatre
Botanic Station
Vernon Street
McClure Street

Botanic Road
Sports Club

University Street
Queen's Film Theatre
University Avenue
University Avenue
Rugby Ave.
Hatfield St.
Ormeau Road

Ormeau
Park

Queen's University
Whitla Hall
Rugby Rd.

B o t a n i c
Ulster Museum
G a r d e n s
Strandmillis Embankment
Ormeau Bridge
Ormeau Road
Ravenhill Road

St. Peter's
Dublin, Armagh, Enniskillen
Dublin, Armagh, Enniskillen

Giant's Ring   Newcastle

© Baedeker

Renaissance palazzo (1898–1906) designed by Sir Brumwell Thomas, with corner towers, a massive dome and magnificent banqueting hall. In front of it are statues of Queen Victoria (see Famous People) and prominent citizens of Belfast, and on the west side is the War Memorial in a **Garden of Remembrance**. There is also a sculptured group commemorating the sinking of the Titanic, the ill-fated liner having been launched from Belfast's Harland and Wolff shipyard in 1912.

On the north of the square stands the **Linen Hall Library** (1788), with an exhibition on the history of linen manufacture.

Donegall Square and the adjoining streets, particularly **Royal Avenue**, are the city's main shopping streets, with large department stores.

St Anne's Cathedral	To the north, by way of Royal Avenue and Church Street, is St Anne's Cathedral, the principal church of the (Anglican) Church of Ireland, begun in 1898 (architect Sir Thomas Drew). A Neo-Romanesque building of the basilican type, it has three fine west doorways decorated with sculpture. The baptismal chapel has a mosaic ceiling made of hundreds of thousands of tiny pieces of glass. In the chapel is the tomb of Sir Edward Carson (died 1935), leader of the Ulster Unionists.
Other churches	Among several other churches worth visiting are St Patrick's Pro-Cathedral (Roman Catholic; late 19th c. pre-Raphaelite tryptich) in Upper Donegall Street, the Tudor-style St Malachy's (Roman Catholic; 1848) in Alfred Street, and in Corporation Street the Sinclair Seamen's Presbyterian Church, consecrated in 1853, which now houses a maritime museum.
★ Opera House, ★ Crown Liquor Saloon	West of the City Hall in Great Victoria Street stands the very ornate Opera House with, opposite, the "Crown Liquor Saloon", a Victorian pub. Old gas lamps lend added atmosphere to the latter's elaborately furnished rooms. Both Opera House and pub are well worth seeing.
Custom House	Figures of Britannia, Neptune and Mercury adorn the Custom House (1854–57) beside the River Lagan north-east of the City Hall.
Albert Memorial	Situated a few steps from the High Street the Albert Memorial Clock Tower was built in 1869 as a memorial to Queen Victoria's husband, the Prince Consort. The tower is often called "the Big Ben of Belfast" because of its similarity to the famous London landmark, which houses Big Ben.
Transport Museum	The Transport Museum in Witham Street has a collection of steam locomotives, trams and vintage cars.
Botanic Gardens	For feet made weary by pavements the Botanic Gardens in the south of the city offer welcome relief, the main attraction being the elegant palm house with plants more than a hundred years old.
Ulster Museum	Also located in the Gardens is the Ulster Museum, with substantial displays from Celtic and Early Christian times as well as a collection of gold and silver items recovered from the wreck of the "Girona", flagship of the Spanish Armada, which sank off the Giant's Causeway in 1588. With works by Brueghel, Turner (see Famous People) and Gainsborough among others, the museum art gallery is particularly strong in 17th and 18th c. European painting in addition to modern Irish art. The sections of the museum devoted to natural and industrial history are also full of interest. The portraits of prominent persons of Northern Irish descent, including ten American presidents, testify to the scale of Irish emigration down the centuries, particularly to the United States.
Queen's University	A short distance north of the Botanic Gardens are the Tudor-style buildings of the Queen's University, founded in 1845 and an independent

Belfast City Hall

institution since 1909. Charles Lanyon's red-brick campus was modelled on Magdalen College, Oxford (see entry) and incorporates a history museum.

To the north of the city, in addition to various parks, sports grounds and golf courses, lie the Zoological Gardens – in a lovely setting with beautiful views – and Belfast Castle (1870), once the home of Lord Shaftesbury but now a restaurant. Cave Hill (1182 ft), volcanic in origin, has a profile supposed to resemble Napoleon's. In good weather the climb to the top of the hill is rewarded with splendid views of the city, Lough Neagh to the west and the Irish Sea coast to the east, with the Isle of Man (see entry) in the far distance.

Zoological Gardens, Belfast Castle, Cave Hill

3 miles east, in the suburb of Stormont, stands the imposing Classical-style building erected in 1928–32 to house the Northern Ireland Parliament. In front of it is a monument to Sir Edward Carson.

Stormont

The open-air Ulster Folk and Transport Museum, in the spacious grounds of Cultra Manor about 7½ miles north, comprises a collection of 18th c. farmhouses, cottages and artisans' workshops painstakingly reconstructed brick by brick. There is also an indoor transport museum. A recently opened rail gallery is the largest of its kind in Ireland.

★ Ulster Folk and Transport Museum

Surroundings

There are several different ways of getting to Lough Neagh, which with an area of 150 sq. miles, is the largest lake in Northern Ireland (18 miles long, 11 miles wide and 39 ft at its deepest). Ten rivers flow into the lake which is well stocked with fish. There is no road running round the lough,

Lough Neagh

The Opera House

nor even a good footpath, the lough shores being low and overgrown with vegetation. The best view of the lough is from Glenavy, where boats can be rented in summer. 5 miles west of Glenavy is the beautiful Ram's Island.

Antrim

One route to Lough Neagh is via Antrim (pop. 8500), the town from which the county and beautiful area of coast both take their name. It is situated at the outflow of the Sixmilewater into the lough. Antrim Castle with its Tudor-style gateway (1622), has been burned down and rebuilt several times. The gardens were designed by Le Nitre, who laid out the gardens at Versailles.

One of the best preserved round towers in Ireland stands in the grounds of ★**Steeple House**, ¾ mile north-east of the town. 90 ft high, it was built in the 10th c.

North of Belfast Lough

Along the northern and southern shores of Belfast Lough – the broad inlet on which the city lies – are a series of popular seaside resorts. The coast immediately north of the lough is particularly beautiful. On the lough's north side, about half-way along (7 miles), is **Carrickfergus**, quite a considerable port before being displaced by Belfast. It is noted for its excellently preserved Norman **castle** (military museum) perched on a spur of black basalt originally surrounded by water except on its north side. Intended for the defence of Belfast Lough, the castle was built between 1180 and 1205 by the Norman nobleman John de Courcy and was taken by King John in 1210 after a year-long siege. In the 18th c. it served as a gaol and arsenal. The most notable features are the massive Keep (with a magnificent Norman Great Hall on the third floor and fine views from the top), the Gatehouse flanked by two towers and a number of ʾannon of the 16th to 19th centuries.

From Carrickfergus a particularly lovely section of coast road runs by way of **Whitehead**, a popular seaside resort at the mouth of Belfast Lough, to **Island Magee**, a peninsula 7 miles long and 2 miles wide. A striking feature on the east side of the peninsula is the Gobbins, a stretch of basalt cliffs 253 ft high containing a number of caves. There are numerous legends associated with the cliffs and caves. At the end of the peninsula can be seen a megalithic chambered tomb (dolmen).

Quarries and cement works disfigure the coast road to Larne (pop. 18,200), a busy industrial town and seaside resort on Lough Larne. There are notable remains of Olderfleet Castle (13th–14th c.; three-storey keep).

Larne

From Larne there are ferry services to Scotland (Stanraer and Cairnryan) and also a ferry to Island Magee.

A romantic and beautiful stretch of road leads from Larne to Cushendun. Having passed through the Black Cave Tunnel, the road rounds Ballygalley Head with its great basalt crags. **Ballygalley** is a popular seaside resort with an old castle, now a hotel. From here to **Glenarm**, a little port at the mouth of the River Glenarm, the road is flanked by white limestone cliffs. The next seaside resort is **Carnlough**, with a small harbour and good sandy beach.

Waterfoot, at the nearer end of Red Bay on the Antrim coast, is delightfully situated, encircled amphitheatre-like by sandstone cliffs at the mouth of **Glenariff** (one of the loveliest of the nine Glens of Antrim). Just beyond Cushendun are the little resort **Cushendall** and the better known **Cushendun**.

The road along the south side of Belfast Lough, continuing down the coast, also passes through lovely scenery and a number of attractive little towns and villages. **Holywood**, a suburb of Belfast, has remains of a 12th c. Franciscan Friary called Sanctus Boscus (Holy Wood), hence its name.

South of Belfast Lough

From here the road continues via Crawfordsburn to Bangor (pop. 55,000), the most popular of Northern Ireland's seaside resorts, with wide sandy beaches, beautiful promenades and plentiful facilities for sport and entertainment. Features of interest are the Castle and Castle Park, and the Abbey Church, on the site of a once powerful monastery founded in 555. On the way to Bangor, Helen's Tower, near Crawfordsburn, should not be missed. Beyond Bangor Copeland Island can be seen out to sea.

Bangor

Further south, at Donaghadee, is the start of the 20 mile long **Ards Peninsula**. From Donaghadee a road runs along the Irish Sea coast to Ballywalter (beautiful beach), Ballyhalbert and finally Cloghy, where it turns inland to **Portaferry** on the peninsula's southern tip. There is a ferry service between Portaferry and Strangford on the mainland.

From Portaferry there is also a road round to Strangford, starting out as the A20 and skirting the west side of the peninsula by the shores of **Strangford Lough**. After passing through **Ardkeen** (ruined castle) and Kircubbin, the road comes to **Grey Abbey**, with remains of a Cistercian abbey founded in 1193, one of the best preserved in Ireland. Notable features are the fine Perpendicular windows and the magnificent west doorway.

The road then continues via Mount Stewart House and Gardens (beautiful park with many dwarf trees), to **Newtownards**, noted for its linen and a good base from which to explore the coastal scenery and the Mourne Mountains to the south. It has a Town Hall of 1770 and a ruined Dominican church (1244).

From here there is a direct route back to Belfast; alternatively the road south can be taken to the whiskey-distilling town of Comber and on down the west side of Strangford Lough to Downpatrick (21 miles). Garden-lovers will prefer Saintfield, the route which turns away from the lough via the little town of Saintfield, allowing a visit to the beautiful **Rowallane Gardens** with their many rare flowers and plants.

On the west shore of the lough is the resort of **Killyleagh** (birthplace of Sir Hans Sloane, founder of the British Museum). Hilltop Castle overlooks the town which has a Jacobean parish church. The scenery is very beautiful, with the Mourne Mountains shimmering blue in the distance.

Downpatrick

Downpatrick (pop. 8200) is the county town of Co. Down. Here in 432 St Patrick began the conversion of Ireland, having landed at Saul, 2 miles further north, where he built his first church and where he is said to have died – although the granite stone in the churchyard does not appear to date from this period. Downpatrick Cathedral was built in 1790 on the remains of an earlier church; the font and some of the capitals came from the older church.

More interesting than the direct route to Clough is the road round the coast via **Strangford**, an old Viking settlement in a beautiful situation on Strangford Lough. The strategic importance of this particular area is evident from the fact that there are four 16th c. Anglo-Norman castles in the immediate vicinity. Audley Castle (*c.* 1500) is open to visitors.

No fewer than seven castles protected the little village of **Ardglass**, once an important harbour but now principally a fishing village. One of them, Jordan Castle, has considerable remains, including a square keep. West of Killough is a very attractive beach.

★ Scenic road from St John's Point to Newry

Beginning at St John's Point a superbly scenic road makes its way along what is surely the loveliest stretch of coast in Northern Ireland to Newry (39 miles), then on round the wide bay of Dundrum, large areas of which are exposed at low tide, to Newcastle. **Dundrum** is a picturesque fishing village with good sandy beaches and an interesting tower surrounded by a moat, the remains of an old castle, built by John de Courcy in 1240 and razed to the ground by Cromwell (see Famous People) in 1642.

Newcastle (pop. 6200) offers all the amenities of a seaside resort, including a very good golf course. It lies at the western end of Dundrum Bay at the foot of **Slieve Donard** (2796 ft), the highest of the **Mourne Mountains** and the second highest in Ireland. The climb takes about two hours and in fine weather is rewarded with magnificent views from the top, extending as far as the Scottish coast.

Beyond Newcastle the road begins to ascend, with the sea on the left and the ever-changing backdrop of the Mourne Mountains (the home of many rare plants) on the right. It passes through some quiet little fishing and farming villages including Glasdrumman and Annalong, from which Rocky Mountain, Slieve Bignian and a number of other peaks between 1700–2450 ft, can all be climbed.

Kilkeel is a favourite haunt of anglers, with good catches to be had not only from the sea and the River Kilkeel but also nearby Carlingford Lough. Around Kilkeel are a number of prehistoric chambered tombs.

Between Greencastle on the north side and Greenore on the south, **Carlingford Lough** cuts deep inland, with a road along either shore.

The road from Kilkeel to Hilltown in contrast, cuts through the Mourne Mountains, with steep gradients. **Hilltown**, in the shadow of the northwest side of the range, is a good base from which to climb and walk in the hills, richly coloured with the changing hues of their granites and schists.

On the north side of Carlingford Lough, surrounded by woodland (mainly oaks), is **Rostrevor**, a charming and peaceful little holiday resort (boating, pony-trekking, fishing, walking).

Newry

The port and industrial town of Newry (pop. 19,000) lies on the River Newry and on a canal, with the Mourne Mountains to the south-east and the Camlough Mountains to the west. The tower of St Patrick's Church, Ireland's first Protestant church, dates from 1578. The neighbouring Cathedral (RC) is Neo-Gothic.

In 1921 the County Constitution was signed in the "Treaty Room" of

Derrymore House near Newry. The thatched 18th c. Georgian manor is well worth a visit.

The road continues via Markethill – with **Gosford Castle**, one of the largest in Ireland – to Armagh.

The cathedral city of Armagh (pop. 13,000), is the seat of the primates of both the Catholic and Anglican Churches of Ireland. It took its name from an Iron Age fort remains of which can be seen 2 miles west. St Patrick built a cathedral here in about 445, but thereafter the town was several times burned down and rebuilt. The site of St Patrick's cathedral is now occupied by the Cathedral of the Church of Ireland, a medieval building restored in 1834–7. The Neo-Gothic Roman Catholic Cathedral (1840–73) is also dedicated to St Patrick. The Protestant Cathedral has a number of notable 17th and 18th c. tombs, the Roman Catholic some interesting mosaics. Nearby are the splendid Georgian Archbishop's Palace and the Diocesan College. Also worth seeing are the Royal School, founded by James I in 1608, the Observatory (1791), and the Court House (1809) by Francis Johnston (1761–1829). Many fine Georgian Houses are found in The Mall, together with the County Museum (local history).

Birmingham   I/K 8

Central England
County: West Midlands
Altitude: 250–750 ft. Population: 1,014,000

Birmingham, popularly known as "Brum", is Britain's second largest city and one of the biggest industrial centres in the world. Its prosperity was based on the engineering, steel (more particularly British Steel) and motor industries, the latter originating with Herbert Austin's factory in 1905 and continuing with British Leyland and now the Rover group. The city also has long manufacturing traditions in armaments, jewellery and foods. The recent history of the legendary "smithy of England", home of Cadbury's chocolate, luxury Jaguar cars and the Austin Mini Cooper, has been one of recurrent economic crisis. The highly impressive International Convention Centre, opened in 1991, symbolises present efforts to revitalise the economy by introducing new forms of industry, especially those in the service sector capable of rapid growth. Plans for regeneration of the city centre include transforming the four-lane inner ring road into a greened boulevard and replacing the Bull Ring, the ugly concrete "temple to consumerism" built in 1964 on the site of the old market place.

Birmingham makes a good base from which to explore the Cotswolds (see entry), the Malvern Hills and the Vale of Evesham. Its numerous canals – there are more in Birmingham than in Venice – are now principally used for pleasure, having in former times carried factory goods and raw materials.

Transport Following a programme of expansion completed in 1991 Birmingham International Airport is now one of the most modern in the world, with bus and rail connections to the city centre and a Maglev (magnetic levitation) monorail link to the National Exhibition Centre (NEC). New Street Station, the city centre mainline railway station, has half-hourly InterCity services to London Euston and good rail connections with all parts of the country.

History The city probably derives its name from the de Bermingham family, lords of the manor of Birmingham from 1150, who in 1166 were granted royal leave to trade and hold a market. Records show that, as early as 1538, the town was already producing knives, tools and nails and in 1639 began to manufacture arms, supplying the Parliamentarian side during

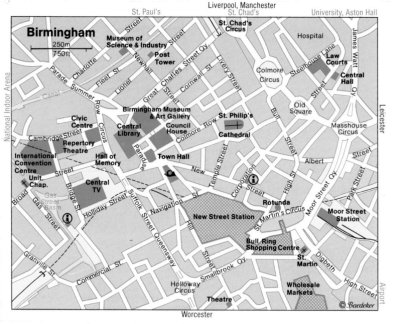

Birmingham

250m
750ft

the English Civil War (1642–46). It was also Birmingham where, between 1774 and 1800, Matthew Boulton and James Watt (see Famous People) perfected the design of the steam engine. This, together with exploitable coal and iron deposits near at hand, accounts more than anything for the city's early rise to industrial pre-eminence. From the end of the 18th c. onwards Birmingham experienced a huge upsurge of economic activity; the Industrial Revolution saw it grow into England's principal centre of commerce and industry, with much the largest concentration of factories.

Sights

Victoria Park

The older public buildings are grouped around Victoria Park. The **Town Hall** (1832–50), a masterpiece of Victorian architecture, takes the form of a Roman temple, with 40 Corinthian columns of Anglesey marble; the large hall can seat 2000. It has been the centre of the city's musical life since the first performance of Mendelssohn's "Elijah" here in 1847, and has one of the finest organs in the country.

Adorning the forecourt are two memorials, one to Queen Victoria and another to the inventor James Watt (see Famous People). Both are the work of Alexander Monro and date from 1899.

The Renaissance-style **Council House** opposite was erected between 1874 and 1879, its clock being affectionately known as "Big Brum". Note the arms of the City of Birmingham with their interesting surround of allegoric figures representing art and industry.

In **Chamberlain Square** (pedestrian precinct), north of the Town Hall, a fountain commemorates Joseph Chamberlain, Lord Mayor of Birmingham from 1873 to 1875. There is also a statue of Joseph Priestley, the discoverer of oxygen, who was minister of the Unitarian church here from 1680 to 1691.

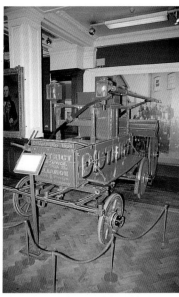

Birmingham Museum: an old fire engine ...   A. Hughes: "The Long Engagement" (1859)

The ⋆ **Central Library** has what is probably the largest Shakespeare collection outside the United States (50,000 volumes in 90 languages). The coin and stamp collections and the archaeological section are also outstanding.

The Birmingham Museum and Art Gallery, designed by H. Yeoville and opened by HRH the Prince of Wales, later Edward VII, in 1885, is one of the finest in the country outside London. Its art treasures include a matchless collection of Pre-Raphaelites (Ford Madox Brown, Arthur Hughes, Dante Gabriel Rossetti and others), as well as paintings from the 17th to 19th c., among them Canaletto's picture of Warwick Castle (1748), Lely's portrait (1654) of Oliver Cromwell (see Famous People), Victorian works by, e.g. David Cox, the Birmingham landscape painter, and modern art – pictures by Wendy Ramshaw and sculptures by Henry Moore (see Famous People), Rodin and James Tower. There are also interesting displays related to the city's history, ranging from medieval coins and historic paintings to Cadbury's chocolate products and turn-of-the-century modes of transport. Othersections are devoted to archaeological finds dating back to the Stone Age and superb 17th to 19th c. silverwork. The Pinto Collection contains 6000 toys and other items (including "love spoons"), all of them made of wood.

⋆⋆ Birmingham Museum and Art Gallery

Close to the Post Office in Newhall Street, the Museum of Science and Industry celebrates Birmingham's industrial history. It has fine collections of machinery and motor cars.

Museum of Science and Industry

A short distance north again, along Newhall Street, lies an area of the city steeped in tradition. Here more than 200 jewellers' workshops and silversmiths are concentrated, chiefly in the vicinity of the Clock Tower on the corner of Vyse Street and Frederick Street and around the Georgian church of St Paul's.

⋆ Jeweller's District

149

Birmingham

Civic Centre

The Civic Centre is located south-west of the Central Library. The **Hall of Memory** opposite Baskerville House (municipal offices) was erected in 1925 to commemorate the 14,000 Birmingham men who lost their lives in the First World War.

Repertory Theatre

On the far side of Centenary Square (pedestrian precinct) near the new International Convention Centre stands Birmingham's celebrated Repertory Theatre with the Studio Theatre adjoining.

★ICC

Opened in 1991 the ultra modern International Convention Centre has eleven conference halls (seating from 30 to 3000 people). Incorporated into the complex are the Hyatt Regency Hotel – a palace of glass – and an elegant Symphony Hall concert hall (with 2200 seat auditorium), the new home of the famous Birmingham Symphony Orchestra with Simon Rattle as principal conductor since 1980.

National Indoor Arena

The National Indoor Arena on the other side of the canal was opened in 1992 accommodating up to 12,000 spectators.

Brindley Place

By the mid 1990s the historic canals south-west of Brindley Place are destined to become the central feature of a modern leisure complex.

Churches

The Palladian-style St Philip's Cathedral built between 1711 and 1715 by Thomas Archer began life as a parish church, being elevated to its present status in 1905. St Martin's Church, just beyond New Street Station, dates from the 13th c. but was rebuilt in the Decorated style between 1872 and 1875. St Chad's, north of the city centre, has the distinction of being the first Roman Catholic church built in Great Britain after the Reformation (by Pugin in 1839–41).

University

Birmingham University was founded in 1900, the Chamberlain Tower

Birmingham: the International Convention Centre (ICC)

(325 ft) being named after the first Chancellor. The University of Aston is of more recent origin, formed when the College of Advanced Technology was granted a charter in 1966. King Edward VI School, east of the University, was established in 1552.

Also situated close to the University is the Barber Institute of Fine Arts. Evolving initially from a private bequest by Lady Barber, the Institute now houses the University's excellent collection of art from the Renaissance to the 20th c. It includes works by Botticelli, Bellini, Tintoretto, Rubens, Rembrandt, Watteau, Manet, Monet, Gainsborough, Constable and Degas.

★Barber Institute of Fine Arts

Just to the south lies Bournville, headquarters of **Cadbury** Bros., the well-known chocolate and cocoa manufacturers established in 1831 (now Cadbury-Schweppes). This attractive suburb started life as a garden village, built by the company for its factory workers in 1895. The 15th c. **Selly Manor Museum** displays old furniture and household equipment.

Further sights

Sarehole Mill in Hall Green is said to have provided J. R. R. Tolkien with inspiration for his book "The Hobbit". The 200 year-old corn mill was converted into a knife factory at the turn of the century and today contains displays illustrating aspects of milling, blade-grinding and English rural pursuits.

Aston Hall, a red-brick Jacobean mansion in the pleasant surroundings of Aston Park, 2½ miles north of the Civic Centre (near "Spaghetti Junction" on the M6), was built by Thomas Holte between 1617 and 1635. From 1818 to 1848 it was the home of James Watt (see Famous People) and is now a museum and art gallery. It has an exceptionally fine oak staircase.

The flower and ornamental gardens of **Cannon Hill Park** in Edgbaston and the glasshouses of the **Harbourne Botanic Gardens** are havens of tranquillity amidst the urban bustle.

Birmingham has many modern **shopping precincts** including Pallasades, The Kings, The Pavilions and the Bull Ring Shopping Centre. The two principal shopping districts are Corporation Street and the area around St Martin's Circus with its old market place and nearby Wholesale Markets.

Situated on the eastern outskirts of the city, just off the M42, the National Exhibition Centre provides a venue for all kinds of trade fairs and shows. Having opened in 1982, by 1993 the 1.3 million sq. ft of exhibition area had been enlarged by a further 0.3 million sq. ft. A Maglev (magnetic levitation) monorail runs between the Centre and Birmingham International Airport a mile or so away.

National Exhibition Centre (NEC)

Surroundings

The ★**Black Country Museum** in Dudley (Tipton Road), about 9 miles west of Birmingham, offers a vivid insight into the history of mining. An old mine-shaft and reconstructed turn-of-the-century industrial community can be inspected at close hand. Interesting trips are also run on the network of canals, in the type of narrow-boat traditionally used for transporting coal.

Dudley

Walsall (12 miles north-west) boasts a unique ★**Lock Museum**, the only such museum in England. The exhibits, some dating from as early as the 16th c., are drawn from all over the world.

Walsall

Bradford-on-Avon   I 9

Southern England
County: Wiltshire
Altitude: 200 ft. Population: 9000

The old wool town of Bradford-on-Avon (Bradford = "Wide Ford") enjoys a picturesque setting on the banks of the River Avon about 8 miles south-east of Bath (see entry). Its narrow streets rise in a series of terraces up the hillside. There is a delightful walk up to the viewpoint at St Mary Tory, starting from the old bridge across the Avon and proceeding via Silver Street, the main shopping street, Market Street with its 17th and 18th c. houses, and Church Street. The latter, passing several fine town houses as it climbs the hill, including Old Church House (1610), Hill House (18th c.) and Abbey House (also 18th c.) leads first to a row of 17th c. weavers' houses in Top Rank Tory and finally to the chapel of St Mary Tory (12th c., restored in 1877) from where there is a marvellous panoramic view. Bradford-upon-Avon's chief tourist attraction, however, is St Lawrence's Church, one of the finest of the small number of Anglo-Saxon churches to have survived more or less intact.

★St Lawrence's

St Lawrence's is believed to have been founded by St Aldhelm (died 709) and is referred to in a document of 705. In 1001 the church became the responsibility of Shaftesbury Abbey, being deconsecrated soon afterwards and put to a succession of different uses (charnel house, cottage, and outbuildings) until its original status became quite forgotten. It was rediscovered in 1856 when, so the story goes, the local vicar, gazing out from a window over the huddle of roofs, recognised the cross-shape of the old church. The buildings adjoining it were subsequently removed, revealing St Lawrence's much as seen today.

The tiny church makes a powerful impression with the simplicity of its architecture and virtual absence of external decoration apart from blind arcades. The tall nave, long and narrow and without aisles, opens into the rectangular chancel by way of a rounded arch. Today the furnishings are plain but traces of paintings have been discovered. The two sculpted angels above the chancel arch date from the 8th c., remnants of a group which would have included a crucified Christ. The original floor is still visible in the chancel while the altar is fashioned from Saxon stone slabs. Three new windows were added in the 19th c. to improve the lighting, the original three being in the porch, nave and chancel.

Avon Bridge

The old stone bridge over the River Avon is truly delightful. Two of its nine arches date from the 13th c., the others from the 17th c. The bridge is made even more special, however, by having a chapel in the centre. This was a place of pilgrimage at one time and later used as a lock-up. Nowadays it serves only for a charming view.

Holy Trinity

Consecrated in 1150 the parish church underwent alteration several times between the 15th and 19th c. Inside are a late medieval wall painting of Mary learning to write, a 13th c. sculpture of a girl in a hood, and a number of tombs of Bradford cloth merchants.

Tithe Barn

The great medieval Tithe Barn once belonged to Shaftesbury Abbey. Built in the early 14th c. it is a masterpiece of medieval joinery, its superbly constructed timber roof truss being supported on massive stone walls. Used originally to store grain it now houses a farm museum.

Lacock

Lacock (10 miles north-east, pop. 1300), a pretty little show-piece village with a market, is today the responsibility of the National Trust. The parish church of St Cyriac's, begun in the 14th c. but only completed in the 17th, is surrounded by numerous late medieval houses and inns.

Lacock Abbey, founded as an Augustinian convent in 1229 and converted to a manor house in 1539, was the home of the Talbot family for hundreds of years. Note in particular the Hall, an early example of Gothic Revival (Neo-Gothic) designed by Sanderson Miller in 1755. There is an interesting museum dedicated to the pioneer of photography William Henry Fox-Talbot (1800–77), inventor of the photographic negative.

Built in 1582 this fine Elizabethan country house (9 miles to the north-east) was purchased by Paul Methuen in the mid 18th c. and sub-sequently handsomely re-appointed. Alterations were made to both house and gardens by a series of celebrated architects – Lancelot "Capability" Brown in about 1760, John Nash in about 1800, and Thomas Bellamy between 1845 and 1849.

★★**Corsham Court**

Its rooms provide a superb setting for a collection of 150 or so price-less objets d'art – paintings, statues, bronzes and furniture. They include works by Lippi, Fra Bartolommeo, Caravaggio, Tintoretto, Veronese, Rubens, van Dyke, Lely, Reynolds and Romney, also décor and furniture by Adam, Chippendale and Thomas Johnson.

17 miles south stands another fine Elizabethan country house, Longleat, built between 1559 and 1578, seat of the Marquis of Bath. The house is a remarkable example of English Early Renaissance architecture distin-guished by the uniformity of treatment accorded its four façades.

★**Longleat House**

Accumulated over a period of 400 years the rich interior furnishings include elegant 17th and 18th c. furniture, silver and porcelain as well as numerous paintings, among the latter being 18th c. hunting scenes by John Wootton.

The beautiful park with its serpentine lake, attractive groups of trees and the world's biggest maze, was landscaped by "Capability" Brown. Also in the grounds are a safari park and a pets' cemetery where animals belonging to generations of the Thynne family lie buried.

Brighton

L 10

Southern England. County: East Sussex
Population: 250,000 (Brighton and Hove)

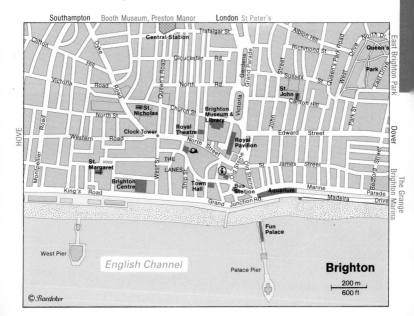

Brighton

200 m
600 ft

© Baedeker

English Channel

Brighton is the largest and best-known seaside resort on the English Channel Coast, an urban centre of population which, together with Hove, spreads for some 6 miles along the pebbled shoreline and over the sometimes steep chalk hills of the South Downs (see entry). Once a fishing village with narrow winding lanes, after 1750 it developed into an elegant watering place where, especially in the 19th c., the English aristocracy and upper classes used to gather. In 1841 it was linked to London by rail. Relaxing under the benign influence of sea air and mineral springs, visitors took leisurely strolls along the boulevards and piers and relaxed in the ballrooms of the fashionable hotels. Reminders of this period still abound: charming Regency terraces, the delightful Palace Pier and the exotic Royal Pavilion, the extraordinary folly created by the flamboyant and eccentric "Prinny", Prince of Wales – later George IV. Today even once fashionable Brighton has surrendered to mass tourism, the 3 mile-long terraced seafront being lined with souvenir shops and amusement arcades. In addition to a full calendar of cultural events there are race meetings in the summer months and the famous Veteran Car Rally in November; there are also several sports stadiums. Over and above the lucrative holiday trade, the resort is highly popular as a conference venue. The University of Sussex, founded in 1961, is located on the outskirts. With Brighton having abandoned any pretensions to being a port, the industrial centre of gravity has shifted west to nearby Shoreham.

Over the centuries the town has played host to many distinguished writers and intellectuals including Samuel Johnson, Jane Austen and William Thackeray (not to mention Prince Pückler in search of a rich wife). Aubrey Beardsley was born here in 1872, and the philosopher Herbert Spencer died here in 1903. Edward Burne-Jones lies buried in the cemetery at neighbouring Rottingdean. The resort has also provided the setting for several well-known literary and other works, Graham

Brighton: the Palace Pier

Brighton: the Royal Pavilion

Greene's "Brighton Rock" (1938) and Attenborough's satirical film "Oh, what a lovely War" (1966) among them.

History First settled by the Anglo-Saxons, Brighthelmstone is mentioned in William the Conqueror's (see Famous People) "Domesday Book" but there- after appears to have been forgotten. In the 16th c. it was a fishing village of about 1500 people living in narrow streets of cottages not unlike the 17th c. ones seen in The Lanes today. In 1750, however, all this changed when Richard Russell, a Lewes doctor, published a book on the virtues of seawater as a treatment for glandular disease. From then on visitors flocked to Brighton as it was now known in their droves. The first ballroom opened in 1766 and in the following year members of the royal family were among those who arrived to take the waters and bathe in the sea. The resort was to prove particularly captivating for the young Prince of Wales (the future King George IV) when he came for the first time in 1783. He fell in love with the beautiful Maria Anne Fitzherbert whom he secretly married in 1785, setting up house in "a superior farmhouse" in the Old Steine. Between 1815 and 1823, some years after his official marriage to Princess Caroline of Brunswick, the prince transformed his residence into a supremely elegant summer palace, the Royal Pavilion. These years, during which the prince was regent for his ailing father, have become known as the Regency Period. They gave rise to a distinctive architecture, the Regency style, determined largely by the prince's highly individual taste. The majority of the buildings on Brighton seafront date from this time, most being three-storeyed and with bright white façades relieved by bay windows and wrought-iron balconies. Further building took place in Victorian times, the great iron Palace Pier protruding far into the sea becoming one of the town's most famous sights. Sadly, in recent years, modern buildings have marred some of the town.

Sights

★★ Royal Pavilion

The Royal Pavilion in the centre of Brighton was built between 1815 and 1823 in the Indian Mogul style, as the summer residence of the Prince of Wales. John Nash was the architect, with Frederick Crace and Robert Jones responsible for the interior. It remains one of the town's principal land-marks. Visitors enter the Pavilion through the Octagon Hall, passing via an antechamber into a long corridor with Chinese ornamentation. Note the fine cast-iron bannisters in imitation of bamboo. To the right of the corridor is the Banqueting Room with its astonishing oriental décor. This includes a chandelier of lotus-shaped lamps protruding from the jaws of six chimerical creatures, all suspended from a silver dragon emerging from a cluster of palm fronds. In the Music Room to the left of the corridor more huge serpents and winged dragons adorn the domed, almost tent-like room (the gas lamps were a technical novelty at the time and evoked considerable wonder). A similar indulgence in the exotic and the extraordinary prevails in the other rooms of the Pavilion, the exception being the prince's own private apartments which are in contrast plain. "Prinny's" passion for splendour provoked a popular outcry, caricaturists ridiculing his lavish life-style and eccentricities of taste. Queen Victoria eventually sold the outrageously extravagant palace for £50,000 to the town, which has been responsible for the building ever since.

The equally distinctive Indian-style stables and riding school which belonged to the palace now house the **Dome Concert Hall** and a museum.

Situated in the former royal stables and riding school the ★**Brighton Museum and Art Gallery** possesses an outstanding collection of Art Deco pieces, with some particularly fine Art Nouveau furniture. There is also a costume gallery with fashions from the 18th c. onwards, a display of old musical instruments, and the excellent Willet Collection of porcelain and ceramics.

Theatre Royal

The Neo-Classical Theatre Royal not far from the museum was built in 1806, although the colonnade was not completed for another twenty years. Many famous actors and actresses including the Kembles, Grimaldi and Sarah Siddons have appeared on its stage, a tradition of good theatre which is still maintained today.

St Nicholas'

A few blocks to the west, at the far end of Church Street, stands the town's original parish church, St Nicholas'. The church itself was begun in the 14th c. but the beautiful Norman font, carved with scenes of the Last Supper, the baptism of Christ and the Legend of St Nicholas, the patron saint of seafarers, dates from about 1160.

★The Lanes

The centre of the old fishing village of Brighthelmstone once stood on the site of the narrow alleyways known as The Lanes, where the charming little 17th c. cottages have mostly been turned into antique shops, boutiques and cafés. Some of the façades are still "weatherboarded", colourfully clad with painted wooden boarding as protection against wind and weather.

Old Steine

The Old Steine, to the east of The Lanes, was at one time the village green. Now it is a well-tended square which extends north to Grand Parade – a magnificent boulevard, lined with trees and planted with flowers – and south towards the promenade. When compared with the stately Neo-Classical façade of Marlborough House (1786), Maria Fitzherbert's house (1804) with its wrought-iron balconies is a perfect illustration of the change of architectural style at the beginning of the 19th c. The same innovation in design is continued by the long rows of Regency houses between Marine Parade and St James Street/St George's Road.

Brighton: the Dome

A short distance north of St James Street, in Carlton Hill, stands the church of St John the Baptist, with the tomb of George IV's beloved Maria Fitzherbert. Following their separation she lived in seclusion in Brighton until her death.

St John the Baptist's

No more than a few paces from the Old Steine lie the seafront and promenade, set off in spectacular fashion by the long iron pier. The original Chain Pier of 1823, immortalised in a painting by Constable (1827), was wrecked by a storm in 1869, while the West Pier (1866), although still standing, is derelict. Only the 1700 ft-long Palace Pier (1891–99) with its voluted ironwork remains in use, jutting out to sea like the upper deck of a steamer on spindly iron legs. The days when the pier was fashionable have long since gone, replaced by a culture of amusement arcades and snack bars.

★ Palace Pier

Magnus Volk's electric **railway** (opened in 1833) runs the length of the eastern section of the seafront from near the Palace Pier to **Brighton Marina**.

Much pleasure can be had simply by taking a walk through the residential areas of Brighton with their Regency-style terraces and squares. West of the centre, going towards Hove, are street after street of houses with round bay windows and iron balconies: Regency Square, Brunswick Terrace, Brunswick Square (1825; facing the sea), and the horseshoe-shaped Adelaide Crescent. Sussex Square, Lewes Crescent (1824) and Arundel Terrace, all east of the centre, are equally worth seeing.

Regency houses

Devoted to natural history the Booth Museum is situated in Dyke Road, in the north-west of the town. In addition to an outstanding collection of stuffed birds displayed in their natural habitats, there are butterflies from all over the world and numerous skeletons of extinct species.

Booth Museum of Natural History

Bristol

Preston Manor | This 18th c. manor house in Preston Road was the home of the Stanford family. Renovated in 1905 it recaptures the atmosphere of life at the turn of the century as well as being a showcase for antiques from earlier periods.

Bristol I 9

Southern England
Unitary Authority of Bristol
Altitude: 355 ft. Population: 385,000

Although the old town centre suffered heavily from bomb damage during the Second World War, Bristol (only 6 miles from the Bristol Channel) retains its charm as a historic port. It also has some fine residential suburbs, balanced, it should be said, by some poorer ones. Having for many years been the home of two of Britain's biggest aero-

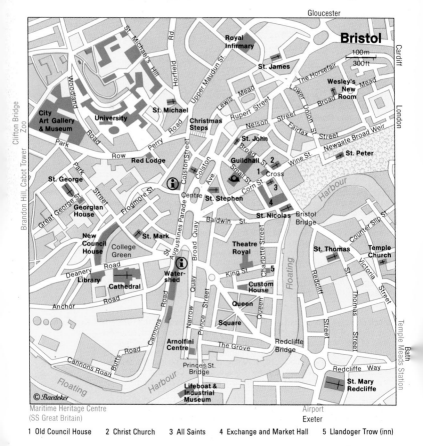

© Baedeker

Maritime Heritage Centre
(SS Great Britain)

Airport
Exeter

1 Old Council House   2 Christ Church   3 All Saints   4 Exchange and Market Hall   5 Llandoger Trow (inn)

nautical companies, Rolls Royce and British Aerospace, both with large engineering plants in the north of the city (and involved in Concorde and the Airbus project), Bristol has turned increasingly for its prosperity to the insurance and service sector (Sun Alliance, Sun Life, Lloyds) and the electronics industry (marked by the arrival in the 80s of firms such as Hewlett Packard and IBM). Food manufacture, tobacco processing, printing and chemicals are also important to the economy. When, because of deeper draught, ships could no longer navigate the narrow River Avon up to Bristol, a new port with modern docks, oil refineries and industrial estates sprang up in the Avonmouth/Royal Portbury area.

The many emigrants for whom the port of Bristol was the gateway to the New World were following in the wake of John Cabot who, in 1497, set sail from Bristol on the expedition which discovered North America. The Cabot Tower was erected on the 400th anniversary of the voyage to honour his achievement. Bristol's three most famous landmarks, however, are the Cathedral, St Mary Redcliffe, and the Clifton Suspension Bridge which spans the tidal Avon.

Transport Access to the airport (8 miles south-west) is by bus or car via the A38. There are good train connections from Bristol to all parts of the country.

History A settlement is known to have existed here as early as the 10th c. From the 12th c. onwards Bristol was a trading centre of considerable importance, being granted county borough status by Edward III in 1373 (a status it retained until incorporated into the new county of Avon in 1974). During the English Civil War the city was the main Royalist base in the West Country. Bristol's later prosperity as a port was based on a triangular pattern of trade: its ships would sail to West Africa laden with English metalware, glass and beads, carry slaves from there to the West Indies (70,000 a year by the end of the 18th c.) and then load up with sugar, rum, coffee, cocoa and tobacco for the return voyage. Following the abolition of slavery, first shipbuilding and then aircraft assembly became the pillars of the economy. Designed by Isambard Kingdom Brunel (1806–59), the SS "Great Britain", built in Bristol in 1838, was the first steamship to make regular crossings of the Atlantic. Brunel, in addition to designing the famous suspension bridge spanning the Avon gorge, was also the engineer in charge of completing the Great Western Railway between London and Bristol.

Sights

Nowadays the bigger freighters and passenger vessels are built further downstream, at large modern yards in Avonmouth and Portbury on the Severn estuary. The old Port of Bristol on the Avon has been given a new and imaginative lease of life, with many wharves and warehouses converted or restored. Traditionally known as the ★**Floating Harbour** it is now an area full of delightful surprises. The old **Watershed warehouses** are alive with little restaurants, cafés and shops while the **Arnolfini Centre**, in a former tea trading house (1832) on the quayside opposite, is a gallery of contemporary art.

Port area

A swing bridge near the Centre provides access to Prince's Wharf on the south side of the harbour. Close by are the **Lifeboat Museum** and **Bristol Industrial Museum** where exhibits include a collection of Rolls Royce aero-engines and a mock-up of a cockpit from Concorde.

The most famous of the harbour area's many bars and taverns is the triple-gabled half-timbered ★**Llandoger Trow** in King Street, built in 1669. Here Alexander Selkirk is said to have told the story of his shipwreck to Daniel Defoe (1660–1731), who immortalised it in "Robinson Crusoe". The Llandoger Trow was also the model for the "Admiral

Bristol

Theatre Royal

Benbow", the inn frequented by Long John Silver in "Treasure Island" by Robert Louis Stevenson (1850–94). Carefully restored in 1991 the tavern is linked by an underpass to the **Theatre Royal** on the opposite side of the street. Opened in 1764 the theatre, now the home of the Bristol Old Vic, is the oldest playhouse in England to have had its stage in continuous use.

Merchants' House

The Merchants' House (1696), a short distance west of the theatre, is the headquarters of the Society of Merchant Venturers of Bristol, founded in 1532.

★St Nicholas'

Two or three blocks north-east from the Theatre Royal, the High Street runs from Bristol Bridge (18th–19th c.) to the Cross. Near the bridge stands the former St Nicholas' Church, now a museum. Among many items of interest are three huge panels ("The Sealing of the Tomb", "The Ascension" and "The Three Marys at the Tomb") comprising a triptych by William Hogarth (see Famous People), painted for the high altar of St Mary Redcliffe in 1756. At the far end of the High Street the intersection of High Street, Corn Street, Broad Street and Wine Street used to be the site of Bristol's High Cross, which today adorns a park in Stourhead (see Shaftesbury, Surroundings).

Covered market

The covered market in the High Street dates from the mid 18th c.

Corn Street
★Exchange

Facing Corn Street and adjoining the covered market at the rear, the Palladian-style Exchange was built between 1740 and 1743 by John Wood the Elder. In front of the building stand four tables, the brass "nails" on which Bristol merchants used to settle their transactions, giving rise to the expression "paying on the nail". The large St Stephen's Church, two blocks to the west, dates from the mid 16th c.

St Stephen's
Old Council
House,
Christ Church

The Old Council House, a Neo-Classical building on the corner of Corn and Broad Streets, was constructed in 1827 by Robert Smirke (1781–1867). Christ Church (1786–90) opposite has an unusual clock.

Guildhall,
St John's

Past the Guildhall (1843–46; on the left), Broad Street ends at St John's Gate, originally part of the old city wall. Above the arch rises the steeple of St John's Church (14th c.; interesting crypt), the body of the church being on a level with the wall.

★Christmas steps

Figures of Brennus and Belinus, mythical founders of Bristol, embellish the arch, beyond which Christmas Street leads to Christmas Steps, an ancient alleyway paved in 1669 and now lined with antique and souvenir shops.

Broadmead

East of St John's Gate, Nelson Street runs through to Broadmead and the nearby shopping centre (pedestrian precinct). Situated just behind Broadmead is **Wesley's New Room** (1739), the world's oldest Methodist Church.

★★St Mary
Redcliffe

When Queen Elizabeth I (see Famous People) visited Bristol in 1574 she described St Mary Redcliffe as "the fairest parish church in England".

Begun in the 13th c. and paid for by wealthy merchants, the church is situated on the south side of the Floating Harbour. It takes its name from the red cliffs on which it stands. The spire, 290 ft high, is a 19th c. addition. The interior is of enchanting elegance with its tall arches, slender clustered pillars and reticulated vaulting. Particularly fine is the hexagonal north porch, with its richly decorated doorway. The wealth and splendour of the church is due to one of the richest merchants of the day, William Canynge, whose tomb can be seen in the south transept. He is commemorated at a special service on Whit Sunday. Also to be found in the church are the memorial tablet and tomb of Admiral Sir William Penn, father of the William Penn who founded Pennsylvania in the USA.

It was in the muniment room of St Mary Redcliffe that Thomas Chatterton (1752–70) claimed to have discovered the poems of an unknown monk named Rowley, poems which he had in fact written himself. The boy poet, born in nearby Redcliffe Way, committed suicide at eighteen. There is a monument to him north-east of the church.

★ Cathedral of the Holy Trinity

Bristol's other famous church is Cathedral of the Holy Trinity, originally the church of an Augustinian house but raised to cathedral status in 1542 when Henry VIII (see Famous People) created a new diocese. Apart from the chapter house nothing remains of the Norman abbey, consecrated in 1165. Construction of the present church spans almost six hundred years. The east end, superbly rebuilt in the Decorated style by Abbot Knowle, dates from between 1298 and 1330. The central tower and transepts were the next to be completed (by 1500), after which building stopped. The nave and towered west façade are 19th c. The cathedral is a hall church, a type unusual in England but quite common, for example, in southern Germany. It is built without triforium or clerestory, the aisles

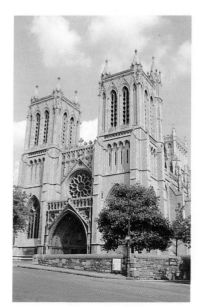

Bristol: Cathedral of the Holy Trinity

Bristol University Tower

and nave being of the same height. The Decorated style is seen most clearly in the clusters of pillars and the ribbed vaulting.

The most splendid feature of the church is the ★★**Choir** (rebuilt in 1298), a structure of inspired lightness displaying an entirely new feeling for space. The choir-stalls are modern but have misericords of about 1520. There are two Lady Chapels, one in Early English style (1210–20) adjoining the north transept and a later one (1298–1330) at the east end, still with its original altarpiece and 14th c. windows. In the south aisle are unusual stellate tombs containing the remains of various distinguished abbots. The Berkeley Chapel contains a rare 15th c. brass chandelier.

The rectangular ★**Chapter House** (c. 1150–70) is also noteworthy, with typical late-Norman decoration – zigzags, fish-scale pattern and interlacing – on the walls.

The gateway with Norman arcades opposite the west front of the cathedral belonged to the old Augustinian abbey.

St Mark's Chapel

Another fine church is St Mark's Chapel or the Lord Mayor's Chapel, originally the chapel of a hospital founded by the Fitzharding family in 1220. The aisle is Early English (late 13th c.) the rest Perpendicular (15th and late 16th c.) with many elements typical of the Gothic style.

University area

The **University**, established in 1909, is situated in Clifton, a popular residential district with a number of fine Georgian houses. The 200 ft late-Gothic tower, built to commemorate the University's founding benefactors, Sir G. A. and H. H. Wills (of the famous Wills tobacco company), is one of Bristol's most prominent landmarks.

Housed in the group of Victorian buildings west of the University is the **City Art Gallery and Museum**. Several of its collections are of special interest, including the oriental collection, the collection of Old Masters and the section devoted to Brunel and his many technical achievements.

Also worth seeing in this part of the city are the **Red Lodge**, with old furniture and a particularly fine Elizabethan room, and the elegantly furnished **Georgian House** (18th c.) a little further to the west.

Foster's Almshouses in Colston Street, completed in 1861, are likewise worth visiting, a pleasing mixture of Tudor and French Gothic elements with patterned masonry, external galleries and a cylindrical staircase of wood.

★SS "Great Britain" Maritime Heritage Centre

The SS "Great Britain", Brunel's famous steamship, lies in Great Western Dock near Gas Ferry Road. Launched in 1843 she was the first vessel built in Bristol to have an iron hull and screw propulsion. The nearby Maritime Heritage Centre provides an interesting insight into the history of Bristol's shipbuilding and maritime trade.

Clifton Suspension Bridge

No visitor should leave Bristol without seeing the famous Clifton Suspension Bridge. It spans the 260 ft deep Avon Gorge on the west side of the limestone plateau known as Clifton Down and Durdham Down. Measuring 702 ft between the piers the bridge was completed in 1864, 33 years after Brunel (died 1859) had first submitted his prize-winning plans.

Zoo Gardens

East of the suspension bridge lies the Bristol Zoo Gardens, notable particularly for their monkey enclosure and aquariums.

Blaise Hamlet

The little thatched almhouses (1811) of Blaise Hamlet in Henbury (4 miles north-north-west) make a charming picture. Designed by John Nash they are now a museum.

Surroundings

Clevedon

Clevedon (pop. 14,300) is a quiet seaside resort in a small bay. William Thackeray (1811–63) was a frequent guest at Clevedon Court, a 14th c.

Bristol: Christ Chruch clock   *Clifton Suspension Bridge*

manor house, where he wrote part of "Vanity Fair" (1848). The journey from Bristol to Clevedon can be made by boat.

Weston-super-Mare (pop. 57,600), one of the largest seaside resorts in England, can also be reached from Bristol by boat. Lying lower down the Severn estuary, on the Bristol Channel, it has a 2 mile-long beach, beautiful parks, excellent sports and recreational facilities and a boating lake. The crescents and terraces so characteristic of the town were built in the 19th c. The Woodspring Museum offers a fascinating account of Weston's history.

Weston-super-Mare

In Yatton and Congressbury, between Clevedon and Weston-super-Mare, there are interesting Perpendicular churches. The uninhabited islands of Steep Holm and Flat Holm in the Bristol Channel are chiefly of interest to ornithologists, being the haunt of countless seabirds.

**Steep Holm
Flat Holm**

Cambridge   M 8

Southern England. County: Cambridgeshire
Altitude: 34 ft. Population: 103,000

Cambridge, university city and county town (of Cambridgeshire), lies on the River Cam. Life in the city is dominated by the 31 colleges, most being rich in tradition and each having a special quality of its own. There are also a number of medieval churches and several excellent museums. The lovely college grounds, gardens and parks along the riverside make up the beautiful Backs. Punting on the river is one of summer's delights.
History In Roman times there was a small town here on the north bank

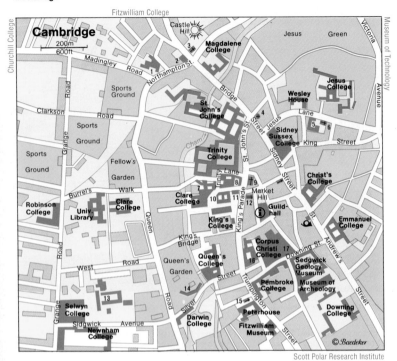

Fitzwilliam College

Churchill College

Cambridge

200m
600ft

Castle Hill

Madingley Road

Northampton St.

Jesus Green

Magdalene College

Sports Ground

Clarkson Road

Grange Road

Sports Ground

Sports Ground

Fellow's Garden

Burrels Walk

Robinson College

Univ. Library

Clare College

St. John's College

Bridge

Cham

Trinity College

Trinity Lane

Jesus College

Wesley House

Jesus Lane

Sidney Sussex College

St. John's St.

King Street

Christ's College

Sidney Street

Market Hill

Guildhall

Emmanuel College

Clare College

King's Parade

King's College

King's Bridge

Queen's Garden

Queen's College

Silver Street

Corpus Christi College

Downing St.

Sedgwick Geology Museum

St. Andrew's St.

Pembroke College

Museum of Archeology

West Road

Queen Road

Darwin College

Trumpington Road

Peterhouse

Fitzwilliam Museum

Downing College

Downing Street

Selwyn College

Sidgwick Avenue

Newnham College

Grange Road

Silver Street

© Baedeker

Scott Polar Research Institute

Victoria Avenue

Museum of Technology

1 Westminster College	7 Trinity Hall	13 University Arts Buildings, Museum of Classical Archaeology
2 Folk Museum	8 Gonville and Caius College	14 Fisher Court
3 St. Giles	9 St. Michael	15 St. Mary the Less
4 Round Church	10 Old Schools	16 Whipple Museum
5 Westscott House	11 Senate House	17 Zoology Museum
6 All Saints	12 St. Mary the Great	

of the Cam. In those days the river was known (and upstream of Silver Street bridge is still known today) as the Granta. To the Saxons consequently the town was Grantebrycg, which later (c. 1125) became Cantebruge. Later still, in Chaucer, it appears as Chambrugge. Even before 1318 when the university was founded, Cambridge was famous for its annual wool fair. Its position on the principal trade route between eastern and central England brought early prosperity to the town (in the 17th c. the Stourbridge Fair was the largest in the country).

The first "schools", attached initially to monasteries, were probably established in the 12th c. by immigrant scholars from Paris. The first college, Peterhouse, was founded in 1284. Despite its romantic medieval character Cambridge is a thoroughly modern town with all the usual amenities.

Sights

★★ Cambridge Colleges

Oxford (see entry) and Cambridge are the English universities (see Introduction), best known in Europe. Both were founded in the mid 13th c. – Oxford slightly earlier than Cambridge, for which reason it is always

Cambridge: the "Mathematical Bridge" at Queens' College

referred to first – and both today have some 10,000 students. In the Middle Ages students went up to the two universities at the age of 14 or 15, earning the title of Master of Grammar after three years (the "trivium" of Latin grammar, rhetoric and logic) and Master of Arts after another four years (the "quadrivium" of arithmetic, geometry, astronomy and music). A doctorate in theology, law or medicine required additional years of study.

The colleges were laid out according to monastic tradition, with cloister-like courts, a large dining hall and a chapel. Access is usually through a gatehouse or "Porter's Lodge". Because the colleges are first and foremost academic institutions, rather than museums, visitors may find themselves turned away, e.g. at exam time or on other such occasions.

The oldest college in Cambridge, **Peterhouse College**, was founded by Hugh de Balsam, Bishop of Ely, in 1284. It is one of the smallest colleges. The Hall and store-room on the south side of Old Court are the earliest of the original 13th c. buildings. Among those who studied here were Cardinal Beaufort, the chemist Henry Cavendish, the physicist Lord Kelvin and the poet Thomas Gray (1716–71).

The nearby 13th–14th c. church of St Mary the Less (Little St Mary) was originally dedicated to St Peter and was the college chapel for over 300 years. Inside the church, a memorial tablet to Godfrey Washington, priest and member of Peterhouse, bears the arms of the Washington family (on which the flag of the United States was based).

Across Trumpington Street from Peterhouse stands **Pembroke College**, founded in 1347 by the Countess of Pembroke but much altered since. The chapel (1663–65) was Wren's first work, later extended by George Gilbert Scott in 1881. Pembroke has produced many bishops and poets, the most celebrated being Edmund Spenser (*c.* 1552–99). The reformist bishop Nicholas Ridley, burned at the stake in Oxford, and the statesman William Pitt also took their degrees here.

Cambridge: the magnificent building of King's College Chapel

★**Queens' College**, in Silver Street, founded in 1448 by Andrew Dockett under the patronage of Margaret of Anjou, wife of Henry VI, and then re-founded in 1465 by Elizabeth Woodville, wife of Edward IV, has the most complete medieval buildings of all the colleges. A magnificent crenellated gateway leads to the red brick First Court dating from the period of foundation, with the Hall (decorated by William Morris), Library and Old Chapel. On the wall is a sundial of 1733. Cloister Court (*c.* 1460) has the President's Lodge, a handsome half-timbered building (1460–95), on its north side. (Queens' is the only college headed by a President, all the other college heads being known as Masters.) To the left, off Cloister Court, is the small Pump Court, with the Erasmus Tower above the rooms occupied by Erasmus when he taught Greek here (1511–14). To the north are Walnut Tree Court (1618) and Friars Court with Sir Basil Spence's Erasmus Building (1961) and the Victorian chapel (1889–91). Beyond Cloister Court the wooden Mathematical Bridge – a 1902 reconstruction of the original bridge built in 1749 – leads over the Cam to the lovely college gardens. The bridge is so-called because it was built without nails, relying for its strength on meticulous calculation.

Corpus Christi College in Trumpington Street was founded in 1352 "by the townspeople for the townspeople". Old Court dates back to 1377, although since restored. The library contains valuable manuscripts and incunabula collected by Matthew Parker, Archbishop of Canterbury c. 1550. The adjoining St Benet's Church was the original college chapel and has a late-Saxon tower. The dramatists Christopher Marlowe (1564–93) and John Fletcher (1579–1625) were notable members of the college.

Trumpington Street runs into King's Parade, on the left-hand side of which stands ★**King's College**, founded in 1441 by Henry VI and the earliest of the royal foundations. King's College Chapel (1446–1515), built of white Yorkshire limestone, is the finest building in Cambridge, a masterpiece of Late-Gothic architecture. The rest of the buildings date from the 18th to 20th c. At the rear of the Fellows' Building a huge expanse of lawn extends down to the river where, from King's Bridge, there are lovely views along the Backs. Among the many distinguished alumni of the college were the writer Horace Walpole (1717–97), the poet Rupert Brooke and the economist Lord Keynes. Women students were admitted to the college for the first time in 1969.

★★**King's College Chapel**, a hall church 290 ft long, 45 ft wide and 80 ft high, is renowned for its twelve-bay interior in the Perpendicular style.

Cambridge: the Great Court of Trinity College

It has breathtaking fan vaulting by John Wastell (1512–15), and lovely Perpendicular tracery in the windows and on the walls. The stained glass windows (1515–31; west window 19th c.), embellished with Tudor coats of arms, are noted particularly for the cycle on the life of Mary, Jesus and the Apostles. The wooden organ screen (1533–36), organ case (1686) and choir-stalls (16th–17th c.) are lavishly carved. The altarpiece is a painting by Rubens, the "Adoration of the Magi" (1634), presented to the college by A. E. Allnatt in 1961. Visitors are recommended to attend Evensong, when the famous King's College Choir sings.

Beyond King's stands the **Senate House**, a Palladian building by James Gibbs (1722–30), with delicate plaster and woodwork and numerous statues. It is used for important academic occasions and ceremonies such as the conferment of degrees. Other buildings in the court, among them the Old Schools (14th–15th and 18th–19th c.), are occupied by university offices.

St Mary the Great (Great St Mary's), opposite the Senate House, is both parish and University church. Built in the 15th c. it has a very fine interior. The galleries were added in 1739 at a time when university sermons, given by great scholars, attracted huge congregations. The gallery used by masters and fellows of colleges was ironically referred to as "Golgotha". The tower (erected in 1608) is famous for its view.

★**Trinity Hall** in Trinity Lane was founded in 1350 by William Bateman, Bishop of Norwich. It has an old Elizabethan library preserved in its original condition, with books chained to shelves.

★**Clare College**, next to Trinity Hall, was first founded in 1326 as University Hall. Bad management necessitated its re-founding by Lady Elizabeth de Clare in 1338. In 1638, following a fire, work started on rebuilding the college in its present Renaissance style, seen at its loveliest in First Court. The delightful Clare Bridge (1640) crosses the Cam to the Fellows' Garden. Distinguished past members include the reformer Hugh Latimer, who was burned at the stake at Oxford, and the Elizabethan dramatist Robert Greene.

Facing Trinity Street, **Caius College** (pronounced "Keys"), or Gonville and Caius College to give it its full name, was founded in 1348 by

167

Edmund Gonville, vicar-general of the diocese of Ely, and enlarged after 1558 by Dr John Caius, physician to Edward VI and Queen Mary. It still has a strong medical tradition today.

Caius has three gates which together symbolise the student's academic "path". The college is entered from Trinity Street through the Gate of Humility, leading into Tree Court (1868–70). From there the Gate of Virtue gives access to Caius Court (completed in 1567), from which, finally, the Gate of Honour (1575) opens onto the Senate House opposite where degrees are conferred.

★**Trinity College** was established in 1546 by Henry VIII (see Famous People). It was created by the merger of several older colleges, including Michaelhouse (1324) and King's Hall, the latter dating from 1337 in the reign of Edward III to whom the Great Gate (1535) is dedicated. Thomas Nevile, Master of Trinity from 1593 to 1615, removed the statue of Edward III from its position on the street side of the gate and replaced it with one of Henry VIII as the college's founder and benefactor. Edward's statue now stands on the clock tower near the chapel. On the inner side of the Great Gate there are statues of James I, his wife Anne of Denmark, and their son, the young Prince Charles, while a statue of Elizabeth I (see Famous People) stands above the Queen's Gate on the south side of the Court. Beyond King Edward's Gate (1418), parts of the old King's Hall buildings are still identifiable. Trinity Great Court, measuring 336 × 228 ft, is the largest in Cambridge and was laid out around 1600. The well (c. 1610) used to provide the college's drinking water. A passage leads into Nevile's Court, completed in 1614. The chapel with its statues of distinguished scholars was begun under Mary Tudor.

The library was built by Wren (1676–90). The old oak bookcases have fine limewood carvings by Grinling Gibbons. Trinity can claim more distinguished former members than any other college: statesmen including Balfour, Sir Austen Chamberlain, Stanley Baldwin and

"Bridge of Sighs" at St John's College ...   *... and the chapel*

Nehru; poets and writers, among them George Herbert, Abraham Cowley, Dryden, and Edward Fitzgerald; the historian G. M. Trevelyan; the philosopher Bertrand Russell; and scientists such as Galton, Clerk-Maxwell, Thomson, Gowland Hopkins, Rayleigh, Eddington, Ernest Rutherford and Isaac Newton (see Famous People for the last two). Edward VII and George VI were also at Trinity. From New Court, or King's Court (1823–25), there is a bridge over the Cam, with a beautiful view of the Backs. A magnificent avenue of limes leads to the College Grounds.

★**St John's College**, in St John's Street, was erected on the site of an old monastery hospital. The college was founded in 1511 by Lady Margaret Beaufort, mother of Henry VII. A richly ornamented gateway opens into First Court, a fine example of Tudor architecture. The Chapel, built by Sir George Gilbert (1836–39), contains stalls and monuments from its predecessor. The dining hall of 1519, known simply as "The Hall", was enlarged in sympathy with later buildings in 1826. It has a fine hammerbeam roof, beautiful panelling and some good portraits. The Combination Room has a splendid plaster ceiling with festoons of vines. Second Court, built by Ralph Symons between 1598 and 1602, is exceptionally attractive with its mellow brickwork. Third Court dates from 1669–71 and includes the Library (1623–24) on its north side. From here the Bridge of Sighs (by Henry Hutchinson; 1831) leads over the Cam into New Court (1826–31) and the College Grounds. The Cam can be re-crossed by way of the Old Bridge (1709–12).

Among the many notable members of St John's were the dramatist Ben Jonson (1573–1637) and the Lakeland poet William Wordsworth (1770–1850) in whose famous "Prelude" there occurs a description of his college rooms.

Magdalene College (pronounced "Maudlen") is the only one of the old colleges to be built on the west side of the Cam. Originally established as a Benedictine college in 1428 it was re-founded during the dissolution by Lord Audley in 1542. First Court retains its charming 15th c. character. The Pepys Library in Second Court, a handsome building dating from the second half of the 17th c., contains the library of more than 3000 volumes and valuable manuscripts bequeathed to his old college by Samuel Pepys (1633–1703).

The foundation stone of ★**Jesus College** was laid in 1496 by John Alcock, on a site which at that time was outside the city walls. The college, situated east of the Round Church, in Jesus Lane, incorporates parts of the old Benedictine nunnery of St Radegund, founded in the early 12th c. The entrance is by a fine gateway built by Alcock. The Chapel, formerly the conventual church, is Early English (mid 13th c.). The stained glass windows (19th c.) are by Ford Madox Brown and Burne-Jones. On the east side of the court is the façade of the old chapter house (c. 1230). Among famous alumni were Archbishop Cranmer, the writer Laurence Sterne, the economist Thomas Robert Malthus and the poet Samuel Taylor Coleridge.

Facing St Andrew's Street, some little way south of Jesus College, **Christ's College**, like St John's, was founded by Lady Margaret Beaufort (1505). Its foundation marked a step on the way towards the modern university, for students were allowed to attend lectures at Christ's without being members of the college. The buildings have been drastically modernised. The Chapel (dedicated in 1510) has panelling of 1703 and old stained glass. Notable members of Christ's include Milton (who is supposed to have planted the mulberry tree which still grows in the garden) and the naturalist Charles Robert Darwin (see Famous People).

Emmanuel College, further along St Andrew's Street, was founded in 1584 by Sir Walter Mildmay and incorporates parts of a former Dominican priory. The college produced a number of Protestant ministers, many of whom emigrated to America, including some of the Pilgrim Fathers. The Chapel and cloister are by Wren (1668–74). A window in the Chapel commemorates John Harvard, the principal founder of Harvard University in Massachusetts.

★ Fitzwilliam Museum

Fitzwilliam Museum

The most famous museum in Cambridge – which no visitor should miss – is the Fitzwilliam Museum in Trumpington Street, a Neo-Classical building in Portland stone (1837–48), the masterpiece of its architect George Basevi. The original collection was bequeathed to the University by the 7th Viscount Fitzwilliam (died 1816). The Museum contains a magnificent collection of English pottery and china, Greek, Roman and Egyptian antiquities, and illuminated manuscripts. The exceptionally fine gallery has works by Hogarth, Gainsborough and Turner as well as the Impressionists and Dutch Masters of the Baroque (Rembrandt, Van Dyck, Rubens, Frans Hals and others).

University Library

The University Library with its collection of more than 1½ million volumes can also be visited. Situated on the far side of the Cam in Burrell's Walk, it occupies a modern building by Sir Giles Scott, completed in 1934.

★ Church of the Holy Sepulchre

Better known as the Round Church, the Church of the Holy Sepulchre in Bridge Street is one of the few Norman round churches in England (*c.* 1131, the rectangular chancel being 15th c.). It was drastically restored in 1841. Bridge Street leads to the Great Bridge, an iron structure of 1823. From the far side of the Cam there is a good view of the picturesque Fisher's Lane.

Other museums

The **Folk Museum** has a wide-ranging collection of everyday items – domestic equipment, commercial paraphernalia, tools and implements of various trades – reflecting Cambridgeshire life in centuries past.

The **Sedgwick Museum of Geology** (historic collections of fossils, minerals, etc.), the **University Museum of Zoology** (birds, insects, marine animals) and the **Whipple Science Museum** (history of science, including numerous scientific instruments) belong to the science faculties of the University.

On display in the **Scott Polar Research Institute** are relics and memorabilia from various Polar expeditions, including, e.g. letters, diaries and photos of Scott's ill-fated journey to the South Pole.

Surroundings

Grantchester

In addition to delightful walks along the Backs, through the beautiful college grounds on the west bank of the Cam, there is also a pleasant riverside path across the fields to Grantchester (2½ miles), a favourite haunt of Byron and Rupert Brooke and a popular outing by punt.

Trumpington

The nearby village of Trumpington has a war memorial by Eric Gill and a 14th c. church with the second oldest memorial brass in England (for Sir Roger de Trumpington, 1289).

Impington

Impington Hall at Impington, 3 miles north of Cambridge, once belonged to the Pepys family. Impington College, designed by Walter Gropius and Maxwell Fry, was built between 1936 and 1939.

Newmarket, Mecca of English horseracing, lies 10 miles north-east of Cambridge. The ★**National Horseracing Museum** in the High Street has numerous exhibits relating to the history of the Turf, one of the most popular sports in Britain. The collection includes paintings of famous horses and jockeys, old saddles and tack and trophies. There are several stables actually in the town, not to mention the famous racecourse and training "gallops" close by.

Newmarket

Bury St Edmunds (27 miles north-east), burial place of King – later Saint – Edmund, boasts an 11th c. abbey with five massive gate-towers. The abbey was noted in the Middle Ages for its illuminated manuscripts, one of which, the "Bury Bible" is now in the keeping of Corpus Christi College in Cambridge.

Bury St Edmunds

Moyses Hall, built by a Jewish merchant in the 12th c., is believed to be the oldest surviving dwelling house in East Anglia. Today its rooms are used for the display of Bronze Age archaeological finds, medieval artefacts and a 13th c. monk's chronicle. St James' Cathedral, begun around 1500, became a cathedral only in 1914. St Mary's Church (15th c.) contains many memorials, among them the tomb of Mary Tudor (died 1533), sister of Henry VIII (see Famous People).

★**Ickworth House**, just 4 miles south-west of Bury St Edmunds, was begun in 1796 by the Irish architect Francis Sandy and completed by the Marquis of Bristol in 1830. The mansion contains fine period furniture and a magnificent collection of silver. There is a superb park laid out by "Capability" Brown.

Huntingdon (18 miles north-west), an old and pleasant town on the River Ouse, is famous as the birthplace of Oliver Cromwell (born 1599). Like Samuel Pepys after him, Cromwell attended the local grammar school, the Norman front of which has survived and where today a number of portraits and memorabilia of the **Cromwell** family can be seen.

Huntingdon

All Saints' Church (15th c., Late Perpendicular) preserves the parish registers of St John's Church (destroyed), with a record of Cromwell's birth and baptism. Only foundations remain of a former Norman castle. A 14th c. bridge links Huntingdon to Godmanchester. Between the bridge and the market-place is a house in which the poet William Cowper lived from 1765 to 1767.

1 mile south-west of Huntingdon stands **Hinchingbrooke House**, now a school. The site was originally occupied by a Benedictine nunnery founded in the 11th c. which, at the dissolution of the monasteries, passed into the hands of the Cromwell family. In 1560 they converted the old building into a splendid mansion, incorporating parts of the church and the chapter house. In 1644 the house was sold to the Montagu family. The terraced gardens were laid out by Edward Montagu following his elevation to the Earldom of Sandwich.

15 miles south-east is the pretty little town of Saffron Walden, in a beautiful setting. The name comes from the saffron obtained from the yellow crocuses which were grown here. The town (pop. 11,900) has a long history, evidenced by the discovery of a large Saxon cemetery. There are only scanty remains of the old Norman castle. Some of the old houses offer well-preserved examples of the technique known as pargeting (timber framing with a plaster facing, often patterned; the best example is the Sun Inn). There is an interesting museum and a fine church, St Mary's (c. 1450–1525). Near the museum, on Castle Hill, is the largest turf-cut maze in Britain, with four round "bastions"; its origin is unknown.

Saffron Walden

1 mile to the west of Saffron Walden lies **Audley End**, a splendid Jacobean mansion built by Thomas Howard, Earl of Suffolk, between 1603 and 1616. Some of the rooms are exceptionally fine.

Finchingfield (pop. 1100), within easy reach from Saffron Walden, is one of the most picturesque and attractive villages in England, with many old houses, a sturdy Norman church tower and an old windmill.

Canterbury

Southern England. County: Kent
Altitude: 59 ft. Population: 36,500

Canterbury, a busy market town still blessed with some of its medieval character, lies picturesquely situated on the River Stour, at the heart of a predominantly agricultural region. It is known principally as the see of the Archbishop of Canterbury, Primate of All England and head of the Anglican Church. Indeed Canterbury is rightly regarded as the cradle of English Christianity – it was here that St Augustine (not to be confused with the even more famous Father of the Church, Bishop Augustine of Hippo in Africa) made his first converts while on his mission to the pagan Anglo-Saxons, and where, in 597, he became the first bishop. His burial place in St Augustine's Abbey, just outside the city walls, was for centuries a much revered shrine until, following the murder of Thomas Becket (see Famous People) in 1170 and his canonisation soon afterwards, the neighbouring cathedral came to overshadow it. The pilgrims who flocked to Becket's tomb brought enduring cultural and economic benefits in their wake. Today the city is a colourful blend of urban vitality and religious tradition, attracting 2½ million visitors a year.

History

In Roman times Canterbury was known as Darovernon or Durovernum, later being christened Cantwaraburg (town of the people of Kent) by the Saxons. There is evidence of a church here even before the pagan King Ethelbert of Kent (560-616) married Bertha, Christian daughter of the Frankish King Haribert. It was this church which St Augustine re-founded, following his successful missionising among the Saxons. From then on the history of Canterbury has been linked inextricably with that of the Church. It was another Archbishop of Canterbury, St Dunstan (959–988), who revived Christian culture in England after the ravages of

Canterbury Cathedral

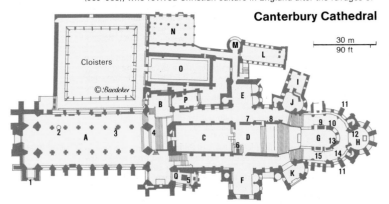

30 m
90 ft

Cloisters

©Baedeker

A	Nave	M	Water tower		
B	Site of Becket's murder	N	Library	6	Archbishop's throne
C	Choir	O	Chapter House	7	Tomb of Archbishop Chichele
D	Presbytery	P	Lady Chapel	8	Tomb of Archbishop Bouchier
E	North-east Transept	Q	St Michael's Chapel	9	Tomb of Henry IV
F	South-east Transept			10	Tomb of Dean Wotton
G	Trinity Chapel	1	South-west entrance	11	Miracle Window
H	Corona ("Becket's Crown")	2	Font	12	Tomb of Cardinal Pole
I	Treasury	3	Pulpit	13	Site of the Becket Shrine from
J	St Andrew's Chapel	4	Choir Screen		1220 to 1538
K	St Anselm's Chapel	5	Tomb of Lady Margaret Holland,	14	Tomb of Cardinal Odet de Coligny
L	Howleiana Library		Earl of Somerset, Duke of Clarence	15	Tomb of the Black Prince

the Viking incursions. His less fortunate successor Alphegus (1005–12) was murdered while held prisoner by the Danes, thus providing Canterbury with yet another martyr. In the year after the Norman Conquest, Canterbury's old Saxon church burned down, leaving Archbishop Lanfranc, appointed by William the Conqueror (see Famous People), with the task of building a new cathedral. Later this too suffered a similar fate (only the crypt has survived).

Archbishop Thomas Becket, a friend of the Angevin-Plantagenet Henry II (1154–89) since youth, had at first to be persuaded by Henry to accept the post. Once installed, however, Becket saw it as his duty to defend the interests of the Church against the king. In December 1170, after returning to Canterbury from a period of voluntary exile in France, Becket was murdered by four of Henry's knights in the north-west transept of the Cathedral. The martyr's blood was immediately pronounced miraculous and for centuries thereafter pilgrims flocked to his shrine.

This widespread veneration of Thomas Becket ended with the Reformation. Henry VIII (see Famous People) ordered a posthumous trial at which Becket was found guilty of high treason. His shrine was destroyed, his remains ignominiously thrown into the river, and any reminder of him obliterated. Interest in the rebellious churchman, less easily suppressed, has survived unbroken to the present day. During the Second World War Canterbury suffered considerable damage, but the Cathedral remained unscathed.

Canterbury Cathedral – Christ Church – reflects the changing architectural styles of five centuries. When the earlier Anglo-Saxon episcopal church burned down in 1067, the first Norman archbishop, Lanfranc (1070–77), built a replacement modelled on the Abbey of St Etienne in his home town of Caen. Lanfranc's cathedral quickly proved too small and St Anselm (Archbishop from 1093–1109) embarked upon the enlargement of the choir. This work continued under Priors Ernulf and Conrad, the new church being finally consecrated in 1130. Less than fifty years later, in 1174, it too was severely damaged by fire, rebuilding commencing in the hands of the French master mason Guillaume de Sens. His soaring three-bay arrangement with pointed arches marked the introduction from France into England of the Early Gothic style; his double transept moreover became a distinctive feature of the English Gothic cathedral. When in 1178 an accident made it impossible for the French William to continue, William the Englishman took over the reins, completing the choir – very much as seen today – in 1184. At the end of the 14th c. the Norman nave was pulled down, being rebuilt (1405) by the royal architect Henry Yevele in the High Gothic style. Replacement of the west transepts followed, completed in 1468, during which time, in 1434, the west façade also acquired its south-west tower (the old north-west tower, built by Lanfranc, was replaced by a copy of the south-west tower in 1832). Finally, in 1502, the tall, Late-Gothic central tower was erected over the crossing, crowning the unusually proportioned cathedral with its extended choir.

The precincts are normally entered through Christ Church Gate, a Perpendicular gatehouse (1517) with a Baroque oak doorway (c. 1660). To appreciate the overall dimensions of the cathedral it is best to begin by walking the whole length of the building, its scale being easily lost sight of once inside the labyrinthine interior. At the same time the various different architectural phases and peculiarities of style can most readily be identified, from the Romanesque (the Norman apses and groined arches, the 12th c. staircase tower of the south-east transept) to the Late Gothic (the nave with its characteristic tracery and buttresses, and the tall central tower).

Entering the Cathedral via the south-west porch (restored in 1862), the tall, light nave and aisles are revealed, with their cluster pillars, Gothic

★★Canterbury
Cathedral

Tour

Canterbury Cathedral: St Augustine's Chair... ... and an archbishop's tomb

tracery windows and ornate ribbed vaulting. Note in particular the west window with its extraordinary tracery and 15th c. stained glass. Afterwards, following the line of pillars on the north side of the nave, proceed past the font (1639, restored) and pulpit (1898) towards the ★**Choir Screen** (1411–30), its magnificent stone-work decorated with angels carrying shields and the crowned figures of six monarchs (from left to right) Henry V, Richard II, Ethelbert of Kent, Edward the Confessor, Henry IV and Henry VI.

The north-west transept to the left of the choir screen is the site of **The Martyrdom**, scene of Thomas Becket's murder on December 29th 1170; also of the Altar of the Sword's Point (the blade of the sword which killed Becket was broken by the force of the blow). The fine stained glass north-west window (1482) depicts Edward IV and his family at prayer.

Continue up the steps into the **Ambulatory**. Here sections of the Norman walls still survive and much of the glass in the windows is medieval in origin. A faded fresco, relic of the colourful murals with which the cathedral was once adorned, recounts the story of St Eustace. The choir-stalls were made in 1682, the archbishop's throne in 1840. The so-called St Augustine's Chair, upon which the Archbishops of Canterbury are traditionally enthroned, is thought to date in fact from the beginning of the 13th c.

Opposite the opening of the north-east transept – the triforium of which is formed by a Norman clerestory (pre 1174) – stands the magnificent **Tomb of Archbishop Henry Chichele**, founder of All Souls College, Oxford (see entry). The Archbishop is represented twice in effigy, first in the full splendour of his archiepiscopal robes and then again as a naked corpse – a poignant symbol of the transience of earthly goods. A few paces away is the marble **Tomb of Cardinal Thomas Bourchier** (died 1486), staunch supporter of the House of York during the Wars of the Roses. St Andrew's Chapel, diagonally opposite on the left, is particularly noteworthy for its Norman architecture, here preserved almost intact.

Ahead are steps leading, on the right, to ★**Trinity Chapel** where, from 1220 until its destruction in 1538, stood St Thomas Becket's golden shrine. Once or twice a day the heavy lid of the shrine would be raised with the aid of a block and tackle, to allow suitably awestruck and reverential pilgrims a glimpse of the gem-encrusted casket containing Becket's remains. Note the elegant sobriety of the Early Gothic choir (1184), the first example of the style to be seen in England. The columns of dark Purbeck marble contrast handsomely with the much lighter arcades below the colonnaded triforium, above which fine articulated ribs support the vaulting. In the north (left-hand) ambulatory of the Chapel are the alabaster tomb of Henry IV (died 1413) and his wife Joan of Navarre (died 1437) and, near by, the Renaissance tomb (1567) of the first post-Reformation Dean of Canterbury, Nicholas Wotton, who is shown at prayer. The walls of the choir on both sides of the Corona (the circular chapel at the far east end) are ★Stained glass embellished with superb late 12th and 13th c. stained glass windows. Known as the ★**Miracle Windows** they depict scenes from Becket's life and works. The ★**Corona** itself ("Becket's Crown"), with its early 13th c. biblical window, once housed a reliquary containing the severed fragment of the saint's skull. On the left inside the chapel is the tomb of Cardinal Reginald Pole, the last Roman Catholic Archbishop of Canterbury, who was appointed at the time of the short-lived English Counter-Reformation under Queen Mary I (1553–58).

Between the piers of the south ambulatory of Trinity Chapel is the **Tomb of Cardinal Odet de Coligny**, Huguenot Archbishop of Toulouse who was reputedly poisoned by a Catholic servant during a visit to England in 1571. Opposite lies Archbishop Hubert Walter (died 1205), on whose shoulders much political responsibility rested in the days of Richard the Lionheart and King John.

In the chapel itself, near to where Becket's shrine once stood, is the ★**Tomb of Edward, the Black Prince**, eldest son of Edward III and a true knight, famous for his courageous pursuit of the English cause during the Hundred Years' War. He died in 1376 at the age of 46, becoming familiar to posterity from his brass effigy and his armour (shield, gauntlets, etc.) which hangs above the tomb.

Steps worn by pilgrims' knees lead down into the south choir aisle where, on the left, stands **St Anselm's Chapel**, dedicated to Anselm of Canterbury (1033–1109), Archbishop from 1094 until his death and a famous Scholastic philosopher and mystic. His support for the papacy during the Investiture controversy brought him into conflict with the English crown. The fresco of St Paul and the serpent (about 1160) high up in the apse is a superlative example of Romanesque wall painting.

In the south-west transept the lovely **South Window** has late 12th c. stained glass which originally graced the choir. **St Michael's Chapel** adjoining has very fine tombs (15th–17th c.) with reclining effigies, including those of Lady Margaret Holland (1437) with the Earl of Somerset and Duke of Clarence at her side, and Thomas Thornhurst (1627).

On the way to the entrance to the crypt (north-west transept), pause at the crossing to admire the elaborate early 16th c. fan-vaulting beneath **Bell Harry**, the cathedral's magnificent central tower.

The large Norman **Crypt** (built about 1100, enlarged after 1174) is the oldest part of the cathedral. In addition to traces of Romanesque wall paintings (c. 1130) note, in St Gabriel's Chapel in particular, the pillars with their splendidly carved Norman capitals (pre-1130) and decorated shafts. The striking variety of motifs (animals, plant ornamentation, demons) reveals influences from as far afield as Lombardy, Byzantium and the Islamic middle-east.

The spacious **Cloister**, a good example of the Perpendicular style (1397–1411), has elaborate vaulting, the more than 800 bosses being brightly painted with faces and coats of arms.

Canterbury

The early 15th c. **Chapter House**, with its beautiful barrel vaulting of Irish bog oak, was the original setting for T. S. Eliot's "Murder in the Cathedral" when first performed in 1935.

Cathedral Close
Green Court

The most interesting of the numerous buildings in the Close lie north of the cathedral, grouped around the Green Court, a quiet square with, in the north-west corner, a roofed Norman external staircase leading up to the King's School Hall. Also of great interest (when open) is the Norman Water Tower, once part of an ingenious water supply and sewage disposal system which ensured that epidemics were virtually unknown in the Close.

King's School

King's School, situated in the northern corner of the Close, was founded by Henry VIII in 1541 – although, being a centre of Anglo-Saxon culture from as early as 600, there had been a school at Canterbury for centuries before that. Among the King's School's many famous pupils were the Canterbury-born dramatist Christopher Marlowe (1564-93), William Harvey (1578–1657), discoverer of the circulation of the blood, and William Somerset Maugham (1874–1965) whose novel "Of Human Bondage" includes a portrayal of life in the school.

St Augustine's
Abbey and
College

St Augustine's College (1846–48), located not far from the cathedral, outside the city walls, harbours the remains of the abbey founded by St Augustine in 604. St Augustine's Gate and the Cemetery Gate date from the 13th c., but are partly destroyed. The foundations of the old abbey church and the graves of St Augustine, King Ethelbert and his wife Queen Bertha have been revealed by excavation. There are also excavated remains of the early Saxon St Pancras' Church, incorporating much Roman material.

★ Old City

Christ Church Gate leads from the Close into the pedestrianised area of the Old City, where numerous ★ **timber-framed buildings** survive. An unbroken row of particularly fine houses, with typical over-hanging upper floors, can be seen in the narrow and busy Mercery Lane. Coming out of Mercery Lane into the High Street, note the Tudor "Queen Elizabeth's Guest Chamber" diagonally opposite, with its attractive pargetting. On the corner of the lane stands "The Chequer of the Hope", successor to the pilgrim hostel mentioned by Chaucer in the "Canterbury Tales" (only a fragment of the medieval original survives). To the right, along the High Street, past Eastbridge Hospital (founded about 1180, extended in the 17th c.) and beyond the bridge over the Stour (with a good view of the picturesque old Weavers' Houses, the homes in the second half of the 16th c. of immigrant Huguenot families), lies the **Westgate** (1375–81) with its round corner towers, portcullis and drawbridge. The impressive gateway now houses a history museum; there is a fine view of the cathedral from the top.

Canterbury
Heritage Museum

Anyone eager to learn more about the history of Canterbury should visit the Canterbury Heritage Museum, in imposing old buildings in Stour Street. On the way, Greyfriars, the remnants of a former Franciscan monastery founded in the 13th c., can be seen on the other side of the river.

Canterbury Tales
Museum

A visit to the Canterbury Tales Museum in St Margaret's Street can also be thoroughly recommended. As the name implies the museum is dedicated to Chaucer and his times.

St Thomas'
Cemetery

Among those who lie buried in St Thomas' Cemetery is the novelist Joseph Conrad (1857–1924).

Castle

Only the stump of the keep survives from Canterbury's 11th c. Norman castle, situated on the south-west edge of the Old Town. Just to the east of the castle, a well-preserved section of city wall skirts Dane John Gardens, named after the still unexplained mound/tumulus known as Dane John. Also in the Gardens are a memorial to Christopher Marlowe, and the "Invicta" (1830), a locomotive built by Robert Stephenson (see Famous People).

Situated outside the city centre, beyond St Augustine's Abbey, St Martin's Church, the "mother church of England", is one of the oldest surviving English churches, believed to have been built originally for Queen Bertha. Numerous Roman bricks are incorporated into the Anglo-Saxon choir. Inside there is a Norman font.

★ St Martin's

Surroundings

Encircled by orchards this attractive village lies 4 miles east of Canterbury. St Mary's Church (late 14th c.) has an Art Nouveau stained glass window by Arild Rosenkrantz depicting the Annunciation (1896).

Wickhambreaux

The flint and sandstone parish church of St Nicholas in Barfreston (7 miles south-east) is a gem of Norman architecture (12th c.), with remarkable exterior decoration. The tympanum above the south door has a mandorla with a figure of the seated Christ, framed by curling tendrils and smaller figures of angels, people and animals. The archivolts are also elaborately carved with medallions depicting animals playing musical instruments and people engaged in seasonal tasks. Likewise notable are the wheel window in the chancel arch, decorated with animal heads, and the adjacent eaves, carved with demons' faces to scare away evil spirits.

Barfreston

The delightful village of Chilham (7 miles) south-west of Canterbury) has a picturesque village green known as "The Square", around which stand ancient timber-framed houses. St Mary's, the parish church, contains some magnificent tombs. Chilham Castle, built in 1616, is not open to the public. The park, landscaped by "Capability" Brown, is open, however, and well worth the walk round – including seeing the eagles and falcons.

Chilham

Faversham (9 miles north-west) is also known for its 16th c. buildings. Among them are the Guildhall on the marketplace, the former Queen Elizabeth's Grammar School, and Ardens House (80 Abbey Street), named after Thomas Arden who was murdered in his home by his wife in 1551.

Faversham

Cardiff · Caerdydd   H 9

Wales/Cymru. County: South Glamorgan
Altitude: 49 ft. Population: 290,000

In 1956 the modern city of Cardiff/Caerdydd became the first ever official capital of Wales (Cymru). It lies on the wide estuary of the Severn and is traversed by two much smaller rivers, the Taff and the Rhymmey. An important port, it has been a university town since 1893 and is the cultural as well as the economic centre of Wales. Cardiff makes an excellent base from which to explore the many interesting places in South Wales (see entry).
   The Romans were responsible for the opening chapter of Cardiff's **history**, establishing a fort here in the 1st c. AD It was in the ruins of this old fort that, in 1090, the Norman baron Robert Fitzhamon erected the first castle. The settlement around the castle quickly grew into a borough, being granted its charter in 1147. Cardiff's period of greatest

prosperity began at the turn of the 19th c. when, in 1794, the 1st Marquis of Bute built the Glamorganshire Canal to the nearby Myrthyr Tydfil coalfield (the canal has since been filled in). In 1839 the 2nd Marquis expanded the harbour, constructing huge docks for shipping the Welsh coal. Soon "King Coal" was also being brought from the Valleys by rail, and the port of Cardiff became the biggest exporter of coal and iron in the world. In 1801 only about 1000 people were living in the city; by 1901 the number had risen to more than 160,000. Today coal is imported rather than exported. Allied Steel and Wire, the city's biggest steel manufacturer, remains one of its major employers, but new growth industries, mainly in the service sector, have for the most part replaced coal and steel.

Transport The airport is situated some 12 miles south-west of the city centre, with transfers being made by bus. There are good rail connections from the Central Station to London and Birmingham via Bristol (see entries).

Sights

Civic Centre

The imposing Civic Centre was the first of its kind in Britain. Among the public buildings ranged around Cathays Park are the Neo-Baroque City Hall (1904), with a bell-tower and a dome crowned by the Welsh dragon. The Marble Hall is decorated with historical figures from the story of Wales. In the centre of the complex is a War Memorial. Other buildings in the Civic Centre include the University College of South Wales, the Law Courts and many government offices.

National
Museum of Wales

The National Museum of Wales was founded in 1907 to "tell the world about Wales, and the Welsh about their own country". It contains

Cardiff: the Neo-Baroque City Hall

A bastion in the castle

National Museum: skeleton of dinosaur ...   ... M. Brown: King René's honeymoon

important early Christian material, archaeological collections, exhibits illustrating the development of industry, and pre-industrial crafts and implements. The Art Gallery provides an excellent survey of the work of Welsh and English painters such as Madox Brown, Wilson, Lawrence, Constable and Gainsborough. Major works by artists of other nationalities include, e.g. landscapes by Nicolas Poussin and Claude Lorrain.

Llandaff Cathedral was founded in the time of Bishop Urban (1107–34). The main part of the Cathedral dates from the 13th c.; the north-west tower was rebuilt in the 15th c. Later the whole Cathedral fell into a dilapidated state, and in 1734 an "Italian temple" was built within its walls by John Wood of Bath. The Cathedral was severely damaged during the last war (1941), but has since been restored. It contains a notable figure of "Christ in Majesty" by Epstein.

Llandaff Cathedral

The Castle in the centre of the city, stands on a site once occupied by a Roman fort; part of the Roman walls, the polygon bastions (4th c.) and the north gate have been preserved and partially restored. Cardiff Castle is really three castles in one, because in 1090 a new fortress was built on an artificial motte by Robert Fitzhamon. His successor, finding it too small, added a new range of richly decorated buildings. After the upheavals of the Civil War the Castle fell into disrepair. Between 1865 and 1920 the whole complex was rebuilt at vast expense but maintaining its original appearance. As well as State Apartments there is a library and a military museum.

Cardiff Castle

In Greyfriars Road can be seen the foundations of Greyfriars Church (1280) and the ruins of a mansion built on the site of the friary after the Reformation.

Greyfriars Church

Living room of an ironworker (c. 1805) ...   *... and a house in the Welsh Folk museum*

Theatre and Sport

Cardiff is well supplied with good shops. Queen Street, the busiest pedestrian precinct in Wales, is also the site of **St David's Hall**, a conference centre accommodating up to 2000 people.

Cardiff has a municipal theatre, the **New Theatre**, as well as the **Sherman Theatre** in Senghenydd Road and a puppet theatre, the **Caricature Theatre**, in Station Terrace. The city also offers a wide range of entertainments and sports facilities of all kinds, including a golf course and a riding centre. Below Castle Bridge, on the river, is the **Cardiff Arms Park** National Rugby Stadium, where international and club matches take place.

Cardiff Bay

Since the beginning of the 1990s almost 2700 acres of former dockland have been re-developed, creating housing, offices, restaurants, theatres, sports grounds and parks. The **Welsh Industrial and Maritime Museum** in Bute Street graphically records the evolution of power generation for the region's industry, from the water-wheel to steam engines, steam turbines and jet propulsion. The adjacent rail and maritime exhibition provides an equally fascinating insight into the development of transport in the country's famous "capital of coal".

The neighbouring **Techniquest** offers visitors the opportunity for some "hands-on" experience of science and technology today.

★ ★ Welsh Folk Museum

Set in exceptionally beautiful parkland 4 miles west of St Fagan's, the open-air Welsh Folk Museum has an intriguing collection of buildings such as cottages, farmhouses, workshops and mills, together with gardens, costumes, equipment and much more, bring the living and working conditions of the past vividly to life.

Surroundings

Caerphilly Castle

7½ miles north of Cardiff is the industrial town of Caerphilly (pop.

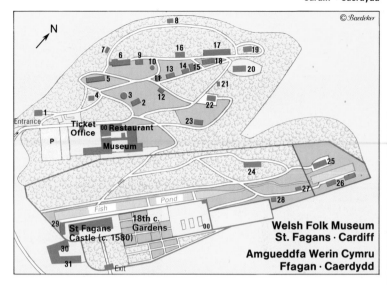

© Baedeker

Welsh Folk Museum
St. Fagans · Cardiff

Amgueddfa Werin Cymru
Ffagan · Caerdydd

1 Llwyn-yr-eos:
   farmhouse (c. 1820)
2 Kennixton:
   cottage from
   Llangennydd Gower,
   West Glamorgan (c. 1610)
3 Hendre Ifan Prosser:
   round pigsty from Mid
   Glamorgan (18th c.)
4 Melin Bompren:
   water-driven grain mill
   from Cross Inn, Dyfed
   (1852–53)
5 Hendre'r-ywydd:
   cottage from
   Llangynhafal, Clwyd
   (1508)
6 Tannery from Rhayader,
   Powys
7 Deheufryn Farm:
   gorse-mill from Dolwen,
   Clwyd (c. 1842)
8 Y Garreg Fawr:
   cottage from Waunfawr,
   Gwynedd (1544)
9 Pottery from Ewenni, Mid
   Glamorgan (kiln c. 1900)
10 Cockpit from the Hawk
   and Buckle Inn, Denbigh,
   Clwyd (17th c.)
11 Tollhouse from
   Pemparcau, Aberystwyth,
   Dyfed (1772)
12 Llanifadyn:
   cottage from Rhostryfan,
   Gwynedd (1762)
13 Derwen:
   bakehouse from Thespian
   Street in Aberystwyth,
   Dyfed (1900)

14 Saddlery from St Clears,
   Dyfed (1926–82)
15 St Mary's National
   School from Maestir,
   Lampeter, Dyfed
   (1880–1916)
16 Gwalia:
   shops from Ogmore
   Vale, Mid Glamorgan
   (1880)
17 Rhyd-y-Car:
   iron-workers' houses
   from Merthyr Tydfil,
   Mid Glamorgan (1805,
   1855, 1895, 1925, 1955,
   1985)
18 Smithy from Llawr-y-
   Gllyn, Llanidloes, Powys
   (18th c.)
19 Hendre-wen:
   barn from Llanrwst,
   Gwynedd (c.
   1600)
20 Cilewent:
   cottage from
   Llansantffraid
   Cwmteuddwr,
   Rhayader, Powys
   (orig. 15th c.)
21 Hay-shed from
   Maentwrog, Gwynedd
   (19th c.)
22 Abernodwydd:
   half-timbered cottage
   from Llangadfan, Powys
   (1678)
23 Capel Pen-rhiw:
   Unitarian chapel from
   Dre-fach, Felindre,
   Dyfed (1772)

24 Stryt Llydan:
   barn from Penley,
   Clwyd (c. 1550)
25 Esgair Moel:
   wool factory from
   Llanwrtyd, Powys
   (c. 1760)
26 Boat-house and
   net-house, with nets and
   other fishing
   equipment
27 Summerhouse from
   Bute Park in Cardiff,
   South Glamorgan
   (c. 1880)
28 Cider-mill and press
29 Demonstration of
   cooper's work
30 Demonstrations of
   wood-turning
31 Coach-house
   (c. 1860)
00 Toilets

MUSEUM

Gallery of Material
Culture

Costume Gallery

Agricultural Gallery

Agricultural Vehicles
Gallery

181

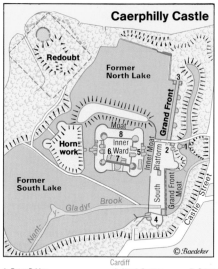

Caerphilly Castle

Cardiff

1 Draw Bridge
2 Gateway to Grand Front
3 North Postern
4 South Postern
5 Gateway to Outer Ward
6 Gateway to Inner Ward
7 Great Hall and Kitchen
8 Outer Ward

28,700), with another mighty castle, once again excellently restored. The town itself, which is also known for its tasty Caerphilly cheese, offers little else of interest. The castle, built to consolidate the English hold on the area in the face of opposition from Llywelyn ap Gruffydd, Prince of Wales, was begun between 1268 and 1271 by Baron Gilbert de Clare. It has the most elaborate defensive system of any British castle. It was enlarged several times and presents a formidable and imposing aspect, with its two drawbridges, massive walls, round towers and moat. However, there are virtually no interior furnishings.

Along the coast between Cardiff and Swansea are a number of small **seaside resorts**. Nearest to Cardiff (5 miles south) – indeed almost a suburb of the city – is Penarth (pop. 22,500), which has a shingle beach and offers excellent facilities for water skiing, sailing and fishing, as well as wide scope for attractive cliff walks. One such walk leads south to secluded Ranny Bay, St Mary's Well Bay at Lavernock and on to Sully with its offshore island, which can be reached on foot at low tide. Sully is a popular resort, with a sandy beach and cliffs.

Carlisle   I 6

Northern England
County: Cumbria
Altitude: 66 ft. Population: 72,200

Carlisle, an old border town on the River Eden and now county town of Cumbria, is mainly an industrial centre and a road and rail junction. In addition to historic buildings such as the cathedral, the Norman castle and the nearby Hadrian's Wall, the city also has a good modern shop-

ping centre. The lovely Scottish border country to the north (see
Southern Uplands) and the magical Lake District to the south are both
within easy reach.

History Hadrian's Wall ran just north of Carlisle, through what is now the
suburb of Stanwix, where the Roman fortifications crossed the river. The
fort later developed into the Romano-British town of Luguvalium. In the
11th and 12th centuries the Scots claimed the town, but after it was fortified by William Rufus had little chance of taking it. In 1645, however,
Carlisle did fall to a Scottish army under General Leslie after an eight
month-long siege. In November 1745 the city was taken again, this time
by the Young Pretender, Prince Charles Edward Stuart (Bonnie Prince
Charlie), without a shot being fired. It was retaken by George II's son, the
Duke of Cumberland, after the Prince's resounding defeat at Culloden
the following year.

Sights

The Cathedral was originally the church of an Augustinian priory
founded in 1102, and was made the see of a bishop by Henry I in 1133.
The south transept and the two bays of the nave are Norman (1123). The
beautiful choir was rebuilt in the Decorated style after a fire in 1292, but
was not completed until 1362. The north transept and central tower,
destroyed in a later fire, were rebuilt between 1400 and 1419. The great
east window in the choir is particularly fine. Completed in 1380 and measuring 62 ft by 33 ft, it comprises a Doom, or representation of the Last
Judgment.
    The choir-stalls, with 46 misericords, date from 1400 to 1433 and are
carved with scenes from the lives of saints. The delicately carved capitals of the Early English-style pillars depict the labours of the months.
The nave suffered serious damage in the 17th c. and was shortened. The
oak pulpit dates from 1599. Sir Walter Scott (see Famous People) was
married in the cathedral in 1797.
    In the **Cathedral precinct** are a gatehouse of 1527, a tower of 1510, a
number of Georgian houses and the Chapter Library in the Fratry, a
superb early 14th c. hall which was remodelled about 1500.

★ Cathedral

The Market Place is adorned with an old **Market Cross** (Carel Cross)
erected in 1682, from where in 1745 Bonnie Prince Charlie is said to have
proclaimed his father king. Opposite stands the **Town or Moot Hall**
(1717) in which city council meetings continued to be held until moved
to the new Civic Centre in 1964. The **Guildhall**, also called Redness Hall
after Richard de Redness, a merchant who owned the building from
1377 to 1399, was for centuries the meeting-house of the eight trade
guilds of Carlisle.

Market Place

Between the Market Place and the Castle, both Castle Street and Fisher
Street contain many fine Georgian houses. **Tullie House** in Castle Street
is of particular interest. Built in 1689 in the Jacobean Renaissance style,
by a family of German extraction who originally arrived in England to
work in the Keswick (see Lake District) gold and silver mines, the house
became a museum and art school in 1893. Between 1989 and 1991 it was
completely restored, a new wing being added at the same time. The
Museum possesses a comprehensive collection of prehistoric and
Roman finds from the Border area, documents relating to the many battles fought between the English and the Scots from the 14th to the 17th
c., and an exhibition specifically devoted to Bonnie Prince Charlie and
1745, a year of great significance in the nation's history. There is also a
well-presented collection of the region's flora and fauna. The adjoining
Art Gallery contains some 2000 works (17th–20th c.) including paintings
by Paul Nash, Sam Bough and Peter Blake.

Castle Street

Carlisle

★Carlisle Castle | The first castle was built by William Rufus in about 1092, providing protection against the ever-troublesome Scots; the present castle, with its magnificent Norman keep, took shape in the course of several subsequent stages of rebuilding. It now houses the regimental **Museum of the King's Own Royal Border Regiment**. Not only the Keep but also the 13th c. Ireby Tower and 14th c. Captain's Tower are extremely impressive. Visitors can see the dungeons in which more than 300 Scottish prisoners were held in 1745, as well as various mementoes of Mary Queen of Scots (see Famous People), imprisoned in the 14th c. Queen Mary's Tower for two months in 1568.

From the Castle there is a good view of the town. A section of the old **city walls**, including a sallyport (a gateway for mounting surprise attacks against besieging troops), can still be seen nearby in West Walls.

Citadel | The Citadel was originally constructed between 1541 and 1543 to secure the city's southern approaches, the engineer in charge being a Moravian, Stefan von Haschenperg. The massive towers seen today were built in the 19th c. by Sir Robert Smirke when the old Citadel was converted into Courthouses.

Outside the gate stands a statue of William, Earl of Lonsdale (1792–1844), a Lord Lieutenant of Cumberland and Westmorland.

Surroundings

Gretna Green | Since Carlisle is only 8 miles from the Scottish border it is easy to visit Gretna Green (9 miles north-west), famous at one time for its runaway marriages conducted by the village blacksmith. A visit can be conveniently combined with a tour of the ★**Southern Uplands** (see entry).

★Lanercost Priory | 12 miles north-east of Carlisle is Lanercost Priory, a former Augustinian

Inside Carlisle Cathedral

Lonsdale Monument outside the Citadel

Carlisle Castle

house founded by William de Vaux in 1166. The choir (1175) and transepts (1220) of the church are roofless, but the nave, dating from the first third of the 13th c., is still used as the parish church. The Jupiter Altar is made of stone taken from Hadrian's Wall. Note also the handsome arcading and the stained glass window by Edward Burne-Jones.

Nearby, beyond the attractive medieval bridge over the Irthing, is the entrance to Naworth Castle, the magnificent seat of the Earl of Carlisle, which dates from 1335. Particularly fine are the Great Hall and the Library, which has a Burne-Jones chimneypiece. The tower (*c.* 1350) is named after Lord William Howard, son of the Duke of Norfolk, who converted the castle into a country house (seen only by prior arrangement).

Naworth Castle

Channel Islands · Iles Normandes   I/K 11

The Channel Islands (French name: Iles Normandes) attract over half a million British holidaymakers every year. They lie in the Gulf of St Malo, at distances of between 10 and 30 miles from the French coast. Alderney, the island nearest to Great Britain, is by contrast 50 miles from the English coast. The largest of these "dependent territories" directly under the control of the Crown, is Jersey, followed in order of size by Guernsey, Alderney, Sark, Herm, Jethou and a number of tiny uninhabited islets and clusters of rocks.

Although each of the islands has its own character, they all have one thing in common, the mildness of their climate. Jersey is famed for its early potatoes and tomatoes, Guernsey for grapes, tomatoes and flowers. They all share, too, the advantage of having lower taxes and duties than mainland Britain, so that alcohol, cigarettes and many luxury articles are very reasonably priced – one of the reasons for the islands' popularity. In more than a geographical sense they are half way between Britain and France: their language is English but full of French expressions, their cuisine is largely French, and their whole way of life, particularly in summer, has a lively southern quality about it. Strolling through one of the larger places, with the shops open until late in the evening, a visitor might well imagine himself in Italy or southern France. With all these attractions it is hardly surprising that the Channel Islands are crowded with visitors during the summer months, the streets as busy as those of a large city. The high point of the season is the Battle of the Flowers in Jersey at the end of July, and holiday accommodation for this period must be booked a year in advance.

Like the Isle of Man (see entry), the Channel Islands are a **Crown possession**, remnants of the old Duchy of Normandy, the greater part of which was lost to Philip II of France in 1204. Since that time the islands have jealously preserved their autonomy, retaining the right to a considerable degree of self-government and a number of other privileges, such as issuing their own coins and banknotes. The Queen, as feudal overlord, is represented by a Lieutenant-Governor. The parliaments of Jersey and Guernsey are known as "States", Alderney's as the "States Assembly". Sark still has its medieval "Chief Pleas" presided over by a hereditary seigneur or dame.

Transport There are excellent air services to Guernsey and Jersey from London and several other major English cities. Guernsey Airport lies 3 miles from St Peter Port; Jersey's international airport at St Peter is situated 5 miles from St Helier. Services to The Blaye, the airport on Alderney, are very much more restricted. In summer there are daily ferry crossings from Torquay for Alderney, from Weymouth, Portsmouth and Torbay for Guernsey, and from Poole and Weymouth for Jersey. Ferries also run to the Channel Islands from Cherbourg and St Malo. There are busy ferry and air services between the islands.

History Excavations have shown that the Channel Islands were inhabited three thousand years before the Christian era. The Romans certainly occupied some of the islands, and Jersey appears in the records as "Caesarea". In the 6th c. Christianity was brought to the islands by St Helier (after whom the chief town of Jersey is named) and St Sampson. In 932 the islands became part of the Duchy of Normandy, remaining in English hands when most of the Duchy was lost to France in 1204. During the Second World War they were occupied by German forces from June 1940 to May 1945. Mementoes of this period can be seen in the German Occupation Museum and many other small museums.

Tour of the islands Visitors who want to get to know the islands properly and are not simply going for the golf or bathing, should allow at least a week, preferably longer. A good programme for a week's visit (which unfortunately does not leave time for the very attractive island of Herm) would be as follows: 2 days on Guernsey, with St Peter Port and the east and north coasts on the first day and the west and south-west coasts on the second; on the 3rd day Sark (by boat); on the 4th day Alderney (though if necessary this could be omitted); on the 5th, 6th and 7th days Jersey, covering at least St Helier, Gorey and Mont Orgueil, La Hougue Bie and the north and south-west coasts.

★**Jersey**

Jersey (pop. 82,000) extends over 11 miles from east to west and 7 miles from north to south. The north coast has the more striking scenery, with a chain of high cliffs, rocky inlets and caves; the other coasts are flatter and more densely populated. Few visitors find their way along the very narrow roads into the interior, an area of intensive vegetable-growing and farming. There is a particularly pleasant footpath which runs along

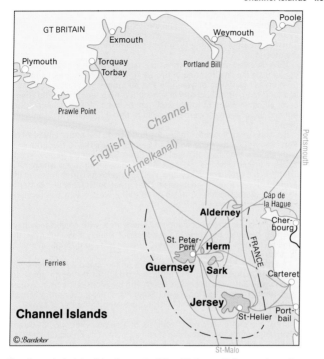

the disused stretch of track – part of the old Jersey Railway – from St Aubin lighthouse to Corbière Point on the south-west tip of the island.

The chief town, St Helier (pop. 29,900), is magnificently situated on wide St Aubin's Bay. It is a lively town, full of atmosphere and charm, having largely kept its Victorian character. On a small rocky island outside the harbour, reached by ferry or by causeway, stands Elizabeth Castle, built during the reign of Elizabeth I (see Famous People). Charles II took refuge there on several occasions. On an adjoining rock, St Helier, the 6th c. apostle of Christianity, is said to have had his hermitage. Fort Regent – now a modern leisure complex with sports facilities and conference halls – used to guard the landward side of the town. In Royal Square, in the centre of St Helier, are the Town Church (10th c.), the Royal Court House, the States' Chamber (administrative building), the Library and a gilded statue of George II. The Jersey Museum in Pier Street has interesting archaeological and art historical collections, the adjoining art gallery being devoted to local artists. Gorey is between 5 and 7 miles from St Helier according to the route chosen. The coastal road is the more beautiful; the alternative route passes through Grouville, a pretty little holiday resort with a splendidly situated golf course.

St Helier

Gorey, on the same bay as Grouville, is a charming little town with a row of picturesque houses along the harbour. It is dominated by the formidable ★ **Mont Orgueil Castle**, a magnificent example of medieval military engineering from the reign of King John.

Inland from Gorey is Jersey's principal tourist "sight" – ★★ **La Hougue**

East Coast

Bie, a large burial mound topped by two chapels, the Norman chapel of Notre Dame de Clarté (12th c.) and the Jerusalem Chapel erected in 1520 by Dean Mabon. The crypt of the latter contains a replica of the tomb of Christ in the Church of the Holy Sepulchre in Jerusalem. Excavation of the mound in

1924 revealed one of the largest passage graves in Europe, probably dating from the late Iron Age or Bronze Age (2000 BC or earlier) and built from stones weighing between 25 and 30 tonnes. It consists of a passage 46 ft long, an oval chamber almost 6 ft high, and three side chambers, all constructed of undressed granite slabs. When archaeologists opened the grave they were dismayed to find it had already been plundered.

Beyond Gorey the coast road runs first beside the pretty bay of **Anne Port**, then round the wide sweep of **St Catherine's Bay**, a favourite spot with anglers, and past the secluded Rozel Bay with its narrow sandy beach. Further west lies the large Bouley Bay, inland from which, near Trinity, is the excellent **Jersey Zoo**, well known for its commitment to the preservation of threatened species. The Carnation Nursery and **Butterfly Farm** (St Mary), another 3 miles or so to the west, has a spectacularly colourful collection of exotic butterflies.

North coast

The north coast is romantic and much indented, with small sandy bays nestling between the rocks. To the west of Bouley Bay, however, the road no longer runs close to the sea, passing instead through an area of lonely, unspoiled scenery.

A little way inland is the highest point on the island, **Les Platons** (485 ft). Other features along this attractive stretch of the north coast are Bonne Nuit Bay, with its shingle beach and the Mont Mado granite quarries; St John's Bay; La Houle cave; Sorel Point, the most northerly point on the island; the waterfall of Les Mouriers; and a number of caves.

West coast

Almost the entire west coast consists of a single, wide bay, **St Ouen's Bay**, familiar to experienced surfers on account of its breakers. Many traditional craft workshops (making pottery, leather goods and jewellery) are found in the area.

St Peter has a **Vintage Car Museum** with a collection of old cars, motorcycles and military vehicles.

South-west coast

St Aubin, on the sandy **St Aubin's Bay** on the island's south-west coast, is a very popular holiday resort, with a small harbour and a castle built on a crag.

St Brelade's Bay, the next bay west, is the site of one of the oldest churches on the island, dating in part from 1042.

Built during the Second World War, the **German Underground Hospital** in the centre of the island makes an unusual but interesting tourist attraction.

★ Guernsey

Guernsey (pop. 55,500) is only about half the size of Jersey but even more densely populated. The cliffs on the south coast rise to 270 ft, from where the land falls gradually away towards the north. The island's numerous restaurants, with a reputation for delectable cuisine from across Europe, have earned Guernsey the nickname "Gourmet Island".

St Peter Port

The narrow streets and alleyways of Guernsey's capital St Peter Port (pop. 16,000) climb steeply from the harbour to the highest point of the town, commanding a splendid view. Many of the houses are Regency in style, giving St Peter Port a pleasant old-world air. On a small island connected by the Castle Pier stands Castle Cornet, founded in 1150 but in its present form largely Elizabethan. Today it houses several museums, the Royal Guernsey Militia Museum, the Guernsey Maritime History Museum, a Royal Air Force Museum and the Art Gallery and Armoury. The pulpit of the Town Church is 12th c., the chapel 15th c. From 1859 to

Corbière Point, the south-western tip of Guernsey

1870 Hauteville House was the home of the French writer Victor Hugo (1802–85), at the time a political refugee from France; it contains mementoes of the poet and furniture of the period.

On the east coast of the island are a number of **Martello towers** as well as the ruined Vale Castle, the early Norman Vale Church, and a large passage grave. East coast

The south coast is interesting and attractive, with cliffs and caves. The largest of the caves is **Creux Mahie**, 200 ft long. **Corbière Point** is of interest to geologists, with green veins in the pink and grey granite. ★South coast

On the west coast lies the very beautiful Rocquaine Bay. The island of **Lihou**, linked to the mainland by a causeway, has remains of a 12th c. priory. West coast

The small island of Herm lies about 3 miles north-east of St Peter Port. Although the resident population is only about 100, Herm attracts up to 3000 visitors a day during the summer. The island has a hotel, a number of old stone-built houses converted into holiday homes, and a camp site. Many species of rare flowers and plants thrive in the moderate climate; also, more than 200 different kinds of shell are found at Shell Beach on the north coast. ★Herm

Tom Thumb Village, its houses lovingly restored, provides a charming diversion.

The even smaller island of Jethou between Herm and Guernsey is private but can be visited. Jethou

Sark, the jewel of the Channel Islands, is the smallest of the main ★★Sark

islands, with a population of about 500. It is unique in having largely preserved the old feudal system which once prevailed on all the islands,
ruled in effect by one man, grandson of the Dame of Sark. Boats ply
daily in summer from Guernsey and (less frequently) from Jersey,
returning the same evening. The landing place is at La Maseline on the
east side of the island.

From La Maseline a steep track winds its way up the cliffs to the little
hamlet of **La Colinette**, the island's main settlement, with a school, a
church, an old manor house, a windmill (on the highest point) and of
course, inns. There are a number of small guest houses scattered about
the island. There are few roads and no cars, but the principal features of
interest can easily be reached on foot.

The most rewarding walk is south-west to the part of the island known
as **Little Sark**, over the rocky isthmus called La Coupée. After the last
war a new track was constructed across this narrow and rugged neck of
land which falls steeply more than 250 ft to the sea. The path leads to
Port Gorey and two very famous rock pools, the Bath of Venus and the
Pool of Adonis; both offer good bathing at low tide.

Off the west coast of Sark lies the privately owned island of **Brecqhou**.
Beneath the bizarrely shaped cliffs overlooking Brecqhou are the interesting Gouliot Caves, filled with sea anemones, etc. but only accessible
at low water. A path off to the left leads to the fishing harbour of **Havre
Gosselin**, although there is little fishing done on Sark nowadays. **Dixcart
Bay**, on the south-east side of the island, is another picturesque spot,
where most of the island's holiday accommodation is found. Le Creux
Derrible is a cave with a natural, 180 ft cleft in its roof; the cave itself can
only be reached at low tide, through two rock arches. There are a
number of other smaller caves and plenty of interesting rock scenery,
best seen by boat.

*Alderney

Alderney (pop. 2100), most northerly of the Channel Islands and the
least visited because of its remoteness, is only 4 miles long and 1 mile
wide. Its economy is based on vegetable and flower growing as well as
tourism. The almost treeless island has beautiful sandy bays between
much indented cliffs and rugged tors.

The little town of **St Anne**, 1 mile from the harbour, dates from the
15th c. It has something of a French air, with cobbled streets, inns, snug-
looking pubs and shops. In Telegraph Bay are two interestingly coloured
rocks known as the Two Sisters.

The uninhabited **Burhou**, to the north, 1 mile offshore, is a bird
reserve; it can be visited by boat except in the nesting season.

Chester

Western England. County: Cheshire
Altitude: 69 ft. Population: 70,200

Chester, county town of Cheshire, is situated on the edge of the North
Wales lowland, on the north bank of the River Dee 7 miles from its
mouth. The city is an important traffic junction, through which passes
the Chester Canal linking Liverpool and Manchester (see entries). The
inner Old Town, designated a conservation area in 1960, still retains its
old city walls, as well as large numbers of well-preserved half-timbered
houses and the remarkably beautiful Rows, two-tier medieval arcades of
shops. Its attractive bridges and parks and its walks along the walls and
by the river make Chester a pearl among English cities.

The surrounding countryside is chiefly given over to agriculture,
mainly potato growing, pig rearing and dairy farming, producing in particular the renowned Cheshire cheese. Salt mining, textiles and light
industry are among the more important secondary activities. British

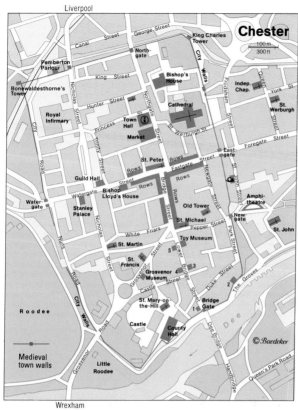

Liverpool

King Charles Tower

Chester

100 m
300 ft

Canal Street
George Street
Northgate
Pemberton Parlour
King Street
Bishop's House
Indep. Chap.
York St.
Bonewaldesthorne's Tower
Nicholas Street
Hunter Street
Northgate Street
Cathedral
Frodsham Street
St. Werburgh
Royal Infirmary
Town Hall
St. Werburgh St.
Foregate Street
Princess Street
Market
Trinity Street
St. Peter Rows
Rows
Eastgate Street
Eastgate
Guild Hall
Rows
Newgate Street
St. John Street
Bishop Lloyd's House
Watergate
Rows
Bridge Street
Amphitheatre
Watergate
Stanley Palace
Old Tower
Newgate
Nuns Road
Nicholas Street
White Friars
St. Michael
Pepper Street
Park Street
St. John
St. Martin
Toy Museum
5
Grosvenor Street
St. Francis
Grosvenor Museum
4
3
Lower Bridge Street
Duke Street
The Groves
Castle Street
2
Roodee
City Walls Road
St. Mary-on-the-Hill
Bridge Street
Bridge Gate
1
Dee
Castle
County Hall
Dee Bridge
© Baedeker
Medieval town walls
Grosvenor Road
Little Roodee
Handbridge
Queen's Park Road

Wrexham

1 Bear and Billet Inn 2 Wishing Steps 3 Tudor House 4 The Old King's Head 5 Falcon House

Aerospace employs about 4000 workers manufacturing Airbus parts. Service industries, shopping centres and tourism are other economic mainstays of the town.

History For four hundred years, from AD 60 onwards, "Deva" (Castra Devana), the Roman camp on the River Dee, was the headquarters of the famous XX Legion. Once the Romans had departed, however, there followed centuries of decline, with periodic occupation by hostile Vikings, Danes and Scots. Eventually, so the Anglo-Saxon Chronicle of 907 records, Legeceaster (town of the legions) was rebuilt by Aethelflaed, a daughter of Alfred the Great, and in 972 the rulers of Wales, Ireland and the Isle of Man all gathered there to pay tribute to the Saxon king Edgar. The town stoutly resisted the Norman Conquest, suffering in consequence. In 1071 its fortunes again revived under the virtually independent rule of the Earl of Chester. From the 12th to 14th c. the west coast river port played an important role in maritime trade with Ireland, Scotland, Spain and France, commercial prosperity bringing with it a cultural flowering. In particular, from the end of the 14th c., the town's merchant guilds put on regular public performances of mystery plays, an early form of English drama. At the end of the 15th c., however, the harbour began to silt up, impoverishing the town; not even Henry VII's grant of new privileges under the Great Charter of 1501 could arrest the decline. During the English Civil War the citizens of Chester remained faithful to the Crown, even offering Charles I refuge. But in 1646 they too were forced to surrender to Parliamentary troops following a five-month siege. The opening of Liverpool's first lock-controlled basin in 1715 marked the end of any hopes Chester had of re-establishing itself as a port. Since the 18th and 19th centuries the town has come to play a key role in the home market for agrarian products.

★★Old City

A first impression of the Old City can be gained from a walk along the town walls. Built mostly of red sandstone they follow the line of the Roman walls, except in the south and west where they extend to the banks of the river to take in the Castle. The complete circuit is about 2 miles. The four main gates – the North- and Eastgates, the Bridgegate and the Watergate – were rebuilt in the 18th and 19th c.

Start at the steps by the **Eastgate** entrance to the Old City (rebuilt in 1769) with its clock erected in 1897 on the occasion of Queen Victoria's (see Famous People) Diamond Jubilee. On proceeding northwards a fine view of the cathedral soon opens up. Further along, in the north-east corner of the walls, stands the **Phoenix Tower** – or King Charles' Tower – (restored 1658) from where in 1645 Charles I is said to have watched his troops defeated at Rowton Moor. The tower is the most interesting of those surviving and houses a small Civil War museum. Along the next, northern, section of the walls, traces of the Roman foundations can be seen. Beyond Northgate, beside the canal which took the place of the old moat running along outside the walls, are a watch-tower, known as **Morgan's Mount**, and the semicircular Goblin Tower or **"Pemberton's Parlour"** from which vantage point a sailmaker called Pemberton apparently used to keep a watchful eye on his workforce. The solid sandstone

Chester: the East Gate

Strolling in The Rows

Water Tower (c. 1325) in the north-west corner also makes a fine view-point, with some Roman remains visible in the garden below. Outside the west walls, on what was once part of Chester's old port, lies the race-course known as the Roodee. There has been horse-racing here at least since 1609. Just beyond it there is a gap in the walls where they are breached by Grosvenor Road. This then crosses **Grosvenor Bridge** which, when built in 1832, had the greatest span of any single-arched stone bridge in England (200 ft).

In the south-west corner of the walls is the **Castle**. The buildings now occupied by the Assize Courts, County Hall, etc. date from the 19th c., the only really old edifice being Agricola's Tower (13th c.), part of which contains the Museum of the Cheshire Regiment.

A little more than half-way along the walls on the south side stands the **Bridgegate**, leading to the Old Dee Bridge (13th c.). Beyond the gate, at the point where the walls turn north, are the ★**Wishing Steps**; anyone who runs up and down the steps twice without drawing breath will, it is said, have their wish fulfilled. Afterwards the walls run alongside Park Street, with, opposite, a row of six pretty 17th c. half-timbered houses. A little further on is the **Newgate** (built 1938), outside which are gardens where, since 1949, Roman finds from excavations in the city have been displayed. Beyond Newgate the walls continue back to the starting point at Eastgate.

One of Chester's most striking and distinctive features are its Rows, galleried walkways with shops, etc., running the length of the stone and half-timbered buildings, usually at first floor level. Originally dating from the early 14th c., all have in varying degrees been restored or rebuilt on several occasions since. They are believed to have evolved from houses and shops which, being erected on the site of Roman ruins, were built partly in front of the piles of rubble and partly on top, linked together by some form of pergola. These Rows are found in all four of the town's main streets which, following the Roman town plan, meet at right angles at the market cross. In Eastgate Street, Bridge Street and Watergate Street the galleries run along at first-floor level, in Northgate Street mostly at ground level. Visits can be made to the shops, cafés, houses and offices, or a stroll taken in town, without having to worry too much about the weather. The many unexpected little nooks and crannies, especially in Eastgate Street, add further to their charm. ★★The Rows

Watergate Street has several exceptionally fine half-timbered houses, including God's Providence House (1652) – the inhabitants of which were spared the plague – and Bishop Lloyd's House (early 17th c.) with beautiful carving on the front. Leche House (1579), a short distance away, also has elaborate half-timbering, as does the richly decorated Stanley Palace (1591, extended c. 1700). The Guildhall Museum (visits by appointment only) contains an interesting exhibition relating to Chester's merchant guilds. ★★Watergate Street

Equally delightful are the rows of half-timbered houses in Lower Bridge Street, in particular Falcon House (17th c.), Tudor House (16th c., believed to be the oldest dwelling house in the town), the Old King's Head Hotel (17th c.) and the Bear and Billet (1664), a four-storeyed half-timbered inn near the Bridgegate. ★★Lower Bridge Street/Bridge Street

13 Lower Bridge Street houses a ★**toy museum** with not only a splendid collection of dolls made between 1860 and 1950 but also the largest collection of Matchbox model cars in the world.

Remains of a Roman bath were discovered at 39 Bridge Street. Proceeding northwards, Chester's 19th c. Town Hall is situated about half way along Northgate Street, beside the Market Square. Across the road the **Abbey Gate** (14th c.) leads to **Abbey Square**, with houses dating from about 1760.

Half-timbered buildings at the corner of Westgate and Bridge Street

★ Chester
Cathedral

The Cathedral is reached from either Northgate Street or the winding St Werburgh Street. Records show that, around 958, the site was occupied by a church and shrine dedicated to St Werburgh (died *c.* 700), abbess daughter of King Wulfhere of Mercia. A little over a century later, having regard no doubt to the salvation of his not altogether guiltless soul, Hugh Lupus, first Norman Earl of Chester, replaced it with a Benedictine abbey. This in turn became a cathedral when, following the Dissolution, a new diocese was created by Henry VIII in 1541.

Part of the Norman church survives in the north transept. The Lady Chapel and Chapter House are Early Gothic (post 1240), most of the choir High Gothic (1280–1315), and the tower, west front and upper part of the nave Late Gothic (1485–90). The entire building was restored by Sir Gilbert Scott between 1868 and 1899. On entry via the south-west porch, the three-aisle pillared nave (14th–16th c.) of the Gothic basilica is most striking. The west end incorporates several features of interest: the baptistery, another relic of the Norman church, contains a 6th c. Venetian font brought to Chester in the 19th c. from a village near Venice; the Consistory Court, though less visually impressive, is nevertheless unique in England.

Leaving the west end, continue along the south aisle, past the massive south transept (14th c.) which, with its three aisles, was used as a parish church (St Oswald's), to reach the Early Decorated ★ **Choir**, undoubtedly the finest part of the Cathedral. The late 14th c. choir-stalls are superbly carved, with 48 droll misericords and an old abbot's seat inscribed with the Tree of Jesse. Part of a 14th c. shrine to St Werburgh can be seen in the Lady Chapel.

Somewhat unusually, the cloister (rebuilt in the 19th c.) and the several surviving **abbey buildings** grouped around it, are found on the cathedral's north side. The Chapter House and its vestibule are both Early English. In the refectory the hammerbeam roof is modern, having been completed in 1939; the stone lector's pulpit on the other hand, approached by a flight of steps set in the wall, is again Early English. The plain undercroft is Norman.

The open space just outside Newgate, now the Amphitheatre Gardens, was once the site of the largest Roman amphitheatre in England, capable of accommodating over 7000 spectators.

Amphitheatre

The nearby St John's Church, some of which dates from the late 19th c., also retains part of a 12th c. Norman church, in particular the still impressive nave. The triforium is Transitional (c. 1200). The original choir and Lady Chapel were destroyed when the central tower collapsed and are now no more than picturesque ruins.

St John's

The Grosvenor Museum boasts an exceptionally fine collection of Roman antiquities. Special displays illustrate the life of a Roman legionary and the Roman fortification of Britain.

Grosvenor Museum

Chester's pleasant zoo, in Upton, about 1½ miles north of the city centre, can be highly recommended.

Zoo

Chichester L 10

Southern England
County: West Sussex
Altitude: 43 ft. Population: 26,000

Chichester, county town of West Sussex, is situated between the South Downs and the coast. It has a pleasant Old Town of Roman origin and a Late Romanesque-Early Gothic cathedral. Chichester Harbour, sheltered by sandbanks and the low-lying Hayling Island, offers ideal conditions for sailing in its many inlets and attractive little bays.

History Regnum – or Noviomagus Regnensium – was established by the Romans at the intersection of two important roads. In Saxon times it became known as Cisseceastre. The cathedral was founded in the 11th c. when, following the Norman Conquest, the town became an episcopal see. In the 14th and 15th c. Chichester experienced a period of great prosperity, being transformed by the wool trade into a thriving port. Today it is the centre for the surrounding region, an area which remains predominantly agricultural in character.

In 1075, re-organisation of the diocese following the Norman Conquest saw Chichester elevated to an episcopal see. Work is thought to have started on the cathedral in about 1088, and records show the choir to have been consecrated in 1108. Building, however, continued right up to the 15th c., passing through several phases of evolution in the Romanesque and Gothic styles. By 1123 the east end of the Norman nave and the transepts had been constructed; and by mid century the four west bays of the nave and the lower storey of the south-west tower were also complete. A fire in 1186 caused the wooden roof to be replaced by Early Gothic ribbed vaulting. The south-west tower was finished at the beginning of the 13th c., the spire over the crossing around 1400. To house the cathedral's heavy bells a detached belfry was built early in the 15th c. Even this was to prove inadequate, however, collapsing in 1861 and being rebuilt five years later.
   The interior of the Late Norman/Early Gothic Trinity Cathedral is furnished with a wealth of medieval and modern art. The **font** (1983), seen to the right on entering the west porch, is by John Skelton; it is executed in Cornish stone with a copper basin. The third side chapel off the south

*Chichester Cathedral

195

A window by Marc Chagall in the North Choir aisle of Chichester Cathedral

aisle contains a monument to Agnes Cromwell by the Neo-Classical sculptor John Flaxman; the altar-cloth with the icon of the heavenly light is the work of Cecil Collins. The **pulpit** (1966) in the nave was made by Robert Potter and Geoffrey Clarke, using reinforced concrete, aluminium and leather-covered wood; the choir-screen in contrast is Late Gothic and dates from 1475. Both transepts are embellished with interesting 16th c. paintings by a local artist Lambert Barnard, reflecting aspects of the cathedral's history.

In the **South Choir** aisle are two exceptionally fine Romanesque stone panels (*c*. 1130-40) depicting with quite extraordinary expressiveness the Arrival of Christ at Bethany and the Raising of Lazarus. The panels are reckoned among the finest examples of Norman sculpture seen in England. A tapestry by John Piper on the theme of the Trinity adorns the altar-screen. The tomb of St Richard, Bishop of Chichester from 1245 to 1253, in the **Retrochoir**, used to attract many pilgrims in the Middle Ages. The shrine, having been destroyed in 1538, was restored in 1984-85 with a tapestry by U. Becker-Schirmer and altar decoration by G. Clarke. In the south-east corner of the choir hangs Graham Sutherland's painting "Noli me Tangere" (1962). The Lady Chapel has 12th–14th c. ornamentation and a ceiling painting by Lambert Barnard (1533). In the **North Choir** aisle is an impressive stained glass window in bright shades of red by Marc Chagall, inspired by the 150th psalm "In Praise of God". Set into the floor of the north transept can be seen the tomb of the composer Gustav Holst (1874–34). A door in the east wall of the transept leads through to the Treasury.

The irregularly-shaped **cloister** on the south side of the cathedral allows excellent views of the spire and nave. The statue on the grass beside the nave is by Henry Moore.

Bishop's Palace   Situated close south-west of the cathedral, the Bishop's Palace has kitchens and a private chapel dating from medieval times. The chapel boasts one of the finest surviving paintings of the Winchester school (12th c.; see Winchester), depicting the Virgin and Child with angels.

Chichester's late-Gothic Market Cross stands a short distance east of the cathedral, at the point where, still true to the original Roman grid pattern, the city's four principal thoroughfares, North, East, South and West Streets, intersect. The octagonal Cross in the Flamboyant style is open on all eight sides. North and South Pallant, off East Street, contain a number of fine old houses. Pallant House (North Pallant) incorporates a small but excellent gallery of modern art, including works by Sutherland, Moore, Nicholson, Severini, Leger and Klee.

Market Cross

Pallant House

St Mary's Hospital, a 13th c. almshouse in St Mary's Square, is well worth seeing for its old sleeping quarters, living rooms and interesting chapel.

St Mary's Hospital

The Guildhall Museum in Priory Park is also of considerable interest, containing – mainly Roman – archaeological finds.

Guildhall

West of Chichester lies Chichester Harbour with an attractive and distinctive landscape of its own – an area of waterways and marshland with large numbers of waterfowl, thatched cottages, little sandy bays and reed-fringed shores.

Surroundings

On one of the Harbour's many creeks stands the village of **Bosham** (about 4 miles west of Chichester; pop. 2800), with a church dating from Saxon times. The tower and pulpit are Saxon, other parts are 13th c. The church is depicted on the Bayeux tapestry; it was from here that Harold set sail in 1064 on his unsuccessful mission to Normandy.

The foundations of **Fishbourne Roman Palace** (c. AD 75; 1 mile west of

Chichester: the late-Gothic Market Cross

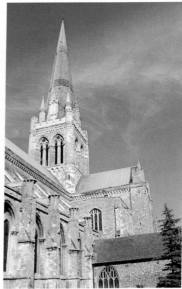

Chichester Cathedral

Chichester) were excavated mainly between 1960 and 1968. The unusually large building, 16,000 ft in area, every one of its 100 or so rooms once paved with mosaics, would originally have stood at the water's edge. It is thought to have belonged to a Celtic tribal chief called Cogidubnus, who became a trusted friend and ally of the Romans. The numerous Roman pavements uncovered illustrate a range of mosaic techniques and variations in quality; there is also an interesting and informative museum about life in Roman Britain.

Goodwood House, seat of the Duke of Richmond, is situated 3½ miles north-east of Chichester. The house was built between 1790 and 1800, mainly by James Wyatt, and contains fine furniture and pictures including works by Canaletto and Van Dyck. The large park incorporates a racecourse where the well-known Goodwood Races are held at the end of July.

Chiltern Hills   K 9

Southern England
Counties: Oxfordshire, Buckinghamshire and Hertfordshire

The Chilterns are a range of chalk hills, mainly in Buckinghamshire and Oxfordshire, rising to heights of up to 850 ft. Unlike similar hills elsewhere in England, they are well wooded, with some of the finest stands of beeches in the country, and offer excellent walking. The abundant supplies of good timber led to the establishment of the furniture-making industry in this area.

Although they are no great height, the Chilterns were in earlier centuries a considerable barrier to communications between London and the north-west. A road ran along the northern fringes of the hills, but on the south side much of the traffic was carried by the Thames. The main traffic routes followed – and still follow – the valleys. One of the earliest roads from London led by way of Watford into the hills and then continued by Berkhamsted and Tring to Aylesbury, situated at the lowest point in the hills. A second road ran from Amersham into the pretty Misbourne valley, by way of Little and Great Missenden, still charming villages. The third cut across the hills and followed the Wye valley from Bradenham by way of Princes Risborough to Bledlow and Whiteleaf. At Bledlow and Whiteleaf are crosses of unknown origin carved in the chalk crags.

A 7th c. manuscript bewails the solitude and desolation of the Chiltern Hills. The ease of modern travel has brought considerable change since then, fuelled by the continuing expansion of London and the desire of wealthy Londoners for a house in the country: but there are still parts of the Chilterns which show little change, and many charming little towns and villages.

Aylesbury

A good centre from which to explore the Chilterns is Aylesbury (pop. 51,900), county town of Buckinghamshire, with a large Market Square and attractive old half-timbered houses. St Mary's Church (13th c.) has an unusual spire and a fine Lady Chapel and misericords.

Waddesdon Manor, 6 miles north-west, was built in 1880–89 for Baron Ferdinand de Rothschild. The house contains a magnificent collection of French furniture, 18th c. Gobelin tapestries, Sèvres porcelain and superb paintings, including works by Rubens, Reynolds and Gainsborough. There are also fine manuscripts and a library. The gardens are considered a masterpiece in their own right.

Claydon House (8 miles north-west), seat of the Verney family, dates from the 16th c. Enlarged between 1752 and 1768, some of its rooms boast sumptuous Rococo and New Gothic stucco work. The Chinese Room in particular is worth seeing.

6 miles south-east lies **Wendover** (pop. 6300), with many fine half-timbered houses. **Coombe Hill**, 1½ miles to the west of the town, is the highest point in the Chilterns (845 ft), with delightful views of the Thames, the town of Aylesbury and the magnificent woods around **Chequers Court**, a historic Tudor mansion (1566) situated 2 miles to the southwest, was presented to the nation in 1917 by Lord Lee of Fareham, for use as a country residence by the Prime Minister of the day.

Amersham (pop. 21,300) is a favourite residential town at the foot of the Chilterns, in the Misbourne valley. The wide High Street has many handsome 17th and 18th c. houses. Other features of interest are the market hall (1682), Drake's Almshouse (hospital; 1657) and the Town Hall.

Amersham

High Wycombe (pop. 59,000), in a narrow valley in the Chilterns, has many furniture factories. The large parish church of All Saints, in the centre of town, dates from the 13th c. but has been much rebuilt and restored. There are two handsome 18th c. buildings, the Guildhall (1757) and the Market Hall, renovated by Robert Adam in 1761. The Art Gallery and Museum contains an interesting collection of furniture and tools. Wycombe Abbey, built in 1795, is now occupied by a girls' school. The village of **West Wycombe**, 2 miles west of High Wycombe, dating from the 15th–18th c., belongs to the National Trust, which is committed to preserving its distinctive character. West Wycombe Park, a country house built in 1698 and altered in the Palladian style between 1765 and 1780, has beautiful spacious grounds landscaped by Humphrey Repton, with a lake, a pavilion and small temples. On the hill above the town stands a hexagonal mausoleum built by the eccentric Sir Francis Dashwood, founder of the Hell-Fire Club.

★High Wycombe

Hughenden Manor (1½ miles north of High Wycombe) was the home of Benjamin Disraeli, one of the British Empire's greatest statesmen and a gifted novelist (see Famous People). He died in the house, which still contains much of his furniture, books and other memorabilia, and is buried in the local churchyard.

Fingest is a charming little village in a fold in the Chilterns, with beautiful views of the hills. It has a notable church with a Norman tower.

Berkhamsted (pop. 16,800), an attractive town set in a lush green valley in the hills, makes another good base from which to explore the Chilterns. Little is left of the castle in which William the Conqueror (see Famous People) received the homage of the Anglo-Saxon dukes and bishops before his coronation in Westminster Abbey. Berkhamsted School, founded in 1541, has some fine Tudor buildings. The religious poet William Cowper (1731–1800) was born in the town.

Berkhamsted

Ashridge (3 miles north) is a large mansion designed by James Wyatt. Now occupied by a college, it has a lovely park with a magnificent avenue of beeches.

Ivinghoe, the village which suggested to Scott the name of his novel "Ivanhoe", has an interesting church with fine woodcarving. In view from the top of Ivinghoe Beacon (904 ft) with its wide panorama of the Chilterns, are the historic old Ivinghoe windmill (1627; the oldest post mill in the country), and the white lion cut in the chalk which acts as a beacon for Whipsnade Zoo.

Whipsnade Wild Animal Park, the largest zoo of its kind (600 acres), was established in 1927–31. The park itself is of great scenic beauty, in addition to being well stocked with animals. The outline of a lion was cut in the chalk on the north side as a warning signal to aircraft. A narrow-gauge railway runs through part of the park.

★Whipsnade Zoo

Dunstable (pop. 48,400), at the foot of Dunstable Downs, 3½ miles from Whipsnade, makes a very worthwhile excursion. The church of St Peter and St Paul originally belonged to an abbey founded in 1131 and has a

Dunstable

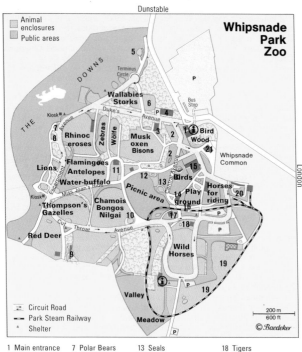

Dunstable

Whipsnade
Park
Zoo

Animal enclosures
Public areas

1	Main entrance	7	Polar Bears	13	Seals	18	Tigers
2	Elephants	8	Kodiak bears	14	Sealions	19	Camels,
3	Monkeys	9	Hippopotamuses	15	Cloisters		Yaks,
4	Cheetahs	10	Flamingoes		Cafeteria		Red deer
5	Penguins	11	Giraffes	16	Park railway station	20	Steam-engine display
6	Bears	12	Red Pandas	17	Café by the lake	21	Administration

Norman nave; the ornate north-west porch dates from the 13th c. It was here in 1533 that Archbishop Cranmer granted Henry VIII (see Famous People) his divorce from Catherine of Aragon, foreshadowing legislation in 1534 installing Henry as the supreme head of an independent Anglican Church.

★ **Woburn Abbey**

Woburn Abbey (9 miles north-west) draws many thousands of visitors every year, most of them attracted by the varied range of entertainment it offers – a wild animal kingdom, sports facilities, playgrounds and amusement park, boating, cafés and restaurants, antique market, etc. The house itself, seat of the Duke of Bedford, is a huge mansion dating from 1746–47, built on the site of an earlier Cistercian abbey. The decoration of the state apartments was the work of Henry Holland (1802). The mansion is a treasure-house of art, with valuable 18th c. furniture, silver and porcelain, and a richly stocked picture gallery (works by Holbein, Van Dyck, Rembrandt, Gainsborough, Reynolds, Canaletto, Velasquez, et al.)

Goring

As the place-name "Vineyards" indicates, vines used to be cultivated here at Goring in the southern foothills of the Chilterns. Here too is the geographical feature known as "the Goring Gap" where the Thames has cut its way through the chalk. Just north of Goring the Icknield Way, the

Romans' ancient strategic highway along the northern slopes of the Chilterns, is crossed by the massive earthworks known as Grim's Dyke (or Ditch), the purpose of which remains obscure. St Birinus, who missionised Wessex, converting its pagan king Cynegils to Christianity in 634, has given his name to one of the hills.

Colchester   M 9

Eastern England
County: Essex
Altitude: 107 ft. Population: 87,500

Colchester, situated not far from the East Coast about 50 miles north-east of London (see entry), can claim to be the oldest town in Britain, having been a Celtic capital even before the Romans came. It is now famous for its rose nurseries and its excellent oysters from the oyster beds in the estuary of the River Colne. It is an attractive town with many fine old buildings of various periods. Extensive excavation has unearthed, among other things, the best-preserved Roman walls in Britain.

The site has a long **history** of settlement, extending back at least to the Bronze Age. In about 40 BC, recognising its strategic value, Cunobelinus (Shakespeare's hero Cymbeline), chief of the Catuvellauni, moved his capital to Colchester (Camuldonum) from what is now St Albans (see entry). The Romans captured the town in AD 44 during the reign of Claudius, but in 61–62 it was sacked by the Iceni from Norfolk under Boudica (Boadicea). When the Normans arrived Colchester had a population of some 2000 and several churches, and still preserved part of its Roman walls. In modern times excavation has revealed the ancient British town, the Roman camp and the later Roman "Colonia". In 1648 the town was taken by Parliamentary forces under Fairfax after a 76 day siege. Like 16th c. immigrant Flemish weavers before them, Huguenot refugees settling in Colchester in the early 18th c. brought their silk weaving skills to the local wool and cloth trade, thus making an important contribution to the town's increasing prosperity. It was the Huguenots also who introduced flower-growing.

The 20 ft-high Roman walls, begun under Vespasian, are some 9 ft thick and enclose an area of about 1000 × 1500 ft. Of the original six gates only the imposing ★**Balkerne Gate**, the west gate of the Roman town, still survives in part.

The Walls

A hundred metres or so east of the Balkerne Gate lies the western end of the broad, handsomely-built High Street, in which can be seen the **Town Hall** (by John Belcher, 1892–1902). On the tower is a bronze figure of St Helen, who according to local tradition was the daughter of "Old King Cole" of Colchester. The king himself is said to be buried in a mound in the Dykes area on the outskirts of the town.

High Street

The district immediately north of the Town Hall is known as the **"Dutch Quarter"**, with a number of pretty little houses with pointed gables. At the end of the 16th c. Flemish refugees fleeing religious persecution made their homes here. Their cloth, particularly a special kind of flannel called "boi", quickly became renowned.

The ★**Castle**, also on the north side of the High Street but further along, was built by William the Conqueror (see Famous People) in about 1080. Some Roman bricks were used in its construction. Fortified by massive 13 ft walls, it has the largest Norman keep in England (115 × 164 ft). The outstanding Castle Museum houses most of the area's Romano-British finds (including pottery, coins, statues and glass). Castle Park, through which flows the River Colne, contains another section of the Roman walls.

Hollytrees Museum	Nearby, in a Georgian mansion (1718) called Hollytrees, there is a very fine collection of toys, costumes and old jewellery.
St Martin's Church	St Martin's Church in West Stockwell Street dates mainly from the 14th c.; the tower, now destroyed, was also constructed partly of Roman bricks.
St Botolph's Priory	Queen Street leads to St Botolph's Street and the ruins of St Botolph's Priory, the first Augustinian house in England (founded post-1093). The only remains are some still impressive arcading from the church, also built from Roman material.
St John's Abbey	Further to the south, in Stanwell Street, stands St John's Abbey Gate, the remains of a Benedictine monastery founded by Eudo in 1096 (and restored in the 15th c.).
Holy Trinity	On the way back to the High Street the Scheregate Steps mark the line of the old Roman walls. Holy Trinity Church in Trinity Street has a Saxon tower incorporating Roman bricks. Inside there are exhibits showing town and country life in the Colchester area over the last two hundred years.
★Siege House	Siege House, an ancient half-timbered house (now a restaurant) in East Hill, still bears traces of artillery fire from the 1648 siege.
Bourne Mill	Just outside the town (1 mile south) stands picturesque Bourne Mill. The extravagantly ornamented gabling (1591) is typical of the style of the Dutch immigrants who built and operated the water-mill, converted later to a corn mill.

Cornwall   F/G 9/10

South-west England. County: Cornwall

Cornwall (pop. 450,000; area: 1370 sq. miles), in the extreme south-west corner of the country, is a much favoured holiday location. Its attraction lies in its many sites of great – and often bizarre – natural beauty, its cliffs and moors, subtropical parks and gardens, delightful sandy beaches, picturesque fishing villages and old mining communities, together with the myriad myths and legends which surround them.

History The first settlement of the region was from Brittany, by folk of the megalithic culture. From the Bronze Age onwards tin mining led to the establishment of vigorous and far-flung trading links. Later, the Romans too exploited the area's mineral wealth. It took until the 9th c. before the Anglo-Saxon kings were able to assert their authority over Cornwall. In 1068 William the Conqueror (see Famous People) named his half brother Roger de Mortain 1st Earl of Cornwall, with possessions extending as far as Somerset and Devon. In 1337 Edward III created the duchy of Cornwall for his son Edward, the Black Prince. Ever since 1503 the title of Duke of Cornwall has traditionally been taken by the heir to the British throne, together with the right to the income from the duchy.
Cornwall's churches are often dedicated to saints largely unknown in the rest of Britain, the region having been first converted to Christianity by Irish-Welsh monks.

Economy "Fish, tin and copper", so says an old toast, were the foundation on which, for hundreds of years, Cornwall's wealth rested. For many Cornishmen, however, they brought in only a modest livelihood; others lived by smuggling and looting shipwrecks. In the late 18th and

19th c. heavy industrial demand led to extensive exploitation of Cornish mineral deposits and the county became the world's foremost producer of tin and copper. From 1920 onwards, however, it faced increasingly intense competition from the Far East. Miners were forced to emigrate as mines shut down and engine-houses fell into disrepair. In many places ruins blighting the landscape are a stark reminder of past prosperity. Over the years the huge shoals of pilchards have also dwindled, so that fishing too has declined. Today tourism, vegetables and flowers grown in the mild climate of the south coast, the slate from quarries near Delabole and the china clay extracted around St Austell are the main sources of income.

The people of Cornwall have always taken pride in their Celtic ancestry. The **Cornish language**, closely related to Breton, nevertheless died out at the end of the 18th c. The efforts now being made to revive it are hampered by the lack of any substantial body of Cornish literature, the written legacy passed down since 1400 being very fragmentary. The old language survives chiefly in the form of place-names, in particular those with the prefix "tre" (home), "lan" (church), "pen" (end, spit of land") or "pol" (bay). It was these which inspired Sir Walter Scott's well-known jingle: "By Tre-, Pol- and Pen-/Ye shall know the Cornishman.

Folk dance and folk music festivals, May Day celebrations derived from old fertility rites, a unique form of wrestling, Cornish pasties (pastry filled with meat and vegetables) and saffron buns are just a few of Cornwall's specialities.

Heading west from Plymouth (see entry) across the River Tamar into Cornwall the first place of interest is the small town of St Germans. In Saxon times, up until 1050, the twin-towered, former monastery church of St Germanus was the seat of a bishop. It has a marvellous Norman west porch with decorated archivolts and zigzag ornamentation.

St Germans

Cliffs on the West Coast of Cornwall

Arthur and Guinevere

The legendary cycle of King Arthur (or Artus) and his Knights of the Round Table has its origins in the far south-west of the British Isles, in what are now the counties of Devon, Cornwall and Somerset. Here, historians are agreed, at the end of the 5th/early part of the 6th c., lived a Breton military leader who confronted the Anglo-Saxon invaders from the east, defeating them in battle at Mons Badonicus in 516.

At this point however history ends and legend begins, a legend which has immortalised in the figure of Arthur the archetype of a Christian king and the embodiment of all the knightly virtues. The first mention of this mythical Arthur, as "dux bellorum", appears in the "Historia Britonum", written about 800 and attributed to Nennius. But it was the Benedictine monk Geoffrey of Monmouth who first transformed Arthur into a figure of profound cultural significance when, in his "Historia Regum Britanniae" (1132–35), he embellished facts relating to the historical king with fiction drawn from Breton fables and folk tales. Geoffrey's Arthur is the son of the Breton king Uther Pendragon and Ygerne, wife of the Duke of Cornwall. Brought up by the wizard Merlin, he takes the throne at the age of fifteen, marrying the beautiful Guinevere, a Roman. Having extended his rule throughout Britain, twelve years of peace ensue. He then embarks with an army for mainland Europe where his knight Gawain defeats the Roman emperor Lucius. Standing on the threshold of Rome, Arthur receives word that his nephew Mordred has abducted Guinevere and siezed power. Returning home he catches up with Mordred at Camlann, killing him in single combat and being himself mortally wounded. He does not however die, but is "carried away" to the island of Avalon. His legendary sword Excalibur disappears, embedded immovably in a rock at the bottom of a lake.

Geoffrey's fable inspired a succession of literary works. In his "Roman de Brut" (1155), the Anglo-Norman poet Wace introduced several new elements which have remained essential strands of the myth ever since. – Healed in Avalon by the sorceress Morgan, for example, Arthur awaits the day when he can return and liberate Britain. But Wace's chief contribution was the introduction of the Round Table of 28 knights. Thereafter, the adventures of Gawain, Galahad, Percival and Lancelot, based on exploits in Celtic-Irish mythology, overshadowed the original Arthurian story. Assuming a dynamism of their own, they opened up new narrative fields. The figure of the king becomes merely the embodiment of chivalrous ideals, and is even on occasion ridiculed – as the husband cuckolded by the lovers in the story of Lancelot and Guinevere for example. Onto this already much embroidered version of the Arthurian story,

A Tudor reproduction of King Arthur's Round Table in the Great Hall of Winchester

Chrétien de Troyes grafted the further legend of the Holy Grail, elevating the search for the mystical chalice into the most sacred duty of King Arthur's knights. From the 12th to the 14th c. de Troyes' "Conte de Graal" (1175) inspired a number of other writers in France while also proving very influential in Germany, where the most notable interpretations were Hartmann von Aue's "Ivein", "Erec" and "Lanzelot" and Wolfram von Eschenbach's "Parsifal". Wolfram transformed what had up to then been an adventure story into a "character" novel, by taking the spiritual metamorphosis of the madcap Percival as his principal theme. It was in England however that the Arthurian legend achieved its most vivid rendering, in Sir Thomas Malory's "Morte d'Arthur" (1470). The myth has continued to exercise a powerful influence on the literary imagination even in more recent times, as in the 19th c. Alfred Lord Tennyson's famous poetry cycle "Idylls of the King" (1859–88), Mark Twain's satire on contemporary culture in "A Connecticut Yankee in King Arthur's Court" (1889) and Richard Wagner's operas "Tristan and Isolde" and "Parsifal". The present century has seen Jean Cocteau's play "Les Chevaliers de la Table Ronde" (1924) which, while based on the love affair of Guinevere and Lancelot, removes the trappings of magic from the story, and the American writer Hal Foster's comic epic featuring Prince Eisenherz at the Round Table. Other examples include the film "Excalibur" by John Boorman and Marion Zimmer Bradley's novel "The Mists of Avalon".

Anyone setting off today in search of King Arthur will find no shortage of places shrouded in mystery. Their authenticity however is quite another matter, and many sites are a disappointment, with nothing to see but an artificial mound. Tintagel Castle lays claim to being Arthur's birthplace, three other castles, Castle Killibury,

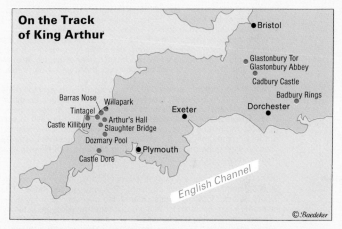

On the Track of King Arthur

- Bristol
- Glastonbury Tor
- Glastonbury Abbey
- Cadbury Castle
- Badbury Rings
- Barras Nose
- Willapark
- Tintagel
- Arthur's Hall
- Castle Killibury
- Slaughter Bridge
- Exeter
- Dorchester
- Dozmary Pool
- Plymouth
- Castle Dore

English Channel

© Baedeker

Barras Nose and Willapark, to being the legendary Killiwick where he spent his youth. Close to Bodmin Moor there is a hunting lodge called Arthur's Hall. Two of the most famous Arthurian knights – Galahad and Tristan (Tristram) – are reputed to have come from the British Atlantis, Lyonesse, assumed to be the now sunken land-bridge between the Scilly Isles and the mainland. Many people have claimed to see the remains of ancient walls uncovered at low tide. It was in Castle Dore, on the south coast, that King Mark brooded over Tristan's and Isolde's love. Three miles away stands Tristram's Stone, alleged to be Tristan's burialplace. Experts now agree on Cadbury Castle in Somerset as the site of Arthur's castle Camelot. Some miles to the north-west stands Glastonbury Tor, beneath which the Holy Grail is said to have been buried by Joseph of Arimathea. Joseph also founded Glastonbury Abbey, where a stone square stands over what is claimed to be Arthur's and Guinevere's grave. Some say Arthur's victory over the Anglo-Saxons took place near the Badbury Rings in Dorset, others at Liddington Castle in Wiltshire. The scene of his final battle is likewise disputed, the alternatives including Camelot (i.e. Cadbury) or Slaughterbridge near Camelford. Not far from the latter is Arthur's Tomb where, according to yet another tradition, the king lies buried. It is said that Excalibur still waits to be reclaimed by its owner at the bottom of Dozmary Pool on Bodmin Moor.

Cornwall

There are two fine windows, the east window (1869) by William Morris and the south window, on the theme of the Virtues, by Edward Burne-Jones. Note too the splendid monument (18th c.) to Edward Eliot by the sculptor John Rysbrack.

★ **Antony House**   Built in the 18th c., Antony House, home of the Carew family (7 miles south-east) is also worth visiting. Situated on the Tamar estuary, it contains Queen Anne furnishings, a portrait by Edward Bower of Charles I painted just prior to his execution, other portraits by Reynolds and gardens beautifully landscaped by Humphrey Repton.

Looe   Looe (20 miles west; pop. 4500), straddling the mouth of the River Looe, boasts a lovely sandy beach and an attractively presented Cornish Museum.

★ **Polperro**   Polperro (6 miles west), an old Cornish fishing village squeezed between two steep and rocky headlands, is always crowded with visitors during the summer. The painter Oskar Kokoschka spent his years of exile here. The Museum of Smuggling recalls the darker side of Polperro's past when it was a smugglers' haven.

Fowey   Fowey (10 miles west; pop. 2150) was once a considerable seaport, home port of the notorious "Fowey Gallants", ships of war and privateers much feared in medieval times. With its many old houses it remains a picture-postcard town. The 15th c. St Nicholas' Church, dedicated to the patron saint of seafarers, has a fine Norman font. It is built on a site previously occupied by two much earlier churches, St Goran's (7th c.) and St Finnbarus', which latter was destroyed. Noah's Ark, an Elizabethan half-timbered house, contains a small local museum.

A fairly long but thoroughly delightful footpath leads past the ruins of the castle built by Henry VIII (see Famous People) to defend the harbour, to **Gribbin Head**, from where there is a magnificent panoramic view.

The **Tristan Stone** (1 mile north), a monolith dating from 550 BC, claims to be the tombstone of the hero of the medieval epic. A few kilometres further north are remains of Iron Age earthworks known as **Castle Dore**, likewise said to be the ramparts of King Mark's castle from the same Tristan story.

St Austell   In the 18th c., the ancient market town of St Austell (9 miles west; pop. 36,000), dominated by the imposing and very ornate tower of Holy Trinity Church (15th c.), leapt suddenly into prominence in the national economy when the chemist William Cookworthy discovered china clay deposits there. Mining continues today, providing the big Derby (see entry), Minton and Worcester (see entry) potteries with a crucial raw material for their fine porcelain, although many other industrial processes use china clay as well. Every tonne of kaolin extracted produces 9 tonnes of waste, and the white spoil heaps, ironically christened the "Cornish Alps", are a distinctive feature of the local landscape (there is a particularly good view from the hill-top parish church at St Dennis, about 6 miles north-west of St Austell). The Wheal Martyn Museum, north of St Austell, has a fascinating section on china clay extraction, including a restored 19th c. clayworks. The cliff scenery of the coast around St Austell Bay is exceptional.

★ **Mevagissey**   The picturesque setting of the fishing village of Mevagissey (6 miles south), with its narrow alleyways and quaint slate houses, guarantees its popularity as a summer resort.

Veryan   Caerhays Castle is one of the sights of interest on the way to Veryan (9 miles south-west; pop. 880), a delightful village noted for its eight, most unusual, whitewashed roundhouses, with conical roofs, Gothic windows and crosses.

The church of St Just-in-Roseland (13th–15th c., restored in the 19th c.) stands in a charming estuarine setting near the village of St Just (5 miles south). Surrounded by a lovely garden the church is built on an ancient Celtic cult site.

★ **St Just**

Like Pendennis Castle on the other side of the river, the castle (1540–43) at St Mawes (2 miles south) was one of a series of fortresses built by Henry VIII to secure the south coast of England against attack by France. From St Anthony Head, the southernmost point of the Roseland peninsula, a splendid panoramic view unfolds.

St Mawes

Trewithen House (4 miles north), an 18th c. country mansion near Probus, is famous for its exceptionally beautiful landscape gardens, with a special rhododendron arboretum, more than 30 varieties of camellia and 40 different kinds of magnolia.

★ **Trewithen House**

In the Middle Ages Truro (6 miles north-west; pop. 17,800) was one of the four Cornish "Stannary" towns where smelted tin was weighed, stamped and taxed. When the separate diocese of Cornwall was created in 1876, it became both the episcopal see and administrative centre for the county. The town is dominated by the tall spire of J. L. Pearson's Neo-Gothic cathedral (1880–1910), around which stand a cluster of Georgian houses. The Royal Cornwall Museum and Art Gallery has an excellent collection of minerals (including gold finds dating from the Iron Age) as well as pottery, porcelain and furniture, also paintings by John Opie (1761–1807), one of Cornwall's most distinguished portrait painters. Particularly noteworthy is Godfrey Kneller's portrait of the Cornish "giant" Anthony Paine, 7 ft 4¼in. in height and the tallest soldier in King Charles II's army. Another section is devoted to Cornish wrestling.

Truro

Flourishing in the exceptionally mild climate of southern Cornwall, ★ **Trelissick Garden** (4 miles south), laid out between 1937 and 1955, is one of the loveliest subtropical gardens in England. The manor house dates from 1825.

Although blessed with a fine natural harbour, Falmouth (9 miles south) has largely surrendered its historic status as a seaport, catering instead for leisure craft and holidaymakers. The town enjoys the mildest winter climate in England. Pendennis Castle (1544–46), built by Henry VIII as a defence against invasion from France, still stands guard over the bay, looking across the River Fowey to St Mawes Castle (1540–43) and commanding several other fine vistas.

Falmouth

There is another treat in store for garden lovers at the magnificent ★ **Glendurgan Garden** (5 miles south) with its many different varieties of tree, rare conifers, rhododendrons and meadow flowers.

The Lizard peninsula (12 miles south) is the most southerly point of Britain. The landscape of steep and rugged coasts, fishing villages and sandy bays, retains something of its ancient character, its beauty owed to the rocks of which it is formed. Green serpentine mixed in with gneiss and red granite, often clothed with gorse and heather, contributes to a delightful medley of colour. For centuries the fisherfolk of the Lizard made a lucrative second living from the spoils of reef piracy, looting the many ships wrecked on the treacherous rocky shores. The first lighthouse on Lizard Point, the southern tip of the peninsula, was only constructed in 1752. Near the village of Mullion a small obelisk-shaped tower commemorates Guglielmo Marconi (1874–1937), the inventor of wireless telegraphy, who made the first successful trans-Atlantic radio transmission from here in 1901. The village of Lizard is a popular seaside resort where the local green serpentine is always one of the favourite souvenirs. Spectacular natural scenery abounds along the 5 miles of sand and pebble beach at Porthleven Sands, and on the cliff path from

★ **The Lizard**

St Michael's Mount

Lizard Point to Kynance Cove (sandy beach) and Mullion Point. The parish church (15th–16th c.) at Mullion is of interest, not only for its 13th c. font and carved 16th c. pews, but also for the dog-flap in the south porch, which enabled the local sheepdogs to run in and out minding their flocks while their masters attended church.

Helston

On May 8th each year Helston (8 miles; pop. 10,800) is the scene of the traditional Furry (or Floral) Dance, centre-piece of a folk festival with participants in period costume. At other times this medieval "Stannary" town, where smelted tin was once weighed and taxed, is a quiet market town, with many 18th and 19th c. buildings and a folk museum in the Old Butter Market.

Godolphin House

This Tudor country house (8 miles north-west) belonged to the powerful Godolphin family. Francis Godolphin (1534–1608) in particular wielded considerable influence, investing heavily in the tin mines. Staunch supporters of the Stuart cause, the family later gave shelter to the fugitive Charles II.

★ St Michael's Mount

In 1050 Edward the Confessor made a gift of St Michael's Mount (6 miles west) to the Benedictine monks of Mont St Michel in Normandy, who thereby acquired a sister monastery on the 230 ft-high granite rock. In 1425 the monastery reverted to the Crown, being transformed into a fortress for the defence of the bay. After the Civil War it came into the possession of the St Aubyn family, in whose hands it remained until taken over by the National Trust in 1954. Generally speaking the setting of St Michael's Mount is more attractive than its buildings. It can be reached on foot at low tide but otherwise by boat. A steep path takes visitors up to the 15th c. tower, after inspecting which a number of rooms with 17th and 18th c. furnishings can also be seen.

Penzance (3 miles west; pop. 18,500), the largest of the towns on the Cornish Riviera, is a lively resort and shopping centre which attracts visitors in the winter months as well as in the summer. At one time it was an important market town and seaport. Sacked by the Spaniards in 1595, it degenerated into little more than a haven for smugglers where, in the 18th c., the freebooters were even able to appoint the mayor – a period memorably recalled in Gilbert and Sullivan's comic opera "The Pirates of Penzance". Subtropical plants are everywhere in evidence, particularly in Morrab Gardens and Penlee Park but also along the attractive promenade. The main street, Market Jew Street, climbs from the railway station to Market House (1836–38), next to which stands a statue of Humphrey Davy, inventor of the miner's safety lamp. Chapel Street has several interesting buildings, among them the Egyptian House (c. 1835; a strange piece of architectural exotica), the Union Hotel from where the first public announcement of Nelson's victory at Trafalgar was made, and the "Admiral Benbow", an old smugglers' tavern.

★ **Penzance**

From Penzance there are ferry and helicopter services to the Scilly Isles (see entry).

North-west of Penzance (4 miles) are found several prehistoric monuments and remains, among them **Lanyon Quoit**, a Neolithic chambered tomb dating from 4000 BC, and the village at ★ **Chysauster** where eight houses, built between 100 BC and AD 250, stand in two rows. Other prehistoric stone relics in the area include Men-an-Tol and Chun Castle.

The early 19th c. Romantic admiration for nature found delightful expression in ★ **Trengwainton Garden** (2 miles north-west of Penzance), many of the plants, such as the special varieties of magnolia, being seen nowhere else in England. The rhododendrons are at their best in early summer, adding a brilliant riot of colour.

Like Penzance, the fishing village of Mousehole (pronounced "muzzle", 5 miles south-west) was razed by the Spaniards in 1595. The miseries subsequently endured by its inhabitants must have helped preserve their Cornishness, since the old Celtic language was still spoken here into the 18th c. A tombstone in the church, dated 1709, bears a Cornish inscription. Today Mousehole is very much a tourist village.

Mousehole

More prehistoric remains are found near Lamorna village (4 miles south-west) and the very attractive Lamorna Cove. The "Merry Maidens" and the "Pipers" are a circle of fifteen megaliths, about 13 ft high, and nine stones, about 3 ft high. Legend holds them to be dancers and musicians turned to stone for making merry on a Sunday.

Lamorna

The village of St Buryan (3 miles west; pop. 3200) nestles in the shadow of its 14th c. fortified church, with a granite tower 98 ft high (excellent view). Among several features of interest are the Celtic crosses and small porch outside and the 15th c. font and slate tombstone (17th c.) inside.

St Buryan

The open-air Minack Theatre not far from Porthcurno (3 miles southwest) was created in 1932. Performances take place from the end of May to September against a splendid backdrop of attractive coastal scenery. The nearby Logan Rock (rocking-stone) offers a magnificent view.

Porthcurno

Land's End is the most westerly point of England – apart, that is, from the Scilly Isles (see entry), visible from the headland in clear weather. The often bizarre granite rock formations carved in the 200 ft-high wave-battered cliffs are best seen from the clifftop walk. During the summer months Land's End attracts large numbers of visitors and a fee is charged for access.

★ **Land's End**

The rather dismal industrial landscape of the former tin-mining town of St Just (6 miles north) is in sharp contrast to the magnificence of the scenery at nearby Cape Cornwall, where there is another opportunity to enjoy a walk along the cliffs.

Cape Cornwall

Zennor

Around the village of Zennor (8 miles north-east), where D. H. Lawrence and Frieda von Richthofen briefly resided in 1916, are a number of very ancient dolmens, the most impressive being the Zennor Quoit.

★St Ives

Both the town of St Ives (5 miles north-east; pop. 9500) and its parish church are named after St Ia, a female Irish missionary who brought Christianity to the area in the 5th c. Up until the 19th c. the inhabitants chiefly lived by harvesting pilchards from the sea. In 1883 St Ives was "discovered" by the painter James Whistler and his pupil Walter Sickert, in whose footsteps numerous other artists have since followed. The architect and still-life painter Ben Nicholson, his wife the sculptress Barbara Hepworth (1903–75), and the potter Bernard Leach are among the famous 20th c. artists to have made their homes there. The Barbara Hepworth Museum and Sculpture Garden has an excellent collection of her abstract sculptures. Another work by Hepworth, "Madonna and Child" (1953), adorns the Lady Chapel of the 15th c. St Ia's Church, which also boasts a modern font. The new Tate Gallery, which exhibits modern art related to Cornwall, adds further to the interest of the town.

Redruth, Camborne

The years since 1920 have seen Redruth and Camborne (13 miles north-east; combined pop. 27,000) surrender their one-time leadership of the copper and tin mining industries to the Far East. In the 17th and 18th centuries a number of famous Non-conformist preachers, including the Quaker George Fox (1624–91) and the Methodist John Wesley (1703–91), were active among the mine workers. Some of the old mines in the area have been turned into leisure attractions (Poldark Tin Mine). Typical old engine-houses, equipped with the high-pressure steam engines which once made Cornish tin mining so highly productive, can still be seen in the Cornish Engines Museum at Pool.

Perranporth

Once a fishing village and haunt of smugglers, Perranporth (10 miles north-east) is now a popular holiday resort with over 3 miles of sandy coastline. A pleasant path leads to the 7th c. St Piran's Oratory which for hundreds of years lay buried in the sands (St Piran was an Irish saint reputed to have crossed the sea on a millstone). A second, equally pleasant path goes to St Agnes Beacon, a lighthouse standing 690 ft above the sea and enjoying magnificent all-round views.

Newquay

Newquay (8 miles north-east; pop. 15,400) is one Cornwall's best-loved resorts, its sandy beaches proving irresistible to large numbers of holidaymakers. Beautifully situated on the open Fistral Bay, the town has a great many Victorian buildings and offers a variety of interesting excursions in the surrounding area. These include visits to the remains of a 9th–11th c. Celtic village at Mawgan Porth, the intriguing rock scenery of the coastal nature reserve at Bedruthan Steps, and Trerice Manor, an Elizabethan manor with a fine 16th c. stucco ceiling.

Padstow

Padstow (11 miles; pop. 2800) on the Camel estuary was at one time the only safe harbour on the north Cornish coast. It was sacked by the Vikings in 981. Over four hundred years earlier, in the 6th c., St Petroc had brought Christianity to the area. The 13th c. parish church, dedicated to the saint, has a 15th c. font carved with apostles and angels by the Master of St Endellion (see below). Some 16th c. stone houses – one being Raleigh Court where Sir Walter Raleigh collected taxes while an official of the Crown – still stand on the North and South Quays of the harbour, from which considerable tonnages of fish and china clay were once shipped. Both the walk over the cliffs to Trevone (charming sandy bay) and the boat trip along the rocky coast make pleasant outings. The May Day dance festival known as the Padstow 'Obby 'Oss (Hobby Horse) is a great attraction, involving a procession, horses, both real and imitation, and music making.

"Tea time" in Lanhydrock House

The Perpendicular parish church in the small village of St Endellion (13 **St Endellion**
miles north-east; pop. 1150) has outstanding stone carving by the crafts-
man known as the Master of St Endellion (15th c.)

The town of Bodmin (10 miles south-east; pop. 12,000) replaced **Bodmin**
Launceston as county town of Cornwall in 1835. Its origins go back to a
monastery founded by the missionary St Petroc who, arriving in the area
around 530, remained until his death in 564. The present parish church
(1469–72), dedicated to the saint, is the largest in the county. It possesses one of the most beautiful Norman fonts (12th c.) in Cornwall, supported by four cherubim and decorated with the tree of life and
allegories of Good (east side) and Evil (west side). There are also two
German panel paintings (*c.* 1500), a magnificent marble monument to
Prior Thomas Vivian (1533), and numerous slate tomb-slabs, including
that of Richard Durant, his two wives and 20 children (1632).
★ **Lanhydrock House**, 3 miles south of Bodmin, is well worth visiting.
Originally a Jacobean manor, it was largely rebuilt after a fire in 1881. The
north wing, however, survived undamaged and has a superb plaster ceiling (*c.* 1642) decorated with scenes from the Old Testament. The drawing
room has 18th furnishings, including a portrait by George Romney, the
morning room splendid tapestries from the Mortlake works (17th c.). The
old kitchen fittings and equipment are a delight for anyone interested in
cookery. A magnificent avenue of yews enhances the lovely park.

Together with Liskeard, Helston and Truro, Lostwithiel (6 miles south) **Lostwithiel**
was one of the four Cornish "Stannary" towns where tin could be
weighed and stamped. The parish church, St Bartholomew's, has an
interesting 14th c. font with carvings showing falconry and wildlife.
Lostwithiel's chief attraction, however, is Restormel Castle, a massive
ruined fortress (12th–13th c.) perched high above the River Fowey.

Tintagel: King Arthur's "Castle" ...   *... and the Victorian Post Office*

★**Bodmin Moor**	Bodmin Moor (6 miles north-east of Bodmin), an area of barren, craggy moorland crowned with granite tors, lies at the heart of the narrow Cornish peninsula. It is a fascinating landscape, offering excellent walking. The highest point is Brown Willy (1375 ft), from which there are extensive views. The moor is dotted with standing stones and other monuments of various periods. The inn at Bolventor, a small village in the centre of the Moor, achieved fame as the "Jamaica Inn" of Daphne du Maurier's (1907–89) novel of that name. Cornwall often features in her work.
★**St Neot**	The village of St Neot, on the southern edge of the Moor, has a parish church (1425) with twelve outstanding 15th and 16th c. stained glass windows.
Altarnun	On the north side of the Moor, the 15th c. parish church at Altarnun (pop. 2200) is dedicated to St Nona, mother of St David of Wales. A 6th c. Celtic cross in the graveyard below the 108 ft tower recalls the saint's missionary activities. Inside the church are a Norman font, decorated with rosettes and bearded faces; some particularly noteworthy early 16th c. benches, beautifully carved with a mixture of religious and secular motifs (e.g. the Passion, bagpipe players, male sirens, etc.); and a fine, wide, 15th c. choir screen.
Camelford	The tiny, legend-surrounded, market town of Camelford (13 miles north of Bodmin; pop. 1880) is assumed by many to be Camelot, where King Arthur had his court. It is also the location of the very interesting North Cornwall Museum of Rural Life.
Tintagel	Tintagel (8 miles north-west) is probably the best known village in Cornwall, thanks to its association with the story of King Arthur and the

Holy Grail. The link with the Arthurian legend was first made by Geoffrey of Monmouth in his "Historia Regum Britanniae" (1136), in which **Tintagel Castle** is said to be King Arthur's birthplace. Since then numerous other writers have followed Geoffrey's lead. Little remains now to inspire the imagination; only a few pieces of wall from the castle which Reginald, Earl of Cornwall, bastard son of Henry I, built on the storm-swept cliffs in about 1145, and some ruins of a 6th c. monastery.

Of rather greater interest at Tintagel are the ★**Victorian Post Office**, in a much weathered 14th c. stone house with slate roof, and the parish church, standing alone a short distance from the village. The old post office in particular is always crowded with visitors in summer.

There is a beautiful clifftop walk to Boscastle, squeezed between cliffs constantly lashed by the waves. One of the old grey houses with tall slate roofs contains a Museum of Witchcraft.

Boscastle

Bude (18 miles north-east; pop. 6000) is a modern resort with a long sandy beach. If the sea is rough take care when walking along the breakwater, especially at high tide. Compass Point is well-known for its splendid views.

Bude

Stratton (2 miles east; pop. 1288), an ancient village with some thatched cottages and a market, boasts a 14th–15th c. parish church. Inside are a very fine Norman font, a pulpit made in 1544, and an east window by Burne-Jones (19th c.).

Stratton

Morwenstow (6 miles north; pop. 620), most northerly village in Cornwall, also possesses an interesting little church, St John the Baptist. Standing in solitary splendour on the cliffs, it has a lovely columned Norman porch. Robert Stephen Hawker (1803–75), an eccentric clergyman, built the vicarage, giving it unusual chimneys modelled on the church towers of places he had lived. He was also known for his dedicated ministry to the unfortunate victims of shipwreck.

Morwenstow

Until 1835, Launceston (24 miles south-east; pop. 6100) was Cornwall's county town. Founded in medieval times, it grew up in the shadow of the huge Norman castle, which stood guarding the border with Devon. The now ruined castle was begun soon after the Conquest by William's half brother, Robert de Mortain, first Earl of Cornwall. In the town, intricately carved reliefs decorate the granite exterior of St Mary Magdalene (1511) – coats of arms, palm leaves and flowers, and, in a niche below the east window, the reclining figure of Mary with instrument-playing angels. Inside the church are some interesting stone and bronze tombstones and an early 16th c. polychrome wooden pulpit.

Launceston

Cotehele House (14 miles south-east), a mainly Tudor manor-house with some earlier (15th c.) gates and towers, has original furnishings dating back to Stuart times; also 17th–18th c. tapestries. The spacious terraced garden is charming.

★**Cotehele House**

Leaving Cornwall for Devon at the end of the tour, head either east towards the famous Dartmoor (see entry) or south to the port of Plymouth (see entry) and the coast.

Cotswolds   I 9

Southern England. County: Oxfordshire

The Cotswolds, a range of low limestone hills forming the watershed between the Thames and Severn basins, lie between the M4 (London to Bristol) and A40 (Oxford to Gloucester), bounded on the west by the M5. They extend from Chipping Campden in the north to Bath in the south, a distance of some 55 miles, and are 24 miles across from east to west, reaching a maximum height of 1070 ft. Fully justifying their designation as "an area of outstanding natural beauty", they provide splendid walking country, where beech woods alternate with pastureland grazed by vast flocks of sheep renowned for the quality of their wool.

Sheep-farming has a long tradition in the Cotswolds, having been introduced in the 12th c. by the monastic houses. Wool brought prosperity to the region, a prosperity still reflected today in the splendid churches paid for by wealthy wool-merchants, and the trim villages and little towns. Nearly all are built of the local honey-coloured, weather-resistant oolitic limestone, as are the low walls which divide the fields – though many of these have been removed with the expansion of wheat-growing at the expense of sheep-farming.

Cirencester

Cirencester (pop. 16,100), an ancient city at the meeting-place of five Roman roads, makes a good starting point for tours through some interesting parts of the Cotswolds. Much Roman material, the fruits of excavation, can be seen in the excellent Corinium Museum. In medieval times Cirencester was the largest wool market in England, a fact reflected in its having one of the richest and finest parish churches in the country, St John the Baptist, with an imposing tower (c. 1400). Particularly notable is the beautifully carved three-storeyed south porch; there is also fine fan vaulting in St Catherine's Chapel and some good stained glass. Cirencester Park, home of Earl Bathurst, has beautiful grounds, with a 5 mile-long avenue of chestnut trees. Not far away is another mansion, Barnsley House, dating from 1657, the beautiful garden of which is well worth a visit.

Cirencester: the Parish Church of St John the Baptist

From Cirencester the A419 runs west through Oakley Woods, passes close to Sapperton, with Daneway House, a manor-house of the 14th–17th c., and then enters the ★ **"Golden Valley"** of the Stroudwater, with many cloth factories. Stroud (pop. 20,100), a lively modern town 12 miles from Cirencester, was once a prominent centre of the textile trade. 2 miles south is **Woodchester**, with an old Dominican abbey and large Roman villa, the latter having been excavated to reveal well-preserved mosaic floors.

Stroud

4 miles north of Stroud on the A46 lies Painswick (pop. 1750), with many handsome stone-built houses dating from the great days of the wool trade. The churchyard boasts more than a hundred fine yews.

Painswick

6 miles beyond Painswick on the A46 a short detour can be made to Birdlip on the A417. From here, on the crest of the Cotswolds' steep western escarpment, there is a beautiful view of the Severn valley.

Birdlip

The A46 continues north-east to Cheltenham (see Gloucester). Take the B4632 to Winchcombe (13 miles; pop. 4500), an attractive old Cotswolds town built of grey sandstone. The church, in the Late Perpendicular style (1490), contains carvings from the earlier Benedictine abbey (founded *c.* 800), of which nothing now remains.

Close by stands **Sudeley Castle**, once the home of Henry VIII's widow Catherine Parr (died 1548), who later married Lord Seymour of Sudeley; it stands in very beautiful gardens.

★ **Cheltenham**

South-east of Winchcombe, on a hilltop some 1000 ft high, is Belas Knap, a Neolithic chambered cairn.

Belas Knap

2 miles north-east is Hailes Abbey, once a great Cistercian house but now reduced to only a few scanty remains. Adjoining is a small archaeological museum.

Hailes Abbey

3 miles further along the B4632 in the direction of Broadway a visit can be made to two picturesque little villages, Stanton, with a street lined by 16th–17th c. houses, many of them lovingly restored, and the equally attractive Stanway. Both villages have Tudor manor-houses.

Stanton, Stanway

Broadway (pop. 2000), at the foot of the Cotswolds, is a good centre from which to explore the surrounding area on foot, with the added lure of picturesque old inns and numerous antique shops. With its wide, busy main street and its many Elizabethan houses, Broadway is one of the most attractive of the Cotswold towns. Among the finest houses are Abbot's Grange, the Tudor House, and the Lygon Arms.

From Broadway the A44 runs south-east, soon climbing in the direction of Stow-on-the-Wold. At nearby Guiting Power the **Cotswold Farm Park** has a collection of rare British breeds. **Fish Hill** (1024 ft), with the Beacon Tower, is famous for its panoramic views; it is said that in good weather thirteen counties can be seen.

From the A44, here following a fairly winding course, a side road goes off left to Chipping Campden, the most northerly point in the Cotswolds and one of the prettiest and most appealing little towns in England.

★ **Broadway**

Chipping Campden (pop. 2000) was once the centre of the wool trade, home in the 14th and 15th c. to many wealthy wool-merchants, who built themselves magnificent houses in the town. The finest (late 14th c.) belonged to William Grevel, referred to by a commemorative brass in the 15th c. church as "the flower of the merchants of all England". Other outstanding buildings are the Town Hall, the Woolstaplers' Hall (partly 14th c.), the old Grammar School (1628), the Market Hall (1625) and the late 14th c. almshouses. 3 miles north is Hidcote Manor, with a beautiful garden.

Chipping Campden

Rejoining the A44 the route then continues by way of **Chastleton House**, a large Jacobean mansion built by a wool merchant in about 1610, with beautiful old furniture and other items of interest, set in a magnificent garden, to Chipping Norton, another wool town.

Chipping Norton

Some 3 miles outside the town are the ★ **Rollright Stones**, a famous Bronze Age stone circle, less impressive than the larger monuments at Avebury and Stonehenge (see entries) but in a very beautiful setting. There are about 70 stones in the main circle, known as the King's men, together with a burial chamber called the Whispering Knights and the isolated King Stone.

Stow-on-the-Wold

West of Chipping Norton is Stow-on-the-Wold (pop. 1600), a small town situated at the meeting-place of eight roads, with a spacious market square in which several big sheep markets are held every year. **Abbotswood**, 1 mile west, is famous for its beautiful park. The return to Cirencester (10 miles) is by way of Northleach and Chedworth Roman Villa (AD 180–350; 4½ miles south), one of the best preserved in the country, with mosaic floors, baths, hypocausts and a museum containing finds from the site.

Tetbury

The carefully restored **Close Hotel** in Tetbury (3 miles south-west of Cirencester) was once the home (known as "The Close") of Sir Thomas Estcourt, a wealthy wool merchant. Over 400 years old, it is a splendid example of a stone-built Cotswold manor-house.

Malmesbury

Malmesbury (5 miles south-east; pop. 2900), another small wool town, was the birthplace of the philosopher Thomas Hobbes (1588–1679). High Street and Horsefair Street both have attractive 17th c. gabled houses and there is also a fine medieval market cross (c. 1500). St John's

Tetbury: "The Close"

Hospital dates from the mid 13th c. The most noteworthy building in the town, however, is the Abbey Church, remnant of Malmesbury's once powerful Benedictine abbey. Its history can almost certainly be traced back to an even earlier foundation, dating from the end of the 7th c. – the first abbot was St Adhelm who died in 709 – and later rebuilt by King Athelstan (died 940) whose alleged tomb can be seen in the church. All that now survives of the old Benedictine abbey church are six of the original nine bays of the Norman-Early English nave (c. 1150). The central tower collapsed in the 16th c., followed by the west tower, after which the east end too fell into ruin. The columned Norman south porch with its quite outstanding sculptures remains as the show-piece of the church today. The Saxon font and the organ (1714) also deserve mention.

About 10 miles further south, Chippenham (pop. 19,000) is the site of one of the biggest livestock markets in the country. The town has many 16th and 17th c. half-timbered houses, of which the finest is the Old Yelde Hall (16th c.) on the Market Place. Until 1841 it was the town hall and is now the local history museum. Also worth seeing are the handsome Ivy House (about 1730; Bath Road) and the Late-Gothic St Andrew's Church, altered in the 19th c. The South Chapel contains tombs of the Hungerford family. **Chippenham**

Neighbouring Castle Combe (5 miles west) is one of the prettiest Cotswold villages, with rows of picturesque medieval houses, a 13th–15th c. parish church (St Andrew's; 14th c. font), the elegant Manor House (14th–18th c.; now a hotel) and, contrasting with it, Water Lane and the old weavers' houses. ★Castle Combe

Sheldon Manor (2 miles west of Chippenham) is famous for its collection of Nailsea glass as well as for its roses.

Coventry   K 8

Central England. County: West Midlands
Altitude: 295 ft. Population: 335,000

Coventry, a centre of the British textiles trade ever since the Middle Ages, also has a long tradition in the motor and aeronautical industries, for which reason it was targeted by the German Luftwaffe early in the Second World War. A massive bombing raid in 1940 left the city centre almost completely destroyed. Of the old Cathedral nothing but a few fragments remained. They are now incorporated into the new Cathedral built after the war, an acknowledged masterpiece of modern architecture. The rebuilding of the city itself, with fine open squares, wide streets and pedestrian zones, is an excellent example of contemporary town planning.

History Coventry grew up in the 11th c. under the protection of a monastic house founded by Leofric, Earl of Mercia. Tradition has it that the Earl's wife, Lady Godiva, interceded with her hard-hearted husband on behalf of the people of Coventry, for relief from the heavy taxes he imposed. He in turn agreed to lighten his demands, if she rode naked through the streets of the town. This she did, the grateful citizens steadfastly refusing to peer from their windows, with the single exception of "Peeping Tom" who later recounted the story. By the 14th c. Coventry's woollen industry had already established a reputation for its trade fairs; soon it prospered further, developing into a major textile centre. In the 17th c., however, the economy began to decline, a process which continued until engineering, in the shape of sewing machine, bicycle and motor manufacture, brought about a revival of its fortunes in the mid 19th c.

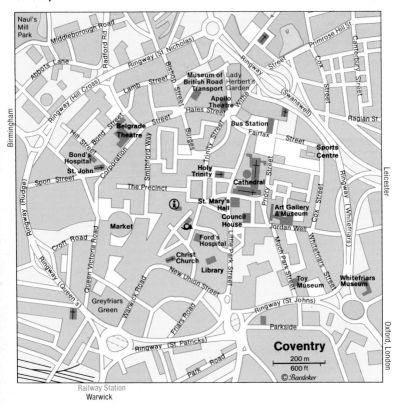

Railway Station
Warwick

Broadgate	The traditional centre of the city, Broadgate, has been replanned as a spacious square, with a statue of Lady Godiva (by W. Reid Dick) in the centre. Broadgate House, at the south-west end of the square, has a clock on which Lady Godiva appears on the stroke of the hour, with Peeping Tom at a window above.
Holy Trinity Church	Holy Trinity Church, at the north-east corner of Broadgate, has one of the three slender spires which are Coventry's best known landmarks. The spire of Holy Trinity, constructed in 1166, is 327 ft high. The church, in Perpendicular style, has very beautiful windows, a stone pulpit of about 1470 and interesting tapestries woven for the coronation of Elizabeth II. Priory Row, close by, is a charming little street of half-timbered houses. Behind Holy Trinity rise the new Cathedral and the ruins of the old.
★★Coventry Cathedral	The **old Cathedral**, originally one of the largest parish churches in England (Perpendicular; 1373–1433), was elevated to cathedral status only in 1918. After the bombing only parts of the external walls survived, together with the slender, 303 ft-high spire, still a glorious example of Late-Gothic embellishment. At the east end, a cross fashioned from two charred beams is a poignant symbol and reminder of the devastation. The sacristies were rebuilt after the war with the help of young German volunteers.

Coventry Cathedral

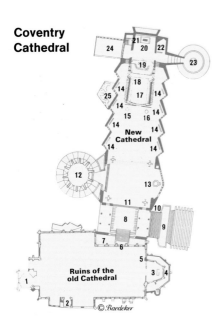

1 Tower
2 Haigh Chapel
3 Cross made from charred beams
4 International Centre
5 Figure of Christ
6 Queen's Staircase
7 Entrance to the Crypt
8 Porch
9 St Michael's Steps
10 St Michael and Lucifer
11 Engraved glass screen
12 Chapel of Unity
13 Font
14 Tablets of the Word
15 Pulpit
16 Lectern
17 Choir
18 Bishop's throne
19 High Altar
20 Lady Chapel
21 Tapestry
22 Chapel of Christ in Gethsemane
23 Chapel of Christ the Servant (Chapel of Industry)
24 Refectory
25 Ruins of the Benedictine Monastery

A tall, canopied porch on the north side links the old cathedral ruins with the modern ★★St Michael's Cathedral, designed by Sir Basil Spence and erected between 1956 and 1962. At the south-east end, on the outer wall of the nave, to the right of the entrance, is a bronze by Jacob Epstein, "St Michael subduing the Devil". The nave itself, 420 ft long and orientated north-south, can seat a congregation of 2000. The walls are built in zigzag fashion, the offset concrete panels alternating with windows facing towards the altar. The vast concrete ceiling is broken up by the diamond pattern of its ribs.

Taking the place of the usual west end is a huge glass screen, engraved with figures of angels, saints and patriarchs by John Hutton. Its effect is to create a striking visual link both with the old cathedral ruins and the people going about their business in the streets of the town. Another most impressive feature of the interior is the baptistery, with a font hewn from a rough stone block brought from Bethlehem, and a great stained glass window, the **Sunburst Window**, by John Piper, centred on the radiant sun which symbolises the Holy Ghost. The ten stained glass panels in the walls of the nave, designed by Lawrence Lee, Geoffrey Clark and Keith New, are set at an angle so as to be fully visible only from the Choir. In their spectrum of colours, from yellow through red to blue and violet, they symbolise the journey of man from birth through death to resurrection. Geoffrey Clarke's "Cross of Nails" behind the altar is made out of three medieval nails from the ruined cathedral, yet another powerful symbol, this time of reconciliation. At the north end hangs a huge **tapestry** (75 × 38 ft) in glowing colour showing Christ in Glory surrounded by four beasts mentioned in the Revelation of St John. Designed by Graham Sutherland, it was woven near Aubusson in France.

The **Chapel of Unity** is intended to represent accord between the Church of England and the Free Churches. The mosaic floor was a gift from the Church of Sweden; the stained glass windows came from Germany.

St Mary's Hall	One building fortunate enough to survive the bombing was the 15th c. St Mary's Hall immediately south of the cathedral, headquarters of the Merchants' Guild since 1342. The Great Hall (1394–1414) has impressive oak vaulting and a tapestry believed to depict Henry VII's visit to Coventry in 1500. **Caesar's Tower** (13th c.; adjoining the Hall) was rebuilt after war damage.
★ Ford's Hospital	The most interesting of the surviving half-timbered buildings is Ford's Hospital in Greyfriars Lane, an almshouse for five poor married couples. Founded in 1509 it was restored in 1953.
Greyfriars Abbey	Of Greyfriars Monastery, destroyed in 1539, there survives only the beautiful steeple, now incorporated in Christ Church. The dormitory and cloister of the Whitefriars Monastery have been restored and house a local museum. Bablake Old School (1560) is also worth seeing.
★ Bond's Hospital	The picturesque Bond's Hospital, a half-timbered almshouse for elderly men was founded in 1506. A small section of the town walls of 1356 has been preserved between Cook Street Gate and Swanswell Gate, the only two of the town's original twelve gates which survive.
Herbert Art Gallery and Museum	As well as works by native British painters, the Herbert Art Gallery and Museum has sections on local social and folk history, the early stages of industrialisation in the Coventry area, and documents on the history of Coventry itself.
British Road Transport Museum	The British Road Transport Museum provides a fascinating account of the history of road transport in Britain.

Surroundings

★ **Kenilworth Castle**	Kenilworth Castle (5 miles south-west) was built in 1120 by Geoffrey de Clinton, Treasurer of England in the reign of Henry I, and enlarged by Elizabeth I's favourite Robert Dudley, Earl of Leicester. The castle, constructed of red sandstone, was formerly surrounded by a lake. Elizabeth often stayed here, Leicester on one occasion arranging for her the three week-long entertainment described in Sir Walter Scott's "Kenilworth". The friendship lasted until the Earl's death in 1588; his tomb is in St Mary's Church in Warwick. Even in ruin the castle is highly impressive, with its walls and towers surrounding the bailey, the old half-timbered stables and the Norman keep. The Great Hall, the White Hall, the private apartments and the Audience Chamber all date from the period when the castle belonged to the Earls and Dukes of Lancaster. The parish church of Kenilworth, with a Norman doorway, adjoins the remains of Kenilworth Priory, founded in 1126 by Geoffrey de Clinton.

Dartmoor   G/H 10

South-west England. County: Devon

In most people's minds, mention of Dartmoor conjures up images of wild ponies, the notorious prison at Princetown, and Sir Arthur Conan Doyle's "The Hound of the Baskervilles". It covers by far the greater part of south-west Devon, an area rich in legend and redolent with history, where the barren hills with their granite outcrops (tors) display a rugged grandeur. The desolate wastes of moor and heathland average some 90 in. of rainfall a year, considerably more than most other parts of England. In 1949, 365 sq. miles of the former royal hunting preserve were designated a national park, extending from Okehampton in the north to

Ivybridge in the south, and from Bovey Tracey in the east to Tavistock in the west. The highest points are "High Willhays" (2038 ft) and "Yes Tor" (2021 ft) near Okehampton. In addition to the vast moorland, the special charm of the scenery lies in its delightful valleys and numerous little rivers and streams, including the East and West Dart from which Dartmoor takes its name. The brooding relics of prehistory, ruins of abandoned mine workings from the early industrial era, and, above all, the impenetrable character of the moor itself, frequently blanketed in mist, have combined to give Dartmoor its rather sinister reputation and made it the subject of a host of legends and eerie ghost stories.

There are only two major roads across Dartmoor – one from Tavistock to Ashburton, the other from Yelverton by way of Princetown and Two Bridges (where it crosses the first road) to Moretonhampstead.

Postbridge "clapper bridge"

One of Dartmoor's principal features are its **"tors"**, the granite outcrops, often eroded into bizarre shapes, which jut up from the moorland. These were the source of many of the stones used in prehistoric times to make the chamber tombs, cairns and stone circles which are so numerous on Dartmoor. The true origin of some of these ancient structures is in fact unknown, several previously believed to be prehistoric having been shown to be more recent. There is similar uncertainty about the age of some of the **"clapper bridges"**, thought at one time to date from the Bronze Age (the word "clapper" derives from the Saxon word "cleaca" meaning "big stone"). The bridges consist of granite slabs spanning the river in a series of rectilinear arches.

Dartmoor's many **prehistoric sites** rank high among its attractions. One of the best preserved Bronze Age settlements can be seen at Grimspound near Manaton, where 24 circular huts are enclosed by a 10 ft-wide wall. Remains of another early village have been discovered at Great Tor. At Merrivale, near Princetown, are a menhir and several stone circles and alignments. Green Hill Row, 7 miles north-west of South Brent, is probably the longest series of burials, with more than 70 stones.

A Dartmoor Pony

Although allowed to run free throughout the year on the open moorland, the shaggy-coated **Dartmoor ponies** actually belong to various farms. The earliest known reference to these small moorland horses is by Aelfwold, Saxon Bishop of Crediton, in 1012. For centuries, until replaced by motor vehicles at the end of the 19th c., they were used as beasts of burden, carrying not only wool and granite but also lead, tin and copper from the Dartmoor mines. At one time they were somewhat larger, cross-breeding with e.g. Shetlands, thoroughbreds and hackneys having resulted in the smaller, hardy strain of mostly brown, black and grey pony. The ponies should not be fed.

Dartmoor

Note: A number of footpaths cross the National Park. It goes without saying that lighting fires is forbidden and all rubbish must be removed. Those intending to walk on the moors should heed the advice issued by the National Park authorities as regards carrying detailed maps and a compass, keeping strictly to the signposted routes and taking adequate clothing, etc.; anyone unfamiliar with the area can easily become lost. It should be remembered also that the weather can change very quickly. Car drivers must expect to encounter sheep and ponies on the road.

Moreton-hampstead, Chagford

Moretonhampstead and Chagford (pop. 1500 and 1250 respectively) are good bases from which to explore the surrounding area by car or on foot. Moretonhampstead is a small market town with a 17th c. covered market, interesting almshouses dating from 1637, and a granite church (St Andrew's). Chagford (4 miles west), on the headwaters of the River Teign close to several high granite tors, also boasts a granite church.

Situated about 2½ miles east of Chagford is Britain's newest castle, constructed between 1911 and 1930 by Sir Edwin Lutyens for a wealthy tea merchant called Julius Drewe. Built of granite, the 200 ft-long ★**Castle Drogo** has a generally medieval air, while incorporating a mixture of Norman, Romanesque, Tudor and modern elements.

Bovey Tracey

Bovey Tracey (pop. 3850), south-east of Moretonhampstead, is a popular holiday place in the Bovey Valley, with pottery and hand weaving workshops.

Postbridge

From Moretonhampstead the B3212 runs south-west to Postbridge (8 miles), where the best known of Dartmoor's ★**clapper bridges** spans the River Dart. It is now thought to have been built in the 13th c.

Bennett's Cross

The granite Bennett's Cross on the B3212 just before Postbridge is also believed to be over 500 years old.

"Tors" on Dartmoor

A drawing room in Castle Drogo

Chagford: the Parish Church   *Bennett's Cross*

En route to Postbridge a very worthwhile detour can be made south to the delightful little village of Widecombe-in-the-Moor at the foot of Hameldown Beacon (1706 ft). Immortalised in the old ballad "Widdicombe Fair", the village consists of a cluster of charming thatched cottages encircling the large St Pancras' Church (sometimes referred to as "the Cathedral of the Moor"). Church House (16th c.) has at various times been a brewery and the village school.

★ **Widecombe-in-the-Moor**

More very picturesque cottages can be seen at Buckland-in-the-Moor, a short distance further south.

Buckland-in-the-Moor

7 miles south-west of Postbridge, the two principal roads across Dartmoor meet at Two Bridges. From here a very pleasant walk goes to Wistman's Wood, an oak wood nature reserve extending for about ½ mile along the banks of the Dart.

Two Bridges

There is another walk through the lovely Cowsic valley to the ancient village of Lydford, founded in Saxon times and a place of considerable standing in the Middle Ages on account of its tin mines. At one time the Keep of Lydford's now ruined 12th c. castle was used as a prison, the first of Dartmoor's prisons but no less notorious than the later one at Princetown.

Lydford

South of Lydford nature provides some spectacular scenery in the shape of the deep, 1½ mile-long Lydford Gorge and White Lady Waterfall, where the River Lyd plummets more than 90 ft. It was here in the 17th c. that Roger Rowe's Gubbin gang wrought so much mischief, vividly described in Charles Kingsley's novel "Westward Ho" (1855).

★ **Lydford Gorge**

Princetown, the largest community on Dartmoor, is also the site of Britain's best known **prison**. Built in 1806 by French prisoners of war, it

Princetown

has served since 1850 as a penitentiary for "lifers". Details of the prison's history are available from the information office in Princetown Town Hall. St Michael's Church (completed 1813) was built by inmates of the prison. Sir Arthur Conan Doyle wrote "The Hound of the Baskervilles" in what was then the Dutchy Hotel, now the Nature Conservancy Council's information centre.

Buckland Abbey
8 miles south-west of Lydford, beyond Yelverton, stands Buckland Abbey, a former Cistercian house, founded 1278, and gifted in 1541 to Sir Richard Grenville, whose grandson made it into a country house. In 1581 it was bought by Sir Francis Drake (died 1596). It is now a museum housing an exhibition about the abbey and items of naval history, with memorabilia of Drake, including Drake's Drum.

Tavistock
In former days Tavistock (5 miles north-west) prospered through a combination of tin and wool; St Eustace's (14th/15th c.) and the Guildhall (1848) were both built by subscription from local tin barons and clothmakers. On the Plymouth (see entry) road, just south-west of the town, a statue (1883) by J. E. Boehm commemorates Sir Francis Drake, born at nearby Crowndale Farm in 1540.

Ashburton
Ashburton (pop. 3550), on the southern edge of Dartmoor, also flourished in the heydey of tin-mining and the woollen trade. A number of interesting buildings survive, including some handsome 17th and 18th c. houses and a 14th–15th c. granite church with a very beautiful tower.

Buckfast Abbey
From Ashburton a detour can be made to Totnes, which lies off Dartmoor. The road passes close to Buckfastleigh (pop. 2530) and Buckfast Abbey, on the banks of the Dart. Originally a Benedictine foundation (1018), the abbey was taken over by the Cistercians in 1147. In 1882 the Benedictines re-established themselves there, subsequently building a large new church (1907–37).

Totnes
Totnes (pop. 5700), further down the Dart valley, is an interesting old town of narrow winding streets and gabled houses. Parts of the old town walls have been preserved, including the East and North Gates. The Guildhall (rebuilt 1611), is a relic of the Norman abbey. St Mary's Church (mid 15th c.) has a notable west tower and a very beautiful rood-screen. The main surviving feature of the castle is the Norman keep, from which there is a fine view. The town was formerly an important wool town and is still a busy shopping centre for the whole surrounding area. There are boats from Totnes to Dartmouth.

Derby   K 8

Central England
County: Derby
Altitude: 200 ft. Population: 218,000

Derby is an industrial city noted mainly for its Rolls-Royce works and large china manufactories. It lies on the west bank of the Derwent not far from its junction with the Trent. The town flourished during the Industrial Revolution of the 18th c. and preserves many buildings of that period, particularly in the centre. It has a notable cathedral. Derby is a good centre from which to explore the Peak District (see entry), now a national park.

History The Roman fort of Derventio lay on the opposite bank of the Derwent at Little Chester. In 1715 John Lombe built the first silk-mill in England here, and in 1756 William Duesbury founded the first porcelain manufactory. Thereafter silk and porcelain brought the town prosperity, and it grew rapidly. In 1877 the Royal Crown Derby Porcelain Company was established, reviving the manufacture of porcelain. Derby's involvement in the motor industry began in 1906 with the founding of Rolls-Royce by Frederick Henry Royce; the company began exporting cars almost immediately.

The church of All Saints became the Cathedral in 1927. The tower, built 1508–27, is 210 ft high; the church itself was remodelled by James Gibbs in 1722–25. It contains the tombs of Bess of Hardwick (Elizabeth Countess of Shrewsbury, died 1608) and Henry Cavendish.

Cathedral

The museum has several interesting sections. One is devoted to the town's history and includes a Bonnie Prince Charles Room, with wood panelling from Exeter House where the Young Pretender lodged in 1745. Others cover the growth of technology, with e.g. a model of the Midland Railway, local archaeology, and the region's flora and fauna. The adjoining art gallery has a collection of 24 paintings by local artist Joseph Wright (1734–97), or Wright of Derby as he is usually known; also displays of precious porcelain.

Derby Museum and Art Gallery

The Market Place, Irongate and Friargate, the latter spanned by a Victorian railway bridge, all retain some fine Georgian houses. The modern Eagle Centre with its shops, market and theatre makes a stark contrast. Also noteworthy are the County Hall (1660) and Assembly Rooms (1764). The Industrial Museum (a short distance north-west; Rolls-Royce aero engines, etc.) occupies a former silk mill founded in 1717. Entrance is through an elaborate wrought iron gate (1728) by Robert Blakewell.

Kedleston Hall (4½ miles north-west; near Quarndon), home of the Curzon family, is probably the finest Adam house in England, having been refashioned by Robert and James Adam in about 1760. Its principal feature is the great marble hall, with 20 pink alabaster pillars; there is much fine furniture by Chippendale and other leading cabinet-makers of the day. The north front, with six Corinthian columns, was built by James Paine at the end of the 17th c. Also worth seeing are the "Indian Museum" and the chapel (12th c.).

★Kedleston Hall

The open-air tram museum at Crich (12½ miles north) carries the visitor back to an almost forgotten era. Its collection of more than 40 horse-drawn, steam-powered and electric trams, gathered together from all over the world, provides a unique glimpse into the history of the tram from 1873 to 1953.

★National Tramway Museum

Melbourne (6 miles south; pop. 3600), a charming little town, possesses a very beautiful Early Norman church (St Michael and St Mary) with three towers.

Melbourne Hall, a seat of the Marquis of Lothian, dates from the 16th c., but with an 18th c. extension. The art collection and furniture are well worth the visit, as also is the magnificent park with rare old trees.

Melbourne

Repton (8 miles south-west of Derby; pop. 1850) is noted for its public school, founded in 1557. The **School Museum**, housed in part of a 12th c. Augustinian priory incorporated into the school buildings, contains interesting exhibits relating to the history of the village. St Wystan's Church has a Late Saxon crypt (10th c.).
Foremark Hall, a Palladian mansion in Foremark (2 miles east of Repton), was built in 1760. The 17th c. St Saviour's Church (Perpendicular exterior) is also noteworthy, having a three-tier pulpit and wrought-iron choir screens by Robert Bakewell.

Repton

Burton-upon-Trent

Burton-upon-Trent (10 miles south-west of Derby; pop. 59,000) is a famous brewing town. The monks of Burton Abbey (founded 1002, now almost completely destroyed) were the first to appreciate the excellent beer-making qualities of its water, a discovery which in later centuries led to the establishment of numerous breweries.

Sudbury Hall

As well as being superbly appointed, Sudbury Hall (17th c.; 12 miles west) contains a Museum of Childhood with a marvellous collection of old toys.

Stoke-on-Trent

Stoke-on-Trent (15 miles north-west), a conurbation created in 1910 by the amalgamation of six towns, lies at the heart of the Potteries, the area where Britain's ceramics industry is based. Many internationally famous porcelain manufacturers, including Wedgwood, Royal Doulton and Spode, have their roots here. Several companies offer factory tours; visitors can watch British porcelain being made using traditional as well as modern methods.

Opened in 1981, the ★**City Museum** and adjoining **Art Gallery** (in Bethesda Street, Hanley) possess what must be one of the finest collections of English pottery and ceramics to be seen anywhere. The **Gladstone Pottery Museum**, in Uttoxeter Road, Longton, occupies an early Victorian ceramics factory which still has its original workshops and bottle-ovens.

The 1000 ft-deep galleries of the **Chatterley Whitfield Mining Museum** offer a fascinating insight into the harsh realities of coal mining. British Coal's national collection of mining artefacts is also housed in the museum. The combined effects of geological problems, declining demand and cheap foreign competition closed the pit in 1977, even though its high grade anthracite was some of the best in Britain.

Alton Towers

Alton Towers, an amusement park, has more than 100 attractions, with something for everybody, young and old.

Biddulph Grange Garden is a haven of peace in comparison, a Victorian park laid out in 1845 and reopened in 1991.

Dorchester

I 10

Southern England
County: Dorset
Altitude: 250 ft. Population: 14,000

Dorchester, the county town of Dorset, is situated in a chalk valley of the River Frome. It makes an ideal centre from which to explore the beauties of the Dorset countryside, whether by car or on foot. Although relatively small, the town boasts a past overflowing with incident, from prehistory (Maiden Castle hill-fort), through Roman times to the 17th and 19th centuries when it was the scene of several notorious executions and trials. Dorchester is also closely associated with the poet and novelist Thomas Hardy (1840–1928) who living locally, made "Casterbridge" and the surrounding area the setting for his work. Hardy's cottage in Higher Bockhampton is now a museum.

History Dorchester's prehistoric roots lie in Maiden Castle, but the town itself, on the banks of the Frome, was founded by the Romans in about AD 50. Called Durnovaria, it evolved during the 2nd c. into an important garrison and market town (the typical Roman grid system of streets still survives as a reminder). By AD 800 Dorchester, now part of the kingdom of Wessex, had developed into a major centre for trade, its status confirmed by the existence of a mint. From the late 11th c. the Normans also fostered its economic growth, encouraging cloth manufacture in particular. Dorchester's subsequent history was foreshadowed in 1337 when, for the first time, reference is made to a judicial court in the town. During the Civil War the townsfolk took the Parliamentarian side; later they threw their weight behind the Duke of Monmouth, Protestant pretender to Charles II's throne. For this many of them paid dearly when, at the so-called "Bloody Assizes" in 1685, the notorious Judge Jeffreys condemned more than 300 of Monmouth's supporters to death or lengthy periods of imprisonment. In the 17th and 18th centuries trade and agriculture stagnated, as a result of which some inhabitants emigrated to America, founding New Dorchester near Boston. The economy recovered somewhat in the 19th c., the town's delightful "period" house-fronts mainly dating from this time. The old town walls were demolished long ago, their line being marked today by the tree-lined Walks.

Sights

High West Street leads to the oldest part of the town, with remains of the Roman walls visible in Albert Road (south) and a 4th c. Roman town house in Northernhay (north-west). As well as the quite interesting **Town Hall** (1847), High East Street, High West Street and Cornhill/South Street (pedestrianised) boast numerous picturesque 17th–19th c. houses and inns. Note especially the King's Arms and Borough Arms in High East Street (both 17th c.), and the Antelope Hotel in South Street (16th–19th c.) where, during the Bloody Assizes, Charles II's Lord Chief Justice, Judge Jeffreys, presided over the trial of Protestant supporters of Monmouth's rebellion.

Old town

Near by stands an **obelisk** erected in 1784 on the site of the old town pump, still called Town Pump. In High West Street, St Peter's Church, built in the 12th c. but greatly altered in the 19th, has a monument in the churchyard to William Barnes (1800–86), a local schoolmaster who wrote poetry in the Dorset dialect; the interior of the church contains tombs of various 14th c. knights. The **Victorian Corn Exchange** (1847–48), opposite the east end of St Peter's, served many different purposes: prison, covered market and courts. Judge Jeffrey's Lodgings across the street were linked by secret passageway to the courtroom in the Antelope Hotel.

Old Crown Court

The **Old Shire Hall**, a hundred yards or so along High West Street, contains the **Old Crown Court**, scene in 1834 of another notorious Dorchester trial, this time of the Tolpuddle Martyrs. The six men had formed an association in an attempt to secure better wages for farmworkers. This constituted a challenge to the vested interests of oppressive landowners. Found guilty of conspiracy, they were sentenced to seven years hard labour in Australia. Two years later, after prolonged public outcry and fierce parliamentary debate, they were pardoned. To commemorate the affair, regarded as a milestone in British Trade Union history, the courtroom has been turned into the Tolpuddle Memorial.

Thomas Hardy's Cottage

St George's Church, on the site of a Roman cemetery in Fordington in the east, has an interesting south porch, with a small Norman tympanon depicting the dragon-slaying St George. Two Art Nouveau windows (1903–13) by William Morris embellish the transept.

The **Dorset County Museum** (High West Street), in a pleasant Victorian building with an unusual exhibition hall of iron construction, comprises a geological section, many pre-Roman finds (including from Maiden Castle), and collections from the Roman and medieval periods. In addition there are memorabilia of Admiral Sir Thomas Masterman Hardy, once Flag Officer to Nelson; also of the local poet William Barnes, of the Victorian sculptor Alfred Stevens and, last but by no means least, of Thomas Hardy, including his study, removed here from his home. The novelist was born on June 2nd 1840 in nearby Higher Bockhampton, where his modest birthplace, now called **Hardy's Cottage**, can be visited. He later moved to Max Gate, a house in Arlington Avenue, off the Wareham road, where he lived until his death. Hardy's novels are a socio-historical commentary on life in his native Dorset.

All Saints Church at the end of High East Street has been converted into a museum housing the county's principal archaeological collections. Reflecting 100,000 years of history and prehistory, they include finds from Maiden Castle, Mount Pleasant and Greyhound Yard.

Among the many notable items in the very fine collection of the **Dorset Military Museum** in Bridport Road, is Adolf Hitler's desk, removed by men of the regiment from the Berlin Chancellery in 1945.

Maumbury Rings

The Maumbury Rings in Weymouth Avenue (south-west of the town centre) were originally a Neolithic stone circle. The Romans incorporated them into an amphitheatre large enough to accommodate 10,000 spectators, comprising an oval stadium measuring some 207 × 164 ft.

During the English Civil War it was used as a fort, and in the 18th c. for public executions.

Surroundings

Maiden Castle (2 miles south-west) is rightly considered one of the most impressive prehistoric fortified settlements in the country. A tour of the site takes a good hour, with information boards posted along the way. The principal feature is a huge, oval-shaped Iron-Age hill-fort (*c.* 500 BC), its main axis being around 2625 ft in length. This is surrounded by four massive earth ramparts, topped at one time by palisades, and in places still standing 80 ft high. The site also includes a Neolithic Long Mound (*c.* 2800 BC) and the foundation walls of a Romano-British temple (*c.* AD 370).

Maiden Castle

8 miles north of Dorchester, at Cerne Abbas, is another fascinating relic of the past – the **Cerne Giant**, a huge male figure, 180 ft from head to foot, hewn in the chalk hillside. The origin and significance of the figure remain obscure; possibly it was associated with some as yet unknown fertility rite. Similarities with Roman portrayals of the god Hercules suggest the Giant may perhaps date from the early Roman period in Britain.
    The village of Cerne Abbas has a fine gatehouse formerly belonging to a Benedictine abbey; also a tithe barn and, opposite the church, a number of Tudor cottages.

Cerne Abbas

Milton Abbas (10 miles north-east) is an exceptionally attractive 18th c. "model" village, built largely out of self-interest in 1786 by Joseph Damer, 1st Earl of Dorchester. Because the nearby village of Middleton interfered with the view from his country-house (a converted abbey), he went to the extraordinary lengths of having it demolished, moving its inhabitants to a picturesque new village of thatch-roofed houses. The Earl's house, Milton Abbey, is now a school. The abbey itself was founded by King Athelstan (*c.* 935), fulfilling a vow made when he defeated the Danes; the surviving buildings are all 14th–15th c. In addition to a 15th c. painting of its founder, the abbey church contains the tomb of the Earl and Countess of Dorchester, designed by Robert Adam (1775) and movingly executed in stone by Agostino Carlini.

Milton Abbas

Athelhampton Hall (6 miles north-east), a 15th c. country-house with 19th c. formal **French garden**, was built by Sir William Martyn, sometime Lord Mayor of London. It is a fine example of the Perpendicular style in secular architecture. The Great Hall is especially magnificent, with linen-fold panelling, superb timbered roof and an oriel window with heraldic

Athelhampton Hall

Athelhampton Hall

glass. The rooms are filled with fine furniture, works of art, porcelain and glass from the 15th to the 19th c.

★★**Montacute House**

Montacute House (22 miles north-west), a delightful Elizabethan country mansion, was built by Thomas Phelips, Speaker of the House of Commons in the reign of James I. The house was probably begun in 1588 and completed around 1600. It is built of the mellow, locally quarried, Ham Hill stone, as also is Montacute village. The E-shaped three-storeyed building has large bay windows with many lights, curved gables and unusually tall and decorative chimneys. Statues of famous historical figures adorn niches in the walls. The rooms, with opulent 17th–18th c. furnishings, include the Great Hall where a plaster frieze tells the story of a husband deceived. Lord Curzon's Room on the first floor commemorates the famous statesman, who rented the house between 1915 and 1920. The Long Gallery, 60 ft from end to end, originally used for social functions such as games and dancing, is now hung with portraits of Tudor and Stuart luminaries, including some outstanding works on loan from the National Portrait Gallery in London. The superb gardens are one of the very few surviving examples of Early Jacobean scenic design.

Yeovilton

The **Fleet Air Arm Museum** near Yeovilton (26 miles north-west, reached via the A37 and A3151) has a collection of more than 40 naval aircraft past and present, including a number which saw action in the 1982 Falklands War. On some days there are also flying displays.

Cadbury Castle

Cadbury Castle, a prehistoric settlement commanding a splendid vista over the surrounding countryside, lies off the A303 near Sparkford (29 miles north).

The large Iron Age hill-fort, in use over a considerable period, was finally abandoned after the Roman occupation in AD 43. Local names such as River Cam, Queen's Camel, etc. gave rise to the idea that this was where the battle of Camlann took place, and hence that King Arthur was responsible for the fort. It has also been suggested as the site of Camelot, the Arthurian royal court.

Bere Regis

The village of Bere Regis (10 miles north-east), where in Saxon times King John had a hunting lodge, still retains its original Romanesque church (St John the Baptist; 12th c.). Among several remarkable features are the late 15th c. tie beams, the ends of which, projecting into the nave, are elaborately carved with life-size figures of the apostles, each picked out in rich colours. Four roof bosses above the centre aisle depict – starting with the head at the east end – Cardinal John Morton (1420–1500), Archbishop of Canterbury, who donated the ceiling; his cardinal coat of arms; the Tudor Rose (in honour of Henry VII, whose Lord Chancellor he was); and a ribbon-like decoration symbolising settlement of the quarrel between the Houses of Lancaster and York. (This was achieved through the marriage of Henry Tudor (Henry VII) to Elizabeth of York, a marriage which Morton arranged.) The Norman capitals are also particularly charming; note for example the poor headache sufferer. The south aisle contains the 14th c. burial chapel and tomb of the Turberville family, the inspiration for Thomas Hardy's novel "Tess of the d'Urbervilles".

Sherborne

Sherborne (19 miles north; pop. 7400) still retains some of its medieval village architecture. It became a bishopric in 705 and was for a time the capital of Wessex. The abbey school is now a highly regarded public school.

The **Abbey** has a splendid Late Norman south porch, remains of the old Benedictine abbey (about 1170), a Norman crossing arch and an Early English Lady Chapel. These apart it is mainly Perpendicular in style, having been extensively rebuilt in the 15th c. The fan vaulting is among the most beautiful and finely articulated in England. The canopied choir-stalls and the misericords date from the 15th c. Two

Anglo-Saxon kings are said to lie buried here; if true, their tombs have not survived. The bell known as "Great Tom" hanging in the tower was a gift from Cardinal Wolsey. Some of the former monastic buildings are now incorporated into the school. The Almshouse (1437) still has its original 15th c. chapel, hall and sleeping quarters.

Sherborne's two **castles**, one in ruins, stand opposite each other in the attractive setting of a deer park. Only the Norman gatehouse and a tower remain of the 11th c. castle, erected by Roger, Bishop of Salisbury. The later Sherborne Castle was built between 1592 and 1603 by Sir Walter Raleigh, who made it his home.

Neighbouring Yeovil (pop. 26,400) is a bustling market town, the centre of an agricultural area of apple orchards, farmland and ancient villages. The handsome Early Perpendicular St John's Church has an unusual copper lectern and several rather curious bosses (including some carved with African masks from the time of the Crusades). Nearby, the Museum of South Somerset in Handford contains exhibits from Yeovil's history and reconstructions of a Roman kitchen and dining-room   **Yeovil**

Dundee   H/I 4

Scotland
Region: Tayside
Altitude: 285 ft. Population: 175,000

Dundee, Scotland's fourth largest city, lies along the north side of the Firth of Tay. It was known at one time for jute, journalism and jam, all of which played a prominent role in its development. The famous jute factories and weaving mills, which together with shipbuilding formed the basis of the city's prosperity, have now all but disappeared. So too have the large printing works. Jam and marmalade-making continues, but to a much lesser extent than before. Expansion of the service sector, the opening in 1987 of a 118 acre high-technology park, product specialisation and investment in new industries have brought about a much-needed revitalisation and diversification of the local economy. The presence of such companies as US textile firms Levi Strauss and Gore (particularly the latter, manufacturing their Goretex waterproof fabric) and many now well-established small and medium-sized businesses in the biotechnological, precision engineering and instrument making fields (producing e.g. insulators, medical instruments, CAD/CAM computer systems, etc.), testify to the success of this regenerative strategy. The city environment has also been improved, by redeveloping the docks and waterfront with offices and leisure facilities and transforming the Dons Road commercial area into a shopping and residential district.

The first and now notorious railway bridge carrying the Edinburgh to Dundee line across the Tay, was constructed between 1872 and 1878 by Thomas Bouch. At the time it was the longest bridge in the world, with a total span of almost 2 miles. During a storm in 1879 it collapsed, taking a crowded train with it into the depths. The present Tay Rail Bridge, opened nine years later, still provides the best view of the city.

Having been subject to much conflict over the years Dundee has preserved few old buildings. The scenery in the nearby Grampian Mountains (see entry), however, is some of the finest in Britain.

Sights

The city centre was largely rebuilt after the Second World War. The sole surviving medieval building is the beautiful 154 ft-high tower of St Mary's Church in Nethergate, built in the 15th c.   St Mary Tower

231

McManus Galleries	Albert Square is dominated by the Victorian building housing the McManus Galleries. The art collection includes European masters and 19th and 20th c. Scottish painters and there is also an interesting exhibition on local history from the early period to the present day.
★★ "Discovery"	The Royal Research Ship "Discovery", used by Captain R. F. Scott on his first expedition to the Antarctic in 1901–04, is moored on Riverside Drive west of Tay Bridge Road. Now beautifully restored, the ship in which the 30 men set out for the south polar icecap has become the town's new waterfront landmark. The ★**Discovery Point Visitor Centre**, opened in 1993, provides an intriguing insight into the fascinating world of the Antarctic and a record of Scott's expedition.
"Unicorn"	Also open to visitors is H.M. Frigate "Unicorn", moored in Victoria Dock on the east side of the Tay Bridge. Launched in 1824, the 46-gun frigate is the oldest British naval vessel still afloat.
Camperdown Wildlife Centre	This wildlife park 4 miles north-west of the town centre features Scottish fauna past and present, including brown bears, wolves, pine martens and native species of bird – pheasants, golden eagles, etc.

Surroundings

Perth	Perth (22 miles west; pop. 43,000), once the capital of Scotland, and scene of many historic events, is well worth visiting. Traditionally known as "the Fair City", it stands at the inner end of the Firth of Tay, between two wide expanses of green parkland called the North Inch and South Inch. It is and has long been a thriving commercial centre.
	St John's Church was the scene in 1559 of a fiery sermon against idolatry by John Knox. The preacher from Edinburgh (see entry) aroused his

Royal Research Ship "Discovery"

H.M. Frigate "Unicorn"

Scone Palace

audience to such a fervour of iconoclasm that a host of works of art were destroyed.

For a city which was Scotland's capital until the 15th c., Perth has surprisingly few historic buildings. The **Fair Maid's House** in Curfew Row, immortalised by Sir Walter Scott (see Famous People) in "The Fair Maid of Perth", is now a craft shop.

An excellent **nature trail** leads to the top of Kinnoul Hill (729 ft), culminating in an outstanding view.

Huntingtower Castle (2 miles west of Perth), formerly called Ruthven, comprises two 15th c. towers linked by a later building. The hall is embellished with wall and ceiling paintings. According to legend a daughter of the house, in fear of being found with her lover, leapt from one tower to the other, since when it has been known as Maiden's Leap.

⋆ **Scone Palace** (2 miles north of Perth) stands close to the site of the long demolished Scone Abbey. It was here that the Scottish kings, from Kenneth II to James VI, were traditionally crowned, after Kenneth MacAlpine had brought the celebrated coronation Stone of Destiny to Scone in the 9th c. Carried off to England by Edward I in 1297, the Stone of Scone as it is more usually called, was placed under the Coronation Chair in London's Westminster Abbey, where it remains to this day. At one time the Stone rested on Mote Hill which, so tradition holds, was raised with earth from all the continents.

The sturdy-looking palace, built in the 19th c., is the seat of the Earl of Mansfield, portraits of whose ancestors hang in the Long Gallery. The exterior is particularly impressive in autumn when the creeper-covered walls turn a dark shade of red. It is a positive treasure-house inside, with a magnificent collection of porcelain (Meissen, Sèvres and Derby services, etc.), exceptionally fine Chippendale furniture, 17th and 18th c. ivories, and highly unusual papier-mâché work (*c.* 1730) by the Martin brothers of Paris.

The park is every bit as remarkable for its rare species of tree. One of those who worked as a gardener here in the 19th c. was the botanist David Douglas. He later went to America, discovering the species of spruce which bears his name.

Crieff

The **Highland Trust Museum** in Burrell Street, Crieff (17 miles west of Perth) displays traditional methods of weaving and other crafts prac-

tised in the Highlands.

Crieff's ★**Glenturret Whisky Distillery**, founded in 1775, has a good claim to be Scotland's oldest, although the Littlemille Distillery in Bowling (Dumbarton-shire) and the Strathisla Distillery in Keith (Banffshire) also began operating about this time. Whether first or not, Glenturret, also known as "The Hosh", is certainly one of the smallest distilleries in Scotland, with just two stills producing 1760 galls of malt whisky a year. This is left to mature in oak casks for at least eight years.

Glenturret Distillery

Durham   K 6

Northern England. County: Durham
Altitude: 167 ft. Population: 40,000

The old centre of this ancient county town, with its magnificent cathedral and castle perched high above a loop of the River Wear, is a never-to-be-forgotten sight. First fortified in Roman days, the medieval city stood for centuries as a bulwark against the Scots, while the superb Norman cathedral drew a multitude of pilgrims to St Cuthbert's tomb. Coal mining brought Durham into the industrial age. The city makes a good base for excursions into a region extending from the Pennines to the North Sea coast.

Although the area of County Durham – bounded by the rivers Tyne and Tees – had long been settled, little is known of its **history** prior to Roman times. Durham was then part of a region under Celtic rule, the territory of the Brigantae, into which the Romans advanced at the end of the 1st c. Later they called a halt to further encroachment north, preferring to consolidate their hold behind the security of Hadrian's Wall (see entry). Durham's next mention in documentary sources occurs in the 10th c. when, in 945, the monks of Lindisfarne were driven from their monastery by Viking raiders. They bore St Cuthbert's remains away with them and, guided by a divine sign, fixed eventually on a new resting place at "dunholm" (hill island). In 1017, after receiving a gift of land from the Danish overlord, work began on a church. The Norman Conquest met with strong resistance in northern England; but once successful, Walcher de Lorraine was appointed bishop. In 1092 his successor, Bishop William St Carileph, demolished the existing church, clearing the site for the present cathedral. As rulers of a frontier outpost constantly threatened by the Scots, the bishops of Durham enjoyed sovereign-like status. Together with the title of Prince-Bishop went the power to raise their own armies, establish their own judicial courts, mint coins, levy taxes and grant political asylum. Strategically positioned on the route to Scotland, and profiting from the powerful attraction for pilgrims of St Cuthbert's shrine, the city quickly prospered; the surround-

Durham Cathedral

A Norman capital in the castle

ing countryside became divided into large estates on which feudal barons erected splendid castles. From the early modern period onwards mineral-based industries came to play an increasingly important role. Pitheads and chimneys in time dotted the landscape, and the steel and shipbuilding industries flourished. In the 19th c. the population was swelled by an influx of immigrant workers; industrialists built grand houses, working class districts grew up, and trade unions were founded (the annual Durham Miners' Gala is still a major event in the calendar). As mining has declined, more and more service-sector businesses have relocated in the city.

Whether approached from the narrow streets of the Old City across Palace Green, or from the banks of the Wear over Prebend's Bridge, the cathedral is an awe-inspiring sight. Completion of this, one of the great Anglo-Norman churches, took only a relatively short span of time, with few subsequent alterations. The nave, north and south transepts and four west bays of the choir were all built between 1093 and 1133. By 1175 the Galilee Chapel had been added to the west end, and between 1217 and 1222 the two west towers were raised. Between 1242 and 1280 the east end was modified, the Chapel of the Nine Altars replacing the existing apse. Finally, in 1490, the central tower was partly rebuilt.

★★ Durham Cathedral

Visitors enter the cathedral by the **North-west door** (12th c.), famous for its sanctuary knocker. In medieval times fugitives would knock here, hoping to find sanctuary in the cathedral. A constant watch was kept by a guard posted in a little room above.

The Norman **nave** astonishes just through its size – 200 ft long, almost 40 ft wide and 72 ft in height; massive piers and columns support the vaulted ceiling, one of the earliest in England. The use of ribbed vaulting and buttressing marked a turning point in vault construction, anticipating techniques perfected later in Gothic architecture. The zigzag mould-

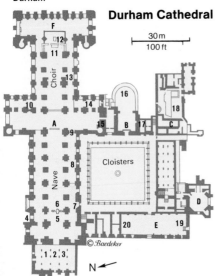

Durham Cathedral

30 m
100 ft

A Crossing Tower
B Chapterhouse
C Crypt
D Kitchen
E Dormitory
F Chapel of the Nine Altars

1 12th c. painting of St Cuthbert and King Oswald
2 "Crucifixion" (13th c.)
3 Tomb of the Venerable Bede
4 North doorway, with door-knocker
5 Font
6 Black Marble cross
7 Miners' Memorial
8 Votive chapel of the Nevilles
9 Barrington Statue
10 St Gregory's Chapel
11 High Altar
12 Tomb of St Cuthbert
13 Bishop's throne
14 Light Infantry Memorial Chapel
15 Prior Castell's Clock
16 Prior's Chair
17 Prison
18 Deanery
19 Restaurant, bookshop
20 Treasury

ing on the arches and spiral decoration of the columns soften the otherwise strict and uncluttered lines, without lessening in any degree the visual dominance of the altar. The ornamentation of the columns echoes the twisted pillars of the holy temple in Jerusalem, which were also copied by Bernini for the altar tabernacle of St Peter's in Rome. In the Middle Ages there were also echoes of the heavenly Jerusalem, in the form of paintings, long since vanished. Women were not normally admitted to the nave, except to the font at the west end. A black marble cross in the floor of the second bay marks the point beyond which they were not allowed to pass.

To the right of the entrance, built on to the original west façade, is the ★ **Galilee Chapel**. The graceful columns and arches of this Late Romanesque-Norman masterpiece are reminiscent of Moorish architecture, familiar to the Normans from their Mediterranean wanderings. The 12th c. paintings on the east wall probably depict St Cuthbert (north side) and St Oswald (south). The chapel also contains the tomb of the Venerable Bede (died 735), "the monk of Jarrow", learned author of the celebrated "Ecclesiastical History of the English People". Originally interred at Jarrow, his remains were stolen and brought here in 1022, the purpose being to enhance Durham's own collection of relics.

Returning to the nave, in the south aisle, the **Miners' Memorial** (1947) and associated 17th c. frieze of the Passion commemorate the men of Durham's premier industry.

Further along the aisle in the **Neville Chantry**, the more easterly of the grave effigies is that of Ralph Neville (died 1367), victor of the Battle of Neville Cross (1346), who fought with and captured the Scottish king, David II. The Nevilles were the first lay persons to be interred in the cathedral. In contrast to the practice elsewhere, requiem masses were not used in Durham as a means of raising funds for building.

At the corner of the aisle and south transept stands a statue of Bishop Barrington (1734–1826), penultimate holder of the title of Prince-Bishop. An enlightened man, he not only patronised the arts but also founded a co-operative society and fostered improvements in agriculture. The

Miners' Memorial in Durham Cathedral

great tower over the crossing has beautiful ribbed vaulting. To the right, on the end wall of the Prior Castell's south transept, is **Prior Castell's Clock** (early 16th c.). The chancel, ahead, has 17th c. choir stalls.

The **Bishop's throne** (14th c.), "the highest in Christendom" is ensconced above the memorial and tomb of Bishop Hatfield (1345–81), founder of Durham College and of Trinity College, Oxford (see entry).

The Chapel of the Nine Altars, a sympathetic Gothic replacement (1242–80) for the original Norman apse, contains the **Shrine of Saint Cuthbert** (died 687). The tomb was broken open in 1827; some of the relics found in it can be seen in the cathedral Treasury.

The early 15th c. cloisters are entered from the east via the Late Norman Prior's Doorway. On the west side, the **Monks' Dormitory** (1398–1404) houses an important collection of sculptures including Saxon crosses, Roman altars and stonework from St Cuthbert's tomb, while the Treasury contains early manuscripts (8th c. onwards) and textile fragments, among the oldest examples of such handwork found in England. The refectory (south side) was converted into a library in 1648. The octagonal kitchen, with fine vaulting, dates from 1366–70; it remained in use, without interruption, until 1940.

Having been built as a fortress by the Earl of Northumberland in 1072, Durham Castle, on the far side of Palace Green from the cathedral, was presented by William the Conqueror to the prince-bishops of Durham, whose feudal residence it then became. The most interesting rooms are the Norman chapel (1080; with delightful archaic capitals), the large dining-hall (*c.* 1300), the kitchen with its fireplace and pantry (1499), and the bishop's apartments. Since 1832 the spacious castle has been part of Durham's University College.

★Durham Castle

The Old Fulling Mill (archaeological museum) houses finds from the

Fulling Mill

237

Roman, Anglo-Saxon and Norman periods unearthed by excavations in the city centre.

Oriental Museum

The University of Durham's Oriental Museum on Elvet Hill, just a short distance from the old city centre, has excellent art and archaeological collections gathered from the Near and Far East (including China, Japan and Egypt).

East Coast/South East Coast   M/N 8/9

Southern England
Counties: Kent, Essex, Suffolk, Norfolk and Lincolnshire

The east and south-east coasts of England extend from the Thames estuary, by way of the Wash, to the south side of the River Humber, and have along their length many well-known and popular seaside resorts as well as a number of important ports. The topographical pattern of this long stretch of coast is very varied – sometimes bounded by easily eroded cliffs, elsewhere fringed by sandy beaches, often by fertile fenland reclaimed from the sea. Many hundreds of miles of embankments and dykes protect this land, much of it lying only just above sea level. This part of the English coast is sinking all the time: over the last 2000 years it has become lower by something in the order of 39–42 ft. In spite of the length of the coast there are only a few harbours deep enough to take tankers and other large vessels.

Isle of Thanet
Margate

Together with Cliftonville, Margate (pop. 49,100) is one of the most popular resorts on the Isle of Thanet – today more of a peninsula than an isle. Attracting mainly Londoners, it has miles of fine sandy beaches, good entertainment facilities, including the Bembon Brothers' leisure park, a theatre, a concert hall and amusement park. Architectural highlights include splendid 19th c. crescents, a number of very fine houses such as the Tudor House (16th c.) in King Street and the Limes and India House (18th c.) in Hawley Street, and the painstakingly restored buildings of Salmestone Grange in Nash Road. The church of St John the Baptist in the High Street contains an interesting collection of brasses, some of which are highly unusual; note in particular the brass skeleton commemorating Richard Notfelde (died 1446).

Broadstairs

From Margate a lovely path runs along the cliffs to Broadstairs (5 miles), where Charles Dickens (see Famous People) wrote some of his work, including "David Copperfield" (1850), in the real Bleak House. The house is now a ★**Dickens Museum** dedicated to the great man of letters, whose memory is further celebrated during the week-long Dickens Festival held every year in June. Throughout the seven days, old and young alike dress in Victorian costume and there are Victorian-style parties and balls.

Westgate-on-Sea,
Birchington

Westgate-on-Sea and Birchington are two smaller resorts retaining something of their old-fashioned charm. The Powell-Cotton Museum in Birchington has well-presented natural history and ethnographic collections. Here the sandy beaches are separated by stretches of chalk cliff.

There is an interesting walk to **Reculver**, site of Regulbium, a Roman fort of the 3rd c. It once protected the wide and important (because navigable) Wantsum channel which, joining up with the River Stour, separated the Isle of Thanet from the mainland.

Whitstable

Whitstable (pop. 26,200) is known to gourmets the world over on account of its excellent oysters. There is evidence of the existence of oyster-beds here for at least 2000 years. The Whitstable to Canterbury (see entry) railway line, built by George Stephenson (see Famous People) in 1830, was the first passenger line in the world. The town has some attractive old houses, a shingle beach and a small yacht harbour.

Isle of Sheppey

The Isle of Sheppey, approximately 17 sq. miles in area, is separated from the mainland by the channel known as The Swale, spanned by a bridge carrying the A249. The abbey church of St Mary and St Sexburga at Minster was founded in 673; the present building is 13th–15th c. and has some interesting tombs. The Early English-style church of St Henry and St Elizabeth in Sheerness, completed in 1864, was designed by Edward Welby Pugin. Not far away from the coast road stands the extraordinary "Folly Ship and Shore", a house constructed in about 1850 from the remains of a stranded ship. The Isle abounds with camping sites, holiday camps and chalets.

Southend-on-Sea

Southend-on-Sea (pop. 155,800), on the northern side of the Thames estuary, forms with Leigh-on-Sea, Prittlewell and Westcliff a sizeable town which could almost be regarded as a suburb of London. It is a very popular seaside resort, with a famous pier 1½ miles long, constructed around the turn of the century; at low tide the sea retreats for almost a mile. Despite stretching for more than 6 miles, the beach can be very crowded at weekends. The town takes great pride in its Assembly Rooms. There are regular river excursions.

At nearby **Prittlewell**, part of a former **Cluniac priory** survives, dating back to about the 11th c. A museum of local and natural history, including archaeological finds, is housed in buildings added in the 19th c.

The ruins of the 13th–14th c. **Hadleigh Castle**, just to the west, were famously captured by John Constable in a romantic painting which now hangs in the Tate Gallery in London (see entry). The castle affords an extensive view over the Thames estuary and marshes.

Clacton-on-Sea

Clacton-on-Sea (pop. 36,500), with a gently sloping beach 7 miles long, is particularly suitable for families with children. It has everything hoped for in a modern seaside resort – a pier (built in 1873), a splendid promenade, beautiful parks, a golf course and a wide range of entertainments.

Harwich

Harwich (pop. including Dovercourt: 14,200) is a busy port which handles a large part of the ferry traffic to and from the Continent. The old town, situated at the mouths of the Rivers Orwell and Stour, bears the marks of its long seafaring tradition. Nelson (see Famous People) was a frequent visitor to the old Three Cups Inn. The town has many fine Georgian houses, including the red-brick Guildhall (1769).

Dovercourt is a neat Victorian suburb with charming little houses.

Felixstowe

Felixstowe (pop. 19,800), facing Harwich on the north shore of the approximately 10 mile-long tidal estuary, is an important container terminal as well as a popular seaside resort with a beautiful promenade, public gardens and entertainment facilities. Built on cliffs the town occupies an almost island-like position between the sea to the southeast, the River Deben to the north, and the wide Orwell estuary to the south, which the latter must be crossed by ferry, since there is no bridge.

Orford

Beyond Felixstowe, Hollesley Bay runs north to Orford Ness and the old port of Orford (pop. 650), now a quiet little village on the Ore, which flows parallel to the coast, behind the Ness, for more than 12 miles. The moated castle (1165–76) has a polygonal keep. The church has a ruined Norman tower and choir. Orford Ness is a nature reserve where many seabirds nest.

Aldeburgh

The small town of Aldeburgh (pop. 2870) on Aldeburgh Bay was a considerable port from the 15th to the 17th c. From this period

239

A colourful promenade at Felixstowe

date the Moot Hall (1520–40) and a number of picturesque old houses. Aldeburgh is now a popular seaside resort, internationally known for its Music Festival held in June and featuring the works of Benjamin Britten (see Famous People), a former resident. The town is also much favoured by anglers, as is Thorpeness, 2 miles north, which, in addition to sea-angling, offers freshwater fishing in a large mere.

Southwold

With its charming old cottages Southwold (pop. 2230), situated on a hill overlooking the sea, surrounded by extensive areas of green, is a typical old-world English town. The church is a fine example of the flint and stone masonry frequently found in Suffolk. The town is becoming increasingly popular as a holiday resort.

Lowestoft

Lowestoft (pop. 59,400) is the most easterly town in England. As well as being a popular seaside resort with a good sandy beach, it is also a busy fishing port and centre of the fish-processing industry (although the golden days of the herring fisheries are long since past). Among the town's thriving enterprises today is Brooke Yachts International, a boat-yard specialising in luxury craft. The town is well known to the art world, not only from the watercolour "Lowestoft" by William Turner (see Famous People), but more especially from the delightful Lowestoft porcelain manufactured here between 1756 and 1803. The **fish market** adds to the life and colour of the town, as do the narrow lanes in the older part.

North of Lowestoft lies the **Pleasurewood Hills American Theme Park**, with a variety of fairground-style rides and other entertainments (including American sealion and parrot shows, etc.).

Great Yarmouth

Great Yarmouth (pop. 52,700) is situated on a narrow spit of land between the sea and the River Yare, from which latter the town takes its name. Having in the past owed its development to the herring fishing industry, it is now primarily a pleasant, modern, seaside holiday resort, with a 6 mile long sandy beach, an attractive promenade, three piers and a wide range of amusements. The Yare is navigable by seagoing vessels right up into the town, and the harbour makes a busy scene. Great Yarmouth is also a good base from which to visit the delightful Norfolk Broads. There are regular horse-race meetings during the summer.

Yarmouth's ⋆**"Rows"** are a characteristic feature of the older part of the town. Before their numbers were substantially reduced by bombing during the last war, there were 120 or so of these very narrow lanes. Narrowest of all is Kitty Witches Row, in the area between Hall Quay and the Market Place. The ancient, carefully restored Tollhouse in Middlegate Street, and the 17th c. Old Merchant's House, are now museums. On South Quay there are several fine old houses; No. 4 contains the pleasing Elizabethan House Museum (furniture and other everyday effects from the 16th to the 19th c.). At the end of the street is the Town Hall (1883). The Maritime Museum for East Anglia in Marine Parade has exhibits on the sea and the fishing industry, as well as the most recent industry – oil and gas in the North Sea.

St Nicholas' Church is the second largest parish church in the country, exceeded only by Holy Trinity Church in Hull. Having been completely burned out during the war, the façade is now the only 12th c. survival. The churchyard is enclosed by parts of the **old town walls**, of which the nearby King Henry's Tower and the Blackfriars Tower are also remains. Close to the church is the interesting old Fishermen's Hospital (1702).

Many enjoyable trips can be made from Great Yarmouth to interesting places in the surrounding area. These include **Burgh Castle**, 3 miles south-west of the adjoining, quieter seaside resort of Gorleston. Built in about AD 300 the fortress, which has three walls remaining, stands above Breydon Water, the confluence of the Yare, Waveney and Bure. Known to its builders as Gariannonum, it was one of the Roman forts on the "Saxon shore".

Happisburgh

North of the little coastal places of Caister, Winterton and Sea Palling, on the edge of the Norfolk Broads, Happisburgh is a picturesque village with a fine Perpendicular church. At Bacton, 3 miles north-west, are the ruins of **Bromholm Priory** (1113).

Mundesley-on-Sea

Mundesley-on-Sea (pop. 1600) is a small, rather select seaside resort with a beautiful clean beach. Prices, accordingly, tend to be high. Inland lie several villages with interesting churches, including Knapton, Trunch and Paston.

Cromer

Cromer (pop. 5500) is the best known seaside resort on the North Norfolk coast, with every amenity and facility needed for an enjoyable holiday – a lengthy beach, cliffs, a golf course, a variety of amusements and, inland, the Norfolk Broads. The cliffs, formed from strata of the Cromer Forest Bed, are a happy hunting ground for fossil-collectors at low tide. The Perpendicular parish church has a magnificent 160 ft-high tower.

Completed in 1620, the delightful **Felbrigg Hall** (3 miles south-west), home of the Wyndham family, is well worth visiting. The church in the pleasant park contains tomb slabs dating from the 16th to the 17th c.

Blickling Hall (10 miles south-west) should be on everyone's list, a superb Jacobean mansion, begun by Jacob Lyminge and completed by Thomas Ivory in 1770. Notable even among so many exceptional features is the stucco work, on the staircase and on the ceiling of the 125 ft Long Gallery; also outstanding are the beautiful gardens.

Sheringham

West of Cromer, but still on the long stretch of cliffs extending for some 30 miles south as far as Happisburgh, stands Sheringham (pop. 5100), known among other things for its golf course.

Sheringham Hall (1812–17; south-west) is another country house worth visiting. A Regency mansion, it has a lovely park, and gardens with terraces and fine espaliers. Both house and gardens were the work of Humphrey Repton, who is commemorated in one of the rooms.

The country inland from here is beautifully wooded, with the ruins of Beeston Priory on the edge of the woods. West of Sheringham, where the coastline describes a wide arc, lies an expanse of flat marshland.

Blakeney Point

Blakeney Point, a narrow tongue of land covered with tussock grass and sand-dunes, is the nesting-place of countless water birds and a port of call for many migrants. It is now a nature reserve where wildlife and rare plants are protected. Salthouse Broad, to the east, is also a nature reserve. Permission for bird-watching can be obtained on application to Point House, Morston.

Hunstanton

Further west still along the A149, Hunstanton (consisting of Old Hunstanton and New Hunstanton; pop. 4200), offers a magnificent view of the Wash such as can be had from nowhere else. The huge shallow-water inlet is the remnant of an even more extensive arm of the sea, which once also covered what are now the Fens (see entry). Hunstanton is a quiet modern seaside resort with a good sandy beach. The cliffs are of interest to geologists for their variegated colouring (red and white limestone, reddish-brown sandstone). The church in Old Hunstanton (Decorated) contains some fine monuments.

King's Lynn

See entry

Skegness

There are no seaside resorts on the Wash itself, large areas of which dry out completely at low tide and which measurements show to be steadily silting up. The next resort of any consequence is Skegness (pop. 13,600), which has attracted holidaymakers since 1785. It has a pier 1854 ft long and a wide range of entertainments. South of the town, on Gibralter Point, is a bird reserve with a bird-watching station.

Mablethorpe, Sutton-on-Sea

Mablethorpe and Sutton-on-Sea (combined pop. 5500) are less crowded resorts. The poet Alfred Lord Tennyson (1809–92) spent his childhood here, when Sutton was a mere village amongst lonely sand-dunes.

Cleethorpes

Cleethorpes (pop. 33,300) has grown from a small fishing village into a popular seaside resort, with a beach of fine sand, a promenade and a swimming pool. The parish church, Holy Trinity and St Mary, has a Saxon west tower, Norman nave and Early English choir.

Grimsby

Grimsby (pop. 91,500), immediately adjoining Cleethorpes, at the mouth of the Humber, is England's foremost fishing port. It is also an important industrial town with extensive docks. According to the 14th c. "Lay of Havelock the Dane", Grimsby is so named after a fisherman called Grim, who saved the life of the king's son here.

The early morning auction in the **fish market** makes a lively and interesting spectacle. The **Doughty Museum**, located in the Town Hall, has more than 60 18th–19th c. ship models and a fine collection of Chinese porcelain.

Edinburgh   H 5

Scotland. Region: Lothian
Altitude: 197 ft. Population: 435,000

Edinburgh, capital and cultural centre of Scotland since the 15th c., is one of the most beautiful cities in the world. It has been called the "Athens of the North" by virtue of its rich cultural tradition. As well as hosting the world-famous Edinburgh International Festival the city boasts several first class museums and art galleries together with a great number of buildings and monuments of historical interest. Edinburgh is really two towns, the Old Town and the New. The Old Town huddles in the shelter of the great Castle high on its rocky perch, a maze of narrow lanes, ancient tenements and yards through which the famous "Royal Mile" descends, linking the Castle at one end and the Palace of Holyroodhouse at the other. The Georgian New Town in contrast is a masterpiece of 18th c. town planning, characterised by wide streets, elegant façades and spacious squares. Today Edinburgh has numerous highly successful service industries, and the George Street area in particular is one of Europe's major centres for finance and investment.

Transport Edinburgh lies within easy reach of Glasgow (see entry) via the M8 Motorway and Perth via the A90. The small Edinburgh Airport is located 7 miles west of the city centre. There are good rail services from Waverley Station, situated in the heart of the city, between Princes Street and the "Royal Mile".

Virtually nothing is known of Edinburgh's **history** at the time of the Roman occupation or before. According to legend the Picts built a fort on the volcanic castle crag in the 5th c. The site gained strategic importance once the Angles from Northumberland had overrun Lothian; the Gaelic name "Dunedin" (dun = hill) is thought to derive from Edwin, King of Northumbria (617–633). The town was probably retaken by the Scoto-Picts when they advanced south in the mid 10th c. Michael Canmore (1057–93) built a castle on the rock, and his wife, St Margaret, a chapel. By 1329, when Robert the Bruce granted Edinburgh its first charter, together with the port of Leith, there was quite a large settlement on the ridge below the castle. After the loss of Berwick in 1482 Edinburgh – by then an important centre of trade and craft industry – became capital of Scotland, although the Scottish kings still frequently resided elsewhere. Following the Act of Union in 1707 which left Scotland without a separate parliament, Edinburgh's political importance declined, but it remained a town of considerable consequence, particularly in the intellectual and cultural field. The University became a leading centre for research, and numerous literary figures and artists made their homes here. At the beginning of the 19th c. the Nor'Loch (or North Loch), the area now occupied by Princes Street Gardens, was drained, and three bridges built (North Bridge, George IV Bridge and Waverley Bridge) to link the Old Town with the New. In 1996 Edinburgh became the second city of Great Britain to be included in the UNESCO list of world cultural heritage.

Edinburgh Castle

★★Old Town

★Edinburgh
Castle

The dominant feature of Edinburgh's skyline is the Castle, visible from many parts of the city and itself offering a magnificent vantage point from which to view the rest of Edinburgh. After crossing the spacious Esplanade, the venue in August of the annual Military Tattoo, the visitor enters the Castle by a drawbridge over the waterless moat. At the entrance are bronze figures of two national heroes, Robert the Bruce, crowned king in 1306, who won a decisive victory over Edward II of England (see Famous People) at Bannockburn in 1314, and William Wallace (c. 1270–1305), who led the struggle against Edward I of England and was captured and executed by his adversary.

From here the roadway runs up to the Portcullis Gate, below the state prison, better known as **Argyll's Tower**, because the Marquis of Argyll was confined there in the 17th c. Beyond the Gate, built on the highest point of the Rock, is the Citadel or King's Bastion (443 ft).

Here too is **St Margaret's Chapel**, consecrated in 1090 and thought to be the oldest building in Edinburgh. Although very small (only 17 × 11 ft), it is an interesting example of Early Norman architecture; it was restored on Queen Victoria's orders in 1853, and again in 1934. Near the Half Moon Battery is the modern gun used for firing Edinburgh's "One O'Clock Gun", the time signal which booms out over the city at one o'clock in the afternoon every day except Sunday. At the same time, on Calton Hill, a time-ball on the Nelson Monument is lowered.

National War
Memorial

The National War Memorial, built in 1927 by Sir Robert Lorimer, is a very impressive and moving building to the decoration of which a number of notable artists contributed. It contains memorials to all the Scottish regiments, and even to the animals who also played their part. In the cen-

Bust of Mary Stuart   *... and knightly armour*

tral shrine is a silver casket containing a Roll of Honour with the names of 150,000 Scottish fallen.

Around the other sides of Crown Square are grouped historic apart-ments: the bedroom of Mary Queen of Scots (see Famous People) where, in 1566, the future James VI of Scotland and I of England was born; the Crown Room, in which are displayed the ancient regalia of Scotland – the Sceptre, the Sword of State (1501), a present from Pope Julius II to James IV, and the Crown, the latter made in 1540 from Scottish gold; and the Great Hall, with a comprehensive collection of weaponry and armour. The casemates below were used as prisons and still retain a forbidding air.

Crown Square

Scottish regimental uniforms and a variety of war relics can be seen in the **Scottish United Services Museum** on the west side of the square.

Among the many fine cannon on view in the casemates is the huge **"Mons Meg"**, cast in Mons in 1449, with a range of up to 2 miles.

Running through the heart of the Old Town are four historic streets which, stretching from the Castle to Holyroodhouse, make up Edinburgh's "Royal Mile". On either side are clusters of tall tenement blocks, anything from six to eleven storeys high, evoking the days when people of all social classes were often housed beneath a single roof. Now shops, pubs and restaurants are an additional attraction, making the Mile a delightful place to stroll.

★★Royal Mile

Right at the top, on Castlehill, the **Outlook Tower** built by Sir Patrick Geddes incorporates a 19th c. **camera obscura**.

Castlehill

Diagonally opposite stands the ★ **Scotch Whisky Heritage Centre**, a shrine dedicated to "uisge beatha", Scotland's national liquor. Electric-powered "time cars" carry visitors on a journey into the past, providing an entertaining insight into the social and industrial history of this most famous of Scottish institutions. Notable incidents from the days of smuggling and prohibition, the processes traditionally used in the pro-duction of "Single Malt" and "Blended" whiskies and the stories of famous distilleries all find a place in this imaginative presentation.

Tolbooth St John's Church, a few steps further on, contains a chair which belonged to the great Scottish reformer John Knox (c. 1505–72), a disciple of Calvin.

The carefully restored ★ **Gladstone's Land** (c. 1620), on the left hand side of the Lawnmarket, is an old merchant's house with elaborately painted ceilings.

Lawnmarket

Lady Stair's House (1622) in the adjacent ★ **Lady Stair's Close** contains a small museum with memorabilia of the novelist Sir Walter Scott, the poet Robert Burns (see Famous People for both) and the author Robert Louis Stevenson (1850–94); Stevenson, like Scott, was born in Edinburgh.

Other interesting old houses are to be seen opposite in the 16th c. **Riddle's Court**, which has an intriguing staircase tower, and also in **Brodie's Close**. The latter was named after a tradesman Francis Brodie whose double life is said to have inspired Stevenson's novel "Dr Jekyll and Mr Hyde".

Granite setts in the shape of a heart, let into the pavement in front of St Giles' Cathedral, mark the site where, for more than 400 years, the **Old Tolbooth Prison** stood. The prison plays a central part in Scott's novel "The Heart of Midlothian".

High Street

★ **St Giles' Cathedral**, Edinburgh's principal church, was begun at the end of the 14th c., replacing an earlier building burnt down in 1385 during a raid by the English king Richard II. Of this latter church, a door-way and part of the choir still survive. The central tower (161 ft; com-pleted in 1495) is highly distinctive, being topped by eight flying

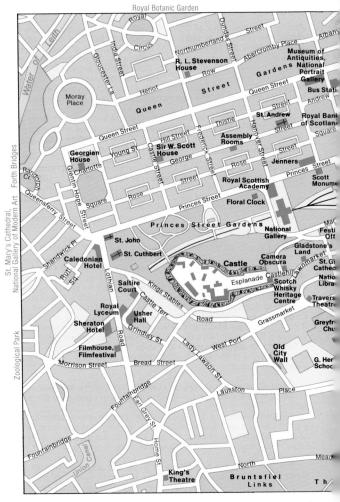

buttresses forming a crown spire. The Chapel of the Most Ancient and Most Noble Order of the Thistle, designed in 1911 by Sir Robert Lorimer, is a superb example of modern Gothic, with ornately carved woodwork. The Order of Thistle is one of the oldest knightly orders in Europe. West of the chapel is the Preston aisle, with the royal pew. In the south aisle is the pre-Reformation Vesper Bell. The church contains numerous monuments commemorating eminent Scots, the Marquis of Montrose (1612–50) and Robert Louis Stephenson among them. The four octagonal piers supporting the tower are believed to date from the Norman church of 1120. Although St Giles' is usually referred to as a cathedral, it was actually a cathedral only for a short period in the 17th c.

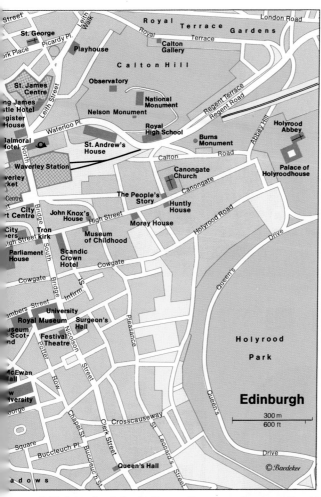

Behind the church lies **Parliament Square**, on the site of the old churchyard in which the fiery reformer John Knox was almost certainly buried in 1572. The lead equestrian statue of Charles II (1685) in the square is thought to be the oldest of the kind in Britain.

Parliament House, where the Scottish Parliament met from 1639 until the union of the two parliaments in 1707, was built in 1632–40, although considerably altered in 1808. The Hall is especially noteworthy, 122 ft long, with a fine hammerbeam roof and containing a statue of Sir Walter Scott, Chief Justice here from 1806 to 1830. The buildings are now occupied by the High Court of Justiciary and the Court of Session. The Signet Library, adjoining, was designed by

St Giles' Cathedral in the Royal Mile

Museum of Childhood in the High Street

House of John Knox

William Stark, the Upper Library (1822) in particular being something of an architectural masterpiece.

East of St Giles' stands the **Mercat Cross**, from which, ever since the Middle Ages, the accession of a new monarch has been proclaimed.

On the other side of the High Street are the **City Chambers**, headquarters of municipal administration since 1811, with a cenotaph commemorating the dead of two World Wars.

The ★ **Museum of Childhood**, further down the High Street, on the right, was created 30 years ago by Patrick Murray. Five floors are occupied by displays of old toys, including model railways, automated toys, dolls and games from all over the world.

Across the street, in Chalmers Close, is the restored part of the former Trinity College (1460), rubbings can be made from copies of old brasses.

The house directly opposite the Museum of Childhood, built in about 1490, was one of three in which **John Knox** lived during his years as minister of St Giles' (the other two no longer survive). Inside is an exhibition dedicated to the great reformer.

Continuing as Canongate, the Royal Mile next passes through the once very fashionable Canongate district. **Huntly** (or Hammermen's) House, which dates from the 16th c., contains a local history museum with collections of Edinburgh silver, ceramics and glass ware, etc. Canongate

On the other side of the road stands the picturesque **Canongate Tolbooth** (1591) with its turreted steeple and projecting clock. Formerly the City Hall, it now houses the **People's Story**, a museum which tells of the life and work of Edinburgh people since the late 18th c. Models, photos and everyday articles of all kinds are used to illustrate the development of industry, commerce and various trades.

Many distinguished Scots, including the economist Adam Smith (1723–90), lie buried in the churchyard of the neighbouring **Canongate Church** (1688).

Off to the left towards the foot of Canongate runs ★ **White Horse Close**, a typically narrow Old Town passage dating back to the 17th c. The White Horse Inn, more than 300 years old, was formerly a mail-coach staging post, with stabling for about 100 horses.

High on the list of Edinburgh's principal sights, the Palace of Holyroodhouse has been the scene of many important events in Scottish history – the marriages of James III and James IV, and of Mary Stuart to Lord Darnley; also the coronations of James V and Charles I. Holyrood is now the official Edinburgh residence of her Majesty the Queen and therefore closed to the public for a time in summer. ★★ Palace of Holyroodhouse

Beginning as an abbey founded in 1128, Holyroodhouse evolved only gradually into the royal residence of today. The first palace was built by James IV, who extended the original abbey guesthouse. This was largely burned down in 1544, and after being rebuilt was again devastated by fire in 1630. The present building was mostly erected between 1670 and 1679, the architect being Sir William Bruce.

The oldest part of the palace, having escaped the fire of 1544, contains Queen Mary's Apartments. Visitors are also taken through a sequence of splendid state apartments, filled with valuable furniture, tapestries and pictures. The Picture Gallery displays a series of portraits of Scottish kings painted by a 17th c. Dutch artist. The Chapel Royal is now a ruin, the sole remaining relic of Holyrood Abbey. The roof of the chapel collapsed in the 18th c. Rebuilding work at the east end revealed a number of ancient gravestones.

In front of the palace stands a 20 ft-high fountain embellished with ornate Renaissance figures and Late-Gothic decoration. The 640 acres of grounds at the rear contain a curious 17th c. sundial. To the west, at the foot of Abbeyhill, is a small building with a pyramidal roof known as Queen Mary's Bath House. Here, according to tradition, the queen bathed in wine to preserve her beauty. Beyond the palace lies Holyrood Park, the highest point of which, the 820 ft volcanic cone called "Arthur's Seat", offers magnificent views over the city and the Firth of Forth. Below the summit are the precipitous Salisbury Crags, dropping sheer for almost 650 ft.

⋆ Grassmarket
and Greyfriars

The picturesque Grassmarket, first mentioned in a document of 1477, has been at the heart of commerce in the Old Town since the Middle Ages. The **White Hart Inn**, on the north side of the market, played host to many an illustrious guest, including the poets Robert Burns (see Famous People) and William Wordsworth. Around it today are a number of other well- known restaurants and pubs. At the east end of the Grassmarket Edinburgh's smallest and most avant-garde theatre, the Traverse, stands on the corner leading into Cowgate.

Opposite the theatre, Candlemakers Row curves gently southwards to **Greyfriars Church** (17th c.). The churchyard, the oldest in Edinburgh, contains the graves of many prominent Scots.

Near by in the Row stands a small fountain with a much-loved statue of Greyfriars Bobby. In 1858, having followed his master John Grey's coffin to its burialplace in the graveyard, the faithful Skye terrier refused to leave. A kennel was built for him, where he devotedly kept watch until his own death fourteen years later. Baroness Burdett Coutts, deeply moved by the story, had the statue erected.

Greyfriars Bobby

A short distance east, in Chambers Street, the renowned **Royal Museum of Scotland** occupies an imposing Victorian building of 1861–88. The museum has extensive archaeological, ethnographical, natural history and technology departments, also a particularly fine collection of primitive art. In 1771 Sir Walter Scott was born in a house near by, which has since been taken down.

The **University of Edinburgh** is Scotland's premier seat of learning, justifiably proud of its long and distinguished academic tradition. Although the university was founded in 1583, the oldest surviving buildings date only from the end of the 18th and beginning of the 19th centuries. The Classical-style Old College, with elaborately furnished rooms in the Upper Library, was designed by Robert Adam; Sir Rowland Anderson added the huge dome in 1883. In front of the building stands a memorial to the inventor James Watt (see Famous People). Expansion in the present century has brought several additions, including the King's Buildings (1928) in West Mains. The former Heriot Watt College became Edinburgh's second university in 1966.

New Town

⋆ Princes Street

Edinburgh's busiest street is Princes Street, on the southern edge of New Town. Almost a mile in length, it has colourful gardens, elegant shops, and many famous restaurants and hotels.

Scottish Tartan
Museum

Located in the Scotch House Shop (3941 Princes Street), the Scottish Tartan Museum established in 1997 has tartans and clan history on display.

Waverley Station
North Bridge

North Bridge, beyond Waverley Station, connects the Old and New Towns (see map p. 246–7).

Scott Monument

A spiral staircase of 287 steps leads up to the top of the 200 ft-high monument to the writer Sir Walter Scott Monument. The marble statue of

Scott, his favourite dog Maida at his feet, is the work of Sir John Steel. A further 60 figures depict characters from Scott's novels and Scottish history.

Another memorial near by commemorates the Scottish doctor and explorer David Livingstone (see Famous People).

Livingstone Memorial

The Mound, half way along Princes Street, provides a second route up to the Old Town. On its east side can be seen the Neo-Classical building of the **Royal Scottish Academy**, designed by William Henry Playfair. On the opposite corner, in Princes Street Gardens, is a **floral clock** – one of the oldest in the world – which is replanted every year.

The Mound

Next to the Academy, the ★**National Gallery**, also designed by Playfair, possesses an exceedingly fine collection of paintings, including works by Raphael, Rubens, Rembrandt, Goya, van Gogh, Titian, El Greco, Van Dyck, a number of French Impressionists, Constable, Gainsborough (see Famous People), Raeburn, McTaggert and Noel Paton.

The Scottish National Gallery of Modern Art, situated west of Princes Street, in Belford Road, has a large collection of works by 19th and 20th c. artists such as Matisse, Braque, Klee, Picasso and the Surrealists Magritte, Miro, Max Ernst and Giacometti. Among British artists and sculptors represented are Henry Moore (see Famous People), Matthew Smith, David Hockney and the "Scottish Colourists" including Peploe, Cadell Hunter and Fergusson.

Scottish National Gallery of Modern Art

The Scottish National Portrait Gallery at the east end of Queen Street (north of Princes Street) has portraits of notable figures in Scottish history from the 16th c. onwards, e.g. Robert Burns, James Watt and Sir Walter Scott (see Famous People for all three). The artists whose work is

Scottish National Portrait Gallery

North Bridge, a central rendezvous

Nelson Monument on Calton Hill

on view include many famous names such as Reynolds, Epstein, Kokoschka and Gainsborough.

★Museum of Antiquities

The Museum of Antiquities was originally founded by the eccentric 11th Earl of Buchan (1742–1829); since 1891 the collection has been housed in its present building, shared with the National Portrait Gallery. Artefacts and works of art occupy three floors, with displays of Neolithic tools (4000–2500 BC), early Pictish stone sculptures (10th–7th c. BC), Pictish silver discovered on St Ninian's Isle (see Shetland Islands), the Hunterston Brooch, and 8th c. Celtic ornamental work. As well as a reconstruction of the late Neolithic village at Skara Brae (see Orkney Islands) there are numerous Roman finds, including pieces of the Antonine Wall (see entry); also the Traprain treasure (5th c. BC), discovered in 1919, and extensive collections of Scottish costumes and gold and silver work.

★Charlotte Square

The Neo-Classical façades on the north side of Charlotte Square, completed in 1791, are considered by many to be Robert Adam's finest masterpiece. The ★ **Georgian House** (No. 7) is now a museum providing a fascinating glimpse into the life of a well-to-do family at the end of the 18th c.

★Royal Botanic Garden

The Royal Botanic Garden, situated to the north of the town centre, is the second largest of its kind in Britain. Within its 69 acres are a herbarium, a palm-house, a tropical house with exotic orchids and Amazonas lilies, a cactus and succulent collection, and an alpine house. As well as an arboretum with huge and rare old trees, there are also magnificent azalea and rhododendron beds and a rock garden. The exhibition hall regularly holds temporary displays.

Calton Hill

Calton Hill offers excellent views of the city. At its foot stands the **Royal High School** (13th c.), where Sir Walter Scott was a pupil.

National Gallery of Scotland

A monument opposite in Regent Road commemorates Scotland's national poet **Robert Burns** (see Famous People).

On Calton Hill itself the most impressive building is the **National Monument**, erected in memory of the Scots who fell in the Napoleonic campaigns. First mooted in 1816, a year after the Battle of Waterloo, designs for a Parthenon-style memorial were drawn up in 1822 by William Henry Playfair. Work started but was never completed.

The **Nelson Monument** a short distance away, honouring the victor of Trafalgar (see Famous People, Lord Nelson), was unveiled in 1816. The time-ball is lowered simultaneously with the One O'Clock Gun fired from the Castle.

Additional sights on Calton Hill include the **City Observatory** and two further monuments, one to the philosopher Dugald Stewart (1753–1828), the other to the mathematician John Playfair (1748–1819).

Edinburgh's port at the mouth of the Water of Leith in the Firth of Forth was left to decay for a long while in the wake of the shipyard crisis until a major rehabilitation project brought new hope. Today the houses around Shore, Constitution and Bernard Street are back to their former glory; they include the old customs house and St. Andrew Lamb's House in Burgess Street which was built by a rich merchant in the 17th c.

Leith

The **Clan Tartan Centre** in Bangor Road 70–74 shows computerised genealogical research of clan history and tartans.

Surroundings

The 14th c. Craigmillar Castle (2 miles south-east) was a favourite residence of Mary Queen of Scots.

Craigmillar Castle

About 5 miles south of Edinburgh lies the mining village of Roslin, popularised in 1800 by Scott's "Lay of the Last Minstrel". The 15th c. village chapel, erected by William Sinclair, is notable for its ornate masonry work and allegorical sculptures – especially the famous "Dance of Death" and the late-Gothic "Prentice Pillar".

Roslin

Another very pleasant excursion is to Haddington and the Lammermuir Hills (10 miles). Much of the counties of Midlothian and West Lothian is industrialised, but East Lothian is still almost entirely agricultural, with fertile red soil and red sandstone houses. Haddington can be reached directly from Edinburgh on the A1, but the more attractive route is the longer one passing through the little coastal towns on the Firth of Forth – Prestonpans, with a fine Mercat Cross, and Aberlady (pop. 700), a quiet little place with a sandy beach and the Aberlady Bay nature reserve (many sea-birds). From here Haddington is a 6 mile drive south. Alternatively it is possible to continue along the coast by way of Gullane (famous golf course) and the little village of Dirleton where there are remains of a very large 13th c. castle, to **North Berwick** (pop. 5100), a trim seaside resort with another two golf courses. Robert Louis Stephenson spent several summers here as a child. There are boat trips to the little offshore islands, in particular the Bass Rock (350 ft), the nesting-place of countless sea-birds.

Haddington and the Lammermuir Hills

3 miles east of North Berwick is the magnificently situated ★**Tantallon Castle** (1374), with ramparts, moat, corner towers and central gatehouse.

From Tantallon the road turns south, heading inland to Whitekirk and then **East Linton** (pop. 850), a picturesque little town on the Tyne. The river, flowing through a small gorge, is crossed by a 16th c. bridge.

The former RAF airfield at East Fortune, a few miles north-west, is now the ★**Museum of Flight** with a collection of more than 30 old planes. Among them are a 1930 De Havilland Puss Moth, 1934 Weir W-2, Supermarine Spitfire and a Sea Hawk.

About 2 miles south-west of East Linton stands the 13th c. **Hailes Castle**, destroyed by Cromwell (see Famous People) in 1650. The narrow dungeons in the two towers are grim-looking even today. Behind it is Traprain Law (724 ft) where, in 1919, a hoard of 4th c. Roman silver coins was found.

Haddington (pop. 8200), formerly county town of East Lothian, is attractively situated on the Tyne, here spanned by two fine 16th c. bridges. The ancient town has a large number of carefully restored houses, very pleasing to the eye, mainly in the High Street. The Neo-Classical Town House (1748) was designed by William Adam, the 170 ft-high spire being added by Gillespie Graham in 1831. The 14th c. parish church, known locally as the "Lamp of Lothian", still has the original central tower, nave and west front. There are three notable 17th c. mansions – Haddington House, Bothwell Castle and Moat House. The restored stepped gables and pantile roofs in the 18th c. Mitchell's Close keep faithfully to the originals.

To the south of Haddington lie the **Lammermuir Hills**, gently rounded and up to 1750 ft in height, with some good trout streams. The little town of Gifford makes a convenient base from which to explore the hills. Nearby are the remains of Yester Castle, which features in Scott's "Marmion". In the hills is Nunraw Castle (17th c.) which also plays a part in one of his novels, "The Bride of Lammermoor"; it is now incorporated into the Cistercian abbey. For anyone returning to Edinburgh from Gifford, the B6355 offers a more leisurely alternative to the A1.

Standing surrounded by acres of cornfields, the **Glenkinchie Distillery** at Pencaitland (5 miles west of Gifford), founded in 1835, is noted for its classic malt whiskies. The upstairs drying floor on which the fermented barley used to be spread out to dry, closed down in 1968, now houses a whisky museum.

★ **Scottish Mining Museum**

The Scottish Mining Museum, consisting of two former pits, provides a fascinating glimpse into the history of the mining industry in Scotland.

The old **Prestongrange Pit** at Prestonpans to the east of Edinburgh is reached on the B1348 via Musselburgh. The underground galleries vividly convey the harshness of the environment in which miners work. The powerful machinery used to extract the coal is also immensely impressive.

Just as instructive is a visit to the ★ **Lady Victoria Colliery**, situated 10 miles south-east of Edinburgh and reached via the A7 to Newtongrange. Once the show-piece of the Scottish coalfields while in operation from 1890 to 1981, the old shaft and pit-head are being turned into a museum. The Grant Richie machine, used to extract coal from depths of almost

Winding machinery in the Lady Victoria Colliery Museum

The Forth Railway Bridge

1650 ft, is already on show. The pit was named after the wife of Lord Lothian, who once owned it.

See entry

Southern Uplands

Many places of interest lie on the drive west around the Firth of Forth, returning to Edinburgh via the spectacular Forth Road Bridge. The first port of call should be the village of Dalmeny, which boasts the finest ★**Norman church** in Scotland. Built in the second half of the 12th c. it has an ornately decorated south porch and superb wood carvings in the interior.

Dalmeny

South Queensferry (pop. 7500) lies in the shadow of the two great bridges across the Firth. Designed by Sir John Fowler and Sir Benjamin Baker, and erected in the 1880s, the massive tubular steel structure of the ★★**Forth Railway Bridge**, 8298 ft long, the track 148 ft above the water, is a masterpiece of civil engineering. The ★★**Forth Road Bridge**, opened in 1964, its span of 5745 ft making it one of the longest suspension bridges in Europe, seems almost flimsy by comparison.

Queensferry

Hawes Ferry Inn in Queensferry features in several of Scott's works. St Mary's Church (founded in 1330), the only Carmelite church in Britain still in use, has a 16th c. tower.

Hopetoun House (3 miles west), a magnificent Baroque mansion, was built between 1696 and 1754 by William Bruce and his sons. It has an elaborate two-storey façade, flanked on both sides by crescent-shaped colonnades and pavilions. The state apartments have ornate stucco ceilings and are sumptuously appointed with 18th and 19th c. furnishings. Among many notable paintings in the picture gallery are Canaletto's "Doge's Palace and the Campanile on the Canale Grande in Venice", and a portrait of Jane, Countess of Hopetoun, by Gainsborough (see Famous People). The early 19th c. Meissen and Derby services in the porcelain collection are also exceptional.

★**Hopetoun House**

Some 6½ miles further on lies the ancient town of Linlithgow (pop. 4300). Here there are some well preserved buildings from the 16th c. with two of major importance. The first, picturesquely situated on a small loch, is the famous **Linlithgow Palace** in which Mary Queen of Scots (see Famous People) was born in 1542. The Palace

★**Linlithgow**

dates from the 15th c. In the courtyard is a fountain erected in the 16th c. by James V, a copy of which stands in the forecourt of the Palace of Hollyroodhouse in Edinburgh. The 100 ft-long Great Hall has a magnificent fireplace installed at the beginning of the 15th c. in the reign of James I; 23 ft wide, it is divided into three compartments.

The second of Linlithgow's important historic buildings is ⋆**St Michael's Church**, the largest parish church still surviving from the pre-Reformation period. First consecrated in the 13th c., it was rebuilt after 1424 and eventually completed in the mid 16th c. The nave (1497) and the choir (1531) are particularly fine; notable also is the tracery in St Catherine's aisle.

⋆**Culross**

Culross is located on the enchanting Fife Peninsula, the very picture of an old Scottish burgh. It is noted for its numerous exceptionally fine houses dating from 1600 to 1800. Very much in evidence are typical white and grey washed walls, red pantiled roofs, crow-stepped gables and outside staircases (the entrances to the picturesque Little Houses being mainly on the first floor). Two buildings which particularly stand out are the Town House (1626) with its elegant double staircase and the mansion known as the Palace, originally the home of a wealthy merchant, Sir George Bruce. Begun in 1597 and completed in 1611 it has beautifully painted beam ceilings and an interesting terraced garden. The present church consists of the choir and central tower of an abbey church founded in 1217.

Dunfermline

Dunfermline is famous as the historical capital of Scotland – Malcolm III was resident here during the second half of the 11th c. Later it became a prosperous coal mining area and the world centre for the damast trade. The steel tycoon and philanthropist Andrew Carnegie (1835–1919) had a lasting effect on the town of his birth. The **Carnegie Birthplace Museum** in Moodie Street relates the dream career of the poor weaver's son who became one of the richest industrialists of his era – his story is often quoted as an example of the "American dream".

The **Benedictine Abbey** has its roots in the 11th c.; its church is the work of the masters of Durham. The grave of Robert the Bruce, the victor of the decisive Battle of Bannockburn and Scotland's national hero, was discovered by chance in 1818 and is indicated by a brass plate beneath the pulpit.

Kirkcaldy

Kirkcaldy (pop. 52,400) is an industrial town and coal-shipping port, associated in particular with the manufacture of linoleum. It was the birthplace of the architect Robert Adam (1728–92) who, along with his brother, was the creator of the Neo-Classical style with which their names are almost synonymous. It was also the birthplace of Adam Smith (1723–90), founder of the classical school of political economy. "The Wealth of Nations", written while he was serving here as a customs official and published in 1776, quickly became the bible of the free-trade movement. The Industrial and Social History Museum in Forth House has, amongst other things, interesting displays relating to the history of linoleum manufacture.

Falkland Palace

Situated just under 10 miles north of Kirkcaldy, at the foot of the Lomond Hills, Falkland Palace, owned since 1952 by the National Trust for Scotland, was at one time a favourite hunting seat of the Stuarts. Although begun in the 15th c., the buildings in their present aspect date from 1540. Mary Stuart (see Famous People) was a regular visitor. The Flemish tapestries in the Royal Chapel, and the Early Renaissance courtyard façade (south wing) are especially note-

Picturesque houses ...   *... and the Town Hall in Culross*

worthy. The real tennis court in the grounds was constructed in 1539.

Beyond Kirkcaldy the A955 hugs the coast of the Fife peninsula on its way to **Wemyss**, a pleasant seaside resort, and then on through **Coaltown** and **Buckhaven** to **Leven**. From here the A915 and 917 skirt the shallow curve of Largo Bay to the holiday resort of **Elie** (population, with Earlsferry: 950) which has an attractive harbour, pretty gabled houses and pleasant beach.

★East coast of Fife

Next come two more, equally charming fishing villages, also very popular with tourists. The first, ★**St Monance**, boasts an interesting Gothic parish church and quaint Little Houses, much in favour among artists as homes. **Pittenweem** also has a cluster of delightful houses around its old harbour, and a parish church with a solid tower (1592). The small Isle of May out in the Firth is a nature reserve.

Anstruther (pop. 3300), a few miles further on, is an important fishing port with a Scottish Fisheries Museum. The manse, the oldest in Scotland still occupied, bears the date 1590. About 9 miles beyond Anstruther lies **St Andrew's Bay** (see entry).

The return to Edinburgh is via the A91 and M90, with a short stop at Kinross, close to Loch Leven, famous for its pink trout. On one of the two islands in the loch stands Loch Leven Castle in which Mary Queen of Scots (see Famous People) was imprisoned for almost a year before making her escape with the help of William Douglas. Her nocturnal flight was spun into a romantic tale by Sir Walter Scott in his novel "The Abbot" (1820). On the other side of the island are the remains of St Serf's Priory. – From Kinross it is a straight run back to Edinburgh by way of the Forth Road Bridge.

Kinross

257

Eurotunnel

Region: Southern England. County: Kent

A new and fast transport system between England and France is now available to the traveller with the Eurotunnel, opened in 1994, which crosses under the Channel between Coquelles near the French port of Calais and Folkestone in the English county of Kent.

From the two terminals, both equipped with restaurants and shops, there is direct access to the respective motorway systems: on the French side exit 13 to the A16, and on the English exit 11a to the M20.

History The first plans to establish a fixed link between Great Britain and the continent were made by the Frenchman Nicholas Desmeret as early as 1751. In 1802 Albert Mathieu, one of Napoleon's engineers, drew up plans. The first British plans are attributed to Sir John Hawkshaw, who envisaged a tunnel in about 1870. A further 25 reports followed but all were abandoned for financial or military reasons. The first excavations on two separate railway tunnels between the Shakespeare Cliff west of Dover and Sangatte west of Calais were started in 1880 but work was halted after the first 2000 m on grounds of national security. All subsequent suggested routes centred on the already established route. In 1970 a tunnel project which was to be up to 90 per cent state-funded was abandoned in the mid-Seventies owing to the economic recession.

In Autumn 1981 an Anglo-French project group was set up, the assessment of the various suggested links involving tunnels and bridges followed and at the beginning of 1986 both governments decided on the Eurotunnel project and the franchise was signed in Paris in 1987. At the end of 1990 breakthrough in the service tunnel was completed, followed in 1991 by the main tunnel. In 1992 a border stone was located in the middle of the tunnel to mark the common border between the two countries that since 1994 finally have a "land connection". Although sensors and computers monitor all train movements the safety systems failed in November 1996 and a burning train destroyed a section of the southern tunnel about 11 miles from the French coast, which then had to be shut down.

★★**Eurotunnel** Eurotunnel acting as the Anglo-French holding company of Channel Tunnel Group Ltd. and France-Manche SA is the client and operating

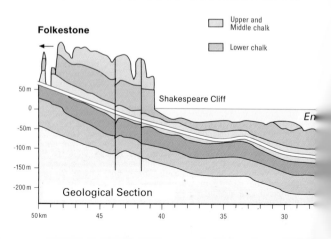

Folkestone

Upper and Middle chalk

Lower chalk

Shakespeare Cliff

En

50 m

0

-50m

-100 m

-150 m

-200 m

Geological Section

50 km   45   40   35   30

Eurotunnel

Rail tunnel   **Service tunnel**   **Rail tunnel**

4,8 m   © *Baedeker*   7,6 m

15 m   15 m

authority of the Channel tunnel, which has no state funding (costs approx. £10 billion funded by 225 banks and 750,000 private investors). Its monopoly on the franchise for the "fixed link" expires in 2042.

Although the Tunnel's image has suffered since the fire at the end of 1996 and the operator has had substantial financial problems, by now almost 50 per cent of transit traffic between England and France goes through Europe's longest railway tunnel – where most ferries need a good hour longer. Considering the growing passenger traffic between the island and the continent, which doubled over the last decade, according to the most recent forecasts the ferry companies should be able to retain a profitable share of the market. In the year 2003, 150 million people are expected to cross the Channel. The market leaders Stena Line and P & O Ferries have increased their channel crossings substantially since the tunnel fire, Hover Speed and P & O have doubled their daily crossings between Calais and Dover. Whilst the ferry companies have already reacted with shorter boarding times, new ships and simpler tariffs, emphasising the sea journey as an experience in itself, the main argument for a tunnel crossing is the time advantage and also the independence from the uncertain weather conditions. Anybody who has travelled with Eurostar or Le Shuttle is normally enthusiastic. Following connection to the European high-speed rail network, journey times to the big cities of continental Europe have reduced considerably; the journey from London to Paris, for example, takes less than four hours and from London to Frankfurt less than five hours, an attractive alternative to air travel.

The 31 mile-long channel tunnel consists of two parallel tunnels   Construction

Eurotunnel

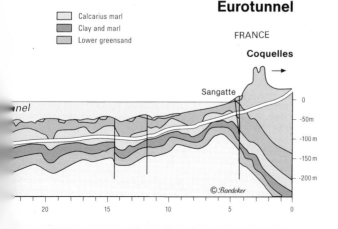

Calcarius marl
Clay and marl
Lower greensand

FRANCE

Coquelles

Sangatte

nel

0
-50m
-100 m
-150 m
-200 m

© *Baedeker*

20   15   10   5   0

Eurotunnel: Folkstone Visitor Centre

A boring machine used in construction

each with a diameter of 25 ft. Between the two single-track tunnels each carrying a one-way shuttle train is a service tunnel with a diameter of 16 ft which is connected to the main tunnels at a distance of 1230 ft. The three separate tunnels which are made from 720,000 prefabricated reinforced concrete segments are set in clayey, impermeable limestone marl between 131 ft and 246 ft below the sea bed, the deepest point at 377 ft below sea level is 8 miles from the coast.

The shuttle service carries passengers and vehicles 24 hours a day, goods traffic is handled separately. Whereas buses and lorries are only transported on one level the carriages for the remaining vehicles are equipped with two loading levels. The trains operate every 15 to 20 minutes during the day, every 30 to 60 minutes at night, the actual journey time being 35 minutes. The boarding times can be kept to a minimum because the British immigration controls take place in France and vice versa so that the total time spent in the Eurotunnel system from departure to driving up to the road is estimated to be about an hour. Fares are not much higher than the channel ferries.

On the ferries the crossing itself compares at 75 minutes with the whole process taking 2½ to 3 hours. Whereas tunnel users can only stretch their legs in the carriage, on the ferry passengers can wander around the deck, shop and have a meal.

Exeter   H 10

Region: Southern England

County: Devon
Altitude: 165 ft. Population: 96,500

Exeter, the old county town of Devon, has retained its historic charm despite its growth in size and importance. Roman town walls, the medieval cathedral quarter, rows of Tudor and Stuart houses, handsome communal buildings and numerous parks and gardens make up the townscape of this city which is a centre of modern service industries. The surrounding Devon countryside is one of England's richest areas of pastureland and is famous for its thick cream and cream cheese; a delicious speciality is the "cream tea", a pot of tea served with small scones topped with cream and jam.

History As early as 1 BC the Dumnonier tribe established a trading settlement at the point where the River Exe ceases to be navigable. In AD 1 the Romans expanded it and extended the important trading and supply route from London to Dorchester as far west as Exeter. About 200 the mighty town walls were built (remains are in the area around Southernhay). In the confusion of the post-Roman period a Saxon monastery was founded near the site of the present-day cathedral, to which, among others, St Bonifatius (d. 745) a missionary to the Germans belonged. Even during the reign of King Alfred Danish invaders repeatedly penetrated from the coast as far as Exeter and sacked the town several times between 876 and 1003. After its reconstruction Edward the Confessor honoured the tireless work of the town's inhabitants by transferring the bishop's seat from Crediton to Exeter.

The town resisted the Norman invasion until 1068 but following an 18 day-long siege it was finally taken by William the Conqueror (see Famous People). Since the 12th c. Exeter has developed because of the river traffic into a flourishing commercial centre. During the Wars of the Roses the town switched its alliance, not always to its advantage, between the Houses of Lancaster and York. In 1497 it withstood an attack by Perkin Warbeck and in the Reformation in 1549 defended itself against the rebels for the introduction of the English Prayer Book. In the Civil War Exeter fell into the hands of the Royalists and was consequently plundered by the Parliamentarian troops so that the citizens reacted by tolerating the secret meetings of the Royalists in the town. The Stuart king Charles II personally visited the town in 1671 to thank it for its support. James II, on the other hand, was less popular with many of Exeter's citizens supporting the Duke of Monmouth instead, for which they were later severely punished. Peace did not prevail again until William III came to the throne. In May 1942 the historic quarter of the town suffered heavy damage in the air raids.

Exeter Cathedral: the Minstrel Gallery

Cathedral nave ...   *... and the clock in the north transept*

Façade Only the two transept towers survive from the Norman church begun in 1112 which preceded the High-Gothic building of the Cathedral of St Peter which was erected between 1257 and 1369. Of particular interest is the west front in the form of a mural on the lower section. Between the doorway and the tracery of the rose window three once colourfully decorated rows of figures represent the new Jerusalem with angels, the kings of the Old Testament seated cross-legged as if in judgment like predecessors of Christ, apostles and prophets.

Main nave In the interior of the triple-naved pillared basilica the tierceron, a long stretch of continuous fan vaulting resting on massive sheaved columns running as far as the east end of the choir, is allegedly the longest ribbed vaulting in the world. It has magnificent keystones and intensifies the particular character of this distinctive longitudinal English Gothic building. On the northern wall of the central nave the **Minstrel Gallery** built by John Grandisson (Bishop from 1327–69) has angels playing musical instruments below baldachins still mostly in the original colours. There are attractive groups of consoles (14th c.) on the pillar beyond the chancel (1687) with a storyteller offering a headstand as a present to the Mother of God on the opposite column of the central nave.

The **Choir** screen with 17th c. paintings was completed in 1325, during the Commonwealth (1649–60) it was walled in, in order that the Independents could use the main nave and the Presbyterians could use the choir for their worship. Of particular interest are the 50 or so misericords from 1230–70 which are integrated into the 19th c. choirstalls, including an elephant with cow's feet, sirens, a king in a cauldron. Close to the high altar is a medieval sedilia (14th c.) with stone baldachins. The lectern in the form of a brass eagle (symbol of John the Baptist) dates from around 1500. The splendid 55 ft-high Bishop's Throne is a masterpiece of Gothic wood carving (1313–17) with panels depicting Bishops Warelwart (d. 1136), Quivil (d. 1291), Stapledon (d. 1326) and Grandisson (d. 1369), the leading architects of the Cathedral. The tombs of various bishops from the 12th to the 16th c. are located in the east choir, the ambulatory and in the Lady Chapel, some in new colourful settings.

Also noteworthy is the large east window (1320–70) with representations of Mary and the Saints, as is the clock in the north transept; the larger face is from the end of the 15th c. and the upper face was added in 1760.

The **Chapterhouse** from 1412 is interesting because of its painted wooden roof truss (1465–78). The modern sculptures (1974) are by Kenneth Carter.

Among its many treasures the **Library** houses the 10th c. "Exeter Codex", with poems by Cynewulf and other Anglo-Saxon writers as well as a copy of the bible which was printed by John Eliot for the Indians in Massachusetts. In the former library are the archives of the Cathedral, going back to the 10th c.

In the Cathedral Close a row of old shops has been preserved, medieval houses of the churchmen, together with the four-storeyed half-timbered building Mol's Coffee House (1598), the small church of St Martin (15th c.) and nearby in St Martin Lane the Ship Inn, an old tavern and meeting place for sailors which is referred to with approval by Sir Francis Drake (see Famous Personalities). A statue of the Anglican theologian Richard Hooker (c. 1554–1600), born in a suburb of Exeter, stands on the green.

Cathedral Close

Cathedral quarter It is just a few minutes' walk from the Cathedral to the pedestrian zone in Princesshay where the entrances to the medieval underground passages have been preserved, or to the High Street, Exeter's main shopping street (pedestrianised). Nearby is the Guildhall, the council or guild house from 1160, 1330 and rebuilt 1466/84) with a portico from 1592. The interior decoration is from the 17th and 19th c., the ceiling of the meeting hall was probably completed in 1470. The small St Pancras Church is the town's oldest sacral building with a chancel from the time of James I and a Norman font.

Old Town

Of the Norman stronghold of **Rougemont Castle** only the moat, the ramparts, Athelstan's Tower (mentioned by Shakespeare in "Richard III") and the gatehouse remain. It is pleasant to walk in Rougemont and the adjoining Northernhay Gardens with their carefully tended greens.

The **Royal Albert Museum and Art Gallery** in Queen Street has a collection of clothing of the past, pottery, some good watercolours and fine products (including silver) by local craftsmen.

Fore Street leads to **St Nicholas's Priory,** the ruins of a Benedictine abbey from 1080 with a Norman crypt and 15th c. kitchen and hall. Close by is Tucker's Hall (1471), the medieval guild house of the weavers, tanners and clothcutters, with its wood-panelling and fireplace from 1638. To the south-east is Stepcote Hill with a charming late-Medieval group of half-timbered houses and the church **St Mary's Steps** with a fine clock (18th c. figures) and a Norman font. Nearby are the remains of an old stone bridge over the Exe (12th c.) which was the former main entrance to the town, West Gate. Not far is the **Customs House** (1681) and the bridge to the **Maritime Museum** with indoor and outdoor exhibitions illustrating in detail the history of seafaring.

Killerton Gardens (7 miles north), a landscaped park of about 1800 with a costume collection in the manor house, are particularly attractive in spring and summer.

Surroundings

Powderham Castle (8 miles south-west) is the seat of the Courtenays, the Earls of Devon. The castle, built in an E-shape in the 16th c. with further extensions (staircase and interior 17/18th c.) is set in a beautiful deer park.

The Fens   L/M 8

Region: Eastern England
Counties: Cambridgeshire, Lincolnshire and Norfolk

The Fens or Fenlands are an area of 1400 sq. miles of marsh and moor around the Wash basin, a dead flat expanse of alluvial land on the East Coast (see entry) watered by the rivers Ouse, Nene, Welland and Witham. There is a distinct difference between the fertile silt fens near to the coast (marsh) and the peat fens (moor) situated further inland.

In the time of Hadrian there were large Roman settlements here engaged in growing corn and winning salt, and the process of draining the Fens was begun by the Romans. Large-scale drainage works were carried out between 1622 and 1656 by a Dutch engineer, Sir Cornelius Vermuyden, thus reclaiming large areas of land for agriculture; in consequence the Fens are now a fertile region growing wheat, sugar beet, vegetables, flowers and potatoes. The drainage system is based on a herringbone pattern of ditches with small channels leading into larger ones and these, in turn, leading into the even larger rivers. Over a period of time the draining off of the water resulted in the moor area sinking so that the peat fens are lower than the silt fens – an example of man changing the natural relief of the land. The water was formerly pumped into the main channels by windmills, as in Holland, and a few windmills can still be seen, for example, at Waltham, Heckington, Alford and Burgh-le-Marsh. Later came steam-driven pumps and these in turn have now been superseded by electric power.

The halophyte-covered foreshore between the dyke and the sea is now earmarked as a nature reserve. There is a visible break where the mudflats begin. To nature-lovers this tranquil green landscape stretch-

A windmill ...   ... in Wicken fen

ing endlessly away to the horizon offers great attractions, with its rare birds, dragonflies, its grazing cattle and sheep, its wide fields and handsome farmhouses.

Also of great interest are the still undrained areas of peat fen, many of which have been left in their original state and are now nature reserves, such as Holme Fen and Woodwalton Fen (with rare butterflies found nowhere else in England).

★Nature reserves

In the ★**Wicken Fen** nature reserve south of Ely, the first British nature reserve from 1899, an area of marshland has been preserved to show the various stages of development and the oldest form of drainage using wind power.

One of the best bases from which to explore the Fens is the charming cathedral city of Ely (pop. 13,200) in Cambridgeshire. The peat found in the surrounding area was used as fuel in salt production and the ensuing trade brought wealth to the town at an early stage, which is reflected in the architecture of its cathedral, the third largest in England. Rising out of the flat fenland, it looks even larger – a landmark visible from far and wide.

Ely

Before the drainage of the Fens, Ely was an island in the midst of the marshland. In the 7th c. St Ethelreda, queen of Northumbria, founded an abbey here, later occupied by the Benedictines. The present building was begun by Simeon, the first Norman abbot, in 1083, and by 1109, when the bishopric of Ely was founded, the eastern part was complete. The western half was completed in 1180–90. In 1322 the Norman crossing tower collapsed. Unlike other churches where this happened – as it did not infrequently – the cathedral was not given a new spire but a unique stone octagon surmounted by an octagonal timber lantern. The new structure, completed in 1342, is of remarkable harmony and beauty.

★★Ely Cathedral

On entering the cathedral through the beautiful west doorway the visi-

Ely Cathedral

tor's first impression is of the astonishing lightness of the 248 ft-long nave, typically Norman in style though it is. This is due to the elaborate articulation of the twelve bays, and also perhaps to the painted ceiling, a 19th c. addition. The Octagon (radius 82 ft) supported by 16 oak trunks, the only structure of its kind in England, is as impressive from the inside as from the exterior. The Norman south-west transept serves as the baptistery. St Edmund's Chapel contains a wall painting from about 1200 and a beautiful 15th c. screen, both restored. The choir has three elegant Decorated bays at the west end. The 59 misericords of the choir stalls (1342) have mostly been renewed. Behind the choir is the chapel (1486–1500) built by Bishop Alcock, patron of Porterhouse and founder of Jesus College, Cambridge (see Cambridge). The Lady Chapel, an admirable example of the Decorated style, contains sculptured scenes from the life of the Virgin, with hundreds of now headless statuettes. In the north cloister is a museum of stained glass.

The surviving conventual buildings are occupied by the King's School, among them the beautiful Prior Crauden's Chapel and the Queen's Hall. The vicarage of St Mary's Church was occupied by Oliver Cromwell (see Famous People) and his family from 1636–47.

From Stuntney (1 mile south-east), where Cromwell had a farm, there is the finest view of the cathedral.

Spalding

Spalding (pop. 18,200) lies in the centre of the bulb-growing area. In spring the fields are full of tulips and daffodils in bloom, attracting crowds of visitors. The trim little town with its brick-built houses is reminiscent of Holland. **Ayscoughfee Hall**, built in 1429 but much altered since then, has a good ornithological collection.

Crowland

Crowland (5 miles south; pop. 2900) is famous for the **Benedictine abbey** which King Ethelbald of Mercia built over the grave of a hermit in the 8th c. Of the church there survive the beautiful 12th c. west front (begun 1170 in Early English Perpendicular style), with old statues; a Norman arch from the crossing; the bell-tower (1427), from which there are extensive views: and the north aisle, now used as the parish church.

The second sight in Crowland is the **Trinity Bridge** with an effigy of Christ which dates from the time when the waterways were the main traffic routes of the Fens. It was built in the mid-14th c. over the junction of two canals, but these have since been diverted and the bridge is now stranded on dry land in the centre of the town.

Boston

Another interesting town is Boston (pop. 33,900). This English town in Lincolnshire gave its name to the American town of Boston in Massachussetts (originally "Botolph's Town"). Lying 6 miles from the mouth of the Witham, it was at one time England's second largest seaport. It is the administrative centre of the Fen district known as "Holland".

★**St Botolph's Church** is one of the largest parish churches in the country and one of the best known for its tower, a landmark visible for miles around with extensive views. It is known as the "Boston Stump" because it took 20 years to build. It has a carillon of 36 bells. There are 64 choir stalls with fine misericords. Boston has maintained its contacts with the United States and the south-west chapel of St Botolph's was restored in the 19th c. by the people of Boston, Massachussetts, in memory of John Cotton, who was vicar here before emigrating to America in 1633.

Glasgow   G 5

Country: Scotland. Region: Strathclyde
Altitude: 46 ft. Population: 690,000
UK City of Architecture and Design 1999

Port Glasgow

Glasgow, situated in the Scottish Lowlands, on both banks of the River Clyde – about 19 miles from its estuary, is Scotland's largest town. Following Athens, Florence, Amsterdam, Berlin and Paris Glasgow was chosen in 1990 as "European City of Culture". In fact in comparison with its proud arch-rival Edinburgh (see Edinburgh) the grey appearance of this inhospitable and rough industrial and commercial metropolis has changed considerably in recent years. The restructuring into a service city has been more successful in Glasgow than in other problem areas of the country, although high unemployment is still dominant in some parts of the city. In the mid-Eighties the new Trade and Congress Centre was opened, old dilapidated buildings on the bank of the Clyde were demolished to make room for gardens and parks and the former dock-yards on the other side of the river were turned into a residential area in 1988. The soot-covered sandstone façades of the Victorian buildings in the city centre have been sandblasted, shopping arcades such as the glass-covered St Enoch Shopping and Entertainment Centre and the elegant Princes Square have been built and the range of cultural activities widened. Nowadays this working-class city seems to combine in its own inimitable way the two elements eagerly sought after by the enlightened tourist: "real life" and "culture". The name Glasgow is derived from the Gaelic term "Glas ghu" (lovely green place) which finds confirmation in the many parks and green areas. Among the multitude of museums and galleries in the city are the world famous Burrell Collection in Pollock Country Park, Glasgow Museum and Art Gallery in Kelvingrove Park with one of the finest municipal art collections in Britain, the renowned McLellan Galleries with their acclaimed changing exhibitions of con-temporary art, the Museum of Transport in Kelvin Hall, the school museum opened in 1990 in Scotland Street School (designed by Mackintosh) and the Gallery of Modern Art which opened in 1996. The Glasgow Citizens Theatre founded in 1942 by James Bridie enjoys an excellent reputation as does the Theatre Royal, the Scottish Opera, the Scottish National Opera and the Scottish Ballet. Some of the events include the colourful May Day celebrations, Streetbiz and international Festivals of Jazz and Folk.

Apart from a few buildings, especially the medieval cathedral, the aspect of the city bears the stamp of the last 200 years. To appreciate Glasgow's urban beauty a closer look is required, for the particular mark of Victorian-Edwardian architecture can be seen as an art form on department stores, banks, insurance companies, hotels, pubs and rail-way stations.

A decisive factor in its earlier development was the dredging of a channel in the Clyde to enable the largest vessels to sail up the river; 200 years ago it was possible to cross the river on foot at low tide. Within the city boundaries eleven bridges and a tunnel link the two sides of the Clyde.

The stunningly beautiful surroundings offer the visitor the choice of the varied scenery of the Scottish Highlands with the North West

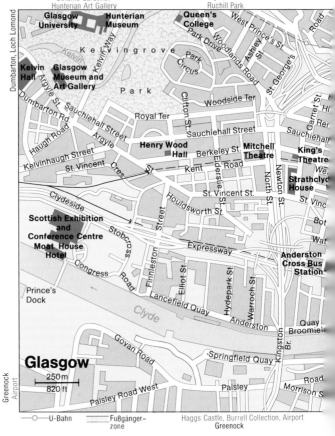

Underground

Pedestrian zone

1 McLellan Galleries
2 Glasgow Film Theatre
3 Savoy Centre
4 Pavilion Theatre
5 Old Athenaeum Theatre
6 St. George's Tron Church
7 Stock Exchange

Highlands, Grampian Mountains and adjoining Southern Uplands (see entries).

Transport Glasgow airport lies 8 miles to the west of the city; access on the M8 motorway. Trains from the south and west terminate at Central Station and from the north and east including Edinburgh (see entry) at Queen Street Station.

Pleasure boats and cruisers and the paddle steamer Waverley depart from Brommielaw Quay (corner of Jamaica Street) by Glasgow Bridge.

History In 543 St Kentigern, also called St Mungo, built a small church on the site of Glasgow. In the 12th c. the cathedral was erected on the site of his grave around which the medieval settlement developed. After

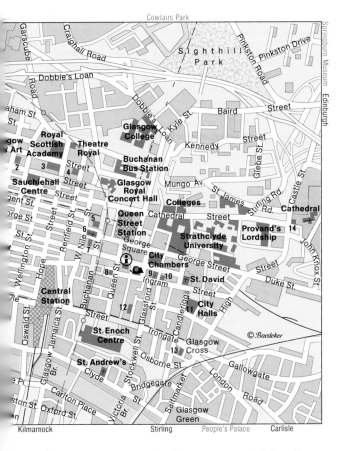

8 Gallery of Modern Art
9 Italian Centre
10 Hutchesons' Hall

11 Ticket Centre
12 Virginia Galleries
13 Tron Theatre

14 St. Mungo Museum
   and Cathedral
   Visitor Centre

the Reformation the town centre was moved to what is today Glasgow Cross, in 1451 Bishop William Turnball conferred the second university in the country upon this trading settlement.

The union of 1707 was followed by a period of economic prosperity brought about by the trade with North America. The clippers of the Glasgow tobacco lords were the fastest ships on the route to Virginia ensuring that Glasgow was in the forefront of the British tobacco trade until the beginning of the American Wars of Independence in 1776. In the same year the economist Adam Smith (1723–90), who had taught at Glasgow University from 1751 to 1763, published his liberal economic theory ("An inquiry into the nature and causes of the wealth of nations") and founded the classical national economy. The middle of the 18th c. saw the heyday of the textile trade, in 1769 the university mechanic

James Watt (see Famous People) invented the steam engine which revolutionised manufacturing, in 1792 the first mechanical looms were built in neighbouring Paisley. Watt was the leading engineer in the dredging of the Clyde estuary to make it navigable to large ships; a 19 mile stretch of river was widened enabling ships to travel as far as Glasgow where heavy industrial sites and docks developed. In 1812 the "Comet", the first seaworthy steamer was launched. By the mid-19th c. 80 per cent of all British steam ships were built on Clydeside and up until the 20th c. the huge luxury transatlantic liners, including the "Queen Elizabeth II" came from Glasgow. The heavy industries of shipbuilding and locomotive building reached their peak at the end of the 19th c., rich businessmen, shipping magnates and cloth manufacturers built churches and public buildings, but little of all this has survived. Another aspect of the economic boom was the drastic population increase in a restricted area which resulted in miserable living conditions. On account of the many jobs in industry Glasgow became the destination for immigrants, a melting pot of all nations but crowded together in ghettoes. As a result of the famine in Ireland and the clearances in the Highlands thousands of Irish and Scottish moved to the Clyde area. The football matches between the two big football clubs Rangers (Scottish Protestant, founded 1888) and Celtic (Irish Catholic; founded 1873) provided an outlet for the increasing religious and social tensions. The infamous slums in the Eastend and south of the Clyde, known as the "Gorbals", were demolished at the end of the 19th c. and replaced by Victorian tenements which were soon also overcrowded. When the slums were again demolished for the second time after the war part of the population moved into the satellite towns of the surrounding area.

The decline in heavy industry on Clydeside led to a considerable drop in the population of Glasgow, further migration was a result of the hub of the Scottish economy moving east (see Aberdeen, Grampian) which led to the decay of urban residential areas in Glasgow. In the Seventies Glasgow's image was still one of smoking factory chimneys and dilapidated housing. Paul McCartney said he liked to perform there because it reminded him of Liverpool with its football hooligans, unemployment, violence and poverty. About 1980 an extensive renovation programme was started in the city centre near the Clyde with associated projects. The 647 acre site of GEAR (Glasgow Eastern Area Renewal) is among the most ambitious attempts in Europe to overcome the problems and decay of inner city areas. Finally, a succession of image-building campaigns, culminating most recently in the choice of Glasgow as UK City of Architecture and Design 1999, have helped strengthen local self-awareness and promote the city both nationally and internationally as a place in which to invest.

Around the turn of the century the so-called Free Style was developed in Glasgow by four Scottish architects: John A. Campbell, Sir John Burnett, James Salomon II and above all **Charles Rennie Mackintosh** (1868–1928). Together with Margaret Macdonald, later to be his wife, her sister Francis and J. H. Macnair Mackintosh formed the group "The Four", the nucleus of the "Glasgow School of Art" which developed a particularly Scottish style of Art Nouveau. The Glasgow School of Art designed by Mackintosh in Renfrew Street is considered to be one of the key works of modern architecture around 1900. Its magnificent synthesis of functional calculation and imaginative decoration was praised by Walter Gropius as the "beginning of a breakthrough". The designer excelled for his interior designs with new proportions and forms based on geometric patterns. "Toshie", who was famous in Germany for his entry in a Darmstadt architectural competition (Art Lover's House, 1901), became the darling of the population of Glasgow. There are copies of his masterpieces everywhere and the Willow Tearoom in Sauchiehall Street, designed and later restored by him, became a mecca for art nouveau fans as did the building of the Scotland Street School Museum of Education, the Hill House in neighbouring Helensburgh and the only recently completed (1989–91) Art

Art nouveau bedroom in Hill House

Lover's House in Bellahouston Park built on Mackintosh's plans from 1901. The only church designed by him is the headquarters and information centre of the Charles Rennie Mackintosh Society (870 Garscube Road).

Sights

In the centre of the city is George Square with 12 statues of famous people including Robert Burns, James Watt, Sir Walter Scott (central statue) and Queen Victoria (for all five see Famous People) together with Thomas Campbell and Sir Robert Peel (1788-1850), Prime Minister and Rector of the University.

*George Square

On the eastern side of the square stands the magnificent town hall, built in 1883 by William Young in Italian Renaissance style. Of particular interest are the loggia the staircase decorated with Breccia and Carrara marble and the banqueting hall which has a beautifully coffered barrel vaulting.

City Chambers

Also on the square is the Merchant's House (1877), seat of the oldest Chamber of Commerce in Great Britain, founded in 1605 (houses an interesting model of a tobacco clipper), the Bank of Scotland and the Head Post Office, all with façades dating from the end of the 19th c.

A few steps south-west the Gallery of Modern Art on Queen Street opened in 1996 with four storeys devoted to contemporary art.

Gallery of Modern Art

Further south Glasgow's popular shopping streets are to be found: **Buchanan Street** (pedestrianised) with the luxurious **Princes Square**, Argyle Street, the Argyle Arcades with Glasgow's oldest restaurant, the sumptuously decorated Sloan's, and St Enoch Centre.

Shopping

Glasgow

Sauchiehall Street

North-east of George Square is Sauchiehall Street, a busy mile of shops, partly pedestrianised.

On the first floor of 217 Sauchiehall Street is the ★**Willow Tearoom** designed by Mackintosh and commissioned by Mrs Catherine Cranston right down to the menus. Following extensive restoration work in 1983 they re-opened and offer delicious teas in a really artistic atmosphere.

A few yards further west the ★**McLellan Galleries** which re-opened in 1990 have excellent exhibitions of modern British artists.

350 Sauchiehall Street is the **Third Eye Centre**, famous as a cultural centre for theatre, music and film. 518 Sauchiehall Street houses the **Regimental Museum of the Royal Highland Fusiliers** (uniforms, weapons, paintings of the history of the regiment).

Glasgow School of Art

In Dalhousie Street, which climbs steeply north, is the art academy designed by Mackintosh in 1876 (entrance in Renfrew Street). This art nouveau building, which was completed in 1909 when the artist was only twenty-eight years old, confirmed his reputation, not only as a master of façade design, but also as an outstanding interior designer; the unconventional library hall is especially interesting.

Tenement House

North-west in Buccleuch Street (No. 145) the Victorian Tenement House provides the visitor with an insight into the way of life of the occupants in the 19th c.

★Cathedral of St Mungo

The most important historic building is the Cathedral in Castle Street, situated to the east of George Square, Scotland's finest Gothic building. Although it is a Scottish Presbyterian church which does not acknowledge the office of bishop, it is known as "Glasgow Cathedral". The square in front with the monument to David Livingstone (see Famous People), was newly laid out in 1990.

Burns Monument in George Square ...   *... and City Chambers*

Wintergarden in the People's Palace   *School museum in Scotland Street*

The crypt dates from the 12th c., the choir and nave are early 13th c., the Lady Chapel and tower are 15th c. additions. Both externally and internally the Cathedral with its clear lines and absence of superfluous decoration has the appearance of a unified whole. The finest part of the building is the crypt, with the tomb of St Mungo, the patron saint of Glasgow, who is believed to have founded the church in the mid-6th c. Other notable features include the pre-Reformation Gothic fan vaulting and a rare rood screen depicting the seven deadly sins. The glass is mainly modern.

The adjoining **Necropolis**, Glasgow's largest cemetery on Fir Park Hill, was laid out in the 18th c. Many wealthy Victorian merchants are buried here with impressive tombs to mark their final resting place; a monument to John Knox has been here since 1825.

The oldest house in Glasgow, Provand's Lordship, is situated opposite the Cathedral. It was built as a hospital in 1471 and now serves as a museum housing furniture from 1500 to 1914.

Provand's Lordship

Opened in 1993, this museum (2 Castle Street) is devoted to the world's religions, their rites and beliefs with regard to life and death.

★Museum of Religious Life and Art

Along the south bank of the Clyde stretches the oldest park in Glasgow, laid out in 1662. A museum in the ★**People's Palace** documents the history of the city, with exhibits on the development of trade and industry, trade unions, the women's movement, entertainment and sport. Tropical and sub-tropical plants are found in the extensive winter gardens.

Glasgow Green

A few yards away the 144 ft-high **Nelson's Monument** towers, erected in 1806 in memory of Lord Nelson (see Famous People).

The Classical church of St Andrew (18th c.) contains impressive choir

St Andrew

stalls made from mahogany which were donated by wealthy merchants.

Barras Market

To the north near London Road is the traditional Barras Market; over 800 stallholders trade here at the weekend.

★Scotland Street

South of the Clyde Mackintosh built a school in Scotland Street in 1906 which was in use until 1979. It is now the **School Museum of Education** with furniture, teaching equipment and materials from Glasgow's schools which illustrate the history of teaching establishments from the Victorian period until 1990.

Scottish Exhibition and Conference Centre

Opened in 1985 the Exhibition and Conference Centre, situated south-east of the city centre on former docks on the bank of the Clyde, can accommodate 10,000 visitors in five halls.

Kelvingrove Park

In the extensive grounds of Kelvingrove Park to the west of the city in the valley of the River Kelvin are a university, a museum and **Kelvin Hall**.

Kelvin Hall is the new location of the extended ★**Museum of Transport** displaying model ships, locomotives, trams, old timers, horse-drawn carriages and a reconstruction of a Glasgow street from 1938.

The neighbouring sports centres provide comprehensive facilities for sporting events and active holidaymakers (athletics, tennis, football).

Glasgow's oldest museum, the **Hunterian Museum and Art Gallery**, was opened in 1807 and houses impressive archaeological, zoological and geological collections. Also worth seeing are the coin gallery, the collection of paintings including works by Rubens, Rembrandt, Whistler, Chardin, Reynolds, Pisarro, Sisley and Mackintosh and the reconstruction of Mackintosh's house with original furniture and his largest collection of paintings, which is integrated into the gallery.

On the northern edge of Kelvingrove Park are the buildings, designed by George Gilbert Scott in 1870, of the famous **University of Glasgow**.

The second University of Strathclyde is not far away, to the north-east of George Square.

★Glasgow Museum and Art Gallery

Every visitor to Glasgow should see the Museum and Art Gallery, opened in 1901, which has one of the finest collections in Britain of pictures by both British and European masters including works by van Gogh, Bellini, Rubens, Botticelli, Rembrandt, Turner, Ben Nicholson and Ben Johnson. The French Impressionists are strongly represented (Degas, Signac, Seurat, Monet, Sisley, Pissarro and Renoir) as are the leading Scottish masters (Horatio McCulloch, Thomas Faed,

Glasgow Museum Building

Robert Herdman, William McTaggart, the brothers David and William Bell Scott, Edward Burne-Jones, William Dyce, Mackintosh, William Gear, Bruce McLean). There are also exhibitions of valuable ancient sculpture, Egyptian reliefs and archaeological finds from Scotland, weapons and equipment, Flemish tapestries and Glasgow jewellery, silver, glass and pottery. Also of interest are the departments about local natural history and ethnography and the history of shipbuilding and navigation on the Clyde estuary.

The Warwick Vase

This fabulous art collection was bequeathed to the city in 1944 by Sir William and Lady Burrell. The design of this modern gallery, situated 4 miles south-west of the city centre in Pollock Country Park and opened by Her Majesty the Queen in 1983, is by Barr Gason, John Meunier and Brit Andreson. Among the 8000 objects are works of art from the Neolithic period to 1900, including Greek and Roman exhibits (bronze and pottery such as the Warwick Vase from the 2nd c.), paintings by Lucas Cranach the Elder, Hans Memling, Cézanne, Delacroix, Manet, Degas and Joseph Craw-

★★Burrell Collection

hall, who was sponsored by Burrell, medieval church fittings (choir stalls, altar pieces, stained glass windows), Chinese works in jade, Indian and Persian carpets, Flemish tapestries, nude figures by Rodin, richly decorated oak-panelled dining room (1500) from Hutton Castle, a doorway from Hornby Castle (16th c.), illuminated manuscripts, English embroidery (16/17th c.), weapons, silver and glass.

Pollock Park is also the location of an impressive manor house of the same name, ancestral home of the Maxwell family. The house designed by William Adam in 1752 contains a marvellous collection of Spanish paintings (including works by El Greco, Goya and Murillo), important works by William Blake and numerous priceless antiques.

Pollock House

The great age of steam locomotives is recreated in the Springburn Museum (Ayr Street).

Springburn Museum

Built by John Maxwell from 1585–87, Haggs Castle (100 St Andrews Drive) has housed a museum for children since 1976. There is a pretty Victorian children's room and a 18th c. cottage.

Haggs Castle

In Calder Park (6 miles south-east of the city centre) the 62 acre Glasgow zoo is an attraction for both old and young alike. Lions, leopards, reptiles, elephants, polar bears and camels are just some of the animals on display.

Zoo

Kibble Palace in the Botanical Gardens off the Great Western Road has a superb collection of orchids and there are relaxing walks through the gardens.

Botanic Gardens

Surroundings

From Glasgow excursions can be made to the Southern Uplands (see entry) in the south and the North-West Highlands (see entry) in the north.

From Gourrock (pop. 11,100) on the Clyde estuary ferries go to the Cowal peninsula; from Ardrossan (pop. 11,350), reached by a scenic coastal road, motor boats go to Arran (see Arran). It is only 15 miles to the "Queen of lakes", Loch Lomond, and not much further to the Trossachs (see Grampian Mountains).

★★Hill House

North-west of Glasgow in Helensburgh, Hill House (Upper Colquhoun Street) is worth a visit. After conceiving Windy Hill house on the opposite bank of the Clyde for his friend William Davidson in 1901 and submitting the plans for Art Lover's House in the same year, Mackintosh designed Hill House on a hill with far-reaching views over the Firth of Clyde for the publisher William Blackie in 1903. It now belongs to the National Trust for Scotland. The exterior decorated with figures reflects the designer's typical art nouveau style and the interior of the building is captivating with furniture mostly designed by Mackintosh.

Renfrew

Paisley, the chief town of the delightful Renfrew District, situated west of Glasgow, is a popular destination for visitors. The history of the world famous "drop-like" Paisley pattern and the development of the local textile industry is illustrated in the Paisley Museum and Art Gallery (High Street); the extensive collection of "Paisley patterned" scarves is of interest.

The looms and weaving equipment in the **Weavers Cottage** of Kilbarchan (Shuttle Street), built in 1763, provide an insight into weaving techniques of the past.

Strathkelvin

The **Forth and Clyde Canal** dating from 1790 winds through the varied

"The Last of the Clans" (Highland Clearances) by Thomas Faed (1865)

countryside of Strathkelvin District, north of Glasgow. In summer there are boat trips on the restored "Ferry Queen".

In the **Barony Chambers of Kirkintilloch** a museum is dedicated to the social and economic development of the region.

Among the attractions of Monkland District are the **Summerlea Heritage Trust of Coatbridge**, with exhibits from illustrating the region's industrial heritage (including steam engines, trams), and the **Drumpellier Country Park** with extensive moorlands, a butterfly farm and a golf course.

The town of Stirling (pop. 37,000), which has been much fought over in the course of history, is strategically situated about 28 miles north-east of Glasgow in the Forth valley at the gateway to the Highlands.

The earliest inhabitants of the site were probably Britons. The town's name is thought to be a corruption of a word meaning "place of strife"; no less than 15 battlefields are to be found in the area around the castle. The history of the castle is closely linked to the House of Stuart. It is an established historical fact that Alexander I died in Stirling Castle in 1124. In 1296 the town was surrendered to the English, but was retaken by the Scots in the following year after Wallace's victory in the battle of Stirling Bridge. The castle was the last to surrender to Edward I. In 1314 the English were finally annihilated by Robert the Bruce (see Famous People) in the battle of Bannockburn. Under the Stuarts Stirling became an important royal residence, and James II (1430), James III (1451) and James V (1512) were born here. In 1543 Maria Stuart (see Famous People) was anointed Mary Queen of Scots in Stirling, where she lived until she went to France. In 1651 the castle was reconquered by the English.

⋆**Stirling Castle**, dominating the town on a high volcanic crag, dates in its present form mainly from the 15th and 16th c. It is approached by way of the Esplanade (statue of Robert Bruce after the battle of Bannockburn) and the outer moat with outworks dating from the reign of Queen Anne. Beyond this is the Gatehouse, flanked by 15th c. round towers, which gives access to the lower square, with Parliament Hall and the Palace, its façade decorated with mythical and allegorical figures. Worth seeing are the "Stirling Heads", 31 remain from the 60 carved oak medallions depicting portraits of the Scottish rulers. On the north side of the Upper Square is the Chapel Royal (1594) built by James VI for the baptism of his son. This Early-Renaissance building contains 17th c. frescos. The garden (Nether Green) to the west of the chapel was laid out in 1532. In the King's Old Buildings is a castle museum. From the north-west part of the ramparts there are fine views.

The **Old Town** features buildings from the 16–18th c. and the Victorian era.

South of the castle, separated from it by a small depression, stands the **Church of the Holy Rude**, with a nave originally built around 1270 in Transitional style and altered in the 15th c. Here Mary was crowned Queen of Scots in 1542 at the age of eight months and in 1567 her son James VI was crowned in this church – the coronation service was performed by the reformer John Knox.

Mar's Wark The ruins of the former town residence of the Earl of Mar were begun in 1570 in Renaissance style and destroyed by the Jacobites in 1746.

The **Argyll's Lodging** town house built by William Alexander of Menstrie, the founder of the Scottish colony of Nova Scotia in North America, was acquired by the Earl of Stirling, Governor of Nova Scotia around 1632. 24 years later the house came into the possession of the Earl of Argyll and retained his name; it is now a youth hostel.

Broad Street, opposite Mar's Wark, leads past Norrie's House (17th c.) to the Tolbooth, built in 1703–06 and extended 1806/11.

There is plenty of opportunity for shopping in **King Street** (pedestrianised) and in Thistle Shopping Centre opposite the station.

On the north side of the town a **medieval stone bridge** (around 1400) spans the Forth, not to be confused with the bridge 300 ft further, which gave its name to the Battle of 1297. About a mile away on the other side of the river is a prominent landmark, the **Wallace Monument**, a square tower (220 ft) erected in 1869 to commemorate the victor of the battle of Stirling Bridge. The exhibition depicts the bitter fight of Sir William Wallace against the English invaders between 1296 and 1298. Thanks to the celluloid epic "Braveheart", filmed with Mel Gibson alias William Wallace and awarded five Oscars in 1996, the Scottish freedom fighter is widely popular today.

Dunblane

The small town of Dunblane (6 miles north of Stirling) has a **cathedral** built by Bishop Clement in 1233. It has an unusual outline as the choir has no lateral aisle or transept, instead the lateral aisles run from the nave, the tower being added to the south aisle. In the interior the Ruskin window and 15th c. choir stalls are of interest.

The **Leighton Library** built in 1687 by Robert Leighton (1611–62) is the oldest private library in Scotland. Following careful restoration it was opened to the public in 1991. It contains over 4500 books in 32 languages.

Doune Motor Museum

Among the extensive collection of old-timers which belong to the Earl of Moray in Doune (pop. 1200; 8 miles north-west of Stirling) there are several Jaguars, Aston Martins and Bentleys, a two-seater MG from 1930, a Morgan Plus Four from 1951, Sunbeam motorcycles from the 1920s and the second oldest Rolls Royce in the world.

Bannockburn Heritage Centre

Some 2 miles south of Stirling on the A872 between the rivers Pelstream and Bannockburn there is some farmland on which in 1314 the famous battle for Scotland's independence took place. Inside a rotunda a flag-pole and the stone "Borestone" mark the spot on which, according to tradition, Robert the Bruce set up headquarters in 1314 before he marched against the English led by Edward II and overcame them in a crushing defeat. The glorious battle assured King Robert I a place as a national hero for all time and has always symbolised national feelings in Scotland. In 1328 England officially recognised the greatest triumph ever gained by the Scots in the Treaty of Northampton.

The historical landscape is dominated by the hill with the bronze statue of King Robert on horseback in his suit of armour with battle axe, looking south for the English regiments. The "Kingdom of the Scots" exhibition at the Bannockburn Heritage Centre (opened 1987) shows in pictures, slides and models the course of Scottish history from the wars of independence until 1603 when, on the death of Elizabeth I, James VI of Scotland became James I of England.

Glastonbury

Region: Southern England
County: Somerset
Altitude: 180 ft
Population: 7100

Glastonbury, situated about 6 miles south-west of Wells, has magnificent ruins of an abbey steeped in legend. A thorn bush which flowers at Christmas grows on the spot where St Joseph of Arimathia is said to have sunk his walking stick into the ground. According to legend Joseph also laid the foundation stone of the first Christian church in the country. He is said to have buried the Holy Grail, the cup which contained the Blood of Christ at the Last Supper, at the foot of Glastonbury Tor, a 526 ft-high hill, from which the Chalice Well with its glistening reddish spring waters flowed. Glastonbury is alleged to be the "Isle of Avalon" of the legend of the Holy Grail, into which the mortally wounded King Arthur disappeared.

Glastonbury Abbey

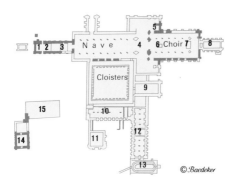

1 St Dunstan's Chapel
2 Lady Chapel
3 Galilee Chapel
4 Central tower
5 Chapel of St Thomas à Becket
6 King Arthur's Tomb
7 High Altar
8 Edgar Chapel
9 Chapter House
10 Refectory
11 Monks' Kitchen
12 Dormitory
13 Lavatory
14 Abbot's Kitchen
15 Abbot's Lodging

History The hills of Glastonbury, referred to by the Celts as Yniswitrin or Avalon, were inhabited as early as prehistoric times. Discoveries in the Lake Village Museum (in the High Street) provide evidence of prehistoric and Ice Age moorland settlements, when the Bristol Channel extended as far inland as here. Boats have been discovered which were used to reach stilt dwellings (lake villages) built on hilltops. They are thought to have been inhabited from the 3rd c. BC until the arrival of the Romans. It remained an island until the surrounding moorland dried out.

Records indicate that a monastery was first founded here in 601. Another followed around 700 founded by Ine, King of the West Saxons. St Dunstan (924–988) who was first a monk and later abbot of this monastery built the first stone church. He is buried here together with the Saxon kings Edmund (d. 975) and Edmund Ironside (d. 1016). A new

★Glastonbury Abbey

Glastonbury: Abbot's Kitchen ...   ... of Glastonbury Abbey

279

Norman church built 1120 was destroyed by fire in 1184. The church underwent expansion between 1186 and the 16th c. In 1539 Henry VIII (see Famous People) had the last abbot of the abbey, Richard Whiting hanged on Glastonbury Tor and the monastery destroyed.

Of the once giant monastery church of St Peter and Paul (580 ft long) the Late-Norman (1184–86) St Mary's Chapel with its interlaced vaulting, doorways decorated with figures and the Joseph Crypt has been more or less preserved. Also remaining are the Galilei Chapel (early 13th c.) and the massive fragments of two crossing tower columns among beautiful trees. A setting in the choir marks the site of King Arthur's grave following the "discovery" of the bones by resourceful relic collectors in 1191 and their removal in 1218 to the choir where they rested until the monastery was dissolved in 1539.

Of the living quarters the large conical Abbot's Kitchen has remained unscathed (1435–40) with the remains of four fireplaces. A small museum contains a model of the grounds of the monastery and other architectural exhibits.

The former abbey barn (14th c.) houses the **Somerset Rural Life Museum**.

Other sights

Two other churches are worth a visit: **St Benignus** from the early 16th c. and **St John the Baptist** with one of the finest church towers of the area. A short stroll around the town can be followed by a walk along Chilkwell Street to the legendary Chalice Well, the spring for the abbey, and then a climb up the nearby ★**Glastonbury Tor**, steeped in legend, to St Michael's Tower (Perpendicular Style) from where there are marvellous views.

Surroundings

Sharpham Manor (2 miles south-west) is the birthplace of the writer Henry Fielding (1707–54) with a door decorated in wrought-iron.

Wells

See entry

Gloucester   I 9

Region: Midlands
County: Gloucestershire
Altitude: 49 ft. Population: 106,500

Gloucester, on the east bank of the River Severn, is the county capital and important industrial centre for the surrounding area. The main attractions are the Norman-Gothic cathedral and the historic 19th c. port.

History In Roman times Gloucester, known as Glevum, was an important fortified town at a ford on the Severn guarding the road into Wales. It was one of four coloniae with special privileges, together with Colchester, Lincoln and York (see entries). The ending "-cester" comes from the Roman "castrum", and the town's four streets meeting at right angles in the centre reflect Roman planning. After the Norman Conquest Gloucester became the seat of a bishop and a favourite residence of Plantagenet kings, Henry III was crowned here in 1216 and Lady Jane Grey proclaimed Queen in 1553. The town gained political importance through the parliamentary meetings between 1378 and 1407 from which the separate sittings of the Lords and Commons developed, which typify England's two chamber parliamentary system. During the English Civil War the town withstood Royalist attacks for one month in 1643 but on capitulation was punished by the razing of the town walls. With the construction of the ship canal to Sharpness Gloucester became an important inland port and the numerous warehouses on the historic docks

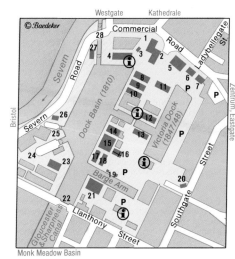

© Baedeker

Monk Meadow Basin

Port of Gloucester

In the south-west of the town are the docks, the construction of which was begun at the turn of the 18th and 19th c. They lie at the end of the Gloucester and Sharpness Canal, originally intended to go as far as Berkeley. The canal runs parallel to the Severn but at a rather higher level in order to avoid the river's considerable variations in level. The various buildings and technical installations are largely preserved in their original state and provide a very good impression of the activity which went on in a 19th c. port. Entrance permits are obtainable from the port office of the British Waterways Board (Commercial Road), but good views can be had from the neighbouring streets (see plan on left).

Historic 19th century port

1 Main entrance
2 Dock Office of British Waterways Board (c. 1830)
3 Tap and drinking fountain (1863)
4 North (Telford) Warehouse
5 City Flour Mills (c. 1850)
6 Regiments of Gloucester Museum
7 Early 19th c. houses
8–10 Robinson and Philpotts Warehouse (end 19th c.)
11–13 Victoria, Britannia and Albert Associated Warehouses
14–15 Albert and Reynolds Mills (c. 1840)
16 Mariners' Chapel (1849)
17–18 Biddle and Shipton Warehouse (beg./mid 19th c.)
19 Old bollards (perhaps a crane base)
20 Weighbridge House
21 Llanthony Warehouse (c. 1870)
22 Llanthony Bridge
23 Alexandra Warehouse (mid 19th c.)
24 Dry dock (1853)
25 Dry dock (before 1843)
26 Pumping house
27 Antiques centre
28 Swing-bridge

illustrate its former economic status. The modern harbour is situated outside the town centre.

The Cathedral was originally the church of an Anglo-Saxon monastery founded by Osric, King of Northumbria, in 681. It became a Benedictine abbey in 1022. The Norman abbots began to build a new monastery church which was consecrated in 1100 and elevated to the status of cathedral by Henry VIII (see Famous People) in 1542. However, its appearance has changed over the centuries. In 1242 the wooden roof of the nave was replaced by Early-Gothic stone vaulting, the eastern part was replaced in the 14th c. in High-Gothic style, the crossing tower in the middle and the Lady Chapel were added at the end of the 15th c. in Late-Gothic style and the west façade was altered.

In contrast to the uniform Gothic exterior of the cathedral the interior of the nave with its massive cylindrical pillars and huge rounded arches up to the vaulting is in Anglo-Norman style. Only beyond the crossing tower are the Gothic filigree architectural forms featured, the south transept is regarded as the forerunner of English Perpendicular style, while the choir with its elaborate vaulting is an example of the later stages of this style. The stained glass of the east window dates from the 14th c. and depicts the coronation of the Virgin. In the choir are numerous important tombs: centrally located is the tomb of Robert of

★ Gloucester Cathedral

Normandy, the eldest son of William the Conqueror (see Famous People), with a reclining figure of the deceased carved in oak (early 13th c.); on the north wall the tomb of the Northumbrian king Osric (d. 729) and the alabaster tomb (1330) with a sculpture of a reclining Edward II, who was murdered after his abdication in 1427 by his wife and her lover in Berkeley Castle and was buried in the abbey church at the instigation of his son Edward III. During the Middle Ages the pilgrimages to the tomb of this martyred king were a profitable source of income. The adjoining Lady Chapel, built between 1470-83, is in Perpendicular style whereas the impressive Norman crypt displays Romanesque features.

The ★**Cloisters** with their fine fan-vaulting were built between 1351–1412 and have the earliest example of fan-vaulting in Britain. On the east side the adjoining **Chapterhouse** (11–15th c.) is Norman apart from the large Perpendicular window. According to tradition William the Conqueror is said to have given the orders for the drawing up of the Domesday Book here, an overview of the property and wealth in his new kingdom. The first sitting of the House of Commons is said to have taken place in this room.

Cathedral grounds

Among the historic buildings around the Cathedral is Abbot's House (11–13th c.). Opposite the west gate (12th c.) the Church of St-Mary-de-Lode, which has a Norman tower, stands on the remains of a Roman villa. In front of it is a monument to John Hooper, bishop of Gloucester and Worcester, who was burned at the stake here in 1555 on the orders of Queen Mary. Tradition has it that he spent his last night in Hooper House (16th c.), which has been preserved in Westgate Street close to numerous fine half- timbered houses from the 15th–16th c. In Northgate Street is the New Inn, built in 1450 for the accommodation of pilgrims.

Museums

In the Folk Museum in Westgate Street old workshops (including those of coachmakers, blacksmiths and carpenters) can be seen, the City Museum and Art Gallery has Roman exhibits, old furniture and exhibitions. The Beatrix Potter Museum (Gloucester Court) contains memorabilia from the animal stories about Peter Rabbit, Tom Kitten and Jemima

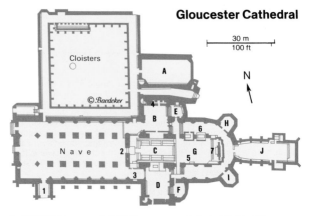

Gloucester Cathedral

30 m
100 ft

N

Cloisters

© Baedeker

A

B

E

H

4

6

Nave   2   C   G   J

5   7

3   D   F

1

A	Chapterhouse	G	Presbytery	3	Tomb of Sir John Bridges
B	North Transept	H	War Memorial Chapel		(14th c.)
C	Choir	I	St Stephen's Chapel	4	Reliquary
D	South Transept	J	Lady Chapel	5	Tomb of Duke Robert Curthose
E	St Paul's Chapel	1	South Doorway	6	Tomb of King Edward II
F	St Andrew's Chapel	2	Altar	7	High Altar

Puddleduck shown in the house of the "Tailor of Gloucester", the setting of Beatrix Potter's famous story.

Berkeley Castle (13 miles south-west) is worth a visit. It is a 12th c. stronghold which is still in the hands of the Berkeley family. An imposing structure built in stone of different colours, it stands commandingly above the Severn, surrounded by beautiful grounds. Visitors are shown the cell in which Edward II was murdered in 1327 for alleged homosexuality by his wife and her lover Mortimer as well as the large 14th c. hall, the old kitchens and the state apartments with beautiful tapestries, silver, furniture and pictures. In the fine Early English parish church are Berkeley family monuments. Dr Edward Jenner (1749–1823), recognised as the pioneer of vaccination, is buried in the churchyard.

Surroundings
★**Berkeley Castle**

Also near here, near Slimbridge Station, are the grounds of the "Wildfowl and Wetlands Trust" with a large collection of waterfowl, founded by Peter Scott.

Slimbridge

Walkers and nature lovers will find ample scope in the Forest of Dean, a wooded area of more than 40 sq. miles lying between the Severn and the Wye. Formerly a royal hunting reserve it now contains little in the way of game.

Forest of Dean

In some areas there are iron and coal workings, particularly around the tiny industrial towns of Coleford and Cinderford. The pits, all small, were worked by "free miners", but most of them are now closed.

One attractive place in the Forest of Dean is **St Briavels**, with a 12th c. castle, now a youth hostel, offering fine views of the surrounding area.

Deerhurst (9 miles north) is a charming little village in the heart of the countryside, with one of the best preserved Saxon churches in the country. St Mary's Church originally belonged to a monastery which is first recorded in 804. The chancel is entirely Saxon: the aisles, arches, roof and clerestory are Norman. The lower half of the tower is Saxon with later long-and-short work; in the east wall is a two-light triangular-headed window. The cylindrical font, with spiral ornament, is also Saxon, dating from the 8th or 9th c.

Deerhurst

Nearby, adjoining a half-timbered house, is Odda's Chapel; a stone found here bears the date 1056, making this the oldest dated chapel in England.

Tewkesbury (7 miles north; pop. 9400) is a charming old-world town with half-timbered houses and ancient inns. It lies near the junction of the Severn with the Avon, with scope for boating on both rivers. A monument commemorates the Battle of Tewkesbury (1471), fought in the "Bloody Meadow" during the War of the Roses.

Tewkesbury

The pride of Tewkesbury is **Tewkesbury Abbey**, one of the finest Norman buildings in the country. Building began in 1092, on the site of an earlier Benedictine house and was completed in 1121. The church is of very similar size and plan to Westminster Abbey. Some of the stone used was imported from France. Particularly impressive features are the massive Norman tower (which can be climbed) and the west front with its recessed arches. In the 14th c. new lierne vaulting was built over the old cylindrical pillars, the new Decorated work harmonising well with the older structure. The transepts are Norman, with 14th c. windows. The choir has Norman pillars, seven splendid windows with stained glass dated before 1430, and choir-stalls with misericords. The finest of the many tombs and monuments is the Beauchamp Chantry (about 1425), built by Isabel le Despenser over the tomb of her first husband Richard Beauchamp, Earl of Worcester. Also notable is the tomb of Hugh le Despenser (d. 1326).

The residential town of Cheltenham (5 miles; pop. 87,200) was made a

Cheltenham

fashionable spa by George III and Wellington. Its many trees give it the aspect of a garden city. There is no finer shopping street in England than the Promenade, and there are numerous other handsome streets of the Regency period. The town has two famous schools, Cheltenham College (founded 1841) and Cheltenham Ladies' College (1853). St Mary's Church has a beautiful rose window. The Art Gallery and Museum in Clarence Street has a good collection of Dutch masters. Cheltenham's many parks include Pittville Park, which contains a lake, the Pumproom and a museum, and Prestbury Park, famous for the National Hunt steeplechases. The Cheltenham festival of Contemporary Music is held in July.

Grampian Mountains   G–I 3/4

Country: Scotland
Region: Grampian

The Grampians are a range of mountains extending across Scotland between the Caledonian Canal in the north and the Clyde valley in the south, with large expanses of heath and moorland. Within the Grampian range are Britain's highest peak, Ben Nevis (4397 ft), Ben Macdhui (4265 ft) and other notable heights. Within the Grampian Highlands is the Cairngorm range, the largest high plateau area in Britain (over 60sq. miles). The whole of the Cairngorm plateau lies over 914 ft, and it has several peaks of over 4000 ft. The predominant vegetation is heather and bracken, with scattered birches and rowans, but there are also considerable areas of pine forest planted by the Forestry Commission. The wild life includes red deer, hares and rabbits as well as large numbers of birds. The rivers of the Grampian region – the Dee, Don, Ythan, Ugie,

River Spey, famous for salmon

Deveron and Spey – are well stocked with fish, and the Spey in particular is famous for its salmon.

Grampian Region, with Aberdeen as its chief town, is a new administrative unit created by the recent local government reform which takes in the old counties of Aberdeen, Kincardine and Banff and part of Moray.

Economy The region is famous for its Aberdeen-Angus beef cattle and thousands of sheep find pasture on the hills while numerous pig-fattening concerns have grown up around the Moray Firth where climatic conditions are favourable. Around a third of Scottish oats and barley are grown here, the latter is grown mainly for the manufacture of whisky – over half of Scotland's 130 distilleries are found in the Grampians.

The finding of oil in the North Sea (some 125 miles east from Aberdeen, see entry) has led to a considerable development of industry in the region, fortunately without spoiling the tourist attractions of the area. The oil boom did not only have the effect of halving the unemployment figures but also raised wages and house prices at the cost of the old-established industries; for example, large parts of the local fishing fleet were transferred to the north-west of Scotland with its low wages.

The chief town in the western part of the Grampian area is Oban (pop. 7500), a popular holiday resort situated in a bay sheltered by the offshore island of Kerrera. From here there are boat trips to Mull and the Hebridean islands and abundant scope for excursions into the surrounding hills and lochs.   **Oban**

Oban has a harbour and is the headquarters of the Royal Highland Yacht Club. Most of the shops, hotels and restaurants are crowded around the railway station which gets quite busy in the summer. Excursions are recommended to Caithness glass factory and Oban whisky distillery built in 1794 which enjoys an excellent reputation. There is good bathing on Ganavan Sands. The best view of the town is from McCaig's Folly, a circular structure built by a 19th c. banker on a hill above the town.

Dunstaffnage Castle (3 miles north) on a crag at the entrance to Loch Etive has three round towers, the 10 ft thick walls dating from the 15th c. when the castle belonged to the Campbell clan. On the ramparts is an old cannon from a Spanish galleon belonging to the Armada which sank in Tobermory Bay (Mull). Flora MacDonald (see Hebrides, Skye) was a prisoner here for a short time. It is said that some of the early Scottish kings were buried in the 13th c. chapel, and it is also claimed – with some improbability – that Dunstaffnage was once capital of Scotland. Tradition also asserts that the Stone of Destiny on which the Scottish kings were crowned for many centuries was kept here, having been brought from Ireland to Iona and from there to Dunstaffnage

Other interesting castles within easy reach of Oban are **Dunollie Castle** (1 mile north) on Loch Linhie, of which only the ivy-covered keep survives and **Castle Stalker** (13 miles north), on a small island in beautiful Loch Creran, with a tower which has been restored. A visit to **Carnasserie Castle**, built mid-16th c., the seat of John Carswell, last bishop of the Isles and abbot of Iona, can be combined with a tour of ★ **Loch Awe**, one of the largest and most beautiful lochs in Scotland, surrounded by wooded hills and dotted with islands and islets. There is a beautiful road down the west side of the loch to Ford, beyond which, on the east side, is Kilneuair church, which appears in the records in 1394 and is said to be haunted. Farther up the east side are the ruins of Fincharn and Ardconnel castles. Beyond Portsonachan the loch becomes wider, and the road runs past Priests' Isle, a former priests' colony and Inisbail, which once had a Cistercian priory. There is a monument commemorating Duncan Ban McIntyre (1724–1812), one of the Highland bards.

One of the finest and most popular sea trips from Oban is to Iona and Staffa, skirting the east coast of the island of Mull (see Inner Hebrides).

Loch Fyne, home fo the Campbells

This offers magnificent views, with Duart Castle and a tower commemorating the novelist William Black (1841–98) straight ahead, to the east Ben Nevis, the highest mountain in Britain, the Glencoe peaks and Loch Linnhe, with countless islands and islets. The route continues past Loch Aline, with Kinlochaine Tower, followed by Manse of Fiunary, Salen and Aros Castle, with a fine view of Ben More, at 3171 ft Mull's highest peak.

Inveraray

A quiet little town which makes a good base for the exploration of the southern and western Highlands is Inveraray (pop. 490), situated on **Loch Fyne** surrounded by wooded hills. Inveraray features in the novels by Scott (see Famous People), who was a great admirer of the ★**castle**, stories by Robert Louis Stevenson and in works by local writer Neil Munro. This classical castle, seat of the Dukes of Argyll, leaders of the Campbell clan, was built in the mid-18th c. based on plans by Robert Morris on the foundations of a medieval castle which the Duke of Argyll had demolished. There is much of interest in the interior of this castle which was badly damaged by fire in 1975 but since restored: tapestries by Robert Mylne and paintings by Gainsborough, Ramsay and Raeburn. There is also a park and the old and new prison is a museum documenting the history of Scottish criminality from the 16th to the 19th c.

A beautiful road leads to Essachosan Glen or Lovers' Glen. Also very beautiful is **Glen Shira**, with the ruins of **Rob Roy's House**, 7 miles northeast. The red-haired pirate Robert MacGregor, better known as Rob Roy, became the Robin Hood of the Highlands through Scott's novels, robbing the rich and giving to the poor like his English counterpart (see Nottingham). The historic MacGregor was actually a cattle dealer whose farm was impounded by the Duke of Montrose, driving the family away and turning Rob Roy into an outlaw, who died peacefully in his own bed in 1734; his grave is in Balquhidder. The Rob Roy & Trossachs Visitor Centre in the rural district of Callander, east of Loch Vennachar has further information on this legendary folk hero. The River Shira, a good trout stream, rises on Beinn Bhuidhe (3106 ft). Just before it flows into Loch Fyne it widens to form the Dubh Loch.

From the head of Loch Fyne a road climbs up to the highest point on the pass, appropriately named "Rest and be Thankful", and then descends to **Loch Long** through picturesque Glen Croe, with a view of the Cobbler or "Ben Arthur" (2891 ft).

The road onward from **Arrochar**, a busy village on Loch Long (2 miles from Loch Lomond) is especially picturesque and make a good starting point for the climb of the Cobbler.

From here a good road bears left to Loch Lomond (2 miles), Britain's largest inland lake and "Queen of Scottish Lakes", with an impressively scenic road running alongside. Its rich fish stocks (trout, salmon, white-fish) make it an angler's paradise. The old folk song "Loch Lomond" is world famous, which tells of two Scottish soldier friends following the Jacobin revolt of 1745, one of whom was to be executed in Carlisle leaving only one to return free along the "bonnie, bonnie banks of Loch Lomond". The melancholy nature of this song has become synonymous with the homesickness felt by emigrants for the Scottish Highlands.

★★**Loch Lomond**

The extensive park of **Balloch Castle** lies on the eastern bank of Loch Lomond; the ground floor of the castle houses an exhibition on the region's development.

Located between Loch Lomond and the Trossachs, the **Queen Elizabeth Forest Park** (24,000 ha) offers marvellous walking routes and nature trails.

To the north-east of Loch Lomond lies the wild and romantic valley of the Trossachs between Loch Katrine and Loch Achray and the two peaks Ben A'an and Ben Venue, hardly an hour's drive from the streets of Glasgow. Trossachs means something like "bristly area". In the early 19th c. the English poets, Taylor Coleridge and William Wordsworth with his sister Dorothy, visited the area and gained inspiration there for their highly romantic works. In 1803 Dorothy Wordsworth noted in her diary: "It was absolutely lonely and everything we glimpsed was loveliness and beauty in perfection." Seven years later the writer Sir Walter Scott was enchanted by the region. The thickly wooded gorges and the story of the MacGregors provided him with an ideal background for his "Lady of the Lake". This adventurous love story featuring Ellen Douglas the clan chief of the MacGregors became a bestseller, inducing even Theodor Fontane to visit the Trossachs in 1858, followed later by Queen Victoria. Today the attraction of Loch Katrine and the Trossachs is unbroken.

★**Trossachs**

Loch Katrine was probably named after the robber clan of the "Catterins" which once frequented the banks of the loch. The small Ellen's Island is named after Scott's heroic "Lady of the Lake". Boat trips on Loch Katrine can be taken from Trossachs Pier on the "Sir Walter Scott", launched in 1900. From here there are pleasant walks in all directions, with views of numerous hills, mountains and lochs.

The figure of Rob Roy (see p. 286) is also linked permanently with the Trossachs. To the east of Loch Venachar detailed information is available on the legendary folk hero and the history of the Trossachs at the **Rob Roy and Trossachs Visitor Centre** on Ancaster Square of the rural settlement of Callander.

Another popular holiday centre in the heart of the Grampian Highlands is Pitlochry (pop. 2600) with the Pitlochry Festival Theatre, the "Theatre in the Hills". Pitlochry, in the Tummel valley, is said to be the geographical centre of Scotland.

Pitlochry

Just beside the town is the artificial **Loch Faskally**, formed in the 1950s by a dam built to provide hydro-electric power. One of the popular sights is the **salmon ladder**, with glass walls through which salmon can be observed making their way upstream. Pitlochry's central situation makes it a good starting point for excursions in all directions.

At the approach to Pitlochry is the **Blair Athol Distillery**, established in 1949 by Bell & Sons (open all year round), which produces an excellent eight and twelve year old single malt whisky.

The interesting drive to ★**Blair Castle** (8 miles north-west) and the castle itself make a visit worthwhile. The beautiful road runs past the approach to the "Queen's View" with a fine view of Loch Tummel and through the famous Pass of Killiecrankie. It was in this breathtaking

Blair Castle, seat of the Duke of Athol

rocky gorge that the English suffered a crushing defeat against the Highlanders led by Viscount Dundee in 1689. Blair Castle, to the north of the little town of Blair Athol, dates from the 13th c. and since the 17th c. has been the seat of the Duke of Athol of Murray clan, the only citizen in Britain with the right, granted by Queen Victoria, to maintain a private army, the Athol Highlanders; colourful parades are held on the last Sunday in May. The interior of the castle gives a good picture of life in Scotland over the last four centuries.

15 miles south-west on the A9 and A827 is **Aberfeldy** on the Urlar Burn near the confluence with the River Tay, with the three waterfalls of Moness. Robert Burns (see Famous People) wrote of the birch woods on the hills "Come let us spend the lightsome days in the birches of Aberfeldy". Today a nature trail leads visitors along the stone steps of the Urlar.

The **distillery** founded here in 1830 by the famous blender John Dewar produces a light peaty malt whisky.

The almost 3937 ft high cone of the **Schiehallion** (20 miles) soars dark brown and bare into the sky. Around 3 hours should be allowed to climb it.

Kinloch Rannoch lies at the foot of the northern slope of the Schiehallion on the bank of **Loch Rannoch**. At one time over 30 clan villages with 2500 members of the MacDonalds, MacGregors, Menzies, Robertsons and Stewarts were clustered around the loch, nowadays only about 400 people live by the lake.

To the west of Loch Laidon stretches **Rannoch Moor**, an inhospitable region yet with a certain magical aura.

The moor borders on the chain of Black Mountains in the south-west with the Buachaille peaks soaring to over 2952 ft on the horizon. **Glencoe** begins here with the White Corries skiing area. Through the Glencoe Pass and before the village of the same name stands the old Clachaig Hotel where the sign "No peddlars and Campbells" is reminiscent of a dark chapter in the history of the clans, the Glencoe massacre. On the morning of the February 13th 1692 the Campbells had murdered their hosts the MacDonalds for hesitating to support the English royal family.

About 12 miles south-east of Pitlochry is the idyllic town of **Dunkeld** with the oldest cathedral in Scotland. Beautifully situated on the banks of the Tay the church was founded in 1107, the building begun in 1318 was destroyed in 1560 by the Reformers shortly after its completion. The nave of this picturesque church is of 15th c. origin but is roofless. The Pict kings lived in Dunkeld, St Columba founded a settlement here in the

6th c. which later received an abbey for Celtic monks. When Kenneth MacAlpin united the riches of the Picts and the Scots in 844 he had residences at Dunkeld and Scone. The present-day town with its attractive marketplace dates from the 17th c. following the destruction of the old settlement by Lowlanders.

In **Hermitage Park**, a small wood near the cathedral, one of the five Tirolean larches still stands which the Duke of Athol had planted in 1738. These trees, which were exotic at that time, were widespread in Scotland until the end of the century. The visitor can enjoy the diversity of trees on the nature trail through the park.

A product of Victorian love of travel, the seven-arched Tay bridge by Thomas Telford connects with the spa town of **Birnam** and its neat houses with pointed gables. It was in Birnamwood that Shakespeare's Macbeth (see Famous People) met his death.

On the A94, the coastal road from Perth (see Dundee, Surroundings) to Montrose, just before Forfar, is one of the finest castles in Scotland, Glamis Castle. This jewel among the romantic castles of Scotland stands in magnificent parkland laid out around 1770 by "Capability" Brown. A long avenue of oak trees leads to the L-shaped baronial style castle, which mainly dates from the late 17th c. There was a castle on the site a thousand years before, the seat of the Earls of Strathmore, the family of the present Queen Mother. According to Shakespeare's tragedy (see Famous People) Macbeth, King of Scotland from 1040 to 1057 and feudal lord of Glamis Castle, murdered Duncan here. Even in the 19th c. visitors were still being shown the deathbed in Duncan's Hall, although the crime happened near Elgin. The castle contains fine furniture, tapestries, pictures and weapons, including portraits of Elizabeth II (see Famous People) and the Queen Mother as the Duchess of York (copy of the portrait by de Laszio). The sleeping quarters of the "Queen Mum" can be visited. In 1930 Princess Margaret, the sister of Queen Elizabeth II was

★★**Glamis Castle**

Glamis Castle

born here; she was the first royal princess born on Scottish soil for over 300 years.

The **Angus Folk Museum** in Kirkwynd Cottages (17th c.) of Glamis has an interesting collection about agricultural history.

The A94 continues through the historic town of Forfar (pop. 10,300), once an important centre of the jute industry in the Strathmore valley, to **Arbroath** (pop. 21,000), a popular seaside resort with its local speciality, "Arbroath Smokies", smoked herring. The red sandstone **Benedictine Abbey** built by William the Lion, of which only ruins exist today, was the scene of an important event in history when nobility and clerics signed a letter to Pope John XXII containing the Declaration of Arbroath declaring Robert the Bruce (see Famous People) to be king. In the rose window of the abbey, known as the "O of Arbroath", beacons were lit to guide the ships at night during the Middle Ages. The restored hall in the former abbot's house is now a museum.

Montrose

The bizarre cliff formations along the coast road north of Arbroath make for a scenic drive to the fishing village of Montrose (pop. 11,000) with a long sandy beach.

Montrose Museum and Art Gallery at Panmure Place has comprehensive collections on the history of the region including Pictish stones, traditional whale fishing equipment and pictures and sculptures by local artists.

Just 4 miles west of Montrose lies the **House of Dun** which was built for Lord David Erskine between 1730 and 1742. The two-storey Palladian-style building was designed by William Adam and inspired by Château d'Issy near Paris. Of particular interest are the allegorical stucco decor of the Grand Salon by Joseph Enzer and the Neo-Baroque dining hall.

Braemar

One of the most popular Highland holiday centres in the Grampians is Braemar (1100 ft; pop. 800) in the valley of the Dee. The highpoint of the year is the **Scottish Highland Games**, ★★"The Royal Highland Gathering" (see Practical Information), held on the first Saturday in September which members of the royal family attend, their summer residence, Balmoral, being only a few miles away. Over 20,000 spectators attend the Games each year, many of them wearing traditional Scottish dress – the ladies in tartan skirts, the men in kilts and plaids. Bagpipes accompany the dancing, while the stripped trunks of young fir trees are thrown from an upright position, a sport which is found only in Scotland, known as "tossing the caber".

The imposing Braemar Castle was begun in 1628 by the Earl of Mar and rebuilt following a fire in the middle of the 18th c. The family residence contains interesting historical finds.

Balmoral

★★**Balmoral Castle**, the Queen's Highland residence, 7 miles north-east of Braemar, is a Victorian mansion in the Scottish Baronial style. The estate was bought by Queen Victoria (see Famous People) in 1852 and renovated by the Aberdeen architect William Smith according to her husband Prince Albert's plans. Visitors are admitted to the parks and galleries when the royal family is not in residence. The best view of this storybook castle of the Royals, set amid old trees, is from the Strathdon Road.

The foundation stone of the parish church of **Crathie** was laid by Queen Victoria in 1893 and the church contains many mementoes of the old queen. The church is attended by members of the royal family when they are at Balmoral so that a crowd often gathers in front of the church before and after the services.

The highest point in the Balmoral Forest is **Lochnagar** (3786 ft), which is often snow-covered. In 1845 John Begg named his ★**Royal Lochnagar Distillery** after it, which draws its water from this wonderful mountain region. When on a visit to the distillery Queen Victoria and her husband were handed the obligatory sample to taste their majesties were so impressed that they appointed Begg official provider to the court, a privilege which the distillery still retains today.

The most popular skiing area in Scotland is north-west of Braemar in the Cairngorm Mountains. The highest point is **Ben Macdhui** (4300 ft), from which there is a magnificent walk over the Cairn Gorm to Glenmore Lodge (6 miles from Aviemore). The Cairn Gorm, which gives its name to the whole area, is only fourth highest, coming after Ban Macdhui, Braeriach (4248 ft) and Cairn Toul (4241 ft). The easiest way to reach the summits is by way of the White Lady chair lift. Between the red granite mountains are a number of lochs, including Loch Avon and Loch an Eilean. The most impressive views are of Braeriach, Cairn Toul and the There is an endless range of fine **mountain walks**, sometimes strenuous; the finest of all, offering splendid views, is the 30 miles from Aviemore over the Lairig Ghru pass to Braemar. There is another walk of about the same length from Braemar to Blair Atholl and a shorter but very attractive one from Aviemore over the Revoan pass and past Loch Avon to the pretty little town of **Nethy Bridge**, with good skiing and fishing and a golf course.

(margin) Cairngorm Mountains

The leading winter sports resort is **Aviemore** (pop. 2400), between the Cairngorms and the Monadhliath Mountains, with many attractive excursions in the area. Aviemore has many leisure amenities as well as hotels, chalets, an ice-skating rink and swimming pools.

The isolated **Loch-an-Eilein** (3 miles south) is of outstanding natural beauty with the enchanted ruined castle of the "Wolf of Badenoch" rising in the centre.

Kingussie (12 miles south-west of Aviemore) is the birthplace of James MacPherson, who translated the ancient Gaelic epic by Ossian, the son of the Scottish king Fingal.

The local open-air **Highland Folk Museum** has an old mill, an 18th c. hunting lodge, a reed and heather covered croft ("Black House") from the Hebrides and an exhibition of traditional life and work in the Scottish Highlands.

The **MacPherson Museum** in neighbouring **Newtonmore** illustrates the turbulent history of the clan and contains a first edition of the "Fingal Translation".

★★Malt Whisky Distilleries (a selection)

For many whisky enthusiasts Scottish malt whisky is associated with the name of Speyside. The "golden triangle" between Grantown-on-Spey, Elgin and Dufftown or Keith has the biggest concentration of malt whisky distilleries in the world; famous names such as Glenfiddich, Glenlivet, Glen Grant and Glenfarclas are found along the Spey valley.

Friends of the "uisge beatha" can follow the signposted Malt Whisky Trail (68 miles) and should visit at least one of the family-owned concerns. Each of the old distilleries offers a different welcome but they all provide a "dram" of pleasurable Scotch to sample.

(margin) ★Malt Whisky Trail

At the point where the A95 heading north from the cosy little town of **Grantown-on-Spey**, with its fine 18 hole golf course, branches off into the Livet valley there is the lovingly restored **Tormore Distillery** with ornate buildings and well kept gardens, now owned by Allied Distillers (visits by arrangement).

The Early-Victorian ★**Glenlivet Distillery**, crowned with pagodas, in the **Livet valley** is testimony of the long history of malt whisky; "The Ballad of the Glenlivet" is documented in the well laid out visitor centre. At the time of the 1715 Jacobite Rebellion, a young Highlander Thomas Smith began to farm here, while also operating a small illegal still. His great grandson George was one of the first people to be granted a dis-

Scotch Whisky

The origins of distilling whisky in Scotland are a secret of history, but it is said that art of distilling was brought to Scotland by the Irish monks. The earliest historical reference is an order by the monk John Cor in 1494 for "eight bolls of malt".

The original Gaelic name "uisge beatha" or "usquebaugh" meaning the "water of life" was shortened during the 18th c. to "usky" and later to "whisk(e)y". The Royal Commission in 1909 used the term "whiskey" to describe all the different products, but today, according to the Oxford English Dictionary, modern commercial language makes the distinction between "Scotch whisky" and "Irish whiskey"; the American Bourbon and Canadian Rye are also spelt with an "e".

The antagonism between England and Scotland is reflected in the last 200 years in the history of whisky. Following the union in 1707 the English customs and excise officials tried to control the production of Scottish whisky which resulted in illicit distilleries and smuggling.

Although the often bloody disputes increased, in 1782 alone 1000 illicit distillers were arrested, the public gave the "sma' stills" moral backing and every second glass of Scotch was the product of an illicit still until new regulations were finally passed in 1823. Various booms and recessions followed.

The French vine pest crisis and resulting brandy shortage in the 1870s increased demand for whisky, on the other hand during both world wars and the American prohibition production almost dried up.

A relic from the prohibition period is the so-called "flatman", an invention of Scottish distillery workers, a small tube, "copper dog" inside the lining of their baggy trousers, through which they could have a swig from the barrel. A later development were the larger flat bottles, carried in the breast pocket, made into a discreet fashion accessory by inventive designers for gentlemen when at the races or at the hunt. Nowadays international companies have increasing control of the whisky industry. The blended whiskies have the largest market share worldwide with the pure malt whiskies enjoying increased popularity more recently.

Even though nowadays chemists can give a detailed description of the various stages in the production of whisky, the fine flavours of Scotch still cannot be explained. Together with a high quality barley the most important components are the special quality of the water in the springs of the Highlands and Lowlands, with their high rainfall, and the aromatic flavour of the peat which gives the distillation its own character.

The first step in the production of malt whisky is malting, whereby the barley is soaked in water and then spread out on the "malting floor" to germinate. The barley is turned frequently to avoid heat development, earlier this was by hand with wooden shovels today it is mechanised. The resulting enzymes convert the starch into sugar in the fermenting process. The germinated barley is placed on the drying floor of the "kiln", a pagoda-style building which has become the symbol of the distilleries. Here the water

Cheers!   *"Slàinte mhath!"*

content is reduced to about 3 per cent, the breakdown of the malted barley stopped and the malt flavoured by peat fires. The dried malt is coarsely ground and then mixed in a "mash tun" with hot water. With constant stirring the soluble starch turns into the "wort" containing the sugar which is in turn cooled and pumped into giant "wash backs" where the yeast is added which turns the sugar into raw alcohol. The result is a liquid similar to beer with an alcohol content of 5–7 per cent.

Now the distillation can begin. It remains unexplained to this day how the firing and shape of the large copper kettles ("pot stills") effects the particular character of the single malt and each distillery keeps to its own traditional shape. During the distillation process the alcohol evaporates and passes through the neck of the kettle into a spiral-shaped cooling tube where the steam condenses. The product of the first stage are the "low wines" containing about 20 per cent alcohol.

The art of the distiller lies in the second stage as only the middle extraction with an alcohol content of about 68 per cent can be collected, while the first and last extractions are mixed back in with the low wines again. The clear spirit is decanted into oak casks where it gains its flavour and golden colour.

According to the law Scotch whisky must mature for at least three years in a customs compound and only water and caramel alcohol can be added at bottling; most malts mature for 8, 12 or 14 years in wooden casks.

"Blended whiskies" are a mixture of Scotch whiskies; their age is determined by that of the youngest single alcohol. Using tulip-shaped "nosing glasses" to smell the whisky the blender chooses his special composition from the wide range of Highland and Speyside malts, the strongly flavoured peaty Islay and Campbelltown malts of the softer Lowland malts.

These malt whiskies are combined with lighter "grain whiskies" – Scottish whiskies made from a mixture of malted and unmalted grains (barley, wheat, maize). Deluxe blends are made from old malt whiskies and matured corn whisky, "vatted malts" are made exclusively from mature malt whiskies.

The best way to drink the delicious elixir has almost become a matter of religion. The addition of ice or soda is regarded as sacrilege. Whether to take in the aroma before sipping a few drops and allow the full flavour of the natural Scottish water to develop remains a matter of personal taste when sampling a "dram" of the legendary "uisge beatha".

Grantown-on-Spey   *Glenfarclas Distillery*

tiller's licence, in 1824. With the support of the Duke of Gordon George Smith built a new distillery, The Glenlivet, which grew to become one of the leading Scottish distilleries. Since 1978 the business has belonged to the Canadian company, Seagram (open March–October).

Also on the banks of the Livet is the **Tamnavulin Distillery** which produces a Single Malt famous for its light smoked flavour. There is a visitor centre in the picturesque old wool mill, to which the business owes its Gaelic name meaning "Mill on the Hill" (open: March to October).

At the confluence of the rivers Spey and Avon the legendary John Smith built the small **Cragganmore Distillery** directly next to the railway line. The house whisky, today owned by United Distillers, ranges among the great "Classic Malts" (open all year round).

For five generations ★**Glenfarclas**, not far from the A95, has been under the ownership of the Grant family. The founder of the distillery in the "valley of the green grass" at the foot of Ben Rinnes was Robert Hay in 1836, from whom John Grant took over the business in 1865. Even today the whisky is still matured for at least ten years in old Spanish sherry barrels (open all year round).

Founded by the Cumming family in 1824 the **Cardhu Distillery** near **Knockando** produces one of the best known malts and has been the leading flagship of United Distillers since 1961. Spring water from the Maannoch Hills is used in the production of the "black rock", as it translates from Gaelic (open all year round).

Reopened in 1947 the **Tamdhu Distillery**, its source Tamdhu Burn rises below the distillery, still malts all its barley in its own large Saladin boxes; Tamdhu has only been available as a single malt since 1976. The original visitor centre in the former railway station is worth seeing.

The small village of **Dufftown**, which developed into the centre of the textile industry under the influence of James Duff, was chosen as the whisky capital by the Grant family and today has nine distilleries.

The distillery founded by William Grant has been owned by the family since the first malt was distilled at ★**Glenfiddich** on Christmas Day 1887. After having worked for 20 years at the Mortlach distillery Grant bought the estate near the source of the Robbie Dubh and together with his seven sons built the distillery. By the fifth generation the well known pure malt whisky was being produced in the striking triangular bottles with the stag label, emblem of the "valley of the deer", the only Scottish Highland malt whisky to be bottled in the distillery. Through their intensive marketing campaign, begun in 1963, of single malt whisky William Grant & Sons Ltd. have contributed considerably to the "rediscovery" of Scottish Malt and today own the Balvenie distillery opposite and the Kinninvie distillery, opened in 1990 with its first malt ready in 1994. As well as a tour of the distillery visitors can watch an interesting film in various languages about the production of Scotch (open all year).

Mortlach Distillery is the oldest in Dufftown. Founded in 1823 it was taken over by George Cowie in 1854, whose name is still on the licence today. It has been modernised several times but the distillery is still coal-fired and has traditional maltings (visits by arrangement).

Also coal-fired is the "old-fashioned" **Strathisla Distillery** in **Keith**, founded in 1746 as Milltown and together with Littelmille (Bowling/Dumbartonshire) in the Lowlands and Glenturret (Crieff/Perthshire) is among the oldest distilleries in the world (open April–September).

Glen Grant Malt is one of the most widely sold single whiskies. This venerable distillery, founded by the brothers James and John Grant in 1840, had already introduced its excellent single malt onto the international market at the beginning of this century (open mid March–September).

Evidence of the importance attributed to the county capital of **Elgin** in the Middle Ages can be seen from the impressive ruins of the former bishop's palace, Spynie Palace. The first 13th c. cathedral building,

Glenfiddich Distillery, still a family firm

295

proudly described by the bishop at that time as the "glory of the kingdom, the delight of foreigners", was destroyed together with the town in 1390 by Alexander Stewart, the "wolf of Badenoch" in retaliation for his excommunication. Further devastation followed later at the hands of the plundering followers of the Reformer John Knox and the troops of Oliver Cromwell (see Famous People). All that remains of the splendour of the "Lantern of the North" are the ruins of the cathedral towers on the edge of the town. The west façade is of French style and the ornate stonework of the octagonal chapterhouse (about 1390) are of particular interest.

Elgin is regarded as the "town of the malt" because large bottling plants such as **Gordon & MacPhail** are located here. From their unrivalled range at 58–60 South Street they can supply a particular Scotch or unusual year of malt whisky.

South of Elgin there are eight distilleries including, as the name suggests, the picturesquely situated **Linkwood distillery** (visits by arrangement), set among woods, and the well known **Glen Moray distillery**, converted from a brewery in 1897 (not open to visitors).

Grantham   L 8

Region: Midlands
County: Lincolnshire
Altitude: 200 ft. Population: 28,600

Grantham is a busy market town in a rich agricultural area, surrounded by areas of pastureland which are reputed to produce some of the best meat, especially sausages, in England. The town is also noted for its gingerbread. The town's most famous daughter is the "Iron Lady" Margaret Thatcher, Great Britain's first woman prime minister, who indelibly shaped the development of the nation between 1979 and 1990. Her birthplace now houses a restaurant called "The Premier". Opposite the

Grantham: Angel and Royal Inn

Guildhall stands a statue of Isaac Newton (1642–1727), who was a pupil at the local grammar school, and the Museum on St Peter's Hill contains many mementoes of the famous philosopher and scientist.

The parish church, St Wulfram's, has a spire 281 ft high, beautiful tracery in the windows, and a 15th c. font. Above the south doorway is a valuable library presented to the church in 1598, with many chained books. Adjoining the church is King's School, where Newton was a pupil, and where he carved his name on a window ledge.

Sights
St Wulfram's

The Angel and Royal Inn (13th c. origin) in the High Street is one of the oldest inns in England. Its illustrious guests included King John, Richard II and Edward VII.

★Angel and Royal Inn

Grantham House, owned by the National Trust, has a 14th c. room occupied by Princess Margaret, daughter of Henry VII, during her journey north in 1503 to marry King James IV of Scotland.

Grantham House

Belvoir Castle (7 miles west) is the imposing seat of the Duke of Rutland. It dates back to Norman times when Robert de Todeni built a castle here. Destroyed in the Civil Wars of the 15th and 17th c. and by a devastating fire in 1806, it was rebuilt by James Wyatt in 1808-16. The castle contains an outstanding collection of pictures including works by Rembrandt, Rubens, Holbein, Poussin and Reynolds, furniture, tapestries and Mortlake wall hangings.

Surroundings
★Belvoir Castle

Belton House (2 miles north) was the elegant seat of Lord Brownlow, built by Christopher Wren in 1688 and later partly rebuilt by James Wyatt. It contains fine carvings by Grinling Gibbons, as well as portraits by old English masters and a valuable silver collection. The church has a Norman font. Belton Tower (1750) stands in the extensive grounds of the park.

Belton House

Woolsthorpe Manor (7 miles south), birthplace of Isaac Newton, is situated near Colsterworth. Adjoining the house is the orchard in which he is supposed to have discovered the law of gravity.

Hadrian's Wall   H-K 5/6

Region: Northern England
Counties: Cumbria and Northern England

Two large works of fortification were built by the Romans against the "Barbarians" of the north. The more northerly of the two was the

Hadrian's Wall

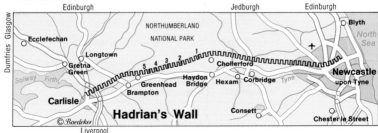

ᒍᒫ Vallum Hadriani   ▮ Roman fort   1 Cilurnum   2 Brocolitia   3 Vercovicium   4 Vindolanda   5 Aesica

Antonine Wall, known as Grim's Dyke from the Firth of Forth to the Firth of Clyde; the other was Hadrian's Wall, marked on some maps as "Roman Wall", which extended from Wallsend near Newcastle upon Tyne (see entry) to Bowness to the west of Carlisle (see entry) on the Solway Firth, a total distance of 73 miles. It was begun in AD 122 by Aulus Platorius Nepos, and completed in 132. The wall was built primarily for defence, but was provided with gates for north-south traffic.

The Wall runs from the Irish Sea to the North Sea, adapting itself to the landscape in wide curves and gentle gradients. It was faced on both sides with small, regularly coursed stones, with a core of rubble and mortar. It was reinforced by a wide ditch, the vallum, on the north side and a rather smaller ditch to the south. The wall was up to 10 ft thick and 20 ft high; now its height is nowhere greater than 6 ft. Along its length there was a series of forts (17–19 in number) accommodating 500 or 1000 men, with barracks and headquarters buildings, storerooms and workshops.

At regular intervals of a Roman mile between the forts were milecastles which no doubt served as lookout posts. Between every two milecastles were two turrets or watchtowers to provide continuous surveillance of the whole frontier and raise the alarm if danger threatened. Along the rear of the Wall ran a military road. The total garrison of the Wall probably amounted to some 10,000 men, who came from all parts of the Roman Empire, including Britain. Small settlements, with shops, inns and temples grew up in the vicinity of the forts.

It is established that the Wall was overrun by the northern tribes on more than one occasion. It was several times renovated and improved, the last occasion being in 369, but in the end it had to be abandoned. In subsequent centuries the Wall was used as a convenient quarry of building material, and Roman stones can be seen in churches and private houses in the area. A walk along the Wall is now a very popular form of recreation, although no one but a specialist or particularly enthusiastic amateur archaeologist would want to traverse its whole length, since for long stretches there is not much to see. The better preserved forts, however, are well worth visiting, and there are considerable sections of the Wall which are still extremely impressive. The most rewarding part is between Chollerford, north of Hexham, (see entry) and Greenhead, within the Northumberland National Park.

Tour

About ½ mile west of **Chollerford** is the best preserved Roman fort, ★**Cilurnum**, designed for a cavalry unit of 500 men. The surviving remains include gates, barrack blocks, the headquarters building, stables, bath-houses and hypocausts (under-floor heating systems). In the entrance hall of Chesters House is an excellent collection of Roman material from the site. On the opposite bank of the North Tyne are considerable remains of a Roman bridge. The church at Chollerton (2½ miles north-east) has monolithic Roman columns in the south arcade (c. 1150) and a Roman altar used as a font.

Going west from Housesteads, beyond Limestone Corner, the Wall runs along the **Great Whin Sill**, a ridge of higher ground which rises to 1230 ft.

At **Carrawburgh** was the fort of **Brocolitia**, where a shrine of Mithras (3rd or early 4th c.) was excavated.

This mystic cult was carried into Germany and Britain by the Roman army from about AD 70. There is a reproduction of the shrine in the Museum of Antiquities in Newcastle upon Tyne (see entry).

At **Sewingshields**, at **Milecastle 35**, the military way leaves the Wall and runs roughly a mile to the south. Those who want to follow the Wall further, therefore, must continue on foot – an effort which is well rewarded by the magnificent scenery.

Housesteads is the fort on the wall which attracts most visitors. Here there has been considerable excavation of the civilian settlement out-

Remains of Hadrian's Wall near Greenhead

side the fort. There are remains of four gates, the headquarters building, granaries, barrack blocks, bath-houses, and infirmary, stables, latrines, workshops and water tanks. The fort was designed for an infantry unit of 1000 men. There is a small museum on the site which belongs to the National Trust.

At **Chesterholm**, 2 miles south, is the fort of ★ **Vindolanda**, with one of the most interesting headquarters buildings and a Roman milestone. The adjoining museum houses writing tablets, textiles and wooden objects from the Roman period.

The Wall, with the well-preserved **Milecastle 37**, runs close to Crag Lough. Then comes one of the best preserved stretches at Steel Rig. At Greatchesters, 5 miles from Housesteads, is the much overgrown fort of **Fort Aesicia**.

Beyond this point the Wall, in places much dilapidated, follows the line of crags known as the "Nine Nicks of Thirlwall" to **Walltown**, with a well-preserved section, and **Carvoran**, near Greenhead, the site of the fort of Banna or Magna.

The ★ **Roman Army Museum** in the former Corvoran farm contains interesting models and reconstructions of the Wall.

Thirlwall Castle, a ruin (1 mile north of Greenhead), was largely built with material from the wall.

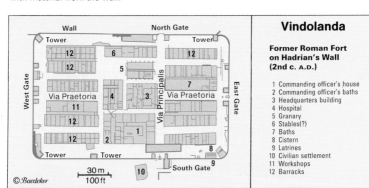

Vindolanda

Former Roman Fort on Hadrian's Wall (2nd c. A.D.)

1 Commanding officer's house
2 Commanding officer's baths
3 Headquarters building
4 Hospital
5 Granary
6 Stables(?)
7 Baths
8 Cistern
9 Latrines
10 Civilian settlement
11 Workshops
12 Barracks

© Baedeker

Not far to the west **Milecastle 48** has well-preserved north and south gates.

Another site worth seeing is **Birdoswald**, the site of one of the largest forts, **Camboglanna**. Here there are very well-preserved stretches of the wall and magnificent views.

Hebrides (Islands)   D–F 2–5

Country: Scotland
Region: Western Isles Area, Highland Region, Strathclyde Region

The Hebrides are a large group of over 500 islands (total area of 281 sq. miles) with their very own character lying off the north-west coast of Scotland, almost 90 of them are inhabited. They are really in fact two groups – those near the coast, the Inner Hebrides, of which the most important and largest are Skye, Mull, Islay, Jura, Rhum, Eigg, Coll and Colonsay, and the 130 mile-long chain of the Outer Hebrides or Western Isles, the main islands are Lewis and Harris (often called "Long Island"), North Uist, Benbecula, South Uist, Eriskay and Barra. Between the Outer and Inner Hebrides are the Minch, the Little Minch and the Sea of the Hebrides. The Outer Hebrides form one of the three Scottish Islands Areas, the Western Isles Area, with the administrative centre in Stornaway, the Inner Hebrides are part of the Highland Region and the Strathclyde region.

The group of islands is formed from pre-Cambrian gneisses, metamorphised slates and rocks of volcanic origin. The windy, cool and damp climate has led to a predominance of Atlantic heaths and moors. The economy is based on cattle rearing, arable farming on small ploughed fields, wool products (especially tweed), fishing and tourism.

Ferries operate all year round between Kyle of Lochalsh on the Scottish mainland and Kyleakin (Skye), Mallaig and Armadale (Skye) with connecting passenger boats to the isle of Eigg and on to Rhum and Muck. In summer there are connections between Mallaig and Kyleakin (Skye) and between Glenelg and Kylerhea (Skye). Passenger boats also sail from Arisaig to Eigg and from Mallaig to Rhum and Canna. Car ferries operate from Uig (Skye) to the Outer Hebrides, Tarbert/Harris (Lewis) and Lochmaddy (North Uist), as well as ships sailing from Oban via Tobermory (Mull) to Castlebay (Barra), Lochboisdale (South Uist), to the isle of Coll and Scarinish (Tiree), and from Ullapool to Stornaway (Lewis); within the Outer Hebrides there are ferry services from Castlebay-Lochboisdale and Lochmaddy-Tarbert. Scalasaig on the isle of Colonsay can be reached by boat from Oban. Car ferries also operate from Kenacraig/Kintyre to Port Ellen and Portaskaig on the isle of Islay; from Portaskaig there is a connection to Feolin Ferry (Jura) and Scalasaig (Colonsay).

In the Inner Hebrides there are **airfields** on Islay and Tiree, in the Outer Hebrides on Lewis, Benbecula and Barra.

Inner Hebrides

★Skye

The largest of the Inner Isles, Skye, now linked to the mainland by a toll bridge (1995), was named "Skúyo" (island of clouds) by the Vikings; in Gaelic it was known as "Eilean Sgiathanach" (winged isle) because of its uneven jagged coastline and "Eilean a Cheo" (misty isle) because of the weather. It is an unspoilt, romantic island with a chain of rugged hills, green valleys and glens, caves, waterfalls and sandy beaches. It is some 50 miles long and between 4 and 15 miles wide; irregularly shaped, with many arms of the sea cutting deep into the land. Among its wide variety of fauna are fish otters and seals, salmon and trout and over 200 species of bird, including a few pairs of rare golden eagles and gannets.

One of the best single malt whiskies in Scotland, the peaty **Talisker**, is produced in the only distillery on the island near Loch Harport, founded in 1830.

Skye is linked with one of the romantic episodes in Scottish history. It concerns the pretender Charles Edward Stuart, affectionately called **"Bonnie Prince Charlie"** by the Scots, who, as a descendant of Maria Stuart (see Famous People) made claim to the throne lost by his grandfather James II. The Prince, who had grown up in Italy, mobilised the Scottish clans against the English who were badly defeated on September 21st 1745 near Prestonpans. Having proclaimed his father James VIII king "Bonnie Prince Charlie" later moved to Edinburgh amid the jubilation of the Highlanders and Scotland was once more Jacobean. In November, as he and his supporters attempted to move south towards London, his luck left him and he had to withdraw to the north until his army was finally decimated on April 16th 1746 at Culloden (see North West Highlands). A prize of £30,000 was placed upon his head causing him to flee and wander for months through the Highlands. He eventually reached South Uist (Outer Hebrides) where he was within a hair's breadth of being captured when the 24 year old farmer's daughter **Flora MacDonald** helped him escape through the English lines, disguised as her servant girl, on a French ship to Skye. It is open to speculation whether she did this for love or pity, but the rest of the story is less spectacular, for the Prince – despite having promised "after all this we shall meet again in St James's Palace" – returned resignedly to Italy and no more was heard from him. Flora was imprisoned in the Tower for high treason, returned to Skye following her pardon, emigrated to America with her seven children returning five years before her death to Trotternish, where her grave has become a tourist attraction. This old story is still kept very much alive in Scotland, especially on Skye, where much of it took place, in songs and ballads with the historic places enjoying high regard. Among them are the island of South Uist with Flora's birthplace, the smaller island of Eriskay further to the south, the spot where Prince Charlie first set foot on Scottish soil, and the Bay of Loch nan Uamh near Arisaig from where the defeated Prince had to leave the country on September 20th 1746 on board a ship ironically named "L'Heureux".

Skye can be reached via a **bridge** (toll) opened in 1995 going from Kyle of Lochalsh across Kyle Akin to **Kyleakin** (pop. 250); this is the main tourist port and has the ruins of Castle Moil. From here there is a road west via Lusa to **Broadford** (pop. 1250), the second largest place on the island (8 miles), a good centre from which to explore the surrounding area.

One of the finest trips from here is to **Loch Scavaig** (15 miles), with magnificent views of **Blaven** (3042 ft) and **Loch Slapin**, and ⋆**Elgol**, a little village with a steep descent to the coast; from the village there is one of the finest views in the country. The incomparably beautiful ⋆Loch Coruisk must be approached by boat. Linked with Loch Scavaig by a river, it lies at the foot of the ⋆**Cuillins** or Coolins, one of the finest climbing areas in Britain, not so much on account of their elevation (the highest point of the 20 peaks being Sgurr Alasdair at 3251 ft) as of their harmonious proportions. The Cuillins are for experienced climbers only, not for beginners. The iron content of the rocks makes compasses unreliable, and a number of climbers have lost their lives here.

The best known peak is **Sgurr nan Gillean** with the climbers' hotel Glen Sligachan a popular base. **Glenbrittle** is a climbing centre with training courses, swimming and boats to Canna, Eigg and Rhum.

Portree (pop. 2000) is the largest place on Skye. To the north are Prince Charlie's Cave and the 164 ft-high black crag, surrounded by smaller rock pinnacles, known as the **Old Man of Storr**. At the northern tip of Skye is the ⋆**Quiraing**, an extraordinary group of bizarrely shaped basalt towers, pinnacles and ledges.

Portree

Tobermory, chief town on the Isle of Mull

Dunvegan (pop. 250), on Loch Dunvegan in western Skye, is famous for its ★**Dunvegan Castle**, the home of the chief of the MacLeod clan, which is reputed to be the oldest castle of the MacLeods, who for centuries waged bloody battles against the MacDonalds of Armadale over who ruled Skye. It is said to have been built in the 9th c.; the tower dates from the 14th c.

From here a road, offering splendid views, runs east to Broadford, via Sligachan and the three basalt columns known as **MacLeod's Maidens**.

Mull

Mull (pop. 2400) is the third largest island of the Hebrides with many footpaths and sport and entertainment facilities (golf, ponytrekking, watersports). The south and east are hilly with peaks rising to over 3000 ft; the hills on the north side are lower.

Tobermory

The capital of the island is Tobermory (pop. 650), an important fishing and ferry port as well as a tourist centre with pretty houses by the harbour. The wreck of the "Florencia", one of the galleons of the Spanish Armada, laden with treasure, lies under the waters of the bay. There are a number of ruined castles in the surrounding area, including Aros Castle and Mingary Castle.

The **Tobermory Distillery** dating from 1798 produces the excellent Ledaig malt.

The **boat trip** via Staffa to Iona past Ulva and the west coast of Mull is highly recommended.

Staffa

Staffa is an uninhabited island which can only be visited in good weather. The main feature of Staffa is ★**Fingal's Cave**, 227 ft long with bizarre rock formations, beautiful colouring and handsome basalt columns. It is named after the Celtic hero, Fingal. The Gaelic name, Uaimh Binn, means "musical wave", referring to the echo of the waves heard inside. A visit to the cave inspired Felix Mendelssohn to compose his famous overture. Here too there is a basalt causeway, like the Giant's Causeway in Northern Ireland (see Londonderry, Surroundings). West of Fingal's Cave is the Boat Cave, which can be reached only by boat.

About 6 miles from Staffa is the island of Iona, with a great historical past. This little island was already a Druid shrine when St Columba landed here in 563. Its original name was "Hy", then "Iona insula". Writers have been inspired by Iona including Wordsworth and Dr Johnson. The Christianisation of Scotland began in Iona when St Columba and his twelve companions founded a monastery. **Iona**

The monastery was destroyed several times by the Vikings but always rebuilt. About 1200 Reginald MacDonald founded a **Benedictine house** on the site of the former monastery church, and from this period survive the 13th c. Norman choir and parts of the chapel.

To the west is the "Street of the Dead" leading to **St Oran's Cemetery**, in which many Scottish kings were buried, and **McLean's Cross**, a richly decorated 15th c. 11 ft high stone cross. Among the more than 60 kings who are said to have been buried here were Macbeth and King Duncan, whom he murdered; the gravestones were thrown into the sea at the Reformation.

St Oran's Chapel, in the cemetery, is the oldest building on the island, erected in the late 11th c. by St Margaret, Malcolm Canmore's queen, probably on the spot where St Columba's first church stood.

On the way to the cathedral, opposite the west door, stands the famous **St Martin's Cross** (12th c.). This cross is 12 ft high and has rich sculptured decoration (figures of the Holy Family).

The **Cathedral**, dedicated to St Mary, is a red granite building begun in the 12th c. and mainly Norman in style; but it was enlarged several times and shows a mingling of different styles. The square tower over the crossing (70 ft high) is borne on four Norman arches. The former nunnery and other buildings associated with the Cathedral have been restored by the Iona Community, members of which live and work on the island during the summer.

The normal population of the island is about 100, living in Baile Mor ("big town"). There are fine views from Dun-I, a hill behind the Cathedral, 332 ft high, from which over 30 islands can be seen.

Islay and Jura, separated only by the narrow Sound of Islay, are almost one island. They can be reached from Oban via Colonsay, or, shorter and faster, from West Talbert. **Islay**

Islay is an unspoiled island with rugged rocks, many bays and sandy beaches. It has two ruined castles and a number of ancient Celtic crosses. The bathing and fishing are excellent. The unofficial capital of the island is Bowmore, the largest place with wide streets and the Killanrow Parish church, built in 1769, the only round church of that period.

Islay has renowned **distilleries** which produce excellent malts. Bowmore has a 200 year-old tradition, Bruichladdich, Scotland's most westerly distillery was founded in 1881 and produces a lighter whisky, as does Bunnahabhain near Port Askaig on the north-eastern tip of the island, where River Margadale flows into the sea; the new Coal Ila distillery is also situated here. Near Port Ellen on the southern tip are Ardberg, closed in 1983 and reopened in 1989, Lagavulin, producer of one the six "Classic Malts" by United, and Laphroaig, the only distillery run by a woman, famous for its distinctive peat-flavoured malt.

The treeless island of Jura (pop. 420, with Colonsay) has hardly been touched by tourism. The highest points are "The Paps" (Scottish slang for breasts; 2571 ft), best climbed from Feolin, where the ferry puts in. In **Jura**

Barnhill Farmhouse, at the north end of the island, Eric Blair, alias George Orwell wrote his futuristic novel "1984" published in 1949.

An illicit distillery is said to have been on the site of the "Isle of Jura" distillery in the hamlet of Craighouse from the beginning of the 16th c. The present-day concern with its exquisite malt whisky dates from 1963.

Colonsay
Oronsay

Named after St Columba and his compatriot St Oran the Hebridean islands of Colonsay and Oronsay are also separated by a narrow channel. At low tide it is possible in two hours to walk across to Oronsay, which has the ruins of a 14th c. priory and a fine 16th c. cross. A Viking grave was found here, with a man and his horse buried in his ship. Oronsay is of interest to botanists for the very rare species of orchids found on the island.

Canna

Of the four islands Eigg, Muck, Rhum and Canna, each inhabited by a few dozen families, the most attractive of the four is the volcanic island of Canna. At the north-east corner of Canna is the notorious Compass Hill, whose iron-bearing basalt rocks used to deflect ships' compasses and put them off their course.

Eigg

On Eigg is an interesting geological feature, the Scuir or Sgurr of Eigg, a towering crag of black pitchstone soaring over 1312 ft.

Rhum

The island of Rhum was identified as a "protected biosphere" by UNESCO in the Eighties with its rich diversity of fauna including red deer, petrels and sea eagles.

Outer Hebrides · Western Isles

The Outer Hebrides are formed from some of the oldest rocks in the world, pre-Cambrian gneiss and granites. The country is fairly feature-less, with great expanses of heath and moorland, few trees, numerous little lochs and simple stone-built houses. The inhabitants live by croft-ing (small-scale farming combined with some fishing) and tourism, except on Harris which is the home of a flourishing tweed industry. Many still speak Gaelic. The islands are mainly of interest to anglers and the archaeologically inclined, who will find here many remains of differ-ent periods of the past.

Lewis
Stornaway

On the most northerly island, Lewis (pop. 16,700), there is only one town – Stornaway (pop. 5500) founded in the 17th c. by the MacKenzie clan from Seaforth, with a good natural harbour which has made it an important fishing port. On the wharf at Arnish Point oil rigs for the oil industry are built. There are air services from Stornaway Airport to Glasgow (see Glasgow). Bus services operate to places all over the island. Stornaway Castle now houses a technical college.

The most notable features of archaeological interest on the island are the ★**Standing Stones of Callernish** (15 miles west), probably the finest stone circle in Scotland, and the ★**Broch of Carloway**, a 164 ft-high defence tower built by the Picts with 10 ft thick walls, also on the west coast.

Harris is part of the main island of Lewis, the principal place is **Tarbert** (pop. 500), port of call for the ferries. From the neighbouring highest summit of the Western Isles, the Clisham (2622 ft) which can con-veniently be climbed from Tarbert, the Scottish mainland can be seen in clear weather. The rest of Harris is also mountainous, with beautiful bays and good bathing beaches.

The island is famous for ★**Harris Tweed**, formerly almost all hand-woven, but now almost exclusively made in small factories. The name "tweed" is a Scottish variation of the French word "toile" (cloth). The famous "orb mark", the globe and Maltese cross symbol of Harris Tweed, is only awarded to wool from Scottish sheep from the islands.

Standing Stones of Callernish, prehistoric circle on the Isle of Lewis

The most southerly point on the island is **Rodel**, with **St Clement's Church** (15th–16th c.), which has fine carving and monuments.

North Uist

To the south of the Sound of Harris is the island of North Uist (pop. 2200) which is linked via Benebecula to South Uist by a dam. This varied rugged landscape has numerous lochs, both salt and fresh water, the indented coastline of bays and peninsulas stretches almost 361 miles. North Uist is particularly rich in wildlife, with red deer, otters and seal lions, and excellent fishing. The inhabitants are primarily small farmers ("crofters") who supplement their income through wool products and harvesting seaweed which is processed into cattlefeed.

The principal township is **Lochmaddy**. The ferry port is the most important centre for the southern islands of the Outer Hebrides. A road runs across the island to Carinish at its southern tip and then by way of a causeway (built in 1960) over the North Ford on to the neighbouring island of Benebecula.

Benebecula

The island of Benebecula, with a population of about 2000, lies between North and South Uist and is now connected to both by road. From Balivanich Airport there are flight connections to Glasgow (see Glasgow), Stornaway (Lewis) and Logonair (Barra). The finest beach on the island is at **Colla Bay**.

South Uist

South Uist has almost 3000 inhabitants and is the second largest island on the Outer Hebrides. The principal place is **Lochboisdale** (pop. 300) which has a harbour. An excellent road runs from the north to the south of the island. The second highest peak, Hecla (1988 ft) offers a rewarding climb. Near Askernish is the island's tourist attraction, popular with visitors from Britain, the birthplace of Flora MacDonald (1727–90), daughter of a local crofter, who helped Bonnie Prince Charlie on his flight from the English in 1746 (see Skye).

Barra

Barra is the most southerly of the larger Outer Hebrides with Logonair airfield. The inhabitants of this 8 miles long and 5 miles wide island speak Gaelic as well as English. There are many trout in the lochs which surround the only hill on the island, Ben Heaval (1260 ft).

Castlebay, the chief town, used to be a flourishing centre for herring fishing, today lobsters and prawns take its place. The medieval Castle Kisimul is picturesquely situated on a rocky islet in the middle of a bay. The MacNeil clan, who have lived here since the 14th c., were regarded as skilful sailors.

Similar in character are the smaller islands to the south, with solitary beaches and often bizarrely shaped cliffs, such as **Vatersay**, **Mingulay** and **Bereneray** with Barra Head, the most southerly point in the Outer Hebrides.

Hereford   I 8

Region: Midlands
County: Hereford and Worcester
Altitude: 197 ft. Population: 48,300

Hereford, on the Wye, was the seat of a bishop as early as the 7th c. and was fortified in the Middle Ages, however, nothing remains of this. Today the town is the centre of a large and prosperous farming region. Hereford cattle are world famous, and farmers come from all over Europe to the livestock auctions here. It is also noted for its cider, more than half the total English output of cider coming from the district. The city is surrounded by extensive apple orchards and hopfields. To the art-lover Hereford's main attractions are its Cathedral and its "Mappa Mundi", one of the oldest maps of the world in existence.

Hereford
Cathedral

The Cathedral, which is dedicated to St Mary and St Ethelbert, was begun in 825 and was the burial place of St Ethelbert, king of East Anglia, who was beheaded by King Offa of Mercia in 794. After being destroyed by the Welsh in 1056 the present day church was rebuilt as a round church by the first Norman bishop Robert de Losinga (1079–95) and Bishop Reynelm (1107–15) added a nave. It displays outstanding examples of the various styles of the Pre-Reformation period. The arches, the piers supporting the tower, most of the south transept and the arches and triforium of the choir are Norman. The Lady Chapel and the crypt are Early English (after 1200), and the north transept was rebuilt between 1250 and 1288 in a style transitional between Early English and Decorated. The tower is Decorated (early 14th c.). The west front collapsed in 1786 and was rebuilt, in rather unsatisfactory style, by James Wyatt and again by John Oldrid Scott in 1902–08.

In the interior the north transept is notable for its tall narrow windows and unusual vaulting. It contains the tombs of Peter of Aiguablanche or Aquablanca (bishop 1240–68) and Thomas de Cantelupe. The south transept is Norman, with Perpendicular windows. In the choir are the bishop's throne and fine choir stalls with 60 misericords (14th c.). To the left of the high altar is a chair which is said to have been used by King Stephen but is probably later. In the choir is the famous **"Mappa Mundi"**, a large map of the world by Richard of Haldingham, representing the world as a circle with Jerusalem at the centre, surrounded by figures of animals and historical and mythological characters. It was drawn up around 1275 in Lincoln (see entry). The crypt (Early English) is the only medieval crypt in England under a Lady Chapel of the same period.

The Cathedral is also noted for its **chained library** of over 1440 volumes, most of which are chained to the shelves so that they can be read but not removed. The collection includes 266 volumes of manuscripts, over 70 of the books were printed before 1500; it also has blocks and printing-presses of 1611. It is housed partly above the north transept and partly above the Bishop's Cloisters, which have very fine tracery.

The town has many handsome old houses and remains of its town walls. Old House, a half-timbered old building from 1621 which is now a museum, is situated in High Town. The collection encompasses memorabilia of David Garrick (1717–79), who was director of Drury Lane Theatre in London from 1747–76 and was born at the Angel Inn in Hereford. He represented the characters of Shakespeare (see Famous People) in a new more human style and wrote several comedies himself. A series of exhibits indicate that other theatrical people had close links with Hereford, Nell Gwynne is said to have been born here and Sarah Siddons (1755–1831) lived in Hereford for some time, as did the Kemble family.

Old House

The City Museum and Art Gallery contains exhibits from the Bronze and Iron Age together with the Roman Castra Magna (5 miles north-west), geological material and pictures by local artists.

City Museum and Art Gallery

The parish church of All Saints is worth a visit. It has fine 15th c. choir stalls and a 15th c. painting of the Annunciation. In accordance with an old custom the 313 books in the library (1715) are chained.

All Saints

Coningsby Hospital or Black Cross Hospital, an early 17th c. building, was designed to accommodate old soldiers, sailors and servants. In the garden there is a Preaching Cross from 1370.

Coningsby Hospital

13 miles south-west is the beautiful parish church of Abbey Dore, set among fruit orchards at the end of the "Golden Valley" of the little River Dore. The church was founded in 1147 as the church of a Cistercian abbey and is in the latest Transitional style. It was restored in the early 17th c. by Viscount Scudamore.

Surroundings Abbey Dore

7 miles south-west is the small but very beautiful Norman church of **Kilpeck**, built about 1120–70, with magnificent carving and a Norman font. The carving shows Scandinavian affinities, which may be attributed to settlers brought here from Kent by Harold (who became Earl of Hereford in 1058).

Ledbury (pop. 3700) is a romantic little town which makes a good base for the exploration of the Malvern Hills (see Worcester, Surroundings). It has many black and white half-timbered houses. The Market House (1633) stands on 16 oak pillars, still those of the original structure. From here a narrow street lined with attractive old houses leads to the large parish church St Michael's and all Angels with its separate tower (13/18th c.). The church shows a variety of different styles from the late 13th and early 14th c., the stained glass is by C. E. Kempe 1895–1904. John Masefield (1878–1967) was born in the town, and Elizabeth Barrett Browning (1806–61) spent part of her childhood here.

Ledbury

Eastnor Castle (1½ miles south-east), built 1812–17 by Sir Robert Smirke, has a good collection of pictures, weaponry and tapestries. It stands in a beautiful park with many rare trees.

Leominster (pronounced Lemster; pop. 8700), is a beautiful old wool town on the River Lugg, situated among orchards and hop-fields. It has a number of black and white half-timbered houses and a triple-aisled church dating from the 12th, 13th and 14th c. Originally belonging to a priory, the church has a Perpendicular tower over the Norman west

Leominster

doorway. In the north choir aisle is a ducking stool, last used in 1809, on which nagging wives were dipped in the river.

Dating from the 14/15th c. and partly rebuilt in the 18th c. **Croft Castle** (5 miles north-west) was built on land which has been held by the Croft family of Domesday for 900 years, since the Norman Conquest until 1957. The furniture (17/18th c.) of this castle with four round corner towers is worth seeing. There are beautiful avenues of trees in the park.

Weobley is a tiny but pretty little village (9 miles south-west; pop. 800). There are an unusually high number of half-timbered houses. The Red Lion dates back to the 13th c. The church, which is mainly 14th c., has a beautiful tower and fine monuments.

Hexham   I 6

Region: Northern England
County: Northumberland
Altitude: 198 ft. Population: 8900

Hexham is situated on a plateau on the south bank of the River Tyne. It lies half way across the narrowest part of England, at roughly the same distance from the North Sea and the Solway Firth. This small market town, which was the seat of a bishop in the 7th c. and was called Hagulstald, is a good base from which to see Hadrian's Wall (see Hadrian's Wall).

★Priory

The priory church stands in the market place. It is also known as the Abbey or St Andrew's Church and is a classic example of Early English architecture (c. 1180–1250). The original church on this site was founded by St Wilfrid of York in 674 as a Benedictine monastery and partly built of stone from Hadrian's Wall. The crypt of this first church has been preserved. Over this crypt the present church, which originally belonged to an Augustinian priory, was built between 1180 and 1250. The nave is modern (1907–09) and the east end of the church was rebuilt in 1858–60 by John Dobson.

The basin of the font in the interior is of Roman origin. In the south transept is a massive "night stair" which led up to the monk's dormitory, now destroyed. At the foot of the stairs are the Acca Cross (about 740) and the tombstone of a Roman cavalryman named Flavinus. In the

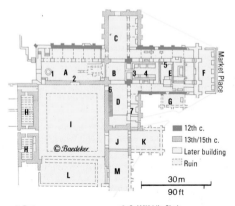

**Hexham
Priory**

A Nave
B Central tower
C North Transept
D South Transept
E Choir
F Chapel of the
   Five Altars
G Chapel
H Cellars
I Cloister
J Vestibule
K Chapterhouse
L Refectory
M Domitory

■ 12th c.
▨ 13th/15th c.
☐ Later building
▨ Ruin

30 m
90 ft

© Baedeker

1 Font
2 Entrance
  to crypt
3 St Wilfrid's Chair
4 Position of 7th and
  12th c. apses
5 Pulpit
6 Roman monument
7 Roman altar

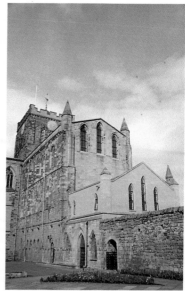

Hexham: Moot Hall ...   *... and Priory Church*

choir the triforium is particularly notable. The church contains many portraits of bishops of *c.* 1500 on the old rood-screen and pulpit. The Saxon bishop's chair probably belonged to St Wilfrid. On the south side of the choir is the chantry of Prior Ogle (d. 1410), on the north side the chantry of Prior Leschman (d. 1491). The most notable part of the church is the ★**crypt** or "Confessio", in which sacred relics were housed. It incorporates stones from Hadrian's Wall, some of them with inscriptions.

Under the choir are the foundations of the apse of **St Peter's Chapel**. Of the priory buildings only a few parts are preserved, among them the lavatory (*c.* 1300), the chapterhouse vestibule (13th c.) and the Priory Gate (*c.* 1600).

The market hall (Shambles) built in 1766 by Sir Walter Blackett is constructed on stone pillars at its northern end and wooden pillars at the southern end. The **Moot Hall** (library), a large defence tower from 1400, was the seat of the sheriffs of the Archbishop of York. The adjoining **Manor Office** (1330–32) served as a prison from the 14th c., today it houses the tourist office. A few yards north is the **Old Grammar School** finished in 1684 and founded by Queen Elizabeth I (see Famous People) in 1599. A number of Tudor and Georgian houses in Market and Beaumont Street are interesting.

Around the market square

Blanchland (10 miles south) is a charming village of barely 200 inhabitants. The drive over high moorland and heath passes Dukesfield Fell (1170 ft). Blanchard is a sleepy little place of stone-built houses dating from the second half of the 18th c., with remains of a Premonstratensian abbey of the 12th c., the choir and north transept of the former church and a gatehouse from around 1500.

Hadrian's Wall (see entry) is also in the vicinity.

Surroundings

Hull · Kingston-upon-Hull   L 7

Region: Northern England
County: Humberside
Altitude: 13 ft. Population: 322,300

The city of Kingston-upon-Hull, usually known simply as Hull, lies on the
north bank of the Humber, which flows into the North Sea 22 miles to the
south-east. Hull is an important sea and ferry port and a busy commercial centre for the region. The university was founded in 1954.

History The town was founded in 1292 by Edward I under the name of
"Wyke-upon-Hull" on both banks of the little River Hull, which flows into
the Humber here. The town was fortified in the 14th c. after receiving its
royal charter in 1299. The refusal by the governor, Sir John Hotham,
to admit Charles I in 1642 was an early act of defiance to royal authority
which played a part in bringing on the Civil War. During the war the town
was several times unsuccessfully besieged by Royalist forces. Centuries
of shipbuilding and fishing led to economic prosperity.

Sights
Queen Victoria
Square

In Queen Victoria Square the **Town Docks Museum** in the former Dock
Offices provides a comprehensive history of seafaring in the town with
numerous model ships, paintings and fishing equipment.

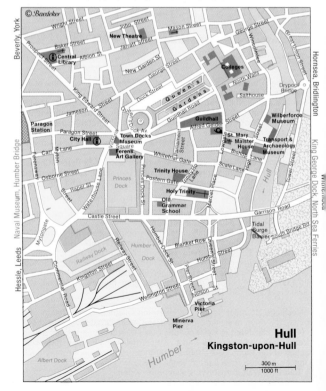

Hull
Kingston-upon-Hull

300 m
1000 ft

The extensive collection in the ★**Ferens Art Gallery**, situated opposite, restored and extended in 1990/91, includes works by Frans Hals, Canaletto and Constable, together with William Hogarth and Henry Moore (for both see Famous People).

Whitefriargate leads to the oldest part of the town by way of Trinity House Lane to Trinity House, founded in 1369 for the care of the sick or needy seamen and from 1456 it was their guild house. In 1787 the first naval school in the world was founded; even today the cadets wear the historic 18th c. naval uniform.

Trinity House

Holy Trinity Church in the market place, which can accommodate a congregation of over 2200, is said to be the largest parish church in the country. It is in Decorated and Perpendicular style, and has a very fine tower and richly decorated Gothic style windows.

★Holy Trinity

The Elizabethan Old Grammar School, south-west of the church, was founded in 1583. Among its most famous pupils were the Puritan writers Andrew Marvell and William Wilberforce (1759–1833), one of the most vigorous opponents of the slave trade, who was MP for Hull and Yorkshire for many years. Since 1988 the school house has housed a museum on local history.

Old Grammar School

25 High Street is Wilberforce's birthplace and now a museum with interesting exhibits from the 18th and 19th c., especially concerning the slave trade. Nos. 23 and 24 are two Georgian houses from the mid-18th c. with fine furniture.

High Street ★Wilberforce House

Not far away is the Transport Museum, opened in 1989, with old coaches, engines, cars and bicycles and the Hull and East Riding Museum, a remarkable archaeological collection from East Yorkshire, including the "Hasholme Boot" from prehistoric times and Roman mosaic floors (4th c.).

★Transport and Archaeology Museum

On the other side of the road stands the merchant's house of the Maister family, built in 1744 in Late-Renaissance style with a Palladian style façade and an artistic wrought-iron banister by Robert Bakewell.

Maister House

The residential house No. 6 was built for the merchant Benjamin Blaydes in 1740 with the original Georgian features restored in the early Seventies.

Blaydes House

In the Middle Ages the harbour stretched between the Drypool Bridge and the River Humber. The old docks have undergone a change of function. Elegant yachts are anchored in the **Marina** in the former Humber and Railway Dock and at Princes Quay. Victoria Pier and Nelson Street were modernised during the Eighties.

In April 1980 the 100 m high **tidal surge barrier** across the Humber was completed which protects the old town from high water.

★Historic Docks

To the west of the town centre the Humber Bridge was opened in 1981, a harmonious blend of technology and aesthetics. At 4954 ft it is the longest suspension bridge in the world without supporting columns.

★Humber Bridge

Isle of ..., Isles of ...

See main place name

311

King's Lynn   M 8

Region: East Anglia. County: Norfolk
Altitude: 16 ft. Population: 37,300

King's Lynn is a typical English town on the east bank of the Ouse, 2½ miles from its outflow into the Wash. It was once the fourth largest town in England and a member of the Hanseatic League. This period of prosperity is still recalled by a 15th c. Hanseatic warehouse. The original name of the town was Lynn: the prefix "King's" was added when Henry VIII granted it the right to hold an additional market. Hence there are two market places in the town, the Tuesday Market and the Saturday Market, around which the older houses are clustered.

Sights
Saturday Market

In Saturday Market, near the river, is the town's principal church, **St Margaret's**, with massive west towers which give it almost the air of a cathedral. It was built by the bishop of Norwich in the 12th c., when the town was known as Bishop's Lynn. The west front is particularly fine. It contains two very fine brasses, probably of Flemish workmanship. These magnificent 14th c. pieces represent a vintage scene and a peacock feast (Peacock Brass).

Opposite the church is the **Guildhall of the Holy Trinity** of 1421, in a striking chequered flint pattern. The treasury in the basement has housed a fine collection of **regalia** since 1978, including a valuable cup and a sword which are said to have belonged to King John. His crown jewels and treasure are supposed to lie buried in the Wash, lost in flight when caught by an unexpectedly high tide. The king died of dysentery a few days later.

Queen Street

In Queen Street are **Thoresby College**, a priests' seminary founded in 1500, with a 17th c. front (now a youth hostel) and **Clifton House**, a Georgian house with an Elizabethan watch-tower.

South of Bridge Street is the **Greenland fishery**, the wooden office of the Greenland sailors built in 1605, testimony from the town's illustrious period when the Greenland sailors set sail from the port of Lynn.

King Street

Leading north from Queen Street is King Street with the former **Custom House**, built in 1683 by Henry Bell in Palladian style with a statue of Charles II above the door.

There are a number of handsome Tudor and Georgian houses in the area around King Street. One of the most picturesque spots is where the old ship canal flows into the Ouse.

Two of the last fishermen's cottages in North Street were lovingly restored in 1991 and now house the **True's Yard Fishing Museum** with displays of traditional fishing equipment.

King Street runs past ⋆**St George's Guildhall** (1406), now used as a theatre and art gallery, to the **Tuesday Market**.

Other streets

A short distance away in St Anne's Street is **St Nicholas's Chapel**, rebuilt in Perpendicular style in 1419. There is interesting window tracery and a late 15th c. brass lectern (not open to the public).

The octagonal late 14th c. **Greyfriars Tower**, reached by way of the High Street and St James's Street, is a relic of a former priory.

To the north in Old Market Street is the **Lynn Museum** with exhibits on local history.

To the east on the Walks the **Red Mount Chapel** can be seen an octagonal brick building, once frequented by pilgrims on their way to Walsingham.

The medieval **South Gate** (mid-15th c.) on the road heading south to London has been preserved.

Sandringham House (8 miles) is a mansion belonging to the Queen. The Neo-Elizabethan house (1867–70) can be visited when the royal family are not in residence. The extensive **park** has magnificent old trees; the azaleas and rhododendrons are particularly attractive when in flower from May to the end of June. The small church has a silver altar and many royal mementoes. Queen Alexandra, George V and George VI died at Sandringham. The **museum**, expanded in 1984, contains hunting trophies and vintage cars belonging to the royal family, including a Daimler Tonneau (1900) which belonged to Edward VII and a Daimler Brougham (1928) of Queen Mary's.

Surroundings
★ Sandringham

The **Snettisham Park Farm** not far to the north provides interesting insights into aspects of country life such as cattle-rearing, wool production and sheep-shearing.

Of this once mighty **Castle Rising** stronghold (4½ miles north-east) there remain a Norman keep and the defensive wall. The parish church is Late-Norman with a beautiful west front.

Trinity Hospital Opposite the church is an almshouse, founded by Henry Howard in 1614 for women. It comprises nine rooms grouped around a courtyard, a communal room and a small chapel. The old ladies who still live there dress in Jacobean costume, red coats and black pointed hats.

Visitors interested in churches should see at least some of the "Seven Churches of Marshland". They are built on the fine sand and silt of the fenland, crossed by lakes and inlets, which was reclaimed from the sea. The churches lie between King's Lynn and Wisbech, 13 miles away, and are mostly built of silver-grey Ancaster stone, in Perpendicular style (Clenchwarton, Terrington St Clement, Walpole St Peter), Perpendicular and Early English (Emneth), Early English (West Walton) and Norman (Walsoken). Walpole St Peter is the "cathedral" of the marshland churches, with a separate tower and 81 very beautiful windows.

Seven Churches
of Marshland

Wisbech (pop. 17,400) is an attractive town which was formerly only 4 miles from the sea but is now 11 miles away. It has a harbour on the Nene and is surrounded by orchards, bulbfields and green fenland. In spring, when the trees are in blossom, and also when the tulips are out it attracts large numbers of visitors. The canals, with houses built along their banks, are reminiscent of Holland. On both banks of the river (North Brink and South Brink) are handsome Georgian houses. Peckover House (1722–26) with beautiful plasterwork and woodwork belongs to the National Trust and is open to the public. Near the bridge is a monument to Thomas Clarkson, an active opponent of the slave trade. Also of interest are the two market places and the parish church of St Peter and St Paul, which has a free-standing 16th c. tower. The Norman castle has long since disappeared, but there is a house built from its stone by Thomas Thurloe, Cromwell's secretary of state. Adjoining it is a museum, one of the oldest in the county, which counts among its treasures the original manuscript of "Great Expectations" by Charles Dickens (see Famous People).

★ Wisbech

Kintyre

F 5

Country: Scotland
Region: Strathclyde

The beautiful Kintyre peninsula lies to the west of the Isle of Arran (see entry); a ferry runs from Lochranza on Arran to Claonaig on Kintyre.

North of Claonaig, Skipness Castle, a 13th c. frontier stronghold of the Clan Campbell, commands extensive views over Kilbrannan Sound.

From Skipness follow the B842 southwards along the peninsula's

Skipness Castle
Campbeltown

almost completely unspoilt east coast to Campbeltown, former clan seat of the Campbells of Argyll and now Kintyre's central market town (pop. 6200). Its prosperity in the 18th and 19th c. was founded mainly on fishing and whisky; the local Springbank Distillery continues to produce an excellent malt.

Machrihanish

Machrihanish golf course (about 5 miles south-west) is known to only a few golfing aficionados.

Southend

Mull of Kintyre lighthouse ("mull" = promontory), west of the village of Southend, has found a niche in musical history as a result of the Paul McCartney song. From the Mull, the Antrim coast of Northern Ireland is easily visible. A "footprint" in the rock in Carskey Bay is said to mark the place where St Columba first trod on Scottish soil.

MacAlister Clan Centre

Back along the A83 to the home of Laird and Lady Glenbarr (Mr and Mrs MacAlister), who themselves conduct visitors around the neat manor house dating from the 18th/19th c. and tell the story of the MacAlister clan.

Gigha Island

From Campbeltown, continue round on the A83 and along the west coast, looking across to the small green island of Gigha (ferry from Tayinloan to Ardminish); chief attraction on the island are the Achamore House Gardens, with a wonderful array of subtropical plants.

Tarbert

Beyond Kennacraig, from where the ferry leaves for Islay (see Hebrides), lies the town of Tarbert. Situated on the narrow neck of land between West Loch Tarbert and Loch Fyne, it is a popular place for watersports and was once a herring fishing port.

Lake District

H/I 6

Region: Northern England
County: Cumbria

The Lake District in Cumbria, much of which (900 sq. miles) was designated a national park in 1951, is an area of incomparable beauty and great variety. With its 16 lakes and numerous small reservoirs it fully justifies the name. Between the lakes are innumerable fells, including 180 over 2000 ft and Scafell Pike (3210 ft), the highest mountain in England. The Lake District covers a distance of some 30 miles from north to south and 25 miles from east to west. At its centre is the little town of Grasmere on the lake of the same name. Five main areas can be distinguished – the southern or Windermere area, the northern or Keswick area, the eastern or Ullswater area and the passes.

Millions of years have contributed to the shaping of the Lake District. Its landscape bears the marks of volcanic eruptions, the Caledonian folding movements, the subsequent submersion by the sea and the resultant deposition of limestone, and finally the glaciers of the Ice Age. From the centre of the area erosion valleys radiate in all directions, and up in the high valleys the water is collected in round basins which feed the lake lower down through a series of mountain streams, waterfalls and rivers. The coast is famous for its large numbers of waterfowl and magnificent gardens. Herons are a common sight, though less abundant than the sheep which roam over the hills. It is a paradise not only for nature-lovers and walkers but also for anglers, yachtsmen and geologists.

During the summer there are regular boat services on Lakes Windermere, Ullswater and Derwentwater. Sailing and rowing, fishing and swimming are possible in most lakes (permit required for fishing).

Lake Windermere

There is an abundance of very attractive footpaths, either going round the lakes (Windermere 27 miles) or radiating from the towns. Walkers and climbers can discover other routes offering new delights using the good maps which are available everywhere; organised tours also operate from many towns.

The Lake District was "discovered" by the poet Thomas Gray (1716–71), who visited the area in 1769 and wrote a book entitled "A Tour in the Lakes". Thereafter many writers and poets sang the praises of the Lakes, in particular William Wordsworth (1770–1850), Dorothy Wordsworth (1771–1855), Robert Southey (1774–1843) and Samuel Taylor Coleridge (1772–1834), who became known as the **Lake Poets**.

Lake Windermere, a glacier lake formed during the Ice Age, is England's largest lake, 10 miles in length and 230 ft deep. At its northern end it is enclosed by rocks; at the southern end it is drained by the River Leven, which flows into Morecambe Bay. Its shores are beautifully wooded, and in some places lined by houses. The largest island, Belle Isle, and some of the smaller ones can be reached by regular boat services. On Ladyholme are the remains of a 13th c. chapel.

★**Lake Windermere**

In Hill Top, near Sawrey the London-born **Beatrix Potter** (1866) wrote her popular series of little books about animals which she illustrated herself, beginning with "The Tales of Peter Rabbit". She spent the last 30 years of her life in the small cottage which is now a museum.

The town of **Windermere** consists of the older part, Bowness-on-Windermere, and the more modern part higher up the hill. The parish church, St Martin's, consecrated in 1483, has been preserved in its Late-Gothic Perpendicular style; the east window of the choir (14/15th c.) is interesting. The National Park Information centre has its headquarters in the High Street.

Windermere

Hawkshead: the Red Lion Hotel ...   *... and Beatrix Potter Gallery*

North of Bowness the **Steamboat Museum** contains old steam and sailing boats, including the "Dolly", built in 1850.

A particularly fine view of the southern part of the Lake District and of Morecambe Bay is to be had from ★**Orrest Head**, reached on a track which runs through Elleray Woods.

★**Hawkshead**

The charming little village of Hawkshead (6 miles west; pop. 660) has picturesque old stone houses around the Market Square, Flag Street and Main Street. The latter is the site of the **Beatrix Potter Gallery**, impressively restored in 1990, with some original drawings by the writer and the Victorian Red Lion Hotel (1850). To the north of the market square are the town hall (1790), the parish church of St Michael and All Angels (15th c.) and the grammar school founded in 1585 by Edwin Sandys, Archbishop of York, at which William Wordsworth was a pupil from 1779–87.

Nearby is **Grizedale Forest** with the Treetops look-out tower.

Coniston

Coniston (pop. 1700) is beautifully situated half a mile from Coniston Water below the jagged peaks of Yewdale Crags. In the churchyard can be seen the grave of John Ruskin (1819–1900), writer and social reformer, whose books, collections, drawings and other possessions are in the **John Ruskin Museum** to the north of the church. His house at Brantwood, 2½ miles away on the east side of the lake, contains drawings and water colours by him.

Coniston Water is a smaller version of Windermere. The most impressive part of the lake is the north end, with Coniston Fells, but the wooded shores are also very attractive. The Old Man of Coniston can be climbed in 1½–2 hours (magnificent views of the surrounding hills).

A popular walk is to the very beautiful **Tarn Hows** (2½ miles north-east). The **Duddon Valley**, celebrated by Wordsworth, can be reached by a footpath which runs over the Walna Scar pass (2000 ft, good views) or by a road, narrow in places, via Broughton-in-Furness.

The best centre for the southern part of the Lake District is Ambleside (5 miles from Windermere; pop. 2560), a typical tourist resort below the Fairfield hills with the interesting Bridge House. Hayes Garden World has magnificent flower beds.

Ambleside

From Ambleside there are lovely walks and excursions – into **Little Langdale**, to Loughrigg Terrace (good view), up Walsfell Pike and **Loughrigg Fell**. The ascent of the Langdale Pikes takes about 1½–2 hours. Dungeon Ghyll is a popular climbing centre.

Rydal (pop. 530) is a quiet little village on the River Rothay at the east end of Rydal Water, 1 mile north-west of Ambleside. The very beautiful **Rydal Water** lies in a sheltered situation below Rydal Fell (2000 ft) and is the first lake to freeze in winter making it popular with skaters.

Rydal Mount was Wordsworth's last home from 1813 until his death in 1850. It contains family portraits and other memorabilia.

Grasmere is a small lake, almost circular in shape, with a lonely green island in the middle. The village of **Grasmere** (pop. 1030) was a great favourite with the Lakeland Poets. Wordsworth lived to the south of the village in ★**Dove Cottage** (now a museum) and is buried here. In the little church of St Oswald (14th to 17th c.), which has a beautiful interior, are memorials to him and other poets.

★**Lake Grasmere**

There are excellent walks from here, e.g. into Easedale and Borrowdale. The impressive **Helvellyn** (3118 ft) can be climbed in 3–3½ hours.

At the foot of Helvellyn is Thirlmere, a reservoir belonging to the city of Manchester, which draws its water from **Haweswater** to the east, a relatively isolated lake, its banks lined with pine woods.

Lake Thirlmere

Ullswater is the second largest lake, offering ideal conditions for sailing and fishing. On the shores of the lake is Gowborrow Park, the scene of Wordsworth's best known poem "Daffodils". Glenriding and Patterdale are beautifully situated on the shores of Lake Ullswater and make excellent centres for walkers.

★**Ullswater**

From Patterdale a very attractive road runs past the Great Mell Fell (1760 ft) to Keswick, one of the most popular Lake District centres (pop. 5000). The town lies on the River Greta, close to Derwentwater, in the middle of a beautiful range of hills, where according to Arthurian legend Sir Gawain came across the green knight. There is an interesting town hall. Greta Hall, now part of the local school, was the home of Coleridge and later of Southey. Further information is available from the **Fitz Park Museum**. The **Pencil Museum** documents the history of the production of pencils and crayons following the discovery of Borrowdale graphite around 1500.

★**Keswick**

Opened in 1989 the ★**Motor Museum** has vehicles on display which have featured in well known films and television series. Among the prize exhibits are the Lotus Esprit Turbo driven by James Bond in "For Your Eyes Only" and his Aston Martin DB 5 from "Goldfinger", the comic duo Laurel and Hardy's 1923 Ford T and the 32 ft-long pink Rolls Royce from the children's television series "Thunderbirds".

Just 2 miles to the east **Castlerigg Stone Circle** (98 ft radius) consists of 38 stones erected in the shape of a circle and estimated to be a place of worship between 4000 to 5000 years old.

There are walks to be recommended from Keswick to **Wasdale Head** via Sty Head Pass (5–6 hours) or via Scarth Gap and Black Sail.

Derwentwater is generally agreed to be the most beautiful of the lakes, with its grandiose backdrop of hills and the wooded crags and green

★★**Derwentwater**

Castlerigg Stone Circle

Lodore Falls

fells which rise from its shores. A number of pretty little islands in the lake invite the visitor to visit them by boat. The River Derwent flows in at one end and out at the other, and the lake is famed for its trout and salmon.

A fine view of the lake can be had from **Castle Head**. There are pleasant trips into ★**Borrowdale**, one of the most beautiful valleys in the Lake Lodore Falls District, or round the lake (10 miles), passing the Falls of Lodore, made famous by Southey's poem. Particular beauty spots in Borrowdale, which is famed for its fine birch trees and its good-quality slate, are Grange-in-Borrowdale and Rosthwaite.

Buttermere Water, Crummock Water

The village of Buttermere lies between Buttermere and Crummock Water, two small lakes belonging to the National Trust, linked by a stream ¾ mile long. ★**Scale Force**, on a stream which flows into Crummock Water, is acknowledged to be the most beautiful waterfall in the Lake District (156 ft high).

To the west in **Cockermouth**, with castle ruins dating from the 13/14th c., **William Wordsworth** was born in 1770. Seven of the rooms in this Georgian townhouse built in 1745 in Main Street are furnished with 18th c. furniture and contain personal belongings of the poet.

Whitehaven Museum has interesting archaeological and geological collections and illustrates the industrial development of the region.

Kendal

Kendal is situated on the east side of the Lake District and there are ruins of a 12th c. castle. ★**Abbot Hall** designed by John Carr in 1759 in Georgian style has a remarkable collection of paintings including portraits by George Romney and Daniel Gardner. Housed in the former stables the Museum of Lakeland Life and Industry provides a comprehensive picture of the history of local crafts and industry.

Art exhibitions, theatrical and musical events are held in the 200 year-old **Brewery Arts Centre**, a former brewery.

No visitor to the Lake District should omit the excursion to Furness Abbey in the wooded "Vale of Deadly Nightshade", 6 miles from Ulverston, in the southern part of the Lake District. This busy town is the birthplace of the comedian Stan Laurel, who is commemorated by a small museum.

★**Furness Abbey** was founded in 1173 by King Stephen for the Benedictine monks, who later adopted Cistercian rule. It was a rich and powerful house, since the abbots held feudal superiority over Furness. At one time it was the second richest Cistercian house in England surpassed only by Fountains Abbey (see Yorkshire Dales). There are extensive ruins of the red sandstone buildings. The transepts, choir and west tower of the church still stand to their full height, but the nave is in ruins. The round-headed arches of the cloister, the Early English chapterhouse, the dormitories and the infirmary are also preserved. The chapel contains two effigies of knights, believed to be the oldest of their kind (12th c.). Large parts of the church also date from the 12th c., only the east end and the west tower were added about 1500.

Lancaster   I 6

Region: Northern England. County: Lancashire
Altitude: 223 ft. Population: 45,500

A visitor to Lancaster has difficulty in realising that through its trade with the West Indies (cotton, rum, tobacco) this port was once more important than Liverpool and gave its name to the royal dynasty of

Lancaster Castle

Lancaster

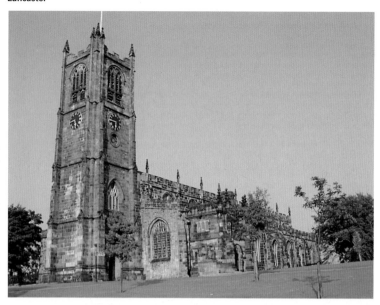

Lancaster: St Mary's Church

Lancaster. Even its former status as county town has been lost to Preston. What remains is a town with many fine buildings which is half old and half modern, the centre of a fertile farming region. Situated on the banks of the Lune the town has a university and some industrial developments. There is ample opportunity for excursions in the surrounding area along the North West Coast (see entry) with Morecambe Bay and the neighbouring Lake District (see entry).

Sights
Castle

The town was originally a Roman foundation, Lun-Castrum, the fort on the River Lune. Later, the Saxons built a wooden tower here, which the Normans replaced with a massive keep in 1102. At the end of the 12th and beginning of the 13th c. the site was expanded with round towers and a wall. Since the 17/18th c. the castle, which rises high above the river, has served as law courts and prison. It has preserved its almost 82 ft-high Norman keep, the Lungess Tower with a small light house known as John o' Gaunt's chair, from which in 1588 the approaching Spanish Armada was sighted. Also interesting are the round Hadrian's Tower (1209, later much altered), the porter's lodge and the Shire Hall (as Lancaster was the county town) with over 600 coats of arms from the 18th c.

St Mary's

St Mary's church, opposite, is mostly Perpendicular in style from the 14th and 15th c. The west doorway is Saxon, the massive tower was added in 1754. The oak-carved choir stalls dating from 1340 and the artistically decorated chancel in Late-Renaissance style are worth seeing.

The Cottage Museum (15 Castle Hill), a tradesman's house built in 1736 and divided into two in 1820, is furnished in the original style.

In the adjoining Meeting House Lane is the Friends' Meeting House of 1690, where the Quakers used to meet, who belonged to the religious community founded by George Fox (1624–91).

Friends' Meeting House

The Georgian Old Town Hall on the Market Square, built 1781–83 and restored in 1873, is now a municipal museum. The historical department with prehistoric and Roman exhibits and an interesting exhibition on the development of local industry together with the department on the King's Own Regiment, stationed in Lancaster since 1880, deserve a special mention.

City Museum

Ashton Memorial

The present-day town hall on Dalton Square was commissioned by Lord Ashton in 1909. Other notable buildings are **St John's Church** (1734) on the North Road, the **Judges' Lodgings Museum** (1620) in Church Street with a childhood museum and the **Custom House** on St George Square which has housed a maritime museum since 1985. **Skerton Bridge** over the Lune constructed by Thomas Harrison 1783–88, was the first road bridge in England to be built without piers. There are good views from the gallery of the **Ashton Memorial** (1909), which stands on a hill in Williamson Park. Opposite in the Palm House there are exotic plants and butterflies.

Other sights

Morecambe (pop. 42,000 including Heysham), situated on the coast in the middle of the bay of the same name, is exceptional not only for its sandy beach and the attractions of a busy seaside town but also for the beautiful countryside of its hinterland. At ebb tide it is possible to walk across **Morecambe Bay** on marked paths. From **Heysham** there are day trips to the Isle of Man (see entry) and boats depart for Belfast (see entry). The 12–14th c. St Peter's Church has Saxon stonework, in the churchyard a Viking gravestone from the 10th c., decorated with animal and human figures, has been preserved.

Surroundings Morecambe

Opened in 1797 the Lancaster Canal, along which goods barges travelled from Preston via Lancaster to Kendal from 1819, is still navigable south towards Preston and north to the eight locks of Tewitfield.

Lancaster Canal

Cockersand Abbey (7½ miles south-west), near the estuary of the Lune, is a Premonstratensian house founded in 1190 with an octagonal chapterhouse. Nearby, on the river, is a bird reserve for wild geese and other water birds.

Cockersand Abbey

The Forest of Bowland is designated as an area of outstanding natural beauty (28 miles south-east). This is an area of moorland with heights ranging between 1000 and 1836 ft. The area is traversed by a number of roads often steep and narrow, which are convenient for walkers and also used by motor traffic. The "Trough of Bowland" is a pass at a height of 1000 ft. There are a number of particularly attractive places in this area, such as Whitewell in the picturesque Hodder valley with trout fishing in the river. Browsholme Hall is a Tudor house (1507) with a notable art collection.

★Forest of Bowland

Leeds   K 7

Region: Northern England
County: West Yorkshire
Altitude: 150 ft. Population: 690,500

The city of Leeds, situated on the River Aire, has a long-established tradition of industry (textiles, furniture, paper, leather, electrical equipment).
Its primary importance is as the regional commercial and financial centre
as well as being the cultural hub of the area. The university enjoys an outstanding reputation, especially the faculties of science and technology.
Leeds is a good shopping centre and has a number of interesting museums, as well as an active musical life. It also has attractive parks and gardens for relaxing walks. York and the Yorkshire Dales (see entries), 25
miles away, are wonderful places to visit.

Transport The north-south M1 motorway and the east-west M621 intersect at Leeds. Leeds-Bradford airport is 8 miles north-west of the city
centre. There are good rail connections to all parts of the country from
City station.

History A ford over the Aire was here in Roman times, the town was
actually founded in the 18th c. with the development of the wool trade.
The first British railway line was constructed to transport the coal from
the mine at Middleton 3 miles away to Leeds in 1758 and the first steam
trains came into operation in 1812. The industrialisation of the 19th c.
brought economic prosperity to Leeds which was based chiefly on textiles and manufacturing.

Sights
City Square

The hub of Leeds is City Square, outside the City Station. In the square
are numerous statues, including figures of the Black Prince (son of
Edward III) and the inventor James Watt (see Famous People).

Victoria Square

Park Row, a business street, leads to Victoria Square, in which stands the

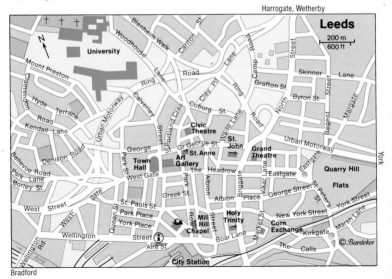

Town Hall, a Palladian building, consecrated in 1858 by Queen Victoria. There is a Corinthian colonnade along the main front which is dominated by a 200 ft-high clock tower. Its ornate Victoria Hall is used for concerts.

On the east side of the square in Calvery Street is the ★**City Art Gallery**, opened in 1888, which has a fine collection of works by British artists, with particular emphasis on the 20th c. English watercolour painting is also well represented with 750 pictures, mainly landscapes, by J. S. Cotman (1782–1842), one of the leading members of the Norwich School (see Norwich). There are also works by Constable and Gainsborough (see Famous People) together with Italian and French masters (including Courbet, Corot, Renoir, Signac). The Henry Moore Sculpture Galleries contain works by the artist (see Famous People) as well as by his contemporaries, including Jacob Epstein and Barbara Hepworth.

Adjoining the Art Gallery is the **City Museum** which has departments of geology, zoology, ethnology and archaeology, including particular material from Yorkshire.

North-east of the Town Hall stands the **Civic Hall**, an imposing build-ing opened by George V in 1933. The towers are decorated with owls, the heraldic emblem of the city.

The best shopping area is to be found in the side streets off the Headrow, the main through-route across the city, laid out in the 1920s. A stroll through the recently restored arcades of the adjoining ★**Victoria quarter** to the south-east is highly recommended. The glass-roofed passage with designer boutiques, fine jewellers and pretty cafés reflects the style of the Victorian era.	Headrow
One of the city's finest churches is St John's in New Briggate, built 1632–34. The church has been preserved almost entirely as it was built and still has the original Renaissance rood-screen, pulpit and stalls.	St John's
The Roman Catholic cathedral in Cookridge Street was built in 1902–04.	St Anne's Cathedral
The Georgian church of Holy Trinity on the river bank in Boar Lane (1721–27) has a very fine tower added by Chantrell in 1831.	Holy Trinity
Between the River Aire and the railway stands the city's oldest parish church, St Peter's, a medieval church rebuilt in 1839–41 in a mixture of Decorated and Perpendicular styles.	St Peter's
The Corn Exchange in Kirkgate is an interesting building. The oval build-ing, built 1861–63 in Victorian style, now houses shops, cafés and restau-rants.	Corn Exchange
A visit to the brewery at Tetley's Brewery Wharf reveals shining copper vats and highlights the interesting history of hops and malt during the last 500 years.	Tetley's Brewery Wharf
This spectacular museum was built to house the royal weapons collec-tion from the Tower of London. Live demonstrations are given using authentic battle gear and hunting costumes, with crossbow shooting and falconry.	Royal Armouries
About 2 miles west of the city centre in Canal Road stands the former wool mill Armley Mills. The history of wool production in Yorkshire from the 18th c. is fascinatingly presented.	Armley Mills
Just 2 miles south of the city is the carefully restored water mill, Thwaite Mill (19th c.), now a museum.	Thwaite Mills
3½ miles north-west, in the Aire valley, is Kirkstall Abbey, a Cistercian	**Surroundings**

★Kirkstall Abbey	house founded in 1152. The picturesque remains include a roofless church with a narrow choir and a ruined Perpendicular tower, and an almost completely preserved chapterhouse. The gatehouse is now part of the Abbey House Museum, with reproductions of houses, shops and workshops illustrating Yorkshire life in earlier days.
Temple Newsam	Temple Newsam (4½ miles east), also owned by the City Corporation, is a 17th c. mansion mainly in Tudor and Jacobean style, on the site of a preceptory of the Knights Templar. It contains valuable old furniture, some by Chippendale, porcelain, ceramics and silver. The house stands in beautiful grounds with marvellous rose bushes and rhododendrons.
★Harewood House	Harewood House, residence of the Earl of Harewood, (8 miles north) is a magnificent three-storey mansion built in 1759–71 based on plans by John Carr. The interior decoration is by Robert Adam, magnificent plasterwork, fine wall and ceiling paintings, many by Angelika Kauffmann, and furniture by Chippendale. As well as an outstanding collection of porcelain it has a large number of valuable paintings, including works by Reynolds, Gainsborough and El Greco (see Famous People). There is a beautiful park designed by "Capability" Brown (see pp. 408–9), with a large lake and the remains of a 12th c. castle. The church contains a number of notable monuments.

Leicester   K 8

Region: Midlands
County: Leicestershire
Altitude: 200 ft. Population: 324,400

Leicester, county town of Leicestershire, is a modern commercial and industrial centre with a long history. It is situated on the River Soar in a region of great scenic attraction. Its traditional industries – hosiery, knitwear and shoe manufacture – have been supplemented in recent years by engineering. It has a variety of churches and other old buildings of many different periods, mostly built in red brick. Cultural interests are well catered for by its museums and art galleries, two theatres and a large concert hall.

Leicester can claim to be the birthplace of modern mass tourism – if the medieval pilgrimages are excluded – since it was here that Thomas Cook organised his first package tour in 1841, a round trip of 30 miles to Loughborough. Thomas Cook travel company is today one of the best known international tour operators.

History Leicester occupies the site of the Roman city of Ratae Coritanorum, of which a number of interesting remains have survived. From 780 to 869 it was the see of a bishop and during the period of Danish rule one of the five boroughs of the Danelaw. The town was fortified by the Normans, and in 1239 passed into the hands of Simon de Montfort, Earl of Leicester. Regarded in Great Britain today as the "father of the English Parliament" his main contribution was insisting important state business be discussed in collective meetings and representatives of the lower orders be included. In the Middle Ages the royal court was regularly held in Leicester, in the 15th c. three Parliaments were held here. Richard III (1452–85), the last of the Plantagenets, spent the night in Leicester the night before the battle of Bosworth, in which he was defeated by Henry Tudor. After the battle his body was brought back and buried in Leicester Abbey; however, after the Dissolution of the monasteries his remains were thrown into the River Soar. Thomas Wolsey (1472–1530; Henry VIII's Lord Chancellor, later dismissed) was also buried here.

In the centre of the city is the **clock tower** from 1866 with figures of Leicester's four principal benefactors.

From here the High Street continues to **St Nicholas's Circle**, the oldest church in the city, with a Norman tower, a Saxon nave and Roman bricks. Close to its west end is the **Jewry Wall**, 79 ft long and 18 ft high, a relic of Roman occupation. Adjoining this are the excavations of the Roman forum and the remains of baths. Beautiful mosaic floors and paving stones are on display in the neighbouring **Museum of Roman Antiquities**.

Also situated on St Nicholas's Circle, Applegate, is the 15th c. **Roger Wygston's House** with a 18th c. façade, now a costume museum.

Sights
High Street and
Applegate

Practically nothing remains of Leicester Castle apart from the earth mound probably le ft by the Normans. Parts of the Great Hall and the cellars are incorporated in the 18th c. County Hall.

The church of **St Mary de Castro** in Castle Street, built in 1107, is partly Norman and partly Early English in style, originally served the castle. It has Late-Norman choir and a fine Early English baptistry.

Castle

The Turret Gateway (1432) leads to Trinity Hospital (an almshouse founded in 1331 and rebuilt in 1901) and to Newarke, where the Newarke Houses Museum is devoted to the historical development of local industry, clocks and towers.

Trinity Hospital,
★Newarke
Houses Museum

In Oxford Street in the porter's lodge is "The Magazine" (early 15th c.), a museum dedicated to the Royal Leicestershire Regiment.

Magazine

Situated in the High Street is St Martin's (Early English and Perpendicular style) which was raised to cathedral status in 1919. Inside is an ornate tomb designed by Joshua Marshall in 1656.

St Martin's

Nearby in Silver Street stands the Guildhall, a 14th c. half-timbered building, which in the Middle Ages belonged to the Corpus Christi guild. During the 15/16th c. the guildhall was rebuilt in Tudor style, since the 17th c. it has been a town hall. Next to the Great Hall there is a notable library dating from 1587 with the Codex Leicestrensis among its treasures, a precious Greek manuscript of the New Testament (15th c.).

★Guildhall

The pedestrianised New Walk leads to the municipal museum and art gallery with works by European masters from the 15th c., including famous German expressionists and French Impressionists, an interesting collection of ceramics, glass and silver and an extensive natural history department about Leicestershire.

Leicester Museum
and Art Gallery

Belgrave Hall in Church Road built 1709–13 in Queen Anne style has a fine collection of historic coaches and agricultural equipment.

Belgrave Hall
Museum

Adjoining the university library (University Road) the Charles Moore Collection of Wind Instruments opened in 1981 has exhibitions of instruments from the 18th and 19th c.

Charles Moore
Collection

St Margaret's church on St Margaret's Way was originally part of the prebend of the bishop of Lincoln. Built in the 13th c. the church was widely reconstructed in the 15th c. in Late-Gothic style. There is notable 19th c. stained glass by Thomas Willement.

St Margaret's

A walk through Abbey Park takes in the ruins of former Augustinian abbey founded in 1143. On its foundations the count of Huntingdon built Cavendish House, which was destroyed in the Civil War.

The Abbey

The Museum of Technology housed in a former pumping works (1891)

Museum of
Technology

in Corporation Road contains, among other exhibits, four balanced-steam engines and a historical transport collection.

Surroundings
Bradgate

The very beautiful **Bradgate Park** (6 miles north-west) with the ruins of the mansion in which Lady Jane Grey (1537–53), the "nine days queen" was born, whom Queen Mary Tudor had executed. In the 12th c. this moor and woodland was a hunting reserve and it has retained much of its original character. It is a popular place for the people of Leicester to visit.

North of Bradgate extends ⋆**Charnwood Forest** once densely wooded, now open heathland. It is excellent walking country consisting of cliffs and rugged landscapes and is dominated by Bardon Hill (912 ft) with good views as far as Derbyshire and the Welsh Marshes. In the past wood from Charnwood was used in the mining of brown coal, the granite quarries of Mountsorrel were worked as far back as in Norman times.

Ashby-de-la-Zouch

The small town of Ashby-de-la-Zouch (pop. 8500) with pretty Tudor houses of the 15/16th c. received its name from the Norman family La Zouch. Only the ruins remain of the former castle, constructed 1461–83 by Lord Hastings, razed in 1648. It featured in the novel "Ivanhoe" by Sir Walter Scott (see Famous People). St Helen's church in Late-Perpendicular style contains ornate tombs of the Huntingdon family from the 16th c.

Castle Donington

9 miles north-east from Ashby-de-la-Zouch there is a **Racing Car Collection** at Castle Donington. The collection includes racing cars dating back to 1911.

Lichfield   K 8

Region: Midlands
County: Staffordshire
Altitude: 266 ft. Population: 25,400

Lichfield, about 25 miles north of the City of Birmingham, is a

Lichfield Cathedral

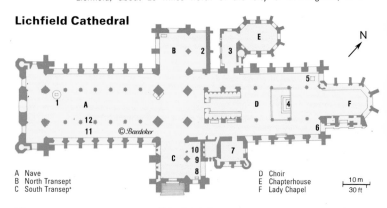

A Nave
B North Transept
C South Transep⁺

D Choir
E Chapterhouse
F Lady Chapel

1 Font
2 St Stephen's Chapel
3 Vestibule
4 High Altar

5 Bishop Ryder's Monument
6 "Sleeping Children"
7 Sacristy
8 St Michael's Chapel

9 David Garrick
10 Samuel Johnson
11 Colonel Anson
12 Earl of Lichfield

quiet and attractive town. Its main attractions are the superb cathedral and its associations with Samuel Johnson (1709–84), the English writer who published his two-volume "Dictionary of the English Language" (1746-55). Until the publication of the "Oxford English Dictionary" (1884) it was the definitive work on vocabulary and pronunciation.

Built of red sandstone the cathedral is dedicated to St Mary and St Chad. This "queen of English minsters" was built on the site of two earlier churches between 1198 and 1325; the first was built by Bishop Hedda around 700, the second probably around the turn of the century. The oldest part is the lower section of the west end of the choir (c. 1198) and the sacristy completed in 1208. The Early English style transepts date from 1220–40, the nave from about 1250 and the Early-Gothic west front from about 1280.

★Lichfield Cathedral

The Lady Chapel and presbytery are from the first half of the 14th c. The church received severe damage during two sieges in 1643 and 1646, restoration began in 1660 and was completed in 1950 with the restoration of the cross on the central tower.

The three elegant spires – a feature unique in England – are known as the "Ladies of the Vale". The west front, notable for the splendid harmony of its composition, is particularly beautiful, with four galleries of niches containing 113 statues of saints; because of the effects of weathering most are modern reproductions. The central door has intricate wrought-iron work by Thomas of Leighton. The entrance to the north aisle, a delicate piece of Early English work, is also very fine.

The interior is notable for its beautiful proportions and the play of colour. The capitals in the nave and the triforium are splendid examples of Early-Gothic. In the aisles are numerous monuments, including a tablet commemorating Lady Mary Wortley Montagu (1689–1762), a pioneer of modern smallpox innoculation.

The **choir** was built in the early English period but partly rebuilt in Decorated style in 1325. The stalls were carved c. 1860 by Samuel Evans of Ellastone, a cousin of George Eliot. In the south aisle is the famous monument of the "Sleeping Children" (1817) by Chantry, the Holy Trinity window above is the original Flemish glass. A medallion commemorates Erasmus Darwin (1731–1802), the botanist, grandfather of Charles Darwin (see Famous People).

The ★**Lady Chapel** was built in 1324 probably after plans by William of Eyton in Decorated style. The nine beautiful stained glass windows depict scenes from the Passion. Seven of them were brought to Lichfield in 1802 from the Cistercian abbey of Herkenrode near Liège. The two most westerly windows are also Flemish work.

Above the elegant **chapterhouse** of 1240 is the **library**, whose greatest treasures are the Irish manuscript gospel "St Chad's Gospel" of 721 and a manuscript of Chaucer's "Canterbury Tales".

The Johnson Birthplace Museum is opposite the market square in Breadmarket Street. The house in which the famous lexicographer was born the son of a bookseller, contains personal memorabilia, books and secondary literature.

Samuel Johnson Birthplace Museum

Opened in 1981 in St Mary's church the Lichfield Heritage and Treasury Centre illustrates the history of the town (costumes, silver, audio-visual display).

Heritage and Treasury Centre

About 3 miles outside the town on the A51 Lichfield to Tamworth Road, near Whittington, the **Staffordshire Regimental Museum** contains numerous uniforms, coats of arms and medals of the North and South Staffordshire regiments.

Surroundings

Lincoln

Location

Region:
Midlands
County:
Lincolnshire
Altitude: 299 ft.
Population:
80,000

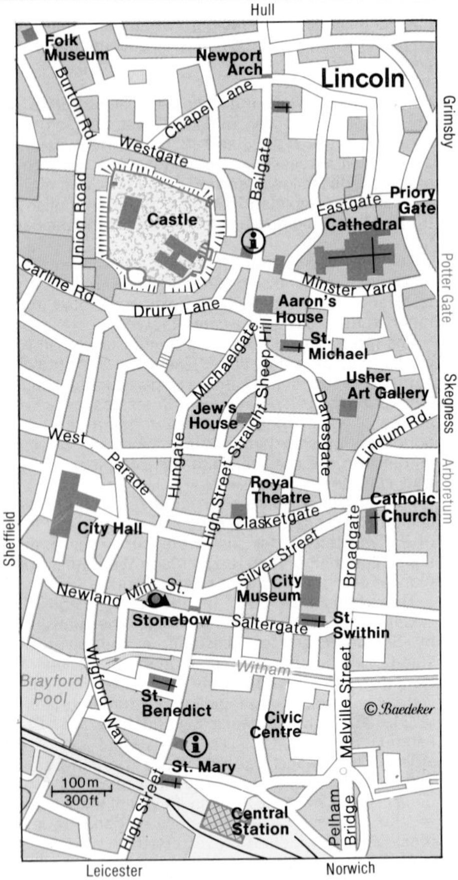

Lincoln, county town of Lincolnshire, is one of the finest of England's old historic cities. It lies on the River Witham which at this point has carved out its course through a ridge of limestone. The town is dominated by its magnificent cathedral, one of the largest in England, which stands on a hill. It also has many handsome medieval houses, remains of Roman town gates and the Norman fortifications.

History In AD 48 the Romans established their first military base for the 9th legion, which in AD 96 became Lindum Colonia (from which the name Lincoln is derived), a town for Roman veterans, and was provided with many public facilities. After the fall of the Roman Empire the Anglo-Saxons penetrated the region. Their kingdom of Lindsey was conquered by the Vikings who expanded Lincoln to an important trading centre from 868 and made it into one of the five boroughs of the Danelaw with a mint. In 1068 the Normans built Lincoln castle as an expression of their newly-acquired domination of the region and soon after in 1072 building began on the cathedral for the largest diocese in England. Lincoln is described in the Domesday Book as a prosperous town with a sizable population of 6000, which led to considerable taxation of its citizens. It became autonomous quite early, the office of mayor (1206) is the oldest in Great Britain. The Magna Carta brought additional privileges for Lincoln. The town developed into an important wool centre and the income from the staple rights and the export of products very much in demand thanks to good trade routes on the Witham and Fossdyke Canal increased the

Lincoln Cathedral, dominating the town

prosperity of the merchants who built themselves handsome houses. However, in 1369 there was economic recession and Lincoln lost the staple rights for wool to other towns with ensuing poverty for the town and in the 16th c. the population had fallen to 2000. Not until the 18th c. did the economy improve as an agricultural centre and by 1831 the population had risen to 12,000. Following its integration into the railway network in 1846 Lincoln became a centre of iron and steel industry. Agricultural machinery, military vehicles and gas turbines were manufactured. Nowadays important industries are the manufacture of semi-conductors, building and construction and services from the tertiary sector.

Sights
Lower town

The busy modern lower town forms a striking contrast with the peaceful and picturesque old town around the cathedral. Starting from the High Street, the first church to be seen is St Peter-at-Gowts, which has a Saxon tower. A short distance away is St Mary's Guildhall (1180–90), a fine example of Norman secular architecture, originally a royal storehouse then a guildhall, with notable Roman excavations. In Akrill's Passage is a notable 15th c. half-timbered house. On the right is the church of St Mary-le-Wigford in Early English style with a Saxon tower. St Mary's Conduit was built in the 16th c. with stone from a Carmelite friary.

Close by, **Brayford Pool**, which is fed by the River Witham, is Lincoln's former inland port. In the 18/19th c. it was an important handling centre for cereals, today the old warehouses have been turned into hotels and restaurants and yachts and motorboats lie at anchor. From the south side there is a splendid view of the cathedral. The river is spanned by the High Bridge which dates from 1160, on the west bank are a number of old half-timbered houses and shops. The **High Street** continues under the Stonebow (15th c.) the medieval south town gate with the Guildhall, the great council chamber, on the floor above it, which reminds the visitor that the office of mayor and sherrif from 1206 and 1409 are among the oldest communal offices in England. The end of the High Street runs into the Strait and then up Steep Hill, which climbs up to the upper town.

Upper Town

Here are to be found the most interesting medieval remains of the Old Town at the foot of Steep Hill is the **Jew's House**, a Norman stone building from about 1170, and the adjoining Jew's Court, probably the remains of a former synagogue from the end of the 12th c. At this time the Jews were influential in Lincoln before being expelled from England in 1290.

Not far away are the old merchant's house Harding House (16th c.), the Harlequin, a half-timbered house which was an inn in the 16th c. and now an antiquarian bookshop, and Aaron's House, a Norman secular building (about 1150). The upper part of Steep Hill is lined with Georgian houses. The traditional pub "The Wig and Mitre" is 14th c. and near Castle Square are other buildings from this period with 19th c. shop fronts.

★★Lincoln
Cathedral

History When the bishop's seat moved from Dorchester-on-Thames to Lincoln Bishop Remigius began work in 1027, which was continued by his successors, on one of the most monumental medieval cathedrals in England in keeping with the largest diocese in the country. This Anglo-Norman cathedral, completed in 1092, was badly damaged by fire in the wooden roof truss in 1141, the restored Romanesque-Norman church was subsequently damaged by an earthquake and was rebuilt by Hugo of Avalon, the French Carthusian monk who was elected bishop in 1186, in Early Gothic style incorporating the undamaged Romanesque parts. The cathedral was completed about half a century later but after the collapse of the crossing tower in 1239 it was rebuilt and with the addition of the Angel Choir in 1280 the original polygonal end of the choir was made straight to become a worthy place for the shrine of the beatified Hugo.

The medieval gateway leads to the imposing twin towered **West façade** which is a mixture of Romanesque and Gothic styles. The central round-arched doorway (about 1150) is Norman with 12th c. frieze-like sculpture depicting scenes from the Old Testament (Noah's Ark, Daniel in the Lion's Den) and dragons in the walls, whereas the statues of kings in judgment in the niches above the main doorway are from the 13th c.

The triple-aisled interior of this Early-Gothic columned basilica is impressive for its length and size with two transepts, and for the contrasting colours of honey-coloured limestone and dark Purbeck marble. In the nave the font is made of black Tournai marble (12th c.) with animal motifs. The other side of the transepts display marvellous Gothic tracery, to the north a round window known as the Eye of the Deacon (about 1200) with medieval stained glass and to the south the Eye of the Bishop (early 14th c.) with pieces of glass from different periods. Legend has it that the Eye of the Deacon watches over his residence whereas the Eye of the Bishop watches over the palace waiting for the gospel from the Holy Ghost. The ambulatory leads to the chapel of Bishop Grosseteste, who was chancellor of the university of Oxford (see entry) in 1214, and to the tombs of Katherine Swynford and her daughter. Katherine Swynford (d. 1403) as the third wife of John of Gaunt ancestor of the present royal family and George Washington, the first president of the USA. The love story of Katherine and John of Gaunt, ancestor of the Tudors, was made popular by Anya Seaton in her novel "Katherine". A wrought-iron gate (13th c.) leads to St Hugh's choir, one of the best example of Early-Gothic architecture (about 1200). The "crazy" vaulting above the choir-stalls has three ribs instead of four leading to the keystone on each truss. It is thought to be the work of the theologian and scientist Robert Grosseteste, who carried out optical experiments before he was made bishop of Winchester in 1235 and following the collapse of the crossing tower in 1239 had the damaged choir truss renovated. The 62 choir-stalls from 1360-80 have wonderful carving, especially the miserichords. The combined sedilia with an Easter sepulchre is a rare example of 14th c. sculpture. The south ambulatory comes to the retro choir known as the Angel Choir (completed about 1280) which gets its name from the 28 angels on the triforium, a Gothic work of great elegance and harmony, which accommodated the shrine of St Hugo. At the top of the second-last pillar to the north is the "Lincoln Imp", which according to legend annoyed the angels in the choir and so was turned to stone. The east window has High-Gothic geometric tracery; a monument below commemorates Queen Eleanor, wife of Edward I, who died near Lincoln. The north ambulatory leads to the cloisters which are 13th c. and have beautifully carved roof bosses. The north side, from which there is one of the finest views of the cathedral, was rebuilt in 1647, together with the library above it.

The adjoining **chapterhouse** is decagonal with its vaulting supported by a central pier; it dates from the middle of the 13th c. Several parliaments met here in the reigns of Edward I and II.

Cathedral Close is very picturesque and has a number of notable buildings, including the remains of the Old Bishop's Palace, Cantilupe Chantry and Vicar's Court (14th c.); a monument commemorates the poet Lord Tennyson, who was born in Somersby in 1809 near Lincoln.

On Castle Hill is the entrance to the mighty castle which was built by William the Conqueror (see Famous People) after an entire quarter of the town had been cleared in 1068; the wooden pallisade was replaced in 1113 by thick defensive walls. In the south-west of the grounds stands the 12th c. keep, known as Lucy Tower, in the north-east corner Cobb Hall, a horse-shoe shaped bastion from the 13th c. There is a good view from the third tower, the Observatory Tower (19th c.). The town's archives in the Old Prison contain a presentation of the Magna Carta from 1215, which was preserved in the Cathedral as one of four existing copies.

Castle

To the north of the castle Bailgate was the centre of the Roman town. Circles mark the positions of the Roman columns and in the cellar of No. 29 (Roman House) the remains of the Roman basilica can be seen. St Paul's church stands on the site of the church built by St Paulinus, who brought Christianity to Lincoln in 627. At the north end of Bailgate is the Newport Arch, one of the two best preserved Roman town gates (1st c.) in England – Balkerne Gate in Colchester (see entry) is less well preserved.

Bailgate

A small section of the Roman town walls can be seen in **East Bight**.

The Usher Art Gallery in the gardens to the south of the cathedral has a fine collection of clocks, jewellery, miniatures and porcelain. The City and County Museum in Broadgate contains many Roman antiquities. The history of the bicycle is documented in the National Cycle Museum in Brayford Wharf North and the Museum of Lincolnshire Life in Burton Road documents local customs.

Museums

Newark-on-Trent (16 miles south-west) is a picturesque little town which is worth a visit. In spite of its name it is not situated directly on the River Trent. Its principal features of interest are the castle of the bishop of Lincoln, in which King John died in 1216, and the Perpendicular church of St Mary Magdalene in the pretty market place, which preserves a beautiful rood screen and a Norman crypt.

**Surroundings
Newark-on-Trent**

Gainsborough (15 miles north; pop. 20,300) is a town with interesting historical associations. King Alfred was married here in 868, and the Danish king Sweyne, died here in his camp in Thonock Park in 1014. During the Civil War the town was the scene of much fighting between Royalist and Parliamentary forces. The Old Hall, part of a medieval manor-house has a handsome roof and an old kitchen. Gainsborough was George Eliot's (1819–80; real name Mary Ann Evans) model for St Ogg's in "The Mill on the Floss", and some of the places she describes can still be identified.

Gainsborough

Liverpool   H/I 7

Region: Midlands. County: Merseyside
Altitude: 184 ft. Population: 775,000

The name Liverpool immediately conjures up the Beatles, the first class
football teams Liverpool FC and Everton FC and the accent of the
"Scousers", as the people of Liverpool are known. The heart of the
Merseyside Conurbation lies on the east bank of the Mersey estuary,
about 3 miles from the open sea. At this point the Mersey is about ¾ mile
wide, opening out inland into a basin 3 miles wide. Liverpool, with one
of the largest harbours in the world not dependent on tides, is a major
port for trans-atlantic shipping. The huge container ships are handled at
the modern docks situated outside the city near Bootle and Birkenhead
on the opposite bank.

This city of superlatives is not only an important trading metropolis,
university town and financial centre. For years it has been trying to
resolve serious structure problems by far-reaching redevelopment programmes, diversification initiatives for industry and incentives for the
tertiary sector. The major employers are the motor companies Ford and
General Motors, the food manufacturers United Biscuits and Nabisco,
Unilever, whose presence dates back over 100 years, Glaxo, Metal Box,
Pilkington Glass and Shell. In 1984 it became a free port. Liverpool's central importance is underlined by the location here of the seats of both
Catholic and Anglican bishops; the Anglican cathedral is one of the
largest churches in Christendom. The city has many handsome historic
administrative and commercial buildings, many gardens and parks and
numerous museums and recreational facilities, including the famous
Walker Art Gallery and the Philharmonic Hall, one of the best concert
halls in Europe.

Transport The airport at Speke (6 miles south-east from the city centre)
is for internal flights only, international flights land at Manchester
International Airport (see Manchester), 30 miles east (motorway). There
are good road and rail connections with Manchester and the rest of
Lancashire; the main railway station is Lime Street station. Birkenhead
can be reached by the Queensway Road Tunnel (parallel to a rail tunnel),
Wallasey by the Kingsway road tunnel. The famous Mersey ferries
operate boat trips for visitors as well as plying between the two banks.
The Liverpool–Manchester Ship Canal, originally constructed for the
transport of cotton, is also navigable.

History The origin of the city's name is unknown, but is traditionally connected with the mythological Liver bird (pronounced "lyver"). This sea
gull or cormorant-like bird figures in the city's coat of arms, carrying a
piece of seaweed in its beak (the symbolic "planta genista" of the
Plantagenets). The name "Liverpool" appears for the first time in a charter of 1173 granted by Henry II, who founded the town and built a castle
here. The port was constructed by King John in 1207. Liverpool's rise in
economic importance is closely connected with the decline of Chester as
a port caused by the silting of its harbour. The first dock on the Mersey
together with the first harbour with locks was opened in 1715, when the
town had a population of some 5000. Liverpool followed Bristol (see
entry) in the lucrative "trading triangle": glass beads, cotton goods, etc.
were exported to Africa, the ships carrying them then conveyed negro
slaves to the West Indies and North America, from where cotton, raw
sugar, tobacco, cocoa, etc. were brought back to England. The regular
shipping services to North America which began in 1840, also contributed to the city's prosperity.

Beatles   Liverpool is the birthplace of the Beatles, whose pop music achieved

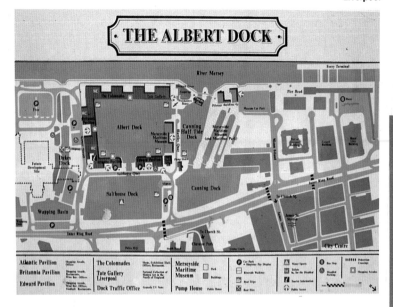

Atlantic Pavilion	Shopping Arcade	The Colonnades	Shops, Exhibition Hall, Offices, Restaurant	Merseyside Maritime Museum	☐ Park	☐ Car Park + Shortstay Pay Display	▲ Water Sports	☐ Bus Stop	‖‖‖‖‖ Pedestrian Crossings
Britannia Pavilion	Shopping Arcade, Restaurants, Wine Bar, Offices	Tate Gallery Liverpool	National Collection of Modern Art in the North of England		☐ Buildings	☐ Riverside Walkway	WC Toilets & for the Disabled	☐ Disabled Parking	☐ Shopping Arcades
Edward Pavilion	Shopping Arcade, Wine Bar, Offices, Football, Restaurant	Dock Traffic Office	Granada T.V. News	Pump House	☐ Public Houses	☐ Boat Trips	☑ Tourist Information		
						☒ Boat Hire	♿ Public Toilet		

world fame in the 1960s. Various tours offer fans the opportunity to follow in their footsteps and visit their former homes (Penny Lane, Strawberry Fields), "The Beatles Story" in Albert Dock and Matthew Street with the rebuilt Cavern Club, where they made their debut on February 21st 1961 (today a discothèque), the Cavern Walks (external murals by Cynthia Lennon), the Memorial Club for John Lennon (see Famous People), the Beatles Shop, bronze statues of the musicians by John Doubleday and Arthur Dooley's controversial statue "The four lads who shook the world". In 1996 Paul McCartney inaugurated the first "entertainment university" for rock and pop music, the Liverpool Institute for Performing Arts, which holds a three-year course and provides an all-round training.

★★Albert Dock

On the waterfront south-west of the inner city is Albert Dock, superbly restored in 1992. Opened in 1846 by Prince Albert and closed in 1972 the inner-city docks of Liverpool were the second largest enclosed docks in Britain of that time, the first to be built without wood using only bricks and iron to reduce the danger of fire. Nearby the old landing stages are reminders of Liverpool's former glory, when luxury liners from America anchored here and the city was a profitable trading centre.

A square block five storeys high surrounds the harbour basin, where once cotton, tobacco and sugar were unloaded. The enormous brick buildings by the Victorian engineer Jesse Hartley (1824–60) are built around an arcaded walkway; its cast Tuscan columns were bollards for mooring the ships. The decoratively restored warehouses with their designer boutiques, offices, restaurants, cafés and museums form a prime example of how to restore decaying inner cities to provide recreational amenities.

An acclaimed branch of the ★Tate Gallery in London has been established in the Albert Dock. As chance would have it the London Tate Gallery, which was founded at the end of the 19th c. with a legacy from the sugar magnate Sir Henry Tate, found new accommodation in the

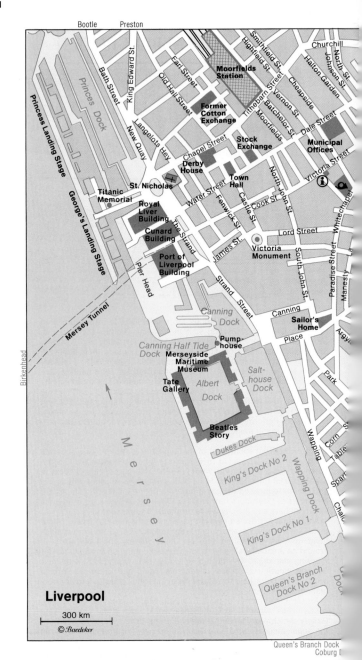

Liverpool

300 km

© Baedeker

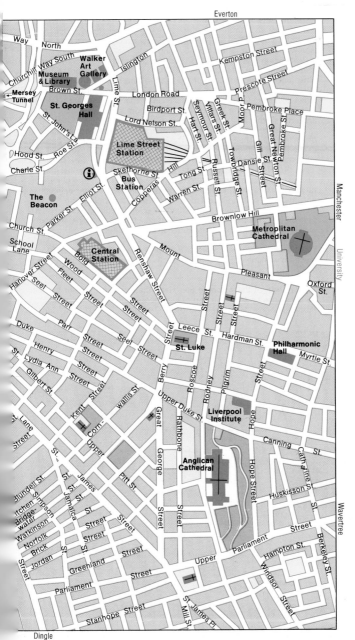

Everton

Way North

Churchill Way South

Churchill Way South

Walker Art Gallery

Museum & Library

Islington

Lime St.

Kempston Street

Prescote Street

Mersey Tunnel

Brown St.

London Road

Birdport St.

St. Georges Hall

St. John's La.

Lord Nelson St.

Seymour St.

Hart St.

Villars St.

Greek St.

Moor St.

Pembroke Place

Pembroke St.

Great Newton St.

Hood St.

Roe St.

Charle St.

Lime Street Station

Skethorne St.

Hill

Tong St.

Russell St.

Towbridge St.

Gill Street

Dansie St.

ⓘ

Bus Station

Copperas

Warren St.

The Beacon

Parker St.

Elliot St.

Brownlow Hill

Church St.

School Lane

Central Station

Renshaw Street

Mount

Metroplitan Cathedral

Pleasant

Oxford St.

Hanover Street

Bold

Wood

Fleet

Seel

Street

Street

Street

Street

Street

Street

Street

Street

Duke

Parr

Leece St.

Hardman St.

Philharmonic Hall

Myrtle St.

Henry

Lydia Ann

Gilbert St.

St.

Seel

Street

Berry

Roscoe

Pilgrim

Street

St. Luke

Rodney

Hope

Kent Street

Wallis St.

Upper Duke St.

Liverpool Institute

St. Lane

Corn-

Upper

Rathbone

George

Anglican Cathedral

Canning

Catharine St.

Hope Street

Huskisson St.

Blundell St.

Kitchen St.

Bridge-water

Simpson

St. James

Jamaica

Pitt. St.

Norfolk

Brick

St.

St.

Street

Street

Street

Street

Upper

Parliament

Hampton St.

Berkeley St.

Watkinson

Jordan

St.

Greenland

Street

Street

Upper

Windsor Street

Street

Parliament

Stanhope Street

St. James Pl.

Mill St.

Manchester

University

Wavertree

Dingle

warehouses where Tate stored the raw sugar before it was refined. The last connection with the inventor of the sugar cube ended in 1981 with the closure of the Tate & Lyle sugar refineries in Liverpool, a fate, which is only too familiar to this once thriving port.

Restoration was the work of Liverpool architect James Stirling who also extended the Tate Gallery on the bank of the Thames for the Turner Museum. The ground floor of the "Tate of the North" has three exhibition halls (total of 4000 sq. m floor space), the first floor has three galleries dedicated to contemporary art. On the second floor are works on loan from the London Tate, on the upper floors are offices, lecture halls and artists' studios.

The neighbouring **Maritime Museum** opened its first permanent exhibition in 1986, "The Emigrants to the New World". It depicts the passage of the seven million emigrants who left the Mersey between 1830 and 1930 for the New World. During the 1840s many Irish were forced to leave their homes because of the famine, in the 50s countless people rushed to Australia in the search for gold and around the turn of the century there were innumerable emigrants to the USA. Other exhibitions document the history of seafaring in Liverpool, beginning with the 13th c. fishing village, through the heyday of the Mersey docks to the modern port development of the 20th c. illustrated by model ships, authentic workshops and historic frigates outside the building.

Beatles Story

The basement of the Britannia Pavilion houses "The Beatles Story" museum with memorabilia, photographs and films of the four Liverpool lads.

From the Waterfront to the Town Hall

To the north of the ★**George Pier Head** the traditional trio of harbour buildings can be seen: the Port of Liverpool Building (administration) in Portland stone designed by Arnold Thornley in 1907, the Cunard

Liverpool: Maritime Museum in Albert Dock

George Pier

Building named after the Canadian Samuel Cunard (Cunard opened the first shipping line Liverpool-Halifax-Boston) and the granite Royal Liver Building by W. A. Thomas (administration).

Nearby the **Titanic Memorial** commemorates the "Heroes in the Engine Room" of the luxury liner which sank in 1912.

Not far to the east of the trio of buildings the **Monument to Queen Victoria** (see Famous People) was unveiled in 1906, designed by F. M. Simpson, the first professor of architecture at Liverpool University.

From here Castle Street leads to the Georgian **Town Hall** (only open to visitors in August), built in 1754 after plans by John Wood of Bath and extended in 1789. The copper cupola is crowned by a statue of Minerva, the Roman goddess of arts and crafts.

The façade of the Classical ★**St George's Hall** (Brown Street) by Harvey Lonsdale Elmes, 1838–54, is decorated with Corinthian columns. The Great Hall, with one of the world's largest organs, is used for concerts and congresses. To the rear are St John's Gardens, in which are statues of prominent Liverpool citizens.

To the north is an imposing group of Neo-Greek buildings, at the west end the **Liverpool Polytechnic Building** (1902: with Liverpool allegories and a Minerva statue).

The adjoining complex contains the Liverpool Museum and the **William Brown Library**, named after a wealthy Liverpool businessman who subsidised the building.

The **Liverpool Museum** contains a variety of collections, covering almost every field of knowledge from archaeology to the sciences. Among them are an interesting collection of model ships and the department of space travel, the famous Ince Blundell Collection (ancient marble) and the Sassoon Collection of carved ivory, and Egyptian, Babylonian and Assyrian antiquities.

City centre

John J Lee: "Sweethearts and Wives" ...   *... in the Walker Art Gallery*

In the adjacent building, named after the Liverpool architect Sir James Picton, are the **Picton Reading Rooms** and the **Hornby Library**.

★★Walker Art Gallery

Liverpool's best known museum, the Walker Art Gallery, (1874–76), was presented to the city by local brewer, Sir Andrew Barclay Walker, who was mayor in 1873. It has a rich collection of works by Italian, Flemish and French masters from the 14th c. to the present, including works by Joos van Cleve ("Virgin and Child", around 1520), Rubens ("The Holy Family", around 1632), Rembrandt (self-portrait, about 1630), by French Impressionists and Rodin. Its display of English painting and sculpture, particularly of the 18th–20th c. is unrivalled by any gallery outside London. It features works by Gainsborough ("Elisabeth, Viscountess Folkestone", 1776), Hogarth ("David Garrick as Richard III", 1745) and Moore, pictures by Marianne Stokes ("Polishing Pans", 1887), Harold Gilman ("Mrs Mounter", 1912) and Nicholas Hillard ("Queen Elizabeth I", 1574) together with a poignant farewell scene at Liverpool's Pier Head by John J. Lee entitled "Sweethearts and Wives" (1860). The John and Peter Moore Exhibition, an important display of contemporary British art is held every alternate year.

Associated with the Walker Gallery is the **Sudley Art Gallery**, in an early 19th c. mansion on Mossley Hill (3 miles south). Mainly English 18th and 19th c. artists such as Gainsborough and Turner are represented.

Museum of Labour History

Opened in 1986 the Merseyside Museum of Labour History, located in the former Lancashire County Sessions House, documents the life of the worker over the last 150 years (changing living and working conditions, struggle for political rights, development of the trade union movement). St John's Centre

The centre point of St John's shopping centre (pedestrianised), which can be reached via Lime Street, is **"The Beacon"**, a 450 ft-high tower with a revolving restaurant and viewing platform with good views.

Next to the shopping centre on Williamson Square is the Playhouse Theatre, England's oldest repertory theatre.

Playhouse
Theatre

Two roads further south in School Lane is the Bluecoat art centre with an excellent gallery and concert hall.

Bluecoat Gallery

Liverpool's possession of two cathedrals, a Roman Catholic as well as an Anglican reflects the high proportion of Roman Catholics of Irish origin in its population compared with other English towns. During the great emigrations in the periods of poverty and famine in Ireland in the 19th and 20th c., Liverpool was the principal port of embarkation for the United States, and many of the emigrants also settled in the city.

★Cathedrals and
University

Building began on the ★**Roman-Catholic Cathedral** in 1928 only ¼ mile from the Anglican cathedral. The original design was for a Neo-Classical building, but only the crypt of this was completed. After the Second World War an architectural competition was held for the completion of the cathedral, the successful design – much more modest than the original plan, which would have produced the second largest church in Christendom, – was by Sir Frederick W. Gibberd, who had worked on the design of Heathrow airport.

The Cathedral, consecrated in 1967, is a massive circular structure centred on a lantern of medieval type and can accommodate a congregation of 3000. Round this cylindrical lantern tower is a huge "tent" 200 ft in diameter, rising sharply to a funnel-shaped drum 270 ft high. Since the Cathedral is built on a hill it has the appearance of a huge lantern rising above the city. The principal structural materials are steel and glass – more glass than in any other cathedral. Opinions differ widely as

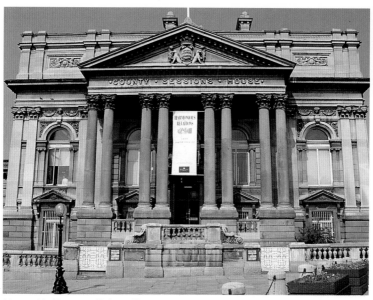

Merseyside Museum of Labour History

Liverpool Roman Catholic Cathedral ...   *... and cargo port*

to whether it is beautiful or not, but it must be conceded that it is striking. It has many nicknames among the local people such as "wigwam", "spaceship" and "Mersey Funnel". The altar, a block of white marble 10 ft long and weighing 10 tonnes, is from Skopje, the capital of Macedonia in former Yugoslavia. The spaces between the 16 supporting piers are occupied by chapels, separated by blue and green glass walls.

Not far to the east the **University** was founded in 1903. The School of Tropical Medicine was the first of its kind in 1899 and is the oldest part of the complex.

The ⋆**Anglican Cathedral**, on St James's Mount, can accommodate a congregation of 2500 and shows a sharp contrast in style to the Catholic Cathedral. It, too, was the result of an architectural competition in 1901, the successful architect was the then 22 year-old Sir Giles Gilbert Scott. When he died in 1960 the church was still not completed; it was finally consecrated in 1978, although services were already held in the building in the 1920s. It has only a single tower, 330 ft high, in place of the twin towers originally planned and is built of red sandstone from Woolton with a copper roof. The tower contains a carillon of some 2500 bells, the largest of which weighs 4 tons. The Willis organ, with 9704 pipes is one of the largest in the world. The Lady Chapel and stained glass are also very interesting.

**Surroundings
Birkenhead**

The residential and industrial town of Birkenhead (pop. 137,800) lies on the west side of the Mersey, linked to Liverpool by tunnels and ferry services. The **Williamson Art Gallery** has an excellent collection of pictures and porcelain, together with much material on the history of the town. Near the tunnel are the ruins of a Benedictine abbey (12th c.) with the chapterhouse, crypt and refectory.

Ellesmere Port

The **Boat Museum** in nearby Ellesmere Port recreates the heyday of the waterways when barges were an important form of goods transport.

Port Sunlight is of interest for the part it played in the history of British **Port Sunlight**
industrial development. The Lever brothers had made a considerable
fortune from soap and founded a model town for their workers on the
estuary of the Mersey in 1888, similar to that of Cadbury near
Birmingham (see entry). They built better schools and training centres.
The ★**Lady Lever Art Gallery** has an excellent collection of Art Nouveau,
18th c. furniture and Wedgwood porcelain, together with works by
Turner (see Famous People) and other English painters.

One of the finest Tudor houses in England is Speke Hall (7 miles east in ★**Speke Hall**
Hale). This half-timbered house on the north bank of the Mersey
(1530–98) is notable for its great hall, its beautiful plasterwork and fine
furniture.

London   L/M 9

Region: Southern England
Altitude: 30 ft
Population: 6.8 million in the Metropolitan County of Greater London

Note: The description of London has been deliberately kept short as the
Baedeker/AA Guide to London is much more detailed.

London, capital of the United Kingdom of Great Britain and Northern
Ireland, seat of the royal family, Parliament and government, lies in a
gently undulating basin enclosed by hills, on both banks of the Thames
some 50 miles above its estuary into the North Sea. The "Greenwich
Meridian", longitude 0°, runs through the London suburb of Greenwich.
London is not only the financial and cultural centre of Great Britain but
also one of the most interesting cities in the world, a real metropolis,
where people from all different countries have made their contribution
to a cultural melting pot which finds expression in music, theatre, dance,
literature, and not least, gastronomy.

The Thames, which follows a winding course through London, divides the   Area and
city into a northern and southern part, with the main tourist sights lying   administration
on the northern bank. The city of London only covers an area of 2.6 sq. km,
about one square mile, thus its name the "Square Mile". It has a resident
population of only about 5000 people and about 400,000 people work here. The
actual area of London (Inner London) – consisting of the City and twelve
surrounding boroughs – covers 120 sq. miles with a population of 3.2 million and together with a ring of twenty further boroughs (Outer London)
make up the Metropolitan County of Greater London with a population of
6.8 million covering 610sq. miles. Including the adjoining suburbs the
number of people in the conurbation of London reaches 12 million.
    London is unique as a metropolis as it is without a unified adminis-
trative body. Until 1986 it was administrated by the Greater London
Council. Responsibility was devolved to the individual boroughs but
New Labour wants to change this now that it is in government.
    The administration of the City of London is based on medieval
attested rights. It consists of 24 Aldermen, who are elected for life, 131
Councilmen, who are elected annually in December to represent the
wards, and finally, the Lord Mayor who is also elected for one year on
Michaelmas Day and is the senior representative of the City. On the day
following his election the Lord Mayor's Show takes place, a colourful
procession through the streets and the new Lord Mayor takes the oath
of office. The representatives of the old craft guilds, the Liverymen, play
an important part in the government of the City. They nominate two candidates to the Aldermen for election as Lord Mayor and elect the
Aldermanic Sheriff and the Lay Sheriff who support the Mayor.

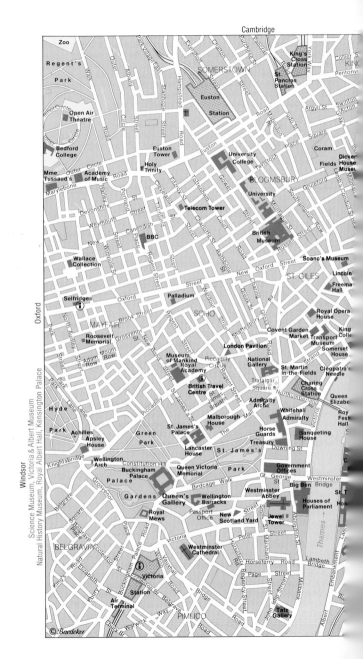

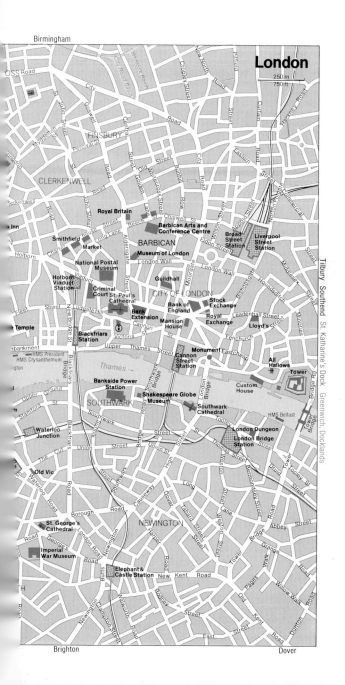

London

Birmingham

250 m
750 ft

OSS Road

City

FINSBURY

CLERKENWELL

Ttkenwell Road

s Inn

Royal Britain

Barbican Arts and
Conference Centre

Smithfield
Market

Holborn

BARBICAN

Broad
Street
Station

Liverpool
Street
Station

Museum of London

National Postal
Museum

London Wall

London Wall

Holborn
Viaduct
Station

Guildhall

Criminal
Court
St. Paul's
Cathedral

CITY OF LONDON

Street

New Bridge St.

Bank of
England

Stock
Exchange

Royal
Exchange

Bank
Extension

Mansion
House

Leadenhall Street

Lloyd's

e Temple

Blackfriars
Station

Victoria

Cannon
St

Fenchurch

Upper   Thames   Street

bankment

HMS President
HMS Crysanthemum
igton

Thames →

Monument Eastcheap

Cannon
Street
Station

All
Hallows

Tower

Bankside Power
Station

Shakespeare Globe
Museum

SOUTHWARK

Custom
House

HMS Belfast

Southwark
Cathedral

Waterloo
Junction

Southwark

Tooley

London Dungeon

London Bridge
Station

Old Vic

Union   Street

Borough   Road

NEWINGTON

St. George's
Cathedral

Long

Imperial
War Museum

Elephant &
Castle Station   New Kent Road

Abbey   Street

Grange

Brighton

Dover

Tilbury Southend St. Katharine's Dock Greenwich, Docklands

London

Culture and science

Over 100 theatres and ensembles, including the world famous Royal Shakespeare Company, two opera houses, six top-class orchestras, numerous museums and collections of international reputation such as the British Museum and the National Gallery earn London its status as a world cultural centre, especially for music. The annual high point of the musical season are the "Proms", the promenade concerts which take place from July to September in the Royal Albert Hall. Musicals have their premières in the theatres of the West End. In numerous less well established concert halls and music bars the "Swinging London" of the Sixties lives on; this was when the city became the centre of beat, pop and rock and the Beatles and Rolling Stones began their careers. The publications "City Limits" and "Time Out" provide the visitor with detailed information on cultural events.

Almost all national newspapers are published in London and it is also the headquarters of the state-owned radio and television company BBC (British Broadcasting Corporation). Three universities, numerous colleges and research institutes are dedicated to the pursuit of knowledge.

Economy

London is with New York and Tokyo one of the world financial centres. Now over 20 per cent of all bank transactions in the world are conducted here and with a daily turnover of $300 billion the city is the largest foreign exchange centre in the world. More than 520 banks and over 500 insurance companies have offices in London. London is also the centre for the world trade in art as represented by the auction houses Sotheby's and Christie's. The increasing attraction of London as a financial centre in the Eighties sparked off a building boom which resulted in spectacular buildings such as the Lloyd's building, the headquarters of the insurance firm, but also the unsuccessful Docklands development. While London became the centre of service and financial companies industrial production declined and moved out of the city. The city's prosperity sank and the rigorous privatisation policy of the former Thatcher government

London: the National Gallery in Trafalgar Square

did one more thing to exacerbate social problems such as high unemployment, a shortage of cheap housing and an inadequate education system and health service.

Traditional industries are textiles, furniture and printing; between the two world wars cement-making, papermaking and vehicle manufacture were established on the lower reaches of the Thames. Since the end of the Second World War a major development has been the establishment of a large refinery and petro-chemical complex at Tilbury, to which the most important docks were transferred. Although numbers are falling the port of London still ranks among the busiest seaports in the world (turnover 1994: 51.7 million tonnes).

There are five **airports** close to London (see Practical Information, Air Travel), two of which are of relevance for the visitor: Heathrow, one of the busiest airports in the world, handling about 47 million passengers annually, and Gatwick which handles chiefly charter flights. An underground rail service operates from Heathrow to the city centre (Piccadilly Line to Piccadilly Circus) as do certain bus lines (A1 to Victoria Station, A2 via Euston Station to Russell Square and night bus 97); from Gatwick British Rail's Gatwick Express and the Green Line bus no. 777 both terminate at Victoria Station.

London has 15 important mainline **stations**. The rail connections to the European mainland depart and terminate at Victoria Station, Liverpool Street Station and Waterloo Station (for the Eurostar services via the Channel Tunnel). Trains for the north depart mainly from Euston, King's Cross and St Pancras Stations, for the west from Paddington and for the south from Victoria, Charing Cross and Waterloo .

Transport

The origins of London go back to the Bronze and Iron Ages. Even Celtic settlers recognised the importance of the site as a gateway between England and the Continent. In the time of the Emperor Claudius four Roman legions led by Aulus Plautius conquer southern England and establish **"Londinium"** on the north bank of the Thames on two hills almost 66 ft high, which today are the sites of Leadenhall Market in the east and St Paul's Cathedral in the west. The name is thought to originate from the Celtic "Llyndun" (= high-lying fort). It was probably the Romans who built the first wooden bridges over the Thames, not far from the present-day London Bridge. Tacitus records the warlike Queen Boadicea who burns down the first Roman settlement in AD 61 with her tribesmen. In the period that follows it is rebuilt with a forum and a Temple of Mithras, the remains of which can still be seen near the Guildhall. About 150 years later town walls are built which occupy roughly the same area as the present-day City. From 240 onwards London is the capital of one of the four Late-Roman provinces. When the British legions are transferred to Germania about 407 it marks the end of the period of Roman rule of Londinium. Around 410 Emperor Honorius gives the British towns their independence and leaves them to the mercy of the Anglo-Saxons.

History

About 449 the **Anglo-Saxons** found the Harbour of "Lundenwic". They strengthen their rule with the victory of Hengist and Eric over the Britons in 457. London becomes the capital of Essex, one of several of their kingdoms, which Egbert of Wessex unites in 827. Following the expulsion of **Danish Vikings**, who burn down Anglo-Saxon London in 851, Alfred the Great makes the rebuilt city the capital of his empire alongside Winchester. Under Knut I London becomes the only capital. He and his successor Edward the Confessor reside in Westminster.

After the Battle of Hastings **William the Conqueror** has himself crowned in Westminster Abbey. Although he guarantees the citizens their rights he builds the White Tower at the Tower of London as a symbol of his power. During the reign of Henry I London is finally established as the capital and asserts its independence. In 1176 the existing wooden bridge is replaced by a stone bridge which lasts more than 650 years. In 1189 the representatives of the Guilds elect Henry Fitzailwyn to be the first Lord Mayor of London.

King John recognises in the **Magna Carta** the right of the guilds to choose the Lord Mayor annually; the king must confirm this appointment. From this arises the custom of the Lord Mayor's Show. Over the following decades the city expands; in 1245 rebuilding of Westminster Abbey begins. The Inns of Court are established during the reign of Edward I. From 1376 the Common Council, which has acted as an informal contact between the Lord Mayor and the Aldermen of the wards, begins to meet regularly. At the end of the 15th c. it becomes an official establishment, elected by the citizens.

During the reign of the **Tudors** the economic growth of London is accelerated. The first trading companies are established, in 1565 Thomas Gresham establishes the London Exchange. At the end of the 16th c. this city of 300,000 inhabitants is the most important trading centre in the world. The 17th c. is characterised primarily by revolt and catastrophe. In 1605 the Catholic Guy Fawkes tries to blow up Parliament ("Gunpowder Plot"). During the **Civil War** London is the focus of the unrest: in 1649 Charles I is beheaded in Whitehall. Following the defeat of Cromwell political calm is restored but the city with a population of half a million, is hit by devastating catastrophes. The **Great Plague** claims over 100,000 victims between 1664 to 1666; hardly is the epidemic over when the **Great Fire** which lasts four days and nights, breaks out devastating four-fifths of the city in September 1666; 100,000 people are made homeless. The rebuilding following this tragedy is still evident today; especially the work of **Sir Christopher Wren**, whose buildings determine the face of London's architecture from 1675 to 1711. Together with numerous secular buildings he builds 53 churches, among them St Paul's Cathedral, one of the emblems of the city. The economy flourishes with the expansion of the British Empire; a visible example of this is the foundation of the Bank of England in 1694.

Under the Hanoverian kings England becomes the leading world power. The first official census in 1801 shows London's population to be 860,000. From 1808 the port is developed. During the reign of **Queen Victoria**, who makes Buckingham Palace the principal royal residence in 1837, London, now the most important city in the empire, expands faster than ever before. This is largely the result of the development of the railways, even the lower-income groups can now live further from their place of work. London is surrounded by a wide ring of Victorian suburbs. Prestigious buildings and improvements to the infrastructure characterise the building boom – work begins in 1840 on the new Houses of Parliament, in 1851 the Great Exhibition housed in Sir Joseph Paxton's Crystal Palace takes place in Hyde Park, in 1863 the first underground train runs from Bishop's Road to Faringdon. This is also one of the darkest chapters of London's history: in 1888 Jack the Ripper terrorises the East End.

During both **world wars** London is the target of German air attacks. 1915 sees the first Zeppelin raid on London. The consequences of the Second World War are far worse: air attacks in 1940/41 and the V1 bombs from June 1944 result in 30,000 deaths, three quarters of all London's buildings are hit. The first high-point of the post-war period is the coronation of Queen Elizabeth in Westminster Abbey in 1953. In the Sixties "Swinging London" is the centre for the new lifestyle of the younger generation. The Greater London Council is established in 1965 (dissolved in 1986). Other important dates of the post-war period are 1982 with the beginning of building in the City and Docklands and 1986 the reform of the London Stock Exchange, which resulted in the "Big Bang". From the early 1970s to the mid-1990s, London became the target of terrorist attacks by the IRA. The Labour Government (since 1997) under Tony Blair has announced that London is to have a unified administrative body once again.

With only **one day** to spend in London you should confine yourself to taking a fairly long walk to see the most important sights. A good starting point is Westminster Bridge below "Big Ben", the clock tower of the Houses of Parliament, behind which rise the towers of Westminster Abbey. Heading north Whitehall, the government quarter, leads past Downing Street and Horse Guards. Behind Horse Guards you can walk through St James's Park to Buckingham Palace. From here the Mall leads to Trafalgar Square, the busiest square in London, dominated by Nelson's Column and the long building of the National Gallery. To the east the Strand leads to the beginning of the City, marked by the dragon of the Temple Bar Memorial. On the right are the tranquil Inns of Court belonging to the Temple. The Strand becomes Fleet Street, the famous (former) newspaper street, which in turn becomes Ludgate Hill. From here you can already recognise the imposing St Paul's Cathedral, passing over Queen Victoria Street to Bank underground station, around which are grouped Mansion House, official residence of the Lord Mayor, the Bank of England and the Royal Exchange. The last part of the walk begins here: through Lombard Street, via Gracechurch Street to the Monument and finally from there down to the Thames to the Tower and nearby Tower Bridge.

Visitors to London who have **more time** at their disposal should definitely include one or more museums. However, a whole day would not be sufficient to see everything in the British Museum. The same applies to the Victoria & Albert Museum with its arts and crafts collection. The art collections of the National Gallery and Tate Gallery are world famous. History lovers will find a wealth of interesting exhibits in the Imperial War Museum or in the Museum of London. Nature lovers are recommended to visit the Natural History Museum or the Science Museum. The Museum of the Moving Image is rather special and a short trip to Greenwich to the National Maritime Museum is highly recommended.

Finally London is also a shopping paradise. There is everything from exclusive gentlemen's tailors to the most unusual junk shops and elegant department stores. The principal shopping areas are Oxford Street and Regent's Street, Kensington and King's Road in Chelsea.

London Tourist Board operates **bus tours** called "Original London Transport Sightseeing Tours". The trips last about one and a half hours and are accompanied by an official guide; recorded tours are available in other languages from the departure point in Baker Street. Other departure points are Haymarket, Marble Arch and Victoria Station. Tickets can be purchased on the buses or from London Tourist Board (see Practical Information). A good way to see London for oneself is from the upper deck of one of London's famous red double-decker buses (lines 9, 11 or 15).

Boat trips along the Thames start from Westminster Pier, Charing Cross Pier or from Tower Pier.

The best means of seeing all the sights in London is by the famous **Underground**, the trains operate at very short intervals between 5.30am and midnight, Sundays from 7.30am to 11pm. The double-decker buses are best avoided during the rush hour – they are crammed full and it is almost quicker to walk. The computerised Docklands Light Railway operates in Docklands. A "travelcard", valid for all types of transport, can be obtained for a week or a month for one or more of the five travel zones. A passport-sized photograph is required except for the one day travelcard. Route maps and timetables are obtainable from mainline underground stations and from London Tourist Board.

The City and the Tower

The nucleus of London was on the north bank of the Thames. The Romans founded their first settlement here and erected fortified walls which ran from the Tower northwards via London Wall street,

Aldersgate and Ludgate down to the Thames and back to the Tower. Today the City is the commercial centre of London with the headquarters of legal and financial institutions.

West City

Underground station
Temple

The best starting point for a walk through the City is from Temple Bar Memorial, a monument crowned with a griffin from 1880, marking the boundary between the City and Westminster. Should the monarch wish to enter the City he/she must (symbolically) ask the Lord Mayor's permission.

★Temple

From the Thames narrow Middle Temple Lane opens up into the precincts of the Temple, former residence of the Knights of the Temple and since 1346 a school of law. In the English legal profession there are barristers who can plead before the higher courts and solicitors who advise their clients and instruct the barristers. The barristers are trained at the Temple, at one of the four Inns of Court: Middle and Inner Temple, Gray's Inn and Lincoln's Inn. The buildings belong to the Inns and consist of student accommodation, libraries, teaching rooms and a dining room.

To the right of Middle Temple Lane are the buildings of the **Middle Temple**. Past members include Sir Walter Raleigh, John Pym and Thomas More. Lawyers and judges still take luncheon in the Middle Temple Hall, built in 1527.

To the left of Middle Temple Lane is the **Inner Temple** with the interesting Temple Church. The original Norman (1185) round church, circular in plan like the Church of the Holy Sepulchre in Jerusalem, had a chancel added in 1240 and was rebuilt by Wren in the 17th c. The church contains nine black marble figures of Temple knights, dating from the 12th and 13th c. The writer Oliver Goldsmith (1728–74) is buried in the adjoining churchyard.

Fleet Street

Fleet Street, the former home of the country's leading newspapers, starts at the Temple Bar Memorial. At the end of the 15th c. the first printing press was established here and the "Daily Courant" was the first newspaper to be published in 1702. Today the street is no longer important as the major newspapers have moved to modern offices on the outskirts of the city. Notable buildings are the Royal Courts of Justice, opposite the Temple, and the traditional pubs "Ye Old Cheshire Cheese" and "Ye Old Cock Tavern".

Old Bailey

Following Fleet Street eastwards leads to the Old Bailey off to the left. Until 1902 this was the site of the infamous Newgate prison when it was replaced by the criminal courts which are known throughout the world as the "Old Bailey".

★St Bartholomew-the-Great

From the Old Bailey it is a short walk to the north-west City. Here on the east side of West Smithfield is hidden the entrance to the oldest parish church in the City, St Batholomew-the-Great. It was founded in 1123 by the monk Rahere, whose tomb together with the font where the painter and Copper engraver William Hogarth was baptised, can be seen inside.

On the other side of the square are the long halls of Smithfield Market, the largest meat market in London.

National Postal Museum

The National Postal Museum is situated in the main post office on King Edward Street. It houses a unique collection of more than 350,000 stamps and postal exhibits from all over the world.

★Museum of London

North-west of the post office, on London Wall, the extensive collections of the Museum of London illustrate the history of the British capital. The

St Paul's Cathedral – a masterpiece of Baroque architecture

prize exhibit is the Lord Mayor's golden coach. An audio-visual show recreates the Great Fire of London (1666).

The magnificent dome of St Paul's dominates the skyline of the City. Together with Big Ben, the Tower and Tower Bridge it is one of the enduring symbols of London. Several churches have preceded the present-day cathedral, which is built on the site of a Roman temple to Diana. The old Gothic cathedral was destroyed in the Great Fire of London in 1666. The rebuilding was entrusted by the city fathers to Sir Christopher Wren, who created his masterpiece here. Building took place on this 557 ft-long and 364 ft-high cathedral crowned by the dome from 1675 to 1711. The left tower houses the largest bell in England, the "Great Paul" cast in 1882 and weighing 17 tonnes.

Inside this high church great Britons are commemorated. All Soul's Chapel at the base of the left tower is a memorial to Lord Kitchener; between the piers of the main nave and the north transept the imposing monument to the Duke of Wellington, the hero of Waterloo. In the north transept are statues of Joshua Reynolds and Dr Samuel Johnson. The choir houses the 17th c. choir-stalls by Grinling Gibbons and in the south choir aisle stands the statue of the poet John Donne, the only sculpture in Old St Paul's to survive the Great Fire.

The entrance to the **Crypt** is in the south-east corner of the area beneath the dome. It contains the tombs of the painters Constable, Turner, Landseer and Reynolds and of Alexander Fleming, who discovered penicillin. The simple tombstone of Christopher Wren bears the Latin inscription "Reader, if you are looking for a monument then look around you". The sarcophogi of Wellington and Admiral Nelson may also be seen; Nelson's coffin was made from the main mast of the French flagship "L'Orient", from the battle of Abukir.

★★St Paul's
Cathedral

Underground station
St Paul's

Opening times
daily 8.30am–4pm
Galleries
10am–4.15pm

Opening times
Mon.–Fri.
10am–4.15pm,
Sat. 11am–4.15pm

St. Paul's Cathedral

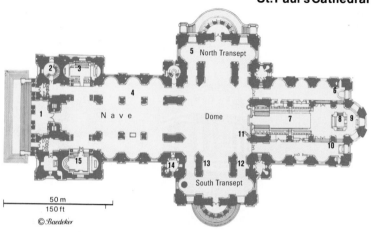

1 West Doorway
2 All Souls Chapel
3 St Dunstan's Chapel
4 Wellington Monument
5 Font

6 Anglican Martyrs' Chapel
7 Choir
8 High Altar
9 American Memorial Chapel
10 Lady Chapel

11 Pulpit
12 Entrance to crypt
13 Nelson Monument
14 To Whispering Gallery, Library and Dome
15 Chapel of St Michael and St George

From the south-west double pier a staircase leads to the galleries which run around the dome. The **Whispering Gallery** is popular with visitors; it is possible to hear even a whisper across the dome's width of 157 ft. From the lantern there are wonderful views of the city.

East city

Underground stations
Mansion House, Bank

North of St Paul's in Gresham Street is the Guildhall, the administrative headquarters of the City of London. The original building dates from 1411 but only sections of the external wall remain; much of it was rebuilt in

★Guildhall

Neo-Gothic style after the Great Fire in 1666. Inside is the Great Hall, the meeting-place of the Common Council, decorated with the banners of the 12 great "livery companies", the old city guilds. There is fine carving in the galleries, a canopied oak dresser houses the City sword and sceptre. Also part of the Guildhall are the Guildhall Art Gallery (London artists), the Guildhall Library (history of London) and the Guildhall Clock Museum with a fine collection of clocks.

St Mary-le-Bow

Heading further east from St Paul's in Cannon Street is Bow Lane, where the church of St Mary-le-Bow is situated, mainly Norman and designed by Wren. With its famous bells it occupies a special place in the affections of Londoners. To be a genuine Cockney you must be born within the sound of Bow bells.

Bank of England

Queen Victoria Street crosses Cannon Street to open out at the junction Bank Station with three of the most important buildings in the City. On the left is the famous Bank of England, founded in 1694 by a Royal Charter as a private company. The original building was designed by Sir John Soane and rebuilt in 1924–39 by Sir Herbert Baker. There is a museum documenting the history and function of the bank.

Guildhall: London's city hall

On the right is Mansion House (1739–53), the official residence of the Lord Mayor. On royal and official processions the Lord Mayor appears on the colonnade of the building.

Mansion House

Straight ahead behind the monument to the Duke of Wellington is the Royal Exchange, now used for fixed interest securities and currency dealing. It was founded in 1566 by Thomas Gresham. The present-day Classical building of the Royal Exchange (1844) is by Sir William Tite. Traditionally from the top of the steps the new monarch is always proclaimed, a declaration of war announced and the conclusion of a peace treaty made known.

★Royal Exchange

The carillon in the tower plays traditional tunes from Great Britain, Australia and Canada. Beyond it to the left rises the modern skyscraper of the Stock Exchange proper.

From Bank Station King William Street leads towards the Thames. Lombard Street branches off to the left, the banking centre of London. It owes its name to the money lenders from Lombardy who traded here in the 13th c.

Lombard Street

At the end of King William Street stands the 202 ft-high stone column called the Monument, erected between 1671 and 1677 and designed by Wren to commemorate the Great Fire. There are good views of the City from the platform.

★Monument

Not far south of the Monument the Thames is spanned by the rather uninteresting modern London Bridge. The Romans put up a wooden bridge not far from here which was replaced in the 12th c. by a stone bridge. This gave way in 1831 to a new bridge, which was sold to an American in 1968 and moved to Lake Havasu in Arizona, USA,

London Bridge

where it spans a dried-out river bed. The present bridge was built in 1973.

Lloyd's of London

From the Monument Gracechurch Street leads to Leadenhall Market, an attractive 19th c. shopping and market arcade. It is directly in front of the futuristic building of the Lloyd's insurance company, one of the most spectacular new developments in London in recent years.

★All-Hallows-by-the-Tower

The route to the Tower runs by the oldest church in London, All-Hallows-by-the-Tower. It was founded in 675 and built in its present form in the 13–15th c.; a Saxon cross has been preserved. It contains an interesting crusading altar which originally stood in Richard I's castle in Palestine and a model of Roman London in the crypt (Undercroft Museum). The parish registers record the baptism of William Penn, the founder of Pennsylvania, and the marriage of John Quincy Adams, the sixth president of the USA.

★Tower Bridge

Tower Bridge is one of the best known landmarks of London. The bridge, with its 200 ft-high towers was built from 1886 to 1894. Both draw-bridges can be raised in 90 seconds to allow large ships to pass through. Nowadays they are electronically operated but the old steam-driven hydraulic machinery is open to visitors. There are interesting exhibitions in both towers tracing the history and outlining the technology of the bridge.

★★Tower of London

Underground station
Tower Hill

Opening times
Summer:
Mon.–Sat.
9am–6pm,
Sun. 10am–6pm;
Winter:
Mon.–Sat.
9am–5pm
Sun. 10am–5pm

The gloomy Tower, the old fortress and former prison, lies outside of the old city walls directly alongside the Thames. It was built as a fortress by William the Conqueror and has been constantly enlarged over the centuries. Nowadays the site consists of the Outer Ward surrounded by a wall with six towers and two bastions, separated from the Inner Ward by a wall with thirteen towers and the main buildings.

The Tower is guarded by the Yeoman Warders who carry out the Ceremony of the Keys every evening at 9.40pm. Visitors who wish to observe this spectacle must apply in writing to The Constable's Office, Tower of London, EC3N 4AB. Six ravens are still kept at the Tower, who, according to legend, can never leave the Tower or else the Empire will fall. The history of the Tower is one of famous prisoners and bloody deeds: the Scottish kings David II and James I, Sir Walter Raleigh, Princess Elizabeth (later to be Queen Elizabeth I) and William Penn were

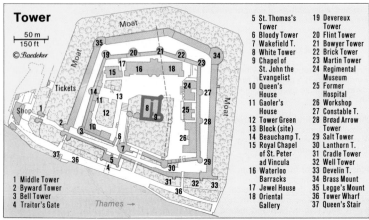

Tower

50 m
150 ft
© Baedeker

Moat

Tickets

Shop

Thames →

1 Middle Tower
2 Byward Tower
3 Bell Tower
4 Traitor's Gate

5 St. Thomas's Tower
6 Bloody Tower
7 Wakefield T.
8 White Tower
9 Chapel of St. John the Evangelist
10 Queen's House
11 Gaoler's House
12 Tower Green
13 Block (site)
14 Beauchamp T.
15 Royal Chapel of St. Peter ad Vincula
16 Waterloo Barracks
17 Jewel House
18 Oriental Gallery

19 Devereux Tower
20 Flint Tower
21 Bowyer Tower
22 Brick Tower
23 Martin Tower
24 Regimental Museum
25 Former Hospital
26 Workshop
27 Constable T.
28 Broad Arrow Tower
29 Salt Tower
30 Lanthorn T.
31 Cradle Tower
32 Well Tower
33 Develin T.
34 Brass Mount
35 Legge's Mount
36 Tower Wharf
37 Queen's Stair

Tower Bridge

Tower Bridge – a well-known London landmark

among those confined; Edward V, Thomas More and Henry VIII's wives Anne Boleyn and Catherine Howard were all executed here.

Among the most important places in the Outer Ward are **Traitor's Gate**, where the prisoners were landed by boat who had been condemned in Westminster; the **Bell Tower** in the south-west corner, where Princess Elizabeth (later to be Elizabeth 1) was imprisoned, and at the entrance to the Inner Ward, the **Bloody Tower**, where Richard III had the two sons of Edward IV murdered in 1483 and Sir Walter Raleigh was held for 13 years; finally Wakefield Tower opposite, where Henry VI is said to have been murdered.

The main buildings of the Tower are found within the **Inner Ward**. First on the left is Queen's House, the residence of the Governor of the Tower, where Anne Boleyn spent her last days, and the Yeoman Gaoler's House. He carried out his bloody work on the Site of Block diagonally opposite. Most executions, however, were carried out outside the precincts of the Tower.

Many of those who met their deaths in the Tower are buried in the **Royal Chapel of St Peter ad Vincula**; they include Thomas More, Anne Boleyn, Catherine Howard and Jane Grey.

To the right is the entrance to the Jewel House in the basement of Waterloo Barracks, where the ★**Crown Jewels** are kept. There is usually a long wait before visitors are allowed to file past the display; photography is prohibited. The most valuable pieces are the Imperial State Crown made for Queen Victoria with the one of the two "Stars of Africa", which were cut from the Cullinan, the largest diamond ever found, and Queen Elizabeth's Crown which bears the most famous diamond in the world, the "Koh-i-Noor" ("Mountain of Light"). The Royal Sceptre contains the other "Star of Africa".

Waterloo Barracks houses a collection of old weapons and equipment; on the eastern side the **Regimental Museum** documents the history of the Royal Fusiliers.

In the centre of the Inner Ward is the majestic **White Tower**, so called because of the white stone from Caen in Normandy with which it was built. This was the first part of the Tower begun during the Norman reign by William the Conqueror in 1078 and completed around 1100. This 91 ft-high tower with its 10–13 ft-thick walls contains weapons and armour from the early Middle Ages to the end of the 16th c., including armour which belonged to Henry VIII, the gilt armour of Charles I and other royal weapons of the Stuarts.

Strand, Holborn, Covent Garden and Bloomsbury

Strand

Underground station
Temple

West of Temple Bar begins the Strand, which connects the City and Westminster along the Thames. Heading towards Westminster we come to one of the many pretty Baroque churches by Christopher Wren, **St Clement Danes**, built in 1681. It is the official church of the Royal Air Force with over 800 crests commemorating those members who lost their lives. The memorial to Air Marshal Arthur Harris ("Bomber Harris"), unveiled in 1992, was the subject of controversy in England as well as in Germany.

Past the church of St Mary-le-Strand, also by Wren and completed in 1717, is the rear of **Somerset House**, built from 1777 to 1786 by Sir William Chambers. From Waterloo Bridge there is a good view of the 657 ft-long façade facing the Thames. The east wing contains the famous **King's College** of the University of London.

The west wing houses the ⋆**Courtauld Institute Galleries'** famous collection of Impressionist and Post-Impressionist paintings, Italian Renaissance and Baroque art and British artists from the 17th–20th c.

Cleopatra's Needle

Looking upstream from Waterloo Bridge the Egyptian obelisk, "Cleopatra's Needle" is visible on the right bank. This 3500 year old specimen from Heliopolis has nothing to do with the beautiful queen, however; it was a present from the Sultan Mohammed Ali to the British monarch.

Holborn

Underground station
Holborn

Another long-established school of law, ⋆**Lincoln's Inn**, is situated in the district of Holborn, north of the Strand. Named after the Earl of Lincoln the school with its large well-tended gardens has been here since 1420. Celebrated members of Lincoln's Inn have been Thomas More, William Pitt, Horace Walpole and William Gladstone.

Sir John Soane's Museum The architect and collector Sir John Soane (1753–1837) lived on the north side of Lincoln's Inn. His house heavily laden with works of art has been left untouched since his death. The collection of paintings including twelve works by Hogarth is particularly interesting as is a real Egyptian mummy.

Covent Garden

Underground station
Covent Garden

For 300 years Covent Garden was a flower and vegetable market and today is a shopping centre with elegant shops and restaurants. In addition two museums attract visitors: in the east corner the **London Transport Museum** with original vehicles and models illustrating the history of public transport in the British capital and the extensive **Theatre Museum**.

A large part of the old market to the north of the central hall was sacrificed for the extensions to the **Royal Opera House** opened in 1732.

On the west side of Covent Garden is **St Paul's Church**. Built in 1633 by Inigo Jones, it is the church for London's actors and up until the closure of the market was the scene of the market traders' harvest festival. The portico facing the market is, in fact, the rear and not the front of the church.

Transport Museum in Covent Garden

One of the busiest squares in London and meeting-place for political demonstrations Trafalgar Square is named after the Spanish Cape Trafalgar off which Admiral Nelson (see Famous People) defeated the Spanish and French fleet on October 22nd 1805. Focal point is Nelson's Column erected in 1840 to 1843 in his honour with his statue on the top. On the base of the monument are four bronze reliefs, cast from French cannons, depicting the four great victories of this national hero.

★★ Trafalgar Square

Underground station
Charing Cross

There has been a church at the north-east corner of the square since 1222. The present-day **St Martin-in-the-fields Church** from 1726 with its fine Corinthian portico was designed by James Gibb, a pupil of Wren. St Martin's is the church of the British Admirality but the Royal Court also belongs to the parish so that the choir has an Admiralty Box and a Royal Box. The chamber orchestra of the Academy of St Martin-in-the-Fields is world famous.

Nelson's Column, Trafalgar Square

The front of the National Gallery, which houses one of the most significant collections of paintings in the world, extends along the entire north side of Trafalgar Square. Designed in 1824 by William Wilkins and completed in 1838 it has been subject to several

★★ National Gallery

Opening times
Daily 10am–6pm
(Wed.10am–9pm)

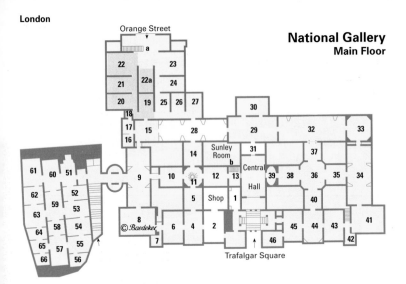

National Gallery
Main Floor

Orange Street

WEST WING (1510–1600)
1 Temporary exhibitions
2 Correggio, Parmingianino
3 Dosso, Garofalo
4 Dosso, Garofalo
5 Holbein, Cranach, Altdorfer
6 Lotto, Moretto, Moroni
7 Tintoretto, El Greco
8 Michelangelo, Sebastiano, Bronzino
9 Titian, Veronese, Tintoretto
10 Venetians
11 Veronese
12 Gossaert, Brueghel
13 Frescoes of Domenichino

NORTH WING (1600 to 1700)
14 Ter Brugghen, Hals
15 Claude, Turner
16 Vermeer, de Hooch
17 Dou, van Mieris
18–22 temporarily closed
23 Dutch
24 Ruisdael, Hobbema
25 Cuyp, Both
26 Hals, Rembrant School

27 Rembrant
28 Ruebens
29 Velázquez, Murillo, Zurbarán
30 van Dyke
32 Carraci, Caravaggio, Guercino

EAST WING (1700 to 1920)
33 Chardin, Fragonard
34 Reynolds, Gainsborough, Turner, Constable
35 Hogarth, Gainsborough, Stubbs
36 British portraits
37 Solimena, Giaquinto
38 Canaletto
39 Guardi, Goya
40 Tiepolo
41 David, Ingres, Delacroix
42 Corot, Friedrich
43 Impressionists
44 Cézanne, Impressionists
45 Seurat, van Gogh
46 Monet, Cézanne

SAINSBURY WING (1260 to 1510)
51 Giotto, Leonardo da Vinci
52 Italian before 1400

53 Italian before 1400, Wilton Diptychon
54 Massaccio, Sassetta
55 Uccello, Pisanello
56 Campin, van Eyck, van der Weyden
57 Crivelli, Tura
58 Botticelli
59 Pollaiuolo, Piero di Cosimo
60 Raffael, Perugino
61 Bellini, Mantegna
62 Dutch and French
63 German
64 Antonello, Bellini
66 Piero della Francesca

a Stairs to gallery A: European paining 1260 to 1920
b Stairs to Galleries B, C, D (temporary exhibitions), E (Italian altar painting) and G (Italian painting of the 16th c., Corregio, Parmigianino)

extensions, including the dome in 1876, which earned it the name "national cruet stand" and the most recent addition, the Sainsbury wing opened in 1991.

The collection can claim to be an almost complete cross-section of works representative of most European schools and periods from the High Middle Ages to the late 19th c. Only the most famous paintings are listed here and it is pointed out that the adjacent plan is subject to change as there are rearrangements from time to time. A computer system ("Micro Gallery") contains detailed information on the exhibits in the gallery.

The new **Sainsbury Wing** donated by the Sainsbury brothers houses paintings from 1260 to 1510 which include works by Fra Angelico, Piero della Francesca ("Baptism of Christ"), Bellini ("La Pieta"), Boticelli, Leonardo da Vinci ("Virgin and Child with St Anna and John the Baptist", "Leonardo Cartoon") and Raffael ("Madonna with Carnations"), Jan van Eyck ("Marriage of Arnolfini"), Hans Memling ("St Mary's Altar") and Hieronymous Bosch ("Christ with a Crown of Thorns").

The **West Wing** houses paintings from 1510 to 1600: Michaelangelo ("Burial of Christ"), Titian ("Venus and Adonis"), Tintoretto, Paolo Veronese, El Greco, Albrecht Dürer ("The Painter's Father"), Hans Holbein the Younger and Peter Bruegel.

The **North Wing** contains paintings from 1600 to 1700: Rubens ("Rape of the Sabines"), van Dyck ("Charles I on horseback"), Frans Hals, Rembrandt ("Saskia and Flora"), Vermeer, Velásquez, Zurbarán, Murillo and Nicolas Poussin.

The **East Wing** contains works from 1700 to 1920: Hogarth, Reynolds, Gainsborough ("The Morning Walk"), Constable ("Haywain"), Turner ("View of Margate"), Watteau, Delacroix, Daumier, Monet ("Waterlily pond"), Manet, Degas ("Dancers"), Cézanne ("Les grandes Baigneuses"), van Gogh ("Sunflowers"), Goya and Canaletto.

The National Portrait Gallery in St Martin's Place has a collection of portraits of famous Britons which may be paintings, sculpture or photographs. There are some outstanding exhibits but the quality of the work is not necessarily decisive.

★★National Portrait Gallery

The works are displayed in chronological order beginning on the top floor. They include the famous life-size cartoon of Henry VIII by Hans Holbein the Younger, Elizabeth I by an unknown artist, self-portraits by Hogarth and Reynolds, a picture of James Cook by John Webber, Sir Walter Scott by Landseer and the Brontë sisters painted by their brother Branwell.

Situated to the north of Covent Garden in the district of Bloomsbury is the British Museum, one of the most famous museums in the world. Founded by an Act of Parliament in 1753 the British Museum is based on the private collections of Sir Robert Cotton, Sir Hans Sloane and Robert Harley, Earl of Oxford. It houses one of the most comprehensive and important art collections from all over the world, all of which cannot be seen in one day. It is therefore recommended to use the plan on p. 258 and the list of exhibits to decide in advance what to see.

British Museum

Underground stations
Tottenham Court Road,
Russell Square

Opening times
Mon.–Sat.
10am–5pm,
Sun. 2.30–6pm

Room 8: the famous "Elgin Marbles", sculptures from the Parthenon in Athens, including the "Horse of Selene" from the east pediment and the largest surviving section of the Parthenon frieze.

Room 12: finds from the Mausoleum at Halicarnassus and the Temple of Artemis at Ephesus.

Rooms 17–26: unique treasures of the Assyrian period including reliefs of a lion hunt dating from the reign of Assurbanipal, reliefs from the Nimrud and Nineveh palaces, and impressive winged figures of bulls with human heads from the Sargon palace.

Room 25: a colossal bust of Rameses II from Thebes West and the Rosetta Stone, a black basalt slab dating from 195 BC; its tri-lingual inscription (in Egyptian hieroglyphs, demotic script and a Greek translation) made possible the decipherment of hieroglyphics.

Room 35: the Mildenhall Treasure, a hoard of Roman silver (4th c.) found in Suffolk.

Room 37: Lindow Man whose mummified body, about 2000 years old, was recovered from a Cheshire bog.

Room 41: Sutton Hoo Treasure – finds from the grave of a 7th c. Anglo-Saxon king.

Room 42: the "Lewis Chessmen", 12th c. Viking chess pieces carved from walrus tusks, from the island of Lewis in the Hebrides.

Rooms 60–62: Egyptian mummies, sarcophagi and papyri, including the famous Books of the Dead (these rooms are currently closed).

London

British Museum

British Library

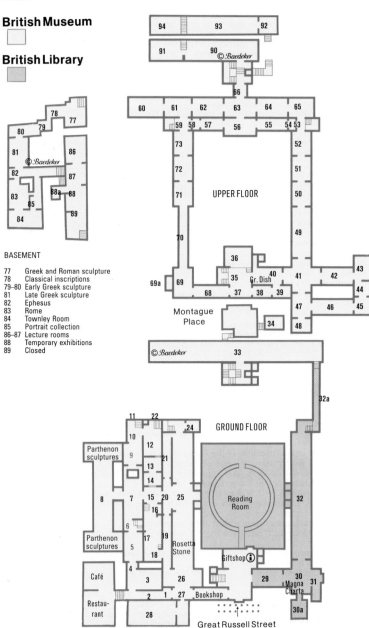

BASEMENT

77	Greek and Roman sculpture
78	Classical inscriptions
79–80	Early Greek sculpture
81	Late Greek sculpture
82	Ephesus
83	Rome
84	Townley Room
85	Portrait collection
86–87	Lecture rooms
88	Temporary exhibitions
89	Closed

GROUND FLOOR
1–2 Greek Bronze Age
3/4 Ancient Greece
3a Early Greek Vases (basement)
5 Greece in 5th c. B.C.
6 Bassae (one flight up)
7 Neirides
8 Parthenon sculpture
9 Caryatids
10 Payava
11 Late Greek vases (one floor up)
12 Mausoleum of Halicarnassus
13/14 Being rearranged
15 Roman art
16 Chorsabad
17 Assyria
19 Nimrod
21 Nineveh
24 Ancient Palestine
25 Large Egyptian sculpture
26 Assyrian Transept
27–28 Temporary exhibitions
29 Grenville Library
30–30a Manuscripts
31 Crawford Room

32 King's Library
33 Art from south and south-east Asia, China, Japan and Korea
33b Temporary exhibitions
33c Old Mexico
34 Islamic art (one floor lower)

UPPER FLOOR
35 Britain in prehistoric and Roman ages
36 Stone Age
37–39 Late pre-history in Europe
40 Britain in Roman times
41–42 Medieval art
43 Medieval pottery and ceramics
44 Clocks, etc.
45 Waddesdon Bequest
46–47 Europe 15th–19th c.
48 Modern art
49 Ancient Persia
50–52 Closed

53–54 Ancient Anatolia
55–56 Early Mesopotamia
57 Ancient Syria
58 Assyrian ivory-work from Minrod
59 South Arabia
60–61 Mummies
62 Grave paintings, papyri
63 Egypt Every-day life
64 Early Egyptian
65 Egypt and Africa
66 Coptic art
68 Greek and Roman bronzes and terracottas
69 Everyday life in ancient Greece and Rome
69a Coins and medals (exhibitions)
70 City and Empire of Rome
71 Italy before the Roman Empire
72 Ancient Cyprus
73 Hellenistic southern Italy
90 Printing and drawings
91 Oriental art
92–94 Japanese collections (one floor up)

Room 70: the so-called "Portland Vase", one of the most exquisite examples of Roman artistry in glass (1st c. BC).

The British Library, which contains 15 million books, is due to move by the turn of the century to new, modern premises near St Pancras Station. This will increase the exhibition area by 40 per cent. The ethno-

British Library

The Egyptian section of the British Museum

graphical department will be moved to the famous circular reading room, where Karl Marx worked on "Das Kapital". In rooms 30 and 30a some of the museum's more exceptional and valuable volumes are exhibited, including two of four copies of Magna Carta and manuscript material by Leonardo da Vinci, Charles Dickens, Horatio Nelson, Isaac Newton, and also the original script of the Beatles' song "Yesterday" by Paul McCartney.

Whitehall, Westminster and St James's

★Whitehall

Underground stations
Charing Cross, Embankment Westminster

Whitehall is not a building but a street which takes its name from the former Whitehall Palace. Today it is synonymous with the British government quarter.

Approaching from Trafalgar Square Admiralty Arch is first on the right followed by the Admiralty building itself by Thomas Ripley.

Immediately to the right are the extensive grounds of **Horse Guards**, built on the site of the old guard house which belonged to Whitehall Palace, and now the headquarters of some government departments. The gate is stoically guarded, despite the attentions of the tourists, by an infantryman and two horsemen of the Household Cavalry. This unit consists of the regiments of the Life Guards (scarlet tunic and white plumed helmets) and the Blues and Royals (blue tunic and red plumed helmet).

The ★**Changing of the Guard** (Mon.–Sat. 11am and Sun. 10am) and the Sunday parade on the parade ground next to St James's Park are among London's greatest tourist attractions. On the other side of the road is the Old War Office, former Ministry of Defence.

To the right of the Old War Office stands ★**Banqueting House**, part of the old Whitehall Palace. In the 13th c. this palace was the seat of the Archbishop of York. Henry VIII had it enlarged and made into a royal residence. Banqueting House served as the banqueting hall of the monarchy but also was the scene of some important events in British history: Henry VIII was married to Anne Boleyn in Whitehall Palace and died here; Oliver Cromwell lived and died within its walls and Charles I was beheaded outside the palace. At the end of the Protectorate Charles II called Parliament to Banqueting House to swear allegiance to him. In 1619 the building burned down and was rebuilt in 1622 by Inigo Jones. After William III transferred his private residence to Kensington Palace, the old palace was destroyed by fire. The most splendid room in the house is the 59 ft-high Banqueting Hall with ceiling paintings by Rubens.

This inconspicuous cul-de-sac is renowned throughout the world: **Downing Street** is the heart of the government quarter. The unprepossessing brick house of No. 10 has been the official residence of the Prime Minister since 1735; it cannot be visited even from outside as the street is closed to the public.

A few yards away from Downing Street the **Cenotaph** ("empty tomb") commemorates those who lost their lives in both world wars, symbolised by the flags and emblems of the army, air force, royal and merchant navy. Whitehall becomes Parliament Street at this point.

At the end of King Charles Street, which follows on, are the **Cabinet War Rooms**. These 19 rooms, situated only a few feet below ground, were used during the Second World War by the British Cabinet and have been left in their original condition.

Parliament Street opens out into **Parliament Square** which is surrounded by statues of British statesmen.

★★Houses of Parliament

Underground station
Westminster

The official name of the Houses of Parliament – The Palace of Westminster – recalls the fact that they occupy the site of the old royal palace. This palace was originally built by Edward the Confessor and enlarged by his successors William the Conqueror and William Rufus. After the royal residence was transferred to Whitehall Palace it served as

Houses of Parliament

the seat of Parliament from 1547, with the House of Commons meeting in St Stephen's Chapel, which no longer exists, until 1834.

The present Houses of Parliament – in Neo-Gothic style to harmonise with the nearby Westminster Abbey – were built between 1840 and 1888 to the design of Sir Charles Barry. They were officially opened in 1852. German air attacks during the Second World War caused heavy damage.

The best view of the imposing **façade** is from the opposite bank of the Thames. "**Big Ben**", on the right, is one of London's most celebrated landmarks. The 320 ft high clock tower owes its name to the bell which was called after Sir Benjamin Hall. The sound of Big Ben has become famous throughout the world as the time signal of the BBC. On the left is the 334 ft-high Victoria Tower. The Union Jack is flown when Parliament is sitting.

The greater part of the **interior**, especially Westminster Hall and the royal rooms, are not open to the public. However, visitors can attend debates in the House of Commons and House of Lords. Admission is by the St Stephen's entrance on the west side and queueing is usually necessary. Admission times for the House of Lords are Mon.–Wed. from 2.30pm (Thu. 3pm) and Fri. from 11am; for the Strangers' Gallery (House of Commons) join the queue at St Stephen's entrance Mon.–Thu. from 4.15pm, Fri. 10am.

House of Commons The members of the government and opposition parties sit opposite one another on rows of benches divided by two red lines – traditionally "two swords' lengths and one foot apart" – which the gentlemen are not allowed to cross. In between them is the Table of the House, on which the mace, the Speaker's sceptre, who presides over sittings in the black chair, is placed.

The **House of Lords** is a sumptuously decorated chamber. The peers sit on red leather benches while the Lord Chancellor sits on the "wool-sack" (named after the woolsacks unloaded in Westminster during the Middle Ages). Opposite is the throne from which the monarch reads the traditional speech on the opening of Parliament.

The **Jewel Tower** in Old Palace Yard facing the Thames is still part of the old Westminster Palace. Until the beginning of the 17th c. it was a repository for the private wealth of the monarch (not the Crown Jewels). It now houses a small museum with relics from the Palace of Westminster.

St Margaret's Church is situated between the Houses of Parliament and Westminster Abbey. It is the official church of the House of Commons and fashionable for weddings among the aristocracy. It dates from the 12/13th c. The main attraction is the Flemish stained glass in

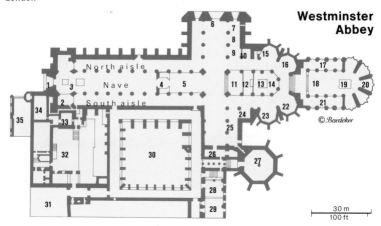

Westminster Abbey

© Baedeker

30 m
100 ft

Collegiate Church of St. Peter in Westminster

1 West Door
2 St George's Chapel
3 Tomb of the Unknown Warrior and memorial to Sir Winston Churchill
4 Organ Gallery
5 Choir
6 North Doorway
7 St Andrew's Chapel
8 St Michael's Chapel
9 Chapel of St John the Evangelist
10 Islip Chapel
11 Sanctuary

12 High Altar
13 St Edward's Chapel
14 Henry V's Chantry Chapel
15 Chapel of St John the Baptist
16 St Paul's Chapel
17 Tomb of Elizabeth I
18 Henry VII's Chapel
19 Tomb of Henry VII
20 RAF Chapel,
   The Battle of Britain
   Memorial Window
21 Tomb of Mary Queen of Scots
22 St Nicholas's Chapel

23 St Edmund's Chapel
24 St Benedict's Chapel
25 Poet's Corner
26 St Faith's Chapel
27 Chapterhouse
28 Chapel of the Pyx
29 Norman undercroft
30 Cloisters
31 Dean's Yard
32 Deanery
33 Jericho Parlour
34 Jerusalem Chamber
35 Bookshop

the east window, presented by Ferdinand and Isabella of Spain on the marriage of Prince Arthur, the elder brother of Henry VIII, to Catherine of Aragón. However, Arthur died before the glass arrived.

★★Westminster Abbey

Opening times
Nave and cloisters:
Mon.–Sat.
8am–6pm,
Wed. until
7.45pm;
Choir, transepts,
Royal chapels:
Mon.–Fri.
9.20am–4pm,
Sat. 9.20am–2pm
and 3.45–5pm

An Anglo-Saxon church dedicated to St Peter is said to have stood on the site of the abbey from the early 7th c. Following its destruction by the Danes Edward the Confessor founded a new church in 1065 as his place of interment and from the time of his burial most British sovereigns were buried here until 1760, as well as numerous prosperous national figures. Westminster Abbey is also the place of coronations and royal weddings; belonging to the Crown it does not come under the authority of any bishop. In the 13th c. Henry III rebuilt Edward's Norman church in a style influenced by French Gothic. After much rebuilding and additional work, some of it carried out by Henry Yvele and Abbot Islip, the church was near completion in 1740 with the construction of the west façade with two 223 ft-high towers by Nicolas Hawksmoor. A masterpiece of Gothic architecture it has the highest Gothic nave in England (102 ft).

The Abbey contains numerous monuments, statues and memorials, of which the most interesting are listed below.

Nave In St George's Chapel to the right of the entrance a portrait of Richard II has been preserved from the 14th c., probably the oldest surviving portrait of an English monarch. In the entrance area is the Tomb of the Unknown Warrior and beyond this in the nave memorial slabs to

Winston Churchill, Neville Chamberlain and David Livingstone, among others. In the south aisle the founder of the Scouting movement Baden Powell, the reformer John Wesley and the Corsican national hero Pasquale Paoli are commemorated; in the north aisle are monuments to William Pitt the Younger, the composer Henry Purcell and Charles Darwin as well as the black sarcophagus of Sir Isaac Newton.

Going left from the north aisle and then in a clockwise direction around the transepts there are monuments in the **North Transept** to William Gladstone, Robert Peel (founder of the "Bobbies") and William Pitt the Elder among others, followed by the three chapels of St Andrew, St Michael and St John; in the **South Transept** on the south wall is the so-called "Poets' Corner" where Walter Scott, Oliver Goldsmith, William Shakespeare, Geoffrey Chaucer, Lord Byron, Charles Dickens, Rudyard Kipling and T. S. Eliot and others are commemorated. Further along the west wall is a memorial to William Thackeray and a statue of George Friedrich Handel. The **Choir** and **Sanctuary** are in the axis of the old Norman church. On the left side of the sanctuary are three notable medieval tombs, including that of Edmund Crouchback (d. 1296), founder of the House of Lancaster. To the right the seats of the clergy are probably installed above the tomb of the Saxon King Sebert (7th c.).

To the left of the sanctuary are the ★★**Royal Chapels**, the tombs of the English rulers. First are the three chapels of the south ambulatory, the last of which contains the tomb of James Watts.

Twelve black marble steps lead to the **Chapel of Henry VII**, a masterpiece of English Perpendicular style, built 1503–19 by Robert Ertue, a church within a church. Over 100 figure and monuments adorn the interior. In the centre is the golden-bronze reclining figure of Henry VII and his wife Elizabeth of York by the Florentine artist Torrigiani, above them are the banners and on either side the choir-stalls of the order of the Knights of Bath. James I, George II and Edward IV are also buried in the chapel. In the left aisle is Innocent's Corner containing the tombs of the three day and two year old daughters of James I, the sons of Edward IV who were murdered in the Tower of London and finally the tombs of Elizabeth I and Mary Tudor. In the right aisle among others are the reclining figures of Mary Stuart and Lady Margaret Douglas, surrounded by her seven children. In front of the right aisle lie Charles II, William II and Queen Anne.

Back in the main part of the Abbey is the **Chapel of Henry V** in which he lies buried with his saddle, helmet and shield from the battle of Agincourt.

This leads on to a room built over the apse of the Norman church, with the wooden **Shrine of Edward the Confessor** (from 1269). On the back wall stands the oak coronation chair of English monarchs. It encloses the Stone of Scone, which represented the power of the Scottish princes, brought back to London by Edward I in 1296 as a symbol of Scotland's subjugation. It was returned to Scotland in 1996. Next to it on the left is the new coronation chair from 1689 and between them the state sword and shield of Edward III. Among those buried here are Edward I, his first wife Eleonore of Aquitaine, Edward III and Richard II who was murdered in 1399.

Leaving the Royal Chapels continue past the chapels of the north ambulatory which all contain the tombs of English nobles. Anne of Cleves, the fourth wife of Henry VIII, is buried in the last chapel.

The **Cloisters** which date back to the 11th c. contain many tombs. The adjoining Dean's Yard (only open Thu.) is said to be one of the oldest gardens in England.

The **Chapterhouse** has vaulting supported on a single pier by Henry of Reims. It is of 13th c. origin as is the wall painting depicting the apocalypse. The House of Commons met here from 1282 to 1547.

The **Pyx Chamber** is part of Edward the Confessor's church and was later a royal treasury, in which was kept the "pyx", a chest containing the trial plates for testing the coinage. It contains the oldest altar in the abbey. Displayed in the Norman Undercroft are seals, charters and wax and wooden effigies.

Westminster Cathedral

To the west of Westminster Abbey is Westminster Cathedral, seat of a cardinal archbishop and together with the cathedral in Liverpool the most important Catholic church in England. It was built on a basilican plan between 1895 and 1903 in Romanesque-Byzantine style. The marble and mosaic decor is very impressive even though it is not complete. Relics in the crypt include a mitre which belonged to Thomas Becket and fragments of the Holy Cross.

★★Tate Gallery

Opening times
Mon.–Sat.
10am–5.50pm,
Sun. 2–5.50pm

Heading south along the Thames from the Houses of Parliament is the Neo-Classical building of the Tate Gallery. The exhibits were built up around the private collection of paintings and sculptures of Sir Henry Tate and present a chronological cross-section of British art from the 16th-20th c. as well as contemporary international art. Outstanding works are "Endymion Porter" (1643/45) by James Dobson, "O the Roast Beef of England/The Gate of Calais" (1748) by William Hogarth (see Famous People), portraits by Peter Lely, "Chain Pier, Brighton" (1826/27) by John Constable, landscapes by Joshua Reynolds and Thomas Gainsborough (see Famous People), pictures by all the famous French Impressionists and works by Georges Braque, Pablo Picasso, Max Ernst and Giorgio de Chirico. Sculptors represented include Aristide Maillol, Auguste Rodin, Ivan Mestrovic, Jacob Epstein and Henry Moore (see Famous People).

The **Clore Gallery**, an interesting annexe by James Stirling opened in 1987, is dedicated to the entire works of the painter **William Turner** (see Famous People).

Tate Gallery

Buckingham Palace

St James's is a very elegant quarter west of Trafalgar Square. The leading London clubs such as the Athenaeum Club are found along Pall Mall – which was the original playing field for the game of paillemaille, a game similar to cricket and popular with the aristocracy in the 17th c. – and around Waterloo Palace and St James's Square. The 131 ft-high monument to the Duke of York towers over Waterloo Place.

At the far end of Pall Mall stands ★**St James's Palace**, the royal palace built during the reign of Henry VIII and designed by Hans Holbein the Younger. After the fire at Whitehall Palace it became the official residence of the monarch in 1619 and foreign ambassadors are still accredited to the "court of St James's". The palace is still the residence of members of the royal family and is not open to visitors who must be satisfied with a view of the Tudor-style Gate House and guards.

Clarence House (1825), part of this complex of buildings, is residence of the Queen Mother; opposite is Lancaster House which is used for government receptions. Behind Lancaster House Buckingham Palace can be seen through the trees of the attractive Green Park.

Since Queen Victoria's accession in 1837 Buckingham Palace has been the London residence of the royal family. It was originally built in 1703 for the Duke of Buckingham and enlarged and rebuilt in 1825 by John Nash and Aston Webb in 1913. The royal family live in the north wing; when the queen is in residence the royal standard flies over the palace. Since 1993 nineteen rooms in the state apartments have been opened to the public for two months in the summer, a period which the Queen spends at Balmoral (see p. 290). The private apartments of the royal family are not available for viewing.

The ★"**Changing of the Guard**" is a popular attraction watched by masses of tourists; it takes place every other day at 11.30am. The monument to Queen Victoria by Aston Webb and Thomas Brock dominates the square in front of the palace.

St James's

Underground stations
Charing Cross, St James's Park, Green Park

★Buckingham Palace

Piccadilly Circus – the heart of the West End

To the left of the palace are the **Royal Mews**, where the magnificent royal coaches can be seen.

East of the palace is ★**St James's Park**, London's most attractive public park. It was laid out by Le Notre for Charles II and was landscaped in 1829 by John Nash. The grand parade The Mall leads back to Trafalgar Square along its northern edge. Set back is Marlborough House, a Commonwealth centre, and the long building of Carlton House Terrace.

West End

Underground stations
Piccadilly Circus, Leicester Square, Oxford Circus Bond Street, Tottenham Court Road

★Piccadilly Circus and surroundings

London's West End is famous not for its historic sights or outstanding museums but for exclusive shops and renowned department stores.

Here are the theatres, cinemas and a myriad of restaurants specialising in local and international cuisine and the no longer notorious district of Soho.

The noisy centre of the West End is Piccadilly Circus which is the "Hub of the World" to Londoners. From here the four main roads Piccadilly, Regent Street, Shaftesbury Avenue and Haymarket radiate into the shopping area and world of theatres and entertainment of the surrounding streets. Huge advertising hoardings illuminate this popular meeting-place by night with the "Eros fountain", although the figure is intended to represent the angel of charity, in honour of the philanthropic Earl of Shaftesbury. The Trocadero Centre is home to the 3D IMAX cinema and in the London Pavilion is the "Rock Circus".

The roads leading off the Circus all have their own individual character: Regent Street with the long-established department store Liberty's and Piccadilly with the no less traditional store Fortnum & Mason are lined with elegant shops whereas one theatre follows another in

Haymarket and Shaftesbury Avenue especially. Piccadilly gets its name from an 18th c. tailor who made the best "pickadilles", high collars with stiff corners.

The most impressive construction in Piccadilly is Burlington Arcade which has been home to the **Royal Academy of Arts**, founded in 1768, since 1869.

The regular exhibitions allow visitors to admire the Academy's greatest treasure, a sculpture by Michaelangelo, the only work by the Italian artist in England.

Burlington Arcade is immediately next to Burlington House. In this very expensive shopping arcade, which is patrolled by the "Beadles", 70 of the finest shops – pipemakers, tobacco shops, gentlemen's outfitters – are to be found.

At the end of Burlington Arcade are Burlington Gardens where the **Museum of Mankind** has temporary exhibitions of the ethnographical collection of the British Museum (see p. 358).

Soho, the district between Regent Street, Shaftesbury Avenue and Oxford Street, still has a notorious reputation as a twilight area and "red light district". However, the number of "porn joints" and strip-clubs has declined and now Soho is better known for its music clubs, delicatessens, restaurants offering a wide range of international cuisine – it has always had an immigrant population – and bars, particularly in Chinatown. There is ample opportunity to have lunch and take a stroll. Many media businesses have established branches here: music and book publishers, recording studios and film companies, exporters and agencies of all kinds.

The most famous street is Carnaby Street which in the Sixties was the place to be in "Swinging London". Now it is just another faceless pedestrian precinct like anywhere else in the world. There are also "real" sights: Karl Marx lived at 28 Dean Street from 1851-56, and Theodore, King of Corsica, is buried in St Anne's Church. Soho Square is a popular meeting place.

Soho

This long, busy and often congested street follows the course of a Roman road. One shop follows another and a visit must include the giant department store, Selfridges.

Marble Arch stands at the west end of Oxford Street. This triumphal arch was designed by John Nash on the model of the Arch of Constantine in Rome and was intended as the main gateway to Buckingham Palace but was found to be too narrow for the royal state coach and so was erected here at Tyburn, the medieval place of execution.

Oxford Street

Marylebone extends north of Oxford Street as far as Regent's Park.

One of its most important thoroughfares is Baker Street, made famous by Sherlock Holmes. His creator Sir Arthur Conan Doyle made his master detective live at No. 221b.

One of London's finest art collections, the ★**Wallace Collection**, is housed in the town house of the Duke of Manchester (18th c.) in Hertford House in Manchester Square. In 25 galleries which reflect the style of the period this valuable collection of the fourth Marquis of Hertford and his son Richard Wallace is displayed. It includes: precious furniture (by Boulle, Cressent and Riesener among others), European weapons and armaments, paintings by Rembrandt ("The Good Samaritan"), van Dyck (portrait of King Philip and his wife), Frans Hals ("The Laughing Cavalier"), Velásquez ("Lady with a Fan"), Titian ("Perseus and Andromeda"), Lawrence ("George IV"), Gainsborough ("Mrs Robinson") and Watteau ("The Music Party") and other works of art (Sèvres porcelain, alabaster reliefs, Italian Renaissance majolica).

Madame Tussaud's Everyone has heard of the famous waxworks exhibition of Marie Tussaud from Alsace, who took wax models from the

Marylebone

Underground stations
Marble Arch, Baker Street

guillotined heads during the French Revolution. These and many more life-size celebrities from all over the world are on show here.

North of Marylebone Road is **Regent's Park**, originally royal hunting grounds laid out by John Nash. There are an open-air theatre, boating lake and areas of grass which every day attract many Londoners. The long-established **zoo** is in the north of the park.

From the relative heights of **Primrose Hill** on the other side of Regent Canal there are good views over the city.

Hyde Park, Kensington and Chelsea

★Hyde Park and Kensington Gardens

Underground stations
Marble Arch, Lancaster Gate, Hyde Park Corner, Knightsbridge

Hyde Park, together with Kensington Gardens to the west, is London's largest open space. The area, originally belonging to Westminster Abbey, was taken over by Henry VIII and made into a deer park. It was thrown open to the public in 1635 who since then have made use of it for relaxation and sport. In the morning it is still quite tranquil in the park with only a few people walking and riding; on summer evenings though the park is often thronged with people. The main entrance to the park in the south-east corner is a triple archway (1828) by Decimus Burton with a reproduction of the Parthenon frieze; on the north-east corner is Marble Arch and the famous Speaker's Corner, where everybody has the right to air their opinions no matter how scurrilous. Particularly on Sundays all kinds of views are expressed. In the centre of the park the Serpentine, a lake laid out in 1730, offers facilities for boating.

At the busy junction of **Hyde Park Corner** on the south-east corner of the park are two memorials to the Duke of Wellington: Apsley House, the London residence of the victor of Waterloo and today open to the public as the **Wellington Museum**, and opposite the monumental Wellington Arch, commemorating Wellington's victory over Napoleon. Facing Apsley House can be seen a bronze equestrian statue of the duke surveying his house with an English grenadier, a Scottish Highlander, a Welsh fuselier and a Northern Irish dragoon keeping guard at the four corners of the pedestal.

The main attraction of Kensington Gardens is ★**Kensington Palace**, which was the private residence of the English monarch from 1689 to 1760 and was the home of the Prince and Princess of Wales until their separation. The state apartments on the first floor with the residential and working quarters of George I, George II, William III and their consorts as well as Queen Victoria, who was born here, are open to the public.

The **Albert Memorial** was erected by Queen Victoria on the southern edge of Kensington Gardens for her consort who died in 1861, Prince Albert of Saxe-Coburg-Gotha. In his hand he holds the catalogue of the "Great Exhibition" of 1851.

Kensington and Knightsbridge

Underground stations
Knightsbridge, High Street Kensington

Kensington and Knightsbridge have quite different attractions: on the one hand there are many interesting museums, on the other the second largest shopping quarter outside of the West End is here – in Kensington around Kensington Church Street and Kensington High Street and in Knightsbridge around the road of the same name and Brompton Road, where ★**Harrod's**, possibly the most famous store in the world, attracts shoppers like a magnet.

Royal Albert Hall

Opposite the Albert Memorial is the elliptical shape of the Royal Albert Hall, the best known concert hall in London. At the time of its completion in 1871 this building with a circumference of 689 ft was regarded as an extraordinarily daring construction. The summer promenade concerts ("proms") take place under its glass dome.

An experience: a visit to the Natural History Museum

Together with the British Museum the Victoria & Albert Museum on the Cromwell Road is the most comprehensive museum in London and similarly it is not possible to try and see everything in one day. At first, a collection of this size appears to be a gigantic conglomeration and may easily overwhelm the visitor. The idea of collecting artistic masterpieces came from Prince Albert and the museum was originally financed from profits from the Great Exhibition of 1851. The foundation stone of the present building was laid by Queen Victoria in 1899 and ten years later it was formerly opened.

★★Victoria and Albert Museum

Opening times
Mon.
noon–5.50pm
Tues.–Sun.
10am–5.50pm
Entrance Fee

The V & A has become one of the world's great art museums. The exhibits are arranged in two groups the **Primary Collections** ("Art and Design": masterpieces in every field of art are brought together by style, period and country of origin) and the **Study Collections** ("Materials and techniques": objects are grouped according to the material used).

The textile and costume departments are of great interest as are the ceramics, porcelain, silver, furniture, Asiatic and Islamic art together with weapons and the heavily insured jewellery department. The collection of paintings includes British miniatures and watercolours, cartoons by Raphael (drawn in 1516 for Pope Leo X) and numerous works by John Constable in the Henry Cole Wing.

Three richly decorated and unfortunately empty rooms on the ground floor, the Morris Room, Gamble Room and Poynter Room once housed the first museum restaurant in England.

The original nucleus of the Natural History Museum was the scientific collection of Sir Hans Sloane which was taken from the British Museum's collection in 1860 and was augmented in 1881 by thousands of new exhibits including those brought back by Joseph Banks, who accompanied James Cook on his voyages of discovery and by Charles

★Natural History Museum

Darwin from his explorations around the world, and presented to the cathedral-like building in Cromwell Road.

Visitors can discover the secrets of nature from interactive displays in many departments. Among the most spectacular displays in the **Life Galleries**, devoted to life forms from all epochs and all parts of the world, are the superb dinosaur gallery, the spiders and "Creepy Crawlies", the ecology section, and the 1.5 to 5 million-year old remains of "Lucy", an early female hominid (Australopithecus) found in Ethiopia in 1974. The museum's exceptional mineral collection includes some 130,000 specimens.

From the newly re-arranged Life Galleries there is direct access to the **Earth Galleries** devoted to geography and geology. Highlights include a large exhibition entitled "The Story of the Earth" and a magnificent collection of gemstones.

★Science
Museum

Further along from the Geological Museum is the Science Museum which documents the history of science, industry, technology and medicine. The departments cover five floors and have exhibits such as historic aeroplanes, vintage cars or gas production. Children can carry out all kinds of experiments in the children's gallery "Launch Pad".

Some of the exhibits on display include Galileo's telescopes, Boulton and Watt's steam engine from 1788, "Puffing Billy", the oldest locomotive from 1813, a typewriter from 1875 with the original keyboard arrangement still in use today, the Apollo 10 space capsule and Soyez spaceship, as well as quite ordinary items such as the oldest known tin can dating from 1823.

Chelsea

Underground station
Sloane Square

King's Road, together with Carnaby Street in Soho (see p. 367) formed the centre of "Swinging London" in the Sixties. It is the main road through the area south of Kensington and is lined with boutiques, pubs and restaurants. The Chelsea Antiques fair in the town hall built in 1887 attracts collectors from all over the world in spring and autumn each year. Chelsea Antiques Market located next to it is open all year.

The **Chelsea Old Church** on the banks of the Thames between Battersea Bridge and Albert Bridge was founded in the 12th c. The chapel named after Thomas More who commissioned it was designed by Holbein; Henry VIII secretly married Jane Seymour in the Lawrence Chapel. Lady Jane Cheyne is buried in the churchyard in a tomb by Bernini, as is Sir Hans Sloane.

Continuing from the church along the Thames towards Westminster are the buildings of the **Chelsea Royal Hospital**. Founded in 1682 probably on the model of the Hôtel des Invalides in Paris, this institution looks after 500 war veterans and invalid soldiers. They still wear the traditional uniforms of the Duke of Marlborough's time, in summer scarlet and in winter dark blue. The decorated rooms and great dining hall are open to visitors. The famous Chelsea flower show takes place in the adjoining gardens. The National Army Museum is also part of the complex.

On the South Bank of the Thames

Southwark and
South Bank

Underground stations
London Bridge,
Waterloo Station

London Bridge links the city with Southwark on the south bank of the Thames. Travellers once used to stay here before going about their business in the City. As Southwark belonged for a long time to the church and was not under the jurisdiction of the City, pubs and prostitution thrived on this bank. Shakespeare's first plays were performed in the courtyard of the George Inn and in 1599 the famous Globe Theatre was opened, which burnt down during a performance in 1613. It has been rebuilt in its original form not far from the original site. Not much of Southwark's past is left today. The warehouses along the Thames have been restored and house restaurants and shops, elsewhere the former disreputable areas of Southwark consist of blocks of flats and building sites.

Approaching Southwark from London Bridge the steel and glass galleries of the Hays Galleria can be seen which belong to the commercial and shopping centre of **London Bridge City** which has developed around London Bridge Station.

Further downstream towards Tower Bridge is moored HMS "Belfast", the last great cruiser of the Royal Navy. The ship came into service in 1938 and was involved in the sea battle at the North Cape in 1943 and the allied landing in Normandy in 1944. After being withdrawn from service in 1963 it was brought to London where it is open to visitors.

HMS "Belfast"

To the right of London Bridge the bell tower of Southwark Cathedral is visible. It is the mother church of the diocese of Southwark and succeeds a monastery built before the 9th c. for which Gifford, Bishop of Winchester built a Norman church in 1106. After this was destroyed by fire Bishop Peter de Rupibus commissioned a new church in 1207 of which the lower part of the tower remains. The present church has undergone much rebuilding and alteration and after Westminster Abbey (see p. 362) is London's finest Gothic church.

★Southwark Cathedral

Left of the entrance can be seen the 13th c. arcading and original 15th c. wooden carving including Judas wearing a kilt. In the north aisle is the tomb of John Gower, friend of Geoffrey Chaucer and court poet to Richard II and Henry IV, his head resting on his three most important books. One of the three ledgers in the north transept is of special interest: the Lockyer Monument to the quack doctor John Lockyer (d. 1672), who claimed that his wonder-working pills were made from sunbeams. Also in the north transept is the Harvard Chapel commemorating John Harvard, founder of the famous American university, who was baptised

The National Theatre

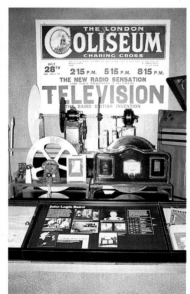

Exhibit in the Museum of the Moving Image

Imperial War Museum: Spitfire, Focke-Wulf 190 and Mustang

here. The north ambulatory also contains beautiful monuments including that of John Trehearne, favourite of James I. The wooden effigy of a knight is from the 13th c. and is the oldest surviving from that period. The choir and retrochoir are among the oldest Gothic work in London.

St Mary Overy Dock

Not far from the cathedral the schooner "Kathleen and May" can be visited in the restored St Mary Overy Dock. The Southwark Heritage Centre has information on the history of the area.

The George Inn

The fruit and vegetable Borough Market has been held opposite Southwark Cathedral since 1851. Borough High Street and the George Inn can be reached by passing through the market. The George Inn is London's oldest remaining waggoner's inn, established in 1676.

South Bank Arts Centre

Close to the south end of Waterloo Bridge is the South Bank Arts Centre. It consists of the three theatres of the **National Theatre**, a modern building built by Denys Lasdun in 1963; the original and lavishly equipped ★**Museum of the Moving Image** which documents the history of film and television and the adjoining **National Film Theatre** which shows films devoted to specific themes or directors; the Hayward Art Gallery, which has exhibits from the modern department of the Tate Gallery (see p. 365); finally the **Royal Festival hall** which seats 3400 and the smaller Queen Elizabeth Hall and Purcell Room.

London Eye

Next to the South Bank Centre in Jubilee Gardens is the massive 135 metre-high British Airways "London Eye". This huge ferris wheel has encountered technical difficulties but is due to open March 2000.

Lambeth

The ★**Imperial War Museum** covers the role of Great Britain in both world wars. It was founded in 1920 and is housed in the former buildings of the Bethlem Royal Hospital in the district of Lambeth which is opposite Westminster. The hub of the museum is the large exhibition hall with aircraft, tanks and artillery from both world wars. In the basement weapons, uniforms, medals and documents illustrate the events of the Second World War. The Blitz Experience gives visitors a vivid impression of air-raid conditions.

Underground stations
Lambeth North

In the southern part of Lambeth is the 12th c. **Lambeth Palace,** for over 700 years the London residence of the Archbishops of Canterbury. Every ten years the Lambeth Conference of Anglican Bishops is held in the Great Hall of the palace.

London's East End

The East End is situated to the east of the City and begins with the areas of Whitechapel and Spitalfields. Even today It is still synonymous with social deprivation. The world described by Dickens in "Oliver Twist" of poverty, terrible living and working conditions, alcohol and prostitution has its origins in the alleys and dives of the East End. It inspired William Hogarth to draw his sequence of pictures "Gin Lane" and "Beer Street" and Henry Fielding's social critique the novel "Tom Jones". William Booth founded the Salvation Army here in 1865 and Jack the Ripper committed his terrible crimes here. Immigrants have lived in the East End since the 17th c., first the French Huguenots, then impoverished farmers from Scotland, Wales and chiefly Ireland, and around the turn of the century East European Jews hoping to find work in the textile factories or in the nearby docks. Today immigrants from the Middle East, Asia and Africa live and work here. There are no real sights as such; Petticoat Lane Market, where literally everything is on sale, is interesting and so is the large collection of dolls and toys in ★**Bethnal Green Museum of Children** north of Whitechapel (Bethnal Green underground station).

Underground station
Tower Hill

On the banks of the Thames east of Tower Bridge (see p. 352) the commercial heart of the Empire once beat. On the docksides of Surrey, Wapping, Limehouse & Poplar, Isle of Dogs and Royal Docks ships from all parts of the Empire used to unload their valuable cargoes of spices, cereals, timber, food and raw materials; many a proud sailing boat was built in the wharves. With the differing demands for a modern port and the building of new port facilities further downstream the docks lost their status in the Sixties and fell into disrepair. The ambitious scheme to redevelop the dockland area was begun in 1982; its aim is to create a giant commercial and residential centre with 200,000 jobs and flats for 115,000 people. The investors were allowed a totally free hand in planning and execution of the scheme by the Thatcher government; free of any restrictions bold, controversial new buildings went up within a few years. Successes include the Financial Times printworks by Nicholas Grimshaw and the residential tower block "The Cascades" by Piers Gough. The other side of the coin is that the long-established residents are faced with rents they cannot afford as the planners were relying on wealthy young businessmen. Meanwhile even this clientele has not rushed to live or shop here. In the evenings the futuristic streets and squares on the Isle of Dogs are almost empty, some of the expensive shops in Tobacco Dock are closed down. The investors in Canary Wharf, the largest office complex in Europe, have also faced problems as space has proved difficult to let. The computer-controlled overhead railway (Docklands Light Railway or DLR) from Bank station is unable to cope with peak demand and does not operate after 9.30pm or at weekends.

Docklands

For visitors however, the DLR is far more interesting than the bus (D9 from Bank) as a way of seeing Docklands. The return journey from

St Catherine's Dock

The "Three Sisters" in Tobacco Dock

Greenwich (across the river from the Island Gardens terminus), can be made by Thames riverboat.

East of the Tower on the south bank the old warehouses of **Butler's Wharf** and the Anchor Brewery have been turned into an exclusive residential and commercial complex. Behind the buildings the narrow street Shad Thames still gives an impression of conditions in Victorian London.

One of the newest museums in London is the adjoining **Design Museum**, situated below the Bramah Tea and Coffee Museum.

★**St Catherine's Dock** opposite Butler's Wharf on the north bank is a successful example of redevelopment. Grouped around the harbour basin with some historic ships (the lightship "Nore") are houses, shops, restaurants and pubs transformed from the old warehouses.

Two threemasters are moored in **Tobacco Dock**: the "Sealark" a pirate ship for children and the "Three Sisters" a floating pirate museum.

The centre of the redevelopment project, the **Isle of Dogs**, can best be viewed from a DLR train. It glides past West India Docks, where Canary Wharf has been built, an office complex with a 734 ft tower, designed by star architect Cesar Pelli. The route takes in Millwall Dock with the office buildings of Harbour Exchange, South Quay Plaza and the London Arena to the terminus Island Gardens.

Greenwich

From Island Gardens the Greenwich Foot Tunnel under the Thames leads to Greenwich. Thames river boats and British Rail (from Charing Cross/London Bridge Station) operate from the City of London to this charming suburb, which is famous throughout the world for the Greenwich Meridian and its part in the history of British seafaring.

Directly next to the pier is the last and most famous of the tea clippers, which transported tea and spices from the Far East to Europe in the 19th c. The **"Cutty Sark"** was built in 1869 and was regarded as the finest and fastest ship of its kind. Not until 1956 was it laid up in dry dock at Greenwich. There is a very interesting exhibition on the old sailing ships in the lower deck.

Not far from the "Cutty Sark" is the smaller "Gipsy Moth IV" in which Sir Francis Chichester sailed single-handed around the world in 1966/67.

To the left of the "Cutty Sark" stands the ★**Royal Naval College**, its long white façade dominating the banks of the Thames. The Royal Naval College occupies a historic site, originally occupied by a palace erected by Edward I and later by the Palace of Placentia built by the Duke of Gloucester in 1428, a favourite residence of Henry VII; Henry VIII married Catherine of Aragón and Anne of Cleves here and also signed the death sentence of Anne Boleyn. His daughters Mary I and Elizabeth I were born in the Palace of Placentia. In the time of Cromwell it was used as a prison. In 1664 John Webb, commissioned by Charles II, began work on a new palace, which was completed by Christopher Wren in 1698.

★★**Queen's House** is one of the most complete mansions in Palladian style. Inigo Jones began the work in 1616 which James I had commissioned as a residence for his wife, Anne of Denmark, but was abandoned after her death. Then in 1629 Charles I had it completed by Inigo Jones for his wife Henrietta Maria. The two wings were added between 1805 and 1816. After renovation lasting six years Queen's House was restored to the former splendour of a royal residence in 1990.

The ★★**National Maritime Museum** has unique exhibits on the history of the British Navy and seafaring in general. The collection begins on the top floor and is arranged chronologically with the rise of Britain as a sea power and the journeys of James Cook. Galleries on the history of the war at sea with Napoleonic France (including Nelson's uniform from the Battle of Trafalgar) and 19th c. expeditions follow; in the basement is a large exhibition on the technology of ships and shipbuilding with the state barge of Mary II from 1689.

"Cutty Sark" in Greenwich dock

Behind Queen's House **Greenwich Park**, laid out by Le Nôtre, rises gently, and is a popular park with Londoners. On the hill the building of the ★**Old Royal Observatory** can be seen, an institution commissioned by Charles I in 1675 which became world-famous and has since been moved to Cambridge. On the top of Flamsteed House a red ball falls from the top of its mast daily at 1pm to enable vessels on the river to regulate their chronometers. The house contains an exhibition of astronomical instruments. The zero meridian which divides the earth into east and west, runs through the Meridian building, marked by a steel rod on the floor. The Equatorial Building houses the largest telescope in Great Britain.

The newest attraction in Greenwich is the **Millennium Dome**, opened on 1 Jan. 2000 and housing exhibits celebrating 2000 years of cultural and technological achievements. The Dome is due to close at the end of the year 2000. Telephone 0870 5000 600 for details.

★**Thames Flood Barrier**

Quite a way downstream from Greenwich is the huge Thames Flood Barrier, which is best seen from the river boats; it was constructed to protect the area from flooding during storms coming from the North Sea. The world's largest flood barrier consists of ten massive steel gates which can be in position within half an hour.

Sights in the outlying area

★**Dulwich College Picture Gallery**

Underground station
Brixton

Barely 6 miles south of the City the atmosphere at Dulwich is surprisingly rural. Dulwich College was the first public gallery in London to open its doors. The nucleus of the gallery was the collection of the Frenchman Noël Desenfans; today it encompasses works of all European schools from the 16th to the 18th c. and has some famous names. The close arrangement of pictures reflects the style of the early 19th c., when Sir P. F. Bourgeois inherited the collection from his friend Desenfans.

National Sports Centre

Underground station
Brixton

One of the great events in London in the 19th c. was the Great Exhibition of 1851 in Hyde Park. The central feature of the Exhibition was the Crystal Palace by Joseph Paxton which was moved to Penge in south London in 1854, but destroyed by fire in 1936. On the same site the **National Sports Centre** was built with a wide choice of sports facilities and a large park whose main attraction is the collection of life-size plaster models of dinosaurs, the only relic of the Great Exhibition.

Wimbledon

Underground station
Wimbledon

The mecca of all tennis fans is also situated in south London. Every summer tens of thousands of them stream to the "All England Lawn Tennis Championship" to watch the contest for the most important tennis trophy of all. It is worth visiting at other times to see the interesting tennis museum and visitors can even enter the sacred Centre Court.

Kew Gardens

Underground station
Kew Bridge

Kew Gardens, the Botanical Gardens on the south bank of the Thames south-west of the city, are a world famous institution. The garden was created in 1759 on the initiative of Princess Augusta, mother of George II. Joseph Banks, a botanist who had accompanied James Cook around the world, was appointed the director during George III's reign. This was the beginning of an era of great scientific expeditions when countless exotic plants were introduced to Kew. The main attraction of Kew gardens are the two massive Victorian glasshouses by Decimus Burton and Richard Turner. The small Kew Palace was occupied by George III during his fits of madness; Queen Victoria spent a great deal of time in Queen's Cottage.

Richmond Park

Further downstream from Kew Gardens lies the largest municipal park in Britain, Richmond Park, in the desirable residential suburb of Richmond.

The park was enclosed by Charles I in 1637 as a deer park; numbers of red and fallow deer still roam around the wooded expanse. Among the attractive features of the park are the Isabella Plantations, the Prince Charles Spinney and the White Lodge, a hunting lodge built for George II, in which Edward VIII was born.

Underground station
Richmond

Hampton Court, perhaps the finest and most interesting of Britain's royal palaces, lies in East Molesley, 15 miles south-west of the city. Hampton Court Palace was built between 1514–20 as the private residence for Cardinal Wolsey, who presented it to Henry VIII in order to secure the king's favour. With the exception of Catherine of Aragón all of Henry VIII's wives lived in the palace; the ghosts of his third wife Jane Seymour and his fifth wife Catherine Howard are said to haunt the palace. Elizabeth I learnt of the defeat of the Spanish Armada in the Channel while staying here. Charles I spent time here both as king and prisoner of Oliver Cromwell. Visitors are shown around not only the State Apartments but the kitchen and cellar as well.

Hampton Court Palace

British Rail
Hampton Court from Waterloo

The extensive park encompasses the king's private gardens and the Tudor and Elizabethan garden. The Great Vine is 200 years old. The Lower Orangery contains Mantegna's "Triumph of Caesar" and another attraction is the famous maze.

Wembley Stadium in north London is to the football fan what Wimbledon is to the tennis enthusiast. Opened in 1923 the stadium can accommodate 78,000 spectators and it is full for the Cup Final, the climax of the football season, in May every year. There are guided tours at 10am daily.

Wembley Stadium

Underground station
Wembley Park

The Royal Air Force Museum occupies the former factory site of the pioneer pilot Claude Graham White in north London. The museum is one of the largest of its kind in the world with three halls displaying over 60 original aircraft from the First and Second World Wars together with a number of documents, medals and equipment from the history of the British Airforce.

Royal Air Force Museum

Underground station
Colindale

Londonderry · Derry   B 5/6

Northern Ireland
County: Londonderry. District: Londonderry
Population: 70,000. Altitude: 46 ft

Londonderry, known to its inhabitants by its original Irish name of Derry, is Northern Ireland's second largest town. Situated where the River Foyle opens out into the sea-lough of the same name, the town has been robbed of part of its natural hinterland of Donegal by the division of Ireland. Nevertheless it remains an important port and industrial centre with a traditional textile industry, but also chemical and mechanical engineering plants and ceramics factories. With its attractive surroundings it is a popular tourist centre and a good base for trips into the Inishowen peninsula and Donegal in the Republic of Ireland. The town itself has an almost completely preserved circuit of medieval walls and a number of interesting old buildings.

History The name Derry is derived from the Irish word "daire", which means oak wood. It is thought that an abbey was founded on the hill in Derry by the missionary, St Columba (St Colmcille; 521–97), who was also founder of other important monasteries and abbeys throughout Ireland and Great Britain, including Durrow, in the interior of Ireland, and Iona (see Hebrides). The abbey was taken over by the Augustines at the end of the Middle Ages. Both it and the settlements thereabouts

Siege of Derry 1688

were attacked and destroyed by the Vikings on numerous occasions during the 9th and 10th c. In the 12th and 13th c. Derry entered its golden period under the MacLochlain dynasty. The colonisation of Ulster was undertaken by James I, who sent out to Derry predominantly Protestant settlers or "planters" from England and Scotland under the guidance of the wealthy London merchant guilds. As a result of this, the town and county were declared a "London settlement" and Derry's name was altered to Londonderry. The massive town walls, which date from this period, were even able to withstand the 105 days' siege by James II's troops in 1688–89. This event is still commemorated by the Orange parades on August 12th. As a consequence of the famines and economic crises in the 18th and 19th c., thousands of Irish emigrants left for America by ship from the harbour at Derry. They included the founders of the colonies of Derry and Londonderry in the American state of New Hampshire. In the middle of the 19th c. the textile industry went through a considerable upturn in activity with the demand for shirts and collars. With the division of Ireland in 1921, Londonderry became a border town. In the more recent past the town has attained an unfortunate notoriety as one of the focal points for the often bloody clashes which have distinguished the conflict in Northern Ireland between Protestants and Catholics.

Warning: Visitors should avoid the "control zones" at all costs. Parking in these areas is in any case forbidden; unattended cars may well be viewed as potential bomb threats and dealt with accordingly. Indeed, the visitor must be prepared for the occasional vehicle check. Pedestrians – and this applies equally to local inhabitants and tourists – must be able to provide evidence of identity if required.

Sights

★Walls

The city walls of Derry are probably the best preserved in the whole of the United Kingdom and remain exactly as they were when they were built in 1618, with the exception of the three gateways which were added later. They form an attractive walk along the perimeter of the Old Town. The Walker Monument on the Royal Bastion provides the best view of the town. Four ancient gateways lead into the town: Butcher's Gate, Ferryquay Gate, Shipquay Gate and Bishop's Gate, the finest of the four.

The history of Derry from the earliest times to the present day is the theme of the **Tower Museum** in one of the towers of the city wall.

The four principal streets of the town run from these gates and meet in the Diamond, which is the name used for their junction (still following the medieval town plan) since the 17th c. The Town Hall originally stood here, but it was destroyed during one of the many sieges of the town and rebuilt elsewhere. The centre of the square is now occupied by the War Memorial.

Diamond

The Old Town contains numbers of Georgian houses, particularly in Shipquay Street, Magazine Street and Bishop Street. The Deanery and the neighbouring Neo-Classical Court House, date from the 19th c. Craft Village is the reconstruction of a turn of the century shopping street, part of the Old Town redevelopment project begun in recent years.

Buildings in Old Town

St Columb's Cathedral (Church of Ireland), which is built in the late Perpendicular style, dates mainly from 1629–36, the tower having been added in 1802. In memory of the men from London who commissioned the building of the cathedral, the main doorway bears the inscription "If Stones could speake/Then Londons prayse/Should sounde who/Built this Church and/Cittie from the grounde". The roof vaulting is carried by corbels with the carved heads of sixteen bishops of Londonderry. Eight of the thirteen bells in the tower date from the 17th c. The bishop's throne incorporates the chair of Bishop Bramhall, who consecrated the church in 1633. The chapterhouse contains relics of the town's history and the locks and keys of the four town gates.

★St Columb's Cathedral

Situated to the north-east of the town walls is the Guildhall, a Neo-Gothic building dating from 1912, which was severely damaged during a bomb attack in 1972, with the result that a large part of its interior has had to be reconstructed. The large Council Chamber, with its splendid oak panelling, and the Treasure Chamber, with its many mementoes of Irish history, are both particularly worth seeing. Also worthy of special mention are the coloured glass windows on which different periods of the town's history are portrayed.

Guildhall

Further to the north from the Guildhall along Strand Road, we reach Magee University College, which forms part of the University of Ulster. It is a Neo-Gothic building dating from 1865, beautifully situated on the River Foyle.

Magee University College

The handsome two-level Craigavon Bridge (1200 ft long), opened by the Lord Mayor of London in 1933, leads over the Foyle to a new and modern suburb of Derry to the south-east.

Craigavon Bridge

A second bridge downstream, Foyle Bridge, was opened to traffic in 1984.

Foyle Bridge

Surroundings

In the grounds of Belmont House School, on the Moville road, there is a large block of gneiss, St Columba's Stone, with two depressions resembling footprints. It is said to have been the coronation stone of the O'Neills, kings of Ulster.

St Columba's Stone

The royal seat of the O'Neills, the Grianan of Aileach, lies west of the town, in the Republic of Ireland. From the old tower, believed to be the oldest building in Ireland, there are magnificent views of Lough Foyle, the mouth of the River Foyle, Lough Swilly and the rocky Inishowen coast in the Republic.

Grianan of Aileach

The two great tourist attractions which can be reached from Derry are the beautiful Antrim coast and the Giant's Causeway. The A2 runs east through the charming villages of Eglinton and Ballykelly to Limavady (18

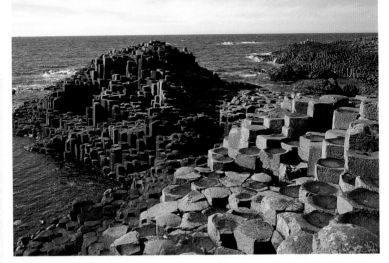

Giant's Causeway

Coleraine

miles; on the left the new Foyle Bridge), an old town in the Roe valley, from which the A37 continues to Coleraine (pop. 16,500), one of the oldest English settlements in the area. This lively town on the River Bann (which is navigable at this point) is noted for its salmon, its whiskey distilleries and its linen factories.

Portstewart

From here the route returns to the coast, coming after 6 miles to Portstewart (pop. 4000), which has beautiful sandy beaches and a picturesque harbour. Portrush, 4 miles to the east, is also good for bathing and has good views across to the offshore Skerry Islands.

The road continues on to the Giant's Causeway, passing the 14th c. Dunauce Castle, built on an isolated crag and linked with the mainland by a bridge.

On the banks of the River Bush lies the oldest whiskey distillery in the world, the ★**Bushmills Distillery**. It is said that as long ago as the 13th c. a "water of life" was produced here by Irish monks. In 1608 the distillery received its licence from James I. Unlike the other distilleries in Ireland, which use unmalted barley to produce their "pot-still whiskey", Bushmills, which is the only malt distillery in Ireland, follows the rules for making Scotch whisky (see p. 296), when making their "single malt". It uses only malted barley, which, moreover, is dried over peat fires, in contrast to the coal fires more usual elsewhere. The result is a light smoky whiskey, which visitors to the distillery get the chance to sample.

★★Giant's Causeway

8 miles further on is one of the great tourist sights of Northern Ireland, the Giant's Causeway, a geological formation of volcanic origin, consisting of a series of some 40,000 vertical basalt columns of prismatic form and varying width and height, their top sides forming stepping stones. Some of the columns have names, like the "Lady's Fan", the "Giant's Organ" and the "Horseshoe". The most imposing part, reached by the Shepherd's Path, is known as the Amphitheatre, with symmetrically

arranged blocks of basalt and columns up to 80 ft high towering out of the sea. Legend has it that the causeway was created by the giant, Finn McCool, an Ulster warrior and Commander of the Royal Army of Ireland. Finn had fallen in love with a giantess on the island of Staffa (see Hebrides) and began to build a path in order to bring his beloved back to Ulster.

The coast road then continues by way of Ballintoy (13 miles) and Cushendun, in the middle of attractive heathland, to **Ballycastle** (pop. 3000), a picturesque little harbour town surrounded by wooded country. From here a boat can be taken to the island of Rathlin, 6½ miles offshore, which was once a Viking stronghold.

The road from Ballycastle to Cushendall, passing the famous Glens of Antrim, is the most beautiful coastal road in Ireland. From Cushendall it is possible to continue along the coast to Belfast (48 miles) or alternatively to return to Derry by the very attractive inland road via Glenariff (A43), Kilrea and Dungiven.

★★**Antrim Coast**

Lough Erne

B 6

Northern Ireland
County: Fermanagh

One of the most attractive inland tourist areas in Northern Ireland is the county of Fermanagh (county town Enniskillen), which includes the large recreational area around the two halves of Lough Erne, probably Ireland's most beautiful lough. It is about 50 miles long and at its point of greatest width measures some 6 miles. The northern half is known as "Lower", the southern as "Upper Lough Erne". The latter is a maze of narrow waterways, inlets and islands and gives the impression of a vast lakeland area, with new twists and turns at every point, rather than a single lake in the conventional sense.

Lough Erne is a bird-watcher's paradise, where grebes, grey herons and swans can be observed, as well as a favourite destination for watersports enthusiasts and anglers, the latter having the opportunity here to land roach, perch, bream, salmon, pike, etc. In summer there are motorboat services on the lough, and it is also possible to hire motor cruisers, which even the most confirmed landlubber can learn to handle in a very short time. The western end of the lough lies almost on the border with the Republic of Ireland and has sluices to regulate the water level.

The A46 runs along the west side of the lough to Enniskillen (pop. 12,500), situated between the two loughs, which are here connected by the River Erne. This lively holiday resort has a good number of old mansions, as well as some delightful parkland scenery, particularly Florence Court and its grounds, the seat of the Counts of Enniskillen, and Castlecoole, a mansion built in the Palladian style by James Wyatt in 1796. Its favourable position on the old trading route between Ulster and Connaught was originally the reason for the choice of Enniskillen as seat of the Maguires, the chieftains of Fermanagh, who had the lough guarded by a fleet of sometimes as many as 1500 boats. A visit to the County Museum in Enniskillen Castle gives a good overview of the historical development of the area. Two other buildings worth seeing are the Anglican Cathedral (17th/18th c.), in which hang the banners of the former royal regiment, and Portora Royal School, founded at the beginning of the 16th c. by Charles I. Former pupils of the school include Oscar Wilde and Samuel Beckett.

★**Enniskillen**

No visitor should omit the trip to the island of Devenish, at the south end of Lower Lough Erne, which has the remains of an abbey founded by St

Devenish Island

Molaise in the 6th c., with a perfectly preserved round tower over 80 ft high, tapering towards the top. There are also fragments of St Mary's Abbey and the Great Church (12th c.) with a cross some 6 ft high.

Boa Island

At the cemetery of Caldragh on the island of Boa, also in Lower Lough Erne and accessible by a bridge, there are two Celtic double-faced sculptures of Janus dating back to the 1st c.

Other excursions

Other holiday resorts in this area are **Ballinamallard**, on the river of the same name (5 miles north-east); the village of **Bellanaleck**, in the heart of the lake district (5 miles south of Enniskillen); **Kesh**, beautifully situated on Lower Lough Erne, with possible excursions to Boa Island and White Island; **Lisbellaw** on Upper Lough Erne, with wool spinning and weaving mills; and **Lisnaskea**, also on Upper Lough Erne, with its ruined Balfour Castle; and the little village of **Belleek**, famous for its long tradition of porcelain manufacture.

Another place of tourist interest is **Omagh** (pop. 8000), the county town of Tyrone, with excellent salmon fishing and good walking in the Sperrin Mountains.

The **Marble Arch Caves**, south-west of Enniskillen and on the northern edge of the Cullcagh Mountains, are worth a visit. Accessible to a depth of some 2100 ft, they contain weird stalactite and stalagmite formations, sinter terraces and waterfalls.

Isle of Man   G 6

The Isle of Man, some 227 sq. miles in area, is situated in the Irish Sea 31 miles from England, about the same distance from Northern Ireland and 16 miles from Scotland. It is a very popular holiday island, with a coastline of more than 100 miles made up partly of sandy bathing beaches and partly of steep cliffs. Most of the island, which is some 33 miles long and 12 miles wide, is undulating and hilly, with a varied scenic pattern of moorland and heath, the dark green of juniper and reedbeds, brown Loghtan sheep grazing on gentle uplands, narrow glens with waterfalls, and areas of woodland. The climate is mild, with the temperature in winter rarely falling below 5°C (41°F).

The Isle of Man does not belong to the United Kingdom, but is a **Crown Dependency**. The island is autonomous and has its own parliament, the Court of Tynwald, which lays claim to being the oldest in the world. In addition it has a range of privileges which have been handed down: its own special system of land tenure, its own constitution (since 1866), as well as the right to levy its own taxes and customs duties under the direct protection of the English crown. The Queen is Sovereign and Lord Proprietor of Man and is represented by a Lieutenant Governor.

The island's legal idiosyncrasies have on numerous occasions attracted the attention not only of London, but also the European Court of Human Rights. Thus the birch is still allowed here as a legal penalty up to the age of 21 and homosexuality is still a punishable offence.

The island's very lenient taxation system, with its low charges and high interest rates, has in the last few years caused large numbers of banks, foreign exchange dealers and investors to settle here. This "wind of change" through the expanding financial sector is most noticeable in the wave of new building which has taken place in the island's capital, Douglas. About a third of the population now lives here. The island has a total population of about 73,000, although in the summer, when the famous TT (Tourist Trophy) motorcycle-race takes place and the colourful assembly of the island's government is held on the Tynwald at St John, the population is swollen by almost half a million holidaymakers.

There are regular **ferry** connections from Douglas to Liverpool and Heysham. The island has its own airline, Manx Air, and provides flight

Typical Tourist Trophy (TT) section

connections from **Ronaldsway Airport** in the south-east of the island with most of the larger English, Scottish and Irish airports.

The Isle of Man has a very interesting **history**. The oldest inhabitants were a hunting and fishing people of the Mesolithic period, c. 2000 B.C. Long before the Romans came to Britain the island was occupied by Celts, to whom the Iron Age forts and the large circular timber-framed huts found here are attributed. The Isle of Man was never occupied by the Romans. St Patrick (d. 463) is believed to have converted the people to Christianity long before St Augustine was sent to Canterbury. Celtic Christianity flourished until the arrival of the Vikings, whose raids began at the end of the 8th c. All these various periods have left their traces on the island, which has much of interest to offer the archaeologically inclined visitor. The island's parliament, the Tynwald, is thought to have its origins in the law-making assemblies established in 979 by the Vikings, who occupied the Kingdom of Man from the 9th to the middle of the 13th c., when it was transferred to Scottish ownership. In 1765 it was acquired by the English crown.

The islanders' fierce sense of independence can be seen in the fact that they think of themselves as **Manx**, rather than English. The old Manx tongue, a member of the Celtic family of languages, has for all practical purposes died out, being preserved only in family and place names. The tailless Manx cat, on the other hand, continues to flourish; originally the result of a mutation, it is now bred to preserve the species.

Yet another legal peculiarity of the island, that of the maximum speed allowed on its public roads, something which has long been restricted in England, has led to the Isle of Man becoming a competition ground for the sport of motorcycle racing. The **Tourist Trophy**, which the Marquis de Mouzilly St Mars presented over 80 years ago as the prize for a touring motorcycle race, has made the island well-known all over the world. The circuit used by the race, which is run every year at the end of May and beginning of June, is in the north of the island and begins and ends at Douglas, the capital, taking in on the way Crosby, St John's, Kirk Michael, Ramsey and the highest point on the island, Snaefell (2036 ft) – a total distance of almost 37 miles. At the almost incredible average speed of 115mph the heavy machines thunder along narrow country lanes, steep downward plunges and sharp curves, the surfaces having treacherous and, as the last few years have repeatedly shown, literally murderous bumps. In spite of the fact that every year the race takes its toll of human lives, and even stars like "Mike the Bike", the popular English racing cyclist Mike Hailwood, have warned publicly about the dangers of the route, the trophy does not seem to have lost any of its fascination for the fans of motorcycle racing. One of the famous Manx riders of recent years is Phil Hogg, who at the end of the 1980s completed the circuit in the fastest time yet achieved of just under 18 minutes.

Douglas

Almost all of the places of any size are on the coast. Douglas (pop. 20,000) lies on a beautiful bay into which flow the little rivers Dhoo and Glass. The Promenade, 2 miles long, is crowded with visitors in summer. The town offers every variety of accommodation, from luxury hotels to the most modest guest houses, and a great range of tourist attractions – large dance-halls, horse-trams, an indoor swimming-pool, a golf-course, a gambling casino. There are a number of handsome buildings, including the Legislative Building, home of the Manx parliament. Of particular interest is the **Manx Museum** in Finch Road, which illustrates the history of the island from the earliest times, with reproductions of rooms and domestic equipment of the past and works by Manx artists. There is an important collection of material of the Celtic and Viking periods, particularly notable for the Manx crosses.

Port Soderick

South of Douglas a beautiful panoramic road runs round Douglas Head to Port Soderick, a popular seaside resort, passing the churches of Braddan (1½ miles) and Onchan (2 miles), which have old crosses.

Ballasalla

The road then continues to Ballasalla (8 miles), with the ruins of a Cistercian house, Rushen Abbey, founded in 1134. This was the last monastery in the British Isles to be dissolved (1540). The old Monks' Bridge is very picturesque.

Langness Derbyhaven

From Ballasalla, which lies inland, the road leads towards the coast, passing Ronaldsway Airport on the left, and comes to the Langness peninsula, which has very beautiful sandy beaches. The little resort of Derbyhaven is noted for an excellent golf-course and for King William's College, founded in 1668, the island's principal school. The little chapel is worth seeing.

Castletown

The next place is Castletown (1½ miles), once capital of the island. **Castle Rushen**, on the site of an earlier Viking stronghold, destroyed in 1313, has played a great part in Manx history. The Castle, once a royal residence, is very well preserved. The clock in the south tower was presented by Elizabeth I (see Famous People) in 1597, and there is also an interesting sundial with 13 dials. Within the walls of the castle, Derby House was built by the 7th Earl of Derby in 1644. From the tower there are far-ranging views. Here too is one of the island's greatest treasures, a Celtic crucifix brought from the little offshore islet, the Calf of Man.

Nautical Museum

The exhibits in the Nautical Museum include models of historic ships and the yacht "The Peggy", which was built by George Quayle in 1791.

Old Grammar School

Adjoining the Manx Museum is the Old Grammar School, which was set up in St Mary's Chapel in 1702. The school was closed in 1930 and today serves as a museum documenting education in the Victorian period.

The road continues round Poolvash Bay and comes to Port St Mary (pop. 1400), a quiet little port and seaside resort. Beyond it extends a very beautiful peninsula, off which, beyond the Calf Sound, lies the Calf of Man. The wild beauty of the scenery can best be enjoyed by walking to Calf Sound (2½ miles) along the cliffs, past Spanish Head.

Port St Mary

The road continues to Cregneish (1½ miles), the most southerly places on the island. On Mull Hill (430 ft) there is a group of six chamber tombs known as the Mull Circle or Meayll Circle. At Cregneish is the ⋆**Manx Village Folk Museum**, a group of thatched cottages with their original furnishings and the implements of various trades and occupations (blacksmithing, fishing, weaving, as well as a shop).

Cregneish

The Calf of Man is a bird reserve with a large population of rare seabirds (over 130 different types), seals and the four-horned Loghtan sheep, so typical of the island. It can be visited outside the nesting season (boat from Port Erin). There are fine views from the highest point (360 ft).

Calf of Man

The picturesque resort of Port Erin (pop. 1800) lies at the head of a deep bay, sheltered by Bradda Head (400 ft). It is the terminal point of a small old-time steam railway from Douglas. The Marine Biological Station has an interesting aquarium. There is a commemorative plaque to a famous Manxman who came from Port Erin: Fletcher Christian, who instigated the famous mutiny on the Bounty; his adversary, Captain Bligh, is said to have been married on the island.

Port Erin

For wild beautiful scenery, a walk along the cliffs to Fleshwick Bay is recommended, continuing to the Niarbyl and Dalby (½ mile inland). In places the cliffs fall sheer down to the sea.

The road from Port Erin to Peel (14 miles) runs via Colby, with a picturesque gorge, Ballabeg, with the Round Table (1000 ft) and the higher South Barrule, Dalby and Glen Maye, with a beautiful waterfall.

Ballabeg

Peel (pop. 3100), halfway up the west coast of the island at the mouth of the little river Neb, is a picturesque fishing port which claims to produce the best kippers in Great Britain.

Peel

Outside the harbour, and linked by a causeway, lies the rocky isle of **St Patrick**, on which are **Peel Castle**, a red sandstone structure surrounded by a wall, and the **Cathedral**, the smallest of all the Anglican ones, dedicated to St Germanus, a disciple of St Patrick. The choir was built in 1226–47, while St Patrick's Chapel probably dates from the 9th c.

Odin's Raven in the boathouse at Peel is the replica of a Viking ship found at Oslo in Norway. The ship was brought over to Man in 1979.

From Peel a beautiful panoramic road runs high above the coast to Kirk Michael (6½ miles), passing White Strand, a fine bathing beach. Kirk Michael, the largest place in the north-west of the island, is beautifully situated between the coast and hills rising to 1600 ft.

Kirk Michael

From Kirk Michael it is possible to continue along the coast, perhaps with a detour to Point of Ayre, but the scenery along this stretch is less attractive, although there are some sand and shingle beaches. It is more interesting to take the inland road, over the wide Ayre plain with its low hills. The road runs past the Curragh, an area of heath and bog, some of which has been brought into cultivation. A mile beyond Ballaugh Bridge is the **Curragh Wild Life Park**. The road then continues via Sulby, a pretty little place in the valley of the river of the same name (with waterfall), to Ramsey.

Ramsey (pop. 4600), in a wide sandy bay, is the second largest place on the island. It is the traditional rival of Douglas, and the inhabitants were delighted when Queen Victoria (see Famous People) landed here in 1847, heavy seas having made it impossible to enter Douglas harbour.

Ramsey

The pier is now called the Queen's Pier. Ramsey offers a variety of pleasant walks – for example to Kirk Maughold, with a 13th c. church.

Laxey

Between Ramsey and Douglas is the little resort of Laxey (pop. 1340), linked to both towns by electric tram – a route of great scenic attraction. From here there is an electric mountain railway up Snaefell, the island's highest point (2036 ft), from which the four countries of Ireland, Scotland, England and Wales can be seen on a clear day. The town's main tourist attraction is the Lady Isabella, a huge ★**water-wheel** 72½ ft in diameter, built in 1854 to pump water out of the lead mines (now disused) of the Great Laxey Mining Company.

The summer house of Duncan Gibb, a Liverpool merchant, has been set up as the **Rural Life Museum** documenting country life in the Victorian era.

St John's

Visitors who are on the island on July 5th should not miss the ★**Tynwald Day ceremony** on the Tynwald Hill at St John's, 8½ miles east of Peel. On this ancient artificial mound, perhaps a Bronze Age burial mound, all the laws passed during the previous year are proclaimed in Manx and English, with traditional ceremonial.

Manchester

Central England
Metropolitan county: Greater Manchester
Altitude: 115 ft. Population of Greater Manchester: 2.8 m

Manchester, the centre of the south-east Lancashire conurbation, is the commercial and cultural capital of the north-west of England. With Salford and eight other municipalities, it forms the metropolitan county of Greater Manchester, in which some three million people now live – after London (see entry) the island's largest conurbation.

Manchester played an important part in the Industrial Revolution and the growth of the workers' movement. Well over 150 years have passed since Friedrich Engels (1820–95), the son of an industrialist from Wuppertal, visited what was then the most important industrial city of the British Empire and later published his dire observations in "Condition of the Working Classes in England". This is still a major work of Communist literature. After the decline of the textile sector about 80 years ago and the disappearance of whole branches of industry, there followed decades of decay and record unemployment before Manchester metamorphosed into an attractive business location and the new "business centre" of the North. Beside major companies like Kellogg's, Heinz, Shell, Siemens and IBM, BBC North and Granada Studios have become established in Manchester, the studios being Britain's largest private film and television producer and instrumental in productions such as the cult film "Four Weddings and A Funeral" (1994). Where chimneys smoked, today the entertainment business reigns. The industrially oriented Castlefield project is probably unique as a municipal open-air museum which now represents the old and new core of the city. In 1994 Manchester was celebrated as the "City of Drama". In 1996 the Nynex Arena was opened – with 16,500 seats it is the largest events hall in Europe. In 2002 Manchester will be hosting the Commonwealth Games. The city has long been an important scene for the pop and rave movements. Its two centres of learning, Victoria University and the technical university UMIST, both rank third on the subsidies list of the Ministry of Education, right after the elite Oxford and Cambridge universities (see entries).

The legendary Old Trafford Stadium of **Manchester United** is an

Manchester – heart of the English workers' movement

absolute must for football fans, Manchester United being for many Mancunians the best team in the world. The glorious history of the club founded 1878 and the cups and trophies of the "Red Devils" can be admired in the United Football Museum.

Transport Manchester lies at the point of intersection of the M6 (north–south) and M62 (east–west) motorways. The international airport is about 9 miles south of the city centre. Trains from the south (London, Birmingham) run into Piccadilly Station, while services from Lancashire, Wales, Scotland, North and West Yorkshire use Victoria Station.

History The Roman settlement of Mancunium was laid out on a flat gravel area. Its rise to prosperity began after Flemish immigrants introduced the manufacture of wool and linen in the 14th c. The extension of the canal network and road links with neighbouring towns and the Pennines, which took place between 1700 and 1750, created the right conditions for the rapid growth of the textile industry. By 1850 the transport infrastructure had been further extended by the creation of railway links, and in 1887–94 this expansion continued with the building of the 35½ mile long Manchester Ship Canal, which made the city navigable to ocean-going vessels (today up to 12,500 tons). Finally an international airport was established, second only to London.

These rail and canal links brought about the concentration of the textile industry in Manchester with its access to the sheep-rearing pastures of the Pennines and a skilled workforce. The first steam-driven spinning machines were the "Spinning Jenny", built by James Hargreaves in 1764, and Samuel Crompton's "Spinning Mule" of 1780. Five years later Edmund Cartwright invented the electric loom, which was however not successfully introduced until 1820. The distribution of the weaving and spinning branches of the industry became in effect a north-south division, with weaving being concentrated in the north of the city, spinning in the south. The cloth manufacturing industry's period of prosperity lasted until the end of the 19th c., whereas in the present century it has been beset by an increasing fall in demand and attendant crises.

The enormous range of **shopping** facilities available in Manchester include the elegant shops of St Anne's Square, King Street and Royal Exchange, and the large covered market halls of Bolton Arcade. As an alternative, the visitor can visit the Galleries Shopping Centre in the centre of Wigan or the smaller shops and businesses of Altrincham.

Just as entertaining and full of variety is a visit to the "Castlefield Urban   Castlefield

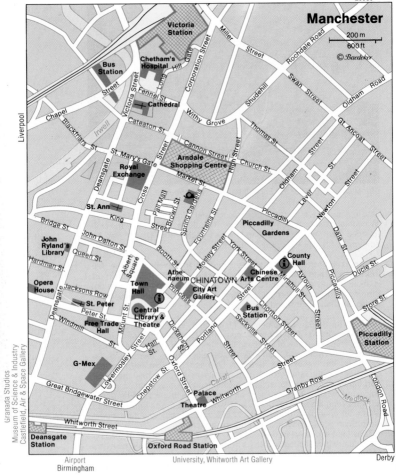

Manchester

200 m
600 ft
© Baedeker

Airport
Birmingham

University, Whitworth Art Gallery

Derby

Heritage Park", to the west of Deansgate Station. A walk among the lovingly restored Victorian houses, including the various new buildings which have been harmoniously added, along the old canals or to the reconstructed Roman fort – all of these things convey in a highly impressive way the history of Manchester from the earliest times to the present day.

★★Museum of
Science and
Industry

This industrial museum on Liverpool Road, Great Britain's "Museum of the Year" in 1990, informs the visitor about a large number of technical advances and innovations. With its twelve galleries it was erected on the site of the world's oldest railway station. In Power Hall (on the corner of Lower Byrom Street) it is possible to admire water and steam-driven machines from the golden period of the textile industry, as well as old steam locomotives, and veteran cars which were manufactured in

*Museum of Science and Industry:
Belsize Car (1912) ...*

... and Roe's triple-decker

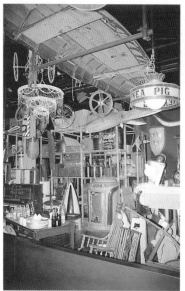

Granada TV studios: property store ...

... and mock-up of 10 Downing Street

Manchester

Manchester (including the Belsize motor car, 1912; Rolls Royce, 1904; Crossley Shelsey 15·7 hp saloon, 1929). The history of the city, from Roman times through the Industrial Revolution to the present day, is documented in the Station Building, which adjoins to the west, while in the Warehouse, a building dating from about 1830 which lies opposite, the creation and development of electricity and energy is explained. To the north of Power Hall in Lower Byrom Street Warehouse, printing and spinning machines can be seen, as well as computers from the very first models to the modern silicon chip. In the "Xperiment" on the upper floor, various models enable the visitor to learn more about the connection between light and energy in an active way.

Air and Space Gallery

On the east side of Lower Byrom Street stands the Air and Space Gallery, the home of numerous aircraft which made history, including a replica of the triple-decker Triplane 1 by A. V. Roe, which in 1909 was, with its 9 hp engine, the first British plane to go up into the sky, and a De Havilland Trident 3 B jet; other attractions include the spacesuit belonging to the astronaut Thomas Stafford and a flight simulator.

★★Granada TV Studios

Pleasure of a special kind is afforded by the two-hour tour of the Granada film studios, which were opened in 1988 and are situated to the north-west of the Museum of Science and Industry. This glimpse of the fascinating world of film and television includes a visit to the properties store, cutting room and various sets (e.g. those for 10 Downing Street and the House of Commons in London, the former Checkpoint Charlie in Berlin, Sherlock Holmes' residence at 221b Baker Street and those used for the popular television series, "Coronation Street") as well as various cinematic presentations, including 3D films.

Roman Fort

To the south, opposite the Air and Space Gallery, the visitor enters the northern gate of the ruins which have been uncovered of the Roman fort, which once existed here and which is now surrounded by lawns.

Waterways

The nearby Bridgewater Canal was constructed in 1759–61 to transport coal from the mines at Worsley to the up-and-coming new town of Manchester. Here, as at the Rochdale Canal, which was opened in 1804, Wigan Pier and Salford Quays to the west, between the River Irwell and the Manchester Ship Canal, many of the old warehouses have been restored and turned into offices, shops, hotels and restaurants. A boat trip on one of the Bridgewater packet boats is particularly recommended.

Castlefield Gallery

To the east of the Air and Space Gallery, the Castlefield Art Gallery has periodic exhibitions of contemporary art.

★Cathedral

The Cathedral, on the banks of the Irwell, is in Perpendicular style and dates mostly from 1422 to 1506. It was raised to cathedral status in 1847. The chapels on both sides of the nave and choir were built between 1486 and 1508, and there were further additions and alterations in almost every subsequent century. Particularly notable are the choir-stalls, with misericords which are among the most richly decorated in the country. The side chapels in the choir have been preserved, unlike those in the nave. St John's Chapel is the chapel of the Manchester Regiment. The little Lady Chapel has a wooden screen of about 1440. The octagonal chapterhouse, built in 1465, has mural paintings by C. Weight (1962) at the entrance, including a figure of Christ in modern dress.

Chetham's Hospital

Chetham's Hospital, just north of the cathedral, dates in part from 1422–61. It was originally a residence for priests of a collegiate foundation, and is now occupied by a music school. Its library is one of the oldest public libraries in England with a stock of over 100,000 books, half of which were printed before 1850.

Manchester Town Hall

The John Rylands Library is housed in a Neo-Gothic building to the south-west in Deansgate. Founded in 1653, it has over five million books and manuscripts and is England's main repository for early printed books.

★John Rylands University Library

The pedestrianised Albert Square is graced by the imposing façade of the Neo-Gothic Town Hall (1868–77), designed by Alfred Waterhouse. From the tower there is an excellent panoramic view, while the Council Chamber and the cycle of paintings by Ford Madox Brown depicting the history of the city merit special attention.

Town Hall

The Central Library next door is a large rotunda by E. Vincent Harris (1934) and houses nine specialised libraries.

Central Library

The Free Trade Hall, opened in 1951 and just a few minutes walk to the south-west in Peter Street, is home to the Hallé Orchestra. First-class concerts are regularly given here.

Free Trade Hall

The centrally situated Great Manchester Exhibition and Event Centre (12,000 sq. yd of exhibition area) is one of the newest such sites in England and is impressive for its size alone. It has been set up in the former buildings of the Victorian railway station on Windmill Street and Mosley Street.

G-Mex

Manchester

Cornhouse

Manchester's Centre for the Visual Arts is at 70 Oxford Street. For those interested in the moving image there are film showings, video and photographic workshops, and temporary exhibitions.

City Art Gallery

The City Art Gallery in Mosley Street possesses one of the largest collections in Britain outside London. The gallery includes works by the pre-Raphaelites, Flemish masters of the 17th c., French impressionists (Gauguin, Manet, Monet, etc.), German artists (Max Ernst), and examples of the work of almost every English artist of any note, including Stubbs, Constable and Turner (see Famous People). The sculpture collection includes works by Rodin, Maillol, Jakob Epstein and Henry Moore ("Mother and Child"; see Famous People).

★Chinatown

Chinatown, the colourful home of one of the largest Chinese communities in Great Britain, is only a stone's throw from the City Art Gallery. The richly decorated Chinese arched gateway which leads into this little district is especially striking. Many shops and restaurants offering a wide range of culinary delicacies (especially from Hong Kong and Peking) have become established in this quarter, while Chinese handicraft can be found at the Chinese Arts Centre in Charlotte Street.

Other museums

There are a number of other museums offering exhibitions on various specialised areas. The **National Museum of Labour History** (103 Princess Street) has interesting displays documenting the workers' movement, the **Jewish Museum** (190 Cheetham Hill) has a collection which deals with the Jewish community in Manchester, while in the **Museum of Transport** (Boyle Street/Cheetham Hill) there are over 60 old buses and other vehicles belonging to the city transport services.

Heaton Hall

Heaton Hall in Prestwich, built in 1772 in the Neo-Classical style by James Wyatt, is also worth visiting for its applied art and elegant furniture.

Platt Hall

Platt Hall, an elegant Georgian house (Wilmslow Road/Rusholme) built in 1764, presents an overview of English fashion and costume from 1600 to the present day.

Wythenshawe Hall

Porcelain, silver and paintings are on display in Wythenshawe Horticultural Centre, a half-timbered mansion.

University

The University of Manchester was founded in 1851 as Owens College, with the help of a bequest of £100,000 by John Owens (1790–1846), a wealthy merchant who left the money for the establishment of a university not subject to ecclesiastical influence. The "Manchester educational precinct" is a large complex which includes a variety of institutes and halls of residence.

Manchester University can claim three Nobel prizewinners: Ernest Rutherford (1871–1939), who put forward the theory of atomic disintegration and laid the foundations of modern atomic physics with his model of the atom (see Famous People); the physician James Chadwick, born in Manchester in 1791, who in 1932 proved the existence of the neutron (Nobel prize 1935); Sir John Cockcroft (1897–1967), one of the leading physicists in British and Canadian atomic research, who worked for a time in Manchester (Nobel prize 1951).

Close by the university is the Manchester Museum with extensive scientific collections. Its Egyptian collection is of particular interest.

Manchester Museum

Near Congleton (16 miles to the south) lies the tiny market town of Marton with a notable half-timbered church, one of the oldest in Europe. The Church of St James and St Paul was founded in 1343. The nave with its wall-paintings, of which just a few are still preserved, dates from this time, whereas the choir was added later, and the bell-tower in 1540. Renovation work carried out in the 19th and early 20th c. removed unnecessary decorations and ensured that this rare jewel of church architecture should be preserved in all its simplicity and charm.

Surroundings
★**Marton**

Another excursion can be made nearby to Little Morton Hall (22 miles to the south), one of the most impressive half-timbered mansions in England, begun around 1480 by Ralph Moreton, with the east wing being added in 1559 by a descendant, the south wing in 1563. Although almost none of the original interior fittings and furnishings have been preserved, the large multi-storeyed building, with its superb half-timbered construction and pretty inner courtyard, moat and garden, offers an excellent glimpse of what rural life was like in 16th c. Cheshire.

★**Little Morton Hall**

See entry

Peak District

Mid Wales

G–H 8

Counties: Powys and Dyfed

The area known as Mid Wales takes in the former counties of Montgomery and Radnor and part of Brecknock, now forming the new county of Powys (county town Llandrindod Wells), the former county of Cardigan, which is now part of Dyfed, and parts of Merioneth and Carmarthen.

The area has a wide variety of scenery, from the great sweep of Cardigan Bay with its sandy beaches to the border regions which were disputed with England for so many centuries. Here can be found farmland and sheep grazing pasture, characteristic half-timbered houses, tiny villages with old stone farmhouses surrounded by green fields in the middle of open heathland where time seems to have stood still.

In general the hills of Mid Wales are lower and less steep than those of South Wales, most of them being gently rounded and undulating. Large reservoirs provide drinking water for the conurbations of Liverpool (see entry) and Birmingham (see entry), but they are not favourably regarded by the Welsh nationalists, who perceive this to be the exploitation of their countryside.

The coast of Mid Wales offers two different types of scenery: sand dunes in the northern half, cliffs with small sandy beaches in the south, the latter providing the opportunity for long and beautiful cliff walks.

South of where the estuary of the River Mawddach opens into Barmouth Bay lies Fairbourne, with the smallest ★**narrow-gauge railway** in the country, the "Great Little Trains of Wales", running along the coast to the Barmouth passenger ferry. Anyone interested in rare butterflies should visit the **Butterfly Farm**.

Fairbourne

Passing the beach resort of Llwyngwril, at the foot of Cadair Idris, the A493 continues to Rhoslefain, where it leaves the coast and goes inland to Llanegryn (2 miles), a quiet little village whose church has a finely carved roof and a Norman font. Nearby is the mansion of **Peniarth**, where the famous Peniarth manuscripts, now in the National Library in Aberystwyth, were collected.

Llwyngwril

Mid Wales

Craig yr Aderyn

The road continues along the windings of the little River Dysynni for 2½ miles to Craig y Aderyn, the nesting-place of large numbers of sea birds, including cormorants. A little further on, the ruins of **Castell y Bere**, perched on a hilltop the far side of Llanfihangel, provide a fairy-tale-like backdrop. The fortress, which dates back to pre-Norman times, was already in ruins by the 14th c.

Abergynolwyn

From there a little road leads over to Abergynolwyn, the terminus of the ★**Talyllyn Railway** from Tywyn, which is claimed to be Wales's oldest narrow-gauge line (opened 1865) and has a width of only 27 in. It used to carry slate from the Abergynolwyn quarries but is now run for the benefit of holidaymakers, who enjoy delightful views of narrow gorges and woodland, with a glimpse of the Dolgoch Falls.

Tywyn

At Tywyn (pop. 4000), the wharf terminus of the line, the coastal road is rejoined. It is a seaside resort with a 3 mile long beach of sand and shingle, a golf-course and a variety of entertainments. In St Cadfan's Church, which is mainly Norman, can be seen ★**Cadfan's Stone**, 7 ft high, with the oldest inscription in the Welsh language written in old uncial lettering (7th/8th c.).

Aberdovey/ Aberdyfi

From here the coast road runs south to the mouth of the River Dovey and the town of Aberdovey/Aberdyfi, a favoured spot among sailing and angling enthusiasts.

Machynlleth

10½ miles up the Dovey valley is Machynlleth (pop. 1900), an attractive little town with broad tree-lined streets, little shops and a tall Victorian clock-tower. In the Middle Ages the rebel Owen Glendower (Owain Glyndwr) held his first parliament in 1404 to govern Wales. Plas Machynlleth, built in 1671, was formerly a residence of Lord Londonderry. Anyone interested in alternative technology should pay a visit to the new Centre for Alternative Technology.

Ynyslas, Borth

From Machynlleth the A487 runs south-west at a distance of some 3 miles from the coast, on which are the little seaside resorts of Ynyslas, at the mouth of the Dovey, and Borth, with a beautiful 3 mile long sandy beach. The road runs through Tre'r Ddol and Tre Taliesin, small villages which are good centres for walking in the Plynlimon range, above the flat coastal area between the Dovey valley and the Vale of Rheidol, and comes to Talybont.

Talybont

Talybont has a number of craft producers, particularly hand-weavers renowned for their tweed. In the old Celtic stone grave behind the village, the bard, Taliesin, the "Homer of Wales", is supposed to be buried.

Aberystwyth

6 miles to the south is Aberystwyth (pop. 13,000), unofficial capital of Mid Wales, situated at the mouth of the rivers Rheidol and Ystwyth (hence the town's name, which in Welsh means "mouth of the Ystwyth"), which join just before reaching the coast. Besides being a university town and a shopping town for Mid Wales, the town is also a popular seaside resort. The university was founded in 1872 as a branch of the National University of Wales (together with Cardiff (see entry) and Bangor). The university theatre Theatr Werin enjoys an outstanding reputation. From the lengthy pier, which extends out parallel with the wide beach, there is a splendid view of Cardigan Bay.

The ★**National Library of Wales** (founded in 1907), in Machynlleth Street, is one of the six libraries of deposit which receive a copy of every book published in Britain. It possesses some 2 million books and many thousands of manuscripts, with particular emphasis on Celtic and Welsh literature. From time to time it puts on special exhibitions displaying some of its treasures, including the "Black Book of Camarthan", the oldest document in Welsh, dating back to 1105.

On Aberystwyth pier

On a rocky crag are the remains of a castle built by Edward I. Near the university is Pen Dinas, the site of a powerful prehistoric hill-fort.

At **Llanfarian**, 3 miles to the south, is **Bryn Eithyn Hall**, with a collection of Welsh furniture, dolls, ship models, etc.

From Aberystwyth there is a beautiful road along the Vale of Rheidol to Devil's Bridge, about 9 miles to the east. Here the River Mynach flows down through a deep gorge in a series of spectacular waterfalls, with a total drop of 300 ft, to join the Rheidol. There are three bridges, the lowest of which, believed to date from the 12th c., is known as the Devil's Bridge. Tradition has it that this bridge was built by a monk from Strata Florida Abbey, 7 miles to the south. The two other bridges were built in 1753 and 1901 (the highest one a rail bridge).

★**Devil's Bridge**

3 miles to the north is Nant y Moch Lake, well stocked with fish. Here there is a nature reserve with a number of waymarked nature trails.

From Aberystwyth to Devil's Bridge there is a narrow-gauge steam railway, covering the 12 miles. It was originally built in 1902 to carry lead from the many mines in the hills, the last of which closed down in 1912.

Nant y Moch

Little is left of Strata Florida Abbey (Welsh "Ystrad Fflur" = valley of flowers), a Cisterian foundation of 1196 near the source of the River Teifi, although it was in its day one of the leading monastic houses in Wales and a great cultural centre. The finest surviving fragment is the west doorway, but there are also remains of the sacristy and chapterhouse as well as a number of tombstones. The medieval Welsh poet Dafydd ap Gwilym is buried here.

Strata Florida Abbey

The road along the Elan valley from Devil's Bridge leads to the pretty little country town of Rhayader, in the upper Wye valley, a popular tourist centre with fine Welsh craft goods to offer (hand-woven cloth, pottery). Here there are facilities for pony trekking in the surrounding hills with their picturesque little lakes. The **Elan Valley** and the Claerwen reservoir, though serving the purposes of water supply, are of great scenic beauty.

Rhayader

From Rhayader we continue east by either the A470 or the A44 to

Llandrindod Wells

reach the county town of Powys, Llandrindod Wells (pop. 4065), the leading spa, of Wales, with magnesium, sulphur, chalybeate and other springs. In its heyday the town attracted some 80,000 visitors every year to take the cure, mainly for rheumatism and gout. From this period it has preserved a legacy of Georgian houses, wide streets, spacious parks and numerous hotels. There are excellent facilities for sport and entertainment, while the museum in Temple Street has an interesting archaeological collection. The golf-course, 1100 ft above sea level, with fine views of the valley below, is one of the highest in Britain. There is good fishing in the River Eithon and the lake in the middle of the town.

Castell Collen

2 miles to the north, at Castell Collen, are the remains of a Roman camp.

Howey

From Llandrindod Wells the A 483 runs south to Builth Wells, where the Irfon flows into the Wye, passing through the quiet little village of Howey. Formerly it was a town of some consequence, with four markets a year, near the drove road on which the cattle were driven from Wales into England.

Builth Wells

Builth Wells is still an important cattle market, the scene of the Welsh Agricultural Society's annual show in July, to which the best cattle in Wales are sent. The town itself was almost completely destroyed by fire in 1691. Of the medieval castle which once stood here practically nothing is left.

Aberedw, Erwood

From Builth Wells the A470 ascends the beautiful Wye valley, passing through Aberedw, with a very fine 15th c. church and its famous rocks, and Erwood, a pretty little place on the Wye, where Henry Mayhew is said to have conceived the idea of "Punch", to the Black Mountains and the Welsh Marches.

Llanrhystyd Llanon, Aberaeron

On the coast south of Aberystwyth are the seaside resorts of Llanrhystyd and Llanon, both with shingle beaches. Then comes Aberaeron, an old fishing port (pop. 1300) with many Georgian houses, at the mouth of the Aeron.

Lampeter

From here it is worth while making an excursion inland to Lampeter, a little market town in the Teifi valley, noted for the horse market in May which attracts buyers and sellers from all over Britain. St David's College (founded 1827), in a fine Neo-Gothic building, has university status and has close associations with Oxford and Cambridge.

Tregaron

10 miles north-east and situated amid beautiful hills is Tregaron, a popular place with summer visitors. For those interested in nature, the high moorland area called the Bog of Tregaron is a nature reserve, covering an area of 500 sq. miles, is well worth visiting.

New Quay

South-west of Aberaeron is New Quay/Cei Newydd (6½ miles), a pleasant seaside resort with plenty of entertainments and a good beach.

Llangranog

Beyond this is Llangranog, most picturesque with its small bay between high cliffs. A path leads to Ynys Lochtyn, with the remains of an old castle.

Aberporth

Aberporth is a very popular resort with a good sandy beach.

Mwnt

A pleasant trip can be made to Mwnt, a charming and secluded beach with beautiful cliff scenery.

Newcastle-upon-Tyne

K 5/6

North-east England. County: Tyne and Wear
Altitude: 89 ft. Population: 210,000

Newcastle is a county town and in an economic as well as cultural sense the capital of the north-east of England. This industrial city stands on the River Tyne, which is here spanned by six bridges and is about 9 miles from its mouth. Newcastle, along with neighbouring towns, has grown into the conurbation of Tyneside. Previously it was an important exporting port, in particular for coal, but this activity has in latter years become drastically reduced, although the importance that coal once had is reflected in the phrase "carrying coals to Newcastle". Newcastle's centres for heavy industry, mechanical engineering, shipbuilding, chemicals and locomotive building today suffer greatly, in common with other large towns in Northern England, from the effects of the industrial structural crisis and the prolonged recession. The newest restructuring attempts are local initiatives which form part of national projects and attract foreign investment, for instance firms set up by the offshore oil industry, such as Press Production, and investors such as Dunlop Armaline and British Telecom Marine.

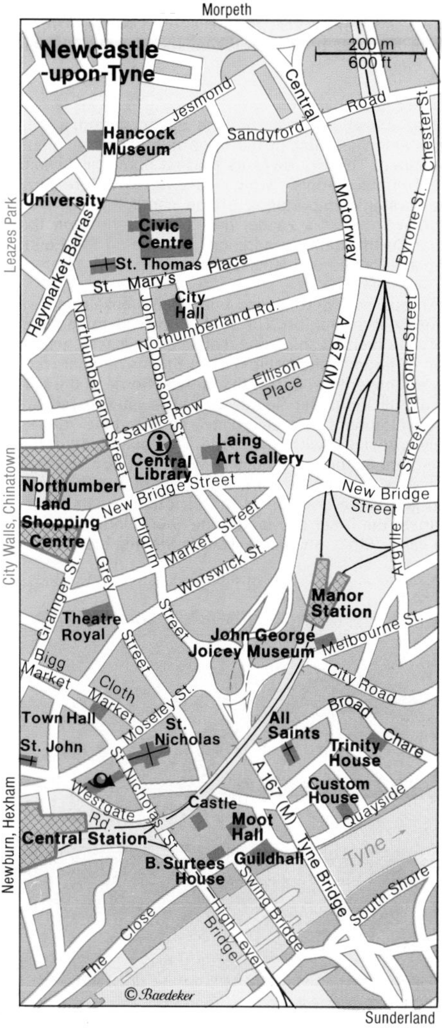

The city centre possesses some noteworthy Vic-

Newcastle-upon-Tyne

torian buildings and historic streets, one of the largest shopping centres in the country around Eldon Square, as well as a number of interesting museums and varied entertainment facilities, including the prestigious performances offered by the Victorian Theatre Royal in Grey Street.

Transport Newcastle Airport is 6 miles to the north-west of the city centre; there are bus and metro connections. From the Central Station there are direct InterCity connections with Scotland, London, Yorkshire, the Midlands, the South-west and Wales. Car ferries from Scandinavia (Bergen, Stavanger, Gothenburg) arrive at the North Shields Ferry Terminal (east of the city centre via the A 1058 and A 19). The ferry "Winston Churchill" runs from Newcastle to Hamburg between April and September. There are also boat trips within the city itself which leave from Quayside Pier.

History In Roman times the city, then called Pons Aelius, was a fort on Hadrian's Wall (see entry), while during the Saxon period it was known as Monk Chester on account of the large number of religious houses which it contained. The city owes its present name to William the Conqueror (see Famous People), who, like Hadrian before him, had recognised the strategic importance of the camp and in 1080 gave his son the order to erect a castle, the "New Castle", on the site of the old Roman fortification. In addition, he ordered the building of the St Nicholas' Cathedral (dedicated to the patron saint of sailors).

The city's most famous period coincided with the establishment of the coal-mining industry in the region. The coal which was mined was transported up the Tyne on small ships or "keels" to Newcastle, where it was transferred on to larger freight ships. Export taxes on coal were the basis for the city's prosperity in Elizabethan times. Some of the pioneering inventions of the Industrial Revolution, especially in railway engineering, the development of electricity and turbine driven machines, are closely associated with Newcastle. The foundation of the famous locomotive-manufacturing industry was laid by George Stephenson (see Famous People) in 1823. The designs for the city's development, which led to the creation of the Victorian streets which even now still dominate the inner city landscape, were undertaken by John Dobson in the early 19th c. and carried out in the first instance by Richard Grainger.

Newcastle: Tyne and Swing Bridges

Sights

Approaching Newcastle from the south, the visitor sees six different bridges spanning the Tyne. The three best known became internationally famous for the revolutionary approach to bridge-building which they enshrined. The oldest is the High Level Bridge, a two-level steel structure almost 165 ft high, the upper level reserved for railway traffic, the lower one for motor vehicles. The bridge was built to plans drawn up in 1849 by Robert Stephenson, son of the legendary locomotive inventor, and was opened by Queen Victoria. The Swing Bridge, which was designed by Sir W. G. Armstrong and opened in 1876, stands on the same site as the "Pons Aelius" built by Roman legionaries. However, the bridge which has the oldest construction and really symbolises the city's identity is the Tyne Bridge, begun in 1925 and officially opened by King George V in 1928. At that time it had the largest arch of any bridge in the world, although only months later this record was usurped by the new Sydney Harbour Bridge in Australia.

★Tyne Bridges

Bessie Surtees House

The Quayside district around the Tyne and High Level Bridges has been redeveloped and many of the old houses have been turned into small hotels, shops and restaurants; on Sundays a pleasant stroll may be taken through the colourful junk market which is held here. On ★**Sandhill** a number of historic buildings can be seen, including the Guildhall (1658, rebuilt in the early 19th c.) and the Merchants' Court with a fireplace dating from 1636. The lovingly restored **Bessie Surtees House** (41–44 Sandhill) consists of two merchant's houses, dating from the 16th/17th c., with a Jacobean façade which has been restored to its original state. Inside, the English Heritage puts on seasonal exhibitions. The building derives its name from the pretty banker's daughter, Bessie Surtees, who fell in love with John Scott, the son of a coal merchant from Love Lane. In 1772, when Bessie's parents tried to forbid the alliance, the couple eloped at night in the fog to Scotland, where they got married. John Scott was later to become a successful lawyer and as Lord Eldon rose to be Lord Chancellor.

Quayside

North of the High Level Bridge on St Nicholas Street the Norman fortified tower bears testimony to the former **"New Castle"**, which was begun in 1080 by Robert Courthose, the eldest son of William the Conqueror, and completed in 1168–72 by Henry II. The late Norman chapel, the "King's Chamber" and the display of archaeological finds are of particular interest, while from the tower there is a fine view.

The gatehouse, which is now separated from the castle by the railway line, is called the **Black Gate**. It was built in 1247 and has been altered several times.

The cathedral is in Mosley Street, which leads off from St Nicholas Street in an easterly direction. This building, which was built mainly in the 14th and 15th c., is not especially large, having only been elevated from the status of parish church to cathedral in 1882. Its lantern tower (almost 197 ft high) was built in 1435–70, the first of four similar buildings existing in Great Britain, and is topped by the strikingly crenellated "Scottish Crown", a spire which is floodlit at night to impressive effect. Features of the interior which are worth seeing include the canopied font and lectern (both dating from 1500), the organ (1676) and the numerous statues (15th/16th, 20th c.), some of them of great interest.

★St Nicholas Cathedral

Earl Grey's Monument

Shopping in the Central Arcade

Victoria Memorial	The statue of Queen Victoria (see Famous People) in St Nicholas Square was the work of Sir Alfred Gilbert (1900).
Chares	To the east of the Tyne Bridge we come to one of the oldest parts of the city, the Chares, with narrow streets and stepped pathways. Of interest are the Custom House (1766) and Trinity House (1721). The **Trinity Maritime Centre** on Broad Chare is housed in a former warehouse dating from the middle of the 19th c. With the help of models of historic ships and the Quayside district, the eventful history of the city and its port is told. The **Church of All Saints**, which was built in the Neo-Classical style by David Stephenson in the 18th c., possesses some elaborate mahogany woodwork and probably the largest brass in England. The latter, which lies on the tomb of Roger Thomton (d. 1429) and his wife (d. 1411), is decorated with 92 figures. Not far away to the north, in the historic building of the Holy Jesus Hospital on City Road, is the **John George Joicey Museum**, which contains various valuable objects connected with local history, as well as an audio-visual show about the flood disaster of 1771 and the Great Fire on Quayside (1854).
★ Grey Street	Joining Mosley Street further to the west is Grey Street, at the north end of which is the 135 ft high column of **Earl Grey's Monument**, a favourite meeting-place in the heart of the city. From the column's viewing platform (164 steps) there is a superb view. The monument which was designed by E. H. Bailey in 1835 in memory of the 2nd Earl Grey, who as Prime Minister had been the architect of the 1832 Reform Bill.
★ Grainger Street	Grainger Street, which also ends at Grey's Monument, is one of the city's

most attractive shopping streets. Richard Grainger (1798–1861) was the main architect responsible for the rebuilding of the city centre in 1830.

An enormous shopping complex has developed around Eldon Square, comprising the shopping centre of the same name, the Central Arcade and the Northumberland Court Shopping Centre. This area has numerous passageways lined with shops, elegant arcades, exclusive designer boutiques, restaurants, cafés and pubs, ideal for looking around at leisure. Those looking for antiques should find a large choice in Vine Lane Market at the end of Northumberland Street.

★Eldon Square

Vine

A short distance to the west of Eldon Square Shopping Centre there is a Chinese district around Stowell Street, famous for its excellent restaurants.

Chinatown

A section of the old medieval city walls, now restored, can be seen running parallel to Stowell Street.

City Walls

The monastic buildings of Blackfriars in Monk Street, which date from the 13th c., today house craft workshops and a restaurant.

Blackfriars

The Laing Art Gallery, to the west of Grey's Monument on Higham Place, was designed by the architects Cackett & Burns Dick, the foundation stone being laid in 1901. The museum contains an extensive collection of paintings and sculptures, including old masters, works by Gauguin, romantic impressions by John Martin and pictures by the British artist, Stanley Spencer, sculptures by Henry Moore (see Famous People), valuable antiques from the 16th–18th c., glassware and ceramics from the Tyneside region, and archaeological finds from Greek and Roman times.

★Laing Art Gallery

Following John Dobson Street to the north, the visitor will immediately reach the Civic Centre, built in the 1960s, whose chimes are based on local tunes. The statue depicting the Tyne river-god is also noteworthy.

Civic Centre

To the north-west on Barras Bridge is the Hancock Museum, with its natural history and ethnology sections, derived from the private collection of Marmaduke Tunstall of Wycliffe. Among the many exhibits there are Egyptian mummies, reproductions of dinosaurs and mammoths, a collection of minerals and fossils. In addition there are zoological collections devoted to mammals, birds and insects, while a geological section explains the history of the area's formation.

Hancock Museum

The complex of buildings which make up the University (founded in 1963) includes a number of interesting museums.

University of Newcastle

The **Museum of Antiquities** in the Quadrangle is noteworthy for its collection, assembled in 1813, of prehistoric, Roman and Anglo-Saxon objects. Of especial interest are the excavation finds and the lifelike model of Hadrian's Wall (see entry), which can be a good source of information before visiting the actual wall itself. There is also a reconstructed altar to Mithras dating from the 3rd c., which was found at Housesteads.

The Percy Building houses the **Greek Museum**, an important collection of Greek and Etruscan vases, terracottas and bronze implements.

The neighbouring **Hatton Gallery** has works by European painters from the 14th to the 18th c. as well as paintings by modern English artists.

Those interested in technology are recommended to go to the extensive materials on display in the **Department of Mining Engineering**, which deal with the coal-mining industry in the region. The hard work and drudgery which went on in the collieries in the middle of the last century are impressively brought to life in the paintings of T. H. Hair.

Among the many exhibits in the Museum of Science and Engineering on Blandford Square, which charts the pioneering achievements of the

Museum of Science and Engineering

401

Imitation mammoths in the Hancock Museum

Museum of Antiquities: Mithras altar replica   *Newcastle University tower*

north-east of England over the last 200 years, there are machines ranging from the traditional windmill and early steam machines to ultra-modern jet turbines. Also on show is the locomotive built by George Stephenson in 1830 for the coal-mines of Killingworth, a model recreating the River Tyne in 1929, as well as various models of ships, including the first turbine-driven steamer in the world, the "Turbinia", designed by Charles Parsons and launched in 1914. Visitors can also gain hands-on experience of some of the objects on display.

Jesmond Dene, a lovely dell in the north-east of the city, linked to Armstrong Park, must be one of the most attractive city parks in the country. "Dene" is the local designation for the type of narrow, glacial meltwater valley which came into being at the end of the last Ice Age. A nature trail has also been laid out in the park, which was made accessible to the general public at the instigation of Lord William Armstrong.

⋆Jesmond Dene

New Forest   K 10

Southern England. County: Hampshire

In spite of its name, the New Forest is by no means new and is not a continuous area of forest, large parts of it being heath and moorland, with a certain amount of agricultural land as well. It extends over an area of some 145sq. miles from Southampton (see entry) to the River Avon at Ringwood.

From the time of William the Conqueror (see Famous People) the New Forest was a royal hunting preserve, while in the 19th c. it was declared a recreational area. Today the forest has been designated a nature conservancy area, even though large tracts of it still belong to the Crown. The wildlife of the forest is symbolised by the famous "New Forest Ponies", which are to be found wherever one goes. Motorists therefore need to proceed slowly and with care, as ponies are likely to stray on to the road at any time.

Extensive re-afforestation is now in progress; a visit in spring can be particularly lovely, when wild flowers are in bloom everywhere, and also when the heather is out. Away from the roads the visitor is able to find real peace and quiet, although occasionally it is possible to come across adders. The Forestry Commission has signs up warning about these snakes, and others alerting people to the dangers posed by areas of marshy land and bog. Besides walking in the forest, it is possible to take a ride in a horse-drawn cart. These are available in Brockenhurst, Burley and on the Butterfly Farm in Ashurst.

A good starting point for a tour of the Forest is Lyndhurst, the unofficial "capital" of the New Forest (pop. 2900). Inside the Victorian parish **Church of St Michael** (1858–69) there are fine capitals decorated with reproductions of leaves and fruit from the New Forest, as well as the tomb of the sculptor John Flaxman and a Neo-Classical fresco of the Wise and Foolish Virgins (1864) by Lord Leighton. Of special note are the large coloured east window and the northern transept window, both the work of Edward Burne-Jones (1862).

Lyndhurst

The road leading north to Cadnam (A337) passes through Minstead, where **Sir Arthur Conan Doyle** is buried.

The **Rufus Stone** (3½ miles north-west of Lyndhurst) was set up in its present position in 1745. It is said to mark the spot where King William Rufus (William II) was killed by an arrow in 1100 while out hunting.

In this area of woodland (2 miles south-west of Lyndhurst) there are romantic old oak-trees, some of them of considerable size.

Minstead

★ Beaulieu Abbey   Well worth a visit is Beaulieu Abbey (8 miles south-east of Lyndhurst). This Cistercian house was founded in 1204 by King John and subsequently dissolved by Henry VIII (see Famous People). Margaret of Anjou and her son found refuge here in 1471. The large gatehouse was converted into a dwelling-house in 1538 and today the Palace House is the seat of Lord Montagu of Beaulieu. In the Early English refectory there is a beautiful reader's pulpit. The principal attraction of the house and park is the ★★National Motor Museum with over 200 vintage and veteran models, as well as racing cars and motorcycles.

Buckler's Hard   Buckler's Hard (3 miles down river from Beaulieu) is a picturesque little place dating from the 17th c. Many famous ships, including "Agamemnon", the flagship of Lord Nelson (see Famous People), were built here between 1750 and 1820, using oak from the New Forest, prior to the advent of iron steamships. This significant chapter in English seafaring history is commemorated by a small Maritime Museum.

★ Exbury Gardens   4 miles south-east of Beaulieu are the very beautiful Exbury Gardens, planted by Edmond de Rothschild (d. 1942).

Northampton   L 8

Central England
County: Northamptonshire
Altitude: 300 ft. Population: 158,000

Location   Northampton, county town of Northamptonshire, is an important industrial town, noted particularly as a centre for the boot and shoe industry. At the end of the 17th c. the town was ravaged by a fire which destroyed many historic old buildings, including some dating from the Saxon and Norman periods. The town, which lies on the northern bank of the River Nene, possesses two important churches and one of the largest market places in England.

History The dispute between Henry II and Thomas Becket in 1164 took place in Northampton Castle, the site of which is now occupied by a railway station. During the Wars of the Roses (1455–85), Lancastrian forces were defeated not far from the town in 1460 and Henry VI was taken prisoner.

Sights
Church of the
Holy Sepulchre   Northampton has one of England's four round churches, the Church of the Holy Sepulchre in Sheep Street, which is modelled on the Church of the Holy Sepulchre in Jerusalem. It originally belonged to a monastic house and was founded by Simon de Senlis, Earl of Northampton (d. 1109), who had taken part in a crusade to the Holy Land. The present nave, eight steps higher than the original one, is in Early English style, the apse is modern, the tower Perpendicular. The interior is highly impressive with its massive Norman piers; the choir, built in 1860–64 under Sir Gilbert Scott, is worth a special look.

Shopping and
entertainments   In the city centre, the shops in the Grosvenor Centre and around the neighbouring Market Square offer an excellent choice. The modern Derngate entertainments complex offers both cultural and sporting events, including the Victorian Theatre Royal.

Other churches   Near the Market Square stands All Saints Church, built after the 1675 fire, with a 14th c. tower which survived the fire. On the front there is a statue of Charles II wearing a toga and a full wig (1712). The Church of St Peter, in Marefair, is a typical example of the richly decorated Middle Norman style (about 1160). St Matthew's Church in Kettering Road is worth a visit for the sake of Henry Moore's "Madonna and Child" (1944) and Graham Sutherland's "Crucifixion" (1946).

The **Central Museum and Art Gallery** in Guildhall Road reflects the town's main industry and contains a collection of footwear from Roman times to the present day. Nearby in Bridge Street there is also the **Leatherwork Museum** (including objects from ancient times to contemporary designs).

Museums

Abington Park (1 mile; on the Wellingborough road out of Northampton) was once the home of Shakespeare's granddaughter, Lady Elizabeth Bernard. The mansion, which dates from the 15th c., was substantially rebuilt in 1740 and is today a museum.

Surroundings
Abington
Museum

Althorp House (6 miles to the north-west) is the seat of the Earl Spencer. The mansion was built in 1573, but its present appearance is owed largely to alterations carried out by Henry Holland at the end of the 18th c. In summer the house is open to the public and visitors can admire the outstanding collection of paintings, which includes works by Reynolds, van Dyck, Kneller and Gainsborough, as well as the valuable porcelain collection.
   The grounds of the house also contain the grave of Princess Diana, the brother of the present Earl of Spencer, and a small memorial museum. Tickets should be pre-booked (tel: 01604 770107).

Althorp House

Castle Ashby (6 miles to the east), former seat of the Marquess of Northampton and now a training and conference centre, is an Elizabethan house with a façade of 1635 and an interesting stone balustrade lettered with the Latin text of Psalm 127. The park, which was designed by "Capability Brown", is well worth seeing.

Castle Ashby

North Devon Coast   G/H 9/10

South-west England. County: Devon

The cliffs of North Devon, buffeted by the Atlantic waves, are widely held to offer the most breathtaking cliff scenery in the whole of Great Britain. These slate formations on the Bristol Channel, differing in age and colour and often much weathered, are impressive in their grandiose beauty. This coastal area combines with the adjoining Exmoor, which rises to a height of 750 ft in Dunkery Beacon, to form a holiday region of great variety, from the lively seaside resorts on the Bristol Channel to the tiny and secluded villages in the heart of the moor.

Barnstaple (pop. 25,000) claims, on the strength of a charter granted in 830, to be the oldest town in England. Situated on the estuary of the River Taw, it is a good centre from which to explore North Devon. There was a harbour here even in Norman times, the bridge across the river being erected in 1273. John Gay, the composer of "The Beggar's Opera", was born here in 1685. Historic buildings, which are also interesting from an architectural point of view, are the Guildhall (1826), Horwood's Almshouses (1674) in Church Lane, Penrose's Almshouses (1627) in Litchdon Street and Salem House (1834) in Trinity Street. The parish church of SS Peter and Paul, unfortunately much altered during its restoration by Gilbert Scott (1866–82) possesses an unusual tower with a crooked spire (13th c.) Also of interest is the Colonnade of the Bristol Merchant Venturers, built in 1708 as a stock exchange, with a statue of Queen Anne. The former St Anne's Chapel houses a local museum with mementoes of John Gay.

Barnstaple

North Devon Coast

Bideford

9 miles south-west is Bideford (pop. 13,000), another old seaport, situated on the estuary of the Torridge with a bridge comprising 24 arches. There are many handsome houses of the 17th, 18th and early 19th c.; the Church of St Mary's is rightly proud of its fine Norman font. On the picturesque quay, a relic of the time when Bideford carried on a thriving trade with America, there is a statue of Charles Kingsley (1819–75), who wrote his famous novel "Westward Ho!" in a house which is now part of the Royal Hotel.

Westward Ho!

Westward Ho!, a seaside resort named after Kingsley's novel, lies 4 miles to the north-west. It has a fine sandy beach 3 miles long and a golf-course.

Lundy Island

Lundy Island, also known as Puffin Island, is a windswept granite islet 11 miles off Hartland Point and can be reached by boat from Bideford, Ilfracombe and Barnstaple. There is also a helicopter connection. The island is 3½ miles long and ½ mile wide and has cliffs towering out of the sea to a height of 500 ft. It was formerly owned by M. C. Harman, who founded a society here to investigate the rare flora and fauna on the island. In 1929 he also gave the island its own currency and stamps, the latter being still valid even today. Large areas of the island, which today belongs to the National Trust, have been set aside as bird reserves. There is evidence of the island's history in the ruins of Marisco Castle, a pirates' stronghold, and Millcombe House (1836).

★★Clovelly

Clovelly is one England's most renowned beauty spots, crowded with visitors in summer. Perched on a narrow ridge of rock which falls steeply away to the sea, the village and its surrounding countryside can best be viewed from the tiny pier or, even better, from the sea. At the end of the village is Yellary Gate, the entrance to the grounds of Clovelly Court,

A puffin on Lundy Island

with attractive walks through delightful scenery, a round trip of some 5 miles and a shorter trip of 3 miles along Hobby Drive.

Woolacombe, situated to the north-west (17 miles), is a pleasant seaside resort with a sandy beach 2 miles long. Excellent walks are possible to three coastal promontories, Baggy Point, Morte Point and Bull Point, which have striking rock formations.

Woolacombe

Ilfracombe (pop. 9500) is the oldest established and most popular seaside resort on the North Devon coast, with a picturesque harbour and good bathing beaches sheltered by towering cliffs. The town, largely built in the last third of the 19th c., differs from other resorts in having been built between hills, the beaches being reached through tunnels in the rock. The old chapel of St Nicholas, on a crag above the harbour, has been converted into a lighthouse. To the west of the town is the attractive Torrs Walk.

Ilfracombe

The beautiful coast road continues east to Watermouth Castle, with fine subtropical gardens, and Combe Martin, where the A399 turns inland on to Exmoor, most of which is now a National Park. Much of the area is cultivated, but there are still expanses of moorland and heath.

Exmoor National Park

The road passes Parracombe on its way to Lynton and Lynmouth (pop. 2000), the latter lying on the coast, the former 400 ft above sea level, near the point where the East and West Lyn join before flowing into the sea. The old word "llyn" means "rushing torrent" and the River Lyn certainly lived up to the name in the great flood of 1952 which destroyed much of Lynmouth, so that the village had to be almost entirely rebuilt. Although the resort is a popular one, the bathing is not particularly good. The beauty of the surrounding countryside, however, more than makes up for this, with particularly attractive spots being the ✴**Valley of Rocks**, **Woody Bay** and **Watersmeet**. Beyond this is the county boundary, the rest of the coastline being in Somerset.

Lynton, Lynmouth

North Downs   L/M 9

South-east England. Counties: Surrey and Kent

The North Downs are a ridge of high ground running parallel to the coast, which extends southwards from the Thames Basin across the counties of Surrey and Kent, from Guildford in the west to the fantastic white chalk cliffs of Dover in the east. The word "downs" in this sense has nothing to do with height, but is linked to the word "dunes". The North Downs are composed of chalk and slope steeply to the north. With the South Downs (see entry), they belong to the Weald system, a geological morphological anticline made of chalk and sandstone. They were formed during the Tertiary Age, at the same time that the Alps were thrust upwards further to the south.
    Running to the west, near Guildford, is the narrow ridge known as the Hog's Back. To the east the North Downs increase steadily in height and breadth, and reach some 900 ft on the Kent border. The downs are popular with walkers, especially at weekends, offering great variety of scenery – pastureland, fertile arable land, occasional areas of heath and scrub and patches of mixed forest – so that they never become monotonous. Five rivers have forced their way through the barrier of chalk and in the valleys lie trim little villages, often surrounded by fruit orchards. One of the main attractions of the area is the large number of castles, stately homes and parks. The footpaths in the region often follow the same course as old trading routes, either across the downs or along the

English Parks

Luxuriant flowers, massive gnarled trees overgrown with ivy, huge exotic ferns, rushing waterfalls, dreamy waterlily ponds, orgies of colour formed by rhododendrons, fuchsias, magnolias, camelias, primulas, violets and other often unknown subtropical plants, framed by expanses of green lawns – all these are typical features which express the aesthetic vision of the English landscaped garden.

Garden of Osborne House (Isle of Wight)

From the medieval monastery garden to the Baroque parkland of the 17th c., the English style of gardening was heavily influenced by the geometric forms bequeathed from French and Italian models. It was not until the beginning of the 18th c. that there was enthusiasm for a more natural - seeming environment, inspired by famous painters such as the Frenchmen Claude Lorrain and Nicolas Poussin, who began to portray their ancient heroes with a background of rugged romantic landscapes. This newly awakened feeling for nature not only inspired the literary circles of Europe to the most wide-ranging treatment of nature and the natural world, but also provided the basis for the outstanding achievements of the English school of landscape painting (Turner, Gainsborough, Reynolds, etc.), and indirectly brought about a special and innovative creative consciousness among English landscape gardeners.

Charles Bridgeman (1680–1738) was probably the first gardener who broke away from the authoritarian rules of symmetrical garden planning around a central axis and sought to preserve the natural charm of the landscape. The "Royal Gardener" designed over 30 private gardens, always taking into account the topographic character of the natural scenery. It was William Kent (1684–1748), however, who raised English landscape gardening to an art form, designing his parks with winding pathways, viewpoints and clearings in which he placed heroic statues, miniature temples and ruins. Claremont Park near London is one of Kent's masterpieces. The most famous landscape gardener of his period, however, was Lancelot Brown (1716–83), who was given the nickname "Capability", as he never ceased to devise new improvements and refinements for each garden that he designed. "Lady Nature's second husband", as he was called by the writer Horace Walpole, had a special instinct for natural beauty. Brown's designs display gentle, undulating contours; his spacious parks are no longer separated by walls from the

Gardens of Penshurst Place

surrounding land, but by ditches; in his landscapes harmoniously placed groups of trees are set off by seemingly natural expanses of water or lawn. Examples of his art are to be found at Stourhead, Bowood House, Sherborne Castle, Petworth House, Longleat House or Milton Abbas. With the romantic park of Blenheim Palace, Brown created the nonpareil of the English "landscape garden", which from 1760 onwards was to point the way for garden architecture all over Europe. America, Asia, and even Africa and Australia were won over by his style of landscape gardening. A fitting successor to the much-copied master emerged in the person of Humphrey Repton (1752–1818). This highly talented artist's innovation was to create terraces joining houses and gardens, which he decorated with lavish floral compositions. His love of detail is reflected in the elaborately organised groups of trees and flowers, usually of many different types, which he placed alongside large expanses of lawn. To complement these, he added picturesque rose and stone gardens, approached by concealed arbours, all of which created the perfect surroundings for those wanting a gentle stroll.

Subsequent "improvements" of many kinds mean that these parks today no longer correspond exactly to the original conception of a "Capability Brown" or a Humphrey Repton. Nevertheless they still continue to exhibit the elegant genial harmony of their creators with their extravagant array of plants and their scrupulously trimmed carpets of lawn. Anyone who has ever come under the fascination of these "Gardens of Eden", will readily understand the very characteristic English love of gardening.

The Regency mansion of Polesden Lacey

foot of the hills, while the Pilgrims' Way follows the old pilgrims' route from Winchester to Canterbury.

Guildford

Guildford (pop. 58,000) in Surrey, is a good base for the western part of the North Downs. Formerly the county town, it is still a favoured residential and shopping town. The ✷ **High Street** is one of the steepest and most picturesque in England, with a number of interesting old buildings. At the top of the street is the Grammar School, founded by Edward VI in 1553, with fine Tudor buildings and a library, the "Chaines Library", so called because it contains 89 books, chained up to prevent theft. Next comes the Jacobean Abbot's Hospital, with a large gatehouse and old furniture, founded by George Abbot, Archbishop of Canterbury, in 1619–22 for twelve men and eight women. The Town Hall, a brick and timber building, was given a new façade, including its famous clock, in 1683. St Mary's Church, near the foot of the hill, is mainly Late Norman (about 1180). Little is left of the old royal castle but the keep (about 1170).

Lewis Carroll (1832–98), the professor of mathematics from Oxford (see entry) and author of world-famous children's books, including "Alice in Wonderland" (1865), lived on and off at **"The Chestnuts"**, a house on Castle Hill. The author's grave, which bears his real name of Charles Lutwidge Dodgson, is to be found on the far side of the River Wye at a cemetery called The Mount.

The influences of Gothic style can be seen in the **Cathedral of the Holy Spirit**, one of the few new cathedrals in England, the foundation stone of which was laid in 1936. As a result of the war the church was not completed and consecrated until 1961.

Clandon Park (3 miles to the east) is the Jacobean seat of the Onslow family, with a mansion which was redesigned in the Palladian style in 1713–29 by Giacomo Leoni. There are richly decorated carpets and stucco ceilings, elaborately crafted furniture and tapestries, and a notable collection of Chinese porcelain birds (17th/18th c.). In the gardens, which were laid out by "Capability" Brown around 1770, there is an Ionian temple (1833) and the "Maori House", which was brought home from New Zealand by a member of the Onslow family who was once a governor there.

One of the most impressive viewpoints on the North Downs can be reached by taking the Leatherhead road (A246) as far as Merrow and then bearing right to Newlands Corner, from where there is a superb view across the flat saddle of the Weald.

★ Newlands Corner

Beyond this is Albury in the valley of the River Tillingbourne (4 miles south-east), with Albury Park, a seat of the Dukes of Northumberland. The house, rebuilt by Augustus Welby Pugin, contains a valuable collection of paintings, clocks and 64 different mantelpieces, which were in part the work of Robert Adam. Following the best Italian models, the park has a Roman bath and a cave inspired by the Grotto of Posilippo in Naples.

★ Albury Park

Further on to the east is Abinger Hammer. The "hammer" is a clock with the figure of a blacksmith, recalling the craftsmen of previous times. The hammers of the clock were once driven by water from the river.

Abinger Hammer

From here a beautiful road runs over the downs to Leith Hill (965 ft), from the top of which it is possible to see as far as London on a good day.

Leith Hill

The attractive Regency mansion of Polesden Lacey is situated just off the A246, a little way south of Great Bookham. The treasures belonging to the estate include the Grenville art collection with paintings by Reynolds, Lawrence, Raeburn and Italian masters of the 14th to 16th c., Flemish tapestries, porcelain from Meissen, Chelsea and Zürich, and valuable Renaissance furniture.

★ Polesden Lacey

Among the attractions of Dorking (5 miles; pop. 23,000) is a visit to the largest vineyard in England, the ★ **Denbies Wine Estate**, with a chance to taste one of 18 different wines produced on this 250 acre estate on the banks of the River Mole. The visitor centre has an interesting display on wine growing (open all year round).

Dorking

Part of the area belongs to the National Trust, including **Flint Cottage**, near **Mickleham**, in which the novelist George Meredith (1828–1909) lived for over 30 years until his death.

To the south is **Juniper Hall**, which at the end of the 18th c. provided

Knole: home of the Sackville family

a place of refuge for French refugees fleeing the Revolution, including Duke Charles Maurice de Talleyrand (1754–1838), who was Foreign Minister of France and represented France at the Congress of Vienna, and the writer Germaine de Staël-Holstein (1766–1817), known as Madame de Staël, whose main work "De l'Allemagne" (1810–13) offered French people the long-standing Romantic idealised picture of the "German poet and thinker".

★**Tunbridge Wells**

Another good centre from which to explore the North Downs is Tunbridge Wells (pop. 45,300), attractively situated on the northern slopes of the Weald. Its chalybeate springs made it a much frequented spa in the 18th c. In 1909 the town's name was changed by royal decree to Royal Tunbridge Wells. Illustrious visitors to the spa have included the dandy "Beau" Nash (see Bath) and the writers Daniel Defoe and John Gay. The main attractions today are the ★**"Pantiles"**, colonnaded cobbled promenades with shops, which have the distinction of being England's first pedestrian zone, and the columned passageways at the spa buildings where people could stroll while drinking the waters.

Sevenoaks

Another possible base is Sevenoaks (pop. 20,000), also attractively situated in the Greensand Hills. Adjoining Sevenoaks School is the entrance to **Knole Park**.

★★Knole, home of the Sackville family, is, with its inner courtyards and galleries, one of the largest and finest country houses in England. Begun in 1456 by Thomas Bourchier, Archbishop of Canterbury, it passed through the hands of the next three archbishops, but was demanded from the fourth, Thomas Cranmer, by Henry VIII (see Famous People), and consequently became crown property. Queen Elizabeth I (see Famous People) gave Knole away to her cousin Thomas Sackville, first Earl of Dorset, who had it considerably enlarged in 1603. Since that time, the house, now the property of the National Trust, has remained practically unaltered both externally and internally. The state apartments, first and foremost the royal bedroom, the ball-room and the Venetian ambassador's room, house an impressive art collection, including almost a dozen pictures by Reynolds, as well as works by Hoppner and Gainsborough, magnificent furniture decorated with gold brocade and pure silver, wonderful Persian carpets (1580), Mortlake tapestries and valuable porcelain. The writer Victoria Sackville-West (1892–1962), who was born at Knole, immortalised the house in her "Edwardians" of 1930; Virginia Woolf chose it as the setting for her novel "Orlando" (1928). A tour of the house is not complete without a stroll through the magnificent parkland with its peacefully grazing deer.

From Sevenoaks or from Tunbridge Wells it is only a few miles to Chiddingstone, a pretty little place with 16th and 17th c. houses and the parish church of St Mary, which was rebuilt in the Jacobean style after a fire. The pseudo-medieval Chiddingstone Castle, which dates from the 17th c., contains a variety of collections, including Stuart relics.

Chiddingstone

Another reminder of a past age of chivalry is ★ **Hever Castle**, situated to the west, which dates from the 13th–15th c., but was rebuilt in 1810 in Gothic style. This moated sandstone castle was where Anne Boleyn, the second wife of King Henry VIII, lived as a young girl. She was beheaded at the Tower of London, both because of her adultery, and merely because she failed to give the king an heir to the throne. There are very few, if any, reminders of this chapter of history at Hever. In 1903 the dilapidated estate was bought by the American William Waldorf Astor and completely restored for him by Frank L. Pearson in the style of the old masters. At the back of the castle, a Tudor village was recreated, and the park was given an Italian look with elaborate Renaissance sculptures. The hedges, clipped to form the shapes of chess figures, are also worth seeing. The grave of Anne Boleyn's father, Sir Thomas Boleyn (d. 1538), is to be found in the Church of St Peter.

Situated to the east of Chiddingstone, the village of Penshurst (5 miles from Tunbridge Wells) is dominated by its church, the old Leicester Arms Hotel on the other side of the street, but most of all by ★ **Penshurst Place**, a Gothic mansion with battlements dating from the middle of the 14th c., which is the seat of the Viscount de L'Isle. Passing its trimmed yew-trees and meticulously planned park, the visitor reaches the grey stone walls of the house, the north and west fronts of which date from 1585, as does the King's Tower. The medieval great hall of 1340 has massive chestnut beams supporting its roof. Its collection of paintings is dominated by pictures of the Sydneys, who once owned the estate. The visitor will also find old vineyards, a farm museum, a toy museum and an adventure playground for children.

Cranbrook (11 miles east of Tunbridge Wells; pop. 5600) is an old weavers' town with one of the largest windmills in England, a church rebuilt in 1430, and a school founded in 1576.

Cranbrook

★ **Sissinghurst Castle**, situated not far to the north-east, is well worth a visit. Of the original Tudor mansion dating from before 1550, only the four-storey gate-tower survives. In 1930 the property was acquired by Victoria Sackville-West (1892–1962), who lived here with her husband, the historian Sir Harold Nicholson. Her study in the tower contains the printing press which was used by Virginia and Leonard Woolf at the beginning of the 1920s to produce the first editions of the later much-famed Hogarth Press.

Nearby, on the edge of the Weald, is the village of Biddenden, where Siamese twins were born around 1500. In memory of these "maids of Biddenden", cakes stamped with a representation of the twins are still eaten here on Easter Monday. The village street boasts not only the

Biddenden

medieval parish church of All Saints, but also two 17th c. red-brick houses, Biddenden Palace and Hendon Hall. The half-timbered building Old Cloth Hall (16th/17th c.) was built for a well-to-do cloth merchant. Catweazle Manor (16th c.) with its hipped roof is also worth seeing.

✶Scotney Castle

The romantic buildings of Scotney Castle are to be found near Lamberhurst (8 miles south-east of Tunbridge Wells). The castle consists of an old 14th c. fortress surrounded by water and parts of two dwelling-houses dating from the 17th and 19th c. A special attraction of the well-kept gardens is the large number of rhododendron bushes.

Maidstone

The county town of Kent, Maidstone (pop. 74,000), is situated about 15 miles east of Sevenoaks. Along the river, and near the parish church of All Saints (1381–96) with its elaborate misericords and superb glass windows (18th c.), there is a fine group of 14th c. houses. The Archbishop's Palace (14th c.), which adjoins the church, once belonged to the archbishops of Canterbury, who made Maidstone their residence until 1538. The exterior steps of the palace and the wainscoted banqueting hall are noteworthy. The 16th c. house known as the Tithe Barn houses a large carriage and coach museum.

The Friary in the village of **Aylesford** (1 miles to the north) is one of the first two Carmelite foundations in England.

✶ ✶Leeds Castle

About 4 miles to the east stands Leeds Castle, in the opinion of Lord Conway "the loveliest castle in the world". The castle gets its name from Led, the prime minister of Ethelbert IV, King of Kent (857). The original Norman fortress was built on two islands in the middle of a lake, now encircled by ducks, Hawaiian geese and black swans. Henry VIII (see Famous People) had the D-shaped, two-storey building turned into a magnificent palace, which was to be used as a royal residence for over 300 years. The main building was completed at the beginning of the 19th c. At the same time a ring of battlements was added to the Maiden's Tower at the eastern end of the island, which dates from the Tudor period. Of note inside the castle are the Banqueting Hall of Henry VIII, with its wonderful ebony floor and carved oak ceiling; the Yellow Room, the silk damask design of which was created by Boudin in 1936; the Thorpe Hall Room, which is an outstanding example of decorative arts in the middle of the 17th c.; and the unique Dog's Collar Museum, with exhibits up to 400 years old. The parkland, extending over an area of some 500 acres (200 ha), contains woodland, Culpeper Garden (surrounded by beech hedges), a labyrinth of 2400 oak-trees, a grotto, the aviary, opened in 1988, with over 100 types of birds, greenhouses, a vineyard and a golf-course.

North-East Coast   K/L 5/6

North-east England
Counties: Humberside, North Yorkshire, Cleveland, Durham, Tyne and Wear and Northumberland

The north-east coast of England extends from north of the Humber estuary near Hull (see entry) to the Scottish border. With one or two exceptions, the seaside resorts here are less well-known and less favoured in terms of climate than resorts in the south of England, but they have the advantage of being less crowded, except perhaps at weekends, and some of them have preserved their original charm and character.

✶Tour of the Coast Withernsea

Withernsea is a resort favoured by the people of Hull (see entry), with a sandy beach which extends along the coast, with interruptions, for miles. There are two fine churches within easy reach, at Hedon (4 miles east of Hull) and Patrington (4 miles south-west of Withernsea). The church at Hedon, with a Decorated nave, an Early English choir and transepts and a Perpendicular tower, is known as the "King of Holderness" (the rich corn-growing area on the plain east of Hull). The church at Patrington, with an imposing tower, is mainly Decorated; it is known as the "Queen of Holderness".

Bridlington (31 miles north; pop. 28,600) is a seaside resort with a long beach which extends south for almost the whole length of Bridlington Bay. In the old town the Priory Church of St Mary, which was begun under Henry VIII, is worth visiting. During the English Reformation period the nave was pulled down and it was not until the middle of the last century that Sir Gilbert Scott completed the restoration of the church. Of note are the Jesse window with its 30 sections and the Early Gothic windows in the nave. It is also worth visiting the nearby Bayle Gate, the gatehouse of the former monastery (1388). The museum of antiquities, which has been set up here, includes a lovingly assembled dolls collection and numerous objects associated with the history of the town. In the town museum in Severby Hall, to the north-east of the centre, there are archaeological finds and a small gallery displaying local art. | **Bridlington**

An outing to ★**Burton Agnes Hall** (6 miles to the south-west) is to be recommended. The mansion, which is a magnificent example of Elizabethan Renaissance architecture, was built in 1598, extended in 1628 by Inigo Jones, and contains valuable furniture and a beautiful collection of French impressionists.

The famous resort of Scarborough (pop. 45,500) owes its name of "Queen of the Yorkshire Coast" to its beautiful sandy beaches. It has been the leading seaside resort in the north of England since 1734, and still preserves its Victorian character. It is well supplied with parks and gardens, cafés and entertainments of all kinds. On the headland between the two beaches is the Castle with a 12th c. keep. The **Church of St Mary** (12th–13th c., Transitional and Early English) is also of interest. Anne Brontë (1820–49), sister of Charlotte and Emily, is buried in the adjoining churchyard. The best view of the town is from Oliver's Mount (500 ft). | ★**Scarborough**

Whitby (pop. 15,800), an old seaport full of tradition, has magnificent beaches of sand, extending to Robin Hood's Bay and beyond. The River Esk flows between the older and newer parts of the town. Whitby was formerly an important whaling station. Captain Cook (see Famous People) served as an apprentice in Grape Lane and began his first Pacific expedition from Whitby. There is a memorial above the harbour to the great seafarer and discoverer. | **Whitby**

The golf-course is breathtakingly situated on high cliffs above the beach, while the best view of the town and coast is to be had from the inappropriately named Khyber Pass.

On top of the cliffs are the towering ruins of ★**Whitby Abbey**, founded in 657 and the venue of the famous Synod of Whitby (664). After being destroyed by the Danes, the Abbey was rebuilt in 1078. The most striking remnant is the 13th/14th c. church, built predominantly in the Early English style. The 199 steps of "Jacob's Ladder" lead to the Norman-Romanesque Church of St Mary's, with a beautiful south door.

Beyond Saltburn-by-the-Sea, a seaside resort favoured by rheumatic sufferers, there is a marvellous stretch of coastline, which includes the rugged Boulby Cliffs, leading to Redcar, a seaside resort with miles of beach, a 3 mile long promenade, a racecourse and a wide range of entertainments. The town also has a museum devoted to fishing and sea rescue. | **Saltburn-by-the-Sea, Redcar**

Tynemouth

The next resort of any size, although not a particularly attractive one, is Tynemouth (pop. 70,000) at the mouth of the River Tyne. It forms a conurbation with North Shields, South Shields, where the Roman fort of Arbeia marks the eastern end of Hadrian's Wall (see entry), and Newcastle-upon-Tyne (see entry). Indeed Tynemouth serves this larger urban area as a residential town and favoured place for weekend outings. The coastline along here is interspersed with many rocks, and on an outlying crag surrounded by water are the remains of the Castle and the ruins of the Priory Church (about 1090), with a fine Early English choir and the completely preserved Percy Chapel (15th c.)

Newcastle-upon-Tyne

See entry

Whitley Bay

Whitley Bay (pop. 40,000) has a much more attractive beach. It is a modern resort with excellent facilities for sport, recreation and entertainment.

Seaton Delaval House

3 miles north is Seaton Sluice, inland from which is Seaton Delaval Hall, seat of Lord Hastings, a gigantic Palladian house built by John Vanbrugh in 1718–29, which contains an excellent collection of furniture and paintings by English masters, including works by Reynolds.

Newbiggin-by-the-Sea

The road continues via Blyth and the pretty village of Bedlington – familiar to dog-lovers because of Bedlington terriers – to the seaside resort of Newbiggin-by-the-Sea, with rock formations, a sandy beach and an impressive church (St Bartholomew's, 13th c.).

Amble

The next stretch of coast, 40 miles long, between Amble and Berwick is designated an area of outstanding natural beauty. The little town of Amble is noted for its boatbuilding.

Warkworth Castle, seat of the Percy family since 1332

Warkworth is prettily situated in a loop of the River Coquet. The **Castle**, which is mentioned in Shakespeare's "Henry IV" (see Famous People), was founded in 1139 and has been in the possession of the Percy family since 1332. Of particular interest are the keep, a later addition, which, despite being without its roof, is well preserved, and the Lion's Tower (1480). St Laurence's Church, largely Norman in style, is also notable.

Warkworth

From here the road continues via Lesbury to Alnmouth, a trim seaside resort and yachting centre. 4 miles inland is Alnwick (pop. 8000), a tiny medieval town situated high above the banks of the River Aln. ⋆ **Alnwick Castle**, seat of the Duke of Northumberland, is a well-preserved example of a medieval fortress. The oldest parts of the castle are the fortified walls, dating from the 12th c., which were strengthened in the 14th c. by the first Lord Percy and given towers. Around this time the massive main gateway was also built, which gave entry to the outer courtyard. In the 18th and 19th c. the castle underwent substantial restoration. Its artistic treasures include French period furniture from the 17th–19th c.; Roman antiquities; a collection of paintings including works by Titian, Palma Vecchio, Sebastiano del Piombo, Tintoretto, Canaletto, van Dyck, William Dobson and Turner (see Famous People); valuable porcelain (including a Meissner dinner service in the dining-room); the state coach of the 3rd Duke of Northumberland and an extensive library with about 8000 volumes, including handwritten prayer books and rare examples of early printing.
    The parish **Church of St Michael** is in the Perpendicular style of the 15th c. and has superb Victorian glass windows.

Alnmouth

The road to the seaside resort of Seahouses runs past Dustanburgh Castle, begun in 1314. Here, with luck, the visitor may find some of the coloured quartz crystals known as "Dustanburgh diamonds" which are used in the manufacture of souvenirs.

Dustanburgh Castle

From Seahouses and the neighbouring village of Bamburgh there are motorboat trips to the uninhabited Farne Islands, a group of some 30 dolerite islets lying between 1½ and 5 miles offshore, now a bird reserve. More than 20 species nest on the islands, which are also the home of seals. During the nesting season only a few of the islands are open to visitors. St Cuthbert spent eight years here as a hermit.

Farne Islands

Bamburgh, once capital of the kingdom of Bernicia, is a pleasant little seaside resort (pop. 600). The enormous ⋆ **Castle**, with its Norman keep, is largely the product of a thorough restoration in the 18th c. **St Aidan's Church** has a very fine crypt and a beautiful 13th c. choir. The popular 19th c. heroine, Grace Darling (1815–42), who rowed out with her father, the lighthouse keeper, to save the crew of the shipwrecked "Forfarshire", is buried in the churchyard.

Bamburgh

11 miles further on is Beal, which is a starting-point for visits to ⋆ **Lindisfarne Priory** on Holy Island, parts of which are a bird sanctuary. At low tide the island can be reached on foot or by car across a causeway (2¾ miles). The island derives its name from the fact that it was very important as an early centre for Christianity. St Aidan was sent here from Iona in order to proselytise the people of Northumbria, and built a small monastery on the island. After the Danes' invasion the monks fled with the remains of St Cuthbert, sixth bishop here, and in 1093 a new Benedictine priory was founded at Lindisfarne. Only a few remains are left of the original fine church, the present building showing for the most part late Norman features (1140–50).
    Standing opposite is the **Lindisfarne Castle**, a fortress built against Scottish attacks in the middle of the 16th c. It was destroyed during the Civil War but was rebuilt in 1902.

⋆ Holy Island

Berwick-upon-Tweed

Bamburgh Castle, a Norman stronghold

Berwick-upon-Tweed

Since 1482 the most northerly town in England has been Berwick-upon-Tweed (pop. 14,000), an old border town which over a period of 300 years changed its allegiance 13 times. For a while it was Scotland's principal seaport. The town is characterised by three large bridges which span the River Tweed. The Berwick or Old Bridge, with 15 arches, dates from 1634, while the Royal Border Bridge (a railway bridge) was built in 1847–50 to plans by Robert Stephenson. The main tourist feature of the town is the ★**Elizabethan ramparts**, which still enclose Berwick on the north and east. In their day a model of their kind throughout Europe, they were built by Sir Richard Lee on the orders of Elizabeth I in 1558–60. With their five bastions they are unique in Britain.

The little **Town Hall** (1761) in Marygate today houses the town museum. The parish **Church of Holy Trinity**, designed in 1652 by the London architect John Young of Blackfriars, has elaborate Venetian windows. The buildings of the **"Barracks"** were constructed in 1717–21 for 600 men and 36 officers and thereby have the distinction of being the oldest garrison in England. Today they house three museums: a regimental museum, the English Heritage military museum and an art gallery which is attached to the Burrell Collection in Glasgow (see entry). Those interested in the history of wine and spirits should also visit the small **Wine and Spirit Museum** in Palace Street East, where home-made liqueur from Lindisfarne (Holy Island) can be sampled.

The **coastal scenery** around Berwick is very fine, with rocks and cliffs, only occasionally interrupted by small bays and harbours. The nearest bathing beach to the town is in the seaside resort of **Spittal**, to the south.

North Wales

G/H 7/8

Region: Wales/Cymru
Counties: Gwynedd and Clwyd

North Wales, one of Britain's oldest established tourist regions, offers an abundance of holiday attractions within a relatively small area. Road signs proclaiming "Croeso i Gymru" ("Welcome to Wales") greet the visitor as he enters the country and bear witness to the warm hospitality of the Welsh. The elegant little town of Llandudno is one of Britain's longest established seaside resorts, and the North Wales coast offers a great variety of scenery, with its spacious beaches and lively bathing resorts, rugged cliffs, little fishing villages and secluded bays. Snowdonia National Park, with Wales' highest mountain, Snowdon (3560 ft) has for centuries attracted climbers and walkers. The Lleyn Peninsula and the Clwydian Range are also designated as "areas of outstanding natural beauty", and there are many historical sites and charming little towns, deep ravines and picturesque valleys, which turn any outing into a voyage of discovery.

North Wales comprises the former counties of Caernarfon and Merioneth, which after reorganisation formed the county of Gwynedd, and the former counties of Denbigh and Flint, which after reorganisation became the county of Clwyd. The Tudor dynasty, which ascended the English throne, originally came from North Wales, while today the British heir to the throne is proclaimed "Prince of Wales" at Caernarfon Castle – the present Prince Charles' investiture took place there in 1969. The nationalist party of Wales, Plaid Cymru, was also founded in North Wales in 1925. In 1966 the party sent its first member of parliament to the House of Commons at Westminster: Gwynfor Evans (b. 1912), a symbolic figure for the newly awakened Welsh nationalism.

Many **Welsh place names** begin with the syllable "llan", which means "church". Other common beginnings are "aber" = "river-mouth"; "afon" = "river"; "bryn" = "hill"; "craig" = "rock"; "llyn" = "lake"; "rhos" = "moorland".

The **Eisteddfod** is the cultural and political high point of the Welsh year, as well as being a national institution full of tradition. The festival has been held every year since 1860, alternating between North and South Wales and always at a different place which, for the duration of the week, becomes the cultural capital of Wales. The ceremony of the "crowning of the bard", which is similar to medieval mastersinger contests, has its origins in a contest first held at Cardigan Castle (see South Wales). In the middle of the 16th c., during the reign of Elizabeth I, this contest became a recognised public competition for poets, subsequently developing into the national festival week which we know today. This contest for the bard's throne, which up to now has always been conducted exclusively in Welsh, includes singing competitions, poetry readings, drama, folk dancing and popular music forms.

A popular **souvenir** from Wales are "lovespoons", hand-carved spoons made of wood, which since the 17th c. have been traditionally given to the beloved as a sign of love and fidelity. These engagement gifts, which are elaborately decorated with initials, hearts (= "my heart

Snowdon Mountain Railway

In Snowdonia National Park

is yours"), anchors (= "lasting power of love"), Celtic crosses (= "wedding"), keys (= "my house belongs to you"), lucky horse-shoes and other symbols, are fashioned from a single piece of wood – sycamore, oak, beech or rowan. Even today these spoons are still a popular present for family occasions, weddings and other occasions, being a mark of affection.

It is still quite an adventure to take a ride on one of the colourful ⋆ **"great little trains of Wales"**, with their ancient locomotives and carriages, which chug across the countryside at full steam, even today. A nostalgic relic of the slate-mining age, when they were used for transporting slate from the mines, these ten narrow-gauge railways now carry millions of visitors every year through some of the most scenically impressive parts of Wales.

⋆⋆ Coast road
Flint

Entering North Wales from Chester, the road runs alongside the Dee estuary through a heavily industrialised area to Flint, an old town which was granted a charter by Edward I in 1284. Edward also built the castle (now ruined), which has an unusual plan with a separate keep surrounded by a moat. The castle, which was begun in 1277, was the first of 17 fortresses which Edward I had built to defend the North Wales coast. It also features in Shakespeare's "Richard II" as the scene of the king's capture by Bolingbroke.

Point of Ayr

At the Point of Ayr a stretch of coastline begins, with sandy beaches and good bathing, which extends to beyond Llanfairfechan. The resorts here offer ample facilities for entertainment and sport, with small yachting harbours and seafront promenades ideal for a long stroll. The resorts include Prestatyn, **Rhyl** with a promenade 3 miles long and Sun Centre, Kinmel Bay and then a series of resorts along the wide sweep of Colwyn

Bay, including the town of **Colwyn Bay** itself, with its annual fishing festival, Rhos-on-Sea and Llandudno.

It is well worth a small detour from Rhyl to **Rhuddlan Castle** in the Vale of Clwyd (3 miles south of Rhyl). This fortress, completed in 1282, was the second largest in the chain of castles which Edward I built in North Wales, and he himself sealed the conquest of Wales here in 1284 in the "Statutes of Rhuddlan". The fortress, which was designed by James of St George on a plan of concentric circles, had a double ring of walls, six massive fortified towers and a protected harbour. It was later razed to the ground by Cromwell's troops.

Another excursion can be made to **St Asaph** (pop. 2522; 6 miles south of Rhyl), a picturesque little town situated between the Rivers Elwy and Clwyd. The village church, only 180 ft long and 70 ft wide, has the distinction of being the smallest medieval cathedral in Britain. It was founded in 560 as a monastery church by St Mungo, who had been expelled from Glasgow (see entry), and was consecrated by his successor, the bishop St Asaph (d. about 596). Although the church was burned down by Owain Glyndwyr in 1402 and rebuilt in the 18th–19th c., it has largely preserved its Decorated style of 1284–1381. The massive crossing tower dates from 1715 (fine views from the top).

There are various monuments commemorating William Morgan, who published the first complete translation of the Bible into Welsh in 1588, and William Salisbury, who was the first person to translate the New Testament into Welsh (1567). The crypt contains a collection of early Welsh translations of the Bible and prayer books, as well as the Greek-Hebrew-Welsh dictionary belonging to the brilliant self-taught scholar, Richard Robert Jones.

The excursion can be continued to Denbigh/Dinbych (6 miles south of St Asaph), which is dominated by its castle, built in 1282 by Henry Lacy, which is another of the fortresses built for Edward I. The castle was on numerous occasions the scene of decisive skirmishes, including one in 1399, when it was Henry ("Hotspur") Percy's headquarters in his campaign against Owain Glyndwyr, and in 1660, when it was one of the last Royalist bastions, being forced to concede defeat to Cromwell's troops after an 11-month siege. The statue over the castle gateway is thought to depict Edward I. The town museum, which is housed in the castle gatehouse, exhibits mementoes of the Denbigh-born journalist Henry Morton Stanley, who tracked down the missing African explorer David Livingstone (see Famous People) by Lake Tanganyika.

Denbigh

Llandudno (pop. 20,000) is one of the most popular seaside resorts in Wales, with two sandy beaches, one on either side of the town, separated by the limestone promontory of Great Orme Head. The more easterly of the two beaches, North Shore, is bounded by another headland, Little Orme. With the advent of tourism in the last century, this Victorian town became a gathering-place for the new middle class, who came here from the nearby industrial regions of Liverpool (see entry) and Manchester (see entry). To date, the magnificent late Victorian pier has been mercifully spared the modern fairground influences – games machines and souvenir stalls – which are so typical of many resorts on the south coast. Mostyn Street, with its shopping arcades, is well worth a visit, and there is a wide range of cultural events and entertainments.

Llandudno

Great Orme's Head (679 ft) can be reached by a cable-car and has a superb panoramic view, while **Little Orme's Head** (463 ft) has beautiful cliff scenery.

West of Llandudno is Conwy Bay, also mainly sandy. Conwy itself (pop. 14,000), situated at the mouth of the River Conwy, is one of the most attractive towns in Wales. It has preserved an almost complete circuit of medieval walls, with three gates and 22 semicircular towers. The ★**Castle**, which was built at the orders of Edward I, is a masterpiece of medieval architecture. 2000 workmen were needed for the construction of this

Conwy

Conwy Castle ...   ... and yacht harbour

imposing fortress, which dates from 1283–89. In 1290 Edward was besieged here by the Welsh, but was finally relieved. The castle, with its 12–15 ft thick walls and eight towers, also played an important part in later history. The Great Hall, 125 ft long, is now roofless, but one of the eight arches which supported the roof has been rebuilt to show the original beauty of the structure. The King's Tower contains a very beautiful oratory.

St Mary's Church, in the centre of the town, occupies the site of an earlier Cistercian abbey and dates mainly from the 13th c. Notable features are the west doorway, a 15th c. font and the monument to Nicholas Hookes, who was his father's 41st child and himself the father of 27 children.

★**Plas Mawr** is headquarters of the "Royal Cambrian Academy of Art", a national art school formed in 1881 by local artists from Cardiff. The building itself, which dates from 1577–80, is a typical example of Elizabethan domestic architecture, with 365 windows and 52 doors. The banqueting hall, with Renaissance stucco decorations, is particularly fine.

A short distance away, on the corner of Castle Street, is the oldest house in the town, **Aberconwy House**, dating from the 15th c. Today it houses exhibitions of antiques.

Penmaenmawr

There is a very beautiful road from Conwy over the Sychnant Pass to Penmaenmawr, a seaside resort particularly favoured by sailing enthusiasts. To the west is the **Penmaenbach promontory** (783 ft). Here there is an interesting history trail, with Druid stone circles and a Stone Age axe factory.

Vale of Conwy

Up the beautiful valley of the River Conwy, at Talcafn Bridge, are the magnificent ★**Bodnant Gardens**, laid out by Henry Pochin in 1875. They are particularly renowned for their rhododendrons, azaleas and camellias, as well as for the rose-garden and rock garden.

Llanrwst

The road continues up the valley to the little market town of Llanrwst (pop. 2700), with its beautiful three-arched bridge thought to be built in

1636 to plans by Inigo Jones, who is also believed to have supplied the design for the nearby Gwydir Uchaf Chapel (1633). The latter contains a stone coffin, supposedly that of Llewelyn the Great (13th c.). **Gwydwr Castle**, on the opposite bank of the Conwy, was originally constructed in the 15th c., but has been rebuilt several times.

The coast road continues from Penmaenmawr via Llanfairfechan, one of the quieter seaside resorts, to Bangor (pop. 13,000), a university town, sailing centre and a good base for trips to the beautiful island of Anglesey (see entry), which is connected to the mainland by Telford's Menai Suspension Bridge. The tiny **Cathedral** was probably founded by Deiniol, the first bishop, in 548. Three earlier churches on the site were destroyed in 1071 by the Normans, in 1282 by Edward I and in 1404 by the Welsh rebel leader, Owain Glyndwyr (1359–1416). The choir was rebuilt about 1496 and the rest of the church in the early 16th c., but the whole building was restored about 1870 by Gilbert Scott. The chapter-house contains interesting old books and manuscripts.

Bangor

The **Museum of Welsh Antiquities** displays old Welsh furniture and costumes, and documents from the 17th–19th c. dealing with local history.

Penrhyn Castle (1 mile to the east), which was built by Thomas Hopper in the Neo-Norman style in 1827–40, is a reminder of the great days of Welsh slate-mining in the 19th c., when the Penrhyn Quarries, belonging to the Pennant family, produced 130,000 tons a year, roughly a quarter of the total Welsh output of slate. It is no surprise therefore to find the grey stone even in evidence inside the castle, with a billiard table, mantelpiece and four-poster bed made of slate.

At Bethesda (4 miles south-east of Bangor in the Ogwen valley) the visitor will find the vast **Penrhyn Quarries**, cut about 1000 ft deep into the mountain, where slate of all different colours is mined, some of which is turned into souvenirs and jewellery.

Bethesda

It is also well worth while climbing the Carnedds, two mountains near here which are named after two Welsh brothers: Carnedd Llewelyn (3484 ft) and Carnedd Dafydd (3426 ft). From these peaks there is a breathtaking view of Snowdownia.

Carnedds

9 miles south-west of Bangor is the county town of Gwynedd, Caernarfon (pop. 12,000), beautifully situated on the Menai Strait at the mouth of the River Seiont. It is a picturesque old town of narrow streets, with old town walls and a magnificent castle. The yachting harbour is also a favourite mooring-place for smart sailing boats, and the town is a good base from which to explore the beauties of the Lleyn Peninsula.

Caernarfon

★★**Caernarfon Castle** was begun by Edward I in 1283 as a seat for his eldest son, Edward of Caernarfon, the first Prince of Wales. The power and might of the throne is symbolised by the great stone eagles on the

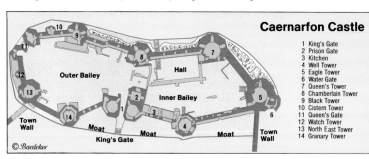

Caernarfon Castle

1 King's Gate
2 Prison Gate
3 Kitchen
4 Well Tower
5 Eagle Tower
6 Water Gate
7 Queen's Tower
8 Chamberlain Tower
9 Black Tower
10 Cistern Tower
11 Queen's Gate
12 Watch Tower
13 North East Tower
14 Granary Tower

© Baedeker

423

Caernarfon Castle, built by Edward 1

Eagle Tower and the layout of the castle walls and towers, which calls to mind the Roman wall at Constantinople. The massive building with its 13 towers and two gates belongs to the most impressive and externally best-preserved medieval fortresses in Europe. It occupies the site of an earlier Norman castle, washed by the waters of the River Seiont and the Menai Strait, while on the landward side it is protected by a moat. The building of the castle took almost 37 years: the Eagle Tower, Queen's Tower and Chamberlain Tower were built between 1285 and 1291, the Black Tower and Queen's Gate 1295–1301, the rest of the structure 1315–22. The castle has had an eventful history and withstood many sieges; more recently, it was the scene of Prince Charles's investiture as Prince of Wales in 1969, an event marked by a special exhibition.

The Roman Fort **Segontium**, south-east of the town, has a museum containing material excavated on the site.

★ **Lleyn Peninsula**

The Lleyn Peninsula (pron. "hleen") was one of the earliest parts of Wales to be settled, with many prehistoric remains, and is one of the strongholds of the Welsh language. It is an area of great natural beauty, with a number of hills. Much of the coastline is rocky, but there are nevertheless a number of small seaside resorts such as Trefor, Nant Gwrtheyrn and Nefyn, Porth Ysgadan, Porth Ychen and Porth Colmon. Porth Oer has an excellent beach, known as the Whistling Sands, because of the noise it makes when walked on.

Situated on the southernmost part of the peninsula, the resort of **Aberdaron** possesses a splendid sandy beach 1½ miles long. From here there is a magnificent cliff-top walk to the most westerly point on the peninsula, Braich-y-Pwll (2½ miles). Y Gegin Fawr, now a café and souvenir shop, was in the 14th c. a rest-house for pilgrims travelling to the offshore island of **Bardsey**, now a bird reserve.

Porth Neigwl, or "Hell's Mouth", is a sandy bay 4 miles long, near which is the village of Llanengan with its interesting 15th c. church. **Abersoch**, with St Tudwal's Islands lying offshore, has two large sandy beaches and is much favoured by water-sports enthusiasts. Llanbedrog, in sheltered Tremadog Bay, and **Pwllheli** both have excellent beaches.

Llanystumdwy

Llanystumdwy is situated on the extensive estuary formed by the rivers Dwyfor and Dwyfach, in a very attractive area which offers excellent walking. The village has the ★ **Lloyd George Memorial Museum** devoted to the politician David Lloyd George (1863–1945). Born in Manchester, he spent his childhood at his uncle's house in Llanystumdwy, after the death of his father. He then worked as a lawyer at the slate harbour of Porthmadog, before going to London as the member of parliament for Caernarfon and advancing to become the leader of the Liberal party and finally Prime Minister. During his period of office he carried out important social reforms. The museum has a large number of mementoes which serve to document the life of this British statesman, who epitomised the Anglo-Welshman. Lloyd George returned in 1944 to the place of his childhood and his grave lies on the banks of the Dwyfor.

Criccieth

Criccieth is a popular seaside resort with a small 13th c. castle, from which there are very fine views. A delicious speciality of Criccieth, which every visitor should sample, is the creamy Cadwalader's Ice Cream.

Porthmadog, Tremadog

At the mouth of the River Glaslyn are the twin towns of Porthmadog and Tremadog (pop. 3420), tiny industrial centres which attained international importance for the shipping of slate and today have developed into seaside resorts with excellent facilities for sport. From Ynys Tywyn, near the harbour, there are wide views of the surrounding area. The poet Shelley (1792–1822) lived for some time in Tremadog; Lawrence of Arabia (1888–1935) was born there.

Porthmadog is also the terminus for the oldest narrow-gauge railway in the world, the **Ffestiniog Railway**, built in 1836 to transport slate from the mines at Blaenau Ffestiniog. It now carries thousands of visitors through the beautiful Ffestiniog valley.

Blaenau Ffestiniog

The centre for the Welsh slate-mining industry is Blaenau Ffestiniog, surrounded by massive, smooth and gleaming waste-heaps left by the slate quarries. Slate, the mineral which dominates this environment, is everywhere in evidence and in every conceivable shade, from the brightest to the darkest silver-grey, providing a cladding for the little terraced

Tremadog Bay

Non-operational rail track

Slate quarrying at Blaenau Ffestiniog

houses, built out of rough stone and granite, which line the main street, and even visible in the enclosures reserved for sheep-grazing.

This long seam of Cambrian slate extends from the Carnedds on the north-west flank of the Snowdon massif as far as Nantlle and was formed during the Palaeozoic period about 600 million years ago. Whereas at Penrhyn and Dinorwc it was possible to mine the slate using open-cast methods, the more unfavourable diagonal seam at Blaenau required tunnels and shafts. Large-scale slate quarrying was begun at the beginning of the 19th c. by the Liverpool mining speculator Samuel Holland at the Oakeley Slate Quarries, his example being immediately followed by other, mainly English entrepreneurs. The layers of slate, after preliminary working, were transported for export through the Vale of Ffestiniog on a narrow-gauge railway to the nearby harbour of Porthmadog. From there the much prized weather-resistant building stone was shipped all over the world. At the height of the slate boom, around the turn of the century, the population of Blaenau almost reached 12,000 and its 18 mines, which employed some 4000 men – almost a quarter of the slate-workers in North Wales – produced some 140,000 tons each year. Today there are just two open-cast mines left which only employ 150 men.

The hard life of the "rock men" is well documented in the **Gloddfa Ganol Slate Museum**, which was opened in 1974 in a former tunnel of Oakeley Quarries. These men prepared for the blasting of the slate by candlelight below ground. The slate was then split into layers above ground by "splitters" and then beaten into the desired sizes by "dressers". Later on this work was carried out by machines.

Also in Tremadog Bay, on a wooded peninsula between Porthmadog and Harlech, is an Italian town in miniature, **Portmeirion**, which is now a holiday colony. Portmeirion was the brainchild of Sir Clough Williams-Ellis (1884–1978), who dreamed of recreating an Italian village in Wales and had it built on his own private promontory, together with a mansion (now a hotel) and Gwylt Gardens.

The village of Harlech (pop. 1300), once the county town of Merioneth, lies on a rocky outcrop of Cambrian origin, towering over the salt marshland of Morfa Harlech. Like the other fortresses built by Edward I, it was intended that it could be supplied from the sea, but today the village lies ½ mile from the shore. The massive **Castle** is like something out of a fairytale and is a symbol of Welsh patriotism. It was conquered by Owain Glyndwr, the last national leader of the Welsh, in 1404 in a struggle against English supremacy, and remained in his hands for almost five years. In 1647 the conquest of Harlech Castle, which had remained true to the Royalists, marked the end of the Civil War. The fortress was designed in 1283–9 by James of St George and is almost a perfect rectangle. Its most striking feature is its three-storey, twin-towered gatehouse, the effect of which is completed by four circular corner towers. From here there is a superb view across Tremadog Bay, to the peaks of Snowdownia and the Lleyn Peninsula.

Harlech

The parish **Church of St Collen's** possesses a magnificent oak roof with carved angels, flowers and animals.

The road from Harlech to Barmouth, some 10 miles in length, passes through an area of great scenic beauty. Inland lies part of Snowdonia National Park, with mountains rising as high as 2462 ft. Rhinog Fawr (2362 ft) is popular with climbers, the starting-point for the ascent being the village of Llanbedr on the Artro, a river well-known among anglers for its trout. The road runs along the foot of the hills, passing through Ardudwy, for many years a centre of the Welsh struggle for independence against England, and Llanaber with its early 13th c. church.

Barmouth/Abermaw is a popular seaside resort situated on a narrow strip of land between the hills and the sea. Charles Darwin (see Famous People) produced part of his treatise on the evolution of man here.

Barmouth

The Mawddach estuary is of great scenic beauty. A road runs along its shores to Dolgellau (10 miles), a town of stone-built and slate-roofed houses beautifully situated in the valley of the Wnion. Around the turn of the century there was a "mini gold-rush" here, when gold was found in some of the mountain streams nearby. The gold used for the wedding rings of the Queen, the Prince of Wales and Princess Diana came from veins of quartz at the Clogau St David's Mine, the hallmark of which carries the Welsh red dragon. Being within reach of so much magnificent scenery, Dolgellau is a favourite base for walks and climbs in the surrounding hills and on Cadair Idris. To gain an initial impression of this beautiful landscape, the visitor is recommended to take the Precipice Walk to Moel Cynwch (1068 ft) and on to Cymmer Abbey, a Cistercian foundation of 1198, of which only the Norman church (restored) has been preserved.

Dolgellau

From Dolgellau there are three routes up ★**Cadair Idris** (2927 ft), the most popular Welsh mountain after Snowdon, and offering even better views. The walk takes between 2½ and 4 hours, depending on the route chosen.

Cadair Idris, the chair of the giant and bard Idris, is a massive ridge 7 miles long, which falls steeply into the Mawddach valley to the northwest but slopes more gently away into outlying hills on the other three sides. The rocks are of considerable geological interest. The four highest peaks – Mynydd Moel, Pen-y-Gader, the Saddle and Tyrau Mawr – range between 1848 and 2927 ft. From the summit there are splendid views in all directions.

Snowdonia is the name given to the mountainous area in the county of Gwynedd, with 14 peaks over 3000 ft, culminating in Snowdon/Yr

★★**Snowdonia**

Wyddfa itself (3560 ft), followed by Crib Goch (3023 ft), Crib-y-Ddysgl or Garnedd Ugain (3493 ft), Lliwedd (2947 ft) and Yr Aran (2451 ft). The best view of the whole group is to be had from Capel Curig, but the peaks themselves can be seen from Porthmadog or the Nantlle valley.

Snowdonia National Park is a more recent creation and covers a much wider area than the traditional Snowdonia, extending inland from the coast between Paenmawr and Caernarfon by way of Bethesda to Bala Lake and Llanfairfechan (see p. 15). Access to a beautiful part of this area, including Snowdon itself, is made easier by the Snowdon Mountain Railway, which starts from **Llanberis** (pop. 2330), in a magnificent setting at the beginning of the Llanberis Pass. The twin lakes of Padarn and Peris have one of the largest pumping stations in Europe for the purpose of supplying water. Between them is Dolbadarn Castle, with a 13th c. round tower, and 2 miles to the south is Bryn Bras Castle.

★★ **Snowdonia National Park**

The workshops of the ★ **Welsh Slate Museum** in Gilfach Ddu were built in 1870 for the slate quarry of Dinorwic, which at the time was the largest in the world, and consists of a huge amphitheatre carved directly into the slopes of the Elidir mountains.

The easiest method of ascending Snowdon from Llanberis is provided by the tiny ★ **Snowdon Mountain Railway**. It steams up to the summit of Snowdon at a speed of little more than 5 miles an hour, passing through Hebron, Halfway and Clogwyn stations. There is a bus service, the "Snowdon Sherpa", serving Porthmadog, Beddgelert, Llanrwst, Betws-y-Coed, Capel Curig, Caernarfon and Llanberis, all good starting-points for trips into Snowdonia. There are National Park information centres at Llanrwst, Llanberis, Blaenau Ffestiniog, Harlech, Bala, Conwy, Aberdyfi and Dolgellau. A variety of waymarked trails, each only a few miles long, enable visitors to become acquainted with the scenery, flora and fauna and geology of the region. There are five waymarked and relatively safe and easy routes to the summit, starting from Llanberis, Pen-y-Pass, Beddgelert, Nant Gwynant and the Snowdon Ranger. The most direct route, albeit the least attractive, is the one from Llanberis; the best ascent is to start from Beddgelert and return to Pen-y-Pass, or vice versa.

Snowdon itself (Welsh: Eryri) comprises many peaks, the highest of which Yr Wyddfa (3560 ft) affords incomparable views in all directions. But there are a large number of other mountains in the area which are also well worth climbing. All over Snowdonia there are good walks and climbs, offering far-ranging views of beautiful mountains and valleys.

★ **Snowdon**

Beddgelert (pop. 500), the village at the confluence of the rivers Colwan and Glaslyn, is one of the most charming little places in Wales, a favourite starting-point for walks and climbs, situated as it is at the junction of three main roads. From Moel Hebog, a 2 hours' climb from here, there is a splendid panoramic view extending out into Cardigan Bay. One road from here descends to Caernarfon, another runs northeast through Nant Gwynant, the valley of the Glaslyn and one of the most beautiful in Wales.

This leads to the delightful little town of **Betws-y-Coed** (pop. 770) (= "temple in the wood"), situated in Gwydyr Forest at the junction of the Conwy, Lledr and Llugwy valleys. This is a very popular holiday place, crowded with visitors in summer. The ruin of Pany Mill and the 15th c. Pont-y-Pair bridge are attractive to look at. The immediate surroundings are very beautiful, with the Fairy Glen, the Swallow Falls and the Conwy waterfalls.

Llyn Ogwen is a beautiful mountain lake with a waterfall (Benglog Falls). Half a mile to the south is **Llyn Idwal**, in which the son of Prince Owain Gwynedd is supposed to have been drowned by his stepfather. High in the mountains is the **Cwm Idwal** nature reserve (Alpine flora), and nearby is an almost inaccessible gorge known as the Devil's Kitchen,

◀ *Harlech Castle – symbol of Welsh patriotism*

Panorama from Snowdon (North Wales)

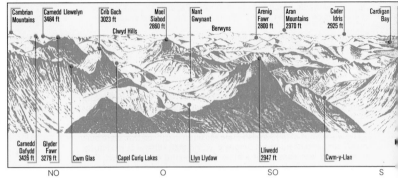

| Cambrian Mountains | Carnedd Llewelyn 3484 ft | Crib Goch 3023 ft | Moel Siabod 2860 ft | Nant Gwynant | Arenig Fawr 2800 ft | Aran Mountains 2970 ft | Cader Idris 2925 ft | Cardigan Bay |

Chwyd Hills   Berwyns

Carnedd Dafydd 3426 ft   Glyder Fawr 3279 ft   Cwm Glas   Capel Curig Lakes   Llyn Llydaw   Lliwedd 2947 ft   Cwm-y-Llan

NO   O   SO   S

6 ft wide and 500 ft deep. This and one or two other spots in Snowdonia are the only habitats in Britain of the rare Snowdon lily, Lloydia serotina, a protected species. At the south end of Llyn Ogwen is the triple peak of **Tryfan** (3010 ft), much favoured by climbers.

The holiday village of **Capel Curig** is a good base for mountaineering and walking in the Snowdonia area, and is also popular with anglers and painters.

On the eastern edge of Snowdonia the A4212 leads to **Bala Lake**, with the little market town of Bala (pop. 1600), a lively holiday place at the foot of the Aran and Berwyn Mountains. Its main attractions are the 4 mile long lake, which offers ideal conditions for sailing and angling, and

The "Ladies of Llangollen" ✫.

... lived in Plas Newydd at Butler Hill

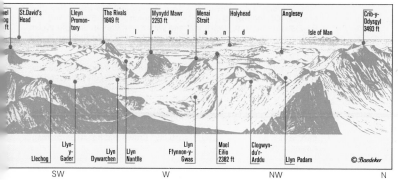

uel og ft	St.David's Head	Lleyn Promontory	The Rivals 1849 ft	Mynydd Mawr 2293 ft	Menai Strait	Holyhead	Anglesey	Isle of Man	Crib-y-Ddysgyl 3493 ft

I r e l a n d

Llyn-y-Gader · Llechog · Llyn Dywarchen · Llyn Nantlle · Llyn Ffynnon-y-Gwas · Moel Eilio 2382 ft · Clogwyn-du'r-Arddu · Llyn Padarn · © *Baedeker*

SW   W   NW   N

the Bala Lake Railway, a narrow-gauge railway which runs along the shore of the lake.

Llangollen

Another very popular holiday resort is Llangollen (pop. 3100), in a beautiful setting on both banks of the River Dee. The romantic landscape in this wooded river valley has been impressively captured by William Turner (see Famous People) in several paintings. Llangollen is famed for the ⋆**International Musical Eisteddfod** held here every summer since 1947, where amateur singers go through their paces alongside famous soloists and choirs from all over the world. Illustrious visitors to the festival have included Yehudi Menuhin, Mstislav Rostropovich and the Vienna Boys Choir.

The 14th c. parish church, **St Collen's**, has a fine carved oak roof with figures of angels, animals and flowers.

The town can thank two capricious ladies for the curious ⋆**Plas Newydd**, a black and white half-timbered house on Butler Hill. Inspired by the ideas coming from Europe of a new sensibility and emotional awareness, Eleanor Butler and her companion Sarah Ponsonby, 16 years older, broke with convention and fled from their family home to England, coming through Wales. The sight of the Dee valley so bewitched the two women that they decided to remain in the "most beautiful country in the world". They occupied a cottage on the edge of the village and lived there together for 50 years, turning the garden into a veritable gem. Between 1789 and 1814 they gave their very simple dwelling its "Gothic" look. The "most famous virgins in Europe", as Prince Pückler respectfully named the two eccentric "Ladies of Llangollen", received many famous people of the period, including the Duke of Gloucester, the Lakeland poet William Wordsworth, Sir Walter Scott (see Famous People) and the actress Sarah Siddons.

The 19 arches of the 984 ft long **Pontcysyllte Aqueduct**, built by Thomas Telford (1795–1805) on the eastern side of the town, span the River Dee in spectacular fashion.

Valle Crucis Abbey

Valle Crucis Abbey, 2 miles to the north, was founded by Prince Madog ap Gruffydd Maelor in 1202 for Cistercian monks. The remains include the west front of the church, with three beautiful 14th c. windows, a pointed arch at the east end, the sacristy, the chapterhouse, the dorter and the fish-pond. In a field a quarter of a mile away is the early 9th c. Eliseg's Pillar, commemorating Eliseg, Prince of Powys, and his victory at the Battle of Bangor, in which he lost his life. From here the road climbs to the Horseshoe Pass (1353 ft) with Moel-y-Gamelin (1897 ft).

431

Welshpool	In the most southerly part of North Wales, close to the border with England, is Welshpool/Trallwng (pop. 7000), former county town of Montgomeryshire. It lies on the River Severn and has many Georgian houses. Of interest are the 14th c. church of St Mary's and the Powysland Museum, Welshpool and with many Roman and old Welsh finds from the region. The **Welshpool and Llanfair Light Railway** is one of the most attractive narrow-gauge railways still in operation.
⋆ **Powis Castle**	Powis Castle, 1 mile to the south, has for over 500 years been the seat of the Earls of Powis. Built of red sandstone, it has largely preserved the appearance of a 13th–14th c. castle in spite of restoration work in the 16th c. The Long Gallery has fine plaster decoration and pieces of early Georgian furniture, while in the Oak Drawing Room there is a portrait of the 1st Earl of Powis by Gainsborough. The terraced gardens were laid out in the early 18th c. with balustrades and arcades and lead into the park, which was designed by "Capability" Brown and boasts some magnificent oak-trees.

North-West Coast   H/I 6/7

North-West England
Counties: Cheshire, Merseyside, Lancashire and Cumbria

The north-west coast of England extends from the Welsh to the Scottish borders. It is a flat region bordered by beaches of fine sand, from which the sea recedes at low tide anything up to 2 miles. Climatically the resorts on this stretch of coast are less favoured than those further south, but inland the scenery is often very beautiful.

Wirral Peninsula	On the Wirral peninsula between the estuaries of the Mersey and the Dee are the resorts of West Kirby and Hoylake, looking across the Dee to North Wales (see entry). Both have long sandy beaches and promenades, and Hoylake is famed for its first-class golf-course.
New Brighton	As its name indicates, New Brighton was originally established in emulation of the popular Sussex resort. It lies on the south side of the Mersey, here almost a mile wide, opposite Liverpool Docks. Although the water is not especially clean, the resort is popular for visitors from the Liverpool–Birkenhead conurbation. The town has one of the largest swimming-pools in Europe, an amusement park and a long promenade extending from Hoylake to beyond Seacombe.
Formby, Ainsdale	Near Formby, which has a good golf-course, is the large Ainsdale nature reserve, with sand-dunes and areas of marsh and brackish water, where rare flora and fauna can be found. Adjoining the reserve is the Southport wildfowl sanctuary.
Southport	Southport (pop. 86,000), a popular seaside resort, prides itself on being England's oldest garden city. It is a town of wide tree-lined streets and beautiful parks and gardens with greenery everywhere. It is very enjoyable to walk down the colourful Lord Street or along the wide beach, with views across the Irish Sea. Every amenity is on offer, including a promenade, pier, swimming-pool, amusement park, salt-water lagoon and several excellent golf-courses.
	Inland from Southport the country is flat and featureless, the only special attraction being **Rufford Old Hall** (8 miles to the east), a late medieval manor-house with a 17th c. and 19th c. wing. It houses the Philip Ashcroft Museum.
Lytham St Anne's	Situated opposite Southport at the mouth of the River Ribble, Lytham St

Anne's (pop. 42,000) is a family holiday resort. Founded in 1875, the town has an especially attractive beach, 6 miles long, with sand-dunes. There are also fine parks and gardens and five good golf-courses.

Blackpool, 5 miles to the north, is the largest holiday resort in the North of England and is still expanding. The bustling town can accommodate over half a million visitors in the summer months at the height of the season. Entertainment for every taste is provided in profusion – golf, zoo, circus, dance-halls, theatres, cinemas, bathing pools (including the enormous "Splashland" complex), a promenade 7 miles long, and three piers, at which pleasure-boats dock. Since 1889 the town's most famous landmark has been the Blackpool Tower, 519 ft high, situated on the beach, which also has an aquarium. The festive illuminations in autumn are a high point of the year for the resort. Other annual events which attract many visitors are the dance and music festivals and the summer agricultural show. Blackpool is also the venue for the annual conference of the Trade Union Congress. It is expected that by 1994 Blackpool will have gained its newest attraction – a roller coaster almost 236 ft high, with a circuit 1 mile in length. It is anticipated that the carriages will plunge down a gradient of 65 degrees and reach a speed of over 60 miles an hour.

★ **Blackpool**

The resort of Fleetwood (pop. 30,500), situated at the mouth of the River Wyre, owes its rise to prominence to the founder of Rossall School, overlooking Morecambe Bay.

Fleetwood

See entry

Lancaster

Grange-over-Sands (pop. 4000) is an elegant and popular resort on Morecambe Bay, with beautiful public gardens and fine golf-courses. It is a good base for visiting the Lakes.

Grange-over-Sands

Cartmel (2 miles to the west), an attractive Georgian village, possesses a fine old church, the Priory Church of St Mary, originally forming part of an Augustinian priory founded by the Earl of Pembroke in 1188. The lower part of the church is Transitional, the upper part of the tower, the nave and most of the windows Perpendicular. The Renaissance stalls date from 1612 to 1613.
    Not far to the west is **Holker Hall**, dating from the 17th/19th c. and formerly the seat of the Dukes of Devonshire. The house, which is surrounded by magnificent parkland, has some interesting wood-carvings by local artists and valuable period furniture.

Cartmel

Seascale (pop. 2000) is a good base for excursions into the Lake District (see entry) of Cumbria. Its church has fine modern glass windows.

Seascale

The most northerly seaside resort on the west coast before the Scottish border is Silloth (pop. 3000), on the Solway Firth, with a good anchorage which led to its foundation in 1855 as a port for Carlisle. This function has been taken over by Port Carlisle, and Silloth is now of importance only as a holiday resort. It has good golf-courses.

Silloth

North-West Highlands
F–H 2–4

Country: Scotland. Region: Highland

The term "North-West Highlands" generally refers to the northernmost third of Scotland, which is separated from the rest of the country and the Grampian Mountains (see entry) by the "Great Glen of Scotland". In

Rhododendrons blooming in the Scottish Highlands

geomorphological terms the Scottish Highlands are split here by the Caledonian fault-line which runs from coast to coast, from Loch Linnhe in the west to the Moray Firth in the east.

Although the mountain ranges which have been formed by this transverse fault rank among the highest in Great Britain, the actual altitudes involved are not that great in absolute terms. The surface effects produced in the Pleistocene period by Ice Age glaciers have led to powerful indentations and depressions in the valleys; while the relief-forming energy has thrown up the Ben Nevis massif which reaches heights in excess of 4000 ft. The mountain ranges to the west of the Caledonian fault-line, which run predominantly from east to west, make a significant contribution to the climatic differences which inform those areas of the Highlands under the influence of the warm Gulf Stream. Because of their direct exposure to depressions coming in off the Atlantic, the north-west coastal areas, with an annual rainfall of around 80 in., are among the wettest parts of Great Britain. The vegetation period here is very short. The soil, being low in nutrients, often composed of podsol or bog, can only naturally support low-growing bushes and heather, while the upper reaches of the mountains have different wild grasses. The only parts of the region which can support intensive agrarian use are the coastal plains around the Moray Firth, the plains of Caithness and one or two coastal areas in the south-west which are protected from the wind and frost.

History The traditional economic and social system which existed in the Scottish Highlands was founded, with the exception of Caithness, on the **clan system**. This consisted of over 170 social groups, occupying remote highland valleys and often separated from one another by considerable distances, which grew barley, oats and potatoes for their own use and reared "black cattle". The clan owned the land communally, with the clan chief in overall command. Each person had rights and duties resulting from his membership of the clan. When the union took place with England to form one sovereign state in 1707, the Highland clans declared total opposition and supported the Scottish pretender to the throne, Bonnie Prince Charlie. After his crushing defeat at Culloden in 1746 the clan system was proscribed and the whole of its area assigned to English administrators. From 1780, however, the estates were in many cases transferred back to clan chiefs loyal to the crown, these now being vested with feudal rights and appointed as "lairds".

The 19th c. began with one of the most calamitous chapters of Scottish social history, which has had lasting effects ever since. Inspired by the example of the highly successful estates in the southern part of the country and the growing demands of the booming English textile industry, the new Highland landowners believed that their most profitable way of combating the prevailing low-wage economy, with its attendant poverty and starvation, was by switching from the traditional labour-intensive system of agriculture to large-scale sheep-rearing. Large numbers of sheep-farmers were prepared to bid up to three times the normal cost of a lease in order to graze their Cheviot and Linton sheep. First of all, however, a large number of the peasant farmers inhabiting these areas had to be resettled in the coastal districts. This enforced and often brutally enacted resettlement of almost two thirds of the existing indigenous population, known as the **"Highland Clearances"**, began in 1807 in Sutherland and lasted for the next seventy years. The result was the almost total evacuation of the Highlands and an overpopulation of the coastal strip. The crofters, who after resettlement were only given the tiniest of plots of land and needed alternative sources of income in order to make ends meet, turned to fishing and gathering seaweed, neither of which really proved to be economic. As a result, large numbers of crofters were forced to emigrate to the industrial regions of Scotland and England and even overseas. Between 1840 and 1860 over 100,000 people abandoned their Scottish homelands.

A gloomy picture of the desperate plight of these exiles has been left us by the contemporary artist Thomas Faed in his painting "The last of the clans" of 1865, which is on display in the Art Museum in Glasgow.

Up until now emigration has continued to take its toll on the whole area, which, with its weak infrastructure, has only seen a small amount of internal migration within regions. However, along the Caledonian rift valley, where state-subsidised trading and industrial ventures have led to some urban growth, an axis of development has been established between Oban and Wick with good transport and a steady growth in population. At the same time the outlying rural areas, with their deficient infrastructure and inadequate alternative sources of income, continue to suffer depopulation, especially among the younger age groups.

Against the background of dwindling natural resources and the socio-economic imbalance caused by the disastrous measures taken in the previous century, the main aim of today's regional planners and the Highlands and Islands Development Board (HIDB), which was established in 1965, is an intensive programme of economic activity. Infrastructural, financial and organisational measures are intended to promote a broader, market- oriented economic base. This will offer both traditional lines of business and newer areas of growth in the region the chance to flourish on a long-term basis. It is hoped in this way that, with the extension of both public and private utilities, the necessary conditions will be created for a stable population growth. Priorities include the improvement and extension of the transport network, changes in the system of crofts and small farms to enable them to meet the demands of the market economy, including the transfer of crofts into private ownership (now possible since 1976) and the foundation of co-operatives, with the overall aim of being in a position to react more positively to

Tartan, Plaid and Kilt

Many travellers have had their imagination captured by the picture of a Scottish Highlander in his kilt, probably blowing his bagpipes, although they are probably unaware of the fact that there are also Lowlanders in Scotland and that the famed bagpipes were not introduced into the country until the 16th c. Before that the instrument associated with the Scots was the Celtic harp.

Even if kilt-wearers are very much in a minority on the streets of Glasgow or Edinburgh, the tartan in all its various forms is omnipresent. To define tartan merely as Scottish checks, would be to underestimate its significance completely. Whereas in the 15th and 16th c. the term was used to refer to woollen clothing from the Highlands, today it serves to describe woollen cloths with patterns derived from a quite strictly laid down sequence of different coloured horizontal and vertical stripes. Depending on the breadth and spacing of these stripes, the expert can say which region the wearer comes from, which clan he may belong to, and sometimes even his social status, although these definite classifications have latterly become rather blurred. Originally a tartan was only made up of natural colours derived from the sheep's wool, and it was not until later that the wool was coloured with plant dyes. Each weaver would have the sequence of colours notched on a piece of wood, thereby retaining the exact pattern of the tartan for the next generation.

The forerunner of the present-day kilt consisted of two swathes of tartan about 16 ft long and 2 ft wide which the wearer would wrap round himself, fastening it with a belt and taking the remainder of the material up across his chest and over his shoulder – in this way he had produced the "plaid" or "féileadh-mor", roughly translated from Gaelic as "folded large". Echoes of this original style of dress can still be found today in the lavish garments of the members of the Pipe Band. Around the beginning of the 18th c. the "féileadh-bheag" ("folded small"), now known universally as the kilt, came into being, probably because the plaid became too cumbersome to prepare and modern garments such as jackets and coats had started to gain currency. In addition, in front of his stomach, the wearer carried, and still carries, his "sporran", a leather bag, which in the course of time became more and more elaborately decorated. Stockings were originally woven using the same tartan, although nowadays they are normally made of just one colour. "Truis", which were worn tightly around the legs to keep warm, are hardly ever seen anymore. However, the "dirk", a thin dagger worn next to the stockings, can still occasionally be seen.

Whereas wearing the tartan is today often merely a whim of fashion, it was once an extremely important part of how a Highlander saw himself. For him it was less to do with the much-vaunted ability to identify other clansmen; it was more a question of his own distinctive tartan being an expression of his links with his area and his clan. Right up to the middle of the 18th c. the clans determined the structure of Scottish society, despite the nominally higher authority of the king, and it was this, more than anything, which caused the English to regard the Scots as an archaic and uncivilised mountain people. The power of the clans was not broken until the defeat of the Scottish pretender to the throne, Bonnie Prince Charlie, in 1746 at the Battle of Culloden. After that the English not only forbade the carrying of arms, but also any wearing of the tartan, something which wounded Scottish pride where it was most sensitive. During the 35 years that the ban was strictly in force, a large part of the tradition was lost and the chiefs of the rebellious clans forfeited all their influence – an important precondition for the "highland clearances", that infamous campaign of resettlement in which whole clans were driven from their glens to the coast, in order to make land available for sheep-grazing. In 1782 the Marquis of Graham was emboldened to ask parliament to allow the wearing of the tartan again. His success was greeted with immense jubilation. But Scotland's actual renaissance and the reassertion of its national identity did not occur until 1822 when George IV became the first monarch since Charles II to visit Edinburgh and actually wore the tartan of the Royal Stewarts. Sir Walter Scott, who played an important part in organising this visit, also made an important contribution, with his poetry, to this image of the Scottish Highlander in his kilt, and when Queen Victoria acquired Balmoral Castle and even had the curtains made up in tartan cloth, a veritable mania broke out, giving the weavers a field day. Entire regiments were equipped with kilts and tartan stockings, even when they did not have any real Scottish tradition (it was only in 1940 that the Queen's Own Cameron Highlanders became the last combat force to discard the kilt). In upper-class families the possession of a "Scottish wardrobe" was considered the height of good taste, even when the tartan was the product of pure imagination. The services of tartan experts, who researched into the history and traditions of the clans, were in considerable demand. One of these experts, whose findings did have some degree of reliability, was James Logan, the son of a merchant family in Aberdeen, who wandered the length and breadth of the Highlands and brought out a standard work on the subject in 1842/45, "The Clans of the Scottish Highlands". But charlatans were also rife, such as, for example, the brothers John and Charles Sobieski Stuart, who claimed to be grandsons of Bonnie Prince Charlie and published the magnificent and colourful book "The Costume of the Clans" in 1845. The contents of this volume were supposedly based on a 16th c. manuscript unearthed in France, although no other person was ever vouchsafed a glance at the document they claimed to have found.

Buchanan (tartan)   MacLeod (tartan)   Royal Stewart (tartan)

Today the tradition is upheld by the Scottish Tartans Society, which sees to it that only tartans which it approves can be declared genuine. There are now more than 1800 different tartans, both those derived from designs belonging to the old clans and completely new creations. Even an everyday handmade kilt on its own will cost around £200, while the rest of the trappings – jacket, shoes, stockings, sporran and other accessories – can cost about another £300. There are renowned kiltmakers established in Edinburgh's Royal Mile and in Huntly Street in Inverness. The potential buyer needs to understand the following things: "old" does not mean that the tartan is necessarily a centuries-old traditional one, but merely that the colours have been made as closely as possible to the old plant dyes, whereas "modern" and "ordinary" refer to the "newer" colours now available.

competition from Europe. Alongside this there has been an extension of inshore fishing, and afforestation of large areas has taken place, not without considerable opposition from environmental groups. Tourism is also being given special emphasis, in particular in the spring and autumn seasons.

Caledonian Canal The geological formation of the Caledonian fault-line facilitated the construction in the first half of the 19th c. of the Caledonian Canal (by Thomas Telford commissioned in 1803), designed to enable fishing boats and small freight vessels to avoid the long and sometimes dangerous voyage by way of the Pentland Firth, between the northernmost tip of the Scottish mainland and the Orkney Islands (see entry). Today much of this transportation is undertaken by rail and heavy goods vehicles, so that now only a few small freight ships still use the canal. At the same time the importance of the waterway for leisure purposes is continually increasing, with hired cabin cruisers, rowing boats and paddle boats enabling the tourist to enjoy the magnificent scenery. Only a third of the total length of the canal has had to be cut through land, the greater part using the beautiful long narrow lochs which now occupy the geological fault. From west to east these lochs are Loch Linnhe, which is really a fjord, i.e. a glaciated valley which has been flooded by the sea; Loch Lochy; the little Loch Oich; and the longest (24 miles) and best known, Loch Ness. The Canal is just over 60 miles in overall length, has a depth of 16 ft, and 29 locks. The most difficult part of the canal-builders' task was to overcome the difference in height between Loch Linnhe, at sea level, and Loch Lochy, which lay 93 ft higher. This was achieved by a triumph of early 19th c. engineering, a series of eight locks known as Neptune's Staircase, each of which spans a height difference of some 8 ft. The terminal points of the Canal are Fort William and Inverness, which are also linked by a good road connection, the A82.

H. Alexander, first up Ben Nevis by car

West Highland Museum

Fort William (pop. 4500) is the main holiday resort in the district of Lochaber and is a favourite base for climbers of Ben Nevis. The fort after which the town is named, which was built in the 17th c. by William of Orange, has long since disappeared. The town's most important sources of employment are the aluminium works, a paper factory and the Ben Nevis whisky distillery, which was founded in 1825 by John Macdonald and is now owned by the Japanese firm of Nikka Distillers.

The tiny ⋆ **West Highland Museum**, which is in Cameron Square, was founded in 1922 and has an interesting collection of furniture, paintings and implements connected with whisky dating from the 19th c., including the Scottish bowls which were used for drinking whisky, called "quaichs", as well as flat bottles, weapons, everyday objects and examples of Highland dress. Of special interest are the historical documents concerning the West Highland Railway, which was opened in 1894, and the various conquerors of Ben Nevis, including Henry Alexander, who became the first motorist to reach the summit in 1911 in a model T Ford.

Fort William

Fort William's principal attraction is undoubtedly Ben Nevis, at 4406 ft the highest point in the whole of Great Britain. There are various theories as to the meaning of the mountain's name, the most likely being "covered in a cap of mist", which is certainly true on many days during the year. The reddish glow given off by the bare mass of granite and porphyry rock at sunset is particularly evocative. The ascent by the path from Aichintee House (2½ miles; car park) is not difficult; it takes about 3½ to 4 hours. Every year in September there is a race up Ben Nevis, the present record standing at 87 minutes. There is a longer and more difficult route by way of Allta a' Mhuillin and the neighbouring summit of ⋆ **Carn Mor Dearg**, affording views of breathtaking beauty. On the summit of Ben Nevis, which resembles a stony desert, there are the remains of a weather station, which ceased operations in 1894, and a hotel, which was closed in 1915. The flat summit falls away gently at first to the south, and then steeply down into Glen Nevis. The neighbouring peak to the east, **Aonach Mor** (4060 ft) can be ascended by a cable-car (base station at Torlundy).

⋆ **Ben Nevis**

The **view** from the summit of Ben Nevis in clear weather is of overwhelming magnificence, extending in all directions for anything up to 150 miles and taking in the Scottish mountains, the Hebridean islands and even the coast of Ireland. Many climbers start their climb in the evening and spend the night on the top (in sleeping-bags, no shelter) in order to see the sun rise. Unfortunately the view – and the climb – can often be spoiled by mist. Indeed, care is needed at all times, as accidents can occur at any time of the year as a result of inadequate equipment or misreading the weather situation. Some of the best and longest climbs are on the north-east face, but these are for experienced climbers only. Detailed descriptions of the paths and routes across the mountain are available from the Scottish Mountaineering Club and the tourist office in Fort William.

A very beautiful panoramic road, the "Road to the Isles", runs westwards from Fort William to Mallaig (42 miles), from which ferries cross to Skye (see Hebrides).

Mallaig

After about 20 miles, going towards the northern end of Loch Shiel, the visitor will come to the Glenfinnan Monument (1815). It is a memorial to Bonnie Prince Charlie, who in August 1745 united the Scottish clans in opposition to the English.

Glenfinnan Monument

The road from Fort William to Inverness is one of the most beautiful panoramic roads in the country. The first stretch, to Spean Bridge, affords magnificent views of the north face of Ben Nevis. Here large-scale engineering works have been carried out to use the water of Loch

⋆⋆ **Road from Fort William to Inverness**

A view across the Scottish Highlands to Ben Nevis

Treig for the production of hydro-electric power. Spean Bridge is a good base for enjoyable walks up Glen Roy. On the banks of the River Lochy are the two castles of Inverlochy, old and new, and nearby the former Glenlochy whisky distillery, which ceased production in 1983.

Loch Arkaig, Loch Lochy, Loch Oich

To the north of Gailochy, where a side-road branches off to Loch Arkaig, the road follows the shore of Loch Lochy, past the cave in which Bonnie Prince Charlie is said to have hidden during his flight after Culloden, and on to Loch Oich, which, with its backdrop of steep mountains and its tiny islands has a highly picturesque setting. A curious monument over a well named Tobar nan Ceann commemorates a bloody incident in the 17th c. when the heads of seven murderers were washed in the well before being presented to the chief of the Macdonell clan.

Invergarry

Invergarry is a popular base for walkers who wish to explore the splendid mountain scenery and also a centre for anglers.

Glen Shiel

From here a magnificent road (A87) runs north-westwards past Loch Garry, Glen Shiel and Loch Duich to the Kyle of Lochalsh, where a bridge connects to the island of Skye (see Hebrides).

★ Loch Ness

Fort Augustus (pop. 890), at the beginning of Loch Ness, is also a popular tourist centre. Named after the English Duke of Cumberland, **Fort Augustus** was built in 1715. The site was used by the Benedictine order to build an abbey in 1876 and a school of considerable reputation. Nowadays the **Great Glen Exhibition** relates the history of the military, the order and ostensible encounters with the legendary monster. The main road to Inverness (A 82) runs along the northern side of Loch Ness, a minor road (B 862/B 852) on the south side. The latter, which passes through Foyers, with its magnificent waterfall, offers the more attractive scenery of the two, but both roads are well wooded.

Halfway along the lake on the northern side, the A82 passes the ruins of the 12th c. **Urquhart Castle**, on a tongue of land projecting into the loch. In the 14th c. stone brickwork was added.

The controversial Loch Ness Monster is first supposed to have been encountered by the Irish missionary, St Columba, in the 6th c., but did not put in another appearance until the building of the A82 along the north shore in 1933. It is still the subject of wild speculation and not just Loch Ness Monster fans keep a careful look-out along the shores. The Official **Loch Ness Monster Exhibition Centre** at Drumnadrochit explains the early history of Scotland with an audio-visual show, and documents the research and evidence connected with "Nessie", including the earliest photographs, underwater recordings using Sonar equipment and the results of the Operation "Deepscan" of 1987, in which various measurements were taken in this lake, which is full of fish and reaches a depth of over 1065 ft. These measurements suggested the possibility of the existence of a monster, or at the very least, did not entirely refute the possible continued existence of such a creature. Outside the visitors' centre, there is a floating bronze statue of the legendary mythical creature, which, if it exists, is thought to be associated with the dinosaur period.

A canal 3 miles long connects the northern end of Loch Ness with Inverness Firth, the tip of the Caledonian Canal (see p. 438).

Inverness

Inverness (pop. 41,000) is the chief town of the Highland Region, which consists of the old counties of Inverness, Nairn, Ross and Cromarty, Sutherland and Caithness. In the 6th c. Inverness was the capital of a Pictish kingdom. In 565 St Columba visited the Pictish ruler Brude here. In the 12th c. Macbeth's banquet, which Shakespeare (see Famous People) immortalised in his play, is supposed to have been taken place at the castle here. This first castle was built by David I in the middle of the 12th c., while 500 years later Cromwell gave the orders for Scone Fort to be erected. In 1715 the proclamation declaring James Francis Edward to be king was issued from the castle, and in 1745–46 the castle was in Loyalist hands for the last time, under Bonnie Prince Charlie – its destruction by the Duke of Cumberland occurring shortly afterwards in the wake of the Battle of Culloden. The present Victorian castle dates

Inverness: Craig Street footbridge ...   *... and Inverness Castle*

Old Leanach Cottage on the Culloden Battlefield

from the first half of the 19th c. Because of its important location at one end of the Great Glen, Inverness is today also a popular and at times very busy tourist centre. The imposing red sandstone buildings which house the local government offices are popularly known as the "Castle", although the one that stood in Macbeth's time was probably situated further to the east. The River Ness is spanned by two suspension bridges in the town. Facing Castle Hill and reached by the Craig Street Footbridge is St Andrew's Cathedral (1871).

The oldest house in Inverness is **Abertarff House** (1592) on Church Street, which has a noteworthy exterior staircase. Today it is the headquarters of the Highland Association, which works to preserve Gaelic culture and the Gaelic language.

This rich historical legacy of the Highlands is documented and illustrated by the natural and social history sections of the **Highland Museum and Art Gallery** at Castle Wynd.

Culloden Battlefield

The desolate expanses of moorland in the valley of the Nairn, about 6 miles to the east of Inverness, are closely connected with one of the decisive dates of Scottish history, April 16th 1746 – the day of the Battle of Culloden, a clash which represented the culmination of centuries of hostilities. The troops of the English government under the Duke of Cumberland defeated the Highlanders' army, which was already exhausted after a long night march, its 5000 or so men amounting to only half the number of troops which the English were able to field. The brief skirmish on Drumossie Moor was followed by the merciless massacre of the surviving Highlanders in the Jacobite army. The ensuing political sanctions later that year led to the total prohibition of the clan system, thereby causing the final destruction of the traditional way of life of the Highlands as well as all hopes of the Stuart line regaining the throne. The only reminders of the momentous event still to be found on the battlefield are Old Leanach Cottage, the old farmhouse where the Gaelic song "Mo Run Gealog" (My youngest and dearest) still rings out, several memorial stones and graves for the fallen of both armies.

Just 10 miles to the north-east of the battlefield of Culloden is Cawdor Castle, which according to Shakespeare (see Famous People) was the scene of the murder of Duncan by Macbeth, Thane of Cawdor, in 1040. This idea is contradicted – as is the Glamis Castle theory (see Grampian Mountains) – by the fact that the castle was not built until the 14th or 15th c. and Duncan actually fell at the hands of Macbeth at the Battle of Elgin. The castle, however, which is today owned by the Campbell family, contains valuable pieces of furniture and extensive literature about Shakespeare, as well as boasting a superb garden.

★ Cawdor Castle

The nearby whisky distillery is one of three Scottish distilleries which are allowed to use the appellation "Royal". The company was set up in 1812 and accorded its royal title by William IV in 1835.

Royal Brackla Distillery

10 miles further on lies Brodie Castle, completed in 1567, which contains valuable furniture, porcelain, paintings, and a magnificent 17th c. plaster ceiling.

Brodie Castle

The Tomatin Distillery is the largest in Scotland, producing around 12 million litres a year in 23 "pot stills". Today, however, it is owned by the Japanese firm, Takara Skuzo & Okurra.

Tomatin Distillery

A highly scenic road runs north from Inverness, following the coast for most of the way, to Scotland's most north-easterly point, John o' Groats, on the Pentland Firth, and then on to Thurso. From Inverness it borders the Beauly Firth until it reaches Beauly, so called (French "beau lieu" =

★ From Inverness to the Pentland Firth
Beauly Priory

A bedchamber ...   *... in Cawdor Castle*

443

"beautiful place") because of the picturesque situation of a priory built here by French monks in the 13th c. The remains include the west doorway and some fine triangular windows.

★ **Black Isle**

The road then crosses the Black Isle, which is actually a peninsula between Beauly and Cromarty Firth, also called Millbuie Isle. This is the most intensively farmed agricultural region in the Highlands.

Fortrose

The most important town in the area is Fortrose, once a considerable port but now mainly a holiday resort with a good golf-course. The 15th c. bell in the bell-tower of the ruined abbey is still rung every evening. Of the small cathedral, the main surviving part is the chapterhouse. Rosemarkie, now a part of Fortrose, is a still older foundation, the site of a 6th c. monastic school. In 1125 David I made it an episcopal see, later transferred to Fortrose.

Cromarty Firth

The onshore oil installations and other trading and industrial establishments located round the Cromarty Firth are evidence of the most recent economic developments which have come about as a result of the advent of the state-subsidised oil industry in this area.

Dingwall

The A835 goes westwards away from the peninsula and comes to Dingwall (pop. 5000), a road and rail junction at the end of the Cromarty Firth. Dingwall was granted the status of a royal burgh in 1226 and is well-known for its school. Of interest are the old town hall, an obelisk near the church commemorating the 1st Earl of Cromarty and Foulis Castle, 5 miles to the north-east. The A835 continues westwards through beautiful scenery to Braemore and Ullapool.

Alness, Invergordon

The main road, the A9, continues north-east via Alness, with the Black Rock of Novar and the Dalmore and Teaninich whisky distilleries, to Invergordon, once an important naval base but now dominated by the oil industry.

Fearn, Tain

After Invergordon the road skirts the edge of the peninsula of Easter Ross, past Fearn, a small farming town with the ruins of a Premonstratensian abbey, and on to Tain, a royal burgh and a pleasant seaside resort on the Dornoch Firth. The Tolbooth, or prison, with its conical roof is worth seeing, as is the nearby 14th c. St Duthus Church. The old chapel on this site was once a popular place of pilgrimage. After Tain the road enters a tunnel under Dornoch Firth and leads on to the town of Dornoch itself.

★ **Glenmorangie Distillery**

The Glenmorangie Distillery was opened in 1843 and since 1918 has been owned by Macdonald and Muir. Its malt whisky has the biggest sales in the whole of Great Britain. The malt whisky is distilled in the highest "pot stills" in Scotland and only bourbon barrels are used to store it.

Bablair Distillery

A short distance to the west of the Dornoch Firth is Bablair, another distillery with a long history.

Dornoch

Dornoch (pop. 1100) is a pretty little town with a much restored 13th c. cathedral (arcading, fine west window). Of the old castle, formerly the bishop's palace, only the tower remains, and this now forms part of a hotel complex. The town has good bathing beaches and golf-courses.

Skibo Castle

Skibo Castle (5 miles to the west) was built in 1898 for the Scots-born American steel king Andrew Carnegie (1835–1919), who gave 350 million dollars for scientific and charitable purposes and founded the Carnegie Institutes, which bear his name.

A collection of curiosities in Dunrobin Castle

From Dornoch the road, for most of its length running close to the sea, continues to Golspie (pop. 1300) with a good beach and an interesting church, and on to Dunrobin Castle, which has a 13th c. square tower. Its priceless contents include an outstanding collection of paintings with works by Canaletto, Reynolds and John Hoppner, Chippendale furniture, Mortlake tapestries, gobelins and a collection of curiosities in the basement, which include kitchen utensils, hunting trophies and a steam-driven fire-extinguisher. It is very pleasant to take a stroll through the beautifully laid out gardens and park with their views over the sea.

★ **Dunrobin Castle**

Brora (pop. 1100), at the mouth of the River Brora, is a popular fishing centre and seaside resort.

It is well worth making a trip to Loch Brora, situated to the west.

The old ★ **whisky distillery** which was opened in Brora in 1819 at the command of the Duke of Sutherland was originally called Clynelish and did not take on its present name of Brora until 1967–68, when new distilling buildings were opened which were exclusively given the name Clynelish. The 14-year-old Single Malt from the new Clynelish Distillery is considered one of the best whiskies produced in the Highlands.

Brora

Helmsdale (12 miles to the north-east) is the next stop, a fishing village

Helmsdale

with a sheltered harbour and a 15th c. castle. 7 miles to the south, before reaching Helmsdale, close to the road, is a very well-preserved broch (stone tower), while there is another one to the north of the town in the direction of Ord of Caithness.

Berriedale

The next stretch of road, to Berriedale (10 miles), is steep and winding, but scenically interesting, with numerous hills and ravines. At Berriedale there is a ruined castle, below which Langwell Water and the Berriedale River flow into the sea. Inland, some distance away, can be seen the peaks of Morven (2313 ft) and Scaraben, somewhat lower.

Dunbeath

Dunbeath (pop. 490), a fishing village with a fine broch, a 15th c. castle and the Lhaidhay Croft Museum, and Latheron, lying to the north with its old bell-tower, seem lost in this hilly region.

Further north, between Lybster and Ulbster, there is a prehistoric stone circle.

Wick

The port of Wick (pop. 8000) has developed as a result of fishing, and more recently, the oil industry. A visit to the Caithness glassworks on Harrow Hill is recommended. On the rocky coast just to the south of the town are the imposing remains of Old Wick Castle, while a natural rock arch known as the Brig o' Tram and a tower called the Old Man of Wick are also well worth seeing. To the north of Wick are the remains of Girnigoe and Sinclair Castles, perched on the cliff-top, with Ackergill Tower nearby.

John o'Groats

From Wick the main road continues inland to Thurso. However the coast road runs north, past Ness Head, to Sinclair's Bay. To the north of the village of Keiss is the 16th c. Bucholie Castle. At John o'Groats on the Pentland Firth we come to the most north-easterly place in Scotland which is accessible by road, its special position being marked by a signpost. Strictly speaking, to reach the very north-easternmost point, it is necessary to continue for another 2 miles to Duncansby Head. John o' Groats itself has nothing to offer, the house belonging to John o'Groats having been long since destroyed, while he himself is buried in Canisbay churchyard. From the cliffs here there is a fine view of the Orkney Islands (see entry).

Thurso

Thurso, the most northerly railway station in Britain, has beautiful views, a ruined castle and the remains of a 13th c. bishop's palace. The town was once the centre of a flourishing trade in Caithness flagstones, but this no longer exists. The local museum is of interest for an interesting mineralogical collection assembled by the geologist Robert Dick (1811–66). From the nearby harbour of Scrabster there is a car ferry service to Stromness (see Orkney Islands).

West part of the North-West Highlands

There is a beautiful road running along the north and west coasts; the north coast section keeps close to the sea for most of the way, the west coast section runs further inland to avoid the numerous indentations of the coast. There are also very attractive roads running inland from east to west, often following the little rivers which traverse these northern Highlands and passing numerous lochs of all sizes.

Loch Shin

One of the largest of these lochs is the centrally located Loch Shin (15 miles long by 2 miles across), which is used for the production of hydroelectric power but also offers good fishing and water sports. At the southern end of the loch is **Lairg** (pop. 1000), which is a good centre for exploring the areas to the north and west, for example, Loch Naver and Altnaharra to the north, with its superb mountain walking, or Loch Loyal and the strangely shaped Ben Loyal (2504 ft). Near Lairg itself is Ben Kilbreck (3154 ft).

The wildly romantic Loch Assynt

Scourie

It is also well worth making a trip along the A 838 and A 894 to the coast at Scourie (44 miles), skirting Loch Merkland, with its rich stocks of fish, and on past Loch More and Loch Stack, also popular with anglers, both splendidly situated amid mountains ranging from 2300–2800 ft.

Ullapool

One of the most popular holiday resorts in the North-West Highlands is Ullapool (pop. 1000), a picturesque fishing village on sheltered Loch Broom. From here there is a ferry service to Stornoway on the island of Lewis (see Hebrides).

Summer Isles

The beautiful Summer Isles, further out to sea from Ullapool, at the mouth of the loch, are delightful to visit, while inland, excursions can be made into the wild and extraordinary scenery stretching over to Loch Assynt, with bizarrely formed peaks and numerous tiny lochs.

★Loch Assynt

There is a good road (A835) to this area via Ledmore, but the scenery is even wilder and more beautiful on the Inverkirkaig road, keeping close to the coast, with the Kirkaig Falls 2 miles to the south. The backdrop of mountains changes all the time, as Ben More Coigach (2438 ft), Cul Beag (2523 ft) and An Stac, usually called Stac Polly (2009 ft), present themselves in different aspects. These are mountains for rock climbers rather than for hill walkers. Then, beyond Loch Lurgain and Loch Bad a' Ghaill, Cul Mor (2787 ft) and Suilven (2399 ft) come into view, the latter from certain points of view resembling a huge sugarloaf. Loch Assynt, noted for its trout, is also surrounded by mountains. The road along the north side of this loch is one of the most beautiful in Scotland, with a magnificent backdrop of mountains and ruined castles.

Lochinver

Around Lochinver there are said to be no fewer than 280 lochs – many of them having no name – which offer excellent fishing. The climate here is very mild, and subtropical plants flourish in Inverewe Gardens (National Trust) near Poolewe, 5 miles north of Gairloch.

Braemore

From Ullapool there is a good road (A835) south-east to Braemore, with the magnificent ★**Corrieshalloch Gorge**, which the 150 ft-high Measach Falls have carved into the landscape.

Norwich

Eastern England
County: Norfolk
Altitude: 60 ft. Population: 140,000

Norwich, county town of Norfolk, lies on the little River Wensum within easy reach of the beautiful Norfolk Broads, which can easily be explored

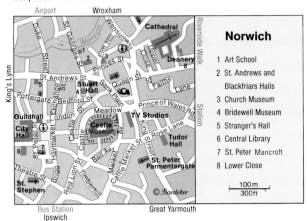

Norwich

1 Art School
2 St. Andrews and Blackfriars Halls
3 Church Museum
4 Bridewell Museum
5 Stranger's Hall
6 Central Library
7 St. Peter Mancroft
8 Lower Close

© Baedeker

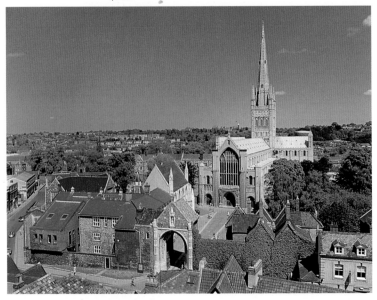

Norwich, the "capital" of East Anglia

by sailing boat, canoe or motor-launch. Norwich has more medieval churches (32 in all) than any other town in the country with the exception of London. Although today it is a bustling business and shopping centre, Norwich has a long tradition as East Anglia's historic capital, and this is reflected in its splendid Norman cathedral and the atmosphere, a product of centuries of history, which is to be found in its old town gateways and winding lanes. The production of mustard, shoes and confectionery is closely associated with Norwich. In more recent times the service sector has steadily grown in importance.

From Tombland, originally a Saxon market-place, there are two gates, St Ethelbert's (1272; upper part restored) and Erpingham (1420), either of which leads into the idyllic tranquillity of the cathedral close with its wealth of historically interesting buildings, including the medieval deanery.

Sights
Tombland

The gleaming white cathedral, dedicated to the Holy Trinity, with a striking spire which is a prominent landmark, has preserved its Norman character better than any other church in England. The building of the cathedral was begun in 1096 by Herbert de Losinga (bishop 1091–1119), who transferred the episcopal see of Thetford to Norwich in 1092. The choir and aisles were completed in 1101, and the nave by his successor Eborard or Everard (bishop 1121–46). The spire collapsed in 1362 and was rebuilt in Decorated style. In the 15th c. the nave and presbytery were re-roofed and a Perpendicular window was inserted in the west front. The spire (315 ft) is the highest in England after Salisbury (see entry).

★★Norwich
Cathedral

The interior has a **nave** with fourteen bays, mainly in the early Norman style, with low massive columns. The windows are Decorated and Perpendicular; the glass is mainly 19th c. Particularly notable is the fine lierne vaulting, with 326 bosses (out of a total of over 800 in the whole cathedral). The **aisles** are also Norman. Two bays of the south aisle were converted into chantry chapels by Bishop Nyx or Nykke (bishop 1501–35). The **transepts** resemble the nave, with beautiful 16th c. vaulting. The choir was rebuilt in the Perpendicular style, but the original apse was preserved. The 62 choir-stalls, with splendid canopies and beautifully carved misericords. date from 1420 to 1480. In the aisles there are a number of tombs, including that of Bishop James Goldwell (1472–99). Behind the high altar is the old stone bishop's throne dating from the 6th or 8th c. (restored 1959).

Norwich Cathedral

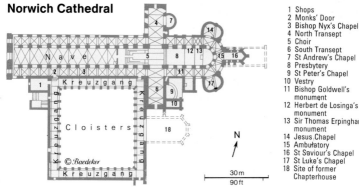

1 Shops
2 Monks' Door
3 Bishop Nyx's Chapel
4 North Transept
5 Choir
6 South Transept
7 St Andrew's Chapel
8 Presbytery
9 St Peter's Chapel
10 Vestry
11 Bishop Goldwell's monument
12 Herbert de Losinga's monument
13 Sir Thomas Erpingham's monument
14 Jesus Chapel
15 Ambulatory
16 St Saviour's Chapel
17 St Luke's Chapel
18 Site of former Chapterhouse

N

30 m
90 ft

© Baedeker

The Monk's Door and the Prior's Door lead through to the two-storey **cloister**, built between 1297 and 1425. Its passageways are full of embellishments in a range of styles from Decorated to Perpendicular and contain more than 400 superb bosses.

The **Bishop's Palace**, with a doorway dating from about 1430, and St John's Chapel (1322) are now part of Norwich School. Formerly named King Edward VI School, it was founded as a monastery school in 1240 and numbers Lord Nelson (see Famous People) and the landscape gardener Humphrey Repton among its past pupils.

★Elm Hill

Below Tombland near the River Wensum, the medieval cobbled street known as Elm Hill branches off. This picturesque little thoroughfare is lined with tiny old houses, many of them now attractive shops.

St Andrew's Hall

Near the top end of Elm Hill are St Andrew's and Blackfriars Halls, originally a large Dominican church, now used for exhibitions and musical events.

Bridewell Museum

Just a short distance away, going south-westwards, in Bridewell Alley is the Bridewell Museum with exhibits devoted to industry and handicrafts in Norfolk, including a display about the silk shawls which were so prized by Queen Victoria.

★Mustard Museum

In the same street the Mustard Museum deals with the 150 years' history of Colman's mustard.

Castle Museum

To the east is the Castle, which was built on an artificial mound, probably about 1160 by Hugh Bigod, Earl of Norfolk. It consists mainly of a Norman keep, which was used until 1884 as a prison and since 1894 has housed a ★**museum**. The interior is set out as a rotunda surrounded by various galleries which contain extensive archaeological sections,

"The Back of the New Mills" by John Crome

natural history dioramas, collections of medieval weapons, glassware and ceramics, as well as a painting collection which includes English and Dutch masters of the 17th and 18th c. and numerous works of the Norwich School.

The founder of the Norwich School of painting was **John Crome** (1768–1821), a weaver's son who was trained as a sign-painter. He devoted himself almost exclusively to painting landscapes of his native area, including the following paintings dating from the beginning of the 19th c. "Carrow Abbey" (1805), "Norwich" and "The Back of the New Mills". One of the most gifted painters of the Norwich School was **John Sell Cotman** (1782–1842), the son of a barber. His masterpieces, which include many etchings and watercolours such as "Devil's Elbow" and "Mousehold Heath", all show a dazzling virtuosity.

To the west of the Castle can be found the spacious market place, which is the site of one of the most notable markets in the county. On the far side are the **City Hall** and the **Guildhall** (1407) with its old windows, now the Tourist Information Office. | Market Place

Strangers' Hall in Charing Cross is a late medieval merchant's house, now a museum, which documents domestic life from the Tudor period through to the Victorian era (costumes, furniture). Suckling House, adjacent to St Andrew's Church, is a handsome example of a medieval town house. The disused church of St Peter Hungate contains a display of religious arts and crafts. One of the most interesting of Norwich's many medieval churches is St George Colegate, built in 1459, with a choir dating from 1498, its interior practically unchanged. The exterior of St Giles is decorated by pebble dash work, something which can be admired on other buildings throughout the city and the rest of Norfolk. | Other sights

The award-winning Sainsbury Centre, part of the University of East Anglia, to the west of the city centre, has displays of modern and primitive art, including works by Picasso, Epstein, Giacometti and Henry Moore (see Famous People). | ★Sainsbury Centre for Visual Arts

A stroll along the Riverside Walk is very relaxing. This follows the River Wensum, to the north-east of the Cathedral, and passes the Cow Tower, part of the city's original medieval fortifications. | Riverside Walk, Cow Tower

A little way to the south is Bishop Bridge (1395), one of the oldest bridges in the country. From Mousehold Heath, north-east of the city, there is a fine general view of the Norwich skyline. | Bishop Bridge

The Britannia Barracks, which are situated on the heath, formerly housed the Royal Norfolk Regimental Museum (uniforms, medals, paintings and silver from 1685 to 1959) but this has now been moved to the Shirehall in Norwich. | Royal Norfolk Regimental Museum

Opened in September 1993, this shopping precinct has been built under the area around the Castle. | Castle Mall

Aylsham (pop. 2500; 14 miles to the north) is an attractive market town with associations with John of Gaunt. | **Surroundings Aylsham**

Blickling Hall (1 mile north-west of Aylsham) is a large red-brick mansion (1616–28), which contains fine furniture and paintings and a magnificent plaster ceiling. In the large park, well planted with trees, are a lake and an 18th c. mausoleum. | **Blickling Hall**

The Norfolk Broads are a fascinating nature reserve, ideal for sailing and boating holidays, which occupy the triangle formed by Yarmouth, Wroxham and Stalham. In the area traversed by the River Yare and its | **Norfolk Broads** tributaries the Ant, Thurne, Bure and Waveney there are about 200 miles of waterways. In the past there were extensive peat-cuttings here, now occupied by shallow lagoons, mostly overgrown with reeds, which were once used for thatching, filling walls and basket-making. Windmills, such as the wooden Boardman's Mill at Ludham, the brick-built Thurne Dyke Windpump on the bank of the Thurne or the 82 ft high Sutton Mill, were once used for drainage and call to mind similar scenery in Holland. Of the "wherries", flat boats used for shipping coal, wood and provisions, which were once typical of the Broads, only four "model ships" still remain. A very impressive picture of the former day-to-day life of the Broadland farmers and eel-fishers is provided by the Victorian photographic pioneer, P. H. Emerson, in his principal work, "Naturalistic Photography", which appeared in 1889. Nature-lovers will find hosts of waterfowl, butterflies, dragonflies and rare flowers, and anglers will be attracted by the large numbers of fish (bream, rudd, roach, perch, pike).

The beauties of the Broads cannot be properly appreciated by road; they must be explored by **boat**. Sailing boats and motor cruisers can be rented and there are various excursion launches which operate trips on the Bure, the Yare and on certain broads.

The largest of the Broads, and one of the most beautiful is ★**Hickling Broad**, with the nearby old Horsey Windmill. The best starting-point for an exploration of this area is Potter Heigham, going upstream on the River Thurne to Martham Broad, Horsey Mere and Hickling Broad, while downstream leads to the River Bure. From there it is possible to continue south-east by way of Breydon Water and the River Waveney to Oulton Broad outside Lowestoft, or westwards through a series of broads to **Wroxham Broad** and the village of Wroxham. Potter Heigham (pop. 690) is usually less crowded than Wroxham. Other good centres from which to explore the Broads are Ranworth and South Walsham, small picturesque villages with interesting churches.

Nottingham   K 7/8

Central England. County: Nottinghamshire
Altitude: 420 ft. Population: 280,000

Nottingham, county town of Nottinghamshire, is built on a number of hills on the north bank of the River Trent. The most important town in the eastern part of the Midlands, Nottingham looks back on a long tradition as an industrial town. Noted in the past for its lace, curtains and stockings, its industry now centres on pharmaceuticals, textiles, mechanical and vehicle building. The town, which since 1948 has had a university, is known as "Queen of the Midlands", on account of its broad streets and parks, such as the Arboretum, Embankment and Colwick Park. It is the focal point of a prosperous and developing region. In addition, the coalfield centred on Nottinghamshire, Derbyshire and South Yorkshire is the largest and most important in England.

The nuclear physicist, George Green (1793–1841), and William Booth, the founder of the Salvation Army (see Famous People), were both born in the suburb of Eastwood. Lord Byron went to school in Nottingham and later lived a short distance north of the town in Newstead Abbey.

Robin Hood

Nottingham is a good base for visiting Sherwood Forest, the scene of the medieval legends concerning Robin Hood, who as an outlaw with Little John and his other "merry men" robbed the rich to pay the poor, finally defeated the scheming Sheriff of Nottingham and was rehabilitated by King Richard. The image of this folk hero is to be found all over the town. The enormous area of woodland which once existed has by now been considerably reduced, although it has managed to retain its atmosphere of daring romantic adventures. Near Edwinstowe, where

Robin Hood in Maid Marian Way...   *... and below the castle*

Robin and "Maid Marian" were married in the presence of the king,
stands the famous old oak, the "Major Oak", which is over 1000 years
old and has a circumference of over 30 ft.

History The town of Snotingaham or Snotengaham was occupied by the
Danes in 868 and became the capital of the five boroughs of the Danelaw
– the others being Derby, Leicester, Lincoln and Stamford (see entries).
In 1068 William the Conqueror (see Famous People) had a castle built
here. Later Nottingham was to become one of Britain's earliest industrial
towns, and as such became a centre of the Luddite riots of 1811–16
aimed at the destruction of the new industrial machinery. The hosiery
industry, which formerly flourished in the whole county, was founded in
Elizabethan times by a local parson who invented the stocking-frame, a
device which was soon adopted throughout the surrounding area.

In the centre of the town is the Old Market Square, the largest in
England, on which the famous Goose Fair was formerly held (it now
takes place on the Forest Recreation Ground). On the east side of the
square is the Neo-Classical **Council House** (by Cecil Howitt, 1929),
crowned by an imposing dome.

Sights
City Centre

North of the town centre are the impressive **Guildhall** (1929) and the
Technical College, both by Cecil Howitt.

The castle, on a rock 133 ft) high, affords a good view of the town.
Outside it are the bronze statues (1952) of **Robin Hood** and his merry
men by the Nottingham-born sculptor James Woodford.

**Nottingham
Castle**

The old castle was destroyed in 1651 by Parliamentary forces and
replaced by an Italian-style palace belonging to the Duke of Newcastle.
This was burned down in 1831 but later rebuilt. Since 1878 it has housed
the ✶**Nottingham Museum and Art Gallery**. Among its treasures there

The Long Gallery in the Castle Museum

are some beautiful Anglo-Saxon brooches (6th c.); medieval ceramics and alabaster carvings; Nottingham stoneware from the 17th and 18th c., including a "love goblet" of 1679; English household silver; drinking glasses of the 17th and 18th c.; an ethnographic gallery (including New Zealand jade jewellery, Burmese bronze statues, Indo-Persian steelware); a collection devoted to the Sherwood Foresters regiment and the fighter pilot, Albert Ball (1896–1917). The picture collection in the Long Gallery includes works by Charles le Brun, Richard Wilson, William Dyce, Marcus Stone, Ben Nicholson and Epstein.

Mortimer's Hole

In the sandstone underneath the town there are a large number of caves, including the 322 ft long "Mortimer's Hole" below the castle, which derived its name in the 16th c. from Roger Mortimer, lover of Queen Isabella, the wife of Edward II.

★Ye Old Trip to Jerusalem

The pub, "Ye Old Trip to Jerusalem" in Castle Road, dates from the 12th c. and ranks as the oldest inn in England. Long-standing tradition and a welcoming atmosphere are combined here in typically British fashion.

★Brewhouse Yard Museum

The row of houses alongside recreates the daily life of Nottingham in the 17th to 19th c. The caves connected to the Brewhouse Yard Museum, which are hewn into the castle rock, once served as a beer cellar and workshops.

★Museum of Costume and Textiles

The costume museum in Castle Gate contains valuable lacework, Renaissance-style embroidery and notable 17th c. wall coverings which were manufactured in Nottinghamshire.

St Mary's

The Church of St Mary in Stoney Street is mainly in the late Perpendicular style. Of interest is its 19th c. glasswork from the workshops of Ward-Hughes and Clayton Bell.

The story of the folk hero is turned into a living legend on a visit to the fantastic model wood at "The Tales of Robin Hood" exhibition centre on Maid Marian Way.

The Castle Boulevard runs west (2 miles) to Highfields Park, which was presented to the town by Lord Trent and is now occupied by the university. Jesse Boot, who became Lord Trent, opened the first of his chain of chemist's shops in Nottingham, and the firm still has a large factory in the area.

Near the university, in a large park, is Wollaton Hall, an Elizabethan mansion (by Robert Smythson, 1580–87) which now houses the Natural History Museum of Nottingham. An industrial museum has been set up in the stables.

9 miles to the north is Newstead Abbey, the family home of Lord Byron, whose tomb is in Newstead parish church. When he inherited the estate he and his mother were too poor to live there. In spite of his debts, however, he came to live in the house after leaving Cambridge, but was obliged to sell the property six years later (1817). The house was originally an Augustinian abbey founded in 1170 by Henry II. Of the original buildings there remain the west front of the church, the refectory, the chapterhouse (now a chapel) and the cloisters. Newstead now belongs to the city of Nottingham, and Byron's rooms have been preserved as they were in his lifetime, with many mementoes of the poet. The garden contains very old and rare trees.

From Newstead it is 1 mile to Hardwick, where there is another fine Elizabethan mansion, Hardwick Hall – "Hardwick Hall, more glass than wall", the contemporary jingle went, for the house has 50 windows and relatively small areas of wall. It was built by Robert Smythson in 1591–97 for Bess of Hardwick (Elizabeth, daughter of John Hardwick), who married four times, her last husband being the 6th Earl of Shrewsbury. Inside the hall there is a rich collection of tapestries, furniture, embroidery and portraits. In the centre of the house is a large two-storey hall, with a magnificent staircase leading to the upper floor. From the house there are beautiful glimpses of the gardens. Close by are the remains of Hardwick Old Hall, with fine plasterwork. In the park, to the north, is Ault Hucknall Church, with the tomb of Thomas Hobbes (1588–1679), the philosopher and author of "Leviathan".

5 miles from Hardwick is Bolsover Castle, originally built by William Peveril in the 11th c. and restored in 1613–17 by Charles Cavendish, son of Bess of Hardwick by her second marriage. Today it is mainly in ruins but contains some fine chimneypieces.

15 miles north-east is Southwell (pop. 6500), a small market town which makes a good base for the exploration of the Robin Hood country. Charles I stayed in the Saracen's Head before giving himself up to the Scots in 1646, thus beginning the long period of imprisonment which ended with his execution. Southwell Minster was begun in the 12th c. and the nave and transepts of this period have been preserved. There are three Norman towers, one over the crossing and two on the west front; the west towers still have their original roofs, in spite of rebuilding after a fire in 1711 and further alterations in 1880. The minster, originally served by a college of secular canons, became a cathedral in 1884. The fine brass lectern was found in a lake in the grounds of Newstead Abbey, where it had probably been thrown for concealment by the monks at the time of the Dissolution of the Monasteries.

The most exquisite part of the minster is the Decorated chapterhouse (13th c.) with its wonderful doorway. A profusion of beautiful naturalis-

The Tales of
Robin Hood

Highfields Park

Wollaton Hall

**Surroundings
Newstead Abbey**

Hardwick Hall

Bolsover Castle

Southwell

tic leaves and flowers, vines and grapes, animals and human figures, have been carved here by an unknown sculptor.

Offa's Dyke   H/I 7–9

Wales (the Welsh Marches bordering England)

Offa's Dyke is an earth rampart built by King Offa of Mercia between 784 and 796 to provide protection for the Anglo-Saxons against Welsh attacks. It extends from the Severn estuary to the Dee, a total distance of some 170 miles.

After defeating Caradoc, a Welsh prince, between Abergele and Rhuddlan (south of Rhyl) Offa built the wall to mark the border between Mercia and Wales. His palace was at Sutton Walls.

The earth rampart was reinforced by a ditch on the Welsh side. It can be followed, with many interruptions, for a distance of more than 140 miles between the estuary of the Dee and the Wye. A second earthwork known as Wat's (or Watt's) Dyke, which is probably of somewhat later origin, runs parallel to Offa's Dyke, 3 miles away, for a distance of some 40 miles from the Dee to the Severn.

Kington

At certain places in England Offa's Dyke is quite well-preserved, enabling the visitor to gain a good idea of what it was like. One such stretch of the Dyke, which has survived almost intact, is near Kington, a small market town near the Welsh border. Kington is also noted for the large sheep market held annually in September.

Knighton

Not far away is Knighton (county of Powys, Wales), a little town set among wooded hills on the River Teme, with well-preserved stretches of the Dyke on either side of the town. Here too there is a large sheep and lamb market in autumn.

Montgomery

Another attractive little town where Offa's Dyke can be seen is Montgomery (pop. 970), 10 miles south of Welshpool. It was formerly the county town (at least in name) of the old county of Montgomeryshire, now part of the new county of Powys. The little town, which has many Elizabethan and Georgian houses, lies off the main road, and its railway station is a mile from the town. It takes its name from Roger de Montgomery, Earl of Shrewsbury (d. about 1093), who conquered Powys. The castle, of which some remains exist above the town (good view), was built by Henry III in 1223. Montgomery was the birthplace of the poet George Herbert (1593–1663), whose brother Lord Herbert of Cherbury (1583–1648), the philosopher, also lived here for a time. In the 13th c. parish church there is a monument to their father. The church also contains an early Norman font, carved misericords and a beautiful rood-screen, probably from the ruined abbey of Chirbury (Shropshire). The Town Hall is in the Georgian style.

Mold

Another well-preserved stretch of the Dyke can be seen at Mold (pop. 7730), county town of Clwyd (Wales). The town has a charming old High Street and a beautiful late 15th c. parish church with its original glass. The painter Richard Wilson (1714–82) is buried there. The town's most famous son is the Welsh writer Daniel Owen, who is commemorated by a statue in the town centre. One mile south of the town, in Cilcain Road, there is a pillar marking the spot where in 430 British forces led by St Germanus, Bishop of Auxerre, defeated the pagan Picts and Scots.

Offa's Dyke Path

Offa's Dyke Path is one of the long-distance paths laid out by the Countryside Commission. The paths are waymarked and described in booklets issued by the Commission.

Orkney Islands   H/I 1/2

Northern Scotland
Region: Orkney Islands

The Orkney Islands lie off the north coast of Scotland and are separated from the mainland by the Pentland Firth. The shortest distance between the two is 6½ miles, between John o' Groats and the southern tip of the island of South Ronaldsay. About 19,000 people live on 18 out of the total number of 67 islands, which are of varying size (14,000 on the main island, which is called Mainland). The islands extend over a distance of 48 miles from north to south and 35 miles from east to west.

A fertile layer of topsoil over the islands' underlying red sandstone, and a mild climate brought about by the Gulf Stream, make for highly productive agriculture. Large fields stretching across gentle hillsides, broken up by marsh, grassland and heathland, are the main features of the Orcadian landscape. Only Hoy, with its steep towering cliffs, is different. Besides agriculture, fishing, particularly for crab and lobster, constitutes an important source of income for the islands. Another important source of employment is the offshore oil industry, which has a large tanker-loading station on the island of Flotta in Scapa Flow.

The Orkneys are a very popular holiday destination for nature-lovers, ramblers and bird-watchers. Anglers and sports fishermen will also find plenty of enjoyment here, as the stock of fish is enormous, both in the sea and in the lakes on the island of Mainland. However, even those in search of sights in the more usual sense of the word, will not be disappointed: it is no surprise that these islands were inhabited in prehistoric times, given their favourable climate and fertile soil. These early inhabitants have left behind plenty of evidence of their occupation, on a scale not normally found in Great Britain. However, many of the Stone Age and Bronze Age sites can only be reached on foot or by bicycle.

On no account should the visitor miss the chance to sample the local malt whisky and other specialities, especially lobster and smoked cheese.

Transport Car ferry Scrabster–Stromness (twice daily in the season) and Aberdeen (see entry)–Stromness (once a week); pedestrian ferry John o'Groats–Burwick (several crossings daily) and Gill's Bay–Burwick (daily every 2 hours); daily connections between the islands and from Stromness to Lerwick (see Shetland Islands); every Sunday, June–August also on Thursday.

Direct flights with British Airways from Aberdeen (see entry) and Inverness (daily except Sun.) and with Loganair also from Aberdeen and Inverness (daily except Sun.) to Kirkwall and between the other islands and with the Shetlands (see entry).

History At the very same time that the pyramids were being built in Egypt, the first settlers on the Orkneys were erecting their simple dwellings. They were driven out by the Picts, who in turn had to yield to conquerors from further north. For hundreds of years the Orkneys, together with the Shetlands, the Hebrides (see entries) and Northern Scotland, belonged to Norway. To this day many names recall this period in the islands' history, and indeed the local culture and traditions are if anything more Nordic than British. Right up until the 17th c. a Norse dialect called "Norn" was spoken here, and the name "Orkney" is thought to derive from the Norse word "orc" (wild bear). The story of the Norwegian rulers ("jarls") of the Orkneys is to be found in the "Orkneyinga Saga". Following the Battle of Largs in 1263 the Norwegians lost their Scottish territories except for the Orkneys and Shetlands. In 1468 King Christian I pledged the islands as security for the dowry of his daughter Margaret on her marriage to James III of

Scotland. The dowry was not paid, and the islands were thereupon annexed by Scotland in 1472. The Scots established their own feudal system on the islanders, who had not previously come into contact with the clan system and had managed their affairs and governed on a communal basis. The islander Patrick Stewart was sentenced to death for his atrocities and executed in Edinburgh in 1615. During the First and Second World Wars the landlocked bay of Scapa Flow was the main base of the British fleet.

Mainland
Kirkwall

Of the 14,000 inhabitants of Mainland, half live in the capital, Kirkwall (Old Norse "kirkjuvagr" = "church bay"), which is situated on a wide bay at the narrowest point of the island. It is a town of narrow streets, and houses built in Norwegian fashion with small windows and gables facing on to the streets.

The most notable building is the large cathedral, dedicated to ★ **St Magnus**, its architecture reminiscent of Trondheim Cathedral in Norway. It was begun in 1137 at the instigation of Jarl Rognvald the Holy, who had it consecrated in the name of his uncle Count Magnus, who was killed on Egilsay in 1116. By the end of the 15th c. the church with its west façade was to all intents and purposes complete, the oldest surviving parts being the transepts and three bays in the choir. The massive Norman columns are notable for being set at irregular distances from one another. King Haakon of Norway was buried here in 1263, but his remains were later transferred to Trondheim. Two skeletons found in pine chests inside two pillars in 1926 are probably the remains of St Magnus (murdered in 1114) and his nephew. The Cathedral of St Magnus and Glasgow Cathedral are the only Scottish churches to have survived the Reformation unscathed.

Near the Cathedral are the ruins of the 13th c. **Bishop's Palace**, in which King Haakon died. The building is connected with **Earl Patrick's Palace**, also in ruins, which was completed by the infamous and hated Patrick Stewart in 1607 and is a fine example of 16th c. secular architecture in Scotland.

Tankerness House was built in 1574 for a lord of the manor, who was also a merchant. The stately home today houses an exhibition about the history of the Orkneys.

A short distance to the south of the town lies ★ **Highland Park Distillery**, the most northerly in Scotland. Its 12-year-old malt whisky is well-balanced, slightly smoky and pleasantly dry.

To the west of Kirkwall on the road to Stromness is the Stone Age chamber tomb known as ★ **Maes Howe** (about 2700 BC), which never fails to astonish by virtue of its enormous size. A 36 ft long, very narrow passage, created by stone slabs up to 16 ft long, leads into the main chamber and its three side-chambers, which were pillaged in the 12th c. by Vikings as runic carvings testify: "Haakon alone created the treasure from this hill" is just one of the many inscriptions. According to others, Norse crusaders took refuge here from a storm.

To the south-west of Kirkwall a crusader built a **Orphir Church** on the bay of Scapa Flow. It is the only round church in Scotland.

Stromness

The second largest town on the island and its most important ferry port is Stromness, situated on the west coast. It possesses two interesting museums: the collection of modern art at the Pier Arts Centre, **Pier Arts Centre** was bequeathed to the town by the collector, Mary Gardiner, while the **Stromness Museum** provides a wealth of information about fishing and the bird life on the island, as well as showing relics of the German fleet which was sunk in Scapa Flow.

The most important prehistoric site on the Orkneys is the Stone Age village of ★ **Skara Brae**, north of Stromness, which is over 5000 years old. The inhabitants at this time, who lived from cattle-rearing and farming, erected ten huts out of flat stones and slabs, which they covered with earth and their waste. Of particular interest at Skara Brae is that the

vestiges of Stone Age interior fittings and furniture have been preserved: bench-type beds of stone slabs filled with straw and another
construction, similarly made out of stone, which resembles a cupboard.
The houses of Skara Brae lay under a thick layer of sand until 1850, and
were only uncovered thanks to a storm. Researchers reckon that these
Stone Age people must have been beset by some natural disaster which
buried their village. Only the skeletons of a young boy and an old man
have been discovered. The most important of the finds are now on display in the National Museum of Antiquities in Edinburgh (see entry).

Another relic of the early inhabitants of the Orkneys is the 5000-year-
old ★**Ring of Brodgar** on Loch Stenness to the north-east of Stromness.
These monoliths, originally numbering 60, of which 27 now survive,
stand upright forming exact subdivisions of a circle. The purpose that
they served has not been properly explained, but the interaction of
water, landscape, clouds and these mysterious stone columns creates a
lasting impression.

Looking in a south-easterly direction from the Ring of Brodgar, the
visitor will see a similar, albeit smaller, group of stones. Of the original
twelve, only four of the **Standing Stones of Stenness** now remain on the
shores of Loch Stenness.

The tidal island of Birsay off the north-west coast of Mainland (only
accessible on foot at low tide) was an important Viking settlement and,
as the erstwhile capital of the islands, was also the first place to have a
church. The remains of their settlement and an Irish-Scottish church are
still to be seen. In the village of Birsay stand the ruins of a 16th palace.

Birsay

On the coast road going eastwards from Birsay can be seen Great
Britain's largest experimental wind farm. Its highest tower has a rotor
measuring 197 ft in diameter.

**Burgar Hill Wind
Turbine Site**

Below the wind turbine site stands Gurness Broch, a Pictish defensive
tower also used as a dwelling, dating from the first half of the first millennium. These windowless "brochs" were constructed out of stones.
They comprise a cylindrical inner building and an outer wall tapering
upwards. Passages and steps used to connect the two.

Gurness Broch

Because of its favourable strategic position, the wide expanse of almost
landlocked sea called Scapa Flow was used as the main base of the
British fleet during the First World War. After the capitulation of the
German Reich, the remaining ships of the German navy, 74 battleships,
cruisers, etc., were interned by the allied powers in the western part of
Scapa Flow, in order to await the completion of the peace treaty. Over
4700 men had to wait on the ships for seven months, without being
allowed to go on land. On June 21st 1919 Admiral von Reuter ordered
the fleet to be scuttled; the men opened the outlets on the ships and then
rowed in their boats to land. The pride of the German Kaiser sank to the
bottom of the sea, to the absolute fury of the Allies. The action turned
out to be a tragic mistake, for the admiral had been under the
impression that Germany had not signed the peace treaty, when in fact
the signing had merely been postponed for a couple of days. News had
been getting through to Scapa Flow, but generally with four days' delay.
Most of the ships were subsequently lifted and scrapped, although to
this day there are still seven German warships at the bottom of Scapa
Flow.

Scapa Flow

In the Second World War the British Home Fleet lay at anchor in Scapa
Flow. On October 14th 1939 the German U-boat 47 managed to enter the
bay and sink the battleship "Royal Oak". Over 800 sailors lost their lives.
The British government thereupon had decommissioned warships
dropped into the sea to form a barrier between Mainland and the islands
of Burray and South Ronaldsay. Italian prisoners of war later constructed
the Churchill Barriers out of cement, thereby creating a permanent link

Orkney: Stone huts more than 5000 years old

between these islands. From the barriers it is possible to see the masts of British ships protruding from the water.

Hoy

Hoy shows a different face from that which is seen on the other Orkney islands. It rises to as much as 1565 ft above sea level and is rugged and mountainous. Its north-west tip is famous for having some of the highest cliffs in Great Britain, **St John's Head**, which drops 1135 ft down to the sea. From here, looking south, can be seen the famous rocky pinnacle of the Old Man of Hoy, towering up 449 ft out of the sea. Around St John's Head there is a nature reserve which provides an ideal vantage point for watching all kinds of sea-birds, such as auks, fulmers and gannets.

South Ronaldsay

The most southerly of the Orkney Islands is reached by the road which crosses the Churchill Barriers. On the tiny little island of Langholm can be seen the Italian Chapel, which Italian prisoners of war erected out of a store-room using corrugated iron and wood, and the **Orkney Wireless Museum** in St Margaret's Hope, which has on display radio equipment and other communications apparatus used by the British Navy.

Rousay, Egilsay

Rousay, an island which lies off the shore of Mainland, is well-known for its many prehistoric graves, including the large burial chamber of **Blackhammer Cairn**, dating from the 3rd c. BC, and Midhowe Cairn. This is also the site of Midhowe Broch, a defensive tower.

On the island of Egilsay, lying to the west of Rousay, St Magnus was murdered. The 12th c. church, built in the Irish style, is dedicated to him.

Papa Westray

Those wanting to see two of the **oldest stone houses** in Europe, will need to go to the tiny island of Papa Westray, right in the north-west corner of the Orkneys. In both of these houses, over 5000 years old, spades, hammers and drills made of whalebone have been found.

Oxford

Central England
County: Oxfordshire. Population: 116,600

Oxford is one of the oldest and most celebrated university towns in Europe and for centuries has rivalled Cambridge (see entry) for academic pre-eminence in England. Its untrammelled spirit of investigation, which permeates the old college walls, its delightful gardens, peaceful courtyards and squares, the hectic bustle of its pedestrian zone, its excellent cultural facilities – all these help to create the town's special atmosphere.

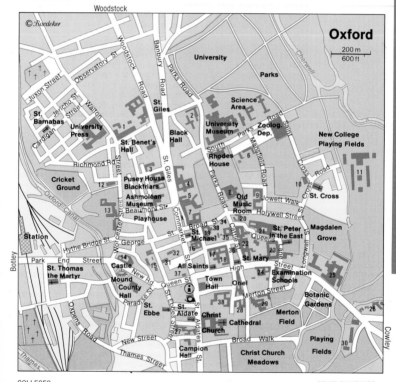

COLLEGES

1 Somerville	11 St. Catherine's	21 New College	31 Frewin Hall
2 Keble	12 Ruskin	22 All Souls	32 Union Soc Rooms
3 Regents Park	13 Worcester	23 Queen's	33 Sheldonian
4 St. John's	14 Nuffield	24 University	Theatre
5 Trinity	15 St. Peter's	25 Magdalen	34 Clarendon
6 Mansfield	16 Jesus	26 Wayneflete	Building
7 Balliol	17 Lincoln	27 Pembroke	35 Bodleian Library
8 Waldham	18 Brasenose	28 Corpus Christi	36 Radcliffe Camera
9 Manchester	19 Exeter	29 Merton	37 Carfax Tower
10 St. Cross	20 Hertford	30 St. Hilda's	38 Peckwater Quad

OTHER BUILDINGS

History The name of the town comes either from its literal meaning, a ford for oxen, or from "Osca's ford". It first appears in the records in 912. The beginnings of the university, on the other hand, are obscure. Oxford gradually became the meeting point of scholars who came together mainly to discuss religious questions. The building of teaching institutions independent of monasteries and churches was begun shortly after 1264, when Merton College was founded. In the years following there were further institutions created leading to the creation of an education system which can claim to form the academic elite of the country and which strives to serve both the need for individuality and the demand for a sense of social responsibility.

The history of the colleges and the resulting University of Oxford was not entirely free of tensions between the academics and the townspeople. In 1355 there were violent clashes, with many students even being killed in tavern brawls, for which the elders of the town had to pay compensation. During the Reformation there was renewed unrest, with many reformers from Cambridge even being burned to death at the stake for their religious beliefs. During the Civil War from 1642 to 1645 Oxford was a Royalist stronghold, but then suffered an economic and academic decline in the period afterwards. Reform of the monastic system of education did not take place until the 19th c., with oral examinations being replaced by written ones, examination degrees being introduced, academics being employed on the basis of scientific reputation, and even if they were married, and finally women being allowed to study, even though they have only been eligible to be awarded academic degrees since 1920.

Of the 57 prime ministers of Great Britain, 24 have come from Oxford: indeed since the Second World War all of them whether Conservative or Socialist, except for Churchill (see Famous People), Callaghan and Major. Famous Oxford graduates have included such diverse luminaries as John Wycliffe, Sir Walter Raleigh, Samuel Johnson, Pope Alexander V, Cecil Rhodes, George Washington's grandfather, Percy Bysshe Shelley, Evelyn Waugh, the Huxley brothers, W. H. Auden and Dorothy Sayers.

Sights

★★Oxford Colleges

Although the centre of Oxford is not large, plenty of time should be allowed for a visit, since there are so many things to see. The main features, of course, are the 40 colleges, which as a rule are only accessible to visitors during the afternoon in term-time. Ever since the 13th c. college buildings have been set out around a quadrangle, subsequently around several inner courtyards, with a gate which could be locked when necessary. They included a chapel, dining-hall, library and rooms for the students and their tutors, so that each college formed an autonomous body.

The four principal streets of the town meet at the intersection known as Carfax, which makes a good starting point for a tour. The 14th c. "Carfax Tower", which is a relic of St Martin's Church (now destroyed), has a good view. Going south down St Algate's Street, past the Town Hall, we come to St Aldate's Church, which dates from about 1318 but has been much altered.

Pembroke College

Beyond this on the right-hand side is Pembroke College, which was founded in 1624, although its origins date back to 1446. It is now housed in Neo-Gothic buildings which date from the 19th c. The critic and lexicographer Samuel Johnson (1709–84) was a student here in 1728–29.

★★Christ Church College

Christ Church dispenses with the nomenclature of "college" and is known as "the House". It is one of the largest colleges and was founded in 1525 by Cardinal Wolsey and re-founded after Wolsey's fall by Henry

Oxford: Christ Church College, founded by Henry VIII

VIII. Tom Tower, which was added by Wren in 1681–82, contains the huge bell weighing over 7 tonnes known as the Great Tom. Every evening at five minutes past nine it peals 101 times (once for each member of the original college). In earlier times the last peal of the bell was the signal for all college gates to be closed.

The main quadrangle of Christ Church, ★**Tom Quad**, with its charming fountain is the largest courtyard in Oxford. The lower tower has a very fine staircase of 1630 with fan vaulting. It leads up to the Hall, a spacious and elegant dining-hall with a magnificent wooden ceiling, which was completed in 1529. It contains portraits of Henry VIII (see Famous People) and distinguished members of the college, including the philosopher John Locke (1632–1704), who was sent down (expelled) for sedition, and William Penn (1644–1718), founder of Pennsylvania, who was also sent down as a Nonconformist, having defended the persecuted Quakers. There are also portraits of many prime ministers and of Lewis Carroll (1832–98), author of "Alice in Wonderland", who under his real name of Charles Lutwidge Dodgson was professor of mathematics in Oxford.

The chapel of Christ Church acquired the status of ★**Cathedral** in 1546 and is administered by a dean. The entrance, easily overlooked, is on the east side of Tom Quad. On the site which it now occupies there was originally a nunnery founded by St Frideswide, a Mercian princess, in the 8th c. The present building, mainly in the Transitional style, dates from the second half of the 12th c. Cardinal Wolsey had part of the nave demolished in order to make space for the college buildings to be extended.

The most striking feature in the interior is the double arcading of the nave which creates an impression of much greater height. This is a feature of the Transitional style. In the middle of the 14th c. the church was extended to the north of the Lady Chapel around the Latin Chapel and large tracery windows were installed in order to give expression to the Gothic feeling for light and space. The choir was created in 1500 with fan vaulting over hanging keystones. In the south transept is the Thomas Becket window (about 1320) and the five glass windows designed by Edward Burne-Jones and made by William Morris in 1871–77. Also of note in the choir aisles and the Latin Chapel is the St Frideswide window (1858); in the Lady Chapel three 14th c. tombs (Lady Montacute, Prior

Sutton, John de Nowers) and the remains of the Frideswide shrine (1289) which was destroyed in the Reformation, as well as the grave of the bishop and philosopher George Berkeley (1681–1735), who gave his name to the town of Berkeley in California. The small cloister is Perpendicular, the entrance to the chapterhouse late Norman, while its interior (the diocesan treasure chamber) is in the Early English style.

At the north-east corner of Tom Quad, beyond the Deanery (in which Charles I lived between 1642 and 1646), is a passage known as **Kill-Canon**, so chilly it was feared that the canons would catch their death of cold. Here stands a statue of Dean Fell (d. 1686), the subject of the famous lines (originally by Tom Brown): "I do not like thee, Doctor Fell, The reason why I cannot tell". The passage leads into **Peckwater Quad**, a Palladian structure designed by Dean Aldrich (1705–13), which has subsequently been completely restored. The Library contains a collection of drawings and mementoes of Cardinal Wolsey.

The new ★**Picture Gallery** beyond it has an outstanding collection of paintings and drawings by old masters, mainly 15th to 17th c. and from Italy, Flanders and France.

Canterbury Quad (by James Wyatt, 1773–78) occupies the site of Canterbury Hall, where Sir Thomas More (1478–1535), the statesman and humanist, was a student. From here Canterbury Gate leads out into Merton Street.

Corpus Christi College	On the right-hand side of Merton Street is Corpus Christi College, founded by Richard Foxe, Bishop of Winchester, in 1517. It is notable particularly for its beautiful gardens, and in the inner courtyard a sundial of 1581 with a pelican, the college symbol, and a perpetual calendar.
Oriel College	Opposite Corpus Christi stands Oriel College, founded by Edward II in 1326. It takes its name from a house known as La Oriole which previously stood on the site. The 16th and 17th c. buildings are well-proportioned, but a newer block built in 1911, with a statue of Cecil Rhodes, a member of the college, is less attractive. The 19th c. Tractarian movement originated in Oriel. It took its name from the "Tracts for the Times" written here by John Henry Newman (1801–90), an Anglican priest who was one of the leaders of the Oxford Movement but became a Catholic in 1845 and was made a cardinal in 1879.
Museum of Modern Art	Near Oriel, in Pembroke Street, is the Museum of Modern Art, established in 1966.
Merton Street	From here Merton Street, one of the oldest and most picturesque streets in the town, leads on to the High Street.
★★Merton College	Merton College is the oldest college still in existence. It was founded in 1264 by Walter de Merton, Chancellor of England and later Bishop of Rochester. Unlike other colleges, it was intended in the first place for secular students. The Chapel consists of a choir of 1277 and a large antechapel of 1414; the tower was added in 1481. Most of the windows of the choir have their original glass (there is a particularly fine Virgin and Child in the east window). The brass lectern of about 1500 is another notable feature. From the front range of buildings a passage leads under the Treasury into the attractive "**Mob Quad**" (about 1380). The 14th c. library in this quadrangle is the oldest in England still in use, with many historic books. Distinguished members of Merton College have included the politician, Lord Randolph Churchill (1849–94), the poet T. S. Eliot (1888–1965) and Max Beerbohm (1872–1956), the English writer and artist.
★★High Street	Merton Street leads into the splendid High Street, a busy street lined

Oxford: Queen's College

A romantic lane

with magnificent buildings. It was described by Wordsworth in a sonnet, and the American writer Nathaniel Hawthorne (1804-64) called it "the finest street in England".

Also situated in the High Street is Magdalen College, which was founded in 1458 by William of Waynflete, Bishop of Winchester, on a site which was then outside the town walls.

★★ Magdalen College

Magdalen Tower, in late Perpendicular style, was built between 1482 and 1504. Under the **Muniment Tower** is the entrance to the Chapel, where evensong is sung by the college's renowned choir during the University term. In the **Founder's Tower** are the state apartments, with early 16th c. tapestries. The passage under this tower leads into the cloisters, with grotesque figures known as "hieroglyphs". Beyond the college stretches a deer park called the Grove. A bridge in the park leads over the Cherwell into the Water Walks, one of which is known as Addison's Walk. (The writer Joseph Addison (1672–1719) was a member of Magdalen, as were Oscar Wilde and King Edward VII.)

Opposite the entrance to Magdalen is the University Botanic Garden, one of the oldest in England, founded in 1621. Plants of every conceivable kind, from all over the world, are to be seen here. The Magdalen Rose Garden was a gift from the Albert and Mary Lasker Foundation of New York (1953) to commemorate the development of penicillin, in which Oxford played a considerable part. The drug was first used in the Radcliffe Infirmary.

University Botanic Gardens

Magdalen Bridge leads across the River Cherwell. It was built in 1772 and widened in 1883. Beyond the bridge, in Cowley Place, is St Hilda's College (1893), the only college exclusively for women.

Magdalen Bridge, St Hilda's College

All Souls College, Oxford

In Iffley Road are the church and mission of the Cowley Fathers and Greyfriars Hall. Returning along the High Street, we come to the Examination Schools (1882), designed by Sir G. T. Jackson, an Oxford architect.

Queen's College

Opposite lies Queen's College, founded in 1340 by Robert de Eglesfield and rebuilt in Palladian style between 1692 and 1730. A statue of Queen Caroline commemorates her gift of £1000 to the college.

★St Edmund's Hall

Queen's Lane leads to St Edmund Hall, the first mention of which is in 1317. It was named after St Edmund of Abingdon, Archbishop of Canterbury (1170–1240), who studied here. This medieval students' hall of residence was for centuries used by The Queen's College, but since 1957 has existed as a separate college. Its tiny inner courtyard with a fountain dates from the 15th c., while the remaining buildings are of later date.

University College

On the south side of High Street is the group of buildings forming University College. Its original name was the Great Hall of the University, but to students it is merely known as "Univ". Although money for the foundation of a college was initially made available as early as 1249, the actual building of the college did not begin until 1280. The buildings which exist today are in the Late Gothic style, some of them not having been erected until the 17th c. In a small domed building there is a marble statue of Shelley, who was expelled from the college for atheism.

Beyond The Queen's College is All Souls College, a college for post-graduate study only, with many members prominent in public life. The college was founded in 1438 by Archbishop Chichele of Canterbury in memory of those who had fallen in the Hundred Years' War. The chapel is particularly notable for its hammer-beam roof (15th c.) with angels. To the north is the Codrington Library, with a sundial by Wren.

★ All Souls
College

The University church, St Mary the Virgin, has a fine Decorated tower (1280–1310). The choir was rebuilt in 1462–66, while the nave and Lady Chapel date from 1490–1503. From the tower there is a very fine view of the town.

University Church

Near the church is Brasenose College, founded in 1509, which derives its name from the brass door-knocker with a lion's head over the gate, while another one dating from the 13th c. can be seen in the hall.

Brasenose
College

The Old Congregation House, to the north-east of the Church of St Mary, is now a chapel. All Saints, at the corner of Turl and High Streets, formerly the City Church, now houses the Library of Lincoln College. The nearby Mitre Hotel was built in the 17th–18th c.

Old Congregation
House
All Saints

North of St Mary's is Radcliffe Square, surrounded by university buildings. The **Radcliffe Camera** (1737–49) is a rotunda designed by James Gibbs (1682–1754), the most prominent representative of the Anglo-Italian style of architecture. It originally housed the Radcliffe Library. The 16-sided room on the ground floor is now a reading room of the Bodleian Library.

Radcliffe Square

The main group of university buildings is on the north side of the square. The Old Schools Quadrangle dates from 1613 to 1618 and is on the site of an earlier building. Since 1884 all these buildings have formed part of the Bodleian Library, the university library and the first public library in the country, founded in 1598 by Sir Thomas Bodley. A copy of every book published in Britain is deposited in the Bodleian, which contains almost 2 million volumes and some 40,000 manuscripts.

Bodleian Library

The Divinity School dates from 1426 to 1480. It possesses a notable ceiling, which was restored by Wren. Charles I's Parliament met here during the Civil War.

Divinity School

A short distance to the north in Cattle Street is the Sheldonian Theatre, Wren's second major building, built in 1664–69, although its windows have been altered since then. The theatre is used on the occasion of the annual Commemoration or Encaenia in the middle of June, when benefactors of the university are honoured and honorary degrees and prizes are conferred.

Sheldonian
Theatre

The Clarendon Building (18th c.), on the east side, is in the Neo-Classical style and houses the university administrative offices. The Old Ashmolean Museum, on the west side, is now a scientific museum. It contains the Lewis Evans and Billmeir collections of early scientific and astronomical instruments, as well as much else. Opposite it is the Bodleian Library Extension (1935–46), with a bookshop and exhibition.

Old Ashmolean
Museum

Nearby, in Holywell Street, is the Holywell Music Room (1748), reputedly the oldest concert hall in the world.

Holywell Music
Room

In Cattle Street, opposite the Bodleian Library, stands Hertford College, on a site previously occupied by Hart Hall, founded in 1301. The Bridge of Sighs over New College Lane joins the old and new buildings of Hertford College.

Hertford College

Oxford: the Sheldonian Theatre

Trinity College

★New College

Not far to the east is the fortress-like New College, which in spite of its name is not new, having been founded in 1379 by William of Wykeham, Bishop of Winchester. Until 1854 only students from Winchester were admitted. The chapel was one of the first examples of the Perpendicular style. The stained glass is mostly 14th c., an exception being the large window in the antechapel, which was painted in 1787 from designs by Sir Joshua Reynolds. Other notable features are the statue of Lazarus by Epstein and memorials to three German members of the college who fell in the war. The choir stalls have the original 14th c. misericords. Choral evensong in the chapel is an occasion not to be missed if opportunity offers. The high hall has fine linenfold panelling. The cloisters, with wood vaulting, and the detached bell-tower date from the 14th c. The beautiful gardens (1711) are bounded on two sides by the old town walls.

Wadham College

Returning along New College Road and turning into Parks Road, we come to Wadham College, little changed since its foundation in 1610. The hall ranks as one of the finest in Oxford, the chapel has good stained glass and the gardens are particularly beautiful. Famous members of Wadham have included Admiral Blake (1599–1657), Admiral of the Fleet under Oliver Cromwell from 1649, and Sir Christopher Wren (1632–1723), the architect of many churches and castles.

Exeter College

In Turl Street is Exeter College, founded by Walter de Stapledon, Bishop of Exeter, in 1314. The college today is characterised by much later building in the Victorian style.

Jesus College

Opposite is Jesus College, founded by Elizabeth I in 1571, which has traditionally had a high proportion of students from Wales. The rear quadrangle (1670) is particularly fine. Members of Jesus College have included the former prime minister, Harold Wilson, the adventurer, Lawrence of Arabia, the dandy, "Beau" Nash, and the chemist, Thomas Vaughan.

To the south is Lincoln College, which was founded in 1427 by Richard Fleming, Bishop of Lincoln, "to defend the true faith". The north quadrangle dates from the period of the original foundation. The chapel, with its numerous wood-carvings, is also of interest. A famous past student was the Methodist preacher, John Wesley (1703–91).

Lincoln College

North of Broad Street, past the New Bodleian Library, lies Trinity College, founded by Sir Thomas Pope in 1555.

Trinity College

Three floors of an adjacent building are devoted to a permanent exhibition on the history of the university, today more than 800 years old.

Oxford Story

Facing Broad Street is Kettell Hall (about 1620). Its beautiful chapel (1691–94), probably by Dean Aldrich, has fine wood-carvings in the style of Grinling Gibbons.

Kettell Hall

The building of Balliol College, situated next to Trinity College, was undertaken in 1263 by John de Balliol, as a penance for having taken the Bishop of Durham prisoner, the foundation of the college being secured with the help of bequests from his wife in 1282. The present buildings are however 19th c. The library has an outstanding collection of medieval manuscripts. Balliol is traditionally preferred by Scottish students.

Balliol College

A cross in St Giles Street marks the spot where the reformers Latimer, Ridley and Cranmer were burned at the stake. They are also commemorated by the Martyrs' Memorial (by Sir George Gilbert Scott, 1841). Nicholas Ridley, Bishop of London, and Hugh Latimer, Bishop of Worcester, were martyred on October 16th 1555 and Thomas Cranmer, Archbishop of Canterbury, on March 21st 1556. Cranmer was examined from September 1555 to February 1556 in the hall of the Divinity School.

Martyrs' Memorial

Also in St Giles, the wide handsome street which runs north from the Martyrs' Memorial, is St John's College, founded in 1555 by Sir Thomas White, a wealthy merchant who was Lord Mayor of London in 1553. Part of the buildings actually consists of the remains of St Bernard's College, a Cistercian establishment built in 1437. The chapel contains the tomb of Archbishop Laud (beheaded 1645), who was member and later master of the college. A fan-vaulted passage leads into Canterbury Quadrangle, mainly built by Laud (1631–36), with attractive colonnades. The gardens are among the most beautiful in Oxford.

St John's College

Farther along St Giles are Regent's Park College (Baptist) and St Benet's Hall (Benedictine). To the right, in Museum Road, is Rhodes House, headquarters of the Rhodes Trust, founded under the will of the South African statesman Cecil Rhodes (1853–1902), which grants some 200 scholarships to Commonwealth and foreign students.

Rhodes House

The University Museum, built in 1855–60 under Ruskin's direction, contains a number of interesting collections, including geological, mineralogical and zoological sections which contain work by Darwin (see Famous People), Burchell and Hope.

University Museum

A pretty bridge over the River Cherwell leads from Manor Road to St Catherine's College, built in 1960–64 on part of Holywell Great Meadow. From the end of South Parks Road there is a pleasant walk along the Cherwell past Parson's Pleasure to a path called Mesopotamia which leads to Magdalen Bridge.

St Catherine's College

The Ashmolean Museum, founded in 1683, is the most important of the four university museums and is the oldest museum in the country. The Neo-Classical building, which was designed by C. R. Rockerell, houses a magnificent collection of art and antiquities, including classical sculp-

★★Ashmolean Museum

ture, Far Eastern art, Greek and Roman pottery and a valuable collection of jewellery.

Worcester College

Worcester College, at the end of Beaumont Street, was founded in 1714. It incorporates parts of Gloucester College, which was founded for Benedictine students in 1283. On the south side of the college site there are six 15th c. cottages, and there are three other cottages on the north side. The college gardens are some of the largest in Oxford and contain a lake.

★ Cornmarket
Street

Cornmarket Street, commonly known as the "Corn", is Oxford's busiest shopping street. On the right-hand side is **St Michael's Church**, with a Saxon, or possibly early Norman tower. The former Crew Inn, where Shakespeare is said to have stayed on the journey between Stratford and London, now contains the offices of the Oxford Preservation Trust.

Somerville
College

Until 1993, when men were finally admitted, Somerville College on Walton Street had been exclusively a women's college since its inception in 1894. Its list of famous members includes Indira Gandhi, Margaret Thatcher, the writer Dorothy Sayers, the Nobel prizewinner for chemistry, Dorothy Hadgkin, and the soprano Kiri te Kanawa.

Surroundings

Iffley

A favourite walk is from Folly Bridge (1½ miles) to Iffley, which has a famous Norman church (1175–82), with a very beautiful west front. The high altar is Early English and many of the windows are 14th and 15th c.

★ Blenheim
Palace

8 miles to the north-west, in Woodstock (pop. 3000), is Blenheim Palace, seat of the dukes of Marlborough, the Spencer-Churchill family, and birthplace of Winston Churchill (see Famous People). The spacious parkland includes a large lake and bridge which can be visited without

Blenheim Palace – home of the Spencer-Churchill family

having to buy an entrance ticket. The magnificent palace, with its economical layout, was built between 1701 and 1724 for John Churchill, 1st Duke of Marlborough, under the direction of the architect, John Vanbrugh, and with the financial support of Queen Anne, who wished to express her thanks to the Duke for his victory in 1704 over the French at the Battle of Blenheim (actually the Battle of Höchstädt). From the main building, with its Neo-Classical columned entrance-hall, quadrantal annexes with crowned corner-towers and colonnades lead to the side wings with their large courtyards, through which the visitor makes his way to the vast courtyard in front of the main building. From here it is possible to walk directly into the gardens with their French Rococo borders and splendid old trees which form part of the English landscaped park created by Lancelot "Capability" Brown. Alternatively the visitor can lose himself among the 200 rooms of the palace itself. Of particular interest are the monumental Great Hall with its painted ceiling (1716) by James Thornhill depicting the Battle of Blenheim, the room commemorating Sir Winston Churchill, the state rooms in all their Baroque splendour with their numerous hanging tapestries (18th c.) depicting battle scenes, elegant pieces of furniture and large numbers of portraits by such masters as van Dyck, Reynolds and Kneller, as well as salon creations by Laguerre. The palace chapel contains a grandiose tomb for the 1st Duke of Marlborough, his wife and children.

Abingdon

6 miles south is Abingdon (pop. 22,000), a charming town on the Thames and formerly the county town of Berkshire, which experienced its heyday during the period of the wool trade. It has a large number of interesting houses and churches, including the old two-storey County Hall (1678–82; now a local museum) and the beautiful St Helen's Church (Perpendicular), with a graceful spire, double aisles and elaborately painted panelling (1390) in the Lady Chapel. Many old hospitals from the period 1446–1797 can be visited, including Christ's Hospital, founded in 1553. There are also some parts left of the once influential Benedictine abbey, which was consecrated in 675 and dissolved in 1538: the Checker Hall (13th c.), the Long Gallery (about 1500) and the abbey doorway (1450).

Peak District I/K 7

Central England
County: Derbyshire

With its attractive scenery the Peak District has always been a recreational area for the people of the surrounding industrial areas: the conurbation of South-east Lancashire centred around Manchester (see entry), the towns of Sheffield and Derby (see entries) and the English pottery industry based at Stoke-on-Trent and Newcastle-under-Lyme.

The name is a misnomer in that it does not refer to steep mountain summits, but is derived from the area's location at the southern end of the Pennine range, the three highest hills in the area being called "The Peak".

People first started coming to the Peak District around the turn of the century in search of relaxation, an escape from their dirty and crowded towns and the chance to breathe in clean air and roam around at will. Their enthusiasm, however, was in many instances dampened by the fact that large tracts of the dramatic moorland scenery in Dark Peak were reserved by their owners for the rearing and hunting of Scottish grouse. It was not until after the Second World War that the idea of setting up national parks gained currency and in 1951 the Peak District was declared the country's first ★ **National Park**. Since then the area has been freely accessible, except for certain days during the shooting season.

This facility is widely enjoyed and consequently at weekends there is heavy traffic on the roads through the park and in summer the pretty valleys are often swarming with visitors. Footpaths have been designated along the banks of the clear streams which flow through the valleys and these are as much an inducement to ramblers as the magnificent views which are to be had from the paths across the high moorland. At the same time, for those keen on mountain climbing there are weird rock formations in Dark Peak. The area is also popular with riding enthusiasts.

The Peak District National Park, which extends over an area of 550 sq. miles, consists of two quite different types of landscape. The northern part, with crags and hilltops rising to heights of over 2000 ft, is made up of magma rocks and chalk surrounded by millstone-grit. This rugged region, which is also known as High Peak or Dark Peak, has typical cotton-grass moorland, heathland with scrub, and dark rocky outcrops. The southerly Low Peak or White Peak is limestone country, often with very curious rock formations, through which rivers have cut their way to form beautiful valleys or "dales". In between can be found lonely farmhouses built out of sandstone or limestone. Characteristic of the area are the stone walls, which began to be built in the 16th c. when the arable fields were turned into grazing land, as it was thought that cattle-rearing would provide a better use of the barren land. Most of the stone walls were constructed in the 18th c., though in recent years they have been partially replaced by electric fences for reasons of economy. An even more recent development has been the recognition that traditional stone walls have a charm and aesthetic value of their own, and there has been a move to preserve them. Parts of the park are wooded, especially in the north, where afforestation has also been undertaken in many places. In addition, this part of the park contains the majority of the 50 or more reservoirs which have been established to provide for water needs of the surrounding industrial areas.

The only reminders of the mining industry, which at one time was the second most important economic activity, are some walled-in tunnels and pieces of jewellery made out of fluorspar, which has the nickname "Blue John". The exploitation of seams of lead began in Roman times, although the first written mention of mining is not found until a document dating from 1288. By the early modern period the deposits had been exhausted right down to the level of the water-table and it was necessary to look for newer, more profitable methods of extracting the ore. Drainage systems and steam engines revolutionised the process, but at the same time made the whole operation more expensive. By the turn of the century the deposits had begun to run out and in 1952 the last mine was shut down.

Transport Three main roads traverse the area between Derby and Manchester. The first route (A52 and A523) skirts the western edge via Leek and Macclesfield, the second route (A6) passes through Matlock and Buxton, while the third (A52/A512/A6) goes via Ashbourne and Buxton.

Buxton

Buxton (pop. 20,000), situated at a height of 1000 ft, is a good centre from which to explore the Peak District. The radioactive springs here were known in Roman times (1st c. BC), and since then many illustrious visitors have come to Buxton, including Mary Queen of Scots (see Famous People). In Higher Buxton, the oldest part of the town, are the Town Hall (1899; Market Place) and the museum (Terrace Road), in which prehistoric and Roman finds are displayed and the development of the town as a spa and resort is documented.

In the beautifully situated ★ **Pavilion Gardens**, the opera house (1905) and the octagonal concert hall (1875) have regular performances, while the large Victorian conservatory with its many tropical plants, a café and the gondola lake, which receives its water from the River Wye, all pro-

Buxton: Pavilion Gardens

vide an attraction for the visitor. For children there is a circular trip on the miniature railway.

Interesting for its architecture is **The Crescent**, which is situated a short distance away. This crescent-shaped street, 316 ft long, was built in 1780–88 out of local sandstone and was designed by John Carr of York, who modelled it on the Royal Crescent in Bath (see entry).

The **Devonshire Royal Hospital** (1859), originally built as a riding school, has a dome 154 ft in diameter; it is now a major centre for the treatment of rheumatic diseases.

Buxton, like other places in the Peak District, is noted for the custom of **"well-dressing"**, said to have originated in the nearby village of Tissington.

The custom, which may well go back to pagan times, involves setting up a sacred image by a spring. The image is made of wood covered with clay and then coated with a mosaic of flower-petals.

In **Grin Low Woods** (Buxton Country Park) Solomon's Temple (1440 ft) offers a panoramic view. The tower was erected in 1896, in memory of Solomon Myrock, on a prehistoric burial mound. Just 20 minutes away on foot is **Poole's Cavern** with its impressive dripstone formations.

It is worth making a trip to **Arbor Low** (9 miles south-east of Buxton), a Neolithic **stone circle** with 50 stones (1200 ft).

The village of Castleton (12 miles north-east) is beautifully situated at the western end of the Hope valley and attracts many visitors in summer. On a rocky crag above the village can be seen **Peveril Castle**, with a massive keep dating back to 1176.

Castleton

Castleton is noted for its ★ **caves**, which are open to visitors throughout the year. The most impressive is Peak Cavern, half a mile long. Also of interest is the Speedwell Mine, in which visitors take a boat trip along an underground gallery half a mile long, passing sinter terraces, waterfalls and fantastic stalactite and stalagmite formations. Blue John Mine is reached by way of the Winnats, a steep and narrow ravine 1 mile long. This cavern is named after the bluish (sometimes also yellow-tinged) type of felspar found here, which can also be seen, in many varying shades of colour, in Treak Cliff and Treak Cliff Cavern.

Chatsworth House

Chatsworth (15 miles to the east), the seat of the Dukes of Devonshire, is one of the great country houses of England. Little remains of the original Elizabethan house which was built in 1555 by Bess of Harwick on the banks of the River Derwent. It was replaced with the present building by William Cavendish, 1st Duke of Devonshire, between 1686 and 1708. A wing was added in the 19th c. by Wyatville. Chatsworth contains a magnificent collection of old masters, sculpture, tapestries, furniture, silver and porcelain (at least 1 hour is needed to walk round). The gardens, designed by Joseph Paxton from 1826 onwards, are delightful, with romantic fountains, spectacular cascades and enchanted pathways, an orangery, rose-garden and tropical greenhouse. The landscaped park surrounding the gardens was designed by "Capability" Brown. There is also a reserve for animals. On a hill behind the house is the Elizabethan hunting tower, from which there is a good view. Near the bridge is Queen Mary's Bower, which serves to commemorate Mary Queen of Scots (see Famous People), who was confined at Chatsworth on several occasions between 1570 and 1581.

Haddon Hall

Haddon Hall (15 miles to the south-east), seat of the Duke of Rutland, has a magnificent setting on a hillside above the Wye. This beautiful stately home was originally a Norman stronghold, and the north-east tower and parts of the chapel date from the late Norman period. The visitor enters by the north-west gate which leads into the Lower Courtyard with its fountains. Of interest inside the castle are the Duke's bedchamber, the medieval banqueting hall with massive wooden vaulting, the chapel

Haddon Hall ...   *... has Flemish gobelins*

with 15th c. wall-paintings and a white marble tomb for Lord Haddon, the brother of the 9th Duke, who died in childhood. The stone ceiling of the dining room is decorated with coats of arms belonging to the family, while its walls are embellished with elaborate wood panelling. The Great Hall (14th c.) is hung with wonderful Flemish tapestries, on which hunting scenes and the five senses (feeling, hearing, seeing, tasting and smelling) are depicted. The wainscoted Long Gallery (110 ft) shows Renaissance influences. The colourful gardens were skilfully remodelled at the beginning of this century.

Bakewell (pop. 4220) is another good base for extended walks in the Peak District. The village lies on the banks of the Wye, here spanned by a medieval bridge (13th c.). In the centre of the little town the Old House Museum exhibits household furniture and fittings from the 16th c. All Saints Church (12th–14th c.) contains a 13th c. font and monuments of the Vernon family.

Bakewell

Monsal Dale (4 miles to the north-west) is a beautiful little valley which will appeal to all lovers of nature.

Monsal Dale

Matlock (pop. 13,700) was a much-frequented spa in the 19th c. and is still a popular resort. It is made up of a number of separate parts – Matlock Bridge, at a medieval bridge over the Derwent; Matlock Bank on the hills; and Matlock Bath, which is situated in the narrow gorge of the Derwent. East of Matlock Bath is High Tor, a limestone crag rising to a height of 400 ft above the river. The 19th c. Riber Castle now has an animal and nature reserve. Rutland Cavern is a cave which was used as far back as Roman times (1st/2nd c.) for lead-mining.

Matlock

About 6 miles south-east of Matlock in Crich is the National Tramway Museum, where a collection of old vehicles can be viewed.

National Tramway Museum

The highest plateau in the Peak District is Kinder Scout (2088 ft), best climbed from the village of Edale in the vale of the same name.

Kinder Scout

The Pennine Way is a well-established, long-distance waymarked footpath for walkers and riders. Other classic walks in the area are through Chee Dale, Wye Dale, Ashwood Dale and Manifold Valley with Thors Cave, in which traces of an Ice Age settlement are still to be found.

Pennine Way

Peterborough   L 8

Central England
County: Cambridgeshire. Population: 113,000

Peterborough is an industrial city attractively situated on the north bank of the River Nene, on the edge of the Fens. Traditionally an agricultural centre, it now has large factories producing diesel engines and other heavy machinery. The principal attraction for visitors is the cathedral, one of the finest Norman churches in England.

History The town, "Peter's borough", grew up round the Saxon monastery of Medehamstede, founded about 655 by the first Christian king of Mercia, on the site now occupied by the cathedral. The monastery was destroyed by the Danes in 870 and rebuilt as a Benedictine foundation by Ethelwold, Bishop of Winchester (963–984) in 972. Rebuilding after a fire in 1116 was completed in 1238. Relics of St Oswald and Thomas Becket (see Famous People) made the abbey into a place of pilgrimage and enabled it to become very wealthy. The fact that it was the site of the grave of Catherine of Aragon, first wife of Henry VIII

475

Peterborough Cathedral

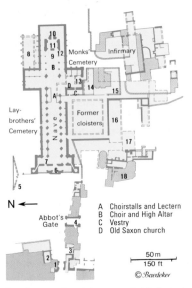

1 Outer Gate
  (St Nicholas Chapel
  above)
2 Chapel of St Thomas
  of Canterbury
3 Prison
4 Knights' Chamber
5 Prior's Gate
6 West Front and entrance
  to the Treasury
7 Portrait of
  Robert Scarlett
8 Site of Lady Chapel
  (destroyed 1651)
9 Tomb of
  Catherine of Aragon
10 New Building (1508)
11 Monks' Stone
12 Site of original burial place
   of Mary Stuart
13 Entrance to the foundations
   of the Saxon church
14 Former Chapterhouse
15 Former monks' dormitory
16 Former monks' refectory
17 Former monastic kitchen
18 Bishop's Palace

A Choirstalls and Lectern
B Choir and High Altar
C Vestry
D Old Saxon church

50 m
150 ft

© Baedeker

(see Famous People), was probably instrumental in saving the abbey from being dissolved and torn down during the Reformation; in 1541 Peterborough was promoted to the status of a cathedral see.

★Peterborough
Cathedral

The monks who in 1118 began rebuilding the abbey in honour of St Peter, St Paul and St Andrew, transported their materials from Barnack in Northamptonshire, just 10 miles away, where they could select the beautiful ivory-coloured stone from their own quarries. The choir was completed by 1140, the transepts and nave by the end of the century. The west front was added between 1200 and 1222 and is one of the most unusual façades of the early Gothic period with its three huge doorways (81 ft high) which form a kind of triumphal arch leading into the church. The façade is flanked by corner towers and the three doorways, which are merely composed of jambstones, are each crowned by a gable of tracery. Behind these the silhouette of the square 15th c. crossing tower can be seen. The Perpendicular porch was added in 1370 as a strengthening device for the pillars.

Circular tour

The interior of the three-aisled columned basilica has retained its Norman appearance, with massive rows of arches, arched galleries decorated with zig-zags, and triple windows in echelon formation as a clerestory. The extremely beautiful painted flat ceiling of 1220 is unique in England (partly restored). In the south side aisle the visitor can admire some most unusual Norman hipped vaulting, which anticipates the Gothic style of ribbed vaulting. On the west wall near the main doorway there is an 18th c. portrait of "Old Scarlett" (1496–1594), sexton and gravedigger, who buried two queens and two generations of citizens in the church. The eagle lectern in the nave is a piece of 15th c. brasswork, the choir stalls date from the end of the 19th c., while the crossing area with its tower was refashioned by Pearson between 1883 and 1886. The north and south transepts display impressive Norman architectural features allied to the original wooden ceiling.

The choir with the high altar and the bishop's throne was redesigned at the end of the 19th c., while the wooden ceiling dates from the 15th c. and is made to look like stone vaulting. In the north section of the choir is the tomb of Catherine of Aragon (1485–1536), queen of Henry VIII (see Famous People), who from 1533 was forced to live separately from the king because of her failure to produce a male heir to the throne. While she was living close to Peterborough as a royal prisoner, Henry VIII, angered at the refusal of the Pope to sanction an annulment of the marriage, broke with Rome and in so doing ushered in the Reformation in England, with the king as head of the Anglican Church. In the south section of the choir there is a plaque marking the tomb of Mary Queen of Scots (see Famous People), who, after her execution at Fotheringhay (Northamptonshire), was interred here. Her remains were subsequently transferred to Westminster Abbey in London in 1612 at the behest of her son James I. Both graves were destroyed by Cromwell's troops. Also of note are the abbots' graves from the 12th and 13th c. in the choir ambulatory, including the marble tomb of Abbot Benedict of Canterbury (d. 1193), who was responsible for the building of the nave and brought the relics of St Thomas Becket to the church.

The retrochoir, also known as the New Building, has splendid fan vaulting (about 1500) and the Hedda Stone, a piece of Saxon sculpture originally made around 780, which was intended to form part of a shrine set up over the mass grave of monks who, along with their abbot Hedda, were murdered in 870 during the Danish invasion.

Of the former **abbey buildings** only Abbot's Lodging, Prior's Lodging and a few old gatehouses still remain, including Knight's Gateway (1302), which used to lead to the Bishop's Palace.

The **Peterborough Museum and Art Gallery** in Priestgate contains among much else archaeological finds and what is thought to be the first portrait of a judge in his robes (16th c.), as well as craftwork produced by French prisoners of war at Norman Cross Prison during the Napoleonic Wars. In the pedestrian area is the enormous covered **Queensgate Shopping Centre**, a marble, glass and steel construction. Nearby St John's Church (1407), the Guildhall (1671) and the Custom's House on the River Nene are among the few historic buildings still remaining in the city.

Other sights

The old market town of Stamford (12 miles to the north-west; pop. 15,800), with its four fine churches, has managed to retain much of its original character. St Mary's has an early Gothic tower with a Decorated broach spire. All Saints Church is also early Gothic with a late Gothic tower and notable brass memorial slabs. St John's (Perpendicular) has fine stained glass and carved oak woodwork. St George's (13th–15th c.) also has fine old stained glass windows.

*Surroundings
Stamford*

The most interesting secular building is Browne's Hospital, founded in 1480, with a Jacobean hall and chapel. The town hall dates from 1777, the former theatre in St Mary's Street from 1769. There are also a large number of fine Elizabethan, Jacobean and Georgian houses.

Burghley House (2 miles south of Stamford), seat of the Marquess of Exeter, is an outstanding example of Elizabethan architecture (1553–87). The mansion was built for William Cecil, Lord Burghley (1520–98), an influential politician during the Elizabethan period. The west front, with its windows, towers and ornamental chimneys, is as delightful as the sumptuous interior fittings, the large number of paintings by Italian and English Baroque painters and the grandiose late 17th c. interior decorations by Louis Laguerre (Bow Room) and Antonio Verrio (Heaven Room). The park surrounding the mansion was created by the famous landscape gardener "Capability" Brown in the 18th c.

Burghley House

Barnack (3 miles to the south-east) is the source of the fine building stone, ranging in colour from ivory-white to yellowish, used in so many

Barnack

churches and houses in this part of the country. It can be seen in the local church, St John the Baptist, built at the beginning of the 11th c. The Saxon tower has an Early English spire, while inside there is an elaborately decorated early Gothic font (13th c.).

Longthorpe

The fortified manor house of Longthorpe (3 miles to the west of Peterborough) has an old 13th c. tower. On the first floor there are wall paintings showing scenes of everyday domestic life, which have survived from the 14th c.

Castor

The tiny village of Castor (pop. 550) is so called because it occupies the site of a Roman camp ("castrum") called Durobrivae. According to the inscription on the doorway, the Norman church was consecrated to St Cyneburga, daughter of King Penda of Mercia, in 1124. Inside the church the 14th c. wall paintings repay close inspection.

Peakirk Wildfowl and Wetlands Trust

Peakirk Wildfowl and Wetlands Trust Gardens (7 miles to the north) belong to the Severn Wildfowl Trust, founded by Sir Peter Scott in 1946 to preserve and maintain Britain's many species of waterfowl.

Plymouth   G 10

South-west England
County: Devon
Altitude: 100 ft. Population: 256,000

Plymouth, situated at the mouth of the River Tamar, which forms the boundary between Devon and Cornwall (see entry), is one of Britain's largest seaports and naval bases, and historically the most important. The defeat of the Spanish Armada off Plymouth marked the beginning of Britain's rise to the status of a world power.

Together with Stonehouse and Devonport, Plymouth has now become a city of considerable size. Bordered by a wide beach, it lies between hills which reach down to the adjoining bays, and the surrounding woodland and meadows combine with extensive parks and gardens to give the city an open and attractive aspect. Famous names connected with British maritime history, such as Sir Francis Drake (see Famous People) and the "Mayflower" are closely associated with Plymouth.

History The city takes its name from the little River Plym and first finds written mention in 1231. The Black Prince sailed from here for France for the last time in 1355, and it was from here that many discoverers and conquerors also set out, among them Sir Francis Drake, the legendary freebooter of Elizabethan times, Sir Walter Raleigh, Hawkins, Martin Frobisher, Admiral Blake and Captain Cook (see Famous People). On July 31st 1588 the Spanish Armada was soundly defeated in Plymouth Sound, with Drake as vice-admiral. On September 6th 1620 the Pilgrim Fathers from Plymouth set sail for America on the "Mayflower". Countless emigrants followed in their steps and made their way to the New World, where today there must be about a dozen towns called Plymouth. During the Second World War the important naval harbour suffered heavy damage, with the result that there are very few historic buildings remaining in the city.

Sights

★ Plymouth Hoe

The finest views of the city and Plymouth Sound are to be had from the Hoe, a spacious park opened in 1817 and traversed by the Promenade, with a prospect extending over the Sound past Drake's

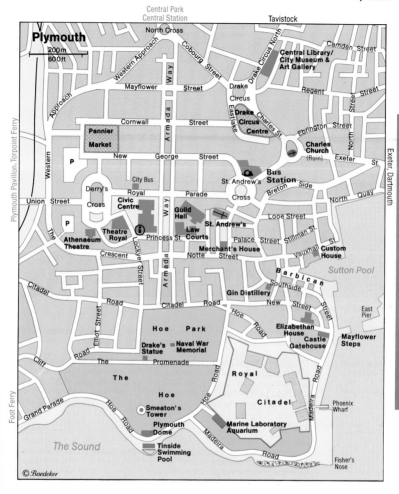

Island as far as the famous lighthouse on Eddystone Rock, 14 miles away. The park has several monuments: the **Armada Monument**, erected in 1888 by Charles May and decorated with Britannia and the coats of arms of all the towns which offered support in the struggle against the Armada; a massive **stone column** (1924) by Sir Robert Lorimer which serves as a naval war memorial; the statue of the circumnavigator **Sir Francis Drake**, holding globe and sword (1884; a copy of the original statue by Joseph Edgar Boehms which stands in a street in Tavistock). The upper part of the former **Smeaton Lighthouse** has been turned into a museum and viewing tower. The lighthouse had to make way for a newer one in 1182 and was dismantled and rebuilt stone by stone.

At the southern end of the Hoe the **Plymouth Dome** has been open

Plymouth: the Royal Citadel

since 1989 and presents the history of the port, from the Elizabethan era to the present day, with the aid of the latest technology.

Royal Citadel / Aquarium

The Royal Citadel, east of the Hoe, was built in 1566–70; its inner court-yard is graced by a statue of George II. At the south-west corner there is an aquarium belonging to the Marine Biological Society, which forms part of a marine laboratory and is well worth visiting. A road runs round the citadel, affording excellent views, including the remains of the old town, with its few remaining old houses.

Sutton Pool

Following Madeira Road, we come to the old harbour, Sutton Pool. Pleasure ships offering excursions around the harbour and Plymouth Sound dock here at Phoenix Wharf. On the **Mayflower Steps**, which is a gateway built in memory of the Pilgrim Fathers, there is a mooring-place for ships crossing over to Drake's Island. A short distance away there is a memorial tablet commemorating the arrival of American aviators Alcock and Brown, who in 1919 were the first persons to cross the Atlantic in a seaplane.

★Barbican

In the narrow streets of the historic quarter of the city, "The Barbican", the visitor can see an excellent example of 16th c. architecture in the **Elizabethan House** on New Street, which has been fitted out exactly as it would have been in Tudor times. In Southside Street the remains of a 14th c. Dominican monastery can still be seen.

Gin Distillery

At the Black Friars Distillery (60, Southside Street) the visitor can learn all about gin production and try a glass of Plymouth Dry Gin.

Armada Way and Royal Parade

The city centre today occupies the area around the two broad avenues, Armada Way and Royal Parade, which adjoin Hoe Park to the north. The main church, **St Andrew's**, stands here; it was built in the second half of the 15th c. and was rebuilt in 1945–57. Sir Martin Frobisher (d. 1594) and Admiral Blake (d. 1657) were both laid to rest here, and there is also a memorial tablet to William Cookworthy, who in 1768 founded the first English porcelain factory. Nearby are the medieval **Prysten House** dating from the 15th c., the Merchants' House, a Tudor building dating from the 16th c., in which a museum of social history is housed, and the Guildhall with its pretty little towers.

Opposite lies the **Civic Centre**, 1958–62, built to designs by J. Stirling (see Famous People), with a 14-storey high rise office building. The viewing platform on the 14th floor provides a breathtaking view of the city and in clear weather it is possible to see as far as Dartmoor (see entry).

On nearby Derry's Cross is the famous **Theatre Royal**, the leading theatre in the town, with the Athenaeum Theatre next door, surrounded by three cinemas.

On the far side of Derry's Cross in Millbay Road, the Plymouth Pavilions opened their doors in 1991. This modern conference and leisure centre also contains a swimming-pool with a wave-machine, an ice-rink and a concert hall which can seat 3000 people.

Plymouth Pavilions

To the north-west of the city centre is Drake Circus Centre, a pedestrian zone with passageways of shops, boutiques and restaurants. The ★**City Museum** is situated here; its exhibits include works of old masters, paintings by Sir Joshua Reynolds, a valuable collection of porcelain and silver, Italian bronze objects and the goblet which Sir Francis Drake was given by Elizabeth I on his return from his three-year voyage around the world.

Drake Circus Centre

Smeaton Lighthouse on The Hoe ...   *... and Sir Francis Drake*

481

Sutton Pool, the old harbour of Plymouth

Devonport

To the west of the city centre, Devonport has many fine old houses, mainly Georgian and Regency. The Royal Dockyard, established in 1691 by William III, can be visited. There is a memorial to the polar explorer, **Robert Falcon Scott**, who was born in Devonport in 1868 and died in 1912 while on an expedition to the South Pole with his ship "Discovery" (today in Dundee (see entry)). Gun Wharf, built between 1718 and 1725 to plans by Vanbrugh, is architecturally interesting.

Surroundings

Mount Edgcumbe

There is a ferry service over to Cremyll in Cornwall (see entry), and the mansion of Mount Edgcumbe, which is over 400 years old and represents a fine example of English interior design in the 18th c. The landscaped park surrounding the house is full of colour and brings together both European plants and more exotic ones from overseas.

★ Cotehele House

Another attractive trip is up the River Tamar to Cotehele (9 miles to the north-west), passing Calstock, with the Morwell Rocks. Cotehele House is an imposing building in the Tudor style, which once belonged to the Earls of Mount Edgcumbe. This medieval mansion, which was built from grey granite between 1485 and 1539, has survived largely unaltered and contains fine furniture, needlework and weapons.

★ Saltram House

Saltram House (3 miles to the east) was begun by John Parker in 1750, its dining-room being designed by Robert Adam in 1768. The house is particularly notable for 14 paintings by Reynolds, who lived in Plympton for a number of years and worked in Devonport. The artist used to like staying at Saltram and painted portraits of the lord of the house and his family. The portrait of the artist himself (1767) which hangs on the stairway is the work of Angelika Kaufmann. Also of interest are the works by Rubens, Stubbs, the American presidential painter Gilbert Stuart and the collections of porcelain and chinoiserie.

★ Antony House

Antony House (5 miles to the west) is also well worth visiting. This Queen Anne mansion is partly 17th c., although it predominantly dates from 1711 to 1721. The rooms make a splendid impression with their exquisite period furniture, but perhaps the principal attraction is the beautiful landscaped park designed by Humphrey Repton.

Portsmouth   K 10

Southern England. County: Hampshire
Altitude: 27 ft. Population: 180,000

The industrial town of Portsmouth, situated on the "island" of Portsea, owes its importance to its magnificent natural harbour. For centuries, from the time of the Armada onwards, it was the principal base of the Royal Navy, while in more recent times Portsmouth has also become the most important naval port in Great Britain; thus in 1981 the town was the port of departure and the marine command headquarters for the British troops in the war against Argentina over the Falkland Islands.

Three famous historic ships provide evidence of past naval might: Lord Nelson's H.M.S. "Victory", the "Mary Rose" of Henry VIII, and the H.M.S. "Warrior", the Royal Navy's first warship.

In the last few years an attempt has begun to be made to address the problem of the town's need to expand – a problem arising from the fact that it is bounded by the sea to the west, south and east, and by Ports Down to the north. Banks of earth and dykes have been built up in order to create new areas of land. In the Hampshire Basin towards Winchester (see entry) the fertile soils with their Tertiary deposits provide excellent conditions for intensive agriculture.

History The strategic importance of this site on the Channel was recognised by the Romans, who built a fort at Portchester, on a promontory just west of Portsmouth – the only Roman fort in Britain or northern Europe which was never destroyed, although frequently captured. The Normans took over the Roman fortress and it was strengthened by Henry II. Richard II had the site extended and built a fortified palace adjoining the keep. In 1415 Henry V assembled his troops here before

W. L. Wyllie: "The Death of Nelson" (1805, in the Royal Naval Museum)

setting sail for France. In the Second World War Portsmouth's strategic importance as a naval base led to large parts of the town being destroyed.

★H.M.S. "Victory"

Figurehead of H.M.S. "Victory"

A visit to the harbour with its magnificent historic frigates is particularly rewarding. A short distance north of the landing stage for ferries to the Isle of Wight (see entry), the visitor will pass the gateway to the old docks. This is the site of Lord Nelson's flagship (see Famous People), which was built in 1765 and is almost 197 ft long, with five decks and 104 cannon. It was lifted from the sea in 1921 and restored. In his hour of victory at the Battle of Trafalgar (1805), barely 20 minutes after he had penetrated the French lines, Vice-admiral Nelson was fatally wounded and died in the cockpit of his legendary ship, H.M.S. "Victory". In the Royal Naval Museum the visitor will find numerous mementoes of Lord Nelson and seafaring in the 18th c. A 46 ft panoramic painting by W. L. Wylie records the course of the Battle of Trafalgar.

★Mary Rose

The "Mary Rose", which formed part of the fleet of Henry VIII (see Famous People), is another ship of great historical interest. This four-decker boat, with its 91 bronze cannon, was built in 1509–10 from best Hampshire oak and enlarged to 700 tonnes in 1536. In 1545, during a sea battle against the French, it sank just a mile and a quarter from its home port. The sea was so rough during this battle that water entered the upper deck of the vessel through the cannon covers and within a short space of time the "Mary Rose" sank to the bottom of the Solent. In 1836 the first divers went down to look for the frigate, and from 1965 onwards the explorations were intensified. Finally, on October 11th 1982, the Tudor ship was lifted from the sea-bottom but it must now wait until 2002 before it can be safely installed in dry surroundings.

H.M.S. "Victory", Lord Nelson's flagship

In June 1987, after eight years of restoration work in Hartlepool, H.M.S. "Warrior" finally returned to Portsmouth. Launched in 1860, this 418 ft long ship (9700 tonnes) ranked in its time as one of the biggest and best equipped warships of its type. It had never actually seen active service when it was taken out of commission after 23 years.

★H.M.S. "Warrior" 1860

Just over the water in Gosport is the Submarine Museum of the Royal Navy. It contains Great Britain's first submarine, H.M. Submarine Torpedo Boat No. 1.

Royal Navy Submarine Museum

The Round Tower (1415) and the Square Tower (1495) have for centuries marked the entrance to the harbour. The Square Tower was originally the residence of the military governor.

Round Tower Square Tower

Of the historic High Street only one building has survived – **Buckingham House** (No. 10), in which the Duke of Buckingham was murdered in 1628. The foundation stone of **St Thomas' Cathedral** was laid in 1185. The chancel and transepts date from Norman times, while the choir is in the late style of Sir Christopher Wren. The south side-aisle of the choir is dedicated to the Royal Navy and this is borne out by the mementoes of the "Mary Rose" and Nelson's "Victory" to be found here. Of interest is the "Mother and Child" by Andrea della Robbia.

High Street

In Old Commercial Road, which can be reached by following Cambridge Road northwards, the visitor will find the Birthplace Museum of Charles Dickens (see Famous People), whose father worked for the navy. The house where Dickens was born was restored in 1970 and contains Regency furniture which belonged to the writer's family. Among the memorabilia are some manuscripts, early copies of his novels, and Dickens' death-bed, which was brought here from his home at Gads Hill in Kent.

Charles Dickens' Birthplace

Museum Road branches off from the High Street in an easterly direction. The Victorian City Museum and Art Gallery with its extensive collections of art and craftwork is situated here. The permanent exhibition entitled "The Story of Portsmouth", which opened in 1991, portrays daily life in the town from the 17th c. through the means of models, realia, photos and videos.

City Museum and Art Gallery

The Sea Life Centre, situated to the south-east on Clarence Esplanade, initiates the visitor into the mysteries of the underwater world.

Sea Life Centre

Close by is the D-Day Museum, opened in 1984, which houses the **Overlord Embroidery**, inspired by the Bayeux Tapestry. This modern 272 ft long tapestry chronicles events in the Second World War from Dunkirk to the Allied landing in Normandy on D-Day, June 6th 1944 (Operation Overlord).

D-Day Museum

The resort of Southsea is now a popular residential suburb of Portsmouth. It has a 3 mile long promenade, from which there is a fine view across to the Isle of Wight (see entry). Southsea was where Sir Arthur Conan Doyle was practising as a doctor when he wrote the first Sherlock Holmes novel "A Study in Scarlet". **Southsea Castle**, which was built by Henry VIII in the middle of the 16th c., contains a number of exhibits connected with the history of the town and military history from Tudor times through to the Victorian era. From the castle walls there is a view across the Solent to the Victorian Spitbank Fort.

Southsea

Old and young alike can enjoy themselves at the futuristic bathing centre known as **"The Pyramids"**, with its fun pools, two large water slides and fitness zones.

The **Natural Science Museum** is housed in Cumberland House, which has recently been renovated. Exhibitions include a section devoted to the flora and fauna of the sea and of marshland areas, as well as a butterfly house with over 100 different species.

In the elegant Victorian officers' mess of **Eastney Barracks** there is a museum offering extensive coverage of the history of the Royal Marines.

Among the best exhibits of the **Industrial Museum** are two mighty steam machines, dating from 1887, which were built by James Watt (see Famous People).

Surroundings
Portchester Castle

Situated on a promontory at the north end of Portsmouth Harbour is Portchester Castle. Construction of the castle, which has 20 ft high ramparts and 20 bastions, was begun in the 3rd c. by the Romans, who named it Portus Adurni. The site was turned into a royal castle at the beginning of the 12th c. under Henry I. At the end of the 14th c., during Richard II's reign, further extensions were added, while Henry V assembled his troops here for the campaign against France.

Titchfield

At Titchfield (19 miles to the north-west), a little place on the River Meon, are to be found the remains of a Premonstratensian abbey founded in 1238 by the Bishop of Winchester. Thomas Wriothesley, 1st Earl of Southampton, who was Henry VIII's Lord Chancellor, converted it into his own residence in 1537, naming it Place House. The fine gatehouse and four towers in the Tudor style still survive. The medieval tiles with their beautiful motives are highly unusual. Shakespeare (see Famous People) was often an honoured guest of the 3rd Earl, to whom the poet dedicated his sonnets.

Richmond   K 6

Northern England. County: North Yorkshire
Altitude: 500 ft. Population: 8000

Richmond is a very picturesque little town, described by the British Council as "typically English". The historic focal point of the old town was the Norman castle, whose spectacular ruins perch on a rock, dominating the banks of the River Swale. Richmond is surrounded by the Pennines and the Yorkshire Dales (see entry) and is a excellent base for nature-lovers and walkers who wish to explore the great open spaces in the vicinity.

History The name of the town comes from the castle ("Riche Mont") built about 1070 by Alan the Red, 1st Earl of Richmond. His extensive possessions, which he held in fee from William the Conqueror (see Famous People), included no fewer than 164 manors and became known as Richmondshire. Henry VII, who inherited the title of earl of Richmond, gave the name to his new palace in Surrey (now Greater London), previously known as Sheen.

Castle

The castle, dating from the 11th c., was impregnable on three sides, thanks to its situation; the fourth side was protected by a massive keep. The best view of the town, which was formerly defended by walls and three gates, is to be had from the top of this 115 ft high keep, which was built between 1150 and 1180.

Market Place

A short way to the north, in the large cobbled market place, is the little church of **Holy Trinity**, surrounded by pretty old houses and small shops.

Green Howards
Museum

In Green Howards Museum over 300 years of the history of the North Yorkshire Regiment are documented.

Poster from 1841

Another special attraction is the lovingly restored Georgian Theatre Royal, which was designed in 1788 by Samuel Butler, who built another five theatre stages within a radius of 31 mile. The auditorium today holds 230. Famous actors suchs as Edmund Kean and Macready once appeared here. Kean joined Butler's theatre ensemble in 1808 at the age of 17 as a singing comedian and "walking gentleman harlequin", before going on to London, where he was to enjoy great success as a classical actor. The long history of theatre and drama is well documented in the theatre museum, which opened in 1979, with historic models, properties, costumes, posters, photos and other mementoes. In the second gallery the visitor can admire the oldest, completely preserved, painted stage set in Great Britain. It was made in 1836 in the workshop of George River Higgins; the number of different trees painted on the backdrop is remarkable.

★Georgian Theatre Royal and Museum

In Ryder's Wynd – the tiny streets in Richmond have the name "wynds" – can be found the Richmondshire Museum, which has exhibits connected with local history from 1071 to the present day (including Anglo-Saxon excavation finds, historic costumes, displays of crafts and industry, children's toys).

Richmondshire Museum

To the north-west near Queen's Road is the Greyfriars Tower (built about 1360–70), which is the last remaining fragment of the former monastery of the Grey Friars order, whose members lived here from the 12th to the 16th c.

Greyfriars Tower

Hand-painted scenery in Richmond Theatrical Museum

St Mary's Church	Going eastwards from the Richmondshire Museum along Station Road, the parish church of St Mary's is reached almost immediately. It contains elaborately carved 16th c. choir stalls, which were originally in Easby Abbey.
Surroundings Swaledale, Wensleydale	Excursions can be made into Swaledale and Wensleydale, two scenically beautiful valleys which lie on the northern edge of the Yorkshire Dales (see entry).
Easby Abbey	An attractive path along the River Swale leads to the extensive and picturesque ruins of Easby Abbey (1 mile), a Premonstratensian abbey founded in 1155. Visitors can see what is left of the refectory, nave and transepts, as well as the east part of the choir. The nearby parish church, St Agatha's, has a copy of the Easby Cross (Anglo-Saxon, about 800; original in the British Museum in London), some fine wall-paintings dating from the middle of the 13th c. and a Norman-Romanesque font.

Rochester   M 9

Southern England. County: Kent
Altitude: 125 ft. Population: 23,500

Rochester lies halfway between London and the Channel ports on the River Medway just inland from where it flows into the North Sea.

The town's official name of City of Rochester-upon-Medway denotes the urban district comprising not just Rochester, but also the neighbouring municipalities of Chatham and Strood. The quiet little town of Rochester is closely linked with the name of Charles Dickens (see Famous People), who spent his childhood in neighbouring Chatham and the last twelve years of his life at Gads Hill, halfway between Rochester and Gravesend. In many of his books locations in Rochester and the surrounding area play an important part; his last work, the unfinished novel "The Mystery of Edwin Drood" is set almost completely in the fictitious town of Cloisterham, which is obviously Rochester.

History Rochester developed from the early Roman settlement of "Durobrivae". It was here that Ethelbert of Kent founded the second episcopal see in England after Canterbury (see entry) in 604. The present cathedral was begun by the Normans, who also added to the town's defences by building a castle. Henry VIII ordered that warships for the English fleet should be built here at the Medway estuary. The Dutch entered the estuary with their ships in 1667 and attacked the dockyard at Rochester. However, for many years after that the docks remained one of the most important places in the country for building naval ships.

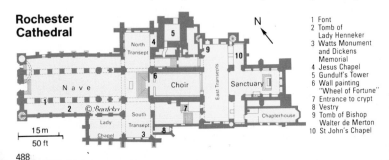

Rochester Cathedral

© Baedeker

15 m
50 ft

1 Font
2 Tomb of Lady Henneker
3 Watts Monument and Dickens Memorial
4 Jesus Chapel
5 Gundulf's Tower
6 Wall painting "Wheel of Fortune"
7 Entrance to crypt
8 Vestry
9 Tomb of Bishop Walter de Merton
10 St John's Chapel

The building of the present cathedral was begun around 1180 by the Norman Bishop Gundulf, who also built the White Tower in London (see entry). It was erected on the foundations of the first episcopal church which had been built under Ethelbert. Gundulf's Tower, on the north side of the cathedral, and the crypt are the two features which survive from this early stage of building. After the consecration of the church in 1130 further building went on until the end of the 13th c., including the addition of the nave and transepts. The central tower was completed in 1343 and in the 16th c. the south-west transept was extended. The most impressive part of the building is the west front, which was finished in 1160. Flanked by two towers and crowned by a late Perpendicular eight-sectioned window, the Norman doorway has two columns on either side, each consisting of a statue: one of King Solomon and the other of the Queen of Sheba. It is the only example in England of a doorway being built employing this device, which was so characteristic of French ecclesiastical architecture of this period. Above the doorway in the tympanum Christ as the ruler of the world is depicted.

★Rochester Cathedral

The groundplan of the original Anglo-Saxon church is discernible in the front part of the north aisle; in the south aisle lies the 18th c. marble tombstone of Lady Ann Henniker, which was designed by Thomas Banks. In the south transept there is a memorial plaque to Charles Dickens and the tomb of Sir Richard Watts. The choir stalls include some of the oldest in England, dating back to 1227. Of special importance in the choir is the fragment of a 13th c. fresco on the north-east pillar, which depicts the "wheel of fortune". The two choir side aisles contain the tombstones of Bishop Hamo de Hythe (d. 1352) and Bishop John de Bradfield (d. 1283). At the north end of the east transept is the tomb of Bishop Walter de Merton. It stands on the site of the tomb of St William of Perth, a Scottish baker, who was murdered here in 1201 while on a pilgrimage to the Holy Land. Magical powers were imputed to his tomb and it developed into a place of pilgrimage. The door of the chapterhouse (14th c.) is another fine feature, with its pictures of a church and a synagogue, and of the four Fathers of the Church and the soul of the church's founder, Bishop Hymo de Hythe. Finally it is possible to descend into the crypt, a major piece of architecture in the Early English style and one of the largest in the country.

A Benedictine monastery was also founded with the cathedral. Three of the four original entrance gates have survived (all of them 15th c.): leading on to the High Street is Chertsey's Gate (as the "Gatehouse" the home of John Jasper in Dickens' "Edwin Drood"); to the right and directly by the cathedral, Deanery Gate, which was used by pilgrims as a shrine for St William; on the south side Prior's Gate, which is extremely well preserved. Also on the south side is Cloister Garth, on the site of the monastery, and Minor Canon Row, a highly attractive row of houses dating from 1723, also immortalised by Dickens in "Edwin Drood".

Monastery

Towering opposite the cathedral is Rochester Castle, construction of which was begun in 1088 on the site of the first Roman fortifications. It is one of the best preserved Norman fortresses in Great Britain. The massive keep, built in 1127, is, at 121 ft, the highest in the country. From its platform there is a magnificent view of the town and the Medway valley. To the south Satis House can be seen, in which Queen Elizabeth I (see Famous People) was a guest in 1573.

★Castle

Walking from the castle in the direction of Rochester Bridge and passing Bridge Chapel (14th c.), we come to the main street of Rochester, the High Street, which boasts several memorable buildings along its length, many of which have found mention in Charles Dickens' novels. The first one, on the left, is the former Bull Inn, over 400 years old, which was renamed the **Royal Victoria and Bull Hotel** after the queen visited it in

High Street

1836. In "Pickwick Papers" it appears as the Bull Hotel, while in "Great Expectations" it is the Blue Boar. Opposite stands the **Guildhall**, built in 1687, which now houses the town museum. On the left, just before the turning into Northgate, is the **Old Corn Exchange**, easily recognisable because of its enormous clock. This building was commissioned by the member of parliament Admiral Sir Cloudesley Shovell in 1706 as the town's meat market and was only converted into a granary in the 19th c. Another "Dickens house", also on the left, is the Elizabethan Watt's Charity or **Poor Travellers House**. This was set up by Richard Watts in 1579 as overnight shelter for six poor travellers, and in so doing he established a tradition which lasted right up to the Second World War. Dickens mentions the house in his Christmas stories. The High Street carries on downhill, past the remains of the medieval town walls, until **Eastgate House** is reached, built in 1590 for Sir Peter Buck, naval officer and mayor of Rochester. The house now houses the ★**Charles Dickens Centre**, in which the writer's works are brought to life by means of modern audio-visual methods. Under the name of "Nun's House" the house also features in "Edwin Drood". In the courtyard can be seen the original Swiss chalet which Dickens was given by the French actor Charles Fechter. Dickens had it installed in Gads Hill and during the summer used to spend most of his time in it. At 144 High Street is the **Kenneth Bills Motor Cycle Museum**, which displays British motor-cycles from 1921 to 1977.

In Crow Lane, which leads off the High Street, stands **Restoration House**, where on May 28th 1660 Charles II spent his first night on English soil after his return from his exile in France. On application at the tourist office it is possible to visit the magnificent interior rooms, which include "Miss Havisham's Room" in Dickens' "Great Expectations". Opposite is **The Vines**, which was once a monastery vineyard.

Surroundings
Chatham

The industrial town of Chatham, which today forms part of Rochester, was the centre for naval shipbuilding on the Medway. For over 400 years warships were built in the famous ★**Royal Navy Dockyard**, including in 1795 Lord Nelson's flagship, H.M.S. "Victory", which today, after extensive restoration, lies at anchor in Portsmouth (see entry). The golden age of naval shipbuilding in the 18th c. has been recreated at considerable expense and today a large exhibition shows the visitor the skills and trades which were needed to build one of the great sailing vessels of the past, while numerous displays give him a picture of the skills of the craftsmen and labourer who worked in the dockyard.

Fort Amherst was initially built in 1756 to provide a defence for the dockyard and in the face of the French threat between 1802 and 1811 it was considerably extended and strengthened. The only cannon shots to fall here were, however, merely fired during extended manoeuvres; Dickens mentions them in "Pickwick Papers". The catacombs and battlement walks of this best preserved of 18th c. British forts can be visited, together with a small museum.

The **Medway Heritage Centre**, housed in St Mary's Church, documents the life of people on the Medway.

From 1817 to 1821 **Charles Dickens** lived at 2 Ordnance Terrace, one of a row of Georgian houses.

Brompton

The Royal Engineers' Museum at Brompton, to the east of Chatham, documents the history of the royal pioneer troops from 1800 to 1845.

Cobham

Situated to the west of Rochester, the pretty village of Cobham is well-known to all readers of "Pickwick Papers" because of the Leather Bottle Inn, to which Tracy Tupman fled. The main attraction of the church of St Mary Magdalene are 18 brass memorial slabs dating from the 14th–16th c., whose pictures of knights, ladies and priests show us a good deal about the dress and weapons of those times. Cobham College was founded in 1382 by Sir John de Cobham and was turned into an old people's home in 1598.

Cobham Hall (built between 1580 and 1670), today a girls' school, is a magnificent late Elizabethan red-brick manor house, with four towers, the typical high chimneys of that period and a gold stucco ceiling (1672) in the Gilt Hall (music room). It is surrounded by a fine park, which is famous for its large rhododendrons.

★Cobham Hall

Over on the north bank of the Medway stands Upnor Castle, an Elizabethan fortress which was built about 1560 to defend the dockyard at Chatham.

Upnor Castle

Gads Hill, the house in which Charles Dickens spent the last twelve years of his life, is in the village of Higham, halfway between Rochester and Gravesend. Even as a child the writer had fallen in love with this house while out on walks with his father and in 1856 he was finally able to buy it. The house is now occupied by a private school, which will however arrange conducted tours.

Gads Hill

Salisbury

K 9

Southern England. County: Wiltshire
Altitude: 150 ft. Population: 37,000

Historically a centre of the cloth industry, Salisbury is the county town of Wiltshire. The town is situated at the point where the Rivers Nadder and Bourne flow into the Avon and is famous for its cathedral, a masterpiece of the early Gothic style.

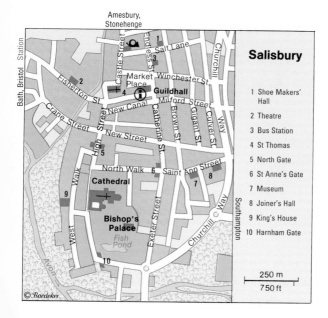

Salisbury

1 Shoe Makers' Hall
2 Theatre
3 Bus Station
4 St Thomas
5 North Gate
6 St Anne's Gate
7 Museum
8 Joiner's Hall
9 King's House
10 Harnham Gate

250 m
750 ft

© Baedeker

491

Salisbury Cathedral, a masterpiece of Early English architecture

History Salisbury dates back to 1220 when the foundation stone was laid for the cathedral, which had been moved here from its previous site at Old Sarum. The chequerboard layout of the town, with enclosed gardens between the houses, was a model for medieval town planning. On receiving market privileges from the king, the bishop built a bridge across the Avon in 1244, thereby creating the right conditions for the town to become a major trading centre, having no less than four market places during the Middle Ages. The town was not, however, granted the privilege of self-government; although the various guilds in the town formed a council, Salisbury was under the jurisdiction of the bishop and the town was not allowed its own higher authority until 1611.

Sights

★★ Salisbury
Cathedral

Salisbury Cathedral is the first major sacred building of the English Gothic period and was built in a relatively short time, from 1220 to 1266, following a single overall plan.

In contrast to the French Gothic cathedrals of the same period, which are lavishly structured and follow definite models, Salisbury Cathedral embodies the more restrained English style in its ground-plan and construction methods. Its elongated shape is typical of this, with the various sections of the church arranged in the order that was definitive for England: nave, long choir, retrochoir, main west transept and east choir transept, the last named being shielded from the choir by false arches. The long, rectangular retrochoir combines with the Lady Chapel, which encloses one end of the longitudinal axis of the cathedral, to form what in England is a separate area, instead of the ambulatory choir which was usual in French cathedrals. In addition the two transepts only possess a single east side-aisle. From the overall impression it is clear that the individual parts of the building were horizontally articulated and completed straight and flat, all rising upwards in equal degrees and at the crossing tower grouped vertically. Even the impact of the façade is subordinate to this basic principle, with its decorative sculptures – of Christ as world ruler with a hierarchy of patriarchs, apostles and saints – providing almost the only architectural embellishment in an otherwise sparsely decorated building.

According to the "Uses of Old Sarum": as early as 1095, self-government for all the cathedrals in the land was made compulsory by Bishop Osmond until the Reformation. The dean was the chairman of the assembly of canons, who all had equal rights; the procantor was the leader of the choir; the chancellor was responsible for administration and the treasurer for the finances.

The **interior**, which is of bright-coloured limestone and darkly gleaming Purbeck marble, displays the horizontal sequencing of the trusses, which is characteristic of English churches, strengthened by continuous ledges, with the effect of considerable depth, instead of the usual upwards extension in the Gothic style. The construction of the walls is divided into three zones, with arches, a gallery-like triforium and a passageway above. A ribbed vault in four parts encloses the nave at a height of only 82 ft. Static difficulties occurred in the middle of the 14th c. with the raising of the crossing tower (404 ft; the highest spire in England). The crossing pillars, whose foundations were on marshy land, began to bend under the massive weight of 6000 tonnes of stone, while the mighty supporting arches which had been inserted at the same time had no effect. To this very day the safety of the tower has constantly necessitated the carrying out of repairs. The interior fittings of the cathedral, which were considerably altered at the end of the 18th c. as a result of restoration measures by James Wyatt, include some elaborate tombstones: those of William Longespee (d. 1226); Sir Richard Mompesson (d. 1627) with his wife; Bishop Giles of Bridport, who consecrated the

A horse-drawn bus in the old part of Salisbury

493

cathedral in 1255; and the brass of Bishop Wyville (d. 1375) as Lord of the Castle.

The High Gothic **Cloister** and the octagonal **Chapterhouse**, the meeting place of the cathedral chapter, both date from the middle of the 14th c. The latter has a single central pillar acting as a vault support, a fine wall-frieze with pictures from the Old Testament and tracery windows divided into four sections with 19th c. glass. Items stored there include the church silver and one of the four original copies in existence of the Magna Carta, the foundation of the British constitution. Other Anglo-Saxon documents and the inspection report on the cathedral tower written by Sir Christopher Wren in 1668 are to be found in the library.

Within the **Cathedral Close** with its green lawns, separated from the rest of the town by its three gateways, there are some notable Elizabethan and Georgian houses dating from the 14th to the 18th c. They were the residences of the dean, ecclesiastical officers and teachers at the cathedral school. Of special interest are Mompesson House, with its elegant interior fittings and wonderful collection of glass, and King's House, which contains the Salisbury and South Wiltshire Museum. This museum has exhibits from Stonehenge (see entry) and Old Sarum, glass, porcelain and ceramic objects, and some landscape paintings by Turner (see Famous People).

Old town centre

To the north of the cathedral we pass through the North Gate, along Crane Bridge Road, and reach the meadows of the River Avon, where there is a fine view of the cathedral, which John Constable captured on canvas in his painting of 1820. Returning to the town centre, we pass the parish church of St Thomas of Canterbury (15th c.) and arrive at the wide market place, which with its 15th c. market cross was the focal point of the old cloth-trading town. Further on to the west is the Guildhall (1788–95), and diagonally opposite to it the Plume of Feathers Inn (15th/17th c.). A little further on in Milford Street we come to the Red Lion Hotel with its fine façade of 1820 and its pretty inner courtyard. Further on, in Gigant Street, is Joiner's Hall, an attractive half-timbered building dating from the 16th c.

Surroundings

Old Sarum

Old Sarum was the precursor of present-day Salisbury. The ruins of the town lie 2 miles to the north of the town centre on a hill which even in prehistoric times was fortified. The Romans built the camp of Sorviodonum on this site, while under the Saxons a town settlement grew up here. William the Conqueror (see Famous People) chose this strategically favourable spot to build a castle and in 1075 moved the episcopal see here from Sherborne. The castle and the cathedral, which was consecrated in 1092, were intended to make Norman claims to overlordship indisputable. It was probably as a result of disputes between clergy and military, coupled with a shortage of water, that the church authorities decided to have a cathedral built on a new site. In 1220 the inhabitants of Old Sarum moved to New Salisbury, where a new town with a cathedral was laid out, following a definite plan, but using building materials from Old Sarum, so that today at Old Sarum only a few remains of the castle within the inner circumference wall can be seen, and the ruined cathedral within the outer wall.

Stonehenge

See entry

Wilton

The old capital of the Saxon kingdom of Wessex, and later of the county of Wiltshire, is situated 3 miles west of Salisbury. The Royal Carpet Factory, founded in 1655, and several other important carpet producers are based in the village. Since the middle of the 17th c. they have taken advantage of the ready supply of local wool and the services of migrant weavers from Flanders and France. The parish church was built in 1843 from plans by Wyatt, following early Christian building models, but with a mixture of styles which is very characteristic of Victorian architecture.

★★ **Wilton House** lies on the edge of the village and is the seat of the Herbert family, the Earls of Pembroke. In 1544 the former abbey building was given by Henry VIII to the general and politician, William Herbert, who was married to the queen's sister. He had the buildings pulled down and a Tudor country mansion built, which in turn was destroyed by a fire in 1647, only the east tower and the Holbein portal (now in the park) being saved. A new house, which from the exterior was of a classical simplicity, was then built under the guiding control of the architect, Inigo Jones, and completed after his death in 1653 by John Webb. The full Baroque splendour of the interior of the new house can best be appreciated in the seven state apartments. A masterpiece of this Baroque style is the white Double Cube Room (66 ft long, 33 ft wide and 33 ft high), decorated with gold-painted flowers and garlands of fruit and rounded off with a brilliantly colourful painted ceiling depicting the Perseus legend. The room is also fascinating for its individual and group portraits which the 4th Earl of Pembroke commissioned from van Dyck between 1632 and 1634. Alongside these likenesses of the Pembroke family there are portraits of Charles I, Queen Henrietta Maria and their three children which are also of considerable interest. The heavy gilded furniture was designed about 100 years later by William Kent and makes a perfect contribution to the overall effect of the room. Hardly less impressive is the Single Cube Room, which is exactly half the size. The painted ceiling has scenes from Sir Philip Sidney's "Arcadia", which he wrote in 1590 while a guest at Wilton House. In the remaining apartments there are other valuable paintings by Hugo van der Goes, Mabuse, Andrea del Sarto, Lorenzo Lotto, Rembrandt, Rubens, Ribera, Reynolds, as well as over 50 gouaches of the Spanish Riding School (1755) by Baron d'Eisenberg, riding master to Emperor Francis I. The landscaped park surrounding the house is also superb, with its magnificent stock of old trees. Another unusual feature, of later date, and one which has been much copied, is the Palladian bridge (1737) over the River Nadder.

Built on top of a sandstone hill, Shaftesbury (19 miles south-west of Salisbury; pop. 4900) is a picturesque little market-town, steeped in the past. King Alfred the Great gave the little town of Shaston its charter and then in 888 founded a Benedictine abbey with an extensive landholding in Shaftesbury, naming his daughter Elgiva as the first abbess. After Edward the Martyr was murdered at Corfe Castle in 979 and the remains of the canonised king were brought to the abbey to be buried, the town became a popular place of pilgrimage with almost a dozen churches. By the 15th c. some 140 nuns were living in the abbey, which had become so prosperous that it was popularly maintained that if the abbess of Shaftesbury were to marry the abbot of Glastonbury (see entry), the offspring would be wealthier than those of the royal family. Small wonder then that Henry VIII should have been quick to dissolve both monastic houses in 1539, confiscate their property and sell off their buildings for demolition. Today only the foundation walls are left as a reminder of the abbey's existence, while in the Abbey Ruins Museum there is a model of the building as it once was, as well as numerous finds from the Middle Ages.

St Peter's is the only one of the twelve medieval churches in the Perpendicular style which has been preserved. It possesses an interesting crypt and a fine doorway.

This **History Museum** is housed in a 19th c. barber's shop and has all kinds of exhibits detailing the history of the town.

Gold Hill is a steep cobbled street picturesquely lined on one side with tiny houses dating from the 16th-18th c., while on the other side there is a 13th c. ochre-coloured wall. At the top (Park Walk, Love Lane) there is

Shaftesbury

a superb view across the Blackmoor Vale to Somerset, and on clear days as far as Glastonbury Tor.

St Giles House

St Giles House, the family seat of the Earls of Shaftesbury, is situated about 15 miles south-west of Salisbury. Anthony Ashley Cooper, 1st Earl of Shaftesbury, was Lord Chancellor in 1672–73, subsequently becoming Leader of the Opposition and in 1679 playing a decisive part in getting the Habeas Corpus Act passed. He was arrested in 1681 and the following year fled the country, taking refuge in Holland. His grandson, Anthony Ashley Cooper (1671–1713), was an important philosopher of the Enlightenment. His doctrine that morality represented the most complete development of man's natural impulses was later to exert a considerable influence on the German poets of the Sturm und Drang movement, notably Schiller.

★★Stourhead House

At Stourhead (26 miles west of Salisbury) we can admire one of the finest English landscaped gardens of the 18th c., which, except for the rhododendrons and magnolias planted in the 19th c., has remained unchanged since the time of its inception. The unique design of the garden includes an artificial lake with caves and landing stages. Surrounding the lake there are hills planted with trees, on which are to be found small classical temples and even the 14th c. Gothic market cross which once stood in Bristol (see entry). A walk through the garden makes the visitor aware of an extremely effective and harmonious connection between "man-made" scenery and open countryside. The park and the stately Palladian mansion were designed in 1721–22 by Colin Campbell for the London banking family of Hoare. Thomas Chippendale provided elegant period furniture for the library, while the painting gallery is adorned with works by Canaletto, Raphael, Nicolas Poussin and Angelika Kaufmann. King Alfred's Tower, which was erected to commemorate the Saxon king, towers over the surrounding parkland and affords a fine panoramic view.

Isles of Scilly   E 11

South-west England. County: Cornwall

The Isles of Scilly lie 25 miles south-west of Land's End, the farthest tip of Cornwall (see entry). As well as five inhabited islands, this archipeligo in the Atlantic encompasses 40 further islands and 150 rock formations with fine-sounding names which offer in part some magnificently beautiful scenery and undisturbed nature. Once a source of terror for seamen, as so many ships were wrecked against the rocky reefs here, the islands are now a holiday paradise boasting a mild climate (the result of their proximity to the Gulf Stream), marvellous sandy beaches, enormous granite formations, charming deciduous forests and moorland. As well as tourism, the 2400 inhabitants live mainly from flower-growing.

Transport From Penzance it is barely three hours by boat (daily except Sunday) or quicker by helicopter to Hugh Town, the tiny capital of the largest island, St Mary's (6 sq. miles). Buses, taxis and bicycles are available on the island for short journeys, while excursion boats cruise between the islands.

History The Isles of Scilly were already settled in the Bronze and Iron Ages. The theory that the Scillies were the northern Tin Islands of antiquity, already known to the Phoenicians, is debated as much as the name "Cassiterides", given to them by Heroditus. To the Romans Sylicanis was an inhospitable foreign post, and even the Vikings only stayed in

Syllanger for a short time. Between AD 400 and 1000 many hermits lived on the islands, while Tresco was home to a community of monks. In 1114 Henry I gave Tresco to Tavistock Abbey to found a Benedictine monastery there. After this the islands were left in peace. Their poor inhabitants lived from fishing, a little agriculture and smuggling. In 1830 Squire Augustus Smith became Lord Proprietor of the islands, after which they experienced a 40-year-long economic heyday. Houses, churches, schools and even five shipyards were built, and flower-growing began.

A large number of St Mary's 1650 inhabitants live in **Hugh Town**, which is surrounded by two sandy bays. The small village museum exhibits finds from early history up to the Christian sea voyages and provides information about the islands' flora and fauna. A 16th–18th c. garrison fort stands on a peninsula offshore from St Mary's. Apart from the octagonal bastion Star Castle (Hotel), the fort can be seen from Garrison Walk. The walls offer wonderful, extensive views.

St Mary's

The ruins of a fort belonging to Henry VIII (see Famous People) are of note. They lie west of Hugh Town and are known as Harry's Walls. Excursions are also available to Telegraph Tower, from where the foot of Bants Carn, a burial chamber dating from the third century BC, and Ancient Village, the remains of an Iron Age village, can be reached. The numerous little fields of flowers, often separated by hedges, are a beautiful sight. A visit to Old Town is also recommended. The east gable of its parish church (founded in the 12th c., restored in the 19th c.) is crowned by a 11th c. stone roof cross. The path to Peninnis Head leads past imposing granite rocks.

Tresco is the second largest of the Scilly Isles. ★**Tresco Abbey** is famous for its subtropical park, laid out in terraces, from which fine views can be enjoyed. Apart from the ruins of the abbey, a collection of figureheads from ships wrecked off the Isles of Scilly can be seen. King Charles' Fort and Cromwell's Castle, both with fortified towers, date from the mid-17th and mid-18th c.

Tresco

St Martin's, rugged in the north and with a flower-bedecked bay in the south, is delightful. A spectacular panoramic view can be enjoyed from St Martin's Head.

St Martin's

St Agnes can claim the second oldest lighthouse in the country (1680). Horse Point is an extremely impressive rock formation.

St Agnes

The smallest of the inhabited islands, Bryher has two attractive bays, Rushy and Hell Bay. The contrast of the small fields of flowers with the steep cliffs and raging sea provides endless fascination.

Bryher

Many of the uninhabited islands are nature reserves, on which visitors can land only with special permission.

Sheffield   K 7

Central England. County: South Yorkshire
Altitude: 230 ft. Population: 530,000

England's fourth-largest city lies approximately 35 miles south of Leeds (see entry) on the River Don, at the foot of the Derbyshire Hills. An industrial city, Sheffield is a popular base from which to explore the Peak District, the favourite recreational area of those living in this conurbation in Central England. Sheffield itself also has a number of well-tended parks and a beautiful green belt area. It is worth visiting the centre of this university town, whose academic institutions have long worked closely

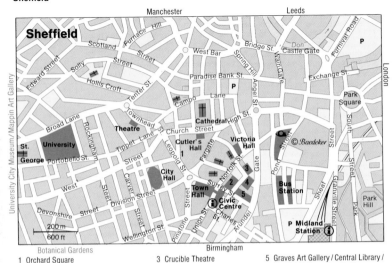

Manchester　　　　　　Leeds

Sheffield

1 Orchard Square
2 Ruskin Art & Craft Gallery

3 Crucible Theatre
4 Lyceum Theatre

5 Graves Art Gallery / Central Library /
Sheffield Information Centre

with local industry. The most recent example of this is the new Technology Park, established to carry out research, which is situated near the technical college. Sheffield is famous for knives, all types of cutting tools, guns and high-grade steel production. As early as about 1478 Chaucer refers in his "Canterbury Tales" to a "Sheffield thwitel", the ancestor of the modern pocket-knife. The knives and other implements were formerly made in home workshops; they are now manufactured in large factories and exported all over the world. Since the early 1980s, recession, a fall in sales and rationalisation have resulted in the loss of more than 70 per cent of jobs in this region; today's leading manufacturers comprise United Engineering Steels, Sheffield Forgemasters, British Steel Stainless, Davy Mackee and Arthur Lee. Another important employer is the confectioner Bassett, subsidiary of the Cadbury-Schweppes Group.

Transport The A1/E 15, M1 and M62 provide good access to the city. Sheffield does not have its own airport, but lies only 45 miles north of East Midlands Airport, 40 miles south of Leeds-Bradford Airport (see entry, Leeds) and 40 miles east of Manchester (see entry) Airport. Sheffield Midland Station offers excellent rail links to the rest of the country.

Sights
Cathedral of St
Peter and St Paul

The cathedral dedicated to St Peter and St Paul stands in Church Street on the site of a parish church founded after 1100 by William de Lovetot, a Norman baron. The new church, built in the late-Gothic Perpendicular style, replaced it in the mid-15th c.; however, only the choir and the tower remain. The nave was built in the late 18th c. and enlarged in 1880. When Sheffield became the see of a bishop in 1914 it was planned to make the present nave the transept of a new and much larger church, but this project was a casualty of the two world wars, leaving the church with an unusual ground plan. In 1966 it was further altered and restored. Note inside the cathedral the font, donated in 1884 by Freemasons, and the marble tomb of the Earl of Shrewsbury (d. 1538), which shows him between his two wives; the elaborately carved alabaster figures were

Sheffield: the Victorian Town Hall

originally painted. The unusual portable sedilla of black oak in St Catherine's Chapel dates from the 15th c. The main decoration is provided by the colourful stained glass windows, fitted at the end of the 1960s, in the Chapterhouse. They depict the history of the town. The Chaucer Window shows the miller of Trumpington (in the Reeve's Tale) with his Sheffield knife.

Opposite the cathedral is Cutlers' Hall, built in 1832 in the Neo-Classic style, the headquarters of the Company of Cutlers. Founded in 1624, it is authorised to grant trade marks for articles reaching appropriate standards of quality; the foundation date continues to be celebrated every year. It has a fine collection of silver dating from 1773 to the present day, made up of one master work from each year, all stamped with the recognised seal of quality awarded by the Sheffield Assay Office. **Cutlers' Hall**

The colourful pedestrian precincts of Orchard Square and Fargate, with their numerous shops, restaurants and pubs, lead south to Surrey Street, site of the Victorian **Town Hall**. This impressive Neo-Renaissance building was erected in 1897 and enlarged in 1910 and 1923. The 193 ft-high tower is topped by a figure of Vulcan, the blacksmith god, holding aloft the arrows he has just forged – a symbol of Sheffield's predominant industry. The tourist office is situated on the ground floor. **Orchard Square, Fargate,**

Surrey Street extends west as Barker's Pool and leads to the City Hall. Designed by Vincent Harris and opened in 1932, its concert hall seats 2700. **City Hall**

East of the Town Hall several museums and theatres line the redesigned Tudor Square. The **Central Library** and **Graves Art Gallery**, opened in 1934, contains an excellent collection of old masters, English art from **★ Tudor Square** the 18th c. to the present day and French artists of the 19th and 20th c., including works by Cézanne, Corot, Picasso and Braque. The Graves Art Gallery is a collection assembled by Dr J. F. Graves, who financed most of the building of the museum and who presented more than 1000 pictures to the city.

Theatres

The **Lyceum Theatre** and the **Crucible Theatre**, both reopened in 1990 after extensive restoration, stand opposite. They mainly stage modern plays.

Ruskin Gallery

The paintings, mineral collection and manuscripts in the Ruskin Gallery (Norfolk Street) were assembled in 1875 by the author John Ruskin (1819–1900); the adjoining Craft Gallery exhibits local crafts.

Castle Market

Castle Market and Castle Square, to the north, are modern shopping centres, partly underground.

Weston Park

The ★**City Museum**, founded in 1874 and now housed in a building erected in 1937, contains a unique collection of British and European cutlery from the 16th c. to the present, together with Bronze Age finds. The adjoining **Mappin Art Gallery** has an excellent collection of 18th and 19th c. English art from the Pre-Raphaelites to Turner (see Famous People).

Untitled Gallery

Excellent changing photographic displays, mainly dealing with local themes, can be seen in the Untitled Gallery in Brown Street (Sheffield 1).

★Kelham Island Industrial Museum

Kelham Island Industrial Museum in Alma Street (Sheffield 3) exhibits steel and silverware dating from three centuries. Craftspeople can be seen at work in the "Little Mesters" workshop. A 1200-hp steam engine is another of the museum's special attractions.

Sheffield High Street

Built at the turn of the century, this museum (West Bar, Sheffield 3) houses a collection of old fire engines, uniforms and equipment.

South Yorkshire Fire Museum

Visitors to the Abbeydale Industrial Hamlet (Abbeydale Road, Sheffield 7; 4 miles south-west of the city), an 18th c. Victorian village, can learn about the traditional production of scythes. The site features workshops, warehouses and workers' cottages.

★Abbeydale Industrial Hamlet

To the east of the village is Beauchief Abbey, which combines the remains of a Premonstratensian abbey founded about 1175 and a chapel built in 1660.

Beauchief Abbey

The National Museum of Popular Music opened in 1999 in Sheffield. The interactive displays chart the history of pop music from Elvis Presley and the Beatles through to the present day. (Open daily 10am–6pm; tel: 0114 296 2626)

Pop Music Museum

Construction of the **Bishop's House Museum** (Meersbrook Park, Sheffield 8) began in the 15th c. and was continued in the 16th/17th c. Its building history is explained in two rooms, other exhibits concern the town's history during the Tudor and Stuart periods.

Eight old locomotives belonging to the **South Yorkshire Steam Railway** await enthusiasts of historic trains in this museum in Barrow Road (Sheffield 9).

The **Bus Museum** in Sheffield Road (Sheffield 9) displays old means of transport, including typically English double-decker buses and pre-war milk floats.

Shepherd Wheel Old grindstones, once used in the production of knives, can be viewed in idyllic Whiteley Woods off Hangingwater Road (Sheffield 11).

Other Museums

Bolsover Castle, 12 miles south-east of the city, stands on a steep hill above the town of Bolsover (population 11,800). This partly ruined Jacobean mansion occupies the site of a manor house built by William Peveril. He was also responsible for the construction of Peveril's Castle at the end of the 11th c. at Castleton, which Sir Walter Scott (see Famous People) immortalised in his novel "Peveril of the Peak". Between 1613 and 1617 Charles Cavendish reconstructed Bolsover Castle's Norman keep and built his new house beside it.

**Surroundings
Bolsover Castle**

Shetland Islands   K/L 0/1

Northern Scotland
Administrative Unit: Shetland Islands Area

The Shetland Islands (or "Zetland" from the Norse "hjaltland"), a group of more than 100 islands, are Britain's most northerly outpost. They lie approximately 100 miles north-east of the north coast of Scotland and share the same latitude as the Norwegian mountains, the southern tip of Greenland, the Gulf of Alaska and southern Siberia. Despite this, the Shetlands, although windy and weather-lashed, do not experience frost, as the Gulf Stream ensures them a reasonably favourable climate. However, the land here cannot be put to as much agricultural use as on the Orkney Islands (see entry). Temperatures vary little.

The islands consist mainly of slate, and offer breathtaking cliff scenery and deeply-indented peaceful bays, the "voes". Most of the larger islands are hilly, the heather and broom-clad hills forming a beautiful contrast with the blue of the sea, the green of the cultivated areas and the valleys, and the brown of the peat bogs. The Shetlands are a popular destination for lovers of raw, sometimes archaic-looking nature. On Fair Isle, Mousa, Noss and at Herma Ness ornithologists can avail themselves of marvellous bird-watching opportunities. Unusual species of otters and seals, now rare in the North Sea, are at home here. Another Shetland animal has become famous all over the world; the tough, shaggy Shetland pony, once used as a draught animal in coal-mines and now the patient friend of all children. Anglers enjoy rich fishing here, and even amateur archaeologists find the area has much to offer.

Economy The 24,000 Shetland Islanders inhabit only twelve of the islands, with more than half of them living on the main island, Mainland. The chief source of income is agriculture, in particular the rearing of sheep for the famous fine ★ **Shetland wool**, from which the no less famous Shetland pullovers and other articles of clothing are knitted. Although these garments continually feature new patterns, care is taken not to stray too far from traditional ones. This line of business is in decline, however, and those wishing to purchase genuine Shetland items are advised to do this on the islands themselves, to avoid buying a factory-made product from the mainland. The patterns of the knitters of Fair Isle, the bird-island occupying a remote position in the Atlantic, are the most famous.

Also of importance are **salmon-farming** and fishing, although the latter has suffered recently from the decline in the number of herring and from pollution caused by offshore boring, particularly since the accident involving a Liberian oil tanker on the south coast in early 1993.

The **North Sea Oil** fields situated between the islands and Norway provide the third source of income. Since the end of the 1970s the oil industry has provided the Shetlands with an enormous boom and the lowest unemployment figures in Scotland, which otherwise has seen a decline in the number of jobs. The character of Mainland has, however, been drastically altered with the introduction of a large airport, new roads, Europe's largest oil port and thousands of foreign oil workers, even though the British Government, in a unique move, allowed the islanders a free hand in negotiations with the oil companies. Meanwhile disillusionment has returned. The number of production workers has been reduced and most of the maintenance flights to the oil rigs now set off from Aberdeen (see entry). The number of Shetlanders working in the oil business has dropped correspondingly.

Norse Heritage The Shetland Islands have retained their Norse inheritance more than the Orkneys. The islanders feel more affinity to Norway and the Faroe Islands than to Great Britain, and their language contains more Norse elements than that of the Orcadians. Their Viking past appears most evident once a year on the last Tuesday in January in Lerwick at the midwinter festival, "Up Helly Aa", when a replica of a Viking longboat is burnt.

Transport Cars can cross to the islands on the Aberdeen-Lerwick (Mon.–Fr.) and Stromness (Orkneys)–Lerwick (Sun., June–Aug., also on Tues.) lines. Ferries link the islands daily. British Airways offer direct flights daily from Aberdeen (see entry), and from Stromness (daily except Sun.). Loganair also flies from Inverness and daily from Edinburgh (see entry).

The Shetland Islands share a considerable amount of their **history** with the Orkney Islands (see entry). Unfortunately, in the last fifteen years the two island groups have developed somewhat differently, the North Sea oil boom having altered the Shetlands considerably more. A major catastrophe occurred in early 1993 when the Liberian oil tanker "Braer" ran aground on the southern tip of the island group in January 1993 spilling 84,500 tonnes of crude oil. This has had a devastating effect on the islands' flora and fauna. It is thought that fishing, salmon farming and cattle breeding, as well as tourism, will take decades to recover from this oil pollution.

Mainland

Mainland, the largest of the islands, is 54 miles long. Its jagged coast has so many fjords and inlets that no spot on the island is more than 3 miles

Lerwick in the Shetlands, the most northerly town in the British Isles

from the sea. Lerwick (pop. 6500), the main town, lies on the east coast, in a bay sheltered by the offshore island of Bressay. Britain's most northerly town, Lerwick was founded by Dutch fishermen who settled here in the 16th c. In addition to providing supplies to the drilling rigs, herring fishing remains one of the town's chief sources of income. The town offers few sights; its attraction lies in its narrow alleyways, which climb upwards from Commercial Road, the main street, to the upper part of town. Shetland Museum, situated here, describes the town's history and character. Fort Charlotte, built in 1655, burnt down by the Dutch in 1672 and not reconstructed by the English until 1781, keeps watch over the harbour. Those wishing to experience "Shetland Fiddling", the local music, should visit The Lounge pub on a Saturday.

Lerwick

Fine views of the harbour and the sea can be enjoyed during a walk around **Loch Clickhimin**, situated a little to the south-west. Clickhimin broch is a very well preserved round defensive tower dating from the Dark Ages.

Scalloway, on the west coast, is the former island capital. The infamous Patrick Stewart (see Orkney Islands) had a castle built here. The town's small museum informs visitors about the "Shetland Bus", a boat which transported Norwegian members of the Resistance from the islands back to their native country.

Scalloway

Walkers can only cross to this small west coast island at low tide. A chapel dedicated to the Scottish patron saint was constructed here in the 7th c. In 1958 valuable Celtic silver treasure was dug up here; it had probably been buried by monks hoping to save it from the Vikings. Only the ruins of the chapel's 12th c. successor can be seen. The treasure is displayed in the National Museum for Antiquities in Edinburgh (see entry).

St Ninian's Isle

503

Shetland Islands

★ Jarlshof

The island's most important sight is Jarlshof on the southern tip of Mainland. Jarlshof is a conglomeration of settlements, whose individual parts date from the Stone Age via the Bronze Age and the Iron Age to the time of the Vikings. Its most recent buildings comprise a 16th c. farm and a country seat, once the property of the notorious Patrick Stewart. A small museum explains the excavations. The name Jarlshof has no historical meaning; it dates from Sir Walter Scott, who gave it to Stewart's house (immortalised in Scott's novel "The Pirate") when he visited the island in 1816.

Shetland Croft House Museum

By returning from Jarlshof in the direction of Lerwick, the Shetland Croft House Museum is reached on the left-hand side of the road at Weiler Dunrossness. Here the lives of 19th c. Shetland inhabitants are portrayed in a typical island farmhouse.

North of the island

Visitors to Mainland are lured to its north by the very romantic natural conditions to be found there. It is not possible to go far by car here as roads often end abruptly, with the coast only accessible on foot. Notable sights include the Esha Ness rock formations on the island's north-west tip, and Rona's Hill, north-east of this, a red granite massif. The island's highest elevation (1486 ft), its summit offers a magnificent view of all the islands. Stenness, a fishing village at the extreme north-west of the island, also has magnificent rock formations and caves, as well as the step-like porphyry rocks called the Gate of Giants. Lunna, on the east coast north of Vidlin, is the site of one of the island's oldest churches. The Norwegian Resistance fighters cast off from Luna on the "Shetland Bus". **Sullom Voe**, situated in a deeply-indented fjord, has a completely different character. It is the largest oil port in Europe and in its harbour, constructed in 1981, the pipelines from the North Sea fields terminate and fill the countless tanks; 60 per cent of British oil requirements are handled here.

Bressay

A very attractive trip from Lerwick in good weather is to the island of Bressay, 1 mile away by boat across the Bressay Sound. Fine views can be enjoyed from the Ward of Bressay. A boat trip through the Orkneyman's Cave at the island's southern end is recommended.

Noss

The uninhabited island of Noss, east of Lerwick, is a wonderful bird reserve. Birds nesting on the cliffs here, which rise to a height of 591 ft, include puffins, storm petrels and northern gannets. Crossings may be undertaken in summer with permission.

Mousa

Mousa lies off the south-east coast opposite Sandwick. It is worth crossing to this island (only in summer with permission) to see the **★Mousa Broch**, Scotland's best-preserved example of a broch (a prehistoric circular stone tower). The broch, known as Mousa Castle, was built in about the year of Christ's birth. It stands approximately 43 ft high and has a circumference of 158 ft at the base. The fireplace was in the middle room, where the cattle were kept. The broch's inhabitants lived and slept in the three surrounding rooms. Europe's largest colony of seals romp on the island's east coast.

Whalsay

A stone house jutting into the water of the harbour on Whalsay, an island in the north-east, is striking. A branch of a 16th c. Hanseatic trading organisation, business people of that period could shelter and store their goods here.

Unst

Unst is the most northerly of the inhabited islands. **Muness Castle**, Britain's northernmost castle stands on the east coast. It was built by Patrick Stewart in 1589. At the island's northern tip the Atlantic thunders against the cliffs of Herma Ness, which are inhabited by tens of thousands of seabirds. The most northerly inhabited place in the British Isles is the rocky islet of Muckle Flugga (200 ft), which is crowned by a light-house.

Only bird-lovers would dare to undertake the adventurous crossing to the island of Foula, which lies 18½ miles off the west coast. They are rewarded with the sight of countless seabirds, in particular a large colony of skuas.

Foula

Fair Isle, lying 27 miles south-west of the southern tip of Mainland in the mid-Atlantic, is of even greater interest to amateur ornithologists. Only 70 people, but hundreds of thousands of birds live here. There have been 340 species observed here: storm petrels, razor-billed auks, terns, puffins, skuas, kittiwakes and many other seabirds, who are joined by countless migratory birds each spring and autumn. A day excursion by ferry from Sumburgh is hardly worthwhile; those travelling here should therefore reserve a bed in the Fair Isle Lodge & Bird Observatory (Fair Isle, Shetland, ZE2 9JU). Camping is forbidden on islands declared as nature reserves.

★Fair Isle

Fair Isle was settled very early on, as shown by a prehistoric wall which divides the island into two. Over the course of centuries a number of ships' companies, whose sailing vessels had been shipwrecked on the cliffs of the Shetlands, were thrown back on land on Fair Isle. Among them were more than 300 men from the "El Gran Griffón", flagship of the Spanish Armada, in 1588. Legend has it that the popular patterns of the knitted Fair Isle pullovers were influenced by the Spanish.

Shrewsbury   I 8

Central England
County: Shropshire
Altitude: 320 ft. Population: 68,000

Shrewsbury, county town of Shropshire, lies on a kind of peninsula in a loop of the Severn, England's longest river, which is spanned here by

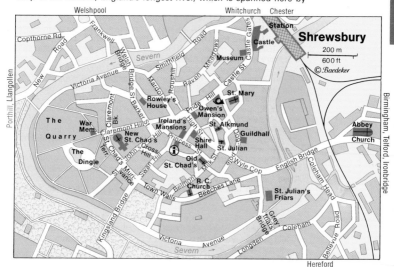

two imposing bridges, the English Bridge and the Welsh Bridge. The old half-timbered houses and narrow streets give this beautiful Tudor town its distinctive atmosphere. As the centre of a wide farming area it is a town full of life and activity, particularly on market days.

History This settlement on the Severn, named Scrobesbyrig by the Anglo-Saxons, had already been founded in the 5th c. and was conquered by King Offa of Mercia at the end of the 8th c. Written reference to Shrewsbury as a settlement of 252 houses grouped around the castle and the four churches was first made in the Domesday Book of 1086. After the Norman Conquest, William the Conqueror gave the estates to his friend Roger de Montgomery and created him the first Earl of Shrewsbury; he subsequently had the castle built in about 1071 and founded Shrewsbury Abbey. For centuries the town was a border fortress on the frontier with Wales, and in 1220 its defences were strengthened by Henry III with the erection of a town wall. Edward I, who based his seat of government in Shrewsbury, conquered Wales in 1283, and had numerous fortresses built along the coast of North Wales (see entry). Edward VI founded the famous Shrewsbury Public School, which counted Charles Robert Darwin (see Famous People) among its former pupils; the satirist Samuel Butler (1612–80) was headmaster of the school for many years. The poet Mary Gladys Webb (1881–1927), who sang the praises of the former county of Shropshire in her work, lies buried in the churchyard.

Castle
The castle, converted into a dwelling-house by Thomas Telford at the end of the 18th c., stands on the north-east narrow side of the town. Laura's Tower, named after the daughter of William Poultney, the owner at that time, affords a fine view across the town. The castle now houses the Shropshire Regimental Museum, displaying uniforms and weapons dating from the time of the Napoleonic Wars.

Churches
The foundation stone of **St Mary's Church** is thought to have been laid 100 years before the Norman Conquest. After its destruction, work began in 1170 on a new church; the present large building is predominantly in the Early English style. The collegiate church, with its graceful spire, is famous for its magnificent 14th and 15th c. glass windows. These include the east window featuring the tree of Jesse, originally located in St Chad's. Equally impressive are the nineteen wooden panels depicting scenes from the life of St Bernhard, which were produced about 1500 by the master of St Severin in Cologne and were later sold to St Mary's by Altenberg Abbey in Saxony. Trinity Chapel, completed in 1630, is embellished with glass windows from St Jaques in Lüttlich.

The *Abbey Church, built from red sandstone and dedicated to St Peter and St Paul, is all that remains of a Benedictine monastery founded by Roger de Montgomery in 1083. By approaching the Abbey from the English Bridge the striking early-Gothic west tower, decorated with a statue of Edward III, can be admired. The large west window, embellished with coats of arms, dates from Richard II's reign. It is also worth viewing James Pearson's altar (1888) and the many tombs, the oldest of which dates from 1300.

St Alkmund Church is named after the son of the king of Northumbria, and is thought to have been founded by Aethelflede, the daughter of Alfred the Great. Only the medieval tower remains; the nave dates from the end of the 18th c. The colourful east window was created by Francis Eginton in 1795.

Old and New
Shrewsbury's oldest church is the 15th c. **Old St Chad's Church** in Belmont. After its tower collapsed in 1788 the congregation decided to build a new church, the New St Chad's. Designed by George Stuart, New St Chad's was officially opened in 1792.

The tower of the former **St Julian's Parish Church** was completed at the end of the 12th c., while the nave was built by T. F. Pritchard in the Classical style at the end of the 18th c. The church now houses a craft centre.

The town contains many well-preserved 16th c. half-timbered buildings, including the Old Market Hall (1596), Owen's Mansion (1592) and Ireland's Mansion (1580). Abbot's House, a typical 15th c. half-timbered house, stands in Butcher's Row, Shrewsbury's oldest street.

Half-timbered Buildings

★**Rowley's House Museum**, an impressive half-timbered house built in 1590 and situated in Barker Street, contains an extensive collection of prehistoric, Roman and medieval finds, including exhibits from the Roman settlement of Viroconium at Wroxeter (including a 12th c. silver mirror), a late-medieval glass window from the Abbey Church and local costumes.

Clive House, an elegant Georgian house only five minutes' walk away on College Hill, houses a porcelain museum with a fine Shropshire collection of 18th and 19th c. Coalport and Caughley pieces. Note also the small collection of watercolours, the Victorian kitchen and other period room settings.

Clive House Museum

A row of old houses line Frankwell Street, which leads north from Welsh Bridge to Charles Darwin's birthplace.

Frankwell

The former quarry, simply called "The Quarry", from which came much of the stone used in the town's buildings from the 16th c. onwards, is now an attractive park with a small lake and a beautiful flower garden, the Dingle.

★Quarry

A magnificent 230 acre park, laid out by Humphrey Repton in 1797, surrounds Attingham, a manor house designed by George Stuart in 1785 for the first Lord Berwick and situated only 4 miles south-east of Shrewsbury. Its expensively-furnished interior contains period furniture and Regency silver, as well as a collection of paintings by Italian and French masters.

Surroundings
★ **Attingham Park**

Wroxeter lies 6 miles south-east on the Severn. Interesting excavations of the Roman station of **Viroconium**, the main town of Brittania Secunda founded in 70 BC, are located here.

Wroxeter

The magnificent Ironbridge Gorge Museum is reached by following the B 4380 further east through the Severn Valley for 13 miles. Ironbridge became famous in 1778 with the construction of the first iron bridge across the Severn. A row of notable museums detailing the Industrial Age now stand here. These include the former warehouses of the Coalbrookdale Company; Rosehill House, with its museum portraying 18th c. daily life; the Tollhouse, which explains the building of the bridge; Blists Hill Open Air Museum, where visitors can experience the Victorian age in the course of a half-hour tour; Coalport China Museum, with its displays on the production of china up until 1930; and Jackfield Tile Museum, in whose workshops tiles were fired and glazed from 1850 to 1960. Abraham Darby's kiln for iron smelting (1709) can also be seen here.

★ ★ **Ironbridge Gorge Museum**

Tong (20 miles east, pop. 6000) is well worth a visit for the sake of its church containing a whole series of fine monuments to members of the Vernon family, and its beautiful fan-vaulting and elaborate wood-carving.

Tong

Boscobel House (16th/17th c.) lies about 3.5 miles to the east. Once the refuge of Charles II after the Battle of Worcester (1651), it has beautiful grounds.

Boscobel House

Bridgnorth

Picturesquely situated on the Severn is Bridgnorth (21 mile south-east, pop. 11,000). A small town of medieval aspect, it has a "High Town" and a "Low Town", 197 ft lower, connected by England's steepest funicular railway. In the High Town is a tower which formed part of the old castle; it leans farther from the vertical than the Leaning Tower of Pisa. The numerous black and white half-timbered houses are in the Queen Anne style. The Neo-Gothic Church of St Leonard has a marvellous 17th c. dragon-beam roof and striking cast-iron plaques.

★**Stokesay Castle**

Romantic Stokesay Castle (22 miles south) was built in the 12th c. for the Norman Say family. In 1280 the wealthy wool merchant Lawrence of Ludlow bought the estate and had it fortified at the behest of Edward I in 1296. Manor House is now one of the best-maintained fortified 13th c. constructions of its type.

Ludlow

Ludlow (29 miles south, pop. 7500) is much visited for its beautiful position on the River Terne and its well-maintained half-timbered houses. The castle was constructed by Roger de Lacy in 1085 to be a defensive fort on the Welsh border. Its oldest part is the almost 66 ft-high Norman keep, from the top of which a fine view can be enjoyed. Building of the parish church of St Laurence began in 1199, but was not completed until the 14th c.; it was partly redesigned during restoration work carried out in the 19th c. by Sir Gilbert Scott and Sir Arthur Bloomfield. Medieval remains include the brightly-coloured 15th c. east window and the large 14th c. Jesse window in the Lady Chapel; the choir stalls embellished with carvings of clerical and worldly themes date from the 14th c.

Southampton K 10

Southern England. County: Hampshire
Altitude: 56 ft. Population: 200,000

The port of Southampton, which has almost amalgamated with Portsmouth (see entry) into a conurbation, lies on a peninsula between the mouths of the River Test in the west and the River Itchen in the east. Its branches of industry include cable works, mechanical engineering, precision engineering, the production of chemicals and synthetic materials, shipbuilding and the service sector.

Although the town suffered much destruction in the Second World War, it has preserved a number of old buildings, including parts of the medieval town walls and two Tudor houses with their characteristic black and white half-timbering. There are excellent shopping facilities both in and out of town. This university town proves a good base for visits to the New Forest and the Isle of Wight (see entries).

Thanks to its favourable position, Southampton is one of the world's best natural harbours. It was used by the Romans during their occupation. The tide rises only 13 ft in Southampton Water, which is of great benefit for shipping. The position of the Isle of Wight not only protects entry to this deep water harbour, but also causes high water in the 9 mile-long mouth of the delta four times a day. This phenomenon occurs thus: the further the water from the Atlantic floods into the English Channel the more the tide spreads out, causing a time delay on the coast – on the south coast of the Isle of Wight of two to three hours. Through this delay the first high tide flooding from the west into the bay is followed two to three hours later by a second high tide from the east.

Until the 1930s Southampton was England's largest port dealing in trans-Atlantic passenger travel. Giant ocean steamers, such as the "Queen Mary", were built in the local shipyards, while hundreds of thousands of emigrants departed the country on ships sailing from here. The "Titanic", whose maiden voyage to New York ended in disaster, was

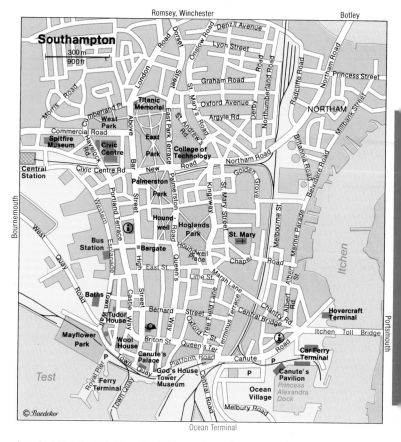

Ocean Terminal

launched here in 1912. Since the 1970s numbers of passengers have steadily declined in the face of competition from cheaper and faster charter flights. Today mainly cruise ships use the port including the two ocean giants P & O's "Canberra" and the "Queen Elizabeth II" belonging to Cunard.

History There was already a harbour here in Roman times, situated a little way inland at Bitterne on the River Itchen. In 1017 Canute was chosen as king here by the Saxons. In 1189 Richard the Lionheart and his knights set sail from here on their way to the third Crusade; and from here Edward III set out in 1345 and Henry V in 1415 for their campaigns in France. On August 5th 1620 the Pilgrim Fathers sailed from here in the "Mayflower". Many troopships departed from this important marine base in both world wars, the reason for the heavy enemy bombing raids of 1940/41.

The best view of the remains of the 14th c. medieval town walls is obtained from the Western Esplanade, also the site of Wind Whistle Tower.

Sights
Town Walls

Southampton

St Michael's	The only remaining medieval church is St Michael's, which stands on Castle Way parallel to the esplanade. Dating from 1070, the church contains Norman relics and a font made of Tournai marble.
★Tudor House Museum	The magnificent Tudor house in St Michael's Square was built in the 16th c. for a wealthy merchant family. Now a museum, it displays exhibits from the Victorian and Edwardian eras, as well as periodic exhibitions about local history.
Mayflower Park	Follow the town walls south to reach Mayflower Park, which lies opposite the Mayflower Memorial to the Pilgrim Fathers.
Wool House, Maritime Museum	Continue a short distance further along Bugle Street to find the Wool House, a 14th c. warehouse, and the Maritime Museum, with its extensive collection relating to the history of the port, including a model of the docks in the 1930s.
Duke of Wellington	Those in need of a rest should visit the Duke of Wellington pub. One of the last Tudor half-timbered houses, it is now a popular meeting place.
God's House Tower Museum	God's House in Winkle Street was founded in the 12th c. as a hospital dedicated to St Julian and was restored in the 19th c. The archaeological museum in 15th c. God's House Tower in Town Quay explains the history of the town from the time of the Roman clausentum via the Anglo-Saxon hamlet to medieval Southampton.
Merchant's House	After extensive restoration work the Merchant's House in French Street (No. 58) was opened in 1988 by English Heritage. The medieval-style house displays traditional crafts.
★Ocean Village	East of the old town the old dockland site of Princess Alexandra Dock has been transformed into a modern leisure and shopping centre. Smart yachts and the SS "Shieldhall", the last steam-driven freighter, are moored in the harbour in front of Canute's Pavilion with its designer boutiques, gourmet restaurants and market halls.
Hall of Aviation	Nearby in Albert Road South the history of aviation in Southampton is told with the help of models, planes and photographs. Showpiece of the exhibition is the "Sandringham" flying boat.
Bargate	High Street leads north from the bank of the Test to the modern town centre. Bargate, at the north end of the street and surrounded on both sides by the shopping centre of the same name, houses a small town museum.
Civic Centre	The Civic Centre was designed by Berry Webber and built between 1930 and 1936 using white Portland stone. The complex contains the town hall, the court, a theatre, a library and a 180 ft-high belltower. Of particular interest to art-lovers is the town's **Art Gallery**, with its interesting selection of old masters and English artists from 1750 to the present day, as well as a valuable collection of ceramics.
Spitfire Museum	The museum to the west in King's Bridge Lane is dedicated to the aeroplane designer R. J. Mitchell, who constructed the Spitfire and the S6 Seaplane.
Above Bar, Titanic Memorial	Continue through the pedestrian precinct Above Bar to its northern end to reach the memorial to the luxury liner the "Titanic", which sank on its first voyage in 1912 after colliding with an iceberg.
Surroundings Netley	At Netley (3 miles south-east; pop. 2300) are the beautifully situated ruins of ★**Netley Abbey**, a Cistercian house founded in 1239. The surviving buildings are mainly Early English.

The yacht harbour at Southampton

★ **Romsey Abbey** stands 8 miles north-west of Southampton in the small market town of Romsey (pop. 13,200). The massive abbey, looking from a distance more like a fortress than a church, was founded in 907 in association with a convent of Benedictine nuns by Elfleda, the grand-daughter of Alfred the Great. A Norman church was built in about 1125, and most of the present building is pure Norman. The east window is Early English (early 14th c.), while the west end, with pointed arches, was built in about 1225. The north transept contains a painted wooden reredos of 1520, the lower half of which portrays the Resurrection, the upper part the Abbess of Romsey. High above the choir arch are two figures of angels which probably formed part of a Crucifixion group. In the southern choir aisle and outside the south transept are two Saxon stone crucifixes.

Romsey

King John's House, east of the church, dates from 1206 and contains a museum.

A statue of the third **Viscount Palmerston** (1784–1865), for many years the British Foreign Secretary and Prime Minister, stands in the market-place.

★ **Broadlands**, his former country seat, lies only ½ mile south. Together with "Capability" Brown's gardens, it was built in 1767. Later ownership of the estate passed to the Mountbatten family; an audio-visual show portrays the life of Lord Mountbatten, the last viceroy and first governor general of India.

South Coast   F 10/11–N 9/10

Southern England

The English South Coast, separated from France by the Straits of Dover and the English Channel, is climatically one of the most favoured parts of Britain. Numerous flourishing subtropical plants adorn the area's many famous seaside resorts, which attract many visitors throughout the year. The scenery between the counties of Kent and Cornwall (see entry) offers great variety. In many places along the eastern part of the coast chalk cliffs rear up from the sea, most strikingly at Dover, the history-laden "Gateway to England". Elsewhere the coast is fringed by marshland, as at Romney Marsh, east of Rye, while opposite the Isle of Wight estuaries and fjord-like inlets cut deep into the land. The limestone of Portland, a peninsula offshore from Weymouth, and a wide surrounding area, worked in enormous quarries, carried the name of Portland cement far beyond the boundaries of Britain and of Europe. Further west, the area around Torbay in the county of Devon earns much praise as the "English Riviera". Beyond the historically-important port of Portsmouth (see entry) the fantastic coastal region of Cornwall (see entry) begins. The English South Coast ends in this county at the aptly-named Land's End.

From Ramsgate to Dover

Ramsgate

The seaside resort of Ramsgate (pop. 37,000) is linked to France (Dunkerque) by ferry. It has grown together with the neighbouring town of Broadstairs into a municipality, and enjoys a very mild climate. The harbour, constructed in 1750, provides moorings for numerous yachts in summer. Ramsgate is a popular seaside resort, with good bathing and abundant entertainment facilities.

The Roman Catholic **St Augustine's Church** on West Cliff is a masterpiece of Neo-Gothic. Built between 1847 and 1851 by A. W. N. Pugin at his own expense, he is buried in the churchyard here. The Grange, the neighbouring house completed in 1843 for the famous supporter of the English Gothic Revival, is adorned with a tower fortified with battlements.

★Sandwich

Sandwich (pop. 5000) still lives on the memory of its glorious past. Although now separated by 2 miles of alluvial land from the sea, it was once one of England's most important seaports, numbered with Dover, Hastings, Romney and Hythe as one of the Cinque Ports. It was also a notorious smugglers' lair. The charming old town contains the remains of the 14th c. medieval town walls, narrow alleyways and a selection of historical buildings. Several 18th c. houses can be seen in Delft Street and King Street. The last of the town's gates stands at the end of Fisher Gate, which dates from 1384. The Guildhall, built at the end of the 16th c. and restored at the beginning of the 20th c, bears the coat of arms of the Cinque Ports: three halved ships and three halved lions. Opposite St Clement's, an Early English church with a Norman tower, stands the Queen Ann palace The Salution (1911). It is also worth viewing the half-timbered house The King's Arms (1592), 17th c. St Peter's Church in Market Street, Manwood Court (1564) and the Old Customs House with its 18th c. brick façade, and St Bartholomew's Hospital with an Early English choir.

The flat coastal strip around Sandwich Bay boasts three first-class ★**golf courses**, where the British Open Championship takes place in some years.

Not to be missed is a visit to ★**Richborough Castle**, 1½ miles north of Sandwich, one of the most important Roman sites in Britain. From this site, called Rutupiae by the Romans, an important channel led to the Regulbium camp at Reculver. The channel entrance (Wantsum) guarded Richborough Fort. In the 3rd c. the fort became part of the defences of the "Saxon Shore". Within the fort is a huge platform which seems to have supported some massive monument. The foundations of a Roman amphitheatre and a pre-Norman chapel have been excavated; finds from the site are exhibited in a small museum.

Along with the castles of neighbouring Sandown and Walmer, **Deal Castle** formed part of the chain of more than 20 castles which Henry VIII (see Famous People) had built along the coast. The fort, formed from six semi-circular defensive constructions, was strengthened by deep ditches and a thick circular wall.

Deal (pop. 27,000) has shipyards rich in tradition, but no real harbour. Ships are loaded and discharged in the Downs, the roadstead between the **Goodwin Sands** (sandbanks 7 miles from the coast) and the coast, and the cargoes then transhipped in smaller boats, called lighters. Although now well marked, the Goodwin Sands have long been a hazard to shipping, with many vessels having gone aground here. Legend has it that the Goodwin Sands were originally the fertile island of Lomea, on which was the castle of Earl Godwin (d. 1053), and that the whole island was submerged in a great storm. With its many old houses, its piers, promenade and golf course, Deal is a popular holiday resort in spite of its shingle beach.

Imposing **Walmer Castle** was declared the residence of the "Lord Warden of the Cinque Ports" in the mid-18th c. One of the most famous people to occupy this position, and consequently the castle, was the Duke of Wellington (see Famous People); the room in which he died can be viewed.

St Margaret's Bay, which also has a shingle beach, is attractively situated below wooded cliffs. Very pleasant coastal paths complement the peaceful refreshing character of the village.

Dover (pop. 34,500), whose famous white cliffs can be seen gleaming from afar, is one of Britain's principal cross-Channel ports. Ferries continuously arrive here throughout the day and night bringing endless streams of visitors on the first step of journeys throughout the country.

★ **Dover**

History All that remains of the Roman settlement of Dudris, founded in about AD 125, is the lighthouse (1st c.) on Castle Hill, and the Roman Painted House, excavated at the beginning of the 1970s and decorated with important frescoes, in New Street. For many centuries Dover was a

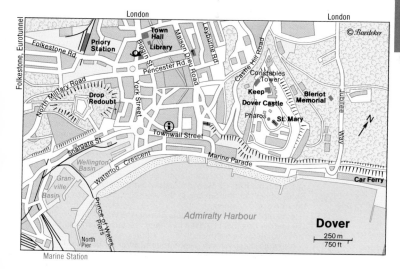

513

Dover: the ferry port

bulwark against attacks from the Continent, until the Second World War, when the town suffered terrible damage because of its role as a marine base.

The steep chalk ★★**White Cliffs**, for long both a proud symbol of the "splendid isolation" of England and also the first sign of home visible from afar for returning sea voyagers, are crowned to the east by the mighty castle. The western cliffs bear Shakespeare's (see Famous People) name. His play "King Lear" ended here, and the much-used quotation invoked by sight of the cliffs "This precious stone set in the silver sea" comes from "Richard II". ★**Dover Castle** is the earliest example in Europe of a concentrically-planned castle. Building of its walls began in 1168 under Henry II on the site of prehistoric ramparts; they were strengthened in the 13th and 14th c. by massive circular constructions. The central Norman keep, built in 1180, houses an extensive local history museum. A special exhibition, comparable to the D-Day Museum in Portsmouth (see entry), concerns events during the Second World War, including the Battle of Britain and D-Day. It also proves interesting to visit the Napoleonic casemates and underground passages reactivated in the Second World War. In clear weather it is possible to see from the castle walls as far as Calais on the French coast, to where the chalk crest extended thousands of years ago. The ruins of the Roman lighthouse, and the church of St Mary in Castle next to Calton's Gate, built from Roman bricks by the Saxons in the year 1000, have been incorporated into the castle complex.

A memorial to the aviator **Louis Blériot** – he was the first to fly across the English Channel in 1909 – has been erected in Northfall Meadow, a small wood to the north-east.

Although most visitors pass through Dover on their way elsewhere, the town is actually of some note, not least for its town hall, the **Maison Dieu Hall**, built in 1203 by Hubert de Brugh as a hostel for pilgrims. The main street has recently become attractively pedestrianised. **"The White Cliff Experience"**, behind the market place, was developed so that people could learn more about the cliffs and important events in the town's history.

From Dover via Brighton to Portsmouth/Southampton

The seaside resort of Folkestone (pop. 50,000) lies 7 miles west of Dover. Hovercraft cross from here to Boulogne in France. Its development into an important seaside resort began in the mid-19th c. with the building of the railway, the reason why the town's characteristic buildings date mainly from the Victorian era. It is worth visiting the Church of St Mary and St Eanswythe, situated in the centre of the old town around the attractive Old High Street. One of the church's windows shows William Harvey, the discoverer of the body's circulatory system, who was born in the town in 1578. The gem of the town is the elegant residential area The Leas with its attractive squares and gardens. It was designed by Decimus Burton in 1843. Sports and leisure facilities are varied and excellent. Refreshing walks can be enjoyed along the wide seafront promenade and the well-tended parkland which extends along the cliff-top, from where there are fine views across to France in clear weather.

Folkestone

The ★ **Eurotunnel Exhibition Centre**, situated in the High Street in the western suburb of Cheriton, explains the construction of the Eurotunnel (see entry) beneath the English Channel, which opened in 1994.

The British **terminal of the tunnel** is reached via the M20 (exit 11a), not far west of Cheriton.

From Hythe onwards the coast is fairly flat: this is the beginning of 49,420 acre Romney Marsh, an area largely devoted to flower growing,

★ **Romney Marsh**

Rye: the Ypres Tower

Romney Marsh

which is particularly beautiful in spring. Flocks of sheep graze every-where here.

Hythe

The small town of Hythe (pop. 14,000) was once one of the Cinque Ports, and acted as an important defensive port during the Napoleonic Wars. The parish church of St Leonard is partly Norman with a splendid chancel; human skulls and bones were discovered in the crypt. The town is traversed by the Royal Military Channel, now a popular meeting place for anglers and amateur ship's captains. It was originally constructed to provide a safe waterway to Rye at a time when there was a threat of invasion by Napoleon.

Hythe is the terminus of the narrow-gauge **Romney and Dymchurch Light Railway** across Romney Marsh to Dungeness on the edge of the Lydd peninsula.

Saltwood Castle, ½ mile away. is a fine Norman stronghold, from which the four knights who murdered Thomas Becket (see Famous People) set out for Canterbury (see entry) in 1170.

★★**Rye**

Rye (pop. 5000) was also one of the privileged Cinque Ports after 1191. Its name means "island", and indeed the town does lie like an island above the flat marshland which has been flooded by the sea more than once. The old town is still partly surrounded by its medieval walls and attracts many artists. Twisty and in some places steep cobbled alleys climb upwards, lined by charming cottages, small craft shops, potteries and very cosy pubs.

For a most rewarding stroll visit enchanting ★**Mermaid Street** with its Old Hospital, a triple-gabled half-timbered 15th/16th c. building and the Mermaid Inn, a 15th c. half-timbered pub rich in tradition – it was once a notorious meeting place for smugglers. At the upper end of the street stands Lamb House, an elegant 18th c. Georgian building in which the American author Henry James (1843–1916) spent the last years of his life and wrote the novels "The Wings of the Dove" (1902) and "The Golden Bowl" (1904). Below the half-timbered houses in the High Street, reached via West Street, Thomas House stands out. Most impressive, however, are the brick-built Old Grammar School (1635) and the George Hotel, constructed at the beginning of the 18th c. In Lion Street, to the left, tea can be taken at "Simon the Pieman's". The house next to this tea-room is named after the dramatist John Fletcher (1579–1625), who came from Rye.

The parish **Church of St Mary**, begun in the 12th c. and renovated several times, stands at the end of Lion Street. A fine view can be enjoyed from the church tower. Its clock, produced in Winchelsea in 1561, is thought to be one of the oldest in the country. The impressive window (1897) in the north aisle is the work of Edward Burne-Jones and William Morris.

Ypres Tower, a former fortress with three semi-circular corner towers, is reached via Church Square. It now houses a museum detailing the history of Rye and the Cinque Ports. From adjoining Canon Gardens there is a fine view across Romney Marsh to the sea.

Winchelsea

Winchelsea, an associated member of the legendary Cinque Ports since 1191, occupies an attractive hilltop position. After its destruction, the town was rebuilt by Edward I in the 13th c., when the streets were laid out on a grid plan around 40 fields. Its economic decline came when the port silted up, and only three of the medieval gates have survived. The town's chief attraction is the incomplete St Thomas' Church, dating from about 1300 and in the early Decorated style. The churchyard contains the tombs of the Adlard family, admirals of the Cinque Ports.

Hastings

The next large seaside resort is Hastings, which together with St Leonards-on-Sea, forms a municipal area with some 75,000 inhabitants. A popular seaside resort, the town is famed as the site of the Battle of

Beachy Head

Weatherproof "net-lofts" in Hastings

Hastings in 1066, which in fact took place at Battle (see entry) 6 miles away. Its importance as one of the Cinque Ports ended with a series of destructive floods and repeated arson attacks by the French at the end of the 14th c. The town experienced another heyday in the 19th c. when it became a seaside resort, taking Brighton (see entry) as its model.

A row of typical ★**"net lofts"** have been retained in the old town. These traditional tall sheds were used by fishermen to store and dry their nets. A coat of black tar helped the horizontally positioned wooden boards to remain weatherproof; known as weatherboarding, this building style is typical of East Sussex and Kent.

Fisherman's Chapel in Rock-a-Nore Street was built in the 19th c. and now houses a **museum** which describes very clearly the development of the local fishing industry. Exhibits include the "Enterprise", the last fishing cutter to be built in Hastings (1909).

Attractive half-timbered houses stand in the narrow High Street and in All Saints Street, with its church of the same name. The remains of the Norman castle, constructed to protect the harbour, are situated on West Hill above the town and can be reached by a funicular railway from George Street. Pelham Crescent, below the castle, was constructed by Joseph Kay between 1824 and 1828. The entrance to St Clement's Caves is near the castle. Hastings seafront promenade is lined with hotels, restaurants and places of entertainment. Next to the pier, completed in 1872, is the Conqueror's Stone at which William the Conqueror (see Famous People) is said to have eaten for the first time in England.

Rudyard Kipling (1865–1936), winner of the Nobel Prize for Literature, lived in 17th c. **Bateman's House**, 1 mile north-west, near Burwash, from 1902 until his death.

See entry

Battle

Bexhill-on-Sea (pop. 37,000) is a trim modern resort with a good golf

Bexhill-on-Sea

course. It is known for its Victorian town houses and for being the first place in Britain to have a motor-racing track (½ miles).

Pevensey Bay

William the Conqueror is supposed to have landed in this small resort in 1066. As all along the coast, Martello towers were erected here between 1805 and 1810 when it was thought that Napoleon might invade.

The Normans built their castle in Pevensey using the remains of a Roman fort, the walls still standing 20 ft high. During the 13th c. the site was strengthened with the addition of a gate tower and circular walls. The Mint House, where coins were minted, was built in 1340 and is now a museum.

★Eastbourne

Eastbourne (pop. 88,000) is one of England's most elegant seaside resorts. Originally a simple fishing village, it was developed in the mid-19th c. by the seventh Duke of Devonshire into a large bathing resort in the Victorian style. A 3 mile-long elegant seafront promenade extends along the wide shingle beach. A marvellous holiday atmosphere is achieved by Grande Parade (mid-19th c.), lined with magnificent white and pastel-shaded houses and luxury hotels, and the brightly-coloured deckchairs on the beach. At the end of the wide mole the iron pier projects far out to sea behind the theatre arena with its music pavilion and winter garden. Eastbourne also boasts several fine parks and numerous leisure facilities. Sports enthusiasts are catered for with more than 60 tennis courts and three golf courses, while the traffic-calmed streets around the High Street offer a colourful array of shops and art and antique galleries. The town's many language schools are famous beyond England, as is the international ladies' tennis tournament held here annually in June. The South Downs Way, a magnificent long distance pathway leading through the South Downs (see entry) of Sussex, begins in Eastbourne.

Eastbourne: the Promenade

Beachy Head (575 ft, 3 miles south-west of the town), a favourite view-point, is picturesquely positioned and can be reached along an attractive footpath. This striking snow-white cliff at the end of the South Downs (see entry) amply justifies its fame, its name not derived from the word "beach", but from the language of the French Normans who called it "beau chef" ("beautiful head"). The 144 ft-tall red and white striped lighthouse at the foot of the chalk cliff is a pleasing contrast. A magnificent cliff path (3½ miles) passes through Cuckmere, Haven and Seaford.

★★ Beachy Head

Seaford also has a number of language schools. The Martello tower at the eastern end of the promenade is the most westerly on the south coast.

Seaford

Among England's most impressive cliff views are those to be gained from the incredible "Seven Sisters": Haven Brow, Short Brow, Rough Brow, Brass Point, Flagstaff Point, Bailey's Brow and Went Hill Brow. The best view of these seven chalk hills, which form part of the foothills of the South Downs, can be enjoyed from Seaford Head.

★ Seven Sisters

Newhaven, at the mouth of the River Ouse, has a large yacht harbour offering a cross-Channel ferry service to Dieppe in France.

Newhaven

See entry

Brighton

To the west, linked up with the outskirts of Brighton, lies Shoreham-by-Sea (pop. 22,000). Seafaring enthusiasts will find models of historic ships and navigation maps in Marlipins Museum, whose façade dates from the 14th c. The town also has two mainly Norman churches, St Nicholas' in Old-Shoreham dates from the mid-12th c., while St Mary de Haura's in New-Shoreham was begun in 1130.

Shoreham-by-Sea

The popular seaside resort of Worthing (pop. 92,000) was discovered at the end of the 18th c. by Princess Amelia, the daughter of George II. Glasshouse cultivation is prevalent here because of the mild climate. The resort has a reasonably good beach, an extensive promenade, an iron mole, a theatre and a concert hall. Exhibits in the museum and art gallery include prehistoric and Roman finds, a Viking ship dating from about 900, 18th c. costumes, 19th c. toys and dolls' houses and works by English artists such as W. Holman Hunt and W. Callow.

Worthing

Littlehampton (pop. 21,000), a resort at the mouth of the River Arun, has a wide coarse-grained beach extending to Bognor Regis and beyond.

Littlehampton

Bognor Regis (pop. 35,000) owes the suffix "Regis" to the fact that George V came here to recuperate in 1929, which gave the resort added attraction – the iron pier had already been opened in 1910. The town offers entertainment facilities for all ages, while the gently sloping beach is very suitable for children.

Bognor Regis

The low-lying peninsula of Selsey Bill lies south of Chichester (see entry). It is very exposed to wind and weather, with parts of it perpetually being washed away by the sea. The resort of Selsey is characterised by colourful holiday houses, as are neighbouring Bracklesham Bay and East Wittering. The much ramified Chichester Harbour and the harbours of West Wittering and Itchenor are popular sailing centres.

Selsey Bill

★From Southampton via Weymouth to Teignmouth

The sailing centre of Lymington (pop. 13,000) is situated 13 miles south-west of Southampton. From here there are ferry services to Yarmouth on the Isle of Wight (see entry).

Lymington

The New Forest (see entry) lies inland and is a marvellous base for outings.

Christchurch

The neighbouring town of Christchurch (pop. 39,000) owes its name to the wide bay along which several seaside resorts have developed. This port lying between the rivers Avon and Stour had already been settled in the Saxon period.

Off the busy main street the ★**Priory Church** (1150) is worth visiting. Its dimensions are more appropriate to a cathedral rather than a parish church (312 ft long). The Norman nave (about 1093) has a beautiful Early English triforium; the north porch dates from about 1300. Notable features of the interior are the 14th c. choir screen, the reredos (completed in the Decorated style in about 1350 but only partially retained) representing the Tree of Jesse, the 12th c. font made of Purbeck marble in the north choir aisle and the tomb of Anne Pugin (d. 1832) in front of Berkeley Chapel. Anne Pugin's husband, the master builder A. W. N. Pugin, donated the main altar. The remains of a 12th c. Norman castle and of Constable's house (about 1160) can also be visited.

Christchurch is especially popular with sailing enthusiasts who like to take their boats round **Hengistbury Head**, a narrow tongue of land which was occupied by early Neolithic settlers and has remains of prehistoric defensive works.

Bournemouth and Poole

The modern seaside resort of Bournemouth (pop. 160,000) has joined with Poole (pop. 120,000) into a long ribbon settlement. Its mild climate makes it a popular resort throughout the year as well as a popular retirement town for the well-to-do. Its many language schools also ensure, however, that young people from all around the world populate this renowned resort. The town's elegant villas, luxury hotels and rows of whitewashed houses are, as in many other South Coast seaside resorts, the product of the Victorian fashion for bathing. Visitors will discover a

Bournemouth: the beach and pier

wealth of shopping and sports facilities here, as well as an extensive range of leisure facilities including the **Pavilion Theatre** and the first-class Bournemouth Symphony Orchestra. They will also marvel at the magnificent greenery of the town's many parks, which culminate in the marvellously-situated **Compton Acres Gardens** at Canford Cliffs to the extreme south of the resort. Steps and two lifts descend to the fine sandy beach complete with **pier** and promenade, which is closed to traffic in summer.

The **Russell-Cotes Art Gallery and Museum** on East Cliff houses an interesting art collection which includes paintings by R. Wilson, Morland and artists of the Victorian period, as well as valuable objets d'art from Japan and Burma. It is also worth visiting **Rothsay Museum** which has English furniture, china and porcelain, and rooms devoted to shipping. **Boscombe Manor** on Beechwood Avenue near Boscombe Pier has been renamed the Shelley Rooms and is dedicated to the romantic poet Percy Bysshe Shelley (1792–1822). Shelley and his wife Mary are buried in St Peter's churchyard.

Bournemouth's cliffs are cut at several points by deep valleys called **chines**; the most impressive of these are Boscombe Chine and Durley Chine.

Poole has a unique natural ★**harbour** with regular passenger and freight sailings, good watersports opportunities and a ferry service to Cherbourg in France. Poole Quay is lined with traditional fishermen's pubs and redeveloped warehouses, now housing shops, pubs and small workshops, such as Poole Pottery.

It is worth exploring the Purbeck peninsula, famous for its Purbeck marble. Sandstone rather than true marble, it is found in many English churches. Ferries cross from Sandbanks to the Isle of Purbeck.

Isle of Purbeck

The small village of Wool (pop. 4300) lies west of Wareham. Its 15th c. bridge spans the River Frome. Next to the bridge stands the Woolbridge, called Wellbridge House by Thomas Hardy.

Wool

Lulworth (5 miles south), with its castle ruins, lies on an almost circular bay called Lulworth Cove. It is worth visiting the ¾ mile-large petrified forest.

There is a **Tank Museum** at Bovington Camp, part of the military training area around Wool and Lulworth. Lawrence of Arabia's country residence can be visited 1 mile north of Bovington Camp.

Lulworth

The enormous ruins of this 12th/13th c. Norman castle are visible from afar. It was here that King Edward the Martyr was murdered in 987 at the instigation of his mother-in-law Elfrieda. Lady Bankes defended Corfe Castle against Parliament in both 1643 and 1645 until betrayal allowed it to be forcibly invaded by parliamentary decree. The village, older than the castle, is very charming.

★**Corfe Castle**

A detour to the seaside resort of Swanage (5 miles south-east; pop. 8200) proves worthwhile. This small town is situated in a sandy bay surrounded by low hills. The approximately 40 tonnes stone globe to be seen here is amazing, as are the stone pillars, façades and towers. Burt, the administrative head of the area, collected much of what was being torn down in London and rebuilt it, if somewhat out of place, in Swanage. This mainly modern resort has a good yacht harbour and attractive old houses, particularly around the millpond.

Swanage

The route returns via Studtland with lovely bays and a Norman church past Corfe Castle to Wareham (10 miles north-west, pop. 27,000), a small town near the mouth of the Frome. All around there are earth walls dating from pre-Roman times. The small restored Anglo-Saxon St Martin's Church contains a statue by Eric Kennington of the legendary

Wareham

T. E. Lawrence dressed as an Arab. In St Mary's Church there is a hexagonal lead font (1100) and the marble sarcophagus of Edward the Martyr.

Dorchester

See entry

Weymouth

The modern seaside resort of Weymouth (pop. 48,000) has grown up around an old seaport in a wide bay with a fine sand and shingle beach. There are ferry services from Weymouth to the Channel Islands (see entry) and to Cherbourg in France. On the promenade is a statue of George III (1760–1820), who was a frequent visitor to the town. Weymouth has a number of handsome Georgian houses and hotels. Several Tudor buildings, complete with 17th c. furniture, stand in Trinity Street. King George III once lived in Gloucester House, now an hotel. Weymouth's old warehouses have been redeveloped and now house small shops, pubs and gourmet restaurants. During the summer months chic yachts and motor boats are moored in the harbour.

Isle of Portland

A pleasant trip is from Weymouth to the Isle of Portland, a peninsula linked with the mainland by Chesil Bank. The island (pop. 12,000) is famous for the grey-white stone mined from its quarries and used in the construction of St Paul's Cathedral in London (see entry) and the UN building in New York. Portland Castle, built by Henry VIII (see Famous People), occupies the site of an earlier Saxon stronghold. Its museum now documents this powerful monarch's defensive forts. South of Easton quarries characterise the landscape. At the southern tip of the island is Portland Bill, with three lighthouses and a bird-watching station.

Chesil Beach, an almost 10 mile-long gravel barrier leading from the north end of the Isle of Portland across to Abbotsbury, forms the protective border of "The Fleet" lagoon, a waterfowl sanctuary with one of Europe's largest variety of species.

Abbotsbury

The remains of an 11th c. Benedictine monastery can be found in Abbotsbury (9 miles west of Weymouth). More famous, however, is the ★ **Swannery**, founded in 1393 and now home to almost 1000 birds. Although swans were eaten as a culinary delicacy at royal banquets until as recently as the 1950s, it is now the lagoon's oysters which enjoy particular popularity among gourmets. It is worth visiting the ★ **Subtropical Gardens** laid out in 1750 by the Earl of Ilchester in a protected valley on the outskirts of Abbotsbury. Palms, bamboo groves, multicoloured exotic plants and lush rhododendrons all flourish here.

Lyme Regis

Lyme Regis (pop. 4500) lies in the middle of the large bay of the same name at the mouth of the Lyme and is surrounded by magnificent cliffs. This small town was the favourite holiday resort of the writer Jane Austen (1775–1817), who made it famous through her novels, such as "Persuasion", published in 1818. The old stone causeway, called the Cobb, is of historic interest. James Scott, Duke of Monmouth, landed here in 1685. He disputed claims to the English throne with his uncle, the later James II, but without success. The resort has charming little alleys and notable Georgian houses, such as Belmont House in Pound Street and the Royal George Hotel in Broad Street.

Those interested in geology should visit the excellent fossil collection in the **Philpot Museum.**.

Coast Road from Lyme Regis to Exeter

The coast road from Lyme Regis to Exeter has many steep gradients and is very narrow in places, but offers a succession of splendid views. In 8 miles it reaches **Seaton** (pop. 4300), a seaside resort with good water-sports facilities, situated at the mouth of the River Axe. **Sidmouth** (pop. 11,000), a fashionable place in the early 19th c., is more sophisticated and more attractive. This small resort's climate is so mild that eucalyptus trees are able to flourish here. The town is sheltered from rough winds by reddish cliffs through which the River Sid – hence the town's name – has cut its way. There are many Regency houses, and above the beach there is a small promenade.

Budleigh Salterton (pop. 4000), at the end of Lyme Bay, is similar in character. Inland lies **East Budleigh**, a typical Devon village, with a pretty church. It is the birthplace of Sir Walter Raleigh (1522–1618), the English seafarer, writer and favourite of Elizabeth I; the Raleigh coat of arms, borne by stags, can be seen on a pew in the 15th c. small parish church of All Saints.

Exmouth (pop. 30,000), at the mouth of the wide estuary of the Exe, has a long shingle beach, with a promenade at the foot of picturesque red cliffs. At low tide outcrops of rocks are exposed along the beach. During the summer the small harbour provides mooring for numerous sailing boats, many of whose owners come from nearby Exeter (see entry).

Exmouth

Dawlish (pop. 8000), on the other side of the Exe estuary, is surrounded by fascinating red cliffs. This more peaceful seaside resort has golden sand and offers good opportunities for bathing.

Dawlish

See entry

Exeter

The Regency resort of Teignmouth (pop. 11,900) lies on a tongue of land at the mouth of the River Teign, and thus enjoys a vista out to sea and over the estuary. The river is spanned by one of the country's longest bridges, which leads to Shaldon, a quiet seaside resort. Strangely-shaped red cliffs, a magnificent beach, a promenade, a pier and parks make Shaldon very popular.

Teignmouth

★★From the "English Riviera" to Cornwall

The approximately 22 mile-long climatically-favoured coastal stretch around Devon's Torbay Bay is known as the "English Riviera". At its centre lies the elegant seaside resort of Torquay, into which the adjoining towns of Paignton and Brixham were incorporated in 1968.

Built on seven hills, the "Queen of the English Riviera", as Torquay is also called, owes its development to the Napoleonic Wars. In anticipation of a French landing, troops were stationed here and houses built for their families.

★★Torquay

There are few remains of earlier periods in Torquay apart from the ruins of **Torre Abbey**, a Premonstratensian abbey founded in 1196. Only the gatehouse (about 1320), the remains of the chapterhouse and the foundations of the church have survived. The municipal art gallery is housed in the former tithe barn, known as the Spanish Barn after a frigate belonging to the Spanish Armada was wrecked off the coast in 1588 and its crew were held prisoner here.

Torquay's situation, sheltered by red cliffs and wooded hills, favours the growth of subtropical plants, and the town's **parks and gardens** are a feast to the eye, with palms and other magnificently-coloured Mediterranean vegetation. Around the busy harbour, into which numerous yachts as well as ferries from Alderney and Guernsey (see Channel Islands) sail in summer, there are many Victorian buildings, most of which were built on the initiative of the Palk family between 1820 and 1860. Higher Terrace, Vaughan Parade and Hesketh Crescent were founded by Jacob Harvey and his sons in the mid-19th c. Agatha Christie spent Christmas Eve 1914, her wedding night, in the famed Grand Hotel. The "Queen of Crime" was born in Torquay more than a hundred years ago. In the manor house next to Torre Abbey a room has been furnished with Christie memorabilia, including an old typewriter, photographs, old furniture and her own bibelots.

Torquay: a bowling green ...   *... and the beach*

A delightful contrast to the Victorian town centre is provided by the old-fashioned suburb of **Cockington**, with its tiny thatched cottages, an old village smithy (14th c.), weaving works and a manor house; those with sufficient time should experience the pleasure of riding to this village in a horse-drawn carriage.

As well as the main **beach** Torre Abbey Sands, those of Babbacombe and Oddicombe are most popular.

Refreshing **cliff walks** lead from Torquay to Anstey's Cove and Peak Tor Cove.

Standing in grounds of 5 acres **Babbacombe Model Village** (scale 1:50) has more than 400 miniature buildings constructed in English styles ranging from traditional thatched cottages to modern town houses.

★**Kent's Cavern**, two dripstone caves with strangely-shaped stalactites, is of particular interest because the remains of what were probably Britain's oldest inhabitants were discovered here. Some of the finds are displayed in the **Torquay museum**.

Paignton

The family holiday resort of Paignton has an attractive promenade and extensive sandy beaches. Carriages pulled by restored steam locomotives depart from the station along the 7 miles of the Torquay and Dartmouth Steam Railway.

Oldway Mansion was commissioned in 1871 by the sewing machine manufacturer Isaac Singer, whose son had the large hall made into a copy of the Hall of Mirrors at Versailles. It is also worth visiting Kirkham House, a lovingly-restored 14th c. town house and medieval Cornton Castle, which stands outside the town.

Brixham

The colourful fishing harbour of Brixham has succeeded in preserving its old charm. Accompanied by the shriek of seagulls, fishing boats continue to return here with their catch, while pilot boats come and go and pleasure- craft await passengers. The British Fisheries Museum in Old Market House near the harbour documents the development of trawlers and trawl fishing; the museum also contains a replica of the "Golden Hinde", a frigate captained by Sir Francis Drake (see Famous People). Sailors' yarns and smuggling stories are recounted in the local seafaring museum.

Dartmouth

The stretch of coast extending south from Brixham as far as Start Point is of great interest and beauty. By crossing the River Dart and continuing via Kingswear (ferry) the idyllically-situated small town of Dartmouth (pop. 6000) is reached. Of its former importance as a marine port – ships sailed from here in 1190 for the crusades, in 1347 for the siege of Calais and in 1588 to fight against the Spanish Armada – only the **Britannia Royal Naval College** bears testimony. Opened in 1905 and situated high above the town, it can count all male members of the Royal Family among its graduates. The pleasant little town has romantic twisty alleyways and picturesque rows of houses around the inner harbour.

Most impressive are the half-timbered buildings in the **Butterwalk** (1635–40), an arcade with graceful sculptures and home to the ★**Town Museum**.

St Saviour's, situated on a hill outside the town and dating from the 13th–15th c.; particularly notable is the 14th c. ironwork on the south door depicting two leopards with the tree of life.

At the mouth of the Dart are **St Petroc's Church** (1641), which in accordance with tradition was built on the site of a chapel dedicated to St Petroc (d. 594), and the 14th/15th c. **Castle**.

Start Bay

The road to Start Point skirts the wide curve of Start Bay. The fertile region between the coast and Dartmoor is known as the South Hams. The road continues via Stoke Fleming, the beautiful bay called Blackpool Sands, and Strete, then south to Slapton Sands, sandbanks largely consisting of shingle which extend for almost 7 miles to Start Point. For the next 1½ miles the road follows Slapton Ley, a freshwater lagoon.

Kingsbridge, Salcombe

Drive through the charming small town of Kingsbury – try to visit its Cooksworthy Museum – to the village of Salcombe (pop. 2000), which has a sheltered yacht harbour, a good sandy beach and gloriously colourful subtropical plants. The village nestles under a steep hill, from which there is a good view of the fjord-like arms of the sea which cut into the land.

Bigbury-on-Sea

Bigbury-on-Sea (pop. 561) lies in a charming setting at the mouth of the Avon in a wide bay with a sandy beach. A causeway leads to **Burgh Island**, on which there is a noted hotel, the superior Burgh Island Hotel.

South Downs   L/M 9/10

Southern England. Counties: West Sussex and East Sussex

The South Downs, like the North Downs which are separated from them by the Weald, comprise a long ridge of chalk hills extending from Eastbourne in the east to beyond Winchester, running almost parallel to the coast. They are magnificent walking country and have been designated as an area of outstanding natural beauty.

"The Downs are sheep, the Weald is corn", so Rudyard Kipling described the humpback pastures of the Downs used for sheep grazing, and he continued in rhyme "You be glad, you are Sussex born". Countless sheep continue to graze amid sparse vegetation on the chalk pastures of the Downs, although some crops are now grown here.

The building stone most often seen in the Downs is flint, which occurs in layers of chalk. It is usually found in walls or on the façades of buildings, used either as a whole pebble ("knitwork") or broken up and laid out in dark shimmering pieces on mortar ("flushwork").

The chalk cliffs were once both famous and infamous for their reef pirates and smugglers. During the 18th c., the heyday of smuggling, approximately one-third of English sea trade slipped through as "free trade", and it is thought that half the gin and almost a third of the tea entering the country was handled by the gangs of smugglers in Kent and Sussex. Neither harsh punishments nor strengthening of the coastguard could stop the well-organised smugglers, until 1840 when the Government finally employed their strongest weapon: a drastic reduction in taxes.

Walkers will enjoy following the ★ **South Downs Way**, which begins in Eastbourne (see South Coast) and encompasses the South Downs and now continues as far as Winchester (see entry).

Circular tour

The A27, which extends along the north side of the South Downs from Eastbourne (see South Coast) to Brighton (see entry), offers a convenient way of obtaining an impression of this range of hills and some of its attractive towns and villages. The first stop should be made at Wilmington (7 miles from Eastbourne), with the remains of a Benedictine priory which now houses a small museum of rural life.

Wilmington

The ★ **Long Man of Wilmington**, a gigantic figure cut out of the chalk hillside and standing out clearly from the grass-covered slope, is a truly impressive sight. It is similar to the Cerne Abbas chalk figure in Dorchester (see entry) but, at a height of more than 230 ft, is a good 33 ft taller. The figure is depicted supporting itself on either side with a staff, like the edges of a picture, and poses a puzzle. Its age and origin are unknown, but it probably dates from Saxon times (7th c.) and represents the heathen god Wotan. This is contradicted by the fact that it has been tolerated for so long by the monks of Wilmington Abbey; perhaps the pious brothers carved it themselves "for fun", as an old verse says. The first reference to this giant chalk figure occurs in 1764.

Alfriston

Picturesque black half-timbered Tudor buildings, leaded oriels, red brick gables and white-painted "weatherboarding" decorate the small village of Alfriston on the banks of the River Cuckmere. The village is dominated by St Andrew's Church, built in the Decorated Style of the 14th c. and standing on an artificial hill on the "Tye", as the Saxons called their village greens. In 1977 the half-timbering was carefully restored by the National Trust, an organisation dedicated to the upkeep of the countryside and rural estates. The notable Star Inn was built in 1520.

Glyndebourne

In Beddington a road turns off north from the A 27 and heads to Glynde and the famous ★ **Glyndebourne Opera House**, which was opened in 1934 by John Christie with a performance of Mozart's "Marriage of Figaro". The performances of opera, mainly by Mozart, but also by composers such as Handel, Richard Strauss, Stravinsky and Benjamin Britten (see Famous People), staged here attract numerous music-lovers from all over the world. The opera-house is at present being rebuilt.

Lewes

Lewes (pop. 15,000), 8 miles north-east of Brighton (see entry), is the county town of East Sussex. It is magnificently situated on the Downs, at the point where the River Ouse has cut its way through the hills. Lewes Castle was built around 1088 to defend this passage. It has a ruined keep (views) and fine flint masonry. The picturesque old town with its steep streets, old half-timbered buildings, Georgian houses and typical flint masonry surrounds the castle. In Barbican House is the **Museum of the Sussex Archaeological Society**, and associated with this is Anne of Cleves' House. The most interesting churches are St Anne's

Arundel Castle overlooking the River Arun

(mainly Norman) and St Michael's, with a round tower. The Town Hall, with a fine oak staircase (1893), contains the **Municipal Museum**.

South-east of the town is **Mount Caburn**, which rises steeply to a height of 490 ft; to the west is **Mount Harry** (639 ft), above the racecourse.

The **University of Sussex**, founded in 1961, lies 4 miles further west. Its main administrative offices are in Stanmer House, a Palladian mansion built between 1720 and 1727; the new buildings were designed by Sir Basil Spence.

Arundel

Arundel (pop. 2400) is picturesquely situated approximately 16 miles west of Brighton (see entry) on the River Arun, at the foot of the South Downs, and is one of the most attractive small towns in southern England. The battlement-crowned ★**Castle**, which dominates views of the town, is the seat of the Dukes of Norfolk. Winding alleys lined with rows of attractive old houses lead upward to the imposing fortress, which was founded in the 11th c. but was completely destroyed in 1644. Since then it has been much altered and restored, most recently between 1890 and 1903. Of the original complex only the gatehouse has survived, the keep is a Norman addition. Together with the Roman-Catholic church of St Philip Neri, which the 15th Duke of Norfolk had Joseph Hansom build in the second half of the 19th c., and the parish church of St Nicholas (14th c.), the castle is a majestic sight across the roofs of the town; the best view can be enjoyed from the wide bend in the Arun. There are beautiful walks along the river, and the Great Park with Swanbourne Lake, and Potter's curiosity museum are also worth visiting.

Amberley

The attractive small village of Amberley lies 6 miles north-east of Arundel. Its early Norman parish church of St Michael contains a 12th c.

font and a notable 15th c. brass by John Wantele. The castle was restored in the early 20th c. and has a massive gatehouse. It is surrounded by a 14th c. medieval circling wall and now functions as a top hotel.

Bignor

Bignor, about 8 miles north of Arundel, has a beautiful thatched 15th c. half-timbered cottage, the **Old Shop**. East of the village is a ★ **Roman villa**, discovered in 1811, with mosaic floors.

Approximately 8 miles east of Bignor stands **Parham House**, an Elizabethan manor house. Visitors are captivated by the wood-panelled Long Gallery with its richly-embellished five-edged 19th c. barrel-vaulted ceiling, and, primarily, by its extensive picture collection. This includes portraits of Zucchero and works by Romney and Gainsborough.

Petworth

Petworth (pop. 2700) is situated about 6 miles north of Bignor. This enchanting little market town on the northern edge of the Downs has many picturesque houses and has become famous for its "great house", ★★ **Petworth House**, seat of the Earls of Egremont. This magnificent country house with its 328 ft-long garden frontage

Oast Houses, a traditional feature of the Weald

gained its present appearance between 1688 and 1696. The extensive garden, designed by "Capability" Brown, is a masterpiece of English landscape gardening. Among the treasures of the house is one of England's most important collections of paintings. William Turner (see Famous People) had a studio here from 1830 to 1837; he loved the local scenery and often painted it. Many of his oil paintings and water-colours can be admired in the Turner Room. The collection also boasts works by Titian and Rogier van der Weyden, Van Dyck, Reynolds and Gainsborough. Marvellous lime wood carvings (1692) by Grinling Gibbons decorate the Carved Room. The excellent collection of ancient sculptures in the North Gallery are no less impressive.

South-east of Petworth, after crossing the River Rother, is the highest point of the Sussex South Downs, **Duncton Hill** or **Littleton Down** (837 ft).

Beyond the hill, on a side road off the A27, lies Boxgrove. Its **Priory Church** (1120–1220) shows the transition from Norman to Early English, and boasts a notable 16th c. ceiling fresco by Lambert Bernard.

Boxgrove

Midhurst (6 miles west of Petworth) is a delightfully-situated small town on the Rother with the enormous ruins of a Tudor manor house; nearby is Cowdray Park with a golf course and attractive trees.

Midhurst

The hilly landscape of the Weald extends between the North and the South Downs, and reaches the coast in the county of Kent, to the east. In this region, often called the "Garden of England", romantic valleys contrast with bright deciduous forests, green pastures, and numerous fruit gardens and hop fields; between these lie attractive villages and small towns, all having managed to retain their own individual charm.

Characteristic of this hop-growing area are the **oast houses**, brick buildings with white pointed roofs on whose floors hops used to be laid out to dry. Many of these oast houses have now been converted into desirable second homes. Other local building traditions were "tile hanging", scale-like wood and brick decoration of houses, and "weatherboarding", wooden slats, brightly painted or made weatherproof with a layer of pitch or tar, fixed to the exterior walls of buildings.

Southern Uplands · Lowlands   F–K 5/6

Scotland
Regions: Strathclyde, Dumfries & Galloway and Borders

The Lowlands extend from the English border approximately to a line running between Glasgow and Edinburgh. Despite their name they can only be considered low in comparison to the Northern Uplands; for this reason the name Southern Uplands is used as much as Lowlands to describe this area. The south-west Lowlands are characterised by single towering peaks such as the Merrick, at 2760 ft southern Scotland's highest mountain. The eastern Lowlands reach a height of approximately 2000 ft. The richly-varied landscape is extremely attractive; just as in the Highlands there are steep cliffs, sandy beaches and lochs full of fish. The contours of the Southern Uplands are gentler than in the Highlands. Impressive contrasts arise through the juxtaposition of bare hills, lush meadows and delightful valleys. High moorland and heathland alternate with fertile arable land; here and there quiet villages and small market towns have evolved. Although the area proves fascinating primarily for walkers and nature-lovers, it also contains many historically interesting sites.

Economy Agriculture, particularly sheep breeding, continues to be a dominant branch of industry here, in combination with the wool and textile industries. The main centres of textile production are Hawick and Galashiels, while Innerleithen and its surroundings are best known for their knitwear. Various mills and textile centres offer tours for interested visitors, and the Scottish Museum of Woollen Textiles in Walkerburn explains the process of cloth production from the rearing of Cheviot sheep to the finished tweed.

Apart from its geographic attractions, two Scottish national poets gave their names to a whole area of land. **"Robert Burns Country"** lies in south-west Scotland and encompasses Alloway, where Burns was born, and Dumfries, where he died. Those following the life and love story of this literary figure along the Burns Trail will come to know the counties of Ayrshire and Dumfries and Galloway, both of which inspired the poet. **"Sir Walter Scott Country"** is the name given to the Tweed valley, the area generally thought of as the Borderland, where the romantic house of this much-read author is situated (for both, see Famous People).

★From Ayr via Dumfries to Gretna Green

Ayr

Throughout the Lowlands there are numerous attractive towns and villages, pleasant places to stay and good centres for tours of the area.

One of the most popular is Ayr (pop. 50,000), on the coast facing the Island of Arran (see entry) and with a long sandy beach. The River Ayr is spanned by two bridges, the "Auld Brig" and the "New Brig". The old one dates from the 13th c., while the new one fulfilled Burns' prophesy of 1788 and had to be rebuilt in 1877.

Alloway

A monument in front of Alloway station commemorates **Robert Burns**, who was born in 1759 in Alloway (2 miles south). The simple thatched cottage in which he was born can be visited. Opposite Alloway's parish church the **Land o'Burns Centre** documents the life and works of the poet.

★Culzean Castle

Continuing south-west along the coast a visit is recommended to the Georgian-style Culzean Castle, with its beautiful gardens. Both were designed by Robert Adams, Scotland's most famous supporter of Classicism, and built between 1777 and 1792. An image of the castle, fortified with battlements, standing on the dramatic steep coast can be found reproduced on the Royal Bank of Scotland's five pound note. Inside visitors are captivated by the elegant rooms, the most impressive of which are the oval stairway with two-storeyed pillar decoration and the richly-embellished Round Salon.

Kirkoswald

Opposite the castle a road leads to Kirkoswald with the cottage, now a museum, of the shoemaker (souter) John Davidson, a friend of Burns during his youth. Souter Johnnie and his drinking-mate Douglas Graham of Shanter Court were immortalised in Burns' daring ballad "Tam o'Shanter"; stone figures of ghosts now populate the garden.

Tarbolton

The road continues past Crossraguel Abbey, the remains of a Cluniac house founded in 1244, and Maybole to Tarbolton, which owes its fame to the fact that Burns founded the Bachelors' Club and became a Freemason here.

Mauchline

Burns lived and married in Mauchline (pop. 3800). Poosie Nansie's Taverne still exists, if considerably altered. The **Burns House Museum** in Castle Street is filled with furniture found by Burns in 1788 for Jean Armour. Outside the town stands the **National Burns Memorial Tower**, opened in 1896, which contains an extensive collection of his work.

The A 713 passes through Dalmellington, and the A712 continues from New Galloway through the magnificent wooded scenery of the Dumfries and Galloway region. Approximately 6 miles west of New Galloway an imposing granite memorial on the banks of Chatteringshaw's Loch commemorates the victory of Robert the Bruce (see Famous People) over the English in March 1307.

Dalmellington

The holiday village of Newton Stewart (pop. 2000) lies a further 6 miles south-west. It has a good golf course and excellent fishing in the River Cree.

Newton Stewart

A worthwhile detour leads via Bargrennan (7 miles north) to Glen Trool with the loch of the same name. From its position high among the hills, there are marvellous panoramic views.

Loch Trool

South of Newton Stewart lies the farmland of the Machars peninsula with a series of prehistoric sites, including in the south-west the Bronze Age stone remains of Drumtrodden and the ruins of the Iron Age fortress, Barsalloch Fort.

Machars Peninsula

The ruins of a 13th c. chapel can be seen on Whithorn Island, at the tip of the south-east coast. It is thought that Bishop Ninian founded the first church on Scottish soil here in Roman times.

St Ninian's Chapel

The A75 continues west from Newton Stewart via Glenluce, with a Cistercian abbey founded in 1192, to Stranraer. About 3 miles before reaching this port, it is worth stopping at **Castle Kennedy**, north of the A75. The castle's gardens are renowned for the blaze of colour produced by its rhododendrons, magnolias and azaleas. Regular ferries ply between **Stranraer** and Larne in Northern Ireland.

Glenluce

Follow the coast road (A75) east from Newton Stewart for 18 miles to reach the ruins of 15th c. Cardoness Castle, the former seat of the McCullochs of Galloway, situated at the head of Fleet Bay.

Cardoness Castle

After a further 10 miles stop next at Kirkcudbright (pop. 2500), at the mouth of the River Dee, which here flows into Kirkcudbright Bay. The village has a 16th/17th c. tollbooth, in which John Paul Jones, founder of the United States navy, was once imprisoned. There are mementoes of him in Stewartry Museum in St Mary Street, which also documents local history. Above the castle are the imposing ruins of 16th c. Maclellan's Castle.

The ruins of **Dundrennan Abbey** (6 miles) still convey some impression of the former splendour of this 12th c. Cistercian foundation. The choir and the transepts have been largely preserved, and there are some interesting monuments. Mary Queen of Scots is said to have spent her last night in Scotland here before seeking refuge in England.

Kirkcudbright

The A75 continues to Castle Douglas. About 3 miles before this small town medieval **Threave Castle** can be seen to the left on an island in the Dee. Its four-storeyed keep was built by Archibald the Grim, Lord of Galloway, between 1639 and 1690.

Laid out during the Victorian era, gloriously colourful **Threave Gardens** (1 mile further on, south of the A75), tempt visitors to take a relaxing stroll.

Castle Douglas

Farther along the beautiful coast road (A75), beyond Dalbeattie, are the enchanting ruins of Sweetheart Abbey, also called New Abbey. This Cistercian abbey was founded in 1273 by Devorgilla, who also established Bailliol College in Oxford (see entry). It is said that she asked to be buried here together with the heart of her husband, John Bailliol – hence the abbey's name. From the summit of the Criffell (1866 ft), to the south-

Sweetheart Abbey

Robert Burns House in Dumfries

Gretna Green – destination for lovelorn runaways

west, there is a marvellous view over the Solway Firth towards the Lake District (see entry).

Dumfries

Dumfries (pop. 30,000) is the main town of the Dumfries and Galloway region. It is another place with Burns connections as the poet spent the last years of his life here. The house in which Burns died in 1796 and where his wife Jean Armour lived until her death in 1834 is now a **museum** containing many mementoes (formerly Mill Vennel, now Burns Street); the **Burns Mausoleum** is situated near St Michael's churchyard. The **Robert Burns Centre** in Mill Road on the banks of the Nith stages extensive exhibitions about the national poet.

The town has a rich history, its first charter having been granted by Robert II in 1395. The old town hall in the centre of the market place was built in 1708, the bridge constructed in 1208 is now for pedestrians only. Regional history is recounted in Dumfries Museum, which also has an observatory.

The ruins of **Lincluden Abbey**, a 15th c. Benedictine house, lie 1½ miles to the north. Princess Margaret, daughter of Robert III, is buried here.

Lochmaben

The holiday resort of Lochmaben (9 miles north) is surrounded by five lakes, and is thus almost an island. Anglers can try their luck in these waters, which are rich in fish. The ruined castle was probably the birth-place of Robert the Bruce (see Famous People), a statue of whom stands in front of the town hall.

★Glenkiln Sculpture Park

A special experience awaits art-lovers in Moniaive (14 miles north-west). A few miles south of the village in remote moorland near the Glenklin estate, and standing half-way up a slope, are the life-size bronze statues "King" and "Queen", the works of Henry Moore (see Famous People). Their owner, Sir William Keswick, has assembled a notable open-air sculpture collection here, which includes works by Rodin, Epstein and Renoir.

Those interested in industrial history should follow the A76 north to Dalpeddar, then turn off on to the B797 just beyond the town and continue north-east to Scotland's highest village, Wanlockhead (32 miles). The village's **Museum of Lead Mining** informs visitors about the heyday of lead production; exhibits include mine shafts, mining equipment, furnished miners' cottages dating from 1740 to 1890, and a collection of the region's minerals.

Wanlockhead

With the discovery of sulphur springs the village of Moffat (20 miles north-east, pop. 2000) developed after the mid-17th c. into a spa resort. Of more importance to economic growth here as in the whole region, however, was sheep breeding. A bronze ram on Colvin Well in the High Street symbolises the wealth of the "Sheep Country" as a result of the wool and cloth trade.

Moffat

The return journey to Dumfries should include a visit to Drumlanrig Castle, the seat of the Douglas clan, the later Dukes of Buccleuch and Queensberry. An avenue of beech trees leads to the castle which is crowned with a number of small Baroque towers. Its portrait gallery includes works by Kneller, van Dyck, Ramsay, Reynolds and Gainsborough.

Drumlanrig Castle

On the final part of the journey to Gretna Green try not to miss Ruthwell and Caerlaverock Castle. Caerlaverock Castle (8 miles south-west), seat of the Maxwell family, dates back to 1270. The triangular ground-plan with its double moat and drawbridge was altered in the 15th c. The buildings around the courtyard date mainly from the 17th c., when the castle was more a residence than a fortress. It is supposed to be the Ellangowan of Scott's "Guy Mannering".

Caerlaverock Castle

Ruthwell should be visited mainly for its runic cross. One of the two most famous Anglo-Saxon runic crosses, it occupies a niche in the church, which appears to have been built to house it. This sandstone cross, probably dating from the 8th c., is 17 ft tall and is carved with reliefs of figures, leaf ornamentation, Latin inscriptions and runic script.

★Ruthwell Cross

The border to England can be crossed at Gretna Green, where the blacksmith used to marry runaway couples in his ★**Blacksmith's Shop**. Gretna Green's world-famous mock marriages began so that couples wanting to marry, but without their parents permission, could do so from the age of sixteen. Scottish law only required a declaration from the young couple in front of two witnesses, whereas in England a marriage without parental consent was only possible after the age of 21 (in 1977 the minimum age was lowered to eighteen). This resulted in numerous races between parents and children taking place on the border road – with both happy and tragic results. It was not until 1940 that these world-famous "anvil marriages" were declared illegal through a change in the law. The romantic myth of these wild unions still attracts "marriage tourists" – in the 1980s alone more than 100 couples a year tied the knot at Gretna Green. The village now has a tartan and tweed shop, craft studios and a carriage museum, whose exhibits include William IV's landau.

Gretna Green

★Borders

Undisturbed nature, breath-taking landscapes, beautiful beaches, busy fishing harbours, secret picturesque mountain villages and a host of imposing castles and other historical sites are all offered by the south-eastern Lowlands, commonly called the Borders. The history of the Border country has been considerably influenced by four abbeys, all founded in the reign of David I (1124–53). Despite many wars and incursions from England these monasteries developed into important economic and cultural centres, and achieved wealth through sheep rearing and crafts.

★Carter Bar

Those entering southern Scotland from the English county of Northumberland on the A68 through the Cheviot Hills will arrive at the border at the top of the Carter Bar pass (1371 ft), where the red lion of the Stuarts greets travellers. Those struck by the magnificent scenery are already beginning to fall in love with Scotland and to understand the affinity that local inhabitants have for their native region.

Jedburgh

The pleasant little town of Jedburgh (pop. 5000), with its 16th c. triple-arched bridge, is reached after 10 miles. The castle became a prison in 1823 and now houses a museum. The main sights are the picturesque remains of ★**Jedburgh Abbey**, founded in about 1118 and destroyed by the English in 1544. The church is still almost completely intact. Its most splendid features are two Norman arches and the west façade with a magnificent rose window, although particular note should be taken of the arcades in the nave and the tracery of the window. Excavations have unearthed on the south side part of the monastery site. The visitors' centre offers insights into the lives of the monks.

★Dryburgh Abbey

The A68 continues to Dryburgh Abbey (8 miles north on the B6404), picturesquely situated between old trees on the banks of the Tweed. The abbey was founded by Hugh de Morville in 1150 for Premonstratensian monks, who were temporarily very wealthy and influential. During the 14th c. the monastery was repeatedly plundered by the English and was finally destroyed in 1544. The remains, in High Gothic style, include the beautiful west doorway, the rose window at the western end of the refectory, the chapterhouse and St Modan's Chapel. St Modan is said to have been the abbot of a monastery which was built on this site in the 6th c. In the north transept Sir Walter Scott is entombed in a granite sarcophagus designed by Chantry.

★Melrose

Melrose (5 miles north; pop. 3000) is a popular base for tours of the Borders. It has a notable old railway station, a motor museum and excellent angling in the Tweed.

★★**Melrose Abbey** is the most magnificent of all the Scottish abbeys, and according to Theodor Fontane is the romantic treasure "certainly of all ruins ... by far the most beautiful and the most gripping". Built of red sandstone in 1136 for Cistercian monks, it was later often devastated and plundered. Some of its stones were used in the construction of other buildings. In spite of these ravages the remains, mostly dating from the 15th c., are still of great splendour. Particularly impressive is the elaborate masonry, the masterly variety in the detailed structure of the capitals and sculptures, which include true-to-life representations of handwork and a fantastic gargoyle shaped like a bagpipe-playing pig. The tracery of the windows in the transepts and the east window is also magnificent. The heart of Robert the Bruce, who facilitated restoring the abbey after its destruction by Edward II, is said to be buried near the high altar. The abbey owes its popularity in part to William Turner's idyllic drawings and Sir Walter Scott's "The Lay of the Last Minstrel", in which the magician Michael Scott composed melancholy verses about Melrose in the moonlight.

Eildon Hills

The character Michael Scott is also linked to the neighbouring Eildon Hills, a three-headed hill whose highest peak attains 1387 ft. The magician is supposed to have caused the devil to split the hill into three. From the top of the Eildons there are wonderful panoramic views.

Beautiful stonework ...   *... of Melrose Abbey*

In neighbouring Newstead a monument on Leaderfoot Hill marks the site of the important Roman station of Trimontium; numerous finds are exhibited in the National Museum of Antiquities in Edinburgh (see entry).

Newstead

Abbotsford forms the heart of "Scott's Country". Sir Walter Scott wrote most of his poems and historical novels in Abbotsford House on the banks of the salmon-rich River Tweed and finally succumbed to his years of overwork here in 1832. As the estate and the ford below the house formerly belonged to Melrose Abbey, Scott decided to call it Abbotsford. Using the royalties from his much-read works Scott had the existing farmhouse renovated between 1817 and 1827 in the style of a Scottish manor house into, as he himself said, "a romance of stone and mortar". A leading architect William Atkinson took responsibility for making the building imaginative, with small oriels and battlement-protected small corner turrets. The entrance is reminiscent of the main doorway of Linlithgow Palace, while the library's elaborate wooden ceiling is a copy of that in Rosslyn Chapel. The house is full of mementoes of Scott and contains, as well as numerous manuscripts, a collection of border ballads, portraits and curiosities such as Bonny Prince Charlie's Scotch glass ("quaich") and what is said to be the outlaw Rob Roy's sword, as well as a notable collection of weapons and armour. Scott's death mask can be seen in the study.

★★Abbotsford

Approximately 3 miles west of Selkirk, where Scott acted as sheriff for more than 30 years, **Bowhill House**, seat of the Dukes of Buccleuch and Queensberry, ought to be visited. The country house's valuable collection of paintings includes works by Canaletto, van Dyck, Raeburn, Reynolds and Gainsborough.

Selkirk

Traquair House

Traquair House, situated 14 miles west of Abbotsford, is one of Scotland's oldest inhabited manor houses. It served the Scottish monarchy as a residence and a hunting lodge from the 10th c. The Bear Gates, iron gates guarded by two stone bears, were closed behind Bonny Prince Charlie in 1745 with the vow that they would only be reopened when a Stuart ascended the throne – as a result they are still closed. Queen Mary is said to have tasted the ale produced by the house's brewery, which is still brewed today following an old recipe, during her visit here in 1566.

Thirlestane Castle

The Border fortress of Thirlestane (1 mile north of Melrose) was built in the 13th c. and renovated for the Maidlands family in the 16th c. The castle is now the seat of the Earls of Lauderdale, and houses the Border Country Life Museum, which vividly chronicles the turbulent history of the Border region.

Kelso

Kelso (10 miles east of Melrose; pop. 4900) is an attractive market town on the Tweed near the mouth of the Teviot. Its ★ **Abbey** was founded in 1128 by monks from Picardy. The largest of the four Border abbeys, it suffered the same fate as the others and became a victim of power and destruction. The transepts and, in particular, the west tower, which is more reminiscent of a castle, are the best-retained parts of this late Norman complex built of red sandstone. Try also to visit the town's market place, in which the curfew is rung every evening from the Court House. The five-arched bridge over the Tweed was constructed in 1803 by John Rennie and offers the most impressive view of the abbey ruins. Every September farmers from all over the world come to Kelso for its famous ram market.

Floors Castle stands at the west end of the town. Built in 1721 by William Adam for the first Duke of Roxburgh, it was sympathetically

Abbotsford: Sir Walter Scott's death mask and his study

536

enlarged about a century later by William H. Playfair. Of particular note are the 17th and 18th c. French period furniture, the fine tapestries, the Chinese and Dresden porcelain and the Victorian collection of birds. A tree in the extensive grounds is supposed to mark the spot where James II was shot during the siege of Roxburgh Castle in 1460.

Roxburgh, formerly of great importance as one of the four royal burghs, is now a small town. The 13th c. town centre has completely disappeared, and only the ruins of the castle (3 miles north-west) now remain.

Roxburgh

Mellerstain House (6 miles north-west of Kelso), built in the Georgian style, was begun by William Adam in 1725 and completed a few years later by his son Robert Adam. In 1909 the terraced garden was given its Italian appearance. The manor house contains valuable period furniture and paintings, including works by Ramsay, Aikman, Nasmyth and Gainsborough.

Mellerstain House

The small Edwardian castle Manderston House (15 miles north-east of Kelso), now owned by the Palmer family, has a magnificent garden with gloriously colourful rhododendrons.

Manderston House

The official name "Stonypath" is to be read on the sign directing visitors to the artist Ian Hamilton Finlay's fantastic gardens at Dunsyre in the sparsely-populated Pentland Hills, some 24 miles south-west of Edinburgh. Finlay himself, however, calls his 4 acre oasis of culture **"Little Sparta"**. With his wife Sue, this garden artist began work here in 1966 on turning an abandoned farm into a magic world of fairy tales, myths and stories. Gorse, lilies and lupins are interspersed with sundials, classical columns and striking stone groups with engraved mottoes. Among the labyrinth of concrete-poetical form and sense references are the visionary stone slabs on the banks of the lake inscribed with the words "The order of the present is the disorder of the future", a pyramid commemorating the Romantic Caspar David Friedrich, the gleaming gold head of the French revolutionary Saint Just, with the inscription "Apollon Terroriste" on its forehead, miniature sculptures of aircraft carriers as a parody of warlike actions and the classical front of an ancient temple for Philomen and Baucis. Finlay has long been known in the international art world.

★ **Stonypath ("Little Sparta")**

The industrial village of New Lanark lies 35 miles south-east of Glasgow on the banks of the River Clyde, which has cut a wide path through the red sandstone here. The village has been classified as a historical monument.

★★ **New Lanark**

By the 19th c. the famous model settlement of the great social reformer **Robert Owen** (1771–1858) was already well-known to those interested in technology and sociology.

Founder of the industrial village was Owen's business-minded father-in-law **David Dale**, whom contemporaries described as being as humorous as he was inventive. The textile businessman Dale came here in 1783 with Richard Arkwright, an expert on industrial spinning mills and for a time Dale's partner. He recognised the special advantage of the village's location: the water-power of the Clyde Falls, combined with Arkwright's new machines, formed the basic prerequisites for the famous cotton spinning mills. Two years later the first factory started up. For a time some 70 per cent of the workers were children whom Dale had brought from the orphanages of Glasgow and Edinburgh but whom, considering the conditions of that time, he cared for in an exemplary fashion.

When Robert Owen took over the factories, cotton spinning was one of the most important industries in England. Owen, who was born in Newton in Wales, came from a simple background. At nineteen he was given control of a cotton factory in Manchester (see entry), the stronghold of industrial capitalism. The industrialist, aware of reform, was convinced of the congruence of the interests of employees and employers. In his opinion good living and working conditions as well as a good education improved not only the welfare but also the efficiency of the workers and were of benefit to the interests of the business. He saw social costs such as those incurred in the building of workers' homes and improvements to the workplace as necessary investments. He had the productivity of each individual worker equally as well controlled as the organisation of his social services. These included insurance against illness and free visits to the doctor as well as the goods obtained wholesale in the village shop, which were sold almost at cost price. Owen paid particular attention to children's education and introduced a privately-financed school system. The Institute for the Formation of Character, which served as both a school house and a cultural centre, opened in 1816 with fourteen teachers and approximately 300 children. Dancing, music and natural history occupied a large part of the timetable. Corporal punishment was forbidden. The working day was finally cut by Owen to ten and a half hours, the minimum age for child workers was set by him at ten.

Through his commitment, which also encompassed involvement in the reform of factory legislation, Owen prompted the first British health and safety at work laws. Later model settlements based themselves on his ideas about social reform. Emboldened by his success in New Lanark, Owen tried to achieve a similar result in 1825 with "New Harmony" in Indiana, USA. This failed after four years, however, because of religious and political differences, and Owen subsequently had to sell his shares in New Lanark.

Up to 25,000 people lived and worked in the multi-storey factories and residential buildings, sandstone constructions with wooden or cast-iron pillars. The production of cotton and textiles, and later also of flax tents, sails and fishing nets, continued until 1968. The site was then sold to a metal exploitation firm and became increasingly run down until finally in 1983 it was placed under protection as an historical monument. After extensive restoration the **Industrial Village** was opened to the public in 1990. However, New Lanark should not remain in existence purely as a museum of industrial and social history; about 100 flats have been extended, the weaving mill and the dyeing works are once more in use and the old factory buildings next to the visitors' centre housed in former spinning mill number three are scheduled to become hotels, trading businesses, and exhibition and conference rooms.

South Wales   F–I 8/9

Wales/Cymru
Counties: Dyfed, Glamorgan and Gwent

South Wales is a popular holiday region, with many seaside resorts, idyllic coastal areas and delightful hills, in which many places bear witness to this country's important past. However, heavy industry here is in crisis. While in 1951 the steelworks of the British Steel Corporation in Port Talbot were prized as being the most modern in Europe, the present recession and structural problems are causing the last two state-subsidised steelworks to face an uncertain future. Along with the traditional heavy industry, other manufacturers, predominantly of chemicals and textiles, have recently settled here, as have computer and electronics firms, all of which are looking to expand. South Wales therefore has many facets. It encompasses the counties of Gwent (formerly Monmouth), Glamorgan (divided into West, Mid and South Glamorgan) and the southern part of Dyfed (the former counties of Carmarthen and Pembroke).

South Wales is a region with a favourable climate. Thanks to the Gulf Stream its winters are mild, there is little rain between January and June, and the coastal area enjoys many hours of sunshine. There are more than 80 beaches, from wide bays to small rock-enclosed coves, many of them almost deserted, others crowded with holidaymakers in summer.

Geologically South Wales mainly comprises ranges of hills running in an east-west direction as in Brittany, in contrast to North Wales with its north-south Caledonian-style formations. The late-Tertiary folding caused by a damp warm climate and extensive denudation through heavy rain and weathering was followed in the Pleistocene period by a glacial coating of the land through three Ice Ages, the Anglian, Wolstonian and Devonian. The glaciation centres were Snowdonia (see North Wales), the Brecon Beacons and the inner Welsh plateaux.

In Anglo-Saxon times Wales was the retreat of the Celts who had arrived in the British Isles in 800 BC, founded the first towns and built fortresses (the "Celtic Hill Forts") on the plateaux. The valleys were also settled by the Romans, who extended the fortresses; they were followed by the Christian Irish, and subsequently the Normans, from whose fortress sites and settlements came today's villages and towns. Characteristic of the settlement and land utilisation of South Wales are individual farms, with groups of trees and intensive agricultural activity immediately surrounding them, otherwise the land is predominantly left as pasture. Only after Henry VIII was the right of inheritance of farms introduced, which led to the reparcelling of the agricultural land within communities, since beforehand gavelkind had always resulted in an increasingly large division of what was owned. In contrast to England, where sheep rearing is mainly carried out for the production of wool, Wales also plays an important part in the provision of meat.

From Chepstow to Swansea

Chepstow (pop. 9000) is picturesquely situated on the River Wye 3 miles above its mouth. Its situation at the most important entrance to Wales from England gave it great significance for centuries, and a large castle was built on a high crag above the town, called Striguil by the Normans. The well-retained castle dates mainly from the time of Edward I, with the keep having been built by the Normans between 1120 and 1230. The walnut tree in the courtyard is said more than 600 years old. The medieval town wall still partly encloses the narrow streets of the old town centre. The 14th c. town gate in Bridge Street now houses a museum devoted to local history and artists from the Wye Valley.

**Chepstow/
Casgwent**

From Chepstow there is an attractive trip northwards up the Wye Valley. After approximately 3 miles turn left into a side road and follow this to its end; from here it is a fifteen minute climb to the top of Wyndcliff (800 ft), with its panoramic views. The charming landscape here is well known for its variety of fauna.

⋆ **Wyndcliff**

Return to the main road and continue for 2 miles north to reach the attractive ruins of Tintern Abbey, whose appearance inspired the "Lake Poet" to write some of his poetry. The abbey is situated on the west bank of the meandering Wye and was founded in 1131 by Walter de Clare for the Cistercian order. The church is in the Decorated style (1270–1325) and measures 228 ft long. Like many other churches, Tintern Abbey fell victim to Henry VIII's securalisation. However, even if the roof, central tower and north wall of the nave have disappeared, the remaining majestic arches with richly embellished tracery on the windows never-theless present a notable appearance and this has been captured in a number of very idyllic paintings by artists including William Turner (see

⋆ **Tintern Abbey**

Tintern Abbey, a Gothic jewel

Famous People). An exhibition in the adjoining visitors' centre explains how the monks used to live.

Caerwent

Situated at Caerwent (4 miles west of Chepstow) is Wales' best-preserved ★**Roman City**. The excavated tribal capital Venta Silurum gives an excellent impression of Roman town planning, since parts of the walls, amphitheatre, baths, shops and town gates have survived from that time. The parish church contains a mosaic and the tomb of a Roman officer.

Prehistoric traces have been found on the **Llan-melin**, a wooded hill, which was probably the main town of Siluria before the founding of Venta Silurum (2½ miles north-west).

All that remains of the former ★**Caldicot Castle** (2½ miles south-west), built in the reign of Edward I, is the massive Norman round tower, now housing a museum.

**Newport/
Casnewydd**

Newport/Casnewydd (pop. 133,000), an important port and Wales' third-largest town, lies at the mouth of the River Usk. At high tide the waters of the Severn Estuary can rise by up to 30 ft here, so the bridges over the Usk – there are five in Newport – have been built especially high. This port and industrial town is home to large chemical and aluminium works. It is worth visiting triple-aisled **St Woolos' Church**, with its 12th c. Norman nave and 15th c. tower. Following its construction the church was awarded the status of a cathedral. Exhibits in the **Museum of Archaeology and Natural History** in Dock Street include artefacts found during excavation of the Roman castles at Caerwent and Caerleon and are particularly worth seeing.

Caerleon

Follow the banks of the Usk for 3 miles north-west to reach the suburb of Caerleon, called Isca Silurum by the Romans, with remains of the fortress of the Second Legion, established about AD 70 and abandoned about AD 140. There are some well-preserved sections of walling, and the amphitheatre is the only one in Britain to have been completely excavated.

See entry

Barry (pop. 43,000) lies 9 miles south-west of the Welsh capital on a narrow peninsula and has several beaches, well-tended parks, a ruined medieval castle, good entertainment facilities, a golf course and a small zoo.

Barry

Extending westwards beyond the airport are a number of small sea-side resorts, including West Aberthwaw, Llanwit Major and Porthcawl, whose sandy beaches attract many day-trippers from Swansea and Port Talbot.

Anyone approaching Port Talbot will probably share the impression of the British historian Roscoe who, while passing through in 1854, wanted to leave "the dirty town of Aberavon" as quickly as possible. An overview of Port Talbot shows a narrow stretch of coast with a bright sandy beach and a narrow bay at the mouth of the Afan, from which a thin densely-populated valley leads inland, steep cliffs falling into the sea, on which rows of houses hang like garlands, all dominated by the smoking chimneys of steelworks and petro-chemical factories, and by warehouses, production lines and electricity grids. This bizarre industrial "beauty" seems to smother the town, but it also lends it a provocative fascination.

Port Talbot

Port Talbot was founded in 1093, shortly after Glamorgan was con-quered by the Normans. Aberavon, as the town was initially called, was first documented in the 12th c., and it received its town charter in 1835 through parliamentary decree. In 1921 the settlements of Aberavon and Margam were combined into Port Talbot. Since administrative reforms the town, which in the meantime bore the name Afan, has comprised the town centre of Aberavon and the communities of Taibach, Margam. Cwmavon, Baglan and Bryn.

In the centre, located half-way up a hill, stands the town's oldest church, **St Mary's**. The new Civic Centre, an attractive administrative complex opposite the bulky purpose-built **Aberfan Shopping Centre**, was opened in 1988. Only a short distance away from the pedestrianised area rows of traditional red-brick two-storey workers houses line Mansel Street, Ty Drawl Street, Court Lane and Oakwood Street. Functionally built with only austere charm, they offer few exceptional features. More spacious are the houses of the "residential people" of Baglan, situated higher up the hill, where the raised social standing is reflected in the dimensions of the architecture. Visitors to Aberavon's almost 2 mile-long sandy **beach** will find an impressive promenade with many enter-tainment facilities.

The town's most famous son is the actor Richard Burton, who came from the suburb of Pontrhydyfen, near Cwmavon. The house in which he was born bears a plaque inscribed to the Hollywood star and stands on a street corner in the Afan Valley, a few miles from **Afan Argoed Country Park**.

The suburbs of Swansea (pop. 187,000), Wales' second-oldest town, whose name is derived from the Welsh Abertawe, extend as far as the Gower Peninsula. This port at the mouth of the Tawe grew in size through the export of iron and coal, and is now an important trading centre, university town and industrial base, even though the regional structural problems are also clearly evident here.

Swansea/ Abertawe

Whenever Wales' largest ★ **market** is held in Swansea, the whole town throbs with visitors, who discover at the brightly-coloured stalls all manner of agricultural products, including varieties of strong Welsh cheese, mussels from nearby Burry Bay, and laver bread, made from seaweed, which is served with oatmeal. Wide Kingsway lies at the heart of the town centre, while the main shopping streets are Union Street, Oxford Street, High Street, Princess Way and Portland Street. There are few historic buildings, the remains of the castle are buried behind modern buildings and only in Castle Street and Castle Lane can medieval masonry still be seen.

Swansea boasts magnificent parks; **Clyne Gardens**, famed for its rhododendrons and azaleas, mounts marvellously-colourful exhibitions in late spring. Boat ponds and play facilities await children at Blackpill Lido.

The **cultural life** of the town, which counts the eloquent poet Dylan Thomas (1914–53) among its sons, is lively, with the theatre and the arts well supported. The **Swansea Music Festival**, the high-point of the town's musical life, takes place every October in the Guildhall, which is decorated with murals by Frank Brangwyn, originally intended for the House of Lords in London. The superior **Grand Theatre** in Singleton Street has its own company, **Brangwyn Hall** is mainly used for concerts. During the summer there is a full programme of variety shows, dancing, concerts and performances for children in the Patti Pavilion near the Guildhall. The **Gower Festival** stages smaller concerts in the surrounding churches annually in July. Among the displays in the **Glynn Vivian Art Gallery** is a marvellous collection of Swansea porcelain.

An attractive quarter has developed around the modern **yacht harbour**, which offers 600 moorings. In addition to the Dylan Thomas Theatre, the quay is lined with small fishermen's pubs and hotels. Working traditional looms can be seen in the industrial and marine museum housed in the Abbey woollen mill, as can part of the former Mumbles railway and museum ships such as the former lightship "Helwick" and the 500 tonne cutter "Katie Ann".

Swansea's long sandy beach offers good watersports facilities. From the Mumbles Pier the White Funnel Fleet operates boat trips, particularly to the attractive Mumbles.

The ★**Mumbles** comprises a wide bay with a long promenade, piers, cafés, restaurants and numerous entertainment facilities, and is a popular destination for the inhabitants of Swansea. On a hill above the Mumbles lie the ruins of Oystermouth Castle (c. 1287) with the gatehouse, great hall and chapel. A prominent lighthouse stands on Mumbles Head, two cliffs from which the area has gained its name.

★★**Gower Peninsula**

The Mumbles form the gateway to the Gower Peninsula, a limestone massif of great scenic beauty. The charming south coast has been classified as an Area of Outstanding Natural Beauty and is a nature reserve which, apart from the towns and villages, is only accessible on foot. There are a number of beaches, while Langland and Caswell Bay are popular sandy beaches, particularly popular among surfers.

The peninsula boasts a mild oceanic climate and good soil on its chalky clay deposits and is thus ideal for agriculture. This is reflected by, among other things, Rhossili's early potatoes and the growing of a variety of crops in the market gardens around Bishopston and Killay. The formerly independent villages of Newton, Killay and Mumbles have been absorbed into Swansea to form a connected area of settlement.

Oxwich

Oxwich has a 3 mile-long sandy beach. There is a nature trail along the coast which offers magnificent views.

Port Eynon

Port Eynon is a popular resort with a sandy beach and dunes and the additional interest of the Culver Hole, a cave once occupied by prehistoric man.

Rhossili

To the west of Port Eynon begins beautiful Mewslade Bay, bordered by Rhossili Bay with its magnificent sandy beach. Rhossili, a small seaside

Collapsed chalk cliffs on the south coast of the Gower Peninsula

resort, is picturesquely situated amid the Rhossili Downs, which climb to a height of 633 ft. Worm's Head, a small isolated ridge of rock, can be reached on foot at low tide (about 1 miles from Rhossili), as can Burry Holms (3 miles north), a small island near the resort of Llangennith.

Penclawdd (Welsh for "mussel") lies east of Whiteford Point. Here, as at Llansaint, Kidwelly, Ferryside and Llanstephan, there are extensive mussel banks.   **Penclawdd**

★The Valleys

In comparison with other British mining areas the Valleys only gained economic importance fairly recently. Mining techniques and productivity levels did not become aligned until the construction of the railways, which linked the Valleys to the ports of Cardiff (see entry), Port Talbot, Briton Ferry, Swansea and Llanelli, and enabled export. In its heyday before First World War South Wales possessed the country's second largest **mining region**.

This region, with an exposed, productive coal-bearing area of 1004 sq. miles, extends westwards in a kidney shape from Newport/Cardiff for about 50 miles, while from north to south it covers an area of approximately 15½ miles. The long syncline is framed by older layers and only selectively overlain by more recent sediments. Through pronounced mountain folding, coal seams found at certain depths experienced extensive fragmentation into individual fields. The quality of the coal ranges from anthracite, glance coal made into hard coal through the process of carbonisation and containing 94 per cent carbon, via lean coal and forge coal to fat coal, which is used for carbonisation. Mining succeeded in the deeper valleys by the use of tunnelling techniques, with flat shafts, while more exposed coal was removed through open-cast mining. On this coal base arose a prospering iron and steel industry, which at the height of the mid-19th c. boom in iron employed more than 15,000 workers in the iron metropolis of Merthyr Tydfil alone.

The decline of "King Coal" and the "Iron King" began in the 1920s, when, after vehement strikes and lockouts, one mine after another had to cease production and the great iron foundries had to close their gates. The problem was compounded by competition from cheap foreign imports, old-fashioned mining and production techniques as well as the difficult location of some coal seams, which made viable mechanised mining difficult. Even the strong community spirit of the Welsh trade unions, which proved itself in 1984/1985 – in Britain's longest miners' strike – and again in 1992 could not prevent the death of the mining industry. Today three pits in the South Welsh valleys with fewer than 1000 miners are the final testimony to the great industrial past, when more than 260,000 men working in about 620 collieries brought in excess of 50 million tons of coal to the surface annually. The steel industry has also been cut back, leaving only minimal works along the south coast of Wales.

Heavy industry, which was based on the initial effect of coal, has left a bad legacy. That the barely landscaped slag heaps are more than just scenic eyesores was made all too clear by the Aberfan disaster of 1966, when one of them, softened by rain, slid downhill and buried a school with 141 children beneath it. Following this the safety of the heaps was increased, and the state approved investments in the rehabilitation of the landscape. Meanwhile some of the heaps have disappeared, with slopes and hills being landscaped, and leisure parks, lakes, new housing areas and business zones being laid out. Educational trails through the mining area provide interested visitors, equipped with protective helmets and miners' lamps, with an insight into these abandoned industries. The process of making good, recultivating and remodelling the valleys, which has begun with varying degrees of success, remains far from complete.

Vale of Neath

The River Neath, which enters the Bristol Channel at Swansea, has carved itself into the exposed carbon layers at a depth of about 1313 ft and in doing so 164 ft and 591 ft above sea-level has cut off powerful coal seams, which in the 18th and 19th c. represented the deciding locational factor for the development of heavy industry. By 1584 Heinz Fosse had already founded the first copper smelting plant in Neath, receiving copper ores from Devon and Cornwall. Until the end of the 19th c. the main industries to evolve here and in the neighbouring Tawe Valley were copper, zinc, iron and steel. These were linked by train and canal to the industrial centres of the coast and to the English market. At the beginning of the 20th c. both the iron and steel works and the mines were increasingly losing their importance faced with cheaper foreign competition. In 1948 the state-run steel industry was concentrated in Port Talbot for reasons of profitability. The "tinplate industry" has meanwhile moved to the hinterland around Valindre and Troshe.

Rhondda Valley

During a journey through the Rhondda Valley visitors cannot fail to notice the idle conveyors and sparsely-grassed slag heaps. The Tre Forest Industrial Park at the entrance to the Rhondda is evidence of the sought-after reincarnation of the valley, whose former economic structure based solely on mining, as in the neighbouring valleys, led to high unemployment and a great exodus of the younger generation. The problem of space in the narrow valleys and the unfavourable conditions for improved transport links make it difficult for new industries and businesses to settle here.

Some of the redundant pits and blast furnaces have been retained for posterity as museums of industrial archaeology. This is also the case in the iron foundry town of **Merthyr Tydfil**, where the local Heritage Trust is trying to retain the relics of the industrial revolution.

Slag heaps in the Rhondda Valley

Visitors at the Big Pit Mining Museum

The development project in Ebbw Vale is evidence of the way in which the former mining area is looking for new perspectives. More than 14,000 miners were once employed here in five pits and an enormous steelworks. The blast furnaces and rolling mills have long been closed, only a galvanising plant still operates. To create attractive incentives for new commercial enterprises 141 acres of old slag heaps around the former steelworks have been cleared since 1983 and the land planted with trees, shrubs and colourful gardens, where the "Garden Festival of Wales" was held in October 1992. After the festival work has continued with the building of new residential houses, office blocks and commercial areas. By the turn of the century the new village, called Victoria, should be ready to offer a home to approximately 2500 people.

Ebbw Vale

"Big Pit" ("Pwll Mawr"), Blaenavon's ironworks, ceased production at the beginning of 1980 after more than a century. Three years later the old blast furnaces and foundries were reopened as a mining museum. Even the tower of the hydraulic lift, with which the ore-laden iron wagons used to be raised on to the loading ramp, has survived. As well as touring the workshops, winding engines and workers' residential area, entry to the 328 ft-deep shaft gives visitors an impression of the hard life of a miner. The tours below ground (warm clothes are recommended) are sometimes led by former miners.

Blaenavon
★Big Pit Mining Museum

From Carmarthen Bay via Pembroke to Cardigan

Carmarthen/Caerfyrddin (pop. 14,000), according to legend the birth-place of the Celtic magician Merlin, lies on the River Towy, 9 miles inland

Carmarthen/ Caerfyrddin

545

from the bay of the same name. It is the county town of Dyfed, which consists of the counties of Carmarthen, Pembroke and Cardigan. The market town was formerly an important seaport, and is now the administrative and cultural centre of this agricultural region. The parish church of St Peter dates mainly from the 14th c.; of the 14th c. town wall and gatehouse only ruins remain. The Guildhall (1766) and the County Museum are worth visiting.

A number of small resorts lie around the wide curve of Carmarthen Bay. Sailors like to meet at **Ferryside**, while at neighbouring **Kidwelly** a 13th c. Norman castle, extended in the reign of Edward I, dominates the Gwendreath Fach estuary.

Laugharne

The small market town of Laugharne (pop. 1300), on the Taf estuary, is famous for its excellent cockles. Laugharne has several 18th c. buildings, including the Town Hall (1746). **Dylan Thomas** called this sleepy nest of 400 souls "the strangest town in Wales" when he and his wife moved into the slate-roofed "Boat House" above the bay at the beginning of 1938. Thomas remained here until his early death. His house has been converted into a museum, while his grave can be found in the village cemetery. The place called "Llareggub" mentioned in Thomas' poems refers to Laugharne.

Pendine

The poorly-overdeveloped seaside resort of Pendine/Pentywyn lies 6 miles south-west. Sir Malcolm Campbell set a world land speed record on Pendine Sands in 1924.

Saundersfoot

The coast road continues to Saundersfoot, a popular yachting centre and the venue of regattas. There is also good sea angling.

Tenby

Tenby/Dinbych y Pysgod (pop. 5220), still with its old town walls, lies on a rocky peninsula at the western end of Carmarthen Bay. This seaside resort, prized at the turn of the century by the artist Augustus John as being "so restful, so colourful and so unspoilt" has a picturesque harbour, around which attractive pastel-coloured houses are grouped, two beautiful sandy beaches, charming narrow alleys, the 15th c., carefully restored **Tudor Merchant's House**, and St Mary's Church, the largest parish church in Wales. Tenby Museum, south of Castle Hill, vividly explains the history of the region.

A very popular outing from Tenby is a boat trip to ⋆**Caldey**, a beautiful island (2½ miles south), which has belonged to Cistercian monks since 1929. The first abbey on this site was founded in 1113, and parts of the 14th and 15th c. buildings remain.

⋆**Manorbier Castle**

The coast road from Tenby continues to the holiday resort of Manorbier (pop. 1100), surrounded by red sandstone cliffs. The medieval castle (1275–1325), standing alone on a hill, paints a romantic picture. This was the birthplace in 1146 of Giraldus Cambrensis, one of the most brilliant thinkers of the Middle Ages, archdeacon of Brecon, protagonist of an independent Welsh Church, adviser on Irish affairs and an excellent orator. He accompanied Archbishop Baldwin of Canterbury on his tour of Wales to gain support for the Third Crusade. This journey gave rise to his best known work, the "Itinerary of Wales", in which he describes Manorbier as the most charming place in Wales.

⋆**Carew Castle**

The impressive ruins of 13th c. Carew Castle (about 6 miles north on the A447) lie on one of the many hills surrounding Milford Haven. Its beautifully carved high cross is thought to date from the 9th c. The church at Carew Cheriton, with a Perpendicular tower, is a fine example of 14th c. sacral architecture.

Pembroke/Penfro

Pembroke/Penfro (pop. 15,300) is a historically important town, with the remains of a 13th c. medieval town wall. Henry Tudor, who later as

Henry VII was the first Welshman to ascend the English throne, was born here in 1457.

The most imposing Norman coastal fortress in Wales towers on the crest of a hill. ★★**Pembroke Castle** was built in 1090 by Arnulf, Earl of Pembroke. From the top of the massive round keep (75 ft) there are magnificent views. Adjoining the keep are the Prison Tower, the Norman Hall and the North Hall, from which a staircase leads down into the huge natural cavern known as the Wogan.

On the hill south-west of the castle stands **Monkton Priory**, a Benedictine house founded at the same time as the castle.

Pembroke Dock (1 miles north) was intended to be one of the largest naval dockyards but was closed down in 1926. Ferries from Rosslare in Ireland now dock here. It is worth paying a visit to **Lamphey Palace**, about 1 mile south-east of Pembroke. The former seat of the Bishops of St David's is surrounded by fruit trees and lush gardens.

Pembroke is an excellent base from which to explore the marvellous scenery of the south-west coast. A particularly delightful walk is along the ★★**Pembrokeshire Coastal Footpath**, laid out in 1970. It covers a distance of 167 miles along the coast from Carmarthen Bay to Cardigan Bay and in doing so crosses the Pembrokeshire Coastal National Park, established in 1952. As walkers pass remote beaches and romantic steep cliffs they are charmed by the unique magic of the landscape; they may also see rare sea birds, such as puffins or razor-billed auks.

★★ Pembrokeshire Coast National Park

Milford Haven (pop. 13,000) is the name both of the town and of one of the most beautiful natural harbours in Britain, the result of deep glacial erosion during the last Ice Age. This industrial town, formerly a naval dockyard, now has one of Europe's largest oil ports, whose importance, however, has continually declined since the discovery of the North Sea oil off the Scottish coast. Milford Haven is also a considerable fishing port, even though water pollution has affected coastal fishing. As well as the large oil-tankers, sailing ships and motor boats dominate the scene in the 20 mile-long, 1–2 mile-wide bay.

Milford Haven

The sheltered sailing harbour of **Dale**, at the entrance to Milford Haven, is surrounded by beaches with fine sand: Musselwick Sands, Martin's Haven, Marloes Sand and Westdale Bay. In 1485 Henry Tudor, pretender to the throne, landed in Dale and marched through Wales to defeat Richard III in the battle of Bosworth Field. He was subsequently crowned as Henry VII.

Westdale Bay, Watwick Bay, Mill Bay and Castlebeach are quiet and uncrowded bathing resorts on a small peninsula near Dale. The tidal currents here make swimming dangerous.

The holiday resort of Newgale (13 miles north) has a 2.4 mile-long sandy beach with views of St Bride's Bay. The romantic Roch Castle perches high on the cliffs some 1½ miles south-east. There is heavy surf on the sea here.

Newgale

Solva is a popular sailing centre and a good base for touring the St David's peninsula.

Solva

St David's/Tyddewi (pop. 1500), a long drawn-out village situated on a remote peninsula at the north end of St Bride's Bay, was for centuries a place of pilgrimage. In 1081 William the Conqueror came here as a pilgrim. St David (Dewi Sant), the patron saint of Wales and twice Archbishop of Canterbury, was supposed to have been born one stormy night on the cliffs south of the village.

St David's/ Tyddewi

The ★**Cathedral**, one of Britain's earliest, was built in a hollow to escape the attentions of marauders from the sea. Consequently from the immediately surrounding area only the tower can be seen. The precincts of the cathedral were enclosed by a wall in the 13th c. The cathedral is mainly Late Norman (end of the 12th c.), but 14th c. rebuilding has given the exterior a Decorated aspect. As in many early churches and cathedrals the original tower collapsed in 1220 and was rebuilt in 1250. The Lady Chapel was added in the Early English period. The west front was given its present form by Sir George Gilbert Scott between 1862 and 1878. While the exterior of the cathedral appears rather sombre and austere, the rich variety of forms within its triple-aisled Norman interior creates an overwhelming effect. The beautiful ceiling of Irish oak was added in the late 15th c. The very fine rood-screen is also 15th c. Of the four arches supporting the tower, the one on the west side dates from before the collapse of the original tower, the three others from after 1220. The choir-stalls, with filigree misericords, and the bishop's throne date from the second half of the 15th c. Bishop Vaughan's Chapel has fine fan-vaulting. The transepts are partly original, partly rebuilt after the collapse of the tower in an Early Gothic style characteristic of South Wales. The relics contained in a small chest in the Trinity Chapel are probably those of St David; his shrine in front of the high altar is empty.

On the north side of the cathedral are the ruins of **St Mary's College**, founded in 1365.

To the west is the ⋆**Bishop's Palace**, with fine arcading, built 1280–1350 for Henry de Gower. The whole building stands on a vaulted undercroft. It is particularly worth visiting the Great Hall, with a handsome porch and rose windows.

South-west of St David's Head can be seen **Ramsey Island**, with Woodwalton Fen and to the north Holme Fen, a nature reserve with rare flora and fauna (permit required to visit). There are remains of a Benedictine abbey on the island.

On the high cliffs of **St David's Head**, the most westerly point in Wales, are the remains of the prehistoric earthwork known as the Warriors' Dyke.

The adjoining land as far as Cardigan, with its rocky coasts, bleak plateaux and narrow valleys, is one of the least spoilt stretches of natural scenery in Wales. It is a thinly populated region mainly devoted to sheep- farming.

Goodwick, Fishguard

In Fishguard Bay are the twin towns of Goodwick and Fishguard (combined pop. 5000). In the old part of Fishguard a huddle of small houses surrounds the beautiful harbour, called Abergwaur, from which ferries depart to Rosslare in Ireland. This setting has become famous since Dylan Thomas' "Under Milk Wood" was filmed here in 1971. The tip of the promontory is dominated by the ruins of a medieval castle. The modern part of the town offers good shopping opportunities. Those interested in Welsh handicrafts should visit the Ateliers Workshop Wales in the centre (Lower Town), while walkers will find many pleasant coastal paths, with numerous fine views. The Pen Caer peninsula, to the north-west, has many prehistoric remains, Iron Age forts and chambered tombs.

Newport

Newport/Trefdraeth (7 miles east) is a pleasant resort on the River Nevern, with the ruins of a 13th c. castle. It offers good beaches, excellent fishing and a golf course.

Pentre Ifan

About 3 miles south-east of Newport, on the edge of the Preseli Hills (Mynydd Preseli), lies Pentre Ifan, Wales's largest Stone Age dolmen.

Carn Ingli Common

Carn Ingli Common, about 1 mile to the south, has remains of an Early Christian settlement. From this area came 33 dolerite stones which were transported to Stonehenge (see entry). In the valley on the other side of the Preseli Hills stands the Gors Fawr, a stone circle similar to that at Stonehenge.

Nevern

At Nevern/Nanhyfer (2 miles east) is St Brynach's Church, dedicated to a

Loom in Dre-Fach Felindre Wool Museum

Raglan Castle, a bardic stronghold

Celtic saint. Visitors should enter the church to see the richly carved Celtic cross, 12½ ft tall.

Cardigan/Aberteifi (pop. 4000) is a busy little market town on the banks of the Teifi (pronounced Tivi), 2½ miles above its mouth. A six-arched bridge, built at the beginning of the 18th c., spans the Teifi, renowned for its salmon and trout, in the town centre. Nearby two round towers from a 13th c. medieval castle can be seen.

    A rewarding excursion is to the picturesque ruins of 13th c. **Cilgerran Castle**, which was built on a high cliff on the south bank of Teifi Valley (3 miles south-east).

Cardigan/ Aberteifi

The Teifi Valley is a traditional base of the Welsh woollen industry. The Museum of the Welsh Woollen Industry in Dre-Fach Felindre informs visitors about the combing and spinning of wool, and about old weaving techniques and patterns.

★**Museum of the Welsh Woollen Industry**

From Brecon Beacons National Park to Monmouth

The Brecon Beacons are one of the most beautiful parts of Wales. Founded in 1957, the national park borders to the west the Black Mountains, with the source of the River Usk, and to the east another mountain range, also called the Black Mountain and famous for its wild ponies. Here the 519 sq. mile national park borders the English county of Hereford and Worcester for 10 miles–15 miles. Most of the mountains are more than 1000 ft high, many reach in excess of 2000 ft. Formed from red sandstone, they look like beacons, hence their name, which may also have been derived from the fires lit on the peaks as signals during the Middle Ages. The landscape features

★★**Brecon Beacons National Park**

native deciduous trees, North American conifers and broad swaths of moorland.

The national park contains many waterfalls, the most famous of which are the **Henryd Falls** at Coelbren. The caves in this area are also of interest, including ★**Dan-yr-Ogof** in the upper part of the Tawe Valley, which is floodlit for the benefit of visitors and which indicates a Bronze Age settlement.

Brecon/Aberhonddu

Brecon/Aberhonddu (pop. 6000), which lends its name to the mountains and the national park, lies in a beautiful setting in the valley of the Usk at its junction with the Honddu and the Tarell. It has many Georgian houses, remains of the medieval town walls and a 12th/13th c. castle, which was razed to the ground in the 17th c. The red sandstone St John's Church (13th/14th c.) became a cathedral in 1933. This fortress-like church is typically Welsh and contains the tomb of Dr Hugh Price, who founded Jesus College in Oxford (see entry) in 1571.

Brecknock Museum in Captain's Walk has important archaeological finds, mainly dating from early Christian times, and a notable natural history collection.

★Hay-on-Wye

About 21 miles north-east of Brecon lies the small border town of Hay-on-Wye (pop. 2000), which Richard Booth, a Welsh nationalist, declared an "independent kingdom" on April 1st 1977. With an eye to publicity the "King of Hay" named it "Booktown", as it has the most books per inhabitant in the world. The antiquarian bookshop belonging to the bibliophile Booth contains more than two million volumes.

Abergavenny

The small market town of Abergavenny on the eastern edge of the national park marks the start of the "Head of the Valleys Road" (A465), which extends along the impressive stretch at the northern end of the "Valleys" as far as Swansea. Built in about 1100, but subsequently renovated several times, the castle now houses a museum devoted to local history.

★Raglan Castle

8 miles further east, imposing Raglan Castle is reached. Originally Norman, but extensively renovated in the 15th c., it is the last surviving medieval fortress in Wales. The hexagonal tower is Norman and offers marvellous views. Towards the end of the 15th c. famous representatives of Welsh poetry and song met at the castle. In 1646 the Marquis of Worcester defended the castle, in which Charles I found refuge, against Fairfax. A little later Cromwell had it torn down.

Monmouth

We finally reach the small town of Monmouth (pop. 7500), which lies on the confluence of the Monrow and Wye, and which has the ruins of a medieval castle, as well as the country's only bridgehouse, which has survived from the 13th c. The town museum in Priory Street stages a special exhibition dedicated to Lord Nelson (see Famous People), which includes his sword and love letters to Lady Hamilton. The ★**Nelson Collection** was started by Lady Llangatock, the mother of Charles Stewart Rolls, the flying pioneer and founder of the Rolls-Royce works who was born in Monmouth. Rolls also achieved the first non-stop return flight across the English Channel in 1910. A monument in Agincourt Square reflects the pride the town feels about its famous son.

St Albans   L 9

Central England
County: Hertfordshire
Altitude: 364 ft. Population: 77,000

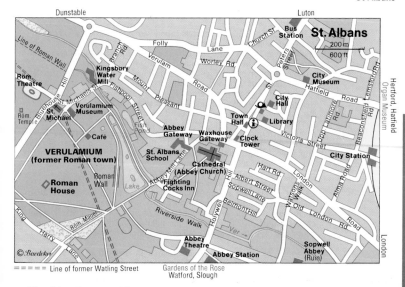

Dunstable · Luton

St. Albans

200 m
600 ft

Folly Lane · Worley Rd · Branch Rd · Verulam Road · Mount Pleasant · Fishpool Street · St Michaels St · Bluehouse Hill · Line of Roman Wall

Kingsbury Water Mill
Rom. Theatre
Rom. Temple
St. Michael
Verulamium Museum
Café
Roman House
VERULAMIUM (former Roman town)
Roman Wall
Lake
Röm. Mauer
King Harry Lane

Fish Pool

St. Albans School
St. Albans Cathedral (Abbey Church)
Abbey Gateway
Waxhouse Gateway
Clock Tower
Town Hall
Library
City Hall
City Museum
Hatfield Road

Church St · St Peter's St · Bus Station

Victoria Street · Hatfield Road · Upper Lattimore Rd · Lower Lattimore Rd · Beaconsfield Rd · Alma Road · Lemsford Rd

Hertford, Hatfield Organ Museum

City Station
City Station

Hart Rd · Albert Street · Sopwell Lane · Belmont Hill · Holywell · London Rd · Old London Rd · Watson · Grove Rd

Abbey Mill Lane
Fighting Cocks Inn
Riverside Walk
Ver

Abbey Theatre
Abbey Station
Sopwell Abbey (Ruin)

London

© Baedeker

===== Line of former Watling Street

Gardens of the Rose
Watford, Slough

The old market town of St Albans lies on a hill above the left bank of the small River Ver, 2 miles north of the London (see entry) circular road (M25). The town attracts particular interest because of its abbey and the old Roman settlement of Verulamium.

History The town owes its name to St Alban, a Roman mercenary, who was converted to Christianity by St Amphibalus and who suffered a martyr's death in 304. His relics were discovered in 793 when Offa, King of Mercia, founded a Benedictine monastery here; this has been the diocesan church of Hertford and Essex since 1872.

At the time of the War of the Roses two decisive battles occurred here in 1455 and 1461 between the House of Lancaster, represented by the red rose, and the House of York, represented by the white rose.

Standing in the centre of the old town is the **Clock Tower**, built between 1403 and 1412 and providing a fine panoramic view. The market place and town hall (1829) are reached a little further on. Continue north from here along St Peter's Street to Hatfield Road, site of the new **St Albans Museum**, which documents the town's history from its beginnings to the present day. Turn east from Hatfield Road along Camp Road to reach the **Organ Museum** with its magnificent collection of mechanical musical instruments, old music boxes and barrel-organs.

The cathedral ★**Abbey Church** stands south of the market place. It formed part of the Benedictine abbey founded by Offa, and, following the abbey's secularisation, became the parish church in 1539. Built between 1077 and 1088, the originally Norman construction was subsequently extended several times.

The western part of the nave was increased between 1214 and 1235, while the monks' chancel was added between 1235 and 1260, and the Lady Chapel between 1308 and 1326. The west front was built by John Grimthorpe from 1879–84, as was the façade of the transept. Only the tower now remains of the original Norman building. With a total length

Sights
Around the
Market Place

551

of 556 ft, St Albans Cathedral is only surpassed in size by Winchester (see entry) Cathedral.

The variety of elements of style found within the cathedral is striking. Immediately inside the west entrance there are a few bays in the Early English style. On the south side of the nave there are five more bays, built after a collapse in 1323. Remains of 13th/14th c. frescoes, including a notable depiction of the crucifixion scene (about 1220), can be seen on the Norman columns flanking the north side.

A beautiful wooden coffered ceiling spans the lay chancel, which is separated from the nave by a rood-screen (about 1350). The ceiling of the crossing is decorated with a painting dating from 1951/52, a copy of the medieval original, whose red and white roses are reminders of the War of the Roses. The large gatehouse (1361) on the south wall is all that remains of the former monastery. The southern section of the transept still contains Saxon balustrades, which were partially lengthened during the Roman Occupation.

The ★**Monks' Chancel** is roofed by ribbed vaulting, which features painted ornamental stucco dating from 1461. The altar wall contains many statues and forms the eastern end of the chancel. It dates originally from 1484 but was renewed between 1884 and 1890. A small chapel stands on either side of the altar wall, with the southern one containing a slab commemorating the abbot Thomas de la Mare (d. 1375).

Behind the altar wall is the ★**Saint's Chapel** (about 1315), which houses the tomb of St Alban. It was reconstructed between 1872 and 1875 from old fragments and its embellishments include depictions of the saint's martyrdom. Special note should be taken of the oak gallery (about 1400), from which pilgrims once used to be able to see the tomb. The tomb of St Amphibalus, who converted St Alban to Christianity, is situated on the north wall of the gallery.

Leave the cathedral in a south-westerly direction and cross the former cathedral garden to reach the **Fighting Cocks Inn**, supposedly Britain's oldest inn. Behind this cross the small River Ver to see the former Roman camp of Verulamium.

★ Verulamium

The first settlement on the site of Verulamium arose in about AD 45. It was the first Roman municipium in Britain and, at the same time, its third-largest town. The ruins of this and a later settlement were used in Norman times as building material for St Alban's monastery.

Excavation work undertaken from 1930 to 1940 unearthed the remains of a fortress, a Roman theatre and a mosaic floor with a hypocaust heating system. Other finds are displayed in the adjoining **Verulamium Museum** in St Michael's Street.

St Michael

Next to the museum on the site of the ancient forum stands the trim St Michael's Church, which features a Norman nave containing the tomb of the philosopher Francis Bacon (1561–1626). Bacon is also commemorated here by a monument.

Kingsbury Water
Mill Museum

By continuing north along St Michael's Street, Kingsbury Water Mill will be reached on the opposite bank of the Ver. Built in the 16th c., the water mill has been restored true to the original and is now used as a museum and to stage art exhibitions and as a restaurant.

Surroundings

Countless varieties of rose grow in the fragrant ★**Gardens of the Rose**, just 2 miles south-west of the town centre.

About 7 miles east of St Albans and close to the old market town of Hatfield (pop. 23,000) stands **Hatfield House**. This imposing Jacobean manor house is surrounded by beautiful parkland and was designed at the beginning of the 17th c. by Robert Lyminge for the Earl of Salisbury. The magnificent interior contains valuable period furniture, paintings and 17th c. tapestries.

St Andrews

Scotland.
Region: Grampian
Altitude: 40 ft
Population: 14,000

The beautiful little town of St Andrews lies on a hill above long sandy beaches, approximately 12 miles south-east of Dundee (see entry). It is known among golfers as the home of the **Royal and Ancient Golf Club**, founded in 1754 and the oldest golf club in the world, whose members have decided the international rules of golf since 1897. The famous British Open championship takes place here every two years on its four eighteen-hole and two nine-hole courses.

The legendary **Old Course** (Par 72) lies next to the sea adjacent to the clubhouse of the Royal and Ancient Golf Club. Originally played over 22 holes, the course was reduced to eighteen holes, nine "out" and nine "in", in 1836.

Essential for all golf fans is a visit to the British Golf Museum. Opened in 1990, it documents the history of the "Alma Mater of Golf" from the Middle Ages to the present in a very interesting way. Golf was first mentioned in 1457, when James II of Scotland banned the sport as attracting too many people away from going to church.

Sights
★★ British Golf Museum

The earliest illustrations of golfing techniques were recorded in 1687 in the diary of the medical student Thomas Kincaid. In the mid-18th c. the first golfing society was established and the rules of the sport set. William IV elevated the Society of St Andrews Golfers to the Royal and Ancient Golf Club in 1834. As well as historical exhibits, the museum displays the various balls, clubs, and rules and techniques of the game, which have evolved during its history. It also provides detailed information about famous championships and legendary male and female golfers, from Tom Morris, father and son, both four-times champion of the Open in the mid-19th c., Harry Vardon, Open champion six times between 1894 and 1914, and Lady Margret Scott, who won the Ladies' Championship three times at the end of the 19th c., to the current golfing greats, including Nick Faldo, winner of the Open at the beginning of the 1990s.

Golf Museum: Famous Winners of the "British Open"

St Andrews

Sacral Buildings

St Andrews played an important role in the history of Scottish churches, which can still be discerned from its churches and monuments. The small town was the see of an archbishop; its cathedral (1160) was once Scotland's largest. Only parts of its gable, walls and gatehouse have survived. It is worth visiting nearby St Rule's, a small 12th c. church with an original chancel and square tower. On Kirkhill are the ruins of another church, the Church of Blessed Mary of the Rocks. Blackfriars Chapel is all that remains of a 16th c. Dominican abbey.

University, Colleges

As well as churches, schools characterise the townscape of St Andrews. It is home to Scotland's oldest university, founded in 1411, which boasts an excellent department of Arabic studies. St Mary's College, opened in 1538, and St Leonard's, opened in 1512, both occupy beautiful old buildings. A school is now housed in Blackfriars Chapel.

The college chapel, formerly St Salvator's Church, contains the pulpit from the town church, from which the reformer John Knox delivered his first sermons.

A rose bush supposedly planted by Mary Stuart (see Famous People) near St Mary's College still blooms. The Martyr's Monument commemorates four reformers, burnt at St Andrews in the 16th c.

Castle

The ruins of a castle built in about 1200 stand on a cliff. Of note are the dungeon, called the "Bottle Dungeon", and an underground escape route.

Rock and Spindle

About 2 miles to the south-east, enjoy a walk to the strangely-shaped basalt pillars, named Rock and Spindle.

St Andrews: The Old Course at the Royal and Ancient Golf Club

Stonehenge

Southern England
County: Wiltshire

Stonehenge is situated 10 miles north of Salisbury (see entry) on the dry chalk elevation of Salisbury Plain, and is Britain's most famous megalithic monument. Together with Woodhenge, the Cursus and other long barrows and round tumuli, it covers a sacral site of some 7.7 sq. miles. Stonehenge ("hanging stones") was built in three phases from about 3000–1500 BC The stone circles visible today date from the Bronze Age, the final building phase. Stonehenge appears to have continued to exist until the Roman era, and was then presumably violently destroyed – whether during the Roman occupation as a measure against the cult of the Druids, or not until the Middle Ages, to prevent the continuance of secret heathen cults, remains unclear. This puzzling phenomenon has inspired various artists, including William Turner and Henry Moore (for both see Famous People), to create remarkable interpretations of the hanging stones. To stop streams of visitors from destroying the site, Stonehenge can now only be viewed from a distance.

Only the gently-curving, originally 6 ft tall enclosing earthwork (diameter 374 ft) dates from the first building phase, which occurred from approximately 3000–2100 BC The earthwork was surrounded by an outer ditch, originally about 6 ft deep, and its entrance was marked by two stone blocks. A short distance from the entrance was the Heel Stone and a free-standing wooden gateway. Around the inner side of the circular earthwork lay a ring of 56 holes, named Aubrey holes after John Aubrey who discovered them in the 17th c. These were used for some centuries as burial sites. The four Station Stones could have been added at the end of this building phase.

With the arrival of **new settlers** from the Beaker culture between 2100 and 2000 BC, the entrance area was extended, parts of the avenue were laid down and the Heel Stone was bordered with a magic circle. Inside the earthwork 4 tonne bluestones, brought from Wales, were positioned in two circles of about 6 ft in diameter, the work stopping, however, halfway through.

In 2000 BC, in the early Bronze Age, construction continued using

Megalithic Place of Worship

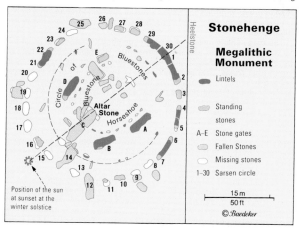

Stonehenge

Megalithic Monument

- ▬ Lintels
- ◠ Standing stones
- A–E Stone gates
- ◠ Fallen Stones
- ◯ Missing stones
- 1–30 Sarsen circle

Circle of Bluestones
Bluestone Horseshoe
Altar Stone
Heelstone

Position of the sun at sunset at the winter solstice

15 m
50 ft

© Baedeker

Stonehenge

Stonehenge, a prehistoric enigma

lavish material and an enormous workforce drawn from various social classes. Sandstone blocks, weighing up to 50 tonnes, were transported to the site from Marlborough Downs, 22 miles away. Used in place of bluestones, they were fitted together into five massive trilithons, the middle one 23 ft high, the others about 3 ft lower, to form the horseshoe-shaped centre of the place of worship. This was enclosed by a lower stone circle, about 14½ ft high, composed of 30 sandstone blocks, each weighing approximately 25 tonnes, with a surrounding entablature of stone slabs, each several feet thick.

Later an attempt was made to arrange the remaining bluestones into two circles on the outside of the sandstone ring, to which ditches, called Y and Z holes, were dug out. Nothing ultimately came of this plan. Stonehenge gained its present appearance in about 1500 BC, when the internal horseshoe-shaped trilithon arrangement was mysteriously repeated with a horseshoe of individually positioned bluestones and a central altar stone. The sandstone circle was given concentric stela-like bluestones.

The megalithic structure at Stonehenge shows evidence of great differences in its origin and its **construction**. The bluestones (a type of basalt) came, according to geological research, from the Preseli Hills in south-west Wales. Their journey covered a distance of 135 miles by sea, using boats reliant on sea and river tides, and by land. The massive sandstone boulders (sarsens) were moved across hilly land at an altitude of 394 ft–591 ft on enormous sledges using rollers, and dragged by about 250 men (on hillsides up to 1000 men) using ropes made from cowhair or woven strips of leather. All the stones were then worked on in front of the site. The sides of the upright stones, which were supposed to point inwards, were smoothed with stone-working tools. The lintels were slightly curved to fit the circular shape of the construction. Mortises for tenons and tongue-and-groove joints were fitted at either end to attach them to the uprights. The massive uprights were then rolled to a prepared hole, tipped in using levers and gradually straightened with the use of ropes, levers and supports. The upper edge was finally smoothed to requirements with stone-working tools and a stone tenon left, on to which the lintel could then be attached. The lintels were slowly raised on permanent timber platforms around the uprights and placed on the tenons.

Why people living 4000 years ago built this place of worship with the use of so much powerful strength and organisation remains an **enigma**. In trying to solve this puzzle archaeologists have put forward numerous controversial theories. It has been interpreted, among other things, as a religious centre used in the cult of the sun because of the exact alignment of the temple with the summer and winter solstice, as a "Stone Age computer" through which astronomical phenomena could be observed and determined, and as an energy centre. The most plausible appears to be a link with the cult of the dead and with sun-worship, if one brings into connection the circular formation of the sacral site with the shape of the sun, an ancient symbol of decline and resurrection.

Stratford-upon-Avon   K 8

Central England. County: Warwickshire
Altitude: 120 ft. Population: 21,000

Stratford-upon-Avon, the small old Elizabethan market town on the River Avon, enjoys worldwide fame as the birthplace of William Shakespeare (see Famous People). The town centre is extensively 16th/17th c. and is surrounded by areas of greenery and charming sections of riverbank, with many attractive rows of half-timbered houses, including Shakespeare's house, where visitors can still follow in the footsteps of the most famous British playwright. The town is internationally famous as a research centre and stage for Shakespeare's works. This culturally-

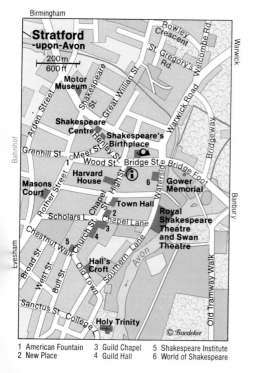

1 American Fountain   3 Guild Chapel   5 Shakespeare Institute
2 New Place   4 Guild Hall   6 World of Shakespeare

Shakespeare's birthplace in Henley Street

blessed setting has repeatedly been used as a backdrop in literature. One of the most recent examples is the detective story "Inspector Jury kisses the Muse", published at the beginning of the 1990s and written by the American authoress Martha Grimes, in which the popular Scotland Yard detective investigates a case of murder in the small historic town.

History The market town of Stratford-upon-Avon, lying on a ford across the Avon, has traditionally been a trading place for the region's agricultural products. The cloth trade led in the Middle Ages to modest affluence for its citizens. Today the town lives primarily by the marketing of its most famous son William Shakespeare (1564–1616) to the tourist industry.

Old Town

Shakespeare's birthplace occupies an isolated position in Henley Street, as the surrounding half-timbered houses have been ripped down to protect it from the risk of fire. The two-storeyed, half-timbered complex with its many gables comprises the house in which Shakespeare was born and the additional houses bought by his father. The interior of Shakespeare's birthplace has remained unaltered and reflects the residential lifestyle of a lower middle-class family in the second half of the 16th c., the period in which Shakespeare grew up as the son of a wool dealer. The rooms have been lovingly arranged with contemporary furniture and contain much memorabilia, including the First Folio edition of his works (1623), and a window on which many illustrious visitors and admirers scratched their names.

Adjoining the birthplace is the modern ★**Shakespeare Centre** (opened 1964), the headquarters of the private Shakespeare Birthplace Trust, founded in 1847. It contains rooms for study and a library.

At the corner of the High Street and Bridge Street stands **Quiney's House**. It was occupied from 1616 to 1662 by the wine merchant Thomas Quiney and his wife Judith, Shakespeare's younger daughter.

Close by, in the High Street, are 16th c. **Garrick Inn**, richly embellished with wood carvings, and **Harvard House**, dating from the same period. This half-timbered house was constructed in 1596 and belonged to the mother of John Harvard (1607–38), founder of the famous Harvard University in Massachusetts, USA.

In the Classical **Town Hall** (1769) nearby stands a statue of Shakespeare, which was presented by David Garrick (1716–79), the famous actor and manager of Drury Lane Theatre in London. Beside the Town Hall is a hotel, partly dating from the 15th c., which bears Shakespeare's name.

A few steps further on in Chapel Street **Nash's House** is now home to the New Place Town Museum, displaying Roman and Saxon finds, as well as mementoes of Shakespeare and Garrick. Thomas Nash, to whom the house belonged, was married to Shakespeare's granddaughter Elizabeth Hall. Next to his house stood New Place, one of the most attractive houses in the town, which Shakespeare bought on May 4th 1597 for the sum of £60. After his return from London in 1611 Shakespeare lived here until his death. The next owner, a priest irritated by the cult of Shakespeare, had the house torn down in 1759. In 1862 the land passed into the ownership of the Shakespeare Trust, which established a marvellous Elizabethan-style garden, Knott Garden, there resembling the one in which Shakespeare is said to have written "The Tempest" in 1611.

The **Guild Chapel** at the corner of Chapel Lane, a single-aisled Gothic church, has a fine wall painting of the Last Judgment of about 1500.

The upper floor of the adjoining Guild Hall, a Tudor half-timbered building, was for centuries used as a grammar school. Shakespeare probably received his school education in these classrooms.

Another Shakespeare research centre is Mason Croft, since 1951 the **Shakespeare Institute** of the University of Birmingham.

A short distance further on into the old town is one of Stratford's most attractive Tudor houses, ★**Hall's Croft**, with its charming garden. This was the home of Dr John Hall, who married Shakespeare's eldest daughter Susanna.

An avenue of lime trees continues to the parish church of **Holy Trinity**, in which lies **Shakespeare's Tomb**. This Gothic construction dates back to the 13th c., but has been considerably altered. The writer's tomb lies in the chancel between the pulpit and the high altar and is marked by a stone bearing Shakespeare's inscription:
"Good friend for Jesus sake forebeare, to digg the dust enclosed heare. Bleste be ye man y'spares the stones and curst be he y'moves my bones."

Holy Trinity

On the wall above the grave is a monument to Shakespeare, set up before 1623, probably the work of the Flemish sculptor Johnson (Geraert Janssen). Close by are the graves of his wife, Anne Hathaway, his daughter, Susanna Hall, his son-in-law, John Hall, and of the first husband of his granddaughter Elizabeth, Thomas Nash. The church also contains the late 15th c. font used in Shakespeare's christening and a copy of the parish registers containing the record of his baptism and burial.

Southern Lane follows the Avon to the Royal Shakespeare Theatre, designed by Elizabeth Scott and built between 1920 and 1932. The old Memorial Theatre, in which almost all of Shakespeare's plays had been produced after 1879, was burnt down. The figures on the façade – Love, Life, Death, Mirth, Faithlessness, War – are by Eric Kennington.

Royal Shakespeare Theatre

The ★**Picture Gallery** on the upper floor contains portraits of Shakespeare and famous actors, as well as costumes and stage-sets.

The Royal Shakespeare Company opened the Swan Theatre in 1936. Its architecture is mock-Elizabethan.

Swan Theatre

The Royal Shakespeare Theatre

World of Shakespeare	The World of Shakespeare, at the end of Waterside, presents audio-visual shows giving an insight into the age of great literature.
Bancroft Gardens	Well-tended Bancroft Gardens now extend along the riverside, featuring Clopton Bridge, a 15th c. stone bridge, and the **Gower Memorial** (1888), actually a memorial to Shakespeare given by the sculptor Lord Ronald Gower and depicting the dramatist sitting in an easy-chair, surrounded by his literary characters Lady Macbeth, Falstaff, Hamlet and Prince Hal.
National Teddy Bear Museum	A completely different attraction for both young and old is the National Teddy Bear Museum, opened in 1988. The toy animal was named after the American president Theodore ("Teddy") Roosevelt, who refused to shoot a young bear while out hunting in 1902. Among the 1000 exhibits assembled from 20 different countries are replicas of popular heroes from children's books, such as Winnie the Pooh, Paddington and Rupert, as well as bears belonging to prominent people, including Humphrey, the bear of ex-Prime Minister Margaret Thatcher, and Teddy Iswlyn, the toy of the former Labour Party leader Neil Kinnock.
Surroundings **★Anne Hathaway's Cottage**	Anne Hathaway's Cottage is situated in Shottery, 1 mile west of the town centre. This country house, a brick building with half-timbering, a thatched roof and a delightful garden, remains in almost the exact state as it was when Shakespeare won the hand of his wife, Anne, here. Until 1899 it was inhabited by descendants of the Hathaway family. Since then it has been furnished again in the style of the 16th/17th c. A small park has been laid out behind the fruit garden. It has been planted with all the trees mentioned in Shakespeare's works.
Mary Arden's House	Shakespeare's mother is said to have lived in Mary Arden's House in Wilmcote (4 miles north-west of Stratford). This magnificent Tudor-style

Anne Hathaway's Cottage

farmhouse now houses a museum devoted to the country customs of the county of Warwickshire.

Charlecote Park

Shakespeare is supposed to have hunted in Charlecote Park (4 miles east), was apparently caught, and lashed as a punishment by Sir Thomas Lucy, whereupon Shakespeare turned him into the somewhat laughable justice of the peace Shallow in "Henry IV". The Lucy family owned the estate after 1247. In 1558 Sir Thomas rebuilt the country seat and received there, among others, Elizabeth I (see Famous People).

Alcester

A popular outing is to Alcester (8 miles west of Stratford; pop. 4500). The town features many old half-timbered houses, including the Old Malt House (about 1500) and the picturesque Town Hall.

★Ragley Hall

Ragley Hall is the distinguished country seat of the Marquis of Hertford. Built in the Palladian style, it lies 1½ miles south-west of Alcester. Built to the design of Robert Hooks between 1679 and 1693, James Gibbs (1682–1754) decorated the salon after 1750 with splendid stucco work. Chippendale furniture, paintings by Rubens and Reynolds, Meissen and Sèvres porcelain embellish the rooms. The 18th c. country garden was created by "Capability" Brown.

Warwick

K 8

Southern England
County: Warwickshire
Altitude: 197 ft. Population: 22,000

The principal town of the county of Warwickshire is an attractive historic town on the River Avon with many old buildings, which has been dominated for 900 years by a defensive fort, Warwick Castle. On weekdays visitors can stroll among the market stalls in Old Square and Jury Street or hunt through one of the many antiques shops.

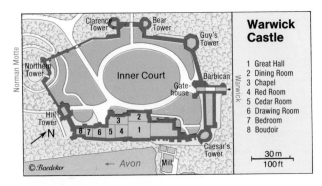

Warwick Castle

1 Great Hall
2 Dining Room
3 Chapel
4 Red Room
5 Cedar Room
6 Drawing Room
7 Bedroom
8 Boudoir

30 m
100 ft

© Baedeker   ← Avon   Mill

History The origins of the town date back to the first Norman fort built here in 1068, although the daughter of Alfred the Great is supposed to have established a fortress here in 915. The powerful Earls of Warwick not only controlled the land surrounding their impenetrable fortress, but also intrigued in English politics, most decisively as "king-makers". In the late Middle Ages this trading town, protected by the fort, became affluent. After a fire in 1694 destroyed most of its medieval buildings, they were carefully reconstructed using the old structures.

Warwick Castle

The massive fortress, crowned with battlements and belonging to the Earls of Warwick, is reached on foot from the modern car parks via the former stable yard (ticket office, restaurant) and the adjoining moat, now an extensive area of parkland with a number of gardens, including a peacock reserve and a rose garden. The inner courtyard of the fortress is entered through the Gate House (1350) complete with the old portcullis. From the courtyard visitors first notice the imposing walls and the towers, which range in height up to 131 ft, all of which can be climbed. The fortifications date from the 16th c., while the fort itself was renovated in the 17th and 18th c. into a castle-like country seat. The magnificent collection of furniture, porcelain, sculptures and paintings by European masters also date from this period. Other additions are the impressive collection of weapons and the wax model museum "A Royal Weekend Party 1898", designed by Madame Tussauds, which is a successful portrayal of the life-style of the British upper class.

Old Town

Situated in the High Street, **Lord Leycester Hospital** was established in 1571 by Robert Dudley, Earl of Leicester, to accommodate twelve ordinary soldiers in a half-timbered house dating from 1383. Many of the streets in the old town still have attractive 17th and 18th c. buildings, including the Court House (Tourist Information) with a Georgian ballroom, Landor House and the Shire Hall, with an octagonal tower lantern. The West Gate has been retained from the old town walls. Guilds have assembled in the early-Gothic St James' Chapel since 1383.

The collegiate church of **★★St Mary** stands in Church Street in the town centre. It was rebuilt (apart from the east end) in 1694 after the great fire and completed in 1704 by Sir William Wilson with the help of Christopher Wren. The most splendid feature of the church is Beauchamp Tower, on the south side of the choir, built in the Perpendicular style (1443–64). The late-medieval windows are mainly original. The tomb of the church's founder, Richard de Beauchamp, Earl of Warwick (1381–1439), can be found in the middle of the chapel. His marble sarcophagus (about 1450) features fourteen mourners, all made of gilded copper, standing in front of the reclining figure of the earl. It is the work of the only well-known English medieval sculptor, John

Massingham. The tomb of the Earl of Leicester, favourite of Elizabeth I (see Famous People), is also here. The choir, completed in 1394, has finely-carved choir stalls (1449), a sedilla, an Easter Sepulchre and the tomb of Thomas Beauchamp (d. 1369). The Norman crypt, dating from 1123, is attractive.

The Market House, built in about 1670 and situated to the west of the market place, now contains the **County Museum**, which boasts an extensive early history department. **St John's House**, a Jacobean manor house on the eastern outskirts of the town, features clothes, furniture and local customs. Oken's House in Castle Street is occupied by an entertaining **Doll and Toy Museum**. | Museums

The bridge across the Avon offers the most beautiful view of Warwick Castle. South of it lies Bridge End, a charming row of houses with half-timbered and stone buildings dating from the late Middle Ages. | Avon Bridge

Royal Leamington Spa (pop. 44,300) lies only 2 miles to the east. It is worth visiting its medicinal springs and the spa gardens, and taking a relaxing stroll in attractive Jephson Gardens and the Pump Room Gardens. | **Surroundings** **Leamington Spa**

Wells 19

Southern England
County: Somerset
Altitude: 128 ft. Population: 9250

Wells, situated 25 miles south-west of Bristol (see entry), is one of the

Wells Cathedral: the west façade

most delightful little towns in England, and is a place in which time seems to stand still. Its population has barely doubled over the course of more than 500 years, while most of its hotels and inns are several hundred years old. Its most impressive construction is the Gothic cathedral with its imposing statue-bedecked west front. Nearby is a charming row of 14th c. houses and the fortress-like Bishop's Palace. The houses of the old town are grouped around the market place, whose stalls enjoy brisk trade on Wednesdays and Saturdays.

History The name Wells is derived from the springs here, which provided water to a monastery founded on this site by Ine, King of Wessex (688–about 726). In 909 it became the see of a bishop, until this was transferred to Bath by the Norman bishop John de Villula in 1088. It was brought back to Wells by Bishop Jocelin (1206–42). Since 1244 the diocese has been known as Bath and Wells.

★★Wells
Cathedral

St Andrew's Cathedral was begun at the end of the 12th c. and was consecrated in 1239 after the first phase of building. It is reached from the market place via Penniless Porch (about 1450), a gateway where the poor used to beg for alms from church-goers. Work continued on the cathedral between 1290 and 1340 with the addition of the central tower to the transept and the Lady Chapel in the chancel. The west towers were completed in the south-west in 1386 and in the north-west in 1421.

The west façade (1220–40) is most magnificent, despite much weathering and the loss of the polychrome frames of the more than 300 figures symbolising the community of the church and the state. In contrast to the distinctive vertical twin-tower façades of French Gothic cathedrals, the English façades display a wider horizontal emphasis, popular since the Romanesque period. Façades and towers are linked in an unusual way, in that the massive towers are positioned next to the side aisles, but in alignment with the end wall of the nave. A combination of narrow lance windows, blind arches and mixed butresses sub-divide the façade. The mid-section of the front is embellished with a gable comprising figures within galleries and pinnacles, while the towers are plain and without ornamentation.

The **interior** of this triple-aisled basilica is simple. A unique feature in the crossing are the double pointed inverted arches. This unorthodox solution was found in 1338 to stop the central tower from collapsing. The capitals in the south-west arm of the transept are particularly charming, with depictions such as a bald-headed man, a man with toothache, a thorn-extractor, and a moral tale: fruit thieves being caught and punished. In the gallery there are numerous statues of bishops (about 1230) and their tombs (14th c.). The chancel shows evidence of late Gothic influence. The unusual carvings, including depictions of animals playing musical instruments, on the misericords (around 1340) of the choir stalls are impressive. The large, stained glass Golden Window (1430) at the end of the chancel depicts the Tree of Jesse, Jesus' line of descent. A famous astronomical clock, constructed in 1392, can be seen in the north-west transept. When it strikes on the hour mounted knights ride into action. Below this is "Christ's Resurrection" by E J Clack.

A few steps further on a staircase (13th/15th c.), decorated with figures of monks bearing columns, leads from the cathedral to the **Chapterhouse** (1360), an octagonal room of consummate perfection whose palm-like vaulting is borne on a single central pier. The surrounding bench was designed for meetings of the members of the cathedral's chapter.

The 15th c. cloister is in the Perpendicular style.

Vicars' Close

This row of forty 14th c. houses built to accommodate cathedral clergy has been marvellously retained and is still inhabited by church employees and students of theology. The chimneys were not built until 1470. The houses are linked to the cathedral via a bridge.

Bishop's Palace

14th c. astronomical clock

Bishop's Palace, surrounded by both a wall and a moat, should also be seen. Begun in 1210, it was restored in the 19th c., and features an inner courtyard, a chapel built by Bishop Burnell, the ruins of New Hall (end 13th c.) and the palace garden with its moat.

Bishop's Palace

The market place and fountain (18th c.) are surrounded by houses of various ages, including a "New Works" group built by Bishop Bekynton in 1453. High Street is the main shopping street, with shops occupying 15th–17th c. houses. The parish church of St Cuthbert (15th c.) has a narrow tower. Its late medieval interior, including a polychrome ceiling, is notable.

Old Town

As long as 60,000 years ago Wookey Hole (2 miles north-west), an impressive series of natural **caves**, offered shelter to wild animals. From the Stone and Iron Ages to the time of the Romans they were inhabited by humans. Water from the River Avon has caused sinter terraces and lakes to form in these enormous dripstone grottoes. Many of the weird limestone formations almost bring to life old legends surrounding witches and ghosts. A small museum exhibiting archaeological finds, a **papermill**, The **Fairground Memories Collection** and **Madame Tussaud's Collection** (a macabre collection of wax heads) are among the attractions here.

Surroundings
★Wookey Hole

The famous cheese town at the foot of the Mendip Hills (10 miles north-west; pop. 2500) is not particularly attractive; in contrast the ★**Cheddar Caves**, magnificent dripstone caves discovered in 1877, are both interesting and overcrowded. **Cheddar Gorge**, approximately 1 mile long and 492 ft deep, is equally as impressive. Cheddar pinks, a type of carnation found only here, bloom throughout the summer.

Cheddar

Isle of Wight (Island)   K 10

Southern England
County: Isle of Wight. Population: 120,000

The Isle of Wight, situated off the south-west coast opposite Portsmouth and Southampton (see entries), measures 23 miles from north to south, is 13 miles long and rises in the south, where chalk and marl cliffs fall steeply in places to the sea, to a height of 775 ft. This entrancing island certainly earns its alternative names "Island of Flowers", "Island of Gardens" and "Diamond in the Sea". In comparison to other parts of Britain the Isle of Wight enjoys an extremely mild climate, although rough winds can sometimes blow in this sailing Mecca. The good weather attracts numerous holidaymakers throughout the year, with the best time for visits being spring, when the flora is lush, and autumn, when the cooler temperatures better suit long walks through the varied landscape. The island is most crowded in August, when the famous regatta week takes place at Cowes.

Wine produced on the island is considered the best in Great Britain, with the wines produced by Adgestone Vineyard, Barton Manor, the small wine-growing estate next to Osborne House, and others repeatedly chosen as "English Wine of the Year".

Transport Car and passenger ferries depart from Portsmouth, Southampton and Lymington. The hovercraft journey from Southsea to Ryde only takes a few minutes. Excursion boats ply their trade around the island during the season – the finest views of the island are to be had from the sea. Bus companies also offer tours of the island. Good roads and public buses ensure easy movement around the island, although visitors should try to make use of the marvellous paths here.

Isle of Wight: Osborne House, at Cowes   *"The Needles", the most westerly point*

History Until approximately 6000 BC the island remained linked to Hampshire on the mainland, and the Solent, now a channel, was a river valley. There is evidence of temporary settlements from after the mid-Stone Age, after the channel between the island and the mainland had opened up. A number of tumuli (including those south of Arreton and Niton Downs, Brook Down and on the south-west coast) date from the beginning of the Bronze Age (about 2000 BC). An Iron Age settlement was found at Chillerton Downs.

The first written mention of the Isle of Wight was made by Sueton, who reported Vespasian's conquest of the island of Vectis in AD 43. Several Roman villas, e.g. at Brading and Newport, show evidence of the Roman way of life. After the Romans departed in about 410 the island is supposed, according to contemporary chronicles, to have belonged first to the kingdom of Wessex, until 1100, when, after the Norman conquest, it was given as a royal favour to the Redvers family. After the family had died out ownership of the island returned to the Crown until 1293 and it was subsequently ruled by royal administrators, while the native islanders earned their money by "free trading", smuggling and the salvage of flotsam and jetsam. The coronation of Henry Beauchamp, Earl of Warwick, by Henry VI as king of the Isle of Wight was of little significance, as this royal favourite died after only seven years. Repeated French attacks laid waste to the island, the final one at the beginning of 1545 destroying Wolverton. The coastal fortresses then built by Henry VIII (see Famous People) at Cowes, Freshwater, Sandown and Yarmouth secured the island thereafter.

In the English Civil War the islanders supported Oliver Cromwell (see Famous People), who imprisoned King Charles I in Carisbrooke Castle from November 1647 until shortly before his execution in London in January 1649. After the restoration of the monarchy the island fell into obscurity from the end of the 17th c. until the Royal Family discovered the Isle of Wight in 1845 as a holiday home. Queen Victoria (see Famous People) often spent summers here with her husband, Prince Albert, who himself planned his summer residence Osborne House in East Cowes.

Since 1890 the island has had the status of a county. Its fertile soil is well used agriculturally, and there are also some small industries here (shipbuilding, construction of small aeroplanes, electrical engineering), which, combined with tourism (in excess of a million visitors a year excluding day-trippers), form the economic base of the island.

★★ Island Tour

The island's main town is Newport (pop. 22,500), situated roughly in the middle, and the centre of administration, business and transport. St James' Square with its statue of Queen Victoria lies at the centre of the town. Nearby stands the old Grammar School (1614), in which Charles I agreed the Treaty of Newport with parliament in 1648. The king's fifteen-year-old daughter, Princess Elizabeth, is buried in St Thomas' Church. She died in 1650 while a prisoner in Carisbrooke Castle and a monument to her by Marochetti was commissioned by Queen Victoria in 1856. The town hall in the High Street was opened in 1816 and is the work of John Nash. Noisy Newport market, held on Tuesdays and Fridays and really a cattle market, attracts many visitors. It is more peaceful in the Roman villa (2nd c.), where mosaic floors, parts of the baths and the hypocaust can be seen.

Newport

★ **Carisbrooke Castle** (1 mile south-west of Newport) is idyllically situated on a hill and stands on the site of a former Roman fort. The keep is Norman (early 12th c.) and offers fine views, while most of the rest of the castle dates from the 13th c. Charles I and his daughter Elizabeth were held captive here in 1647/48; the simple royal rooms can be viewed. The Governor's House contains a museum devoted to the island's history. Behind the house lies the 148 ft-deep castle well.

Cowes, a haven for yachtsmen and women

The 88 acre **Robin Hill Adventure Park** is reached some 3 miles east of Newport. Its attractions include dodgems, a Santa Fe railway, a jungle house and a water garden.

Arreton Manor house dates from 1639 and lies 4 miles south-east of Newport. In addition to pieces of 17th c. furniture, it also has a large collection of dolls. The National Radio Museum is housed in a nearby building.

★**Cowes**

Cowes (pop. 18,900), the island's yachting centre, lies on the mouth of the Medina. This world-famous sailing centre, base of the Royal Yacht Club and with several shipyards, reaches the highpoint of its year with Cowes Week, held on the first weekend in August, and the Admiral's Cup, held every two years. Cowes Castle, built by Henry VIII in 1540, is home to the Royal Yacht Squadron (1815), one of the most famous yacht clubs in the world.

★★**Osborne House**, the former summer residence of Queen Victoria, is situated in East Cowes. This complex of buildings was designed by Prince Albert and built by Thomas Cubitt between 1845 and 1848 in the style of an Italian villa as an asymmetrical site. After Albert's early death Queen Victoria frequently came here and it was at Osborne where she died in 1901. Most of the rooms have remained undisturbed since then. The state apartments, private rooms and the museum in the Swiss Cottage, imported from Switzerland for Albert and Victoria's children, can now be admired as reminders of the Victorian age.

The manor house of the neighbouring wine-producing estate ★**Barton Manor** dates originally partly from the 13th c. and partly from the 16th c. Prince Albert lent the estate, where royal guests of his time lodged, its Victorian flavour and had numerous trees and subtropical plants introduced into its extensive **garden**.

In 1976 Anthony and Alix Goddard began producing **wine** here (mainly from Müller-Thurgau, Gewürztraminer and Schönburger grapes) and now supply in a good year up to 30,000 bottles. Since 1992 a wine "méthode champenoise" has been one of the house's most recommendable products, and can be sampled at a wine tasting.

★**Norris Castle** lies about 1 mile from Osborne House. This Neo-Norman building was constructed in 1799 by James Wyatt for Lord Seymour. Princess Victoria and her mother stayed here in 1831 and 1833.

Quarr Abbey is soon reached by continuing further eastwards. It owes its name to the quarries which provided building material for, among others, Winchester Cathedral.

In 1911 a monastery for French Benedictine monks was built on the site of a demolished abbey dating from 1132. This masterpiece of Expressionist sacral architecture, built of red brick, was designed by Paul Bellot.

From Cowes a road leads via Fishbourne, at the mouth of Wootton Creek, to Ryde (pop. 24,000). The largest town on the island, it boasts wide sandy bays, a pier approximately ½ mile long and a wide variety of entertainments. The town's architecture remains mainly Victorian, and is dominated by the tall tower of All Saints' Church, completed in 1872 and the symbol of Ryde. As a terminal of the frequent ferries coming from the mainland, Ryde is very busy during summer. Out-of-season visitors are catered for by a heated open-air swimming pool.
Ryde

Excellent walks can be enjoyed from Ryde to various destinations, including **Seaview** (4 miles east), a small resort with a good beach and an iron pier 1000 ft long.

Bembridge, a well-kept seaside resort and sailing centre, with a windmill dating from 1700, is reached via St Helens. The Shipwreck Centre tells exciting tales of sunken ships. Pictures and manuscripts by John Ruskin (1819–1900) are displayed in the Ruskin Galleries.
Bembridge

A beautiful cliff walk leads to the **Foreland**, the island's most easterly point, and around Whitecliff Bay to **Culver Cliff**, where there is a statue of the first Earl of Yarborough, founder of the Royal Yacht Club.

Inside Brading's late-Gothic parish church, begun in 1200, there are numerous tombs, including that of Sir John Oglander. A gallery of wax-work figures in the half-timbered house opposite, once owned by Henry VIII, commemorates the island's illustrious guests, including Queen Victoria and the author George Bernard Shaw.
Brading

Near Brading are the remains, including a marvellous mosaic floor, of the largest ★**Roman villa** (3rd c.) on the island. **Nunwell House**, west of Brading, was the seat of the Oglander family after 1522. Sir John Oglander's memoirs of the Civil War and the imprisonment of King Charles I on the Isle of Wight are important reports of their time.

The largest seaside resort on the island is formed by the amalgamation of Sandown and Shanklin (combined pop. 20,500). Popular modern Sandown is especially recommended for children because of its gently sloping **beach**. The town has a golf course and a small zoo in the Victorian Fort Yaverland.
Sandown

The **Museum of Isle of Wight Geology** in the High Street contains an excellent collection of rocks and fossils.

Shanklin adjoins Sandown to the south and is a resort much favoured by artists. The town is idyllically situated in and around a valley. The picturesque Old Town is characterised by thatched cottages with enchanting little front gardens. Shanklin has a good beach, many sports and leisure facilities, and attractive promenade walks. The poet John Keats (1795–1821) lived in Englatine Cottage in the High Street in 1819, and the
★**Shanklin**

Shanklin: thatched cottages in the Old Town

American poet Henry Wadsworth Longfellow (1807–82) also liked to stay in Shanklin.

It is well worth visiting the impressive ravine and cliffs of ★**Shanklin Chine**, the island's longest gorge.

A pleasant walk from Shanklin to Ventnor (4 miles) passes through the village of **Bonchurch**. Both Charles Algernon Swinburne (1837–1909) and the author of the "Blue Lagoon", Henry de Vere Stacpole, grew up here. Both poets are buried in the churchyard of the New St Boniface Church.

★**Winterbourne Hotel** is a charming 18th c. house; Charles Dickens (see Famous People) completed "David Copperfield" here in the last century.

★ **Godshill**

It is also worth making a detour inland from Shanklin to Godshill (4 miles west). This small well-kept village has thatched stone houses, a Methodist chapel dating from 1838, a small natural history museum, a toy museum and medieval St Lawrence's Church (14th c.), with the tombs of members of the Worsley family, and a 15th/16th c. fresco in the South Chapel. The painting "Daniel in the Lions' Den" is probably the work of Rubens or one of his pupils.

Appuldurcombe House

Three-storeyed Appuldurcombe House, built in 1701 for Sir Robert Worsley and partly renovated in 1770 by James Wyatt, is reached by continuing through Godshill Park and across Stenbury Down. The most impressive manor house on the island before its destruction in the Second World War, it has been undergoing extensive renovation since 1988.

Ventnor

Ventnor (pop. 6250), situated on the coast only 3 miles from Shanklin, lies on a series of natural terraces above beautiful beaches. Sheltered on the north by limestone hills, it has the mildest climate on the island and is consequently reputed as an excellent health resort for lung conditions. The best view of the Victorian-style architecture of the town is gained from the pier. The marvellous Ventnor Botanical Gardens, with palms, a rose garden and a view of the Undercliff, a chalk and limestone plateau, are worth visiting. The History of Smuggling Museum in the botanical garden tells island tales dating back to the 13th c.

The steep clay, marl and chalk cliffs which extend along the south-west coastline from St Catherine's Point to Compton Chine are characterised by numerous chines. A good road leads from Ventnor via St Catherine's Point (views) and Blackgang Chine (leisure park) past many small farms and villages, offering many parking opportunites to stop and observe the geological phenomenon of crumbling layers of cliff. The road continues through Chale Bay, Brightstone Bay and Brook and finally arrives in the west at Compton Bay (marl cliffs) and at Freshwater Bay (chalk cliffs).

Freshwater Bay (pop. 5070) lies on the west coast and is a relaxing seaside resort with a beautiful bay. The poet Alfred Lord Tennyson (1809–92) lived here for more than 30 years. His house, in which he received such illustrious guests as Garibaldi, Lewis Carroll, Charles Darwin and the Prince Consort, is now a hotel, Farringford House. All Saints' Church (13th c., restored) has a beautiful late-14th c. brass of the knight Adam de Compton.

Freshwater

Along one of the island's most beautiful pathways from ★★**Freshwater Bay** to Alum Bay, walkers will pass the Tennyson memorial cross, which stands on the summit of High Down. From here there is an unforgettable view of the magnificent coatal scenery and the interplay of colour of the snow white chalk cliffs and the deep blue of the sea. Recommended in good weather is a boat trip to enjoy from the water the entrancing view of Freshwater Cliffs, which soar to heights of 400–500 ft.

Cliff scenery at Freshwater Bay in the Isle of Wight

Today a museum and centre for photography seminars, **Dimbola Lodge**, the house of the expert photographer Julia Margaret Cameron (1815–79), was frequented by the intellectual elite of Victorian England, among them Lord Alfred Tennyson, official poet laureat to Queen Victoria.

★★**Alum Bay**

Alum Bay is a Mecca for geologists: the almost vertical strata of sandstone here are beautifully coloured red, yellow, green and grey, and contrast strikingly with the white of the chalk cliffs. The foot of these steep cliffs can be reached by cable railway; excursion boats wait here for passengers.

★★**The Needles**

The bizarrely-shaped Needles, three massive offshore chalk rocks, lie off the west tip of the island and are an impressive sight. They reach a height of 100 ft. A good view of the Needles can be had from the "Needles Batteries", a fortress complex dating from the end of the 19th c., which was put into use in both First and Second World Wars.

★**Yarmouth**

Yarmouth (pop. 1000) lies on a plateau at the mouth of the West Yar River. It is a delightful village, with a ferry terminus for boats coming from Lymington, and a popular sailing centre.

Attractions include the ruins of a **fortress** (1538–47) with a wedge-shaped bastion dating from the reign of Henry VIII, a small town hall, rebuilt in 1763, and **St James' Parish Church**, with a memorial chapel to Sir Robert Holmes (d. 1692). In 1664 Holmes seized the Dutch possessions in North America, captured New York and became Governor of the Isle of Wight. He had the head of a captured statue of Louis XIV replaced with a sculpture of his own, and had it placed in the chapel for posterity.

Winchester   K 9

Southern England
County: Hampshire
Altitude: 128 ft. Population: 34,000

Winchester, the present county town of Hampshire, was the capital of England from Anglo-Saxon times until the 13th c. The ruins of the royal castle, numerous medieval buldings and one of Europe's longest cathedrals, constructed in the Neo-Gothic style, continue to bear witness to the former political and cultural centre of England, as do the town's achievements in book illumination, which include the unique Winchester Bible.

History The Romans named the town Venta Belgarum, but excavations have revealed the Celtic settlement of Caer Gwent, called the "White Town" after the surrounding chalk hills, which occupied the site since the Bronze Age. At the end of the 5th c. Saxon tribes penetrated the area, drove away the Celtic Britons and founded after 519, under the leadership of Cerdic (d. 534), the Kingdom of Wessex with the main town of Wintanceaster or Winton. During the following period the King of Wessex, mainly under Egbert in 825, assumed leadership of the seven kingdoms in Britain. After the conversion of the West Saxons by Bishop Birinus in 635 a bishop's see was established first in Dorchester in Oxfordshire and after 675 in Winchester. The cathedral was renovated several times in the 9th and 10th c., after which Winchester under Alfred the Great, the ruler of Wessex who was recognised throughout England as king (871–899), became the country's capital. The political importance of the town, coupled with a cultural heyday, was also preserved under the Norman kings, when William the Conqueror (see Famous People) had himself crowned both in London and in Winchester, and the crown jewels and the Domesday Book were kept in Winchester. Only during the reign of Henry III (1216–71) did London finally become the capital of the country. Winchester lost many privileges and sank into obscurity despite many attempts at revival. Arthur, the son and successor of Henry VIII (see Famous People), and Emperor Charles V held a great celebration in the town in 1522, and Charles II commissioned Christopher Wren in 1683 with the building of a royal palace, which was taken down, however, at the end of the 19th c.

The cathedral stands in the centre of the town and is surrounded by lawns. It was built on the site of previous constructions in the Romanesque-Norman style at the end of the 11th c., and was rendered Gothic from the end of the 12th c. until the end of the 14th c. After the Romanesque west front was torn down it was replaced by a façade with dainty flanking towers and a nine-columned tracery window (end 14th c.), which reflects the triple-aisled basilica. The foundations of the pre-ceeding 7th and 10th c. buildings can be seen north of the façade.

Sights
★★Winchester Cathedral

The **interior** makes a striking impact with the balance of its proportions and the successful combination of Romanesque sections of wall (1093) and late-Gothic fan vaulting (begun 1394), mainly in the twelve-bayed **nave** and in the transepts. The bronze statues (1635) of James I and Charles I near the entrance are the work of the sculptor Hubert Le Sueur (1610–43). A notable feature of the cathedral are the numerous **chantries**, funded by donations from allied chapel foundations, where masses were to be chanted. Those of Bishops William of Wykeham and William of Edington in the southern side aisle display Gothic ornamentation. In Prior Silkstede's chapel in the southern transept is the tomb of Isaac Walton (1593–1683), whose book "The Compleat Angler" continues to inspire anglers. The Neo-Gothic rood-screen (1875) was created by George G Scott.

The **Gallery** is reached via steps and through the magnificent wrought-iron grille, Pilgrim's Gate (11th c.). Beforehand it is worth looking at the choir with its wooden fan vaulting (1645) and the tomb of the unpopular William II or William Rufus (d. 1100), son of William the Conqueror. Along the sides of the choir can be seen the tombs of several Saxon and Danish kings, including those of Alfred the Great and his son Edward, as well as those of Canute the Great and his wife Emma. The **Choir** stalls with baldachins and 60 misericords were fashioned in 1310, the choir pulpit in 1520. The sculptured reredos communicates the air of of a typical English medieval sacristy, even if most of the figures were renewed in the 19th c. The richly-decorated chantry of Cardinal

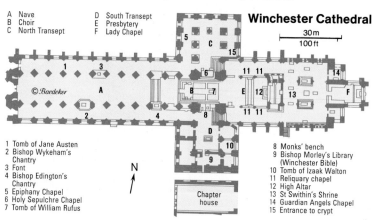

A Nave
B Choir
C North Transept
D South Transept
E Presbytery
F Lady Chapel

Winchester Cathedral

30 m
100 ft

© Baedeker

N

1 Tomb of Jane Austen
2 Bishop Wykeham's Chantry
3 Font
4 Bishop Edington's Chantry
5 Epiphany Chapel
6 Holy Sepulchre Chapel
7 Tomb of William Rufus

8 Monks' bench
9 Bishop Morley's Library (Winchester Bible)
10 Tomb of Izaak Walton
11 Reliquary chapel
12 High Altar
13 St Swithin's Shrine
14 Guardian Angels Chapel
15 Entrance to crypt

Chapter house

Beaufort (d. 1447), opponent of Joan of Arc, is situated in the south gallery. In the actual retrochoir rest the remains of St Swithin (d. 862), whose tomb was greatly revered in the Middle Ages. Bishop Langton (d. 1500) is interred in the south-east chantry. Murals dating from the 16th c. can be seen in the early 13th c. Lady Chapel. The paintings (about 1240, restored later) on the vaulting of the Chapel of the Guardian Angels provide examples of the original decoration; the tomb of the first Earl of Portland (d. 1636) is the work of Le Sueur. In the north ambulatory is the chapel in which Bishop Waynflete (d. 1486) is buried, a little further on is that of Bishop Gardiner with Renaissance decoration and a wooden chair, on which Mary Tudor (Bloody Mary) sat during her wedding with Phillip II of Spain in 1554. Steps lead to the northern transept, where on the left can be seen the Chapel of the Holy Sepulchre, with Romanesque wall-paintings (late 12th c.).

The **Font** of black Tournai marble (1180), decorated with scenes from the life of St Nicholas, stands in the middle of the north aisle.

A brass tablet marks the **Tomb of Jane Austen** (1775–1817), the priest's daughter whose humorous novels, with their lively descriptions of the landed upper middle-class, were not only highly treasured by her contemporaries but also by later writers.

The famous 12th c. ★**Winchester Bible** is kept in the cathedral library in the south transept. Its artistically pictured initials are some of the greatest achievements of book illumination created by the Winchester writing school.

Old Town

North of the cathedral precincts lies the City Museum, which documents the town's history. To the south, via the ruins of the cloister with a view of the imposing nave, whose supporting buttresses date from 1905, are reached the ruins of the medieval deanery and a charming half-timbered corner, which includes Pilgrim's Hall (late 13th c.) with its interesting

Jane Austen's tomb and the Lady Chapel, Winchester Cathedral

hammer-beamed ceiling. The King's Gate leads into College Street, where Wren constructed no. 26/27 as a residence for James II; Wren also built a residence in neighbouring Kingsgate Street for the Duke of Buckingham during the reign of Charles II. College Street continues to the main entrance to Winchester College, passing the house (no. 8) in which the novelist Jane Austen died.

Winchester College was founded in 1382 by William of Wykeham, Bishop of Winchester and has a close association with New College (1379) in Oxford (see entry). It is not only the oldest, but also the most spacious public school with 70 "scholars", who live in the college, and 500 "commoners", who attend daily from their homes. Construction of the college began in 1387, and it was opened in 1394. Two of the original houses, Flint Court and Chamber Court, have been preserved. Seventh Chamber is the oldest school-room in the country. The school chapel has retained its fan-vaulted timber roof, its medieval stained glass, a reredos (1500) and the misericords. Generations of scholars have engraved their names on the pillars of the cloisters. Among its famous old boys are the authors Edward Young (1682–1765) and Anthony Trollope (1815–82), Field Marshal Earl Archibald P. Wavell (1883–1950) and the Labour politician Hugh Gaitskill (1906–63). The War Memorial Cloister, entered from Kingsgate Street, was designed by Sir Herbert Baker in 1924.

College Street, with its view of the medieval wall encircling the cathedral precincts, leads to Wolvesey Palace, the remains of a bishop's palace (rebuilt by Wren), past the ruins of the castle and through attractive **Abbey Gardens**, relics of a 9th c. abbey founded by King Alfred's wife. It leads to the memorial (1901) to King Alfred the Great (871–899) in Broadway, and to the bridge over the Itchen. Near the river is an old mill (17th c.; youth hostel). A charming path continues on the other side of the river further south to **Catherine's Hill**, with the site of a fortress dating from the 3rd c. BC, the foundations of a chapel, and a turf maze over 82 ft long. Walk west from the river via Broadway, with the **Guild Hall** (1871–73, tourist information), the High Street and the pedestrian precinct, with its colonnade of shops, to the 15th c. Butter Cross, which features niches containing statues of saints, King Alfred and Bishop Wykeham. Continue uphill past the former Guild Hall (1713, bank) and the four-storeyed half-timbered Begot House to the impressive 13th c. **West Gate**, which houses a museum of weaponry.

The castle, of which only ruins remain, was built in 1067 during the reign of William the Conqueror, was demolished by parliament in 1644/1647 under the leadership of Oliver Cromwell (see Famous People), and was then completely restored by Wren in 1683 as a residence for Charles II. The regimental museums in the castle grounds document the period at the end of the 19th c. when the castle was used as barracks; the modern building houses the law courts. History has been made in Winchester Castle: at the church assembly held here at Easter 1072 the Archbishop of Canterbury (see entry) secured the precedence in the English church of York (see entry), William the Conqueror had the Treasury established and the Domesday Book kept safe here, and Richard the Lionheart came here in 1194 before his second coronation in the cathedral. The future King Henry III was born in the castle in 1207, Edward I held his first parliament here, and Sir Walter Raleigh was tried in the law hall for conspiring against James I.

Winchester Castle

Only the **Great Hall** (1236), with its columns of Purbeck marble, old stained glass windows and an open wooden roof truss, bears witness to the castle's great past, as does the legendary table-top on the back wall, at which King Arthur is supposed to have held his ★**Round Table**. The "Round Table", completed between 1250 and 1280, which served Edward I (1272–1307) for the glorification of his knighthood, was painted in the Tudor colours in 1522.

Windsor

Hospital of St Cross

England's oldest almshouse, situated about 1 mile south of the town centre, was founded in 1136 by Henry of Blois, Bishop of Winchester and grandson of William the Conqueror, for thirteen poor and pious men. Cardinal Beaufort extended the establishment in 1445 for impoverished nobles. The black robe with a silver crook cross and the purple-red with cardinal's emblem worn by the inhabitants continues to bear witness to the endowments, which at present care for 25 brothers. Their homes are grouped around an inner courtyard, entered through a gate house.

The 15th c. Hall of the Brothers and the kitchen, dating from a later period, should be visited, as should the chapel. The interior of this late Norman-early Gothic sacral building (east choir 1160, west choir 1290) is decorated in the Norman style, and has an original window decorated with a bird's beak in the north transept, and an oak lectern (1507) with a parrot and a heart, symbolising that the preachers of the gospel do not repeat themselves parrot-fashion, but should read with the heart.

At the exit of the Hospital of St Cross visitors can still request the traditional Wayfarers' Dole, a piece of bread and a tankard of beer.

Surroundings Chawton

Those interested in the authoress Jane Austen can visit her retirement home in Chawton (18 miles north-east), where she lived with her mother and her sister from 1809 to 1817. The more than 300-year-old, protected building is now a museum displaying manuscripts, illustrations and other **Austen memorabilia**.

Windsor   L 9

Central England
County: Berkshire
Altitude: 66 ft. Population: 26,300

The small town of Windsor lies on the south bank of the River Thames

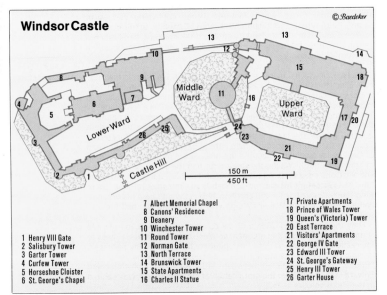

Windsor Castle

© Baedeker

1 Henry VIII Gate
2 Salisbury Tower
3 Garter Tower
4 Curfew Tower
5 Horseshoe Cloister
6 St. George's Chapel
7 Albert Memorial Chapel
8 Canons' Residence
9 Deanery
10 Winchester Tower
11 Round Tower
12 Norman Gate
13 North Terrace
14 Brunswick Tower
15 State Apartments
16 Charles II Statue
17 Private Apartments
18 Prince of Wales Tower
19 Queen's (Victoria) Tower
20 East Terrace
21 Visitors' Apartments
22 George IV Gate
23 Edward III Tower
24 St. George's Gateway
25 Henry III Tower
26 Garter House

Windsor Castle: the Lower Ward

about 22 miles west of London (see entry). It is dominated by its castle, built on a chalk hill, which for more than 900 years has served as the Royal Family's summer home. Windsor Castle is one of the world's most beautiful residences and is also its largest inhabited castle. The royal flag flutters from the top of the Round Tower whenever the Queen stays in Windsor. When she is not here the state apartments can be viewed.

About a dozen monarchs have either added to Windsor Castle or altered it. The founding of the present site dates from the time of Edward III, after William the Conqueror (see Famous People) had had the first castle built in 1078. Henry I, Henry II and Henry III had the castle strengthened by the addition of stone constructions and defensive fortifications. In 1189 the English barons laid siege to the castle and beat the Welsh troops of Prince John, the later King "John Lackland", who had to sign the Magna Carta in 1215 in nearby Runnymede. Edward III, who was born in Windsor, had the old fortress torn down and through William of Wykeham, Bishop of Winchester (see entry), had other fortifications and enlargements, including the Round Tower, carried out. Under Elizabeth I (see Famous People) the north terrace was added. During the reign of Charles II the picturesque castle site was transformed into a comfortable castle home, which following rulers, however, used only seldom. Renewed restoration work using plans drawn up by the architect Sir Geoffrey Wyattville followed under George IV, William IV and Victoria (see Famous People).

★★Windsor Castle

The cost of repairing the damage caused by an extensive fire at the end of 1992 has been estimated at millions of pounds, with the work probably taking several more years.

Edward III established at Windsor Castle in 1348 The Most Noble **Order of the Garter**, the kingdom's highest order. Only 26 knights or ladies may belong to it, although their number can be added to by "extra

The Royals

Has something happened to basic attitudes in Britain? You may well think so when you consider that many Britons now view their Royal family with something less than respect. Since 1992, the "annus horribilis" as the Queen coined it, when a newspaper survey found that 63% of readers would abolish the monarchy if they could, feelings about the royal family have reverted to being not quite so negative. However, merely the fact that such a matter is discussed openly reveals that the British are no longer such resolute supporters of their queen. Two matters in particular are a cause of concern – what do the Royals actually do, and why do they get so much money for it?

The monarch in fact has far less power today than in the past. The Queen could never play a decisive role in political decisions nowadays regardless of the fact that every official act takes place in her name and civil servants swear an oath to her and her descendants. She opens Parliament (with a speech written by the Prime Minister) and discusses the current political situation with him on Tuesdays at 6.30, and she is nominally the supreme commander of the army and head of the Church. On the other hand, she is certainly one of the best informed persons in the country and, unlike politicians, is not subject to the whims of the electorate. In fact, Queen Victoria reigned for over 60 years, George II for 26 years and Elizabeth II celebrated her forty-fifth year on the throne in 1997. The monarch thus symbolises continuity and reliability, features which have been augmented as the actual political power of the monarch has dwindled. Those who support the monarchy today support the British values which are anchored in its splendid history.

There still remains the question of what the Windsors actually do. The Royals' schedules are published daily. The "firm", as Prince Philip rather disrespectfully calls his family, mainly has the job of representation, and not just at major functions: the Queen invites holders of the Order of Merit to lunch, the Prince Consort opens an exhibition, the Prince of Wales unveils a monument, Princess Anne visits a stud, the Duke of York inspects a warship. The other members of the main family – the Queen Mother, Princess Margaret, the Kents and the Gloucesters – are all active as well and generally attend several appointments each day. On such occasions it is clear that the royal family is very popular among the "small" people in particular and everybody, even loyal supporters of Labour, has great respect for the Queen herself. Despite the fact that the Left is purported to be the traditional enemy of the monarchy, Labour's new education programme has merited a nod of approval and a supportive interview from Prince Charles. Nevertheless, Tony Blair will no doubt enquire about the cost-benefit effects of royal activities.

The Royals do cost the British taxpayer a large amount of money. With an estimated private income of £6.5 billion, the Queen is the richest woman in the world. Yet she pays none of her representation expenses. The 400 employees at Buckingham Palace like the footman who takes the Queen's seven corgies and a dachshund for walks, or the Scottish pipe major who circles beneath the Queen's breakfast room playing his bagpipes, the new Royal Yacht, the Royal Train, the Royal Air Force – three aeroplanes and two helicopters – and even the royal palaces: this and still more – over £50m – is paid for out of the public budget. The Queen only runs Balmoral and Sandringham, although the heating bills are paid by the Ministry of the Environment. On the question of money, her subjects' views are clear – many want to abolish all subsidies to the Royals.

The unfortunate love lives and marriages of the Windsors have contributed to bringing about these harsh views, every lurid detail garnished with all manner of speculation being dished up to avid readers by the "royal watchers", journalists employed by the mass-circulation papers to follow the royal family. However civilised the divorces of the Queen's sister Margaret and daughter Anne were, the princes caused a stir: the poker-stiff, heartless Charles was said to mistreat the frail, desperately unhappy Di and be much happier with his polo ponies than with her, and Andrew, called "Randy Andy" because of his eventful past, was deceived by his wife Fergie with a Texan millionaire pictured sucking her big toe. However amusing this may sound, the shamelessness with which the press markets even the smuttiest details and most compromising photos, and the apparent inability of the young royals to get their lives under control are clear signs of the deterioration in the royal reputation.

There used to be more of them – the Royals on the balcony at Buckingham Palace

The unemotional reaction of the Royal family to the death of Princess Diana was also criticised, yet the Queen battles on. Since 1994 she has been paying tax, Anne has married again, Andrew has got divorced, but Charles does not want to give up Camilla Parker Bowles, despite the Queen's wishes. So the Royals have demonstrated that they too are only human. Yet for most Britons they still represent something more than a folklore troop which squanders taxes and functions at best as a tourist attraction. The way for a good subject to act was described by the constitutional theorist Sir Walter Bagehot back in 1867: "Above all things our royalty is to be reverenced, and if you begin to poke about it you cannot reverence it ... Its mystery is its life. We must not let in daylight upon magic."

knights". The order is thought to have been founded at a festival at which a lady of the court lost her garter. This resulted in much laughter and caused Edward to remark that shortly it would be an honour for his knights to receive such a garter. The Most Noble Order of the Garter was an attempt (following King Arthur's Round Table) at the end of the Middle Ages, when the knighthood was already in decline, to establish a select group of brave men and women, who would protect the knightly virtues. The order's insignia comprises on celebratory occasions a chain with the inscription "The George", and at certain events a ribbon with the motto "Honi soit qui mal y pense" (Evil be (to him) who thinks evil of this), which men wear below their left knee and women on their left upper arm.

The castle is built around two courtyards, the **Upper Ward** and the **Lower Ward**, with the Round Tower between them in the Middle Ward. Entrance to the site is through the monumental Henry VIII's Gateway, erected by Henry VIII (see Famous People) in 1511 and displaying elements of Tudor style.

The gateway leads into the Lower Ward, on the far side of which is ★**St George's Chapel**. The chapel of the Knights of the Order of the Garter, it is dedicated to their patron saint, St George. Begun by Edward IV in 1474 and completed by Henry VIII, St George's Chapel is one of the finest examples of late Perpendicular architecture. The façades are decorated with heraldic animals and shields of the ruling houses of Lancaster and York. In the north there are falcons, deer, bulls, black dragons, hinds and greyhounds for the Yorks, in the south lions, unicorns, swans, antelope, panthers and red dragons for the Lancasters. The fan-vaulting in the nave and in the choir is impressive. The stained glass west window (1503–09) features 75 figures, representing the community of the church and the state. The chapel has numerous monuments and many tombs of the English Royal Family and the nobility; the north aisle contains, among others, the tombs of George V and Queen Mary.

Changing of the Guard at Windsor Castle

Windsor: Queen Victoria's monument

Statue of Prince George of Denmark

Of particular splendour in the choir are the stalls (1478–85), carved from Windsor oak, of the Knights of the Order of the Garter, which depict scenes from the life of St George. Behind and above the stalls can be seen the coats of arms, banners and decorative plumes of 700 Knights of the Order. Henry VIII and Jane Seymour, and Charles I are interred in the vault beneath the choir, while Henry VI, Edward IV and his wife, and Edward VII and Queen Alexandra are buried in the sacristy.

The ⋆**Albert Memorial Chapel** was built by Henry VII in 1500 to contain his own tomb, but was not used for this purpose (Henry VII is buried in Westminster Abbey in London (see entry)). Since 1861 the chapel has been dedicated to the memory of Queen Victoria's husband. The interior is elaborately decorated with coloured marble, mosaics and sculptures, and contains the porphyry sarcophagus of the Duke of Clarence (1864–92), the eldest son of Edward VII; the marble figure on the west door depicts the Duke of Albany (d. 1884) wearing Scottish costume.

On the south side of the Lower Ward are the houses of the Military Knights of Windsor, who belong to The Most Noble Order of the Garter. The **Horseshoe Cloisters** (named after their shape) were built between 1479 and 1481 in the half-timbered style. Dean's Cloisters and Canons' Cloisters, the former homes of the dean and the canons, are also very picturesque.

On the north terrace, from which there are fine views, is the entrance to the ⋆**State Apartments**. The rooms were extensively restored by Wyattville; several of them, including the reception room, the Queen's Gallery and the dining hall, have magnificently painted ceilings, the work of Antonio Verno, and wood-carving by Grinling Gibbons. Art treasures found here include a large picture collection (featuring Holbein, Leonardo da Vinci, Raphael, Michelangelo, van Dyck, Rubens, Rembrandt and Canaletto), valuable period furniture and weapons, including, in the Grand Vestibule, the bullet which killed Lord Nelson (see Famous People) in the Battle of Trafalgar. There are also exquisite

French tapestries, porcelain, and glass and silverware. The great fire of 1992 destroyed St George's Hall.

A visit should also be paid to ★**Queen Mary's Dolls' House**, a masterpiece of craftsmanship presented to Queen Mary in 1924.

The **Round Tower**, surrounded on three sides by a deep moat, was originally built by Henry II, and raised to twice its height by Wyattville in 1830. The climb up to a 79 ft-high viewing platform is rewarded by a marvellous panoramic view.

Home Park encloses Windsor Castle to the north and east. Inside the park stand Frogmore House and Mausoleum, in which Queen Victoria is buried together with Prince Albert. **Windsor Great Park** extends along the south side of the castle for 5½ miles and has an impressive stock of red deer.

Town of Windsor

The town of Windsor (pop. 30,000), with its old half-timbered houses and 17th and 18th c. inns, winding alleyways and cobbles, retains in its centre a picturesque medieval appearance. Begun in 1687, the Guildhall was completed by Christopher Wren. Its south face is embellished with a statue of Prince George of Denmark, husband of Queen Anne. The bronze monument to Queen Victoria on Castle Hill was unveiled in 1887.

In 1897 Queen Victoria observed her 60th anniversary as monarch. This event is commemorated by the audio-visual show **"Royalty and Empire"**, situated in Windsor's old railway station. Madame Tussaud's wax figures, old coaches and the Royal Carriage can be seen here.

Inside the Royal Mews in St Albans Street, south of the castle, are displayed some of the **gifts** which have been given to Queen Elizabeth II during her reign. The coach house contains a number of **royal coaches**.

Surroundings
Old Windsor

Old Windsor, 1½ miles south-east, was the seat of the Saxon kings; excavations have uncovered the remains of a building which was probably the palace of Edward the Confessor.

Ascot

Ascot (pop. 7500) lies at the end of Windsor Great Park. For eleven months of the year this small town sleeps, but comes into its own in June with Ascot Week, the great racing occasion which draws many thousands of visitors and is attended by the Royal Family, who drive from Windsor Castle in a procession.

Trips on the
Thames

From Windsor it is possible to undertake several charming trips along the Thames. The Thames is not a monotonous river, but continually branches off and forms islets, resulting in lively parkland scenery. Launches not only take passengers into London, but also to Kingston upon Thames, within the precincts of London (journey time approximately five hours).

To reach Oxford (about 70 miles north-west) it is a two-day journey through very charming scenery. The launches only travel by day, passengers can stay overnight in Wallingford or Henley.

Henley-on-
Thames

Henley-on-Thames occupies an idyllic position on the river between wooded hills, and is famous for the Royal Regatta, which has taken place in the first week of July since its inauguration by Prince Albert in 1839, and which is one of the great social events of the London season. Another traditional ceremony is "swan-upping" in the third week of July. The town has an 18th c. bridge, which spans the wide curve of the Thames, and a row of handsome Georgian houses.

Eton

The small town of Eton (pop. 4500), with the world-famous ★★**Eton College**, is situated on the north side of Windsor Bridge.

Choice of school plays a far greater role in England than in other European countries; those graduating from the "right" school can later find this a decisive factor both socially and in their careers. Eton College is synonymous with English education at its best. Founded in 1440 by

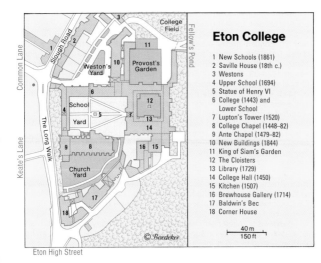

Eton College

1 New Schools (1861)
2 Saville House (18th c.)
3 Westons
4 Upper School (1694)
5 Statue of Henry VI
6 College (1443) and
  Lower School
7 Lupton's Tower (1520)
8 College Chapel (1448–82)
9 Ante Chapel (1479–82)
10 New Buildings (1844)
11 King of Siam's Garden
12 The Cloisters
13 Library (1729)
14 College Hall (1450)
15 Kitchen (1507)
16 Brewhouse Gallery (1714)
17 Baldwin's Bec
18 Corner House

Henry VI, it is the British public school most steeped in tradition. The pupils comprise 70 "collegers", whose position at top of their class entitles them to free study and accommodation, and rather more than 1000 "oppidans" (day boys), who pay fees and live in halls of residence or guest-houses, often supervised by teachers or lecturers. All pupils wear

Eton College

a uniform: cutaway coat and striped trousers. Many very influential men have attended Eton, including Henry Fielding, William Pitt, Percy B. Shelley, William Gladstone, the Duke of Wellington (see Famous People) and 20 English prime ministers. The red-brick main building, which dates from the school's founding, extends around two quadrangles. Most of the buildings opposite are new. The Lower School was established 1624–39, the Upper School between 1689 and 1692. The school chapel is particularly remarkable. Completed in the Perpendicular style in 1441, it is actually only the choir of a church planned to be almost twice this size. It contains old brass plates and, more importantly, some wonderful grisaille paintings (1470–90), depicting scenes from the life of Mary. These were painted over in the second half of the 16th c., but were later restored. A bronze statue of Henry VI stands in the school quadrangle, the work of Francis Bird (1719). A passageway leads from Lupton's Tower (1520) to the cloisters with the hall (1450) and the library (1729).

Runnymede

Runnymede (3 miles south-east) is the name of the small meadow where King John signed the Magna Carta in 1215. There is now a Magna Carta Memorial, and the place attracts large numbers of visitors.

Maidenhead

Maidenhead (6 miles north-west) is a popular holiday resort with many boat clubs. Its railway bridge, opened in 1838, is borne by brick arches with spans up to 131 ft in width.

The Edwardian **Henry Reitlinger Bequest** building houses a notable collection of European and Oriental ceramics.

About 2 miles upstream **Cliveden House** stands high above the river. Until 1966 it was the seat of the Astor family, who bequeathed it to the National Trust in 1942. Since 1986 it has also operated as a hotel. The house is surrounded by Cliveden Woods, charming riverside woods on the Buckinghamshire bank of the Thames.

Burnham Beeches is an attractive area of woodland and heath near Maidenhead, which was bought by the City of London Corporation in 1879 as a place of recreation for Londoners. Dorney Wood, also popular with nature-lovers, has recently been added to it.

Stoke Poges

Stoke Poges (4 miles north) is a place of pilgrimage. Thomas Grey (1716–71) is buried in the attractive churchyard, a statue by Wyatt marking his grave. The landscape which inspired Gray to write his "Elegy Written in a Country Churchyard" has hardly altered. In the church the "Bicycle Window", depicting a man riding a bicycle, should be seen.

Worcester   I 8

Central England. County: Hereford and Worcester
Altitude: 98 ft. Population: 75,000

The town of Worcester lies mainly on the east bank of the River Severn. It is famed both for its piquant Worcestershire Sauce and for its porcelain, which has been manufactured here since 1750. In addition, this county town also possesses a beautiful cathedral and was the site of the last battle between the supporters of the future Charles II and Oliver Cromwell's troops (see Famous People). Unfortunately the town has lost much of its charm as a result of industry and modern development. Its main products, apart from its famous sauce and its porcelain, are gloves (the remnants of a once great textile industry) and metal products.

History The Anglo-Saxons took over a Roman settlement and named it "Wigorna Ceaster". In 680 it became an episcopal see. Bishop Oswald founded the Benedictine abbey here in the 10th c. Worcester was the first town to declare itself for Charles I in the Civil War, and the last to surrender to Cromwell after the war's last battle. This took place on September 3rd 1651 some distance from the town, in which the future Charles II had set up his headquarters. On the same night the king began his flight which ultimately led him to France.

The best view of the cathedral is from the far bank of the Severn. Built of red sandstone, it's exterior was considerably altered during the course of restoration work carried out by Sir George Gilbert Scott between 1857 and 1873. Despite this, the cathedral continues to display all forms of style ranging from Norman to late Perpendicular. During the 10th c. Bishop Oswald built a church on the site of an Anglo-Saxon predecessor. The church was affected so detrimentally by Danish attacks, however, that Bishop Wulfstan (bishop from 1062 until 1095) had it torn down, and a new Norman-style cathedral erected. Of this, following a fire, only the crypt, two niches in the nave, and parts of the walls survive. The choir and the Lady Chapel were built between 1224 and 1260 thanks to generous donations from pilgrims. The north side of the aisle is Decorated, the south side Perpendicular. The central tower, completed in 1347, shows the transition from Decorated to Perpendicular.

Sights
★Worcester Cathedral

No other English church can compete with the continuous, 387 ft-long, vaulting of the otherwise varied **interior**. Bishops' tombs dating from various eras can be found in the side aisles. The ★**Choir** is in the purest Early English style. As at Salisbury (see entry), the slender pillars of Purbeck marble, with their beautifully carved capitals and notable bosses, make an important contribution to the total effect. The choir-stalls (1379) have richly decorated misericords. The central feature of the choir is the tomb of King John ("John Lackland"), who died in Newark in 1216 and who had requested to be buried here. His effigy in Purbeck marble, which dates from about 1240, is believed to be the earliest portrait of an English king, and is the only remaining part of the original tomb. On either side of his head stand sculptures of canonised bishops Oswald and Wulfstan; the lion biting into the tip of the royal sword refers to the loss of power the king had to accept with the signing of the Magna Carta. Prince Arthur, the eldest son of Henry VII, who died in Ludlow in 1502 aged seventeen, is buried in a richly decorated Perpendicular chapel on the right behind King John's tomb. The Lady Chapel not only contains the tombs of bishops Blois and Cantelupe (13th c.), but also a tablet commemorating Isaac Walton's second wife, Anne. Walton (1593–1683) was an important biographer of his time; however, it was not this, but his standard work "The Compleat Angler", still read today, which earned him the highest admiration from disciples of St Peter (i.e. fishermen).

The **Crypt** (1084–92), a relic of the Norman cathedral, has 50 elegant pillars. Here as in the cloister (Perpendicular) the vault has fine bosses. The Tree of Jesse, and angels praying to Mary and her child are portrayed in the **Cloister**.

The **Chapterhouse** is one of the earliest examples of vaulting borne on a single central pillar. The original circular construction dates from 1150, it gained its decagonal exterior in about 1400. The principal relic of the monastic buildings is the **Refectory**, a large hall with a Norman crypt under it. It is now used as the hall of the King's School, which was founded in 1541.

South-east of the cathedral, on the bank of the Worcester-Birmingham Canal, lies the Commandery. It is an impressive Tudor house, built on the site of an old hospital founded by St Wulfstan in 1085. In 1545 it came into the ownership of the Wylde family, and was Charles II's headquarters in 1651 during the deciding battle against Cromwell. The final conflicts raged very close to the house; the Duke of Hamilton, leader of the royalists, was wounded in them, and died in one of the rooms of the Commandery. The Civil War Centre, based in the Commandery, illus-

★Commandery

trates by means of modern audio-visual techniques the cause and the course of the Civil War in England.

★ Royal Worcester Porcelain

Not far south of the cathedral can be found the production site of the royal porcelain manufacturers, founded in 1750, which can be visited. The affiliated Dyson Perrins Museum displays many of the factory's most beautiful pieces.

Tudor House Museum

A 16th c. half-timbered house in Friar Street contains a museum, which, in contrast to its name, documents family life in Victorian Worcester. Nearby stands the very beautifully restored, medieval Greyfriars House.

Guildhall

The imposing Guildhall stands in the High Street. It was built between 1721 and 1723 by Thomas White, a pupil of Wren. Statues of Charles I and Charles II flank the entrance, with their enemy Cromwell hanging by his ears above the door.

King Charles House

Charles II spent the night before the battle in house no. 29, New Street, at the corner of Cornmarket. After the battle had been lost he fled via the back door.

City Museum & Art Gallery

This house in Foregate Street displays art exhibitions and also has departments devoted to natural history, to daily life, and to two old Worcestershire regiments.

**Surroundings
Lower
Broadheath**

The famous composer Sir Edward Elgar (1857–1934), who died in Worcester, was born in Lower Broadheath (3 miles west), near the Terne Valley. The house in which he was born is now open to the public as a museum.

Spetchley Park

Spetchley Park (3 miles south-east) offers pleasantly relaxing walks. It is home to both red deer and fallow deer.

Evesham

Evesham (16 miles south-east) is a pleasant town on both banks of the Avon, in a region famous for its fruit and vegetables. The town has many half-timbered houses. Only the bell-tower (1533) and a gateway remain of a Benedictine abbey founded in 701.

Pershore

Pershore, on the north bank of the Avon, is passed on the way to Evesham. The river is spanned here by a six-arched medieval bridge. The town has preserved a largely Georgian character. The abbey church, originally a Benedictine monastery, has a fine lantern-tower (about 1320), a Norman south transept and a Norman crossing. The choir is Early English, with beautiful vaulting.

Malvern

Malvern (8 miles south-west) occupies an ideal situation on the lower slopes of the Malvern Hills and is one of the most popular spa resorts in England. It consists of several different parts, the centre being Great Malvern.

Despite their relatively moderate height (1000 ft–1400 ft) the ★ **Malvern Hills** offer marvellous views. Their highest point is Worcester Beacon (1395 ft), from which there is an extensive view across the plain and on to Worcester Cathedral, Gloucester and Hereford (see entries). There is a fine walk from Worcester Beacon along the ridge to the Hertfordshire Beacon, with remains of a hill-fort.

In **Great Malvern**, as in the other parts of the town, there are a number of very attractive Victorian houses. The Priory Church, which once belonged to a Benedictine monastery founded by Wulfstan in 1085, has a Perpendicular-style exterior. The nave and some other parts of the interior are early Norman. The tower is modelled on the tower of Gloucester Cathedral. The church is famous for its 15th and 16th c. stained glass windows. The window in the north transept depicts Prince Arthur.

Lower Brockhampton Hall, a moated manor house, lies 8 miles west of
Worcester. A very attractive 14th c. half-timbered building, it has a separate gatehouse. Birtsmoreton Court, 7 miles east, is another moated
manor house.

York   K 7

Northern England
Unitary Authority of York
Altitude: 57 ft. Population: 123,000

York is the former centre of the largest county in Great Britain
(Yorkshire). Although Yorkshire was divided into four individual counties
in 1974, York continues to be the capital city of the north of England,
the counterpart of London. York is also the ecclesiastical capital of the
Church of England, the archbishop of York being second only to the
archbishop of Canterbury (see entry) in the Anglican Church. The Lord
Mayor of this both medieval and modern town also has a special status,
sharing only with the Lord Mayor of London the honorific prefix of
"Right Honorable". The title of the Duke of York is traditionally awarded
to the second eldest son of the Sovereign.

York's fame rests on its amazing sights. York Minster is the largest

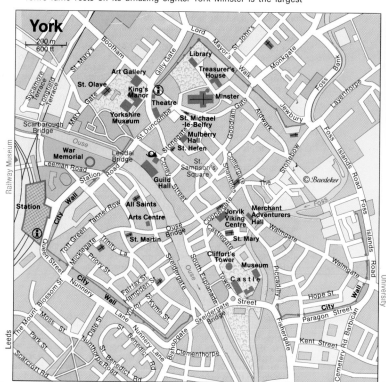

medieval church in England and beyond question one of the most beautiful. Its large amount of medieval stained glass is unique. The townscape is characterised by magnificent half-timbered constructions, three medieval guildhalls, numerous churches and public buildings, and romantic streets. York also has the longest circuit of medieval town walls, approximately 3 miles long. The walls offer a pleasant walk with marvellous views of the city. Several excellent museums enrich the cultural life of the city.

In contrast to other towns, the streets in York are often called "gates" (Stonegate, Petergate, etc.), as in parts of Scandinavia. This is a relic of the Danish occupation. The word which actually means "gate" in other places in England is "bar" in York.

History York was founded by the Romans in AD 71 and called Eburacum. It was the seat of the Ninth and subsequently the Sixth Legion (with 5600 men), and also one of the important military and trading bases in the north of England near the Scottish border. The Romans never succeeded in occupying Scotland. In the 2nd c. Eburacum became a "colonia", an important veteran town and a major cultural centre. Emperor Hadrian visited the town, and two other emperors died here while on visits: Severus in 211, and Constantius Chlorus in 306. The latter's son, Constantine the Great, was proclaimed emperor in Eburacum. Under the Saxons the town, now known as Eofirwic, developed its strategic function. It became both the capital of the Anglian kingdom of Deirta and, as the see of a bishop after 625, its spiritual centre, from which Christianity spread throughout the north of England. Under Alcuin or Ealhwine (735–804) the monastic school gained an international reputation. Alcuin was even summoned by Charlemagne to advise him on the establishment of schools in the Frankish kingdom. After numerous attacks the Vikings finally conquered the town in 866, and made it into their headquarters. They named it Jorvik, from which its present name is derived. The Normans arrived about 200 years after the Vikings, broke the resistance of its citizens and razed the town to the ground. As a result of this none of York's historical buildings is more than 900 years old. After reconstruction York shone even more magnificently than before.

During the Middle Ages York achieved prosperity as a centre of wool-weaving and the cloth trade, as well as through its trade as an international port. The Plantaganet kings, particularly Richard II, used their powers to promote the town. Edward III (1327–77) was the first to bestow the title of Duke of York on one of his younger sons, whose grandson, Duke Richard (1416–60), began the War of the Roses against the House of Lancaster, after they had ruled since 1399. His son ascended the English throne in 1461 as Edward IV, of the House of York. He was succeeded in 1483 by his brother, Richard III, who, two years later, was deposed by the usurper Henry Tudor (Henry VII). During the turmoil of the Reformation a number of the town's churches fell into neglect. Cromwell laid siege to the town during the Civil War, but was able to come to a peaceful agreement with its leaders. The Industrial Revolution passed York by without trace. The coming of the railway finally effected the town's economic growth, which has been continued by the arrival of more than three million tourists a year.

Sights

★★York Minster

The imposing Minster – the name means a monastic church – commemorates the monks who converted those living in the surrounding countryside to Christianity. York Minster is dedicated to St Peter and is worthy of its important diocese, whose bishops sat on the council at Arles in 314. After this its history became shrouded in silence. It was not until the turmoil of the period of the migration of the peoples that the oldest documented (wooden) church was built here for the baptism of

York Minster: the Nave

King Edwin of Northumbria in 627. Succeeding Saxon and Norman constructions were destroyed, and the present cathedral was built in the Gothic style after the 13th c.

The main door in the west front leads into the **Nave**, begun in 1291 and completed after 1350 in the high Gothic style. One of Europe's widest Gothic naves, its wooden vaulting imitates the stone vault which was intended. The central axis is embellished with carved keystones depicting scenes from the lives of Christ and Mary. The impressive eight-columned tracery window (1338) in the west front is inset with a sacral heart (Heart of Yorkshire), the work of the master Robert Ketelbarn, and portrays scenes from the New Testament, as well as apostles and bishops. The shields fixed along the walls of the nave commemorate the nobles who supported Edward I and Edward II in their wars against Scotland. The dragon's head projecting from the gallery is part of a levering device used to raise the cover of the font.

Side Aisles In the north (left-hand) aisle the chapel door, decorated with 14th c. sculptures, in the second bay is notable. A little further along, the Pilgrimage Window (about 1312) can be found above the dragon's head. It shows Peter surrounded by pilgrims, and has some unusual details, such as a cock reading and the funeral of a monkey. Next to this is the radiant 14th c. Bellfounders' Window with its relevant motifs. The Jesse Window (about 1310) in the third bay of the south (right-hand) aisle is also remarkable. It depicts the forerunners of Jesus, including David, Solomon and prophets.

The triple-naved **Choir aisle** was built in the English early Gothic style between 1220 and 1280. The back wall of the north transept features five narrow lancet windows (about 1260). Named the Five Sisters Window by Charles Dickens, its decorative grisaille glass continually fascinates visitors. Continue across the crossing, with its 15th c. vaulted tower, to the

York Minster

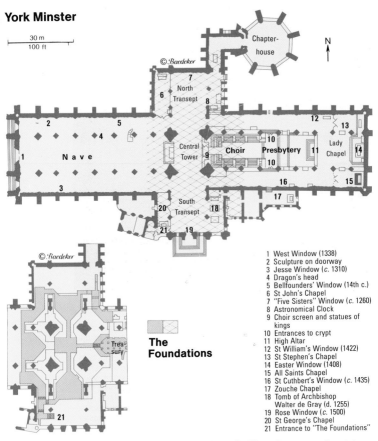

30 m
100 ft

© Baedeker

N

Chapter-house

7

6 North Transept

8

2

5

12

13

4

Central Tower

Choir

Presbytery

11

Lady Chapel

14

1

Nave

9

10

10

16

15

3

South Transept

17

20

18

21

19

© Baedeker

Trea-sury

21

The Foundations

1 West Window (1338)
2 Sculpture on doorway
3 Jesse Window (c. 1310)
4 Dragon's head
5 Bellfounders' Window (14th c.)
6 St John's Chapel
7 "Five Sisters" Window (c. 1260)
8 Astronomical Clock
9 Choir screen and statues of kings
10 Entrances to crypt
11 High Altar
12 St William's Window (1422)
13 St Stephen's Chapel
14 Easter Window (1408)
15 All Saints Chapel
16 St Cuthbert's Window (c. 1435)
17 Zouche Chapel
18 Tomb of Archbishop Walter de Gray (d. 1255)
19 Rose Window (c. 1500)
20 St George's Chapel
21 Entrance to "The Foundations"

rood-screen. This masterpiece of late Gothic sculpture contains statues of fifteen English kings, starting with William I on the left and finishing with Henry VI on the right.

The cathedral's Norman **Choir** was rebuilt in the late 14th c. After a fire in 1829 destroyed the roof and the woodwork (including the choir stalls) they were replaced by copies of the originals. The high altar dates from 1938. St William's Window (1422) in the south gallery depicts scenes from the life of St William, whose shrine in the sacristy was worshipped in the Middle Ages. William Fitzherbert was created Archbishop of York by Pope Eugene III in 1143, was unfairly relieved of his office in 1147, but was reinstated in 1153. During Fitzherbert's triumphal return to York in 1154 the bridge across the Ouse broke under the weight of the specta-tors, but as no one was injured this was taken as a sign of the holiness of the archbishop and he was canonised in 1227. St Cuthbert's Window (about 1435) in the north gallery of the choir forms a counterpart to St William's Window. It portrays events in the life of this saint who was consecrated as archbishop in 685 in the Saxon minster. Behind the choir is the Lady Chapel, with its magnificent east window (about 1408).

Possibly the largest medieval stained glass window in the world, it illustrates parts of the Old Testament. When entering the south transept, which was very badly damaged by fire in 1984, note the marvellous rose window (about 1500). This commemorates the ending of the War of the Roses, fought between the Houses of Lancaster and York for the right of succession to the throne, with the marriage of Henry VII and Elizabeth of York. The tomb of Archbishop Walter de Gray (d. 1255) in the middle chapel is a dignified baldachin tomb featuring a reclining high Gothic figure.

The 12th c. Norman **Crypt** is entered from the presbytery. Here can be seen the remains of the 11th c. apse of the preceeding cathedral, as well as parts of the Eastern Crypt (14th c.). The crypt's valuable contents include the York Virgin (12th c. madonna), the Doomstone (purgatory relief, late 12th c.), decorated 12th c. capitals, the 15th c. font used for the baptism of King Edwin by Bishop Paulinus in 627, and the shrine of St William of York (archbishop, d. 1154), which was brought here in 1972.

Excavations carried out from 1967 to 1972 to strengthen the ★**foundations** of the cathedral around the central tower revealed extensive Roman and Anglo-Saxon structures. After the completion of the work this area was fitted out as a museum and a treasury, containing numerous precious objects including the Horn of Ulf (about 1020) and liturgical utensils dating from the Middle Ages and early modern times.

The vestibule of the ★**Chapterhouse** is reached from the north transept. On entering this part of the cathedral visitors will immediately notice to their left a window (about 1300) depicting kings and queens, and the richly-decorated capitals. The flaying of St Bartholomew can be seen on a capital to the right of the 13th c. door with interlaced decoration leading to the octagonal Chapterhouse (1260–85). The painted woooden vaulted roof (65½ ft in diameter) is self-supporting and was renewed first in 1798 and again in 1976. The fine stall-canopies are impressive, as are the tracery windows, whose glass dates partly from the 13th/14th c. and through which much light pours.

Among the interesting buildings to be found in the cathedral close are half-timbered St William's College (15th c., exhibition on the history of the Minster), the Treasurer's House (17th c. house belonging to the cathedral's treasurer containing numerous antiques) and the Minster Library, which is housed in a 12th/13th c. chapel and has many valuable books and manuscripts. On the south side of the Minster is the church of St Michael-le-Belfrey (rebuilt 1536), which has interesting stained glass windows. A 4th c. Roman column standing behind it commemorates the day when Constantine was proclaimed Roman emperor in York in 306.

★The Minster Close

From the west front of the Minster Duncombe Place leads to the **Museum Gardens**, in which are the remains of St Leonard's Hospital (11th c.) and parts of the Roman fortress with the Multangular Tower, to which the medieval town walls were joined.

★Old Town

The Yorkshire Museum contains important archaeological (mainly Roman and Anglo-Saxon finds), and geological and natural history collections. Medieval sculptures and utensils are exhibited in another branch of the museum including parts of the building of St Mary's Abbey, founded in 1098. The Hospitium (abbey guest house) near the River Ouse has survived. King's Manor (16th/17th c.), where Henry VIII, James I and Charles I stayed when visiting York, has been beautifully restored and now belongs to the university. The City of York Art Gallery in Exhibition Square has a collection of English and European paintings dating from the Middle Ages to modern times. Bootham Bar is one of the medieval city gates. Some attractive Georgian buildings, such as Bootham School, St Peter's School and Ingram's Hospital (1640) stand in the street of the same name.

Yorkshire Museum, City of York Art Gallery

York

York: St William's College

Theatre Royal, ★Stonegate	Follow St Leonard's Place, with its attractive Georgian town residences, past the Theatre Royal, where the actress Sarah Siddons enjoyed great success, and on to Blake Street, site of the elegant 18th c. Assembly Rooms, designed in Neo-Classical style between 1730 and 1736 by Richard Boyle. From here the area between Coney Street and King's Square is a pedestrianised shopping quarter. Nearby St Helen's Church, named in honour of the mother of Emperor Constantine and with 15th c. stained glass windows, and attractive medieval Stonegate are further architectural highlights, as is the Mansion House, designed by Lord Burlington and built in 1725, now the official residence of the Lord Mayor. A gateway gives access to the Guildhall (1449–59, rebuilt after war damage) on the banks of the River Ouse. Other churches worth visiting are St Martin-le-Grand in Coney Street (charming mixture of medieval and modern architecture; Martin's Window), and, a little further away, St Michael's in Spurriergate, which features 12th c. arcades, glass paintings and an 18th c. altarpiece.
All Saints, ★Shambles	All Saints, Pavement, is an old guild church with 14th c. glass paintings, a 16th c. roof, a 17th c. pulpit and interesting tombstones. One road away is the Shambles (derived from the window-sills which were called "shambles"), a narrow dark street of old houses where butchers used to sell their wares, but which is now home to antiques and souvenir shops. King's Square leads to Goodramgate and attractive little Trinity Church (14th c.), with its small garden.
Merchant Taylor's Hall	Bedern Street leads off from Goodramgate and contains 14th c. Bedern Hall, the former dining hall of the choristers. Merchant Taylors' Hall (late 14th c.), the guildhall of the cloth merchants, is situated in Aldwark. At the end of Aldwark is another medieval guildhall, St Anthony's Hall.

Follow The Stonebow past the half-timbered Black Swan Inn (15th c.) to Piccadilly. Here stands Merchant Adventurers' Hall (1357–68), the merchants' and rich tradesmen's most distinguished guildhall. Occupying a position near the River Foss, it has a fine undercroft with oak pillars and a 15th c. chapel. Nearby Fairfax House, in contrast, was the splendid classical town residence of Viscount Fairfax; designed by John Carr and built in about 1762, it contains items detailing 18th c. life. St Denys' Church in Walmgate has 14th/15th c. stained glass windows and a Norman south doorway, while St Margaret's contains a Roman doorway and tower. At the end of the street is Walmgate Bar, one of the city's attractive gates.

Merchant Adventurers' Hall, Fairfax House

A walk along the town walls will leave a lasting impression of the townscape. Built mainly in the 14th c., they follow the line of the Roman walls for much of the way, and incorporate some Roman work. The walls have a total extent of some 3 miles, with six gates or "bars". Four of the old gates have been preserved – Walmgate Bar, Monk Bar and Bootham Bar, all with the original portcullis, and Micklegate Bar, with three figures of knights. Micklegate and Monk Bar can be entered. The stretch of wall between Bootham Bar and Monk Bar offers the finest view of the Minster.

★Town Walls

York Castle, between Fishergate and Skeldergate Bridge, was built of wood by the Normans in 1068, in order to ward off opponents hoping to conquer the north of England, mainly in York. The oldest remaining part is Clifford's Tower, the keep once belonging to Henry III's extensive castle. Constructed in the 13th c. as a replacement for the wooden fortress, it was later named after Roger de Clifford, who was executed here in 1322 as leader of the Lancastrian party. In 1190 about 150 Jews, pursued by a mob incited by the Crusade propaganda against their

York Castle

A Victorian room (c. 1870) in York Castle Museum

people, sought refuge in the old wooden tower and were burnt to death. Prison buildings erected on the site in the 18th c. are now used to house a museum.

★**York Castle Museum** offers a marvellous insight into the English way of life throughout various centuries. It includes Kirkgate, a Victorian street with a number of small shops.

"The York Story"

The history of York is illustrated in the exhibition "The York Story", situated nearby in the former St Margaret's Church in Castlegate.

All Saints,
St Martin-cum-
Gregory

After crossing the Ouse Bridge another quarter containing more historical buildings is reached. It is worth visiting All Saints' Church in North Street to view the 15th c. stained glass windows. Based on the writings of Richard Rolle (about 1300–49), a Yorkshire monk and hermit, and the founder of mysticism in England, they depict the Last Fifteen Days of the World in a series of pictures each of which has an appropriate line of text below it. Try also to see St Martin-cum-Gregory (13th c., 15th and 18th c. stained glass) in Micklegate, where there are some fine Georgian houses, and St Mary's in Bishophill Junior, which has a Saxon tower and an altar by Temple Moore (1856–1920).

Other Museums

The ★**Jorvik Viking Centre** is in Coppergate. This museum documents the daily lives of the Vikings in the 9th/10th c. It includes reconstructions of homes in Danish Jorvik, York's former name, and replicas of early medieval workshops.

York Dungeon, with its bloodthirsty horror show, is in Clifford Street.

The **Museum of Automata** in Tower Street details the history of mechanical objects from the musical box to robots.

Situated in Lower Friargate, the **Friargate Museum**'s collection of wax figures, ranging from Alfred the Great to current models, bring history alive.

Railway Museum: royal wagon ...   *... and historical mail train*

Visitors can themselves take part in excavations at the **Archaeological Research Centre** in St Saviourgate.

The ★**National Railway Museum** in Leeman Road on the outskirts of the city is very interesting. Its impressive array of locomotives and carriages dating from 1820 to the present document the history of this form of transport. Among the exhibits in the large hall, which is laid out like an old-fashioned railway station, are a Victorian mail train from 1838, freight and steam trains dating from the turn of the century, a motorail train and luxurious Edwardian Pullman carriages.

Model railway enthusiasts will greatly enjoy **Rail Rider's World** in York station.

Surroundings

York University, founded in 1963, lies 1½ miles south-east of the city. It was built in the grounds of Heslington Hall, originally an Elizabethan mansion which now accommodates the university's administrative offices.

York University

Beningbrough Hall, an early Georgian country house built by John Bourchier at the beginning of the 18th c., stands approximately 8 miles north-west of York. It contains more than 100 works on loan from the National Portrait Gallery.

Beningbrough Hall

The city of York is an ideal base from which to explore the surrounding area, which offers a wide range of beautiful scenery and historical and artistic interest. Apart from the Yorkshire Dales (see entry), two circular tours are recommended. The first takes in the towns of Beverley and Selby, both famous for their churches.

★ Tour to Beverley & Selby

Leave York by St Lawrence Street and continue along the A1079 until shortly before Hull (see entry). Some 19 miles from York Hayton is reached. Here a detour leads to **Burnby Hall** and its beautiful gardens (2 miles north).

After a total of 29 miles Beverley (population 18,000) is reached. This attractive old market town lies on the foothills of the East Yorkshire Wolds. Its rise to prosperity was based, like other Yorkshire towns, on the wool trade.

Beverley

The impressive ★★**Minster** on the south side of the town was built between 1220 and 1420. The 334 ft-long cathedral was founded by St John of Beverley, Bishop of York (d. 721). The choir and double transepts were completed in the mid-13th c. and are in the purest Early English style. The nave, begun in 1308, is mainly Decorated; the west front with its twin towers, adorned with statues, is Perpendicular. In spite of the mingling of styles the general effect is harmonious, thanks largely to the magnificent carving of the stonework. The west doorway features figures of the Evangelists (early 18th c.). The window above them is in nine sections and is elaborately decorated. The north doorway dates from the early 15th c. Notable features of the nave are the Romanesque font of Frosterley marble, the triforium and the Maiden's Tomb. The main transepts have both east and west aisles. The columns at the east end of the church are of Purbeck marble. The choir is a magnificent example of Early English architecture. The magnificent choir-stalls (1520) have the largest number of misericords in England (68). The canopied Percy Tomb, next to the high altar, is a work of the highest perfection. It is probably the tomb of Eleanor Fitzalan (d. 1328), wife of Lord Percy. The large east window behind the high altar in the Lady Chapel contains some fine old glass dating from 1417.

The marvellous **Market Cross** dates from 1714, while the stuccoed **Guildhall** was built in the 17th c. On the north side of the market place stands **St Mary's**, a cross-shaped church begun in the 12th c. and con-

Selby Abbey

structed both in the Decorated and the Perpendicular styles. Its finest parts are the west front (1380–1411), the choir-stalls and 15th c. misericords, the painted figures of English kings and the rich sculptural decoration. Behind the church is the brick-built **North Bar**, the only one of the original five town gates to survive, and beyond this lies a charming Georgian residential area.

Hull
See entry

Howden
Continue along the A63, in places passing very close to the Humber, to Howden (pop. 2000), a pleasant little town with cobbled streets. Medieval St Peter's Church was built mainly in the 14th c. Its impressive 15th c. tower is 135 ft high. The choir and the chapterhouse fell into ruins in the 17th c. but are well worth examining.

Selby
Follow the A63 for a further 11 miles to reach Selby (pop. 12,000). This small town on the banks of the Ouse has many notable Georgian houses and ★**Selby Abbey**, one of the most attractive abbey churches in England.

The first church on the site belonged to a Benedictine house founded in 1069 – the first major abbey to be established after the Norman Conquest.

The present church, dedicated to St Germanus, was begun in 1100. The central tower collapsed in 1690, damaging the south transept, and both were later rebuilt. After a fire in 1906 caused extensive damage, work began in 1909 to restore the church to its original appearance. Its finest features are the late Norman west front and the north doorway. The east half of the nave is Norman, the west half Transitional. The Decorated choir (1280–1340) is particularly beautiful. Other notable parts are the richly-decorated great east window depicting St Michael, a 14th c. Jesse window and the "Washington Window" (14th c.) in the choir, showing the coat of arms of the family from which America's president George Washington was descended.

From Selby it is 14 miles northwards on the A19 back to York.

Another route leads from York through the delightful scenery of the North York Moors and the Yorkshire Wolds, which rise to heights of up to 800 ft, to the North East Coast (see entry). Formerly this was a vast sheep-grazing region, with only a thin covering of poor soil over the underlying limestone. Recently, however, the soil has been improved and broad swaths of land have become fertile cornfields, variegated by white crags of rock, attractive clumps of woodland and avenues of tall trees.

★★**Yorkshire Wolds, North York Moors**

The A166 leads to **Stamford Bridge**, a tiny village whose claim to fame unfortunately rests on the last great victory of the Saxons, the battle in 1066 in which Harold defeated his brother Tostig and King Harold Hardrada of Norway, who had sailed up the Humber.

From the seaside resort of **Bridlington** a beautiful coast road leads north and can be followed all the way to **Whitby** (see North East Coast) and beyond over the North York Moors, with occasional glimpses of the coast.

The North York Moors National Park extends from the beautiful cliff scenery on the coast into a great expanse of country farther inland, an area of mainly moorland and heath, of pines and broom and a variety of wild flowers. One of the few villages in this sparsely-populated region is Goathland, the terminus of the steam railway operating from Whitby.

North York Moors National Park

The Moors are popular with walkers, many of whom follow the ★**Cleveland Way**, opened in 1969. This 100 mile-long path and bridleway encircles the whole of the national park.

From Scarborough (see North East Coast) the A170 turns inland to the Vale of Pickering. The town of Pickering (17 miles west, population 5000) has a ruined Norman castle with a completely intact encircling wall and three defensive towers (11th/14th c.). The parish church of St Peter and St Paul was also founded during the Norman period. Medieval wall-paintings depicting biblical scenes (mid-15th c.) were found above the arcades of the nave in 1852. They were subsequently painted over but uncovered again after 1880.

Scarborough, Pickering

From Pickering the road continues via Kirbymoorside, with a nature reserve which is particularly beautiful in spring when the wild daffodils bloom, to Helmsley (6 miles west; pop. 1500). Only the keep, the west tower and the moat remain of its 12th c. ruined castle, stone from which was used to build a manor house, now **Duncombe Park**.

Helmsley

Some 3 miles north-west are the magnificent ruins of Rievaulx Abbey, a Cistercian house founded in 1131 by Walter l'Espec, Lord of Helmsley. The remains range in date between the 12th and the mid-13th c. and are mainly Early English in style. They include the choir and transepts of the church, the triforium, the infirmary and the lavatory. On a terrace above the abbey, reached by a steep and narrow path, is a small castle, called the Temple and dating from 1758. From here most impressive views of the ruins and the whole valley can be enjoyed.

★**Rievaulx Abbey**

Returning to Helmsley, take the road which leads via Oswaldkirk, Ampleforth and Byland Abbey to Coxwold (10 miles). **Nunnington Hall**, a large manor house dating from the end of the 16th c., lies on the banks

Oswaldkirk

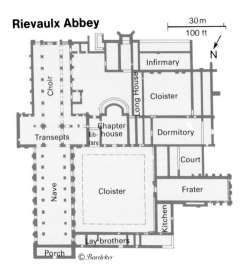

Rievaulx Abbey

30 m
100 ft
N

Infirmary

Choir

Long House

Cloister

Chapter house

Transepts

Lib-rary

Dormitory

Court

Nave

Cloister

Frater

Kitchen

Lay brothers

Porch © *Baedeker*

of the River Rye, 3 miles east of Oswaldkirk. Inside the house can be found fine wooden panelling, valuable tapestries and Chinese porcelain.

Ampleforth

At Ampleforth is a well-known public school, founded in 1802 by English Benedictine monks returning from exile in France. Nearby is a fine modern church designed by Sir Giles Gilbert Scott.

Byland Abbey

Of Byland Abbey, founded in 1177, only the splendid west front of the church, the south transept and the Cistercian house remain.

★Coxwold

Coxwold (population 300) is a charming little village where Laurence Sterne was curate from 1760 until his death in 1768. In **Shandy Hall** he wrote the last part of "Tristram Shandy" and the whole of "Sentimental Journey". His small study is now dedicated to his memory.

Gilling Castle

From Coxwold return via Ampleforth to Gilling Castle (6 miles east), which was built in the 13th c. and renovated in the 16th/18th c. Note the Norman tower and the Great Hall (1575–85), the richly-decorated Elizabethan dining hall with heraldic stained glass windows by Bernard Dinckhoff (1585). The house is now occupied by a school. Visitors can also see the beautiful terraced gardens.

★Castle Howard

Before continuing along the B1257 to Malton (10 miles south-east) a signed detour leads from Slingsby to Castle Howard, a magnificent Palladian mansion built for the third Earl of Carlisle by John Vanbrugh. Both a dramatist and an architect, it was Vanbrugh's first major work, based on plans drawn by Wren. The house is owned by George Howard. Its garden front is particularly fine. The elegant rooms contain paintings, carving by Grinling Gibbons, period furniture and costumes, and valuable vases and statues. The grounds are on a scale to match the house with an impressive family mausoleum, an obelisk, a pyramid and the Temple of the Four Winds (1724–26) by Vanbrugh.

Malton

Malton (pop. 4000) is the last stopping-place on this tour. This little market town on the banks of the Derwent lies in the centre of a large farming area, mainly devoted to corn-growing but also known for the breeding of racehorses. St Michael's Church is a fine Late Norman building with a Perpendicular tower. St Mary's Church, in Old Malton, is all that remains of a Gilbertine priory founded in about 1150. A cross in nearby Orchard Field marks the site of the Roman station of Derventio. Finds excavated from here can be seen in the **Malton Museum** in Market Square.

From Malton follow the A64 for 18 miles south-west to return to York city centre.

Harrogate (pop. 65,000) lies 20 miles west of York and is the most important spa town in the north of England. It owes its fame to the medicinal springs discovered here in the 16th c., which are mainly rich in sulphur and iron. Today Harrogate is primarily a holiday resort and a venue for congresses. Its parks are filled with flowers, often earning the town the title of "Britain's Floral Resort". Harrogate is also a popular residential town, and, although it has little industry, many large firms have their administrative offices here. Harrogate enjoys a good reputation for shopping on account of its elegant boutiques and numerous antiques shops.

*Harrogate

The **Royal Pump Room**, the former pump room above the sulphur spring, has become a museum. It is a pleasure to stroll in the beautiful parks, or on the **Stray**, one of the largest expanses of grass in the world. The **Valley Gardens** in the town centre are magnificent, and **Fountain Court**, with its bubbling springs, should not be missed. **Harlow Hill** offers a fine view across the spa and as far as York and the Humber. Lovers of flowers must visit extensive **Harlow Car Gardens**, which belong to the Horticultural Society. The modern Conference and Exhibition Centre is in King's Road.

Newby Hall (22 miles north-west) is a delightfully situated manor house renovated by Robert Adam in 1770. It is famed for its collection of tapestries and statues, but its gardens are also worth seeing.

Yorkshire Dales   I/K 6

Northern England. County: North Yorkshire

The Yorkshire Dales lie in the north-west of Yorkshire and are a particularly charming area of great natural beauty and variety. The **Yorkshire Dales National Park** takes in Wharfedale, the valley of the River Wharfe, Upper Ribblesdale, Wensleydale, Swaledale and the south side of Teesdale, together with their side valleys. The name "Dales" comes from the Scandinavian word "Thal" and, in contrast to the word "Vale" used generally to mean valley, specifically refers to the boggy valleys fed by rivers flowing down from the Pennines.

The Yorkshire Dales cover an area of about 645 sq. miles and rise to an average height of 600 ft, with individual summits of up to 2000 ft. Common to all the dales is their scanty population, but each has its own particular character. Walking enthusiasts find here an area rich in variety. Ribblesdale is the most dramatic of the dales, with waterfalls and towering crags, interesting caves and large quarries. Swaledale is also wild in parts, with rugged gorges and jagged rocks. Wharfedale, particularly Upper Wharfedale, is a gentler valley of great beauty. Wensleydale, geologically called Yoredale, is wider, with waterfalls and areas of heath.

Lead was mined in the Yorkshire Dales in Roman times, and continued to be worked until the end of the 19th c. when cheap imports made the mines uneconomic. The main economic resource is now agriculture, particularly livestock and cattle-farming. There are also quarries producing some high-quality limestone, which is used for a variety of purposes.

The most southerly valley of the Yorkshire Dales is Wharfedale. Its river of the same name flows north-west of Leeds (see entry). **Bolton Abbey**

Wharfedale

(really a priory), near the village of Beamsley, is a convenient setting-off point for exploring the beautiful scenery here. The most important part of this small but romantic ruin is the 12th c. parish church, which was built in the Early English and Decorated styles. Its west tower was begun in 1520 but never completed. The gatehouse is incorporated in the adjoining Bolton Hall (19th c.), seat of the Dukes of Devonshire.

There are some very fine walks through the surrounding grounds of the **Bolton Estate**. Opposite Bolton Abbey a footbridge and stepping-stones cross the river.

One walk which should not be missed leads along the west bank of the river to the ★**Strid**. Here the Wharfe surges through a gorge which at times is not much more than 3 ft wide. From here the path continues past Pembroke Seat (fine view) to Barden Bridge, about 3 miles from the abbey. Walkers should return from here along the east bank of the river.

The beauties of ★**Upper Wharfedale** can be seen by taking the road along the west bank of the Wharfe past Barden Bridge, built in 1659, and the ruins of 15th c. Barden Tower. Burnsall, attractively situated on the Wharfe and with an old church, is soon reached. The road continues past Grassington (bridge) to Kilnsey, with the formidable Kilnsey Crag, which presents a chalenge to rock-climbers. Visitors to Kilnsey Park can obtain information about the varied landscape of the Dales and try their luck fishing in its trout hatchery. A road leads left through narrow Littondale in the direction of Arncliffe. Great Whernside (2310 ft) can be seen from Kettlewell, some 13 miles from Bolton Abbey. Farther on is Buckden, at the foot of Buckden Pike (about 2297 ft high), where it is possible either to continue along the valley of the Wharfe, called "Langstrothdale" from here on, or to turn off right to Wensleydale.

Skipton

The small town of Skipton to the west of Bolton Abbey lies at the centre of the area extending between Wharfedale and Ribbledale. The Clifford family had an impressive castle with an attractive inner courtyard built here and lived in it from 1307 to 1955. Craven Museum documents the town's history.

Railway enthusiasts are advised to visit the collection of **old locomotives** and carriages assembled at the railway station in the nearby village of **Embsay**. On Sundays throughout the year an old steam train travels from Embsay to Holywell; in July it is also in operation on Saturdays and in August it makes the journey daily.

An excursion can be made north-westwards from Skipton to **Malham**, where visitors can enjoy walks among the very romantic scenery to Malham Cove, a rock formation in the form of an amphitheatre, Gordale Scar, a ravine, and Malham Tarn, a hidden marsh lake.

Wensleydale

Wensleydale is not named after a river but after the small market town of Wensley, south of Richmond (see entry). The stream which flows through it is the Ure or Yore.

Ripon

A good starting-point for tours is Ripon, situated on the Skell, a tributary of the Ure. Ripon is not really part of the true Wensleydale. The town's main attraction is its ★**Cathedral**, originally a monastery founded in 657 by Alchfrith. The cathedral's attraction lies in the variety of styles it incorporates. Its oldest parts, the choir and transepts, date from the time of Roger of Pont (Archbishop of York 1154–81). The Early English west front was constructed between 1220 and 1230; the east end (Decorated) in about 1300. The nave and parts of the central tower are Perpendicular. The interior also shows a variety of styles. The choir shows Transitional, Early English and Decorated work. The triforium is the only one in England to be glazed. Particularly fine are the 34 misericords of the choir-stalls (1489/94). The Anglo-Saxon crypt was built by St Wilfred in 670 as a confessio for the display of relics.

The small town contains many houses, the oldest of which is the former chapel of 14th c. St Anne's Chapel.

Fountains Abbey

One of the most beautiful ruins in Europe is Fountains Abbey, some 4 miles south-west of Ripon. The best way to approach it is through the large park of ★**Studley Royal**, a marvellous example of a Georgian landscaped garden, and over the Skell towards the octagonal tower. The abbey, founded in 1132 for the Cistercian order, then comes into view in all its splendour: one of the largest, most magnificent and best preserved of Britain's ruined abbeys and an excellent illustration of the process by which the dissolved monasteries were converted into private residences. Its name is derived from the several springs which have their source here. The walls have been completely preserved, creating an impressive effect, with a romantic air which is enhanced by the beauty of the setting. The monks acquired considerable wealth through sheep-farming and dealing in wool, and were thus able to finance this splendid building they erected here. The church's nave and transepts are in the Transitional style (1135–47); the tower is Perpendicular. The finest feature is the Chapel of the Nine Altars, in which the pointed arch makes its first appearance in England. Only the cloister has lost its arcading (probably of timber). The extensive monastic buildings, which give the monastery its imposing appearance, have largely been preserved. The chapterhouse, dormitory and lavatory, refectory and kitchen, infirmary and guest houses were provided in duplicate, for monks and lay brothers.

Fountains Hall (1595–1611), partly built with material from the abbey, contains an interesting collection of furniture.

★★**Fountains Abbey**

Jervaulx Abbey (14 miles north-west of Ripon) is another impressive ruined abbey, also in a beautiful riverside setting. It dates from the late 12th and the early 13th c. Little is left of the church, but the extensive monastic buildings of the former Cistercian house can be seen.

★**Jervaulx Abbey**

Middleham   The valley of the Ure is known as Wensleydale only above Jervaulx: and here too its finest scenery begins, with waterfalls and a series of charming little villages on the banks of the river. One of the most beautiful of these is Middleham, with racing stables.

Middleham Castle was once a favourite residence of Richard III. Among its impressive remains is the keep, one of the largest in England.

Wensley   The road continues via Wensley, with its very fine church (Flemish brass of c. 1360 by Simon de Wenslaw) to the well-preserved **Castle Bolton** (1379–97), opulent home of the Scrope family until 1630. Mary Stuart (see Famous People) was held captive here for six months in 1568. Behind the pretty little village of West Witton rises Penhill Beacon (1792 ft). Beyond Aysgarth, 23 miles from Ripon, are three waterfalls, the finest of which is Aysgarth Force, half a mile beyond the bridge.

Hawes   At Hawes (32 miles) a cheese factory making the famous Wensleydale cheese can be visited. The town's new Dales Countryside Museum depicts life in the Dales in earlier times. From Hawes a winding hill road leads to Muker in Swaledale, passing after 2 miles Hardraw Force waterfall, and going over the Buttertubs Pass, named after five deep holes in the rock between 50 ft–100ft.

Kendal   Continue along the bank of the Ure to reach Kendal in Westmoreland, famous for its snuff. Catherine Parr, sixth and final wife of Henry VIII (see Famous People), was born in its now ruined castle.

Swaledale   Swaledale is for the most part rugged and wild. A good base from which to see it is the romantic old town of **Richmond** (see entry). Following the River Swale westwards through ever-changing scenery Reeth is reached after 11 miles.

Reeth   Reeth was a lead-mining centre from Roman times until the end of the 19th c.; the Old Gang Smelting Mill (4 miles north-west of the town) is typical of that era.

Arkengarthdale   At Reeth a hilly moorland road goes off on the right to Arkengarthdale, passing through a number of tiny hamlets.

Barnard Castle   Passing straight through Arkengarthdale follow a road to the right and finally arrive at Barnard Castle, a small old town beautifully situated on the River Tees, with a ruined castle (1112–32) overlooking the river. **Bowes Museum** stands to the east of the town. It was founded by John Bowes and his wife Josephine Coffin-Chevalier, and was modelled on part of the Tuilleries Palace in Paris. It contains an outstanding collection of 18th c. French works of art, including tapestries, ceramics, porcelain, manuscripts, furniture and paintings, as well as a number of old masters, including El Greco and Goya.

Raby Castle, 4 miles north-east of Barnard Castle, is an extremely well-preserved castle, dating from the 14th c. Most of the rooms are now furnished in the style of the 18th and 19th c.; however, the church has remained almost completely unaltered for the past 600 years. Old coaches and fire engines are displayed in a nearby building.

Teesdale   The scenery of Teesdale above Barnard Castle is of great beauty. **High Force** is a 72 ft-high waterfall.

Mickle Fell (2591 ft) in Upper Teesdale is famous for the variety of its flora, which includes Alpine and continental plants as well as species which normally grow farther south. In order to protect these plants nature reserves have been established at Cow Green and adjoining Moor House, and permits are required to enter them.

Practical Information

Accommodation

Self-catering;
Holiday Homes

Self-catering holidays in Britain are becoming increasingly popular, and the British Tourist Authority publishes lists of this type of accommodation. Generally speaking the rates can be as much as 50% cheaper between October and March. Visitors will usually be required to pay a deposit.

Booking Agencies

It is advisable to book well in advance, although there are some organisations where it is possible to make late bookings on arrival.

The Landmark Trust (Shottesbrooke Park, White Waltham, Little Wick Green, Maidenhead, Berkshire SL6 35W; tel. (01628) 825925) was set up by a London banker over 10 years ago to preserve historic buildings. It has over 150 reasonably priced holiday homes on its books, ranging from castles to rented apartments, which are full of character and in unusual settings.

Character Cottages (34 Fore Street, Sidmouth, Devon EX1 8AQ; tel. (01395) 577001) offers over 600 cottages, many of them thatched, in country towns and villages.

Holiday homes are also available from the National Trusts for England and Scotland while Quality Cottages and Country Holidays are organisations which also have accommodation for the disabled on their books. Luxury holiday homes (with possibly a butler) can be rented via Blandings or Castles and Country Estates (information from the British Tourist Authority).

University
campuses

During the summer holidays more than 50 universities and colleges can offer relatively cheap accommodation on their campuses, either as bed and breakfast or self-catering. Details can be obtained from the following addresses:

British Universities Accommodation Consortium Ltd. (BUAC),
P.O. Box H 91, University Park,
Nottingham NG7 2RD; tel. (0115) 9504571

Higher Education Accommodation Consortium (HEAC),
Department H 19, 36 Collegiate Crescent,
Sheffield S10 2BP; tel. (0114) 2683759

Home Exchange

In a home exchange overseas visitors can exchange houses with a British family. There is no rent to pay, just a fee to Home Interchange, the agency that acts as the go-between. The addresses of Home Interchange agents are available from the British Tourist Authority.

Air Travel

International
flights

British Airways, the national airline flying in and out of London

Air Travel

Heathrow, and the other major international airlines provide the United Kingdom with the scheduled flights linking it to the world network. In addition there are a number of budget airlines operating mainly out of Luton and Stansted airports.

Domestic flights

Domestic flights are competed for by British Airways and a number of regional airlines (see below). Besides serving the major airports they also fly to smaller airports such as Aberdeen, Cardiff and Inverness, as well as Guernsey and Jersey in the Channel Islands, the Isle of Man and the Isle of Wight, Benbecula and Lewis in the Hebrides, and Orkney and the Shetlands. The budget airlines also run on some routes.

British Airways operates a super shuttle service out of London to Edinburgh, Glasgow, Manchester and Belfast. Passengers need only arrive ten minutes before departure.

Airlines

British Airways (BA), the national airline, is also one of the major international flight operators, serving destinations throughout the world. London central office: 156 Regent Street, London W1R 5TA; for enquiries and bookings within Great Britain around the clock at local rates tel. (0345) 222111.

British Regional Airlines

Regional airlines, such as Air UK, Aurigny Air Services, British Midland Airways, Brymon Airways, Business Air, GB Airways, Loganair, Maersk Air, Manx Airlines, Suckling Airways and Virgin Atlantic also operate a great many flights within Great Britain and overseas, and usually have their own desks at the airports.

Budget airlines

Budget fares are available to an increasing number of destinations. The major budget airlines are:

Easyjet (from Luton); tel. (0870) 6000000

Ryan Air (from Stansted); tel. (0870) 3331239

Go! (from Stansted); tel. (0845) 6054321

Airports

As national and international air traffic builds up at London Heathrow, one of the world's biggest and busiest airports, the overcrowding is increasingly causing many airlines to fly via nearby Gatwick and to route their freight and charter flights through Luton and Stansted.

London

London Heathrow (15 miles west of Central London);
Links: Heathrow Express to London Paddington

London Gatwick (27 miles south)
Link: Gatwick Express to London Victoria

London City Airport (in Docklands 6 miles east)
Link: Docklands Light Railway and Underground

Stansted Airport (34 miles north-east)
Links: Skytrain to London Liverpool Street

Luton Airport (30 miles north-west)
Link: Luton Flyer train to London Kings Cross and Flightline Bus 757

Belfast

Belfast International Airport, Crumlin (18 miles north-west)
Link: buses to the city centre

Birmingham

Birmingham International Aiport (9 miles south-east)
Link: trains to the city centre

Edinburgh Airport (7 miles west)
Link: buses to the city centre

Edinburgh

Glasgow Airport, Abbotsinch (9 miles west)

Glasgow

Leeds and Bradford Airport (14 miles north-west)
Link: buses to the city centre

Leeds

Liverpool Airport (7 miles south-east)
Link: buses to the city centre

Liverpool

Manchester International Airport (10 miles south)
Link: buses to the city centre

Manchester

Newcastle Airport (6 miles north-west)
Link: Metro and buses to the city centre

Newcastle-upon-Tyne

Bed and Breakfast

Bed and Breakfast, or B&B for short, is a relatively cheap form of overnight accommodation, whether in a farmhouse or private house, where there may be just a couple of rooms, or in a guest house with several rooms and the possibility of an evening meal as well. The rooms are usually pleasant and comfortable, with the celebrated English breakfast to look forward to in the morning.

Signs for this kind of accommodation usually read "Bed and Breakfast", "B&B", or simply "Vacancies".

The price of bed and breakfast is per person and, depending on the season, ranges between £12 and £25 in an ordinary house, £10 and £35 on a farm and £25 and £40 in a guest house.

Prices

There is usually no need to book, simply knock on the door, but anyone wanting to plan their holiday in advance can use the British Tourist Authority's booking service (see Information) or one of the following organisations:

Bookings

Always Welcome Homes, 11 Westerdale Road,
London SE10 0LW; tel. (020) 88580821
(B&B in London, England and Scotland)

Bed and Breakfast (GB) Reservation Office, 96 Bell St.,
Henley-on-Thames, Oxfordshire RG9 2BN; tel. (01491) 578803

Some organisations offer more specialised – and hence somewhat more expensive – B&B addresses:

Special categories

Wolsey Lodges, 9 Market Place,
Hadleigh, Ipswich, Suffolk IP7 5DL; tel. (01473) 822058
(pretty, and often historical, country houses)

Heritage Circle, Meiklemosside,
Fenwick, Ayrshire KA3 6AY; tel. (01560) 600769
(comfortable accommodation in castles, country houses and historic homes)

Boating

Britain's broads, lakes, rivers and canals are very popular with boating enthusiasts. Waterborne holidays range from taking the traditional narrowboats on the canals that criss-cross the heart of England to hiring cabin cruisers on Lough Erne in Northern Ireland or the Caledonian Canal in Scotland, or exploring the broads and rivers of Norfolk. You can take boats down the Thames and its tributaries right into the centre of London, but Scotland's coastal waters require a certain amount of experience.

Narrowboats can be hired in many places. Learning how to handle them does not take long and is a skill soon improved by experience. No licence is required. It is wise to book well in advance, particularly in the peak holiday season when a reservation should be made at least 6 weeks beforehand. Brochures for boating holidays can be obtained from travel agents or a representative of the British Tourist Authority (see Information), and also from

Hoseasons Holidays Ltd
Sunway House, Lowestoft NR32 2LW
tel. (01502) 501010

UK Waterway Holidays (UKWH) Ltd
1 Port Hill, Hertford SG14 1PJ
tel. (01992) 550616

Buses and Coaches

Great Britain has a good network of intercity coach services, with National Express the main coach operator in England and Wales and Scottish Citylink and Caledonian Express the leading operators in Scotland. Within towns and cities and over shorter distances in the rural areas this form of public transport is provided by various types of buses, as opposed to coaches, and these are operated by private companies, local authorities, etc.

Information

National Express, Victoria Coach Station,
National enquiry and reservations; tel. (08705) 808080

Reductions

Visitors from abroad will find it worthwhile getting a discount card, which entitles them to price reductions on all the National Express routes and many of those operated by Caledonian. Children under 16 get this reduction automatically, and students and people over 60 can get cheaper tickets if they hold the Discount Coach Card, valid for 12 months.

The Tourist Trail Pass allows unrestricted travel on all National Express and Caledonian coaches in England, Scotland and Wales for periods of 3, 10, 21 or 30 days.

These bus and coach cards and passes can be bought from the bus company offices in Great Britain and it is worth checking with the local British Tourist Authority representative abroad (see Information) on where they can be obtained outside Great Britain.

Camping and Caravanning

Camping and caravanning are popular British pastimes, so there is no shortage of good camp sites.

Campers from abroad can pay reduced site fees on a number of the large club sites on production of the International Camping Carnet. Caravans and motor caravans are usually accommodated together with tents sited separately. Racecourse sites are something of a British speciality, where camping can be combined with a day at the races.

The brochure "Camping and Caravan Parks" is available from the British Tourist Authority (see Information). Other addresses for useful information include: Information

The Camping and Caravanning Club, Greenfields House, Westwood Way, Coventry, West Midlands CV4 8JH; tel. (01203) 694995

The Caravan Club, East Grinstead House, London Road, East Grinstead, West Sussex RH19 1UA; tel. (01342) 326944

For information about camp sites in the seven forest parks and the New Forest contact:

Forestry Commission, 231 Corstorphine Road,
Edinburgh EH12 7AT; tel. (0131) 3340303

Since there are no suitable camp sites on Jersey and Guernsey in the Channel Islands motor caravans and touring caravans are not allowed unless they are for the disabled; touring caravans are banned on the Isle of Man. Caravan bans

Castles and Historic Sites

The Great British Heritage Pass, obtainable from the British Travel Centre (see Information), will give free admission to more than 600 castles, stately homes, country houses, historic sites, etc., many of which are still in private hands or administered by the National Trust, the National Trust for Scotland, English Heritage and Cadw/Welsh Historic Monuments. These include the eight "treasure houses" – Beaulieu, Blenheim Palace, Broadlands, Castle Howard, Chatsworth, Harewood House, Warwick Castle and Woburn Abbey – and those on the Grand Tour of Scotland – Hopetoun House, Scone Palace and Inverary, Glamis, Cawdor and Blair Castle. Great British
Heritage Pass

The pass can be for a month or a fortnight. It also takes in museums on the "Treasures of Britain" programme, and allows reduced admission at other museums. Many of these places are open all year round but with shorter opening hours between October and March.

This ticket, valid for a week or a fortnight, provides free admission to over 70 castles, abbeys, etc. in Scotland. Information can be obtained from the BTA and:
Historic Scotland, Longmore House, Salisbury Place,
Edinburgh EH9 1SH; tel. (0131) 6688600 Scottish Explorer
Ticket

The Castle Trail in the Grampian Highlands, between Aberdeen and Inverness, takes in sites that come under Historic Scotland and the National Trust for Scotland. A leaflet about the trail, which is signposted throughout, and one entitled "Scotland 1001 Things to See", with information about over 200 Scottish castles and country houses, is obtainable from outlets such as the British Tourist Authority (see Information). Castle Trail

The National Trust in Northern Ireland issues a passport giving free entry to a large number of historic houses, nature parks, gardens, etc. This can be obtained from the Northern Ireland Tourist Board (see Passport of the
National Trust in
Northern Ireland

Information), as can a list, which is free of charge, giving the opening
times of country houses, castles, gardens, museums, etc.

Chemists

Chemists who dispense prescriptions (for which a charge has to be paid)
are often in a special section of a larger pharmacy or drugstore. Opening
times are the same as for other shops, but there will be a list on display
in the window showing which chemists are open for emergencies outside business hours.

Currency

The unit of currency is the pound sterling (£), made up of 100 pence (p,
singular penny). Banknotes are for £5, £10, £20 and £50, and coins are
1p, 2p, 5p, 10p, 20p, 50p, £1, and £2.

Scotland and Northern Ireland each have their own banknotes, issued by
a number of different banks, and since these are not guaranteed means
of payment in England they ought to be exchanged before crossing the
border. Northern Ireland also has some coins from the Republic of
Ireland in circulation. The Isle of Man and the Channel Islands have their
own currency as well. However, "English" coins and banknotes are legal
tender throughout Great Britain and Northern Ireland.

Currency controls | There are no controls on the export or import of foreign currency or ster-
ling.

Cheques and Eurocheques | It is advisable to take Eurocheques or some form of traveller's cheques.
Eurocheques can be used up to a daily limit of £100. Using a Eurocheque
card it is also possible to take out up to £100 a day from AutoBank cash-
points and those displaying the Eurocheque sign.

Credit cards | Credit cards are more widely used for payment in Great Britain than in
many other parts of Europe, and will be accepted by most hotels, restaurants, shops and garages displaying the relevant card sign.

Warning | Be sure to put a stop on credit cards, cheque cards, etc. immediately if
they are lost or stolen. Inform the relevant issuing authority immediately, and keep the receipt for traveller's cheques separately from the
cheques themselves so that replacements can be obtained if necessary.

Banks and Currency Exchange Offices | Currency and traveller's cheques can be exchanged in official bureaux
de change, which often charge quite a high rate of commission, and
most High Street banks. Official banking hours are between 9.30am and
3.30pm, Monday to Friday, but many major banks are now open on
Saturday mornings and for longer hours during the week.

Customs Regulations

European Single Market | The advent of the single market within the European Union in 1993 her-
alded the end of frontier controls for non-commercial travellers between
EU countries. Any European resident going from one EU country into

another can theoretically now bring in an unlimited quantity of items for their personal use, and the same applies on the return journey. However, to put some limit on the amounts brought in and out in a private capacity, a maximum has been indicated. It is possible to exceed this if it is proved to be for private consumption. The controls for non-European residents and those travelling to non-EU countries remain as they were. Duty free shops at airports and on ferries were phased out in June 1999.

Although as an EU member the United Kingdom also wants to make travel to Britain easier it is continuing with its frontier controls for the time being. The suggested maximum amounts for private consumption are listed below. If nothing to declare, use blue channel if provided.

Non-European residents and EU nationals entering Britain can bring in, duty-free, articles for their daily use, items for purposes of tourism, sporting equipment, etc. Residents aged 18 and above from EU countries such as Eire can bring in 800 cigarettes and 400 cigarillos and 200 cigars and 1kg of tobacco, 10 litres of spirits over 22% proof and 20 litres below 22% proof and 90 litres of wine, plus an unlimited amount of perfume and toilet water and other goods and presents up to a total value of £420.

Duty-free items on entry

For items bought in duty-free shops or brought in by non-European residents from countries such as Australia, Canada, New Zealand, South Africa and the USA, the equivalent amounts are 200 cigarettes or 100 cigarillos or 50 cigars or 250g tobacco, and 1 litre of spirits over 22% or 2 litres below 22% and 2 litres of wine, plus 50g of perfume, 0.25 litre of toilet water and other goods and presents up to a value of £32.

The import of meat, fish and certain dairy products is forbidden. Video equipment has to be declared, so the visitor should take proof of purchase. Items which are being imported to be sold in Britain must also be declared. Check with motoring organisations about taking in carphones and walkie-talkies. You are not allowed to bring in cans of petrol or any firearms, flick-knives or gold coins. Shotguns may be brought into Great Britain, apart from Northern Ireland, for up to 30 days without formalities. If you have nothing to declare on entry, take the green channel – the red channel is for people with goods to declare.

Visitors returning home to an EU member country such as Eire can take back duty free the same allowances as they were entitled to bring in to Britain. Visitors returning to Australia can take 250 cigarettes or 250 g of cigars or 250 g of tobacco, 1 litre of spirits or 1 litre of wine, to Canada 200 cigarettes and 50 cigars and 1 kg of tobacco, 1.14 litres of spirits or 1.14 litres of wine, to New Zealand 200 cigarettes or 50 cigars or 250 g of tobacco, 1.125 litres of spirits and 4.5 litres of wine, to South Africa 400 cigarettes and 50 cigars and 250 g of tobacco, 1 litre of spirits and 2 litres of wine, and to the USA 200 cigarettes or 50 cigars or 2 kg of tobacco or proportionate amounts of each, 1 litre of spirits or 1 litre of wine.

Duty-free items on the return home

An export licence is required for controlled drugs, weapons and ammunition, most animals and certain plants and animal products, photographic material over 60 years old and worth more than £200, certain art objects, antiques and collectables. An export licence is required, irrespective of value, for documents, manuscripts and archives (other than printed matter) aged over 50 years and for all archaeological materials. Other goods up to a value of £120 may be exported free of duty.

Export licence

Diplomatic Representation

In Great Britain

High Commission, Australia House, Strand, London WC2B 4LA; tel. (020) 73794334

Australia

Electricity

Canada	High Commission, Macdonald House, 1 Grosvenor Square, London W1X OAB; tel. (020) 72586600
Eire	17 Grosvenor Place, London SW1X 7HR; tel. (020) 72352171
New Zealand	High Commission, New Zealand House, Haymarket, London SW1Y 4TQ; tel. (020) 79308422
South Africa	Embassy, South Africa House, Trafalgar Square, London WC2N 5DP; tel. (020) 79304488
USA	24 Grosvenor Square, London W1A 1AE; tel. (020) 74999000

Electricity

The current in the United Kingdom is 240 volt, 50 cycle AC. Since the type of plug socket will be different from that found in most other countries you will need an adaptor for any electrical appliances that you bring with you.

Emergencies

Dial 999 — For police, fire brigade, or ambulance dial 999, free of charge, from any telephone and ask for the service you require.

Emergency roadside phones — Emergency roadside telephones are located at intervals along all motorways and major trunk roads.
See also Medical Assistance, Motoring.

Events

The following selection is a general indication of the timing of most of the major events and festivals. For further details of dates and venues contact the local tourist information centres (see Information).

January — London: Lord Mayor's New Year's Parade,
London: International Boat Show

February — York (North Yorkshire): Jorvik Viking Festival

March — London: Spring Stampex (postage stamp exhibition)
Cheltenham (Gloucestershire): Cheltenham Gold Cup (race meeting)
London: Chelsea Antiques Fair
London: International Book Fair

Late March–early April — London: Boat Race between Oxford and Cambridge
Harrogate (North Yorkshire): International Youth Music Festival
Liverpool (Merseyside): Aintree Grand National (race meeting)

April — London Marathon
Stratford-upon-Avon (Warwickshire): Start of Royal Shakespeare Company theatre season (until January)
Harrogate (North Yorkshire): International Youth Music Festival, various venues
Devizes to Westminster International Canoe Race
Edinburgh (Lothian): International Festival of Science

and Technology; International Folk Festival
Birmingham (West Midlands): International Antiques Fair
Jersey (Channel Islands): Jersey Jazz Festival

London: Football Association Cup Final in Wembley Stadium	May
Windsor (Berkshire): Royal Windsor Horse Show	
Newmarket (Suffolk): Race Meeting	
Badminton (Avon): Badminton Horse Trials	
Perth (Tayside): Visual Arts Festival	
London: Chelsea Flower Show	
Glasgow (Strathclyde): Mayfest (music and arts festival)	
Orkney: Children's Festival	
Mildenhall, Bury St Edmunds (Suffolk): Mildenhall Air Fête	
Lytham St Anne's (Lancashire): Lytham Trophy (golf tournament)	

Bath (Avon): International Music and Arts Festival (various venues)   May–June
In numerous cathedrals: Cathedral Classics (until July)
Torquay (Devon): English Riviera Dance Festival
May–August
Glyndebourne (East Sussex): Opera Festival
May–September
Chichester (West Sussex): Theatre Festival
London: open-air theatre in Regent's Park
Highland Games at various places in Scotland

Pitlochry (Tayside): Theatre Festival   May–October
Ebbw Vale (Gwent): Garden Festival

Shepton Mallet (Somerset): Royal Bath and West Agricultural Show   June
Douglas (Isle of Man): Tourist Trophy (TT) Motorbike Races
Beverly (Humberside): Folklore Festival
Rochester (Kent): Charles Dickens Festival (various venues)
Epsom (Surrey): Derby Race Meeting
Aldeburgh (Suffolk): Festival of Music and the Arts
Glastonbury (Somerset): Rock Music Festival
Birmingham (West Midlands): Royal International Horse Show
London: Trooping the Colour to mark the Queen's official birthday
Ascot (Berkshire): Ascot Race Meeting
Windsor (Berkshire): the Garter Ceremony at Windsor Castle, service in
  the presence of the Queen and parade of the Household Cavalry and
  Yeomen of the Guard

Bournemouth (Dorset): Music Festival (choirs, bands, orchestras)   June–July
Great Elm (Somerset): Music Festival
Shrewsbury (Shropshire): International Music Festival
Henley-on-Thames (Oxfordshire): Henley Royal Regatta (rowing)

Stamford (Lincolnshire): open air performances by the Stamford   June–August
  Shakespeare Company
London: Academy Summer Show (four private viewings in Burlington
  House, on Piccadilly)

London: Wimbledon All England Lawn Tennis Championships   July
Jersey: Channel Island Surfing Championships
Glasgow (Strathclyde): International Jazz Festival
Llangollen (Clwyd): International Musical Eisteddfod
Cheltenham (Gloucestershire): International Music Festival
Norwich (Norfolk): Lord Mayor's Street Procession
London: City of London Festival
Lisburn (Antrim): Ulster Harp Derby Race Meeting
London: Royal Military Tournament
Silverstone (Northamptonshire): Formula One British Grand Prix

Ferries

	Llanelwedd (Powys): Royal Welsh Agricultural Show
	York (North Yorkshire): Early Music Festival
	King's Lynn (Norfolk): Music and Arts Festival
	Winchester (Hampshire): Southern Cathedrals Festival of Church Music
July–August	Cambridge (Cambridgeshire): Cambridge Folk Festival
	Goodwood (West Sussex): Goodwood Week Race Meeting
	Chichester (West Sussex): International Championship Show Jumping
	Sidmouth (Devon): International Festival of Folk Arts
	Womad, Reading (Berkshire): Womad Festival
	Isle of Wight: Admiral's Cup Regatta and Cowes Week
July–September	London: Henry Wood Promenade Concerts in the Royal Albert Hall
August	Sidmouth (Devon): International Folk Festival
	Llangollen (Clywd) Welsh Folklore Festival
	Edinburgh (Lothian): Edinburgh Military Tattoo
	Aberystwyth (Dyfed) International Welsh Language Festival
	Worcester, Hereford, Gloucester (Herefordshire): Three Choirs Festival
	Conwy (Gwynedd): Regatta
	Ballycastle (Antrim): Oul' Lammas Fair
	Jersey (Channel Islands): Battle of the Flowers
	London: Notting Hill Carnival
	Reading (Berkshire): Rock Festival
August–September	Arundel (West Sussex): Arundel Festival (opera, dance, open-air Shakespeare)
	Edinburgh (Lothian): International Festival and Book Show
September	Braemar (Grampian Region): Braemar Royal Highland Gathering (best known of the Highland Games)
	Salisbury (Wiltshire): Festival of the Arts
	Farnborough (Hampshire): International Air Show (with air displays)
September–November	Blackpool (Lancashire): Blackpool Illuminations
	Sunderland (Tyne and Wear): Sunderland Illuminations
October	Swansea (West Glamorgan): Music and Art Festival
	Colchester (Essex): Oyster Festival
	London: Horse of the Year Show at Wembley
	Cheltenham (Gloucestershire): Literary Festival
	Norwich (Norfolk): Norfolk and Norwich Music and Arts Festival
	Birmingham (West Midlands): British and International Motor Show
October–November	Swansea (West Glamorgan): Festival of Music and the Arts
November	London: State Opening of Parliament by the Queen
	London to Brighton (East Sussex): Veteran car run
	Belfast (Antrim): University Arts Festival
	London: Lord Mayor's Procession and Show
	Edinburgh (Lothian): Winter Antiques Fair
December	Aberdeen (Grampian): Christmas Market Festival
	London: Olympia International Showjumping Championships

Ferries

Ferries to Great Britain

Eire-Great Britain	Dun Laoghaire (Dublin)–Holyhead, daily, Stena Sealink Line

Rosslare–Fishguard, daily, Stena Sealink Line

Esbjerg-Harwich, 3–4 × weekly, Scandinavian Seaways — Denmark–Great Britain

Boulogne-Folkestone, Hoverspeed daily — France–Great Britain
Boulogne–Dover, Hoverspeed daily
Caen–Portsmouth, Brittany Ferries daily
Calais–Dover, Stena Sealink Line, P & O European Ferries, Hoverspeed daily
Cherbourg–Southampton, daily in season, Stena Sealink Line
Cherbourg–Poole, daily in season, Brittany Ferries
Cherbourg–Portsmouth, daily, P & O European Ferries
Dieppe–Newhaven, daily, Stena Sealink Line
Dunkirk–Ramsgate, daily, Sally Ferries
Le Havre–Portsmouth, daily, P & O European Ferries
Roscoff–Plymouth, daily, Brittany Ferries

Guernsey/Jersey–Granville, daily, Emeraude Lines — France–Channel Islands
St Malo–Guernsey (St Peter Port), daily, Emeraude Lines
St Malo–Jersey (St Helier), daily, Emeraude Lines
St Malo–Jersey/Sark/Guernsey/Alderney, daily, Emeraude Lines

Ostend-Ramsgate, daily, Sally Line — Belgium–Great Britain
Zeebrugge–Felixstowe, daily, P & O European Ferries
Zeebrugge–Hull, daily, North Sea Ferries

Hoek van Holland–Harwich, daily, Stena Sealink Line — Netherlands– Great Britain
Rotterdam Europoort–Hull, daily, North Sea Ferries
Vlissingen–Sheerness, daily, Eurolink Ferries

Hamburg–Harwich, 3–4 × weekly, Scandinavian Seaways — Germany–Great Britain
Hamburg–Newcastle, every 4 days (April-Sept.), Scandinavian Seaways

Gothenburg–Newcastle, weekly, Scandinavian Seaways — Sweden–Great Britain
Gothenburg–Harwich, 3–4 × weekly, Scandinavian Seaways

Ferries linking parts of the United Kingdom

Cairnryan–Larne, daily, P & O European Ferries — Mainland, etc.–Northern Ireland
Douglas Isle of Man–Belfast, 2–4 × weekly in season, Isle of Man Steam Packet Co.
Stranraer–Belfast, 4–5 × daily (May–Dec.), Hoverspeed
Stranraer–Larne, daily, Stena Sealink Line

Lymington–Yarmouth, Isle of Wight, daily, Wightlink Ltd. — Mainland–Islands Isle of Wight
Portsmouth–Fishbourne, Isle of Wight, daily, Wightlink Ltd.
Southampton–Cowes, Isle of Wight, daily, Red Funnel Ferries

Penzance–Hugh Town, Scillies, daily in season (except some Sundays), Isles of Scilly Steamship Co. — Scillies

Weymouth–Guernsey–Jersey, daily in season, Condor Ferries — Channel Islands

Fleetwood–Douglas, Isle of Man, once a week (Tuesday) in season, Isle of Man Steam Packet Seaways — Isle of Man
Heysham–Douglas, Isle of Man, daily (less frequent during winter months), Isle of Man Steam Packet Seaways, Sealink
Liverpool–Douglas, Isle of Man, weekly, Isle of Man Steam Packet Seaways

Ferries

Orkneys	Scrabster–Stromness, Orkney, daily in season, P & O Scottish Ferries Aberdeen–Stromness, Orkney, 1–3 × weekly, P & O Scottish Ferries
Shetlands	Aberdeen–Lerwick, Shetland, 5 × weekly, P & O Scottish Ferries
Orkneys–Shetlands	Stromness, Orkney–Lerwick, Shetland, 1–2 × weekly in season, P & O Scottish Ferries
Hebrides Arran	Adrossan–Brodick, Arran, daily, Caledonian MacBrayne Claonaig–Lochranza, Arran, daily, Caledonian MacBrayne Oban–Castlebay, Barra, 3 × weekly, Caledonian MacBrayne
Colonsay	Kennacraig–Colonsay, once a week, Caledonian MacBrayne Oban–Colonsay, 3 × weekly, Caledonian MacBrayne
Gigha	Tayinloan–Gigha, daily in season, Caledonian MacBrayne
Islay	Kennacraig–Port Askaig, Islay, daily, Caledonian MacBrayne Kennacraig–Port Ellen, Islay, daily in season, Caledonian MacBrayne
Lismore	Ullapool–Stornoway, Lewis, 6 × weekly, Caledonian MacBrayne
Lewis	Oban–Lismore, daily except Sun., Caledonian MacBrayne
Mull	Kilchoan–Tobermory, daily except Sun. in season, Caledonian MacBrayne Lochaline–Fishnish, daily, Caledonian MacBrayne Oban–Craignure, daily, Caledonian MacBrayne
Skye	Kyle of Lochalsh–Kyleakin, daily, Caledonian MacBrayne Mallaig–Armadale, daily in season, Caledonian MacBrayne
South Uist	Oban–Lochboisdale, 6 × weekly, Caledonian MacBrayne
Inter-island	Tarbert (Harris)–Lochmaddy (North Uist), 2 × weekly in season, Caledonian MacBrayne Port Askaig, Islay–Feolin, Jura, daily, Western Ferries (Argull) Oban–Tobermory, Mull–Coll–Tiree, 3–4 × weekly, Caledonian MacBrayne Uig, Skye–Lochmaddy, North Uist, daily (except Sunday), Caledonian MacBrayne
Clyde Service	Colintraive–Rhubodach, daily, Caledonian MacBrayne Gourock–Dunoon, daily, Caledonian MacBrayne Largs–Cumbrae Slip, daily, Caledonian MacBrayne Wemyss Bay–Rothesay, daily, Caledonian MacBrayne

Booking Offices

It is advisable to book as much in advance as possible, especially for July and August. Bookings can also be made by travel agents and motoring organisations.

Travel agents and ferry companies will be able to tell you about the size limits for vehicles on their boats.

British Channel Island Ferries	Head Office, Corbiere House, New Quay Road, Poole, Dorset BH15 4DU; tel. (01202) 666900
Brittany Ferries	The Brittany Centre, Wharf Road, Portsmouth PO2 8RU; tel. (023) 92892200; Plymouth Office (0870) 5360360
Caledonian MacBrayne	Ferry Terminal, Gourock PA19 1QP; tel. (01475) 650100

Royal Quays, North Shields, Tyne & Wear NE2 9GE tel. (0191) 2961313	Color Line
Condor Weymouth Ltd., The Quay, Weymouth DT4 8DX tel. (01305) 761551	Condor Ferries
Channel Islands Handling Ltd., Elizabeth Harbour, St Helier, Jersey JE2 3NW; tel. (01534) 66566	Emeraude Lines
The Ferry Terminal, Sheerness Docks, Kent ME12 1RS tel. (01795) 581700	Eurolink Ferries
Hoverspeed Ltd., International Hoverport, Dover CT17 9TG; tel. (01304) 865000	Hoverspeed
P.O. Box 5, Imperial Buildings, Douglas, Isle of Man; tel. (01624) 661661	Isle of Man Steam Packet Seaways
Quay Street, Penzance, Cornwall TR18 4BD; tel. (01736) 362009 and 364013	Isles of Scilly Steamship Co.Ltd.
North Sea Ferries UK, King George Dock, Hedon Rd., Hull HU9 5QA; tel. (01482) 377177	North Sea Ferries
Larne Harbour, Larne, County Antrim, BT40 1AG tel. (0990) 980777	P & O European Ferries
12 Bugle Street, Southampton, Hampshire SO14 2JY; tel. (023) 80333042	Red Funnel Services
York Street, Ramsgate CT11 9DS; tel. (0345) 160000	Sally Ferries
Parkeston Quay, Harwich CO12 4QG; tel. (0990) 333111	Scandinavian Seaways
Eastern Docks, Dover, Kent CT16 1JA; tel. (0990) 711711	SeaFrance
Stena Sealink Ltd., Charter House, P.O. Box 121, Park Street, Ashford, Kent TN24 8EX; tel. (0990) 707070	Stena Sealink Line
Le Shuttle, Eurotunnel, no reservations necessary Information tel. (08000) 969992	Eurotunnel

Food and Drink

Just as people were realising that British cooking, so often spurned
in the past, was much better than its reputation, then the "BSE
scandal" broke. As a result many pubs and restaurants now offer a
range of vegetarian and beef-free dishes. Those who do not rigidly
judge by the yardstick of their own country's cooking will soon discover how self-confident British cuisine and diners have become
during the last few years, even outside the main cities, and that
local specialities are now coming into their own. Many restaurants
also offer fresh fruit and vegetables now. There are a wealth of
alternatives available to those who are not keen to try Yorkshire
pudding, steak and kidney pie, or haggis and they may dine at reasonable prices in numerous Indian, Chinese, Caribbean and Arabic
restaurants.

Food and Drink

Regional dishes

The standard-bearer for a regional cuisine has been the English Tourist Board with its eating-out guide "A Taste of England". Anyone eating in a restaurant displaying its logo can be sure of finding plenty of traditional local dishes on the menu, and the same is true of the guides for the rest of the United Kingdom – "A Taste of Wales", "A Taste of Scotland" and "A Taste of Ulster".

Meals
Morning Tea

Some hotels still serve early morning tea in the bedroom for a small service charge, although there is an increasing tendency to provide tea and coffee-making facilities en suite.

Breakfast

The classic full English breakfast consists of fruit or cereal followed by variations of bacon and eggs, sausages, tomatoes, fried bread and baked beans or mushrooms, accompanied by toast and marmalade and a pot of tea or coffee. Regional breakfast specialities include porridge to start with, and smoked fish such as kippers to follow.

Lunch

Lunch is usually at around 1 o'clock and is often a light meal, particularly if it follows a filling English breakfast. Most people nowadays tend to have a snack of some kind, such as a sandwich or a "Ploughman's" of bread and cheese if eating out in a pub (see Restaurants, Pub Food), but restaurants and hotels also serve three-course meals of soup or cold starter, main course, and a dessert or cheese to follow.

Afternoon tea/High Tea

Afternoon tea is served between 4 and 5pm, accompanied by cake and pastries with perhaps scones, muffins or crumpets. In some homes, especially in the Midlands, the North of England and Scotland, afternoon tea and supper are combined into "high tea", a more substantial meal of meat or egg dishes, salads, etc.

Evening meal

The evening meal in hotels and restaurants is referred to as dinner, as opposed to supper, with four or more courses and the expectation that diners are suitably dressed for the occasion. Many restaurants serving English food stop taking orders after 9.30pm, but it is usually possible to get a meal until much later in other types of establishments such as Indian or Chinese.

Typical British Dishes
Sandwiches

Supposedly invented by the fourth Earl of Sandwich in the 18th c. during a break from the gaming tables, the sandwich has become an English institution like afternoon tea or the traditional pub. The original piece of meat between two slices of white bread has since taken on many different guises, as sold in innumerable sandwich bars, pubs and hotels.

Starters

Starters range from chilled fruit juice, melon, grapefruit cocktail, pâté and various kinds of potted meat, to preparations of fish and shellfish such as prawn cocktail, smoked salmon, mackerel or trout, crab salad, potted shrimp, cockles, winkles, and oysters (the best are from Colchester – "angels on horseback" are oysters rolled up in bacon, grilled and served with toast).

Soup

Soup is another favourite starter, especially in winter, and can vary between thick vegetable soup, cream of tomato, asparagus or mushroom, pea soup with bacon, clear soup made from a meat stock or with vegetables, and local specialities such as Scotch broth, with mutton and pearl barley, and, near the coast, different kinds of fish soup.

Fish

With its island coastline Great Britain is famous for the quality of its fish, and fish and chips has long been the traditional British standby for a ready-cooked meal (see Restaurants, Fish and Chip shops). There are also very many other ways of serving up cod, haddock, halibut, plaice and mackerel, including simply steamed or grilled. Dover sole and Scottish salmon often have pride of place on the menu, but also available are freshwater fish such as trout, carp, bream and pike, and excellent shellfish – mussels, scallops, crab, oysters, etc., with lobster at the top of the price range. East Anglia is famous for its fresh shellfish, and Scotland's north-west Highlands boast particularly good trout and salmon.

British meat is also top quality. The "roast beef of Old England" is famous, usually served with mustard or horseradish sauce, gravy and Yorkshire pudding, but steak and salt beef or silverside is also popular. Lamb tends to be accompanied by mint sauce or redcurrant jelly, and is also delicious as lamb chops. Pork chops are another favourite, while roast pork should come with crispy crackling and apple sauce. Pork also makes tasty sausages and excellent sliced ham. Steak and kidney can either be a pie, with a crust, or in a pudding case of suet pastry.

Other meat dishes include cottage pie (minced meat topped with mashed potatoes), Irish stew (usually stewed cubes of meat and vegetables), Cornish pasties (meat and vegetables in a pastry case), Scotch eggs (hardboiled and encased in sausage meat), and that great Scottish dish, the haggis.

Chicken is popular as a white meat dish, often simply roast with stuffing, with duck and goose less common, although goose or chicken are often also served at Christmas as an alternative to the traditional roast turkey. Wild game is usually only available in the hunting season, which is nationally relatively restricted. Pheasant and partridge tend to come with game chips and cabbage, while grouse from the moors of Scotland are a relatively expensive delicacy in season. Other game dishes include jugged hare and venison, although nowadays the latter tends to be farmed rather than wild.

Meat is usually served with fresh vegetables. These include potatoes (roast, mashed, boiled, or chipped), peas, cabbage, broccoli, carrots, etc. Other traditional accompaniments include Norfolk dumplings and Yorkshire pudding. Another colonial legacy is brown sauce, such as HP or Worcestershire, while tomato sauce and hot-tasting English mustard are other long-standing favourites.

The United Kingdom boasts a whole range of sweets and puddings. Traditional desserts made with cream include syllabub, gooseberry fool, and sherry trifle (jelly, fruit, sherry-soaked sponge fingers, topped with cream and custard). Other favourites with fruit are crumbles with a sweet crumbled topping, fresh fruit salad, and fruit tarts and pies. Steamed puddings usually have a suet dough base and range from jam roly-poly and treacle pudding to Christmas pudding, a highlight of the festive season.

English cheeses include Stilton, Cheddar, Cheshire, Gloucester, and Wensleydale. Wales, besides having its own Caerphilly, has given its name to Welsh rarebit, a delicious savoury of melted cheese on toast blended with beer and mustard or Worcestershire sauce.

The English, Welsh, Scots and Irish are all happily united as a nation of beer-drinkers. Just as driving on the left is typically British, so is the traditional pint of "best bitter". Unlike the rest of Europe, who went over to making the paler, lager-type beers in the mid-19th c., Britain still brews its beer known as "bitter" by top fermentation with the addition of hops, tending to make it much stronger than most other Europeans and non-Europeans are used to. Despite its name, bitter can be quite sweet and fruity. It takes a number of different forms and because it has to mature is usually served unchilled and without much foam to bring out the subtle variations in flavour. Classic versions include bottled "pale ale", "real ale", a keg bitter which has been further matured in the barrel,

Meat

Poultry and Game

Side dishes and sauces

Sweets

Cheese

Drink
Beer

"mild", a dark-brown beer from the barrel, and "brown ale", another dark beer but a bottled version. "Strong ales" are somewhat stronger; in the colder climes of Scotland a favourite brew is the dark and very malty "Scotch Ale".

Stout

Stout is a strong, dark, sweet ale brewed in Ireland from black malt, a bitter served with a creamy head of foam and best represented by the traditional Guinness.

Lager

Lager, the kind of chilled pale beer favoured by Americans and the rest of Europe, is becoming increasingly popular in Britain and is available everywhere.

Wine

Contrary to expectation, England produces some very respectable wine, an art introduced by the Romans and widely practised by the monks in the Middle Ages, drawing on the expertise of the vintners of Bordeaux which belonged to England for some 300 years. This art was lost with Henry VIII's dissolution of the monasteries but has been revived in more recent times and there are about 400 vineyards in the south of England, Wales and East Anglia. They produce mostly white wine (Müller-Thurgau, Riesling, Seyval Blanc, etc.).

Port and Sherry

The traditional apéritif is sherry from Jerez in Spain and of an excellent quality. Port, from Oporto in Portugal, is classically drunk after dinner or with the Stilton cheese; British shippers take most of Portugal's output.

Whisky

See page 292

Other drinks

Local versions of cider include scrumpy from the West Country, while perry, which is rather similar, comes from pears instead of apples. Mead is a wine made from honey, and punch is a hot spiced mixture of alcohol and fruit juice.

Gardens

The British have made gardening a fine art. Their gardens are famous all over the world (see page 408) and great garden designers like "Capability" Brown earned themselves an international reputation. However, in addition to the magnificent formal and kitchen gardens of stately homes many large and small lovingly tended private gardens are also open to the public and well worth a visit. Lists of those which are open to visitors can be obtained from:

National Gardens Scheme, Old Coach House,
Hatchlands Park, East Clandon,
Guildford, Surrey GU4 7RT

Scotland's Gardens Scheme, 31 Castle Terrace,
Edinburgh EH1 2EL

Getting to Great Britain

By Air

Most visitors to Britain, other than those coming from the European Continent or the Republic of Ireland, will arrive by air. Scheduled flights from all over the world by the major airlines operate in and out of international airports such as London's Heathrow and Gatwick, Stansted and Luton, Belfast, Birmingham, Manchester, Glasgow, Edinburgh, etc. (see Air Travel).

Visitors arriving by sea from Ireland and the Continent, whether as foot passengers, by car, rail or bus, have a whole range of ferries to choose from (see Ferries), while anyone wanting to make the transatlantic crossing by sea can still cruise in style, albeit much less frequently, on the great liner, the QE2.

By Sea

"Le Shuttle", which operates through the tunnel between Calais and Folkestone, takes cars and coaches with their passengers. The "Eurostar" express train runs via the tunnel between Brussels or Paris and London.

Eurotunnel

Help for the Disabled

There is increasing awareness in Great Britain of the need to provide proper access for the disabled. Many of the "black cab" taxis, for example, can now take wheelchairs, and most cinemas, theatres, etc. have special loop systems for the hard of hearing. London also has Artsline, a free telephone information service for disabled people on the arts and entertainment in the capital (tel. (020) 73882227). Hotels and guest houses welcome disabled travellers, even though they may not always have special facilities. Specific access guides should be available in most tourist information centres, and more detailed information can be had from the British Tourist Authority (see Information) and, for example:

Holiday Care Service,
2 Old Bank Chambers, Station Road, Horley, Surrey RH6 9UY;
tel. (01293) 774535

Northern Ireland Council on Disability, 2 Annadale Avenue,
Belfast BT7 3JH; tel. (028) 90491011

Hotels

Overnight accommodation in the United Kingdom spans a vast range from the humble bed and breakfast to the very grand hotel or stately home (see below, Castles and Country House Hotels). So far as hotels in particular are concerned they can vary from quaint timbered buildings in country towns through elegant Regency establishments in seaside resorts to the most modern inner city complexes, while travellers of more modest means can usually find a comfortable guest house or a homely B & B (see Accommodation, Bed and Breakfast).

The old coaching inns scattered widely throughout Great Britain are where fresh relays of horses were kept and weary travellers could stay overnight. Many of these mostly small inns are therefore very old and characteristic of their time and place. In the south and east they are often ivy-covered with thatched roofs, while in Wales they have white-washed walls and slate roofs. In Scotland the walls are of natural stone with stepped gables, while in the north and west of England the walls may be timbered and the roofs tiled. If they are cottage style they have small windows set in thick, timber-framed walls, while the Georgian ones have an impressive frontage with tall sash-windows and elegant doorways framed with pillars and porticos. Inns are comfortably furnished without being unduly luxurious and are consequently relatively low-priced. Most have only a few rooms, and the food they serve, which can be very good, is mainly regional. The "Stay at an Inn"

Inns

Hotels

Budget Hotels	brochure is obtainable from the British Tourist Authority (see Information).
Bed & Breakfast	Budget hotels supplying accommodation at reasonable prices are on the increase, usually as part of a chain operation such as Forte Travelodges, Campanile, Travel Inns, etc.
Bookings and Reservations	See entry

It is wise to book in advance, particularly in the peak holiday season, either through a travel agent or with the hotel direct. All Tourist Information Centres (TICs) can provide local accommodation lists and some of them will, for a small charge, make the booking for visitors applying in person. Many TICs operate a Book A Bed Ahead (BABA) service – in Wales a Bed Booking Service – by which a temporary reservation can be made in the locality and for the next destination.

Prices
The price categories given below include a full English breakfast, service charges and VAT, and should only be taken as a general indication. London prices are higher and can often be substantially more than those shown in this list.

Price Categories in this Guide	One Night's Accommodation based on two sharing a double room; singles will be more than half, and sometimes as much as the double rate
A	£160 plus
B	£130–160
C	£100–130
D	£ 60–100
E	under £60

Classification
In England, Scotland and Wales the National Tourist Boards use a system of one to five crowns to classify overnight accommodation according to the standard of facilities and service, with "listed" denoting the minimum category (the classification in Northern Ireland is from A to C). There is also an additional rating of "approved" ("merit" in Northern Ireland), "commended" and "highly recommended".

Hotels and Addresses

Aberdeen	Ardoe House, South Deeside Road, B, 71 r.; Copthorne, Huntly Street, B, 89 r.; Caledonian Thistle, 10 Union Terrace, C, 76 r. At Dyce (airport): Marriott, Overton Circle, Dyce, B, 154 r.
Aberystwyth	Belle Vue Royal, Marine Terrace, C, 34 r.
Ascot	Berystede, Bagshot Road, Sunninghill, B, 91 r.
Bath	★Bath Spa, Sydney Road, A, 100 r.; ★Royal Crescent, 16 Royal Crescent, B, 45 r.; Francis, Queen Square, C, 93 r.; ★Queensberry, Russell Street, C, 29 r.; Duke's, Great Putney Street, D, 24 r.
Battle	★Netherfield Place Country House, Netherfield Road, A, 14 r.; Powder Mills, Powdermill Lane, 25r.
Bedford	The Barns, Cardington Road, D, 49 r. At Clapham: Woodlands Manor, Green Lane, D, 30 r.

Stormont, 587 Upper Newtownards Road, C, 109 r.; Holiday Inn, 106a University Street, D, 114 r.; Jurys Belfast Inn, Fisherwick Place, D, 190 r.   Belfast

Holiday Inn Crowne Plaza, Central Square, B, 284 r.; Swallow, 12 Hagley Road, B, 98 r.; Grand Moat House, Colmore Row, C, 173 r.; Novotel, 70 Broad Street, C, 148 r.; Plough & Harrow, 135 Hagley Road, Edgbaston, C, 44 r.; Thistle, Birmingham City, St Chads, Queensway, C, 133 r.; Strathallan Thistle, 225 Hagley Road, Edgbaston, C, 167 r.; Posthouse, Smallbrook, Queensway, 251 r.   Birmingham
At Adcocks Green: Westley Arms, Westley Road. D, 27 r.
At Hopwood: Westmead, Redditch Road, D, 59 r.

Clifton, Talbot Square, C, 77 r.; Savoy, Queens Promenade, C, 131 r.; Brabyns, Shaftesbury Avenue, North Shore, D, 22 r.   Blackpool

Royal Bath, Bath Road, A, 131 r.; Norfolk Royale, Richmond Hill, B, 95 r.; Chine, Boscombe Spa Road, C, 97 r.; Swallow Highcliffe, St Michael's Road, West Cliff, C, 107 r.   Bournemouth

Wooley Grange, Wooley Green, C, 20 r.; The Swan, 1 Church Street, D, 12 r.   Bradford-on-Avon

Grand, King's Road, A, 200 r.; Imperial, First Avenue, C, 76 r.; Jarvis Norfolk Resort, 149 Kings Road, C, 121 r.; Topps, 17 Regency Square, D, 14 r.   Brighton

Swallow Royal, College Green, B, 242 r.; Avon Gorge, Sion Hill, Clifton, C, 76 r.; Forte Crest, Filton Road, Hambrook, C, 200 r.; Unicorn, Prince Street, C, 245 r.   Bristol
In Almondsbury: Aztec, Aztec West Business Park, B, 109 r.
In Failand: Redwood Lodge and Country Club, Beggar Bush Lane, C, 108 r.

In Calne: Lansdowne Strand, The Strand, D, 21 r.   Calne

Garden House, Granta Place, off Mill Lane, B, 118 r.; Holiday Inn, Downing Street, B, 199 r.; University Arms, Regent Street, B, 115 r.; Gonville, Gonville Place, C, 64 r.; Cambridge Lodge, Huntingdon Road, D, 11 r.; Forte Posthouse, Bridge Road, Impington, D, 118 r.   Cambridge

Chaucer, Ivy Lane, C, 42 r.; Falstaff, 8–12 St Dunstan's Street, C, 23 r.; Canterbury, 71 New Road, D, 27 r.   Canterbury
In Littlebourne: The Bow Window Inn, High Street, D, 8 r.
In Sarre: Crown Inn, Ramsgate Road, D, 12 r.

Cardiff International, Mary Ann Street, B, 143 r.; Cardiff Park, Park Place, B, 119 r.; Moat House, Circle Way East, C, 135 r.; Forte Posthouse, Pentwyn Road, D, 142 r.   Cardiff

Cumbria Park, 32 Scotland Road, Stanwix, C, 49 r.; Swallow Hilltop, London Road, C, 92 r.; County, 9 Botchergate, D, 84 r.   Carlisle
In Kingstown: Forte Posthouse, Parkhouse Road, D, 93 r.

★Gidleigh Park, A, 12 r.   ★Chagford

Golden Valley Thistle, Gloucester Road, B, 124 r.; The Queen's, Promenade, B, 74 r.; Carlton, Parabola Road, C, 63 r.   Cheltenham

★Grosvenor, Eastgate Street, A, 86 r.; Blossoms, St John Street, C, 64 r.; Crabwell Manor, Parkgate Road, Mollington, C, 48 r.; Forte Posthouse, Wrexham Road, D, 105 r.   Chester
In Sealand: The Gateway to Wales, Welsh Road, C, 39 r.

Hotels

Chichester
Chichester Resort, Westhampnett, Roundabout, C, 76 r.; Dolphin & Anchor, West Street, C, 49 r.; Suffolk House, 3 East Row, D, 12 r.

Colchester
George, 116 High Street, C, 47 r.; Red Lion, 43 High Street, C, 24 r. Rose and Crown, D, 27 r.

Coventry
De Vere, Cathedral Square, B, 190 r.; Brooklands Grange, Holyhead Road, C, 30 r.; Forte Crest, Hinckley Road, C, 145 r.; Forte Posthouse, Rye Hill, Allesley, C, 144 r.; Leofric Regal, Broadgate, C, 94 r. In Longford: Novotel, Wilsons Lane, C, 100 r.

Derby
International, 288 Burton Road, C, 44 r.; Midland, Midland Road, C, 49 r. In Littleover: Forte Posthouse, Pastures Hill, C, 62 r.

Dorchester
King's Arms, 30 High East Street, C, 33 r.; Casterbridge, 49 High East Street, D, 15 r.

Dover
Dover Moat House, Townwall Street, C, 80 r.

Dundee
Stakis Earl Grey, Earl Grey Place, B, 102 r.; Angus Thistle, 101 Marketgait, B, 53 r.

Dunkeld
★ Kinnaird, Dalguise, A, 9 r.

Durham
Royal County, Old Elvet, C, 150 r.; Three Tuns Swallow, New Elvet, C, 47 r. In Croxdale: Bridge Toby, C, 46 r.

Eastbourne
Grand, King Edward's Parade, A, 160 r.; Cavendish, 37–40 Grand Parade, B, 114 r.; Wish Tower, King Edward's Parade, C, 65 r.

Edinburgh
★ Balmoral, Princes Street, A, 189 r.; Caledonian, Princes Street, A, 240 r.; ★ Carlton Highland, 1–29 North Bridge, A, 220 r.; George Inter-Continental, 19 George Street, A, 195 r.; Royal Terrace, 18 Royal Terrace, A, 95 r.; Sheraton, 1 Festival Square, A, 263 r.; ★ Channings, South Learmonth Gardens, B, 48 r.; Forte Posthouse, Corstorphine Road, B, 199 r.; Holiday Inn Garden Court, 107 Queensferry Road, B, 119 r.; King James Thistle, St. James Centre, 107 Leith Street, B, 147 r.; ★ Malmaison, 1 Tower Place, Leith, B, 25 r.; Scandic Crown, 80 High Street, B, 228 r.; Albany, 39–43 Albany Street, C, 20 r.; Braid Hills, 134 Braid Road, C, 69 r.; Stakis Grosvenor, Grosvenor Street, C, 136 r.

Eton
Frederick's, Shoppenhangers Road, Maidenhead, B, 37 r.; Holiday Inn, Manor Lane, Maidenhead, B, 190 r.; Thames Riviera, Bridge Road, C, 51 r.; Christopher, 110 High Street, D, 34 r.

Exeter
Royal Clarence, Cathedral Yard, A, 56 r.; Forte Crest, Southern Hay East, B, 169 r.; White Hart, South Street, B, 61 r.; Buckrell Lodge, 157 Topsham Road, C, 54 r.; Countess Wear Lodge, 398 Topsham Road, C, 44 r.; Edgerton Park, Pennsylvania Road, C, 17 r.; Rougemont, Queen Street, C, 90 r.; Red House, 2 Whipton Village Road, D, 12 r.; St. Andrews, 28 Alphington Road, D, 17 r.

Felixstowe
Orwell Moat House, Hamilton Road, B, 60 r.

Glasgow
★ Glasgow Hilton, 1 William Street, A, 319 r.; ★ One Devonshire Gardens, 1 Devonshire Gardens, A, 27 r.; Forte Crest, Bothwell Street, A, 254 r.; Moat House International, Congress Road, A, 284 r.; Holiday Inn, 500 Argyle Street, Anderston, A, 298 r.; Copthorne, George Square, B, 140 r.; Hospitality Inn, 36 Cambridge Street, B, 307 r.; ★ Malmaison, 278 West George Street, B, 21 r.; Crest Glasgow-City, 377-383 Argyle Street, C, 121 r.; Kelvin Park Lorne, 923 Sauchiehall Street, D, 99 r.

George & Pilgrims, 1 High Street, D, 14 r. (15th c. pilgrim inn)   Glastonbury

Forte Posthouse, Crest Way, Barnwood, B, 123 r.   Gloucester
In Upton: St Leonards: Hatton Court, Upton Hill, C, 45 r.; Jarvis Bowden
Hall Hotel & Country Club, Bondend Lane, C, 72 r.

⋆Angel & Royal, High Street, C, 30 r.; Swallow, Swingbridge Road, C, 90   Grantham
r.; Kings, North Parade, D, 22 r.
In Belton: 1–½ miles on the A607: Belton Woods Hotel & Country Club, C,
96 r.

Havelet: Hotel de Havelet, C, 33 r.   Guernsey
St Peter Port: St Pierre Park, Rohais, B, 135 r.

The Angel, Posting House and Livery, 91 High Street, A, 11 r.; Forte Crest,   Guildford
Egerton Road, C, 111 r.

Harrogate Moat House, Kings Road, B, 214 r.; Majestic, Ripon Road, B,   Harrogate
156 r.; Crown, Crown Place, C, 121 r.; St. George Swallow, 1 Ripon Road,
C, 93 r.; Studley, 28 Swan Road, C, 36 r.; Britannia Lodge, 16 Swan Road,
E, 12 r.

Beauport Park, Battle Road, C, 23 r.   Hastings

Belmont Lodge & Golf Course, Belmont Road, C, 30 r; Merton,   Hereford
Commercial Road, D, 19 r.; Travel Inn, Holmer Road, Holmer, E, 40 r.

Beaumont, Beaumont Street, C, 23 r.; County, Priestpopple, D, 9 r.   Hexham

Forte Crest, Castle Street, D, 99 r.; Campanile, Beverley Road, Freetown   Hull
Way, E, 50 r.

Hythe Imperial, Princes Parade, B, 100 r.   Hythe

Kingsmills, Culcabock Road, B, 78 r.; Caledonian, 33 Church Street, C, 106 r.   Inverness

Belstead Brook, Belstead Road, C, 85 r.   Ipswich

Cowes: New Holmwood, Queens Road, Egypt Point, C, 25 r.   Isle of Wight
Shanklin: Fernbank, Highfield Road, D, 24 r.
Seaview: Seaview, High Street, C, 16 r.
Ventnor: Burlington, Bellevue Road, C, 23 r.; The Royal Hotel, Belgrave
Road, C, 55 r.

Rozel Bay: Château la Chaire, C, 14 r.   Jersey
St Aubin: Somerville, Mont du Boulevard, C, 59 r.
St Brelade's Bay: L'Horizon, B, 104 r.
St Helier: Grand, Esplanade, B, 115 r.

Brundholme Country House, Brundholme Road, C, 12 r.; Lyzzick Hall   Keswick
Country House, Under Skiddaw, D, 24 r.
At Portinscale: Derwentwater, C, 52 r.

Butterfly, Beveridge Way, Hardwick Narrows, C, 50 r.; Duke's Head (17th   King's Lynn
c.), Tuesday Market Place, C, 71 r.

Royal Kings Arms, 75 Market Street, C, 55 r.; Forte Posthouse, Waterside   Lancaster
Park, Caton Road, D, 115 r.

Holiday Inn Crowne Plaza, Wellington Street, A, 125 r.; ⋆42 The Calls, 42   Leeds
The Calls, B, 39 r.; Hilton National Leeds City, Neville Street, C, 206 r.;
Merrion Thistle, Merrion Centre, C, 109 r.; Queen's, City Square, C, 190 r.

Hotels

At Headingley: Haley's, Shire Oak Road, C, 22 r.

Leicester	Belmont House, De Montfort Street, C, 44 r.; Holiday Inn, 129 St Nicholas Circle, C, 188 r.; Forte Posthouse, Braunstone Lane East, D, 172 r.
Lichfield	Little Barrow, Beacon Street, C, 24 r.; Angel Croft, 3 Beacon Street, D, 19 r.; The Olde Corner House, Walsall Road, Muckley Corner, D, 11 r.
Lincoln	White Hart, Bailgate, B, 48 r.; Courtyard by Marriott, Brayford Side North, D, 95 r.; Forte Posthouse, Eastgate, D. 70 r.
Liverpool	Atlantic Tower, 30 Chapel Street, B, 226 r.; Moat House, Paradise Street, B, 251 r.; Grange, Holmfield Road, Aigburth, D, 25 r.; Campanile, Chaloner Street, Queen's Dock, E, 78 r.; Travel Inn, Wilson Road, Tarbock, E, 40 r.
Llandudno	Bodysgallen Hall, A, 25 r.; St Tudno, North Parade, C, 21 r.
Llyswen	★Llangoed Hall, A, 23 r.
London West End	★Churchill Inter-Continental, Portman Square, A, 452 r.; ★Claridge's, Brook Street, A, 189 r.; ★Connaught, Carlos Place, A, 90 r.; ★Dorchester, Park Lane, A, 252 r.; Four Seasons, Hamilton Place, Park Lane, A, 227 r.; ★Grosvenor House, 90 Park Lane, A, 454 r.; Hotel Inter-Continental, Hamilton Place, Park Lane, A, 454 r.; ★Lanesborough, Hyde Park Corner, A, 95 r.; ★London Hilton on Park Lane, 22 Park Lane, A, 448 r.; ★London Marriott, Grosvenor Square, A, 223 r.; ★Ritz, 150 Piccadilly, A, 129 r.; ★Athenaeum, 116 Piccadilly, B, 112 r.; ★Britannia Inter-Continental, 42 Grosvenor Square, B, 317 r.; Savoy Court, Granville Place, B, 95 r.; Selfridge, 400 Orchard Street, B, 296 r.; ★Westbury, Conduit Street, B, 244 r.; Bonnington, 92 Southampton Row, C, 215 r.

The beautifully furnished Goring Hotel in London

★Savoy, Strand, A, 200 r.; Waldorf, Aldwych, A, 292 r.; Drury Lane Moat House, 10 Drury Lane, B, 153 r.; Royal Horseguards Thistle, Whitehall Court, B, 376 r.; Strand Palace, Strand, C, 777 r.

Trafalgar Square & The Strand

★Hyde Park, Knightsbridge, A, 185 r.; ★Royal Garden, Kensington High Street, A, 406 r.; Capital, Basil Street, Knightsbridge, B, 94 r.; Copthorne Tara, Scarsdale Place, B, 900 r.; Kensington Palace Thistle, De Vere Gardens, B, 298 r.; London Kensington Hilton, 179 Holland Park Avenue, B, 603 r.; Basil, Basil Street, Knightsbridge, C, 94 r.; Hogarth, 33 Hogarth Road, C, 85 r.; Kensington Close, Wrights Lane, C, 530 r.

Kensington

★The Berkeley, Wilton Place, Knightsbridge, A, 160 r.; Goring, 15 Beeston Place, B, 80 r.; The Halkin, Halkin Street, B, 41 r.; Royal Westminster Thistle, 49 Buckingham Palace Road, B, 134 r.; Rubens, Buckingham Palace Road, C, 188 r.

Belgravia

★Hyatt Carlton Tower, 2 Cadogan Place, A, 224 r.

Chelsea

★The Tower Thistle, St Katherine's Way, B, 808 r.

Tower of London

Copthorne Effingham Park Road, West Park Road, Copthorne, B, 122 r.; ★London Gatwick Airport Hilton, South Terminal, B, 550 r.

Gatwick Airport

Radisson Edwardian International, Bath Road, A, 459 r.; ★Excelsior, Bath Road, West Drayton, B, 839 r.; Holiday Inn Crowne Plaza, Stockley Road, B, 375 r.; ★London Heathrow Hilton, Terminal 4, B, 400 r.; Marriott, Ditton Road, Langley, B, 350 r.; Forte Crest, Sipson Road, West Drayton, C, 569 r.; Novotel, M4 Junction 4, Cherry Lane, C, 178 r.; Forte Posthouse, Bath Road, D, 180 r.

Heathrow Airport

Everglades, Prehen Road, C, 54 r.

Londonderry

Frederick's, Shoppenhangers Road, Maidenhead, B, 37 r.; Holiday Inn, Manor Lane, B, 190 r.; Thames Riviera, At the Bridge, C, 34 r.

Maidenhead

Tudor Park Hotel, Country Club, Ashford Road, Bearsted, B, 119 r.; Grange Moor, 4-8 St Michael's Road, D, 36 r.

Maidstone

Copthorne, Clippers Quay, Salford Quays, B, 166 r.; Holiday Inn Crowne Plaza, Peter Street, B, 303 r.; Portland Thistle, 3-5 Portland Street, B, 205 r.; Victoria & Albert, Water Street, B, 132 r.; Willow Bank, 340-342 Wilmslow Road, Fallowfield, C, 116 r.; Comfort Friendly Inn, Off Hyde Road, Birch Street, W. Gorton, C, 90 r.; Crescent Gate, Park Crescent, Victoria Park, Rusholme, D, 15 r.; Forte Posthouse, Palatine Road, Northenden, D, 198 r.; Mitre, Cathedral Gates, D, 28 r.; Montana, Palatine Road, Withington, D, 22 r.
In Worsley: Novotel, Worsley Brow, C, 119 r.
At Ringway Airport: Manchester Airport Hilton, B, 222 r.

Manchester

★Gosforth Park, High Gosforth Park, A, 178 r.; Copthorne, The Close, Quayside, B, 156 r.; ★Malmaison, CWS Building, Quayside, B, 100 r.; ★Surtees, 12–16 Dean Street, B, 27 r.; Forte Crest, New Bridge Street, C, 166 r.; Imperial, Jesmond Road, C, 130 r.; ★Swallow, Newgate Arcade, C, 93 r.; The County Thistle, Neville Street, C, 115 r.; New Kent, 127 Osborne Road, Jesmond, D, 32 r.

Newcastle-upon-Tyne

Celtic Manor, Coldra Woods, B, 74 r.; Hilton National, Coldra Woods, C, 75 r.; King's, High Street, C, 46 r.

Newport/ Casnewydd

Bristol, Narrowcliff, B, 73 r.; Trebarwith, Trebarwith Cresent, C, 41 r.; Windsor, Mount Wise, C, 44 r.

Swallow, Eagle Drive, A, 122 r.; Holiday Inn Garden Court, Bedford Road,

Northampton

Hotels

C, 104 r.; Westone Moat House, Weston Favell, B, 64 r.; Northampton, 4 Leicester Parade, D, 104 r.

Norwich	Sprowston Manor, Wroxham Road, B, 103 r.; Forte Posthouse, Ipswich Road, C, 116 r.; Nelson, Prince of Wales Road, C, 121 r.; Norwich, 121–131 Boundary Road, C, 102 r. At airport: Airport Ambassador, Norwich Airport, C, 108 r.
Nottingham	Rutland Square, St James's Street, A, 104 r.; Forte Crest, St James's Street, B, 130 r.; Stakis Victoria, Milton Street, C, 166 r.; Strathdon Thistle, 44 Derby Road, C, 69 r.
Orkneys	In Kirkwall on the island Mainland: Ayre, Ayre Road, D, 34 r.; Foveran, St. Ola, D. 8 r.
Oxford	Randolph, Beaumont Street, B, 109 r.; Eastgate, The High, C, 43 r.; Old Parsonage, 1 Banbury Road, C, 30 r.; Bath Place, 4–5 Bath Place, Holywell Street, D, 10 r.
Peterborough	Swallow, Lynch Road, B, 163 r.; Butterfly, Thorpe Meadows, C, 70 r.; Peterborough Moat House, Thorpe Wood, C, 125 r.
Plymouth	Copthorne, Armada Centre, Armada Way, B, 135 r.; Moat House, Armada Way, B, 212 r.; Astor, 14–22 Elliot Street, C, 56 r.; Duke of Cornwall, Millbay Road, C, 70 r.; Novotel, 270 Plymouth Road, C, 100 r.; Campanile, Longbridge Road, Marsh Mills, D, 51 r.; Georgian House, 51 Cathedral Road, The Hoe, D, 10 r.
Poole	Haven, Banks Road, Sandbanks, B, 91 r.; Mansion House, 11 Thames Street, C, 28 r.
Portsmouth	In Cosham: Forte Crest, Pembroke Road, B, 163 r.; Holiday Inn, North Harbour, B, 170 r.; Pendragon, Clarence Parade, B, 49 r.; Keppel's Head, 24–26 The Hard, D, 27 r.
Richmond	Richmond Gate, Richmond Hill, B, 51 r.; Frenchgate, 59–61 Frenchgate, D, 13 r.
Rochester	Bridgewood Manor, Maidstone Road, B, 100 r.; Forte Crest, Maidstone Road, C, 105 r.
Rye	George, High Street, C, 22 r.; ★Mermaid, Mermaid Street, C, 28 r.; ★Jeake's House, Mermaid Street, C, 12 r.
Salisbury	White Hart, 1 St. John Street, C, 68 r.; County, Bridge Street, D, 31 r.; King's Arms, 9 St John Street, D, 15 r.
Scarborough	Wrea Head Country, Scalby, B, 21 r.; Crown, 7–11 Esplanade, B, 77 r.
Scilly Isles	St Martin's: St Martins, B, 22 r.; Tresco: Island, Old Grimsby, B, 40 r.
Shaftesbury	Grosvenor, The Commons, B, 47 r.; Royal Chase, Royal Chase Roundabout, C, 34 r.
Sheffield	Moat House, Chesterfield Road, A, 95 r.; Charnwood, 10 Sharrow Lane, B, 21 r.; Grosvenor House, Charter Square, B, 103 r.; Holiday Inn Royal Victoria, Victoria Station Road, B, 100 r.; Forte Crest, Manchester Road, Broomhill, C, 135 r.
Shetland Islands	Lerwick: Shetland Hotel, Holmsgarth Road, C, 63 r.; Kveldsro House, Greenfield Place, D, 14 r.

Rowton Castle, on A 458, B, 18 r.; Lion, Wyle Cop, C, 59 r.; Prince Rupert, Butcher Row, C, 65 r.

Shrewsbury

Forte Posthouse, Herbert Walker Avenue, B, 132 r.; Polygon, Cumberland Place, B, 119 r.; Southampton Park, Southampton Park, Cumberland Place, B, 71 r.; Dolphin, High Street, C, 73 r.; Southampton Moat House, Highfield Lane, Portswood, C, 66 r.

Southampton

Prince of Wales, Lord Street, B, 105 r.; Scarisbrick, 239 Lord Street, C, 66 r.

Southport

Noke Thistle, Watford Road, B, 111 r.; Sopwell House, Cottonmill Lane, B, 84 r.; St. Michael's Manor, Fishpool Street, C, 26 r.

St. Alban's

★St. Andrews Old Course, Old Station, A, 108 r.; Rusacks, 16 Pilmour Links, B, 48 r.; ★St. Andrews Golf Hotel, 40 The Scores, B, 40 r.; Rufflets, Strathkinness Low Road, C, 20 r.

St. Andrews

Moat House, Etruria Hall, Festival Way, Etruria, B, 147 r.

Stoke-on-Trent

★Creggans Inn, Loch Fyne, B, 21 r.

Strachur

Ettington Park, Alderminster, A, 48 r.; Moat House International, Bridgefoot, A, 247 r.; Welcombe, Warwick Road, A, 76 r.; Alveston Manor, Clopton Bridge, B, 108 r.; Shakespeare, Chapel Street, B, 70 r.; ★Billeslay Manor (2 miles west), A, 41 r.

Stratford-upon-Avon

Holiday Inn, Maritime Quarter, B, 118 r.; Forte Crest, 39 The Kingsway, B, 99 r.; Beaumont, 72-73 Walter Road, C, 17 r.

Swansea/Abertawe

Moat House, Forgegate, Telford Centre, B, 148 r.

Telford

★Imperial Park, Hill Road, A, 150 r.; ★Grand, Seafront, B, 101 r.; Livermead Cliff, Seafront, C, 64 r.; Homers, Warren Road, C, 14 r.

Torquay

★Bishopstrow House, A, 32 r.

Warminster

In Longbridge: Hilton National, Stratford Road, C, 180 r.

Warwick

Swan, 9 Sadler Street, C, 32 r.; Crown, Market Place, D, 15 r.

Wells

Heath Lodge, Danesbury Park, B, 47 r.

Welwyn

Grand Atlantic, Beach Road, B, 76 r.; Royal Pier, 55–57 Birnbeck Road, C, 40 r.

Weston-Super-Mare

Bonchurch: ★Winterbourne, Bonchurch Shute, B, 19 r.; Peacock Vane Country House, Bonchurch Village Road, B, 11 r.; Cowes: New Holmwood, Queens Road, Egypt Point, C, 25 r.; Shanklin: Brunswick, Queens Road, C, 32 r.; Fern Bank, Highfield Road, C, 23 r.

Wight, Isle of

Lainston House, Sparsholt, B, 32 r.; Forte Crest, Paternoster Row, C, 94 r.; Royal, St Peter Street, C, 75 r.; Winchester Moat House, Worthy Lane, C, 72 r.

Winchester

Oakley Court, Windsor Road, Water Oakley, B, 92 r.; The Castle, High Street, C, 104 r.; Aurora Garden, 14 Bolton Avenue, D, 15 r.

Windsor

Fownes Resort, City Walls Road, C, 61 r.; The Giffard, High Street, C, 103 r.; Ye Old Talbot, Friar Street, D, 29 r.

Worcester

Beach, Marine Parade, C, 80 r.; Chatsworth, Steyne, C, 107 r.

Worthing

Hotels

York	Royal York, Station Road, B, 123 r.; York Viking Moat House, North Street, B, 188 r.; Ambassador, The Mount, C, 24 r.; Dean Court, Duncombe Place, C, 40 r.; The Grange, Clifton, C, 29 r.; Middlethorpe Hall, Bishopthorpe Road, C, 30 r.; Mount Royale, The Mount, C, 23 r.; Forte Posthouse, Tadcaster Road, D, 139 r. At Bilbrough, about 5 miles south of city: Bilbrough Manor, C, 12 r.
Castles and Country House Hotels Living like a Lord	Anyone who wants to treat themselves to something really out of the ordinary is well advised to try a few days in one of the many manor houses or castles which have been converted to top-ranking hotels. Even though fairly expensive – the price of a double room with breakfast is between £90 and £200 – the quality and service offered generally make it worthwhile. The historic buildings are furnished with antiques, each with its own particular style. There is a comfortable family atmosphere, sophisticated cuisine and a carefully chosen wine cellar, not to mention the magnificent parkland in which guests may stroll for hours.
★★Castles and Country House Hotels (selection) Langshott Manor	Guests are collected from Gatwick airport by the hotel's own Jaguar (just 10 minutes) to start their stay in the fairytale Langshott Manor begun in 1580. Here the Noble family offers unparalleled hospitality. All the rooms have been carefully furnished with antiques and Christopher conjures up fantastic menus in the best English tradition (Horley, Surrey RH6 9LN, tel. (01293) 786680, fax 783905; 9 r.)
Little Thakeham	Situated in the green hills of the South Downs, this is one of the best examples of fine country houses designed by the British architect Sir Edwin Lutyens who worked early in the 20th c. in the wake of the Arts and Crafts Movement. Tim and Pauline Ractliff have retained the luxurious style and furnished the elegant manor lavishly. The guest can expect a warm atmosphere, delicious cuisine and perfect service (Merrywood Lane, Storrington, West Sussex RH20 3HE, tel. (01903) 744416, fax 745022; 9 r.).
Ockenden Manor	The Elizabethan Ockenden Manor likewise offers marvellous rooms, excellent cuisine and delightful views of the South Downs. For the adventurous the hotel organises balloon trips over West Sussex (Ockenden Lane, Cuckfield, West Sussex RH17 5LD, tel. (01444) 416111, fax 415549; 22 r.).
Amberley Castle	Not far from Arundel is the picturesque Amberley Castle which goes back to the 11th c. Joy and Martin Cummings offer their guests pure luxury with four-poster beds and jacuzzis. The noble 12th c. Queens Room is used for dining (Amberley, West Sussex BN18 9ND, tel. (01798) 831992, fax 831998; 15 r.).
Netherfield Place	Just 3 miles from the historical town of Battle with its famous battlefield of 1066, a jewel of a Georgian manor house was built in 1924: Netherfield Place. Helen and Michael Collier have created an oasis of comfort here with fine cooking and excellent wines (Netherfield Hill, Battle, East Sussex TN33 9PP, tel. (01424) 774455, fax 774024; 14 r.).
Esseborne Manor	Ian Hamilton and his wife took over the famous country hotel Esseborne Manor west of London in 1995. The tastefully furnished rooms offer delightful views of the garden and surrounding farmland – an irresistible invitation to long walks. As the chef comes from Thailand, the menu includes not just British but also Asiatic delicacies (Hurstbourne Tarrant, Andover, Hampshire SP11 0ER, tel. (01264) 736444, fax 736473; 12 r.).
The French Horn	Culinary flights of fancy, romantic dinners by candlelight and relaxing walks along the picturesque banks of the Thames just 18 miles from London's Heathrow Airport during a stay at the elegant French Horn of

the Emmanuel family (Sonning-on-Thames, Berkshire RG4 6TN, tel. (01189) 692204, fax 442210; 16 r.).

Active guests will find swimming pools and tennis courts and 9-hole golf courses at the Chewton Glen sports hotel on the edge of the New Forest. Accommodation is in the elegant manor built in the early 17th c. and converted to the Palladian style in the late 19th c. From the delightful guest rooms there are enchanting views of the parkland (New Milton, Hampshire BH25 6QS, tel. (01425) 275341, fax 272310; 53 r.).

Chewton Glen

A few miles from King's Lynn is the elegant Georgian manor Congham Hall, managed since 1982 by Christine and Trevor Forecast. A prime example of English gardening Christine's fragrant herb garden with over 500 different plants is put to excellent use in the fine catering (Grimston, King's Lynn, Norfolk PE32 1AH, tel. (01485) 600250, fax 601191; 14 r.).

Congham Hall

The Victorian Maison Talbooth at the heart of the Vale of Dedham has ten wonderful suites. It is just 10 minutes by foot to the separate restaurant in a romantic half-timbered building on the River Stour (Dedham, Colchester, Essex CO7 6HN, tel. (01206) 322367, fax 322752; 10 r.).

Maison Talbooth

Since the early 17th c. the noble Plumber Manor has been owned by the Prideaux-Brune family. Gourmets wax lyrical about the imaginative cuisine under the aegis of Brian Prideaux-Brune, the brother of the owner (Sturminster Newton, Dorset DT10 2AF, tel. (01258) 472507, fax 473370; 16 r.).

Plumber Manor

Solid oak panelling, cleverly painted wooden ceilings, old family portraits and cosy four-poster beds are all part of the interior of Lewtrenchard Manor built in 1600, an excellent place from which to explore Dartmoor and the numerous highlights of Devon and Cornwall. The Murrays cosset their guests with delicious cooking and top wines from around the world (Lewdown, near Okehampton, Devon EX20 4PN, tel. (01566) 783256, fax 783332; 8 r.).

Lewtrenchard Manor

Colourful rhododendrons, magnolias and cherries surround the Elizabethan manor house Combe whose history goes back to the 14th c. John and Thérèse Boswell have made this a top address with stylish furniture and exquisite cooking (Gittisham, Devon EX14 0AD, tel. (01404) 42756, fax 46004; 15 r.).

Combe House

Edward Stafford, the third Duke of Buckingham, laid the foundation stone of Thornbury Castle in 1511. Ten years later he was beheaded for treason and the castle passed into the hands of Henry VIII who lodged here with Anne Boleyn in 1535. England's oldest Tudor garden is part of the grounds (Thornbury, South Gloucestershire BS12 1HH, tel. (01454) 281182, fax 416188; 18 r.).

Thornbury Castle

The Elizabethan Greenway Hotel is a insider tip in the Cotswolds. Exquisite antiques and fresh flower arrangements welcome the guest who is very well looked after by David and Valerie White. The wine list reads like a list of the best wines in the world (Shurdington, Cheltenham, Gloucestershire GL51 5UG, tel. (01242) 862352, fax 862780; 19 r.).

The Greenway

The shepherd Michael from the eponymous poem of William Wordsworth, the Lakeland poet, gave the early Victorian manor house in the highly praised Lake District its name. During Wordsworth's most creative years he stayed in Dover cottage which is just a mile distant. Reg Gifford, formerly an antique dealer, has furnished the enchanting country hotel exquisitely. The well chosen wine cellar is also second to none (Grasmere, Ambleside, Cumbria LA22 9RP, tel. (015394) 35496, fax 35765; 14 r.).

Michael's Nook

Hotels

London
Goring Hotel

Even right beside Buckingham Palace in London it is possible to find a top hotel with a country house atmosphere: this is the elegant Goring, one of London's last hotels in family ownership. When O.G. Goring opened the house in March 1910 he was the first in the metropolis to install a private bath and central heating in every guestroom, and today the hotel is still one of London's top addresses. Reserve a room with a view of the garden and enjoy unexpected calm in the heart of the pulsing capital, relax after a long day shopping and enjoy the much praised cuisine in the restaurant (Beeston Place, London SW1W 0JW, tel. (020) 73969000, fax 78344393; 78 r.).

Wales
Maes-y-Neuadd

For over 600 years guests have been to the manor house Maes-y-Neuadd, one of the loveliest Welsh country hotels in the fascinating mountain area of Snowdon. Age-old tradition where exquisite antiques and modern comforts are harmoniously combined. In the Georgian dining room with a panoramic view as far as Tremadoc Bay Peter Jackson serves Welsh lamb, game and delicious fish dishes (Talsamau, near Harlech, Gwynedd LL47 6YA, tel. (01766) 780200, fax 780211; 16 r.).

Scotland
Sunlaws House

In the heart of the Borders the elegant Sunlaws House Hotel belonging to the Duke of Roxburghe, who resides at Floors Castle near by, is one of the first addresses – and itself a rewarding trip. The comfortable rooms have open fires and four-poster beds, fresh salmon is served from the Teviot River of the estate. The plans for the 18-hole championship standard golf course opened in 1997 were drawn up by the well-known architect Dave Thomas (Kelso, Roxburghshire TD5 8JZ, tel. (01573) 450331, fax 450611; 3 miles south-west of Kelso in Heiton/A698; 22 r.).

Balbirnie House

Balbirnie House with its magnificent Long Gallery and first-class library is a jewel from the Georgian period (built 1777). At dinner the gaze will alight on ancient yew hedges and golfing fans will find the hotel has its own golf course (Markinch by Glenrothes, Fife KY7 6NE; tel. (01592) 610066, fax 610529; 30 r.).

Prestonfield House

"Very old fashioned" is the manor house built in 1688 by Sir William Bruce for the Lord Provost of Edinburgh, only five minutes south of the Old Town. Benjamin Franklin and James Boswell were guests in the fine hotel which has been restored faithfully to the original (Priestfield Road, Edinburgh EH6 5UT, tel. (0131) 6683346, fax 6683976; 31 r.).

Cromlix House

David and Ailsa Assenti have furnished the suites in the highly traditional Cromlix Hjouse near Dunblane with exquisite objects and have been careful to retain the original character of the manor house built in 1874; the grounds include a small chapel which provides a wonderful setting for weddings. Dinner is a culinary experience of the highest quality. Anglers will find three trout ponds and the salmon grounds of Allan Water on the 1200ha estate (Kinbuck, Dunblane, Perthshire FK15 9JT, tel. (01786) 822125, fax 825450; 14 r.).

The Gleneagles

The Gleneagles, a palace built in the early 20th c. and owned by Guinness enjoys an international reputation. The enormous 5-star top-class hotel with much space and freedom in the 350ha park offers exclusive premises, three championship golf courses – the third owned by America's Jack Nicklaus – on which every year the Scottish Open is held and an equestrian centre of Captain Mark Philips, country club, brasserie and top restaurants (Auchterarder, Perthshire PH3 1NF, tel. (01764) 662231, fax 662134; 236 r.).

Knockinaam Lodge

On the south-west tip of Dumfries & Galloway, where the unusually mild climate has enabled delightful garden landscapes to come about, lies to the south of Portpatrick the Knockinaam Lodge of

Michael Bricker and Pauline Ashworth. Sir Winston Churchill enjoyed the relaxing calm and during the Second World War chose the hotel sheltered on three sides by steep cliffs as a secret meeting place with General Eisenhower. The premises are more than comfortable; the service and cooking are probably unparalleled – not to mention the wide panoramic view as far as the coast of Ireland (Portpatrick, Wigtownshire DG9 9AD, tel. (01776) 810471, fax 810435; 10 r.).

Private islands always have a special attraction and the small Isle of Eriska north of Oban is no exception. The park and country hotel built in 1884 in the Baronial style seem almost like paradise. In 1973 the Buchanan-Smith family took over the property and created with it a top-class hotel. Absolute comfort combined perfectly with top service and warm hospitality. An additional amenity for active guests is the new leisure tract and swimming pool built in 1995 (Ledaig, Oban, Argyll PA37 1SD, tel. (01631) 720371, fax 720531; 17 r.).

Isle of Eriska

All castles and country house hotels can be booked direct. Other top-class accommodation in castles, manor houses, stately homes and historic residences can be booked through:

Booking Centres

Country Club Hotel Group, Oakley House, Oakley Road, Luton, Beds.
    LU4 9QH, tel. (01582) 422022
The Heritage Circle, Meiklemosside, Fenwick, Ayrshire, KA3 6AY;
    tel. (01560) 600769
Pride of Britain, Esseborne Manor, Hurstbourne Tarrant, Andover,
    Hampshire SP11 0ER, tel. (01264) 736604, fax 736473
Scotts Castle Holidays, 10 Galachlan Shot, Fairmile Head, Edinburgh
    EH10 7JF, tel. (0131) 4454121
Small Luxury Hotels of the World, James House, Bridge Street,
    Leatherhead, Surrey KT22 7EP; tel. (01372) 361873

Information

The British Tourist Authority is responsible for providing tourist information overseas and has offices in the following English-speaking countries:

British Tourist Authority Overseas

Level 16, Gateway, 1 Macquarie Place, Sydney, New South Wales 2000;
tel. (02) 93774400

Australia

Suite 120, 5915 Airport Rd, Mississauga, Ontario, L4V 1T1;
tel. 1 888 VISIT UK (toll free)

Canada

17 th Floor, 151 Queen St, Auckland 1; tel. (09) 3031446

New Zealand

18–19 College Green, Dublin 2;
tel. (1) 6708000

Republic of Ireland

Lancaster Gate, Hyde Park Lane, Hyde Park, Sandton 2196 (visitors)
P.O. Box 41896, Craighall 2024 (postal address)
tel. (11) 3250343

South Africa

Suite 1510, 625 North Michigan Avenue, Chicago, IL 60611;
Suite 450, World Trade Center, 350 South Figueroa Street,
7th Floor, 551 Fifth Avenue, New York, NY 10176–0799;
Information: 1–800–462–2748

USA

National Centres for Tourist Information

British Tourist Authority, Thames Tower, Black's Road, Hammersmith, London W6 9EL;
Written enquiries only.

British Travel Centre, 1 Regent Street, Piccadilly Circus, London SW1 4XT; personal callers only.
Open Mon.–Fri. 9am–6.30pm, Sat. and Sun. 10am–4pm
(with longer opening hours from mid–May to September)
The British Travel Centre brings together the British Tourist Authority, British Rail, American Express, Expotel Hotel Reservations and Edwards & Edwards, and provides a comprehensive information service for visitors travelling in Great Britain.

Tourist Information Centre, Victoria Station Forecourt, London SW1V 1JU; tel. (020) 78248844.
Open Easter–October 8am–7pm daily (shorter opening hours in winter)

England	English Tourist Board, Thames Tower, Black's Road, Hammersmith, London W6 9EL; written enquiries only
Wales/Cymru	Wales Tourist Board, Brunel House, 2 Fitzalan Rd, Cardiff CF2 1UY; tel. (01222) 499909
Wales Tourist Board, London	see British Travel Centre, London
Scotland	Scottish Tourist Board, PO Box 705, Edinburgh EH4 3EU; tel. (0131) 332 2433 Edinburgh and Scotland Information Centre, Waverley Market, 3 Princes Street, Edinburgh EH2 2QP; tel. (0131) 4733800
Northern Ireland	Northern Ireland Tourist Board, c/o Ulster Office, 11 Berkeley Street, London W1X 5AD; tel. (020) 73555040
	Northern Ireland Tourist Board, St Anne's Court, 59 North Street, Belfast BT1 1NB; tel. (028) 90246609

Local Tourist Information Centres

Aberdeen	101 Migvie House, North Silver Street, Aberdeen AB1 1RJ; tel. (01224) 632727
Anglesey	Station Site, Llanfair, LL61 5UJ, Isle of Anglesey; tel. (01248) 713177
Arran	The Pier, Brodick, Isle of Arran; tel. (01770) 302140 and 302401
Avebury	The Great Barn, Brunel Centre, Avebury SN8 1RF; tel. (01672) 539425
Bath	Abbey Chambers, Abbey Church Yard, Bath BA1 1LY; tel. (01225) 477101
Battle	88 High Street, Battle TN33 0AQ; tel. (01424) 773721
Bedford	10 St Paul's Square, Bedford MK40 1SL; tel. (01234) 215226
Belfast	St Anne's Court, 59 North Street, Belfast BT1 1NB; tel. (028) 90246609 Belfast International Airport, Belfast BT29 4AB; tel. (028) 90422888

Convention & Visitor Bureau, 2 City Arcade, Birmingham B2 4TX; tel. (0121) 6432514

Birmingham

The Library, Bridge Street, Bradford-on-Avon BA15 1BY; tel. (01225) 865797

Bradford-on-Avon

St Nicholas Church, Bristol BS1 1UE; tel. (0117) 926 0767

Bristol

Wheeler Street, Cambridge CB2 3QB; tel. (01223) 322640

Cambridge

34 St Margaret's Street, Canterbury CT1 2TG; tel. (01227) 766567

Canterbury

Central Station, Cardiff CF1 1QY; tel. (029) 2027281

Cardiff/Caerdydd

Old Town Hall, Green Market, Carlisle CA3 8JH; tel. (01228) 625600

Carlisle

Alderney: Alderney States Office, Queen Elizabeth Street, St Annes; tel. (01481) 823737 and 822994
Guernsey: Visitor Information Centre, North Plantation, St Peter Port; tel. (01481) 723552 and 723555 (accommodation)
Jersey: Liberation Square, St Helier, tel. (01534) 500777 and 500888 (accommodation)
Sark: Sark Tourist Information Office; tel. (01481) 832345

Channel Islands

Chester Visitor Centre, Vicars Lane, Chester CH1 1QX; tel. (01244) 402111
Town Hall, Northgate Street, Chester CH1 2HJ; tel. (01244) 402111

Chester

St Peter's Market, West Street, Chichester PO19 1AH; tel. (01243) 775888

Chichester

1 Queen Street, Colchester CO1 2PJ; tel. (01206) 282920

Colchester

Bayley Lane, Coventry CV1 5RN; tel. (024) 76832303/4

Coventry

Assembly Rooms, Market Place, Derby DE1 3AH; tel. (01332) 255802

Derby

Unit 11, Antelope Walk, Dorchester DT1 1BW; tel. (01305) 267992

Dorchester

Market Place, Durham DH1 3NJ; tel. (0191) 3843720

Durham

Edinburgh & Scotland Information Centre, 3 Princes Street, Edinburgh EH2 2QP; tel. (0131) 4733800

Edinburgh

Reading: Town Hall, Blagrave Street; tel. (0118) 9566226

Eton

Civic Centre, Paris Street, Exeter EX1 1RP; tel. (01392) 265700

Exeter

35 St Vincent Place, Glasgow G1 2ER; tel. (0141) 2044400

Glasgow

1 The Tribunal, 9 High Street, Glastonbury BA6 9DP; tel. (01458) 832954 and 832949 (accommodation)

Glastonbury

St Michael's Tower, The Cross, Gloucester GL1 1PD; tel. (01452) 421188

Gloucester

The Guildhall Centre, St Peter's Hill, Grantham NG31 6PZ; tel. (01476) 406166

Grantham

Royal Baths Assembly Rooms, Crescent Road, Harrogate HG1 2RR; tel. (01423) 537300

Harrogate

Information

Hereford	1 King Street, Hereford HR4 9BW; tel. (01432) 268430
Hexham	Manor Office, Hallgate, Hexham NE46 1XD; tel. (01434) 605225
Hull	1 Paragon Street, Hull HU3 3NA; tel. (01482) 223559 King George Dock, Hedon Road, Hull HU9 5PR; tel. (01482) 702118
Isle of Man	Tourist Information Centre, Sea Terminal, Douglas IM1 2RH; tel. (01624) 686766
Isle of Wight	The Car Park, South Street, Newport PO30 1JS; tel. (01983) 525450
Lancaster	29 Castle Hill, Lancaster LA1 1YN; tel. (01524) 32878
Leeds	The Arcade, City Station, Leeds LS1 1PL; tel. (0113) 2425242
Leicester	7–9 Every Street, Leicester LE1 6AG; tel. (0116) 2998888
Lichfield	Donegal House, Bore Street, Lichfield WS13 6NE; tel. (01543) 252109
Lincoln	9 Castle Hill, Lincoln LN1 3AA; tel. (01522) 873700
Liverpool	Merseyside Welcome Centre, Clayton Square Shopping Centre, Liverpool L1 1QR; tel. (0151) 709 3631 Atlantic Pavilion, Albert Dock, Liverpool L3 4AA; tel. (0151) 7088854
London	British Travel Centre (see above) London Tourist Board and Convention Centre, Tourist Information Centre, Head Office: Victoria Station Forecourt, SW1; tel. (0839) 123456 and (020) 79322020 (accommodation) London Tourist Board, 26 Grosvenor Gardens, London SW1 0DU (written enquiries)
Londonderry	8 Bishop Street, Londonderry BT48 8PW; tel. (01504) 267284
Manchester	Town Hall Extension, Lloyd Street, Manchester M60 2LA; tel (0161) 2343157 and (0161) 2343158
Newcastle-upon-Tyne	Central Library, Princess Square, Newcastle-upon-Tyne NE99 1DX; tel. (0191) 2610610
Northampton	101 St Giles Square, Northampton NN1 1DA; tel. (01604) 622677
Norwich	The Guildhall, Gaol Hill, NR2 1NF; tel. (01603) 666071
Nottingham	1–4 Smithy Row, Nottingham NG21 2BY; tel. (0115) 9155330
Orkneys	6 Broad Street, Kirkwall KW15 1NX; tel. (01856) 872856
Oxford	The Old School House, Gloucester Green, Oxford OX1 1DA; tel. (01865) 726871
Peterborough	45 Bridge Street, Peterborough PE1 1HA; tel. (01733) 452336
Plymouth	Island House, 9 The Barbican, Plymouth PL1 2LS; tel. (01752) 264849
Portsmouth	The Hard, Portsmouth PO1 3QJ; tel. (023) 92826722
Richmond	Friary Gardens, Victoria Road, Richmond DL10 4AJ; tel. (01748) 850252

Eastgate Cottage, 85 High Street, Rochester ME1 1EW; tel. (01634) 843666 — Rochester

Town Hall, Market Place, St Albans AL3 5DJ; tel. (01727) 864511 — St Albans

Fish Row, Salisbury SP1 1EJ; tel. (01722) 334956 — Salisbury

8 Bell Street, Shaftesbury SP7 8AE; tel. (01747) 853514 — Shaftesbury

Peace Gardens, Sheffield S1 2HH; tel. (0114) 273 4671/2 — Sheffield

Market Cross, Lerwick ZE1 0LU; tel. (01595) 693434 — Shetland Islands

The Music Hall, The Square, Shrewsbury SY1 1LH; tel. (01743) 350761 — Shrewsbury

Above Bar Precinct, Southampton SO9 4XF; tel. (023) 80221106 — Southampton

Bridgefoot, Stratford-upon-Avon, CV37 6GW; tel. (01789) 293127 — Stratford-upon-Avon

Vaughan Parade, Torquay TQ2 5JG; tel. (01803) 297428 — Torquay

The Court House, Jury Street, Warwick CV34 4EW; tel. (01926) 492212 — Warwick

Town Hall, Market Place, Wells BA5 2RB; tel. (01749) 672552 — Wells

Guildhall, The Broadway, Winchester SO23 9LJ; tel. (01962) 840500 — Winchester

24 High St, Windsor SL4 1LH; tel. (01753) 743900 — Windsor

The Guildhall, High Street, Worcester WR1 2EY; tel. (01905) 726311 and 723471 — Worcester

De Grey Rooms, Exhibition Square, York YO1 2HB; tel. (01904) 621756 — York

Insurance

Visitors are strongly advised to ensure that they have adequate holiday insurance, including loss or damage to luggage, loss of currency and jewellery.

Health

Nationals of other European Union countries are entitled to obtain medical care when on holiday in Great Britain. Treatment can be free of charge, but medicines must be paid for. An E111 form should be obtained in the EU country of origin before departure.
Visitors from non-EU countries are recommended, and nationals of EU countries are advised, to take out some form of short-term health insurance providing complete cover and possibly avoiding delays.

Vehicles

Visitors travelling by car should ensure that their insurance covers use of the vehicle throughout the United Kingdom.

See also Travel Documents.

Medical Assistance

Britain has a National Health Service. This provides medical care free of charge for nationals of other European Union countries, but on an emergency basis only for non-EU visitors who should therefore ensure they have some form of health insurance to cover them during their stay (see Insurance). However, prescribed medicines must be paid for, and EU nationals should also bring with them an E111 form from their country of origin. For initial medical treatment go to the surgery of the local GP or "general practitioner" as family practice doctors are called in Britain. EU nationals should make it clear that they will subsequently want to make a claim on their own health funders. Anyone who is taken ill outside a GP's consulting hours should get to the nearest hospital casualty department or, in an acute emergency, dial 999 for an ambulance.

Dentists

Some dentists are part of the National Health Service and a charge is made for emergency treatment.

Motoring

Emergencies

Dial 999 free of charge nationwide for police, fire brigade or ambulance.

Emergency phones are spaced at regular intervals along the motorways.

Breakdown assistance

The Automobile Association (AA) and Royal Automobile Club (RAC) provide breakdown services for members of other affiliated motoring organisations:

Automobile Association; tel. (0800) 887766 (freephone)
Royal Automobile Club: tel. (0800) 828282 (freephone)

Car Rental

The major car rental firms have offices or desks at airports and in all the major cities. There are also local rental companies who will often hire out their vehicles at cheaper rates than the better-known agencies.

Anyone wanting to rent a car must be over 21, or in some cases 23, and have held a driving licence for at least 12 months.

Nationwide Reservations

Avis: tel. (020) 88488733
Europcar: tel. (020) 89505050
Hertz: tel. (020) 86791799
Sixt/Budget: tel. (0800) 181181

Road Traffic Road network

Out of its 224,000 miles of roads the United Kingdom has about 1884 miles of motorway, and is adding more all the time. All major roads are clearly signed and numbered: M, as in M11, indicates motorway, A roads, as in A11, are single or dual carriageway, while B roads (e.g. B 3004) are more minor roads and usually single carriageway. The road network in the South and South-east, Wales and the Midlands is well built up and maintained but tends to thin out north of a line from Liverpool in the north-west to Hull in the east, with fewer trunk roads in the North and in Scotland and minor roads that are often narrow and less well-surfaced in places.

Drive on the left and overtake on the right. If unfamiliar with driving on the left take special care when starting out, particularly when moving away from service stations onto an empty road or negotiating roundabouts.

Traffic Regulations

Traffic rules and regulations are published in the Highway Code, which is available at ports of entry, from bookshops and the motoring organisations. Traffic signs are largely the same as in Europe.

Speed limits

The maximum speed limit on motorways and dual carriageways is 70mph (60mph with a trailer), on other roads outside built-up areas 60

Distances in miles using motorways whenever possible	York	Southampton	Sheffield	Salisbury	Plymouth	Penzance	Oxford	Nottingham	Norwich	Newcastle	Manchester	London	Liverpool	Lincoln	Leicester	Leeds	Inverness	Hull	Gloucester	Glasgow	Edinburgh	Dover	Coventry	Cardiff	Cambridge	Bristol	Birmingham	Aberdeen
Aberdeen	153	539	350	516	610	670	482	379	473	233	334	502	342	377	408	320	105	361	459	141	128	563	418	490	458	492	416	–
Birmingham	129	128	77	112	204	268	64	50	158	205	80	106	93	86	39	110	452	132	53	290	289	180	18	103	100	81	–	416
Bristol	214	76	184	52	199	185	72	141	220	288	161	115	160	176	115	194	539	214	35	366	368	187	91	44	155	–	81	492
Cambridge	150	130	117	134	239	329	82	84	66	230	154	54	170	86	68	194	539	136	119	356	335	123	81	175	–	155	100	458
Cardiff	240	119	179	96	163	228	106	153	236	254	154	159	170	188	138	219	549	230	56	386	385	237	115	–	175	44	103	490
Coventry	126	114	78	96	210	276	50	48	138	204	96	94	110	75	24	113	460	113	57	303	305	164	–	115	81	91	18	418
Dover	264	143	231	157	289	354	128	193	147	345	256	75	273	203	169	260	607	234	180	468	449	–	164	237	123	187	180	563
Edinburgh	194	421	235	397	496	542	357	262	366	110	215	378	216	258	284	202	158	216	333	44	–	449	305	385	335	368	289	128
Glasgow	217	420	247	395	456	545	356	277	385	148	215	397	216	276	302	215	166	254	333	–	44	468	303	386	356	366	290	141
Gloucester	177	126	70	70	156	217	51	111	186	254	95	109	127	137	85	160	505	168	–	333	333	180	57	56	119	35	53	459
Hull	37	245	65	226	355	388	182	90	144	121	95	181	130	44	58	55	387	–	168	254	216	234	113	230	136	214	132	361
Inverness	352	579	390	550	664	703	515	430	498	268	373	536	382	425	460	360	–	387	505	166	158	607	460	549	539	539	452	105
Leeds	24	232	33	215	316	375	168	25	176	98	35	175	75	75	96	–	360	55	160	215	202	260	113	219	194	194	110	320
Leicester	108	162	37	151	283	342	57	25	119	157	67	98	72	51	–	96	460	58	85	302	284	169	24	138	68	115	39	408
Lincoln	75	188	46	128	316	375	73	37	105	158	85	131	118	–	51	75	425	44	137	276	258	203	75	188	86	176	86	377
Liverpool	99	221	72	175	290	283	144	122	220	98	35	203	–	118	72	75	382	130	127	216	216	273	110	170	170	160	93	342
London	193	77	160	84	210	283	57	122	114	283	185	–	203	131	98	175	536	181	109	397	378	75	94	159	54	115	106	502
Manchester	64	208	38	190	267	319	98	63	185	125	–	185	35	85	67	35	373	95	95	215	215	256	96	154	154	161	80	334
Newcastle	84	324	124	304	410	465	260	157	264	–	125	283	98	158	157	98	268	121	254	148	110	345	204	254	230	288	205	233
Norwich	181	221	160	190	343	410	145	122	–	264	185	114	220	105	119	176	498	144	186	385	366	147	138	236	66	220	158	473
Nottingham	77	208	38	190	283	342	98	–	122	157	63	122	122	37	25	25	430	90	111	277	262	193	48	153	84	141	50	379
Oxford	181	67	123	64	213	319	–	98	145	260	98	57	144	73	57	168	515	182	51	356	357	128	50	106	82	72	64	482
Penzance	420	253	346	200	78	–	319	342	410	465	319	283	283	375	342	375	703	388	217	545	542	354	276	228	329	185	268	670
Plymouth	368	151	282	130	–	78	213	283	343	410	267	210	290	316	283	316	664	355	156	456	496	289	210	163	239	199	204	610
Salisbury	262	30	199	–	130	200	64	190	190	304	190	84	175	128	151	215	550	226	70	395	397	157	96	96	134	52	112	516
Sheffield	52	182	–	199	282	346	123	38	160	124	38	160	72	46	37	33	390	65	70	247	235	231	78	179	117	184	77	350
Southampton	245	–	182	30	151	253	67	208	221	324	208	77	221	188	162	232	579	245	126	420	421	143	114	119	130	76	128	539
York	–	245	52	262	368	420	181	77	181	84	64	193	99	75	108	24	352	37	177	217	194	264	126	240	150	214	129	153

637

mph (50 mph with a trailer) and in built-up areas 30 mph. Towing vehicles may not use the outside lane of a three-lane motorway.

Right of way

Traffic on the main road generally has the right of way unless a "Stop" or "Give Way" sign indicates the contrary. At roundabouts give way to the traffic coming from the right already on the roundabout. Motorists must stop at road junctions with unbroken double white lines but may edge forward slowly if the white lines are broken.

Seat belts

Seat belts must be worn in rear seats as well as front seats. Children under 12 may only ride in the rear seats.

Drinking and driving

The blood alcohol limit is 0.8 per millilitre.

Parking

Double yellow lines mean no parking or waiting at any time and a single yellow line means night-time and Sunday parking only. Illegally parked vehicles may be wheel-clamped and only released after a long wait and the payment of a large fine.

Fuel

Although petrol (gasoline) is nowadays sold almost everywhere in litres a few places still show the price in British gallons (1 Imperial Gallon = 4.546 litres). Grades obtainable are Super Fourstar (98 octane), Super (95 octane), leaded and unleaded. Diesel and LPG are also usually obtainable in most places.

Tyre pressure

Tyre pressure is measured in pounds per square inch.

Safety on the Road and Accident Procedure

In Britain vehicles only require third-party insurance.Visitors should in any case obtain a "Green Card" (international insurance certificate) from their normal vehicle insurers (see also Travel Documents). If they are involved in an accident they should also inform their insurers as soon as possible.

However careful a driver you may be accidents can still happen. Whatever the provocation, do not lose your temper, stay calm, keep a clear head and be polite. Take the following steps:

1. **Warn** other drivers there has been an accident by switching on your warning lights and positioning your warning triangle and any flashing lights you may have at an appropriate distance.
2. Apply first aid to anyone who has been **injured** and summon an ambulance if required by getting someone to dial 999.
3. The British **police** will normally only intervene in an accident if someone has been injured. This makes it all the more important to get the names of witnesses if only material damage is involved.
4. Get the **names and addresses** of other parties to the accident as well as the make and registration number of other vehicles involved and the name and number of their insurers.
5. Make sure you collect sources of **evidence** by taking the names and addresses of witnesses, especially anyone not involved, and by making a sketch of the situation at the scene of the accident. Better still, if you have a camera with you take several photographs from different directions.
6. Fill in an **accident report** if you have one and get the other party to sign it. Do not sign any acknowledgement of responsibility.

Opening Times

Opening Times Banks

Banks are usually open Mon.–Fri. 9.30am–3.30pm, but many High Street banks also open on Saturday mornings and for longer hours during the week.

In Scotland most banks close during the lunch hour but also open on Thursdays between 4.30 and 6pm.

Banks in Northern Ireland open at 10am but are also closed at lunchtime.

Shops are usually open Mon.–Sat. 9am–5.30pm, and in the larger towns and cities also until 8pm one night a week, usually Wednesday or Thursday. Supermarkets and some other food shops often stay open until 8pm on weekdays.
Shops

Mon.–Fri. 9am–5.30pm, Sat. 9am–12.30pm.
Post Offices

Following a recent reform the licensing hours for pubs in England, Scotland and Wales may remain open from 11am to 11pm Mon.–Sat. (Northern Ireland from 11.30am), but many landlords still close between 3 and 5pm.
Pubs

Licensing hours on Sundays are traditionally noon to 3pm and 7–10.30pm in England and Wales (but premises can be opened from noon– 10.30pm at the discretion of the landlord), 12.30–2.30pm and 6.30–11pm in Scotland, and 12.30–2.30pm and 7–10pm in Northern Ireland.

Some places in Britain still have early closing one day a week, when shops and some banks shut at 1pm.
Early Closing

Post

Postage stamps are sold in newsagents, service stations and outlets displaying the red sign "We sell postage stamps", as well as post offices. The current cost of a first class stamp is 26p and the rate for letters up to 20g to other countries in the European Union is 30p. For letters and postcards to non-EU destinations the stamps must show the actual postage rate, not just 1st or 2nd (class).
Stamps

Open Mon.–Fri. 9am–5.30pm, Sat. 9am–12.30pm
Post Offices

Public Holidays

Most public holidays in the United Kingdom are also known as "Bank Holidays" but on many of these shops stay open.
England and Wales

New Year's Day (January 1st)
Good Friday
Easter Monday
May Day (first Monday in May)
Spring Bank Holiday (last Monday in May)
August Bank Holiday (last Monday in August)
Christmas Day (December 25th)
Boxing Day (December 26th)

November 5th, Guy Fawkes Day, is not a public holiday but is celebrated in the evening with bonfires and fireworks to commemorate the Gunpowder Plot of 1605.

The Scots do not usually celebrate Good Friday or Boxing Day. In the winter they concentrate instead on Hogmanay, their version of New Year's Eve and New Year's Day, which is even more of a festive occasion than Christmas. Their bank holidays can also be more variable than
Scotland

south of the border, with Spring and Autumn Holidays replacing some of the fixed date bank holidays in England. Scotland also has a number of its own festivals, celebrating the birthday of their national poet with Burns Suppers on January 25th, and their national saint on St Andrew's Day, November 30th.

Northern Ireland

Northern Ireland also has several additional festivals of its own, namely, St Patrick's Day in Catholic communities (March 17th) and Orange Day, in Protestant communities, celebrating the Battle of the Boyne (July 12th).

Railways

British Rail

Great Britain's state railway system has now been privatised and is run by a variety of companies which operate a network of 10,875 miles of railway line linking over 2500 stations. This network, like the road system, is densest in the South and the Midlands. InterCity trains run between all the major cities, supported throughout Britain by an extensive network of connecting services.

Rail Passes

British Rail offers four different passes – the First Class Pass for travel in 1st Class, Standard Class Pass, Senior Pass for senior citizens, and Youth Pass for young people under 26 – valid for unlimited travel in England, Wales and Scotland for periods of four, eight, fifteen and 22 days or one month.
　　The BritRail Flexipass is valid for four days out of eight, eight days out of fifteen and fifteen days out of a month.
The ScotRail Pass is for eight or fifteen days and valid for all British Rail trains inside Scotland.
　　Saver return tickets, etc. are cheap rate tickets for rail travel at certain times during the week.

Royal Scotsman

The "Royal Scotsman" is a historic steam train operating six-day luxury tours out of Edinburgh through the Highlands, taking in castles and stately homes and some of Scotland's famous whisky distilleries.

Restaurants

Restaurant Guides

The many official and semi-official restaurant guides that exist for Great Britain are proof, if any were needed, of how far British cuisine has moved on from its former reputation. In "A Taste of England", "A Taste of Wales", "A Taste of Scotland" and "A Taste of Ulster" the National Tourist Boards publish their own guides to restaurants that keep up the tradition for fine regional dishes. In "Stay at an Inn" the British Tourist Authority lists country inns which provide the kind of meals that make a stay well worthwhile. Other guides include the Consumer Association's "Good Food Guide" and Egon Ronay's "Good Food in Pubs and Bars" and his "Cellnet Guide to Hotels and Restaurants".

Cafés, Coffee Shops, Wine Bars, Sandwich Bars, Tea Rooms

Cafés, coffee shops and tea rooms, which usually close in the late afternoon, are found everywhere throughout the United Kingdom. They serve tea and coffee accompanied by cakes and pastries, as well as lunchtime snacks and sandwiches in many cases. Wine bars serve the same purpose, but are also licensed to sell alcohol. Sandwich bars are a more recent development, selling a wide range of sandwiches and rolls with a great variety of fillings both to take away and eat on the premises.

Snack bars nowadays are increasingly being supplemented by pizza and burger houses, usually franchises operated by the major international chains. There is also a wide range of takeaways, mostly Indian and Chinese, but also Greek, Turkish, Italian, etc.

Snack bars and Takeaways

Fish and chips still reign supreme as the great British takeaway and no place is without its fish and chip shop, complete with salt and vinegar traditionally sprinkled over cod, plaice or, in the North, haddock, fried in batter and eaten out of its greaseproof wrapping.

Fish and chip shops

Besides beer and other alcohol (see Food and Drink) most pubs also serve food, ranging from a simple snack such as crisps and a sandwich or a "Ploughman's" of bread and cheese, to typical British dishes like Steak and Kidney or Shepherd's Pie. A number of pubs also serve restaurant meals in the evening.

Pubs

To get served just go up to the bar, order your drink from the barmaid or barman and pay for it straightaway. There is no need to tip. Most traditional landlords still close between 3 and 5pm. Children under 14 are not allowed onto licensed premises, except in Scotland, but many public houses elsewhere provide family rooms and outdoor areas which cater for children accompanied by adults.

A Selection of Restaurants

Ardoe House, South Deeside Road	Aberdeen
Garlands Restaurant, 7 Edgar Buildings, George Street; Popjoys, Beau Nash House, Sawclose In Box: Clos du Roy, 1 Seven Dials, Saw Close In Colerne: Woods, 9–13 Alfred Street	Bath
Powdermills Hotel, Powdermills Lane	Battle
The Barns Hotel, Cardington Road	Bedford
La Belle Epoque, 103 Great Victoria Street; Nicks Warehouse, 35–39 Hill St.; Roscoff, 7 Lesley House, Shaftesbury Square; Strand, 12 Stranmillis Rd.	Belfast
Sir Edward Elgar, Swallow Hotel, 12 Hagley Road; The Copthorne, Paradise Circus; Plough & Harrow, Hagley Road, Edgbaston	Birmingham
Harveys, 12 Denmark Street; Lettonie, 9 Druid Hill, Stoke Bishop; Bistro Twenty One, 21 Cotham Road South, Kingsdown; Howards, 1A–2A Avon Crescent, Hotwells; Orchid Restaurant, 98 Whiteladies Road; Berkeley Square Hotel, 15 Berkeley Square, Clifton	Bristol
Midsummer House, Midsummer Common	Cambridge
County Hotel, Sullys, High Street	Canterbury
Chikako's, 10–11 Mill Lane; Le Cassoulet, 5 Romilly Crescent, Canton	Cardiff/Caerdydd
Crosby Lodge, High Crosby	Carlisle
Arkle in the Chester Grosvenor Hotel, Eastgate Street; Crabwell Manor Hotel, Parkgate Road, Mollington	Chester
Comme Ca, 67 Broyle Road; The Droveway, 30a Southgate	Chichester
Martha's Vineyard, 18 High Street, Nayland	Colchester

Restaurants

Coventry	Brooklands Grange, Holyhead Road
Derby	Micklover Court Hotel, Etwall Road
Dorchester	Yarlbury Cottage, Lower Bockhampton; The Mock Turtle, 34 High Street West
Durham	Royal County Hotel, Old Elvet
Edinburgh	L'Auberge, 56 St Mary's Street; Martin's, 70 Rose Street, North Lane; Iggs, 15 Jeffrey Street There are restaurants in the following hotels: Balmoral and Caledonian, both in Princes Street; Calton Highland, North Bridge; Channings, South Learmonth Gardens; Dalmahoy, Kirknewton; George, 19–21 George Street; King James Thistle, 107 Leith Street, Norton House, Ingliston
Exeter	Buckerell Lodge, Topsham Road; Ebford House, Exmouth Road; St Olaves Court Hotel, Mary Arches Street
Glasgow	Rogano, 11 Exchange Place; Moat House, Congress Road; One Devonshire Gardens Hotel, 1 Devonshire Gardens; The Town House Hotel, West George Street
Glastonbury	No. 3, 3 Magdalene Street
Gloucester	Carrington in the Hatton Court Hotel, Upton Hill, Upton St Leonards
Grantham	Harry's Place, 17 High Street
Harrogate	La Bergerie, Mount Parade; White House Hotel, 10 Park Parade; Grundy's, 21 Cheltenham Crescent; Miller's The Bistro, 1 Montpellier Mews
Hereford	Governors, at the Merton Hotel, 28 Commercial Road
Hull	Cerutti's (seafood), 10 Nelson Street
Isle of Wight	Seaview: Seaview, High Street
Jersey	Rozel Bay: Château la Chaire; Gorey: Jersey Pottery Restaurant St Brelade's Bay: Lobster Pot, L'Etacq; L'Horizon St Helier: Grand, The Esplanade; Pomme d'Or, Liberation Square St Saviour: Longueville Manor
King's Lynn	Rococo, 11 Saturday Market Place
Lancaster	Forte Posthouse Restaurant, Waterside Park
Leeds	Hayleys, Shire Oak Road; Leodis Brasserie, Victoria Mill, Sovereign Street; Olive Tree, 55 Rodley Lane
Leicester	Belmont House Hotel, De Montfort Street; The Tiffin, 1 De Montfort Street
Lichfield	Thrales, 40–44 Tamworth Street
Lincoln	Wig & Mitre, 29 Steep Hill
Liverpool	Armadillo, 20 Matthew Street; L'Oriel, 14 Water Street

Brown's, Albemarle and Dover Street; Launceston Place, 1A Launceston Place; The Green House, 27a Hay's Mews; Veronica's, 3 Hereford Road, Bayswater; English Garden, 10 Lincoln Street; Lindsay House, 21 Romilly Street; The English House, 3 Milner Street; Wilsons, 236 Blythe Road — London, English cuisine

Alastair Little, 49 Frith Street; Bibendum, 81 Fulham Road; Odins, 27 Devonshire Street — International

Ken Lo's Memories of China, 67–69 Ebury Street and Harbour Yard, Chelsea Harbour; Fung Shing Restaurant, 15 Lisle Street; Good Earth Restaurant, 143–145 Broadway; Imperial City, Royal Exchange, Cornhill; Kai Mayfair, 65 Audley Street; Oriental in the Dorchester Hotel, Park Lane; Zen W3, 83 Hampstead High Street; Zen Central, 20 Queen Street — Chinese

Au Jardin des Gourmets, 5 Greek Street; Boulestin, 1a Henrietta Street; Buchan's, 62 Battersea Bridge Road; Four Seasons Hotel, Hamilton Place; La Tante Claire, 68 Royal Hospital Road; Le Gavroche, 43 Upper Brook Street; Oak Room in Hotel Le Meridien, 21 Piccadilly; Grill Room in the Dorchester Hotel, Park Lane; Les Associés, 172 Park Road; Simply Nico, 48a Rochester Row — French

Kalamara's, 76–78 Inverness Mews; Greek Valley, 130 Boundary Road, St John's Wood — Greek

Bombay Brasserie, Courtfield Close; Salloos, 62 Kinnerton Street; Gopal's, 12 Bateman Street; Indian Connoisseurs, 8 Norfolk Place; The Old Delhi, 48 Kendal Street — Indian

Al San Vincenzo, 30 Connaught Street; Cecconi's, 5a Burlington Gardens; L'Accento, 6 Garway Road; L'Altro, 210 Kensington Park Road — Italian

Suntory, 72–73 St James's Street; Miyama, 38 Clarges Street; Ajimura Japanese Restaurant, 51–53 Shelton Street; City Miyama Restaurant, 17 Godliman Street — Japanese

Jin, 6 Bateman Street — Korean

Albero & Grana, Chelsea Cloisters, 89 Sloane Avenue — Spanish

Anna's Place, 90 Mildmay Park — Swedish

Bahn Thai, 21a Frith Street; Tui, 19 Exhibition Road — Thai

City (Chinese and European), 27 Shipquay Street; Duffy's, (fish, salads), 17 Foyle Street; Inn at the Cross, 171 Glenshane Road; Woodburn, Blackburn Crescent, Waterside — Londonderry

Market, 104 High Street, Smithfield Centre; Little Yang Sing, 17 George Street; Moss Nook, Ringway Road; Woodlands, 33 Shepley Road, Audenshaw; Yang Sing, 34 Princes Street — Manchester

Fisherman's Lodge, 7 Jesmond Dene; 21 Queen Street, Quayside; The Copthorne, The Close, Quayside; Fisherman's Wharf, 15 The Side; Swallow Hotel, Newgate Street — Newcastle-upon-Tyne

St Benedict's Restaurant, 9 St Benedicts; By Appointment, 27 St George's Street; Marco's, 17 Pottergate; Brasted's, 8–10 St Andrews Hill; Greens Seafood, 82 Upper St Giles Street — Norwich

Ginza, 593–595 Mansfield Road; Sonny's, 3 Carlton Street, Hockley — Nottingham

Liaison, 29 Castle Street; Fifteen North Parade, 15 North Parade Avenue; — Oxford

	Munchy Munchy (Indonesian), 6 Park End Street; Bath Place Hotel, 4 & 5 Bath Place; Whites, Turl Street
Orkneys	St Margaret's Hope: Creel, Front Road
Peterborough	Grain Barge, The Quayside, Embankment Road
Plymouth	Chez Nous, 13 Frankfort Gate
Portsmouth	Bistro Montparnasse, 103 Palmerston Road In Cosham: Barnard's, 109 High Street
Rochester	Restaurants in the Bridgewood Manor and Forte Crest Hotels, both on Maidstone Road
Rye	Landgate Bistro, 5–6 Landgate; The Mermaid Inn, Mermaid Street
Salisbury	Milford Hall Hotel, 206 Castle Street
Shaftesbury	La Fleur de Lys, 25 Salisbury Street
Sheffield	Harley Hotel, 334 Glossop Road; Nirmal's (Indian), 189 Glossop Road; Charnwood Hotel, 10 Sharrow Lane
Shrewsbury	Albright, Hussey Hotel, Ellesmere Road
Southampton	De Vere Grand Harbour, West Quay Road; Golden Palace, 17A Above Bar Street
Stratford-upon-Avon	Billesley Manor, Billesley; Shakespeare Hotel, Chapel Street; Stratford House Hotel, Sheep Street; Welcombe Hotel, Warwick Road
Torquay	The Table, 135 Babbacombe Road In Maidencombe: Orestone Manor, Rockhouse Lane
Tetbury	Snooty Fox, Market Place
Wells	Rugantino in the Ancient Gate House Hotel, Sadler Street
Winchester	Hunters, Jewry Street; The Wykeham Arms, 73 Kingsgate Street
Worcester	Brown's, The Old Cornmill, South Quay
York	Melton's, 7 Scarcroft Road; 19 Grape Lane, 19 Grape Lane; Ambassador, 125 The Mount; Middlethorpe Hall, Bishopsthorpe Road; York Pavilion, 45 Main Street, Fulford

Shopping and Souvenirs

Textiles, leather goods	Tweed is probably the most famous of British textiles, especially when made up into a sporty tweed suit, complete with leather elbow patches. Scottish tweed, the best known being Harris tweed, tends to be more finely patterned, while Irish tweed is often bolder and more brightly coloured. Other textile favourites are hard-wearing thick wool jerseys, shirts and overcoats, kilts, plaid wool blankets, paisley shawls and scarves, fine cashmere cardigans and twinsets, Shetland wool sweaters, Irish linen blouses and table linen, sheepskin coats, top quality rainwear, etc. Leather goods include jackets, belts and especially handmade, exclusive footwear.

Tea drinkers can choose between many different blends of their favourite brew, and can find top quality biscuits such as shortbread, chocolate digestives and ginger snaps to go with them, as well as sweet and savoury teatime spreads including jam, marmalade, and gentlemen's relish. Scotland is a mecca for whisky drinkers – the Single Malt Highland whiskies are particularly sought after – while gin is another British speciality. For pipe smokers there are some wonderful tobaccos, and the pipes to smoke them in, although these can be expensive.

Food, drink and tobacco

The Pottery towns in the Midlands around Stoke on Trent are famous for their china produced by world-renowned factories. CDs and records are another good buy, as are umbrellas and walking sticks. Antique silver, jewellery, furniture and other collectables make the kind of souvenir that lasts and appreciates in value, while street markets and junk shops can provide the occasional bargain that is well worth looking for.

Other souvenirs

See entry

Value Added Tax

Sport

Great Britain, in particular England, is the original home of many sports – the British are after all famous for their sportsmanship. Visitors will have plenty of opportunity to take part in their own sports, but can also participate as spectators at the great sporting events, an experience not to be missed.

For information about events in the sporting world check in the daily press. Coverage of sports events is traditionally found on the back page of the national and local daily newspapers.

Spectator Sport

Britain is the birthplace of Association football – or soccer, to give it its popular name – and this is reflected in the United Kingdom's unique position among the world's footballing nations, since it fields four national teams, one each from England, Scotland, Wales and Northern Ireland, in the World Cup and European football championships. Great footballers such as Sir Stanley Matthews and Sir Matt Busby have even earned themselves knighthoods through their footballing skills.

The top league games kick off on Saturdays at 3pm or Wednesdays at 7.30 or 7.45pm, although increasingly these dates and times are changing to meet the demands of television. The grand finale of the season is the Cup Final at Wembley Stadium in May, which is considered a greater achievement for the winner than coming top of the league.

Football (soccer)

Another of Britain's great national sports is cricket, the game of the Commonwealth, which is played in summer at every level from series against national teams from other Commonwealth countries, such as the battle for the Ashes with the Australians, down through county, university and school level, to village and club teams, for whom this particular game, with its complicated rules and scoring system, is a pleasant and sociable pastime, The mecca of all cricketlovers is Lord's Cricket Ground in London, which also has a cricket museum.

Cricket

The sport of curling originated in the Scottish Highlands. Unlike bowls, another similar very British sporting pastime played with polished woods on a velvety smooth green, curling is played on ice and consists of propelling polished lumps of granite (curling stones), weighing over 44 lb, at a target (tee) over a distance of 139 ft.

Curling

Most pubs have its dartboard and darts is the kind of popular game anyone can play. The winner is the first to score 301 or 501, but the skill

Darts

is in hitting the right sections of the board, combining doubles, trebles and bullseyes, to get to the target score first. Television has made professional championship darts a popular spectator sport.

Highland Games

The traditional Highland Games are staged between May and September in various places in Scotland, with Braemar being the best-known venue (see Events). The contestants, in Highland dress, compete in various trials of strength. The most spectacular is tossing the caber, a 20ft long pine trunk that has to be thrown in the air so that it turns full circle and lands upright on its tip. Other events include throwing the hammer, playing the bagpipes and Scottish dancing.

Greyhound racing

Greyhound racing, where dogs chase an artificial hare round the track of a stadium, is a popular spectator sport, although betting with the bookies on the outcome plays an important part.

Horse racing

Ascot, and Epsom with the Derby are internationally famous as flat race meetings usually attended by Royalty, but there are many other race meetings at various courses throughout the country during the racing season. Steeplechasing is when the course includes jumps, and the best known, and most controversial, of these races over the fences is the Grand National at Aintree.

Polo

Polo, in which Britain is one of the leading nations along with Argentina, is another exclusive sport involving horses and, like show jumping and horse racing, is also a favourite with Britain's royal family. Top national players have included Prince Charles, the heir to the throne.

Rugby Football

Another team ball game invented in England, Rugby football, or "rugger", is also a popular spectator sport in Britain and the Commonwealth, and the international games, especially England versus Scotland, can attract as large a crowd, if not larger, as many top football matches.

Snooker

Snooker is a more complicated version of billiards which, like darts, is very much a pub game. Although popular as a game played by the general public, snooker also has its professionals who have achieved star status thanks to frequent television coverage.

Sports for individuals

Anyone who enjoys sporting activity as a participant can find public sports facilities for their use just about everywhere. There is a wide variety of sports centres which offer accommodation as well as tuition. For details of the sporting holidays available contact:

The Sports Council, 16 Upper Woburn Place,
London WC1H 0HA; tel. (020) 73881277

Angling

There are excellent waters for angling throughout the length and breadth of the United Kingdom, but especially in Scotland and Northern Ireland. Angling falls roughly into three categories, game fishing for trout and salmon, coarse fishing for other freshwater fish, and deep sea fishing offshore. Fishing tackle can be rented locally. The British Tourist Authority (see Information) can supply details of the best fishing stretches.

Game Fishing

Game fishing for salmon and trout requires a licence. This can be obtained from fishing tackle centres and shops, some hotels, and the offices of the local fishery board or district. Many trout and salmon waters are privately owned. In England and Wales the trout fishing season begins at the end of March and lasts till the end of September; in Scotland it goes from mid-March to early October and in Northern Ireland usually from March 31st to November 1st, although in Scotland the fishing season limits can vary between late August and late February. The salmon season starts in January and lasts till October. No fishing is permitted in Scotland on a Sunday.

A fishing permit, obtainable from the River Board, is required for coarse fishing in England and Wales but not Northern Ireland. The main fish caught are pike, bream, tench, rudd, roach, perch, carp and eel. The season is from mid-June to mid-March. Coarse fishing is forbidden on the Isle of Man.

Coarse Fishing

The Scottish rivers the Tay, Spey, Dee and Tweed are internationally famous for their salmon and trout-fishing. Other celebrated waters and rivers include England's Lune and Eden in the North-west, the Coquet in the North-east, Rutland Water in the Midlands, and, in Wales, Why Towy, Teifi and Conwy, and the River Sulby on the Isle of Man. The big sea trout are to be had in the lakes of north-west Scotland. The best coarse fishing areas are the River Avon in Hampshire, the Stour in Dorset, the Norfolk Broads and the Fens in East Anglia, and the waters of the Lake District (especially pike and perch), as well as the Scottish lochs and the Welsh lakes and rivers.

Fishing Waters

The top deep sea fishing grounds are in the warmer waters from the Gulf Stream off the West Coast. The season lasts all year round and catches include shark, ray, cod, pollack, hake, bass, grey mullet and sea bream.

Deep Sea Fishing

The British golfer has more than 1800 golf courses to choose from, not including private links and driving ranges. Most of them will also take visiting holidaymakers on payment of the usual fee. The game of golf originated in Scotland, at St Andrews, where the world's oldest golf club, the Royal and Ancient Club of St Andrews, was founded in 1735. The main event of the golfing year is the British Open Golf Championship at Muirfield. Besides the many internationally famous golf courses there are also golfing hotels with their own links.

Golf

The hunting and shooting of game requires a gun licence. Game birds that may be shot during the season, which for grouse begins on the "Glorious 12th" of August, include pheasant, partridge, snipe, red grouse and wild-fowl. Information about the dates of the different seasons, hunting associations, licence conditions, holiday operators, etc. is available from:

Hunting and Shooting

Hook Rise South, Tolworth, Surbiton, Surrey KT6 7NF; tel. (020) 83304411

The Ministry of Agriculture, Fisheries and Food

Bicycles can be hired in many places, and can be carried relatively cheaply on trains, although space is limited, so it is advisable to find out about availability beforehand. For information contact:

London Bicycle Tours, 56 Upper Ground, London SE1; tel. (020) 79286838
Cyclists Touring Club, 69 Meadrow, Godalming,
Surrey GU7 3HS; tel. (01483) 417217

Cycling

Apart from riding schools, where horses can be hired, some travel firms also offer package riding holidays ranging from several days of pony trekking to courses in jumping, dressage and cross-country. For information contact:

Riding

The British Horse Society, Stoneleigh, Kenilworth; tel. (01203) 696697

Holidaymakers can avail themselves of Britain's many tennis courts, both outdoor and under cover. For information about tennis holidays contact any travel agent.

Tennis

Wimbledon is to tennis fans what Lord's Cricket Ground is to lovers of cricket, and its Lawn Tennis Championships in late June/early July are the most famous in the world. These have quite a curious history which dates back to 1877 when the All England Lawn Cricket Club decided to arrange a tournament for the newfangled sport of tennis to raise the money needed for a new roller. This was purchased out of the entry fees and still has pride of place on the club premises. To stand a chance of winning a ticket in the ballot for seats on the Centre Court it is necessary to write as much as a year in advance to:

All England Lawn Tennis Club, Church Road, Wimbledon, London SW19

Climbing and Walking

Many of the United Kingdom's loveliest landscapes are off the beaten track and only accessible on foot. There are some particularly fine long-distance paths in the National Parks, Areas of Outstanding Natural Beauty and on the Heritage Coasts. The best areas for climbing are in Scotland around Ben Nevis and in Wales in Snowdonia. Although the climbing is not unduly difficult the changeable weather is a factor that should never be underestimated, and this applies also to upland walks.

For more experienced walkers there is a network of **long-distance paths**, marked out by signs bearing an acorn. The most taxing route is the Pennine Way, 250 miles long, north from Edale in the Peak District through the wild moorland beauty of the Pennines to Kirk Yetholm on the Scottish border. Offa's Dyke National Trail in the Brecon Beacons traces the route of the fortifications between England and Wales built by the Saxon King of Mercia in the 8th c. It extends for 168 miles from Chepstow in the south to Prestatyn in the north. The Pembrokeshire Coast Path around the western tip of South Wales provides breathtaking views of wild cliffs and sandy beaches, where lovers of birds and plants will be in their element. The Tarka Trail runs for 180 miles through the North Devon moors, while the South Downs Way takes in parts of England's south-east coast. Information about these and other routes is contained in a free leaflet obtainable from the British Tourist Authority (see Information).

Various holiday firms offer walking holidays with accommodation and separate transportation for luggage. Information about these and similar holidays can be obtained from travel agents and:
Ramblers' Association, 1/5 Wandsworth Road,
   London SW8 2XX; tel. (020) 75826878
Countryside Commission, John Dower House, Crescent Place,
   Cheltenham GL50 3RA; tel. (01242) 521381
Scottish Natural Heritage, 12 Hope Terrace,
   Edinburgh EH9 2AS; tel. (0131) 4474748

Taxis

Strictly speaking taxis are "hackney carriage vehicles", which means they can be hailed on the street or pick up passengers from a taxi rank. They have an illuminated "TAXI" or "FOR HIRE" sign on the roof and can be "black cabs" or saloon cars. Taxi fares, which are shown on the meter, are charged per distance covered and start at between £1 and £1.50 for approximately the first mile. Private hire "taxis" or minicabs cannot operate from ranks or pick up in the street. They can only be ordered by telephone or from their office, and do not have set fare rates or meters, so be sure to check in advance how much the journey will cost.

Telephone

British Telecom (BT), Britain's privatised national telephone company, has replaced the familiar red telephone boxes with more modern cubicles. The newer payphones will take any coin, but it is necessary to dial first then insert money when the number responds. Green cubicles take phonecards only. These are obtainable to a value of 20, 40, 100 and 200 units from post offices and most newsagents.

Telephone

Mercury, which is a private telephone company, has blue telephone cubicles which will only take Mercury phonecards.

A cheap rate local 3-minute call costs 5p. Cheap rates apply within the United Kingdom 6pm-8am Monday to Friday and 6pm Friday to 8am Monday, and for international calls weekends and 8pm-8am weekdays. The minimum amount for an international call from a public payphone is £1. A cheap rate 3-minute call to the USA and Canada costs about £1.65.

Call charges

The international telephone code for the United Kingdom is 44. From the United Kingdom to:

International direct telephone codes

Australia: 00 61
New Zealand: 00 64
South Africa: 00 27
Republic of Ireland: 00 353
United States and Canada: 00 1

To call the operator for transfer charge calls or information on telephone codes dial 100.

Operator

For police, fire brigade or ambulance dial 999.

Emergency

For information about United Kingdom numbers call directory enquiries on 192.

Directory enquiries

For information about international numbers call directory enquiries on 153.

Time

In winter, i.e. from the end of October to the end of March, the United Kingdom observes Greenwich Mean Time (5 hours ahead of New York Time). During the rest of the year the clocks are put forward one hour to British Summer Time.

Tipping

The usual tip for carrying luggage is 50–75 pence per piece. In hotels and restaurants where there is no service charge the tip for table service tends to be 10–15% of the bill. Taxi drivers also expect a tip of 10–15%.

Travel Documents

All foreign visitors to the United Kingdom must have a valid passport, unless they are citizens of the Republic of Ireland with which there are no passport controls. In the case of nationals from some Commonwealth countries a visa is required as well, so it is advisable to

Passports

check before departure with the British Consulate or the British Tourist Authority (see Information).

Vehicle
documents

Motorists driving their own car should bring their car registration document and a "Green Card", an international insurance certificate obtainable from their normal vehicle insurers. Cars registered abroad must carry the approved oval sticker for their country of origin. If staying longer than a year they will have to acquire a British driving licence.

Value Added Tax (VAT)

VAT refunds

Value Added Tax (currently 17½%), or VAT for short, is levied on all services and most goods, apart from children's clothing and foodstuffs, everywhere in the United Kingdom but not in the Channel Islands.

As part of the export promotion drive in London and other places some shops can refund the amount of VAT charged on goods for export. For tourists from non-EU countries a simplified procedure for VAT refunds is operated by Europe Tax-free Shopping (ETS) for purchases in excess of £100. Shops operating the Tax-free system can fill in a "Tax Free Cheque" showing the amount of the refund. Once this has been stamped by customs this can be cashed in at one of the ETS cash-pay-outs at ports, airports, train stations, etc.

When to Go

Although London is worth a visit the whole year round, generally speaking the best time to visit Britain as a whole is from June to September, in the longer, sunnier days of summer. In the spring and autumn, however, there is considerably less crowding from other visitors and much pleasure to be had from enjoying the countryside at this time of year. Anyone interested in theatre, concerts, ballet, etc. will find that the cultural season is at its height in the winter half of the year.

Youth Hostels

Great Britain has over 350 youth hostels all offering more than just a cheap bed. Many have recently been modernised and depending on how they are fitted out the price per night for an adult will be from £5–20 and for a person under 18 about £4.

The hostels are usually open 7–10am and 5–11pm, although many stay open longer, whilst in London all youth hostels are open 24 hours a day. In the off-peak season some youth hostels close one or two days a week. The maximum length of stay permitted is four days in London, even with a change of hostel, and three days in the rest of the country. It is wise to book beforehand.

Many hostels stay closed for longer periods in the winter.

Information

Central Booking Service: tel. (020) 72486547
Youth Hostels Association (England and Wales), Trevelyan House, 8 St Stephen's Hill, St Albans, Herts. AL1 2DY; tel. (01727) 855215

Scottish Youth Hostels Association, 7 Glebe Crescent,
Stirling FK8 2JA; tel. (01786) 451181

Youth Hostels Association of Northern Ireland, 22 Donegall Road,
Belfast BT12 5JN; tel. (028) 90324733

Index

Index

Index

Picture credits

Associated Press: 579
Baedeker Archive: 45, 378, 436
British Museum: 358
dpa: 28, 98
Rainer Eisenschmid: 351, 355 (top), 361, 372, 535
Robert Harding: 6/7, 228, 442, 511
Historia-Photo: 60 (r.), 66 (l.)
IFA Bilderteam: 143, 302, 305, 470, 500
Niel Jinkerson/Jarrold Publishing: 448
Helga Lade Bildagentur: 124, 189, 208, 349, 365, 380, 406, 527, 554, 556, 561, 601
Phil Masters: 383
Kai Ulrich Müller: 144, 353, 369, 375, 440, 460, 503, 558
Dr Madeleine Reincke/Helga Cabos: 3 (x2), 5 (x3), 7(x3), 8, 12, 14, 15 (x4), 20 (x2), 31 (x2), 32, 34, 35 (x2), 37, 39, 40, 41, 68, 70, 73, 74, 78 (x2), 80, 82, 83, 84, 85, 86 (x2), 105, 107 (x2), 110, 112 (x2), 113 (x2), 116 (x2), 119 (x2), 122, 126, 127, 130, 135, 136, 138, 149, 150, 154, 155, 157 (x2), 161 (x2), 163 (x2), 165, 166, 168, 170, 174 (x2), 179 (x2), 180 (x2), 182, 184 (x2), 185, 192 (x2), 194, 196, 197 (x2), 203, 204, 211, 212 (x2), 214, 216, 221 (x2), 222 (x2), 223 (x2), 227, 229, 232 (x2), 233, 234, 235 (x2), 237, 243, 244 (x2), 248 (x3), 250, 251 (x2), 252, 254, 255, 257 (x2), 260 (x2), 261, 262, 264, 265, 267, 271, 272 (x2), 273 (x2), 274, 276, 279 (x2), 284, 286, 288, 289, 293, 294 (x2), 295, 296, 299 (x2), 309, 315, 316 (x2), 318, 319, 320, 321, 336, 338 (x2), 339, 340 (x2), 355 (bottom), 364, 371 (x2), 374 (x2), 387, 389 (x4), 391, 392, 395, 398, 399, 400 (x2), 402 (x3), 408, 409, 410/11, 412, 416, 418 (x2), 419, 420, 422 (x2), 424, 425, 426 (x2), 428, 430 (x2), 434, 436, 438 (x2), 441 (x2), 443 (x2), 445, 447, 450, 453 (x2), 454, 463, 465 (x2), 466, 468, 473, 474 (x2), 480, 481 (x2), 482, 483, 484 (x2), 487 (x2), 492, 493, 499, 514, 515 (x2), 517 (x2), 518, 520, 524, 528, 532 (x2), 535 (x2), 536 (x2), 540, 543 (x2), 545 (x2), 549 (x2), 553, 560, 565 (x2), 566 (x2), 568, 570, 571, 574, 577, 580, 581 (x2), 583, 589, 592, 593, 594 (x2), 596, 624
Schuster Bildagentur: 359, 366
Suffolk Coastal District Council: 240
Ullstein-Bilderdienst: 56 (x3), 60 (l. and middle), 67 (x3) 66 (middle and r.)
ZEFA: 6 (bottom), 329

Imprint

365 photographs, 81 maps and plans, 1 large country map

German text: Dr. Madeleine Reincke
General direction: Baedeker-Redaktion (Dr. Madeleine Reincke)
Cartography: Gert Oberländer, Munich; Chistoph Gallus, Hohberg; Mairs Geographischer Verlag GmbH & Co., Ostfildern (large country map)
Editorial work: g-and-w PUBLISHING, Oxfordshire
English translation: Wendy Bell, Julie Bullock, David Cocking, Brenda Ferris, Julie Waller, Crispin Warren, Carole Porter

Front cover: Images Colour Library
Back cover: AA Photo Library (P. Enticknap)

4th English edition 2000

© Baedeker Ostfildern
Original German edition 1998

© 2000 The Automobile Association
English language edition worldwide

Published by AA Publishing (a trading name of Automobile Association Developments Limited, whose registered office is Norfolk House, Priestley Road, Basingstoke, Hampshire RG24 9NY. Registered number 1878835).

Distributed in the United States and Canada by:
Fodor's Travel Publications, Inc.
201 East 50th Street
New York, NY 10022

All rights reserved. No part of this publication may be reproduced, stored in a retrieval system or transmitted in any form by any means – electronic, photocopying, recording or otherwise – unless the written permission of the publisher has been obtained.

The name Baedeker is a registered trade mark.

A CIP catalogue record of this book is available from the British Library.
Licensed user: Mairs Geographischer Verlag GmbH & Co., Ostfildern

Typeset by Fakenham Photosetting Ltd, Fakenham, Norfolk, UK
Printed in Italy by G. Canale & C. S.p.A., Turin

ISBN 0 7495 2408 1